VMware Infrastructure 3
Advanced Technical Design Guide
and
Advanced Operations Guide

Ron Oglesby   Scott Herold   Mike Laverick

VMware Infrastructure 3: Advanced Technical Design Guide
and Advanced Operations Guide

International Standard Book Number (ISBN:)
978-09711510-8-6

Printed in the United States of America by United Graphics,
Inc., Mattoon, IL.

The Brian Madden Company offers discounts of this book when
purchased in bulk. Visit www.brianmadden.com for details.

First printing, June 2008

Authors

Ron Oglesby
Scott Herold
Mike Laverick

Copy Editor

Kim Williams

Publisher

The Brian Madden Company

What's new in this book?

In this book, we have had the pleasure of working with Mike Laverick and adding a complete administration/operations section to the book to take you from design to operations/support and not just leave you "hanging" at design. Beyond that... well, let's just say the whole book was a re-write. If you read the first book you may see a chapter or small section and say to yourself "Hey! I remember that, that was in the last book!" Don't feel cheated, we think there are about 79 pages of information from the first book in this one, and when you have an 800+ page book that isn't a lot of re-used content.

Reader comments about the previous edition of this book

★★★★☆ Reader rating on Amazon.com (37 Reviews)

From Amazon.com:

Excellent job and a must have for VMware ESX engineers, administrators, enthusiasts, and new people who are just starting out with VMware ESX.

Jason Boche

Direct from the reader:

When my VMware SE pulled out a copy of this book to show me some examples of VM networking I knew I should buy my own. I wish I had this book before I started building my first server; it would have save me a lot of time and pain.

George Pampas

The storage section of this book was great. The explanations and writing style that focused on talking to you, not over you, sold me. I can't wait for the next version to come out.

Riley Szyszka

Table Of Contents

Acknowledgements from Ron

I would like to thank Scott, and Mike for working on this book. Both of them are great guys and my guess is that any errors in the book are mine and not theirs. I would also like to note my family that essentially sees me disappear for nights and weekends into the basement or in front of my laptop when writing, thanks for not running me out of the house.

Acknowledgements from Mike

I would like to reiterate my thanks to my partner, Carmel Edwards. She helped me do the initial proofreading of the book before Ron and Scott had their say. She puts up with me talking excitedly about my adventures in virtualization, which must be very tedious for her.

I would also like to thank all of the people on the VMware Community Forums whom I have helped and who have helped me in the last three to four years of using VMware products. Special thanks must go to Steve Beaver, Ken Kline, Alex Mittel, Thomas Bryant and William Boyd.

Lastly, I would like to thank Daryl Swagger, John Troyer and Robert Dell' Imagine, who collectively manage and maintain the Community Forums at VMware.

Acknowledgements from Scott

Well, we've managed to do it again. Before thanking anyone else, I must first thank everyone who has waited patiently while we completed this second book. It's been a long time in the making, and without the amazing amount of demand for a second book it would likely not have happened. Both Ron and Mike also deserve a lot of gratitude for their dedication and willingness to work on this project over the last 2 years. Their perseverance definitely helped keep me going as increased work and travel loads took more and more of my time.

I also want to thank all of the individuals at both Vizioncore and Quest Software for keeping me actively involved in virtualization and allowing me to extend my reach deep into the technology to drive new and innovative ideas forward. I'm glad I can finally provide them with this "Marketing Tool" that they have been patiently awaiting (and promising to customers) for the last 2 years.

Again, I need to extend my eternal gratitude to my mother who taught me to never give up, as well as to my loving wife Leah. Thankfully, the long hours in her classroom provided the extra time necessary for me to write "just one more page".

My final "Thank You" has to go to mother-in-law, who always feels like she gets the short end of the stick for all the effort she feels she's put into these projects. Thanks again to all.

Book 1: Advanced Technical Design Guide

Chapter 1 – Virtualization Overview

This book is an updated version of the original *ESX Server Advanced Technical Design Guide* that was written for ESX 2.x. It has been updated, added to, and re-written to bring it up to speed for ESX 3.0 and Virtual Center 2.0. As was the case with the original book, this book is designed to provide you with practical, real-world information about the use and design of VMware ESX Server systems. In order to study the advanced technical details, we need to ensure that you have a good baseline understanding of VMware ESX features, VMware's other products, and of course virtualization concepts as we know them today.

Even if you've already read and understand our previous book or if you're very familiar with previous versions of ESX or VMware server, we still recommend that you at least skim through this chapter so that you can familiarize yourself with the specific terms and phrasing that we'll use throughout this book.

As you read through this book, you should keep in mind that each chapter was written separately and that it's okay for you to read them out-of-order. Of course if you're new to VMware and virtualization technologies, the chapter sequence will guide you through a logical progression of the components. We'll begin in this chapter with an overview of VMware software solutions.

Virtualization - Today's Favorite Buzz Word

Standing at the RapidApp booth at VMworld this year (VMware's annual conference), I had one of the attendee's approach me and ask "so do you guys really do something with virtualization technology, or are you just another company that throws the word virtual in front of the product and come here?" I laughed. It was funny and any of you that have watched virtualization grow over the past few years understands how funny that really is. Virtualization is the hottest topic around the IT space right now. Virtualize your servers, virtualize your network, virtualize your storage, virtualize your boss... well that last one isn't here yet, but we're working on it.

This book deals with the market leading product ESX Server 3. In this chapter we will give you an overview of where ESX (or as VMware marketing people like to call the whole solution "Virtual Infrastructure 3") fits into the server virtualization space, the type of virtualization it does, and we will try to keep away from all the other "virtual" products.

VMware ESX Server allows for the "virtualization" of x86-based servers. The basic concept is that a single piece of physical hardware is used to host multiple logical or "virtual" servers. The ability to host multiple virtual servers on a single piece of hardware, while simple to understand in theory, can be extremely complex in execution. It should be noted that the idea of virtual servers is nothing new. Look to the UNIX space and you will hear terms like "Frames" and LPARs" and can equate those with Hosts and Virtual Machines. VMware's place in IT shops is driven in the x86 space, where hardware is cheap (compared to UNIX) and generally underutilized.

When VMware technology is used in an environment, a single host allows multiple virtual servers to share the host's physical resources. These resources include processor, memory, network cards, and storage (We'll refer to these four physical resources as the "core four" throughout this book.) This architecture also gives you the ability to "partition" your host to allow for the server's resources to be fully utilized while you migrate multiple physical servers to a single VMware server running multiple virtual servers. (We'll discuss partitioning and migration strategies in much more depth throughout this book.)

So what does this mean to your environment or your business? It depends on what your business looks like and which product from VMware you're thinking about using. Obviously if you're reading this book then you're at least contemplating an ESX Server implementation. But even with ESX you have a number of alternatives on how to deploy and utilize the system. Also, when investigating VMware technology it is unfair to simply look at ESX and why it is used. You can only decide to use ESX instead of GSX or Workstation after you really understand what each product does and where they truly fit. Outside of the VMware suite of products you may also have to look at other virtualization solutions, like those based on XenSource. And to make an informed decision about these solutions you need a better understanding of virtualization technology for x86 servers.

Hardware Virtualization vs. Software

The word virtualization is thrown around a lot these days, and everyone claims his way of virtualizing is better than everyone else's. But to understand what you are getting into you need to understand some basics. The first (and most important) concept you need to grasp is the difference between hardware virtualization and software. Most people in IT are aware that Intel and AMD have released "processor" virtualization technologies for their processor. There is a lot of talk about "moving this or that out of Ring 0 and into a Ring 1." There is also talk about how Intel is working on hardware hypervisors for their network cards, and HBA manufacturers are also creating hypervisors... So what does it all mean?

To make it simple let's look at the processor and two major virtualization "products." First let's look at XenSource (pronounced zen) and Xen based products like Virtual Iron. Xen is basically a free virtual machine monitor (a chunk of software that allows for multiple operating systems to run on a single piece of hardware) that grew out of the Linux community and originally would require a modification of the guest operating system to run properly. There is more detail and strategy on this product in chapter 2, but for now let's just take the basics.

The reason this modification was required was due to the x86 processor architecture and its concepts of security rings (ring 0 through 3). In virtualization the host operating system generally will run at ring level 0, the most secure part of the processor if you will, with Virtual Machines running at ring level 3. Of course operating systems (like Windows or Linux) are written so that they require full control of ring level 0. So when these OS's are run as a guest virtual machine they need to be modified so that the guest OS is not making ring level 0 calls (or in Windows system/kernel calls) to areas of the processor to which it doesn't have access. With the processor virtualization technology that has been introduced, it is basically a hardware change to allow for a "virtual Ring 0" if you will, labeled 'Ring 1.' The idea is that the manufacturer can make changes to move the required instructions up a level (to ring 1) and then the guest OS's are fooled into thinking they have full control of ring 0 all the time.

Before these processors were released, using Xen required that you modified the kernel in the guest OS and host. For Windows shops this was not an option and slowed the adoption of Xen as a virtualization solution. With Xen out, most Windows environments adopted ESX server since it allows the VM to execute against the processors (direct execution) without modifications to the guest OS at all.

ESX did (and does in 3.0) what I like to think of as processor thunking. Remember when you ran 16 bits apps on a 32 bit system, and the process for re-mapping the 16 bit addresses to 32 bit addresses was termed as "thunking." Well I like to think of ESX doing the same thing, but on the processor side. ESX essentially allows the guest OS to see the processor as it is. It then allows direction execution on the processor (even to ring 0) from the guest OS. The trick here is that the ESX kernel also runs at ring level 0, and each time a call from the guest comes down, the kernel essentially has stopped executing itself on ring 0, allowing the execution of the command from the guest (there is a binary translation involved) then sending the results back to the guest and resuming its operations.

This may sound like a ton of overhead, but it's not. Sure there is some, but essentially both forms of virtualization perform about the same, and in either case there is still a need for some type of virtual machine monitor/hypervisor to manage the guests and their access to resources.

Which brings us to our next point, no matter what the hardware manufacturers do (processor, NIC, HBA or Memory), there will, for the foreseeable future, be a hypervisor like Xen or ESX. A software layer will be required to manage all these hardware devices and their unique one-use hypervisors. The decision you have to make is which piece of software to use. Xen and VMware ESX are the two "big name" players with Microsoft Virtual Server following behind until their Longhorn hypervisor is publicly available. We'll get into the difference between hosted and bare metal architectures in the following pages, but at least now you can put to rest the arguments from the guy two cubes over about how you should just wait for the hardware hypervisors to come out and explain the reality of virtualization to him. Since this book is an ESX book we will continue to focus on that from here out.

So what is "virtualization?"

Simply stated, VMware (the company) provides virtualization technology. All of their products (Workstation, ESX Server, and VMware Server) work in more-

or-less the same way. There is a host computer that runs a layer of software that provides or creates virtual machines that x86 operating systems can be installed to. These virtual machines are really just that—complete virtual machines. Within a virtual machine you have hardware like processors, network cards, disks, COM ports, memory, etc. This hardware is presented through BIOS and is configurable just like physical hardware.

If we were to jump ahead a little and look at a virtual Windows server, you would be able to go into device manager and view the network cards, disks, memory, etc..., just like a physical machine. As a matter of fact the whole idea is that the virtualized operating system has no idea that it is on virtual hardware. It just sees hardware as it normally would.

In Chapter 2 we'll go into detail on how virtualization actually takes place with ESX Server, but for now it's just important to understand that from a high level there are a few components that make up any virtualization environment:

1. A host machine/host hardware

2. Virtualization software that provides and manages the virtual environment

3. The virtual machine(s) themselves (or "VM's"—virtual hardware presented to the guest

4. The guest operating system that is installed on the virtual machine

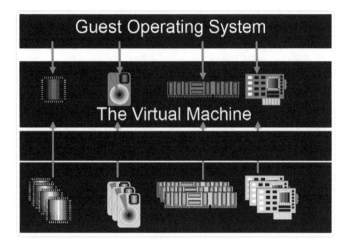

Knowing that each of these four elements must be in place in a virtual environment and understanding that they are distinctly different resources will allow you to understand where different virtualization software is used. Let's examine each of these components a bit before moving into the breakdown of the different virtualization technologies available from VMware and other vendors.

The Host Machine

The host machine in a virtual environment provides the resources to which the virtual machines will eventually have access. Obviously, the more of the resources available the more virtual machines you can host. Or put more directly, "the bigger the host machine, the more virtual machines you can run on it." This really makes sense if you look at Figure 1.1. In Component 1 of the diagram, the host machine has processors, some RAM, a set of disks, and network cards. Assuming that the host is going to use some of each of these core four resources for its own operation, you have what's leftover available for the virtual machines you want to run on it.

For example, let's assume that the host is using 10% of the available processor for itself. That leaves 90% of the CPU available for the virtual machines. If you're only running a single virtual machine (VM) then this may be more than enough. However, if you're trying to run 30 VM's on that host then the hosts "extra" 90% CPU availability will probably lead to a bottleneck.

The other challenge is that since all of the VM's are sharing the same resource (the CPU's in this case), how do you keep them from stepping on each other? This is actually where Component 2 from Figure 1 comes in—the virtualization software.

The Virtualization Software

The virtualization software layer provides each virtual machine access to the host resources. It's also responsible for scheduling the physical resources among the various VM's. This virtualization software is the cornerstone of the entire virtualization environment. It creates the virtual machines for use, manages the resources provided to the VM's, schedules resource usage when there is contention for a specific resource, and provides a management and configuration interface for the VM's.

Again, we can't stress enough that this software is the backbone of the system. The more robust this virtualization software is the better it is at scheduling and sharing physical resources. This leads to more efficient virtual machines.

VMware provides three versions of this virtualization software. The first two—"VMware Workstation" and "VMware Server"—are virtualization software packages that install onto an existing operating system on a host computer. The third version ("VMware ESX Server") is a full operating system in-and-of itself. We'll explore some of the reasons to help you choose which product you should use later in this chapter. The important idea here is to understand that ESX Server is both its own operating system and also the virtualization software (Components 1 and 2 in the model we've been referencing), while VMware Server and Workstation are virtualization software packages that are installed on and rely upon other operating systems.

The Virtual Machine

The term "virtual machine" is often incorrectly used to describe both the virtual machine (Component 3) and the guest operating system (Component 4). For clarity in this book we will not mix the two. The virtual machine is actually the virtual hardware (or the combined virtual hardware and the virtual BIOS) presented to the guest operating systems. It's the software-based virtualization of physical hardware. The guest operating systems that we install into these "machines" are (in most cases) unaware that the hardware they see is virtual. All that the guest OS knows is that it sees this type of processor, that type of network card, this much memory, etc.

It's important to understand that the virtual machine is not the OS but instead the hardware and configurations that are presented to the guest OS.

The Guest Operating System

In case it's not clear by now, the guest OS is the x86-based operating system (Windows, Linux, Novell, DOS, whatever) that's running on a VM. Again, understanding that the guest OS (or "guest machine" or simply "guest") is simply the software (Component 4) that's installed onto a VM (Component 3) will make your life easier when it comes to understanding and troubleshooting your environment.

Once all four of these components are in place you'll have a virtual environment. How this virtual environment performs, is managed, and the types of functionality available in your virtual environment are all dependent on the type of software you're using to provide your virtual environment.

Which Virtualization product which should I use?

Well that's the question isn't it? Since this book is about ESX Server we can probably assume that you've already made your decision. Then again you might be using this book to help make your decision, so we'll go ahead and look at the products and how they fit into the IT world.

Most VMware folks started out using VMware Workstation (simply called "Workstation" by VMware geeks in the community). Workstation allows us to create virtual workstations and servers on our own PC. This lets us create small test environments that we can use to test scripts, new software packages, upgrades, etc. VMware Workstation is perfect for this.

Figure 1.2: Where do the VMware and other Virtualization products fit?

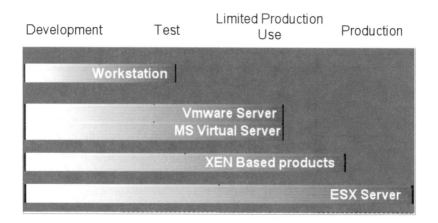

Development   Test   Limited Production   Production
                                          Use

Workstation

Vmware Server
MS Virtual Server

XEN Based products

ESX Server

Of course Workstation has its limitations. Probably the biggest one is that VM's can only run while you're logged into your host workstation. Log off and the VM's shutdown. Also, VMware Workstation is pretty much a local user tool which means that there are really no remote administration capabilities whatsoever. These limitations keep Workstation on the desktops of developers, engineers, and traveling salespeople who have to give multi-server demos off their laptops. No one uses Workstation for production environments.

VMware Server (formerly called "GSX" for short) is a step up from Workstation. Server is basically a software package that installs onto an existing host operating system (either Linux or Windows Server). It offers remote management and remote console access to the VM's, and the various VM's can be configured to run as services without any console interaction required. Its limitation is really that it has to use resources from the host hardware through the host OS. This really limits the scalability and performance of Server.

The reason for this is that with Server, VM's do not have direct access to the hardware. Let's look at an example to see how this can cause a problem. We'll look at memory use. Let's assume you configure 384MB of memory for a VM running on VMware Server for Windows. The "catch" here is that since VMware Server is "just" another Windows application, the VM doesn't get direct access to 384MB of memory. Instead it requests 384MB of memory from Windows and is dependent on the Windows scheduling mechanism.

Sure you'll see the host's memory utilization go up by 384MB (plus some for overhead) when you turn on the VM, but the guest OS has to send all memory requests to Windows. In this case you'll have a host OS managing the "physical" memory for the guest OS. This is on top of the guest OS managing its own memory within the VM.

While this is just a simplified example, it points out some of the inherent limitations with VMware Server that aren't seen in ESX. Does this mean VMware Server isn't a good product? Not at all. It just means that it has limitations stemming from the fact the virtualization software runs on top of a host OS. VMware Server is still used in plenty of environments—especially those that don't require enterprise class scalability for their VM's, those that have a limited numbers of VM's, and those that do not require maximum performance. VMware Server is also frequently found in corporate test labs and is used to allow administrators to get the benefits of a "virtual" test environment without the them needing to know all the ins and outs of a full virtual server OS. Finally, many companies use VMware Server when they don't have the budget to buy ESX-certified hardware or when the VMware champions can't win the political "everything has to run on Windows" battle.

What makes ESX different than VMware Server, Workstation, or even Microsoft's Virtual Server in its current revision?

VMware ESX Server is its own operating system. Unlike VMware Server or Microsoft Virtual Server, ESX is not a software package that installs into a host OS- ESX is the host OS. Engineered from the beginning to be nothing more than a VM host, ESX Server is completely designed to give the VM's the best performance possible and to allow you (the admin) to control and shape the way the host resources are shared and utilized.

So what does using ESX instead of VMware Server or Workstation get you? The answer is simple: performance (more management and recovery features and reliability).

- Performance. ESX Server provides a level of performance for your VM's that simply cannot be found in VMware Server or Workstation. It also allows for more advanced resource allocation, fine tuning of performance, a better VM-to-processor ratio, and more advanced resource sharing.

- Management and Recovery Features. ESX, when used with Virtual Center, allows you to manage the load on your systems by moving a VM to any host in a cluster without downtime. It also has an automated mode where it will move and shift load (by moving VM's) to different hosts in the cluster automatically. In the event of a server failure in the cluster, the VM's will be restarted on the remaining hosts and brought back online within minutes.

- Reliability. VMware published an ESX Server Hardware Compatibility List (HCL). If the hardware you're using for ESX is on the HCL, then you can be confident that everything will work as expected. ESX also lets you get rid of any problems that exist in the host OS since host OS's don't exist with ESX.

In short if you're looking to implement virtual machines on an enterprise level or if you're looking to host a lot of production servers as VM's, then ESX is a great choice.

A 60-second Overview of the ESX Server Architecture

An ESX Server is made up of two core components:

- The ESX Server kernel (called "VMkernel")
- The Service Console

The term "ESX Server" is usually used to describe all of this stuff together.

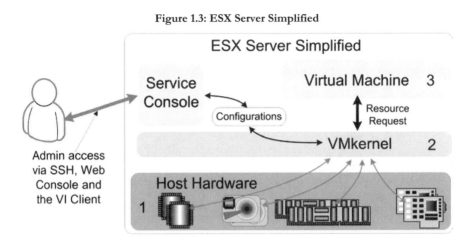

There is quite a bit of confusion in regards to what the Service Console and the VMkernel really are. The service console is a customized Linux 2.4 kernel based on a Redhat Enterprise Linux distribution. The key to understanding the Service Console's relationship to the kernel is that the Console is really just a high priority virtual machine that allows you (though tools) to interact with the VMkernel and manage its configurations. The VMkernel on the other hand is the hypervisor and the real guts of ESX.

In Chapter 2 we'll go into great (and sometimes painful) detail about the VMkernel and the Service Console. For now we just want you to understand the basic architecture so you see how ESX is different from VMware's other two main products.

Referring to Figure 1.3 you can see that the service console is what allows us to interact with this server. This operating system allows us Secure Shell access, supports a web based management console, and allows us to manage the server. But, the service console is not ESX itself, it does not schedule resources or manage hardware access, and basically would be a simple Linux server if it wasn't for the VMkernel.

The VMkernel is what manages/schedules access to specific hardware resources on the host. It is the VMkernel that provides the Virtual Machines into which guest operating systems can be installed. This kernel is what makes ESX different from the other software packages available. The VMkernel allows direct hardware access to the core 4 resources. It manages memory for the VM's, schedules processor time for the VM's, maintains virtual switches for VM network connectivity and schedules access to local and remote storage.

This kernel has been specifically built for this task. Unlike Windows or Linux hosts that have been built to be multi-purpose servers, this kernel's whole purpose is to share and manage access to resources. This makes it extremely light yet extremely powerful. Overhead in VMware ESX is estimated at 3-8%, while overhead for the host in these other OS's is generally 10-20% and sometimes as high as 30% depending on configurations.

The reduction in overhead basically comes from ESX being a "bare metal" product. Unlike the technologies used in workstation, Server or the current *Microsoft products, ESX makes the most of your hardware and has been built from the ground up to provide superb VM performance. Contrast this to the GSX, Workstation and Microsoft Virtual Server products that are really add-ons to operating systems that are built to handle numerous tasks and are not focused on providing high end VM performance.

*- a note here on the Microsoft virtualization product: At the time of writing Microsoft's publicly available virtualization product is MS Virtual Server 2005 R2. This product is an application that runs in a standard Windows 2003 Server environment. Microsoft's road map for virtualization includes a lightweight, bare-metal hypervisor like ESX Server, but at this point it is a road map available to the public and only beta code, so when comparing products we are using currently available technology.

Chapter 2 – Virtual Infrastructure Architecture

VMware is using a different marketing approach this time around with the newest release of their enterprise virtualization platform. With the previous version, each component of the virtual infrastructure was labeled and sold as a separate SKU. This caused quite a bit of confusion to end users trying to build a large-scale infrastructure with exactly what licensing components needed to be purchased to enable all of the features that were required.

To combat this, VMware took a new approach of combining the most used components into a single bundle called VI3, or "VMware Infrastructure 3". We have run into a great number of people that still insist this stands for "Virtual Infrastructure 3", which is definitely not the case[1]. VI3 comes in three different flavors, each of which contains a different level of functionality through enabled components and features. To start things off we want to discuss the available components and features that make up the VI3 suite. Much of this information will not be new to many readers of this book, but you never know, you may learn something.

There is actually a good chance that you will not read the term VI3 outside of the title of this book and this chapter. VI3 has many components that while they do interact with each other they, for the most part, are configured and managed as standalone components that fall well outside the generic umbrella of VI3.

ESX Server

ESX Server 3.0 is the single piece that is absolutely required to run a virtual infrastructure in an environment. The ESX Server component is the virtualiza-

---

[1] Even though it would have made a lot more sense since we feel it is quite foolish to include your company name in an acronym that makes up a product name.

tion software that enables you to actually run virtual machines. It is also the single most complex piece of the VI3 virtualization platform, and as such, will receive a majority of the attention throughout this entire book. We will go into more detail than most individuals will ever need to know about ESX Server throughout the rest of this chapter.

Virtual SMP

Virtual SMP is an add-on module for VI3 that provides the capability to configure multi-processor virtual machines. It is important to point out that you do not need Virtual SMP to use ESX Server itself on a multi-processor host; you only need it to create VMs that use multiple physical host processors. VMware has bumped up the number of processors that can be assigned to a single guest operating system from two to four in VI3. Virtual SMP will be discussed in more detail later in this chapter when we discuss the core 4 resources in depth.

VirtualCenter

VirtualCenter is an integral part of any virtual infrastructure that consists of more than a handful of ESX Servers. The server component of VirtualCenter is not included in the VI3 pricing structure, but VirtualCenter Agents, which are required to communicate with the management server, are. The VirtualCenter Management Server runs on a standalone Windows host and contains a database backend to store configuration and performance data. The VirtualCenter Agents are included with ESX 3 that provide the required communication channel between the ESX hosts and the VirtualCenter Management Server.

As previously mentioned, every VirtualCenter Management Server will require its own license that is independent of the standard VI3 licensing. The good news is that in a vast majority of the VI3 implementations a single management server is more than enough to manage and monitor the entire environment. Many of the advanced features provided by VI3 actually require the use of VirtualCenter. When we discuss the features that VI3 provides we will make sure we indicate which ones do have such a requirement.

The VirtualCenter component is such an important part to a VI3 implementation we will have several chapters in this book that are dedicated to functionality features that are only available if VirtualCenter exists. In addition, a majority of the Administration Book is focused on configuration and management of the entire infrastructure using VirtualCenter components. Chapter 4 is the first chapter that is dedicated to the configuration and use of VirtualCenter.

A High Level Look at the VI3 Features

If you are reading this book there is probably an extremely good chance that you are either using VI3 or you have made a fairly solid decision that VMware will be your platform of choice for your virtual infrastructure. Knowing that, we want to simply highlight the advanced VI3 features that you are probably well aware of in this chapter. Throughout the rest of the book we will discuss the best way to use each of these technologies for a variety of situations. If you notice terms that are unfamiliar to you, please remember this is just a quick primer. Everything will be fully explained in their respective chapters where we discuss them in detail.

VMware VMotion

To this day VMotion remains one of the greatest technologies in virtualization and is probably one of the biggest drivers towards server virtualization. VMotion provides the capability for virtual machines running on a shared storage architecture to have their hardware resources shifted from one host server to another in real time with no impact to the guest operating system. This single technology provides unparalleled levels of availability and allows for hardware and virtualization software management of an entire virtual infrastructure without having to shut down a single virtual machine. Figure 1 shows a simplistic view of how VMotion functions in a typical VI3 environment.

Figure 2- 1: VMotion

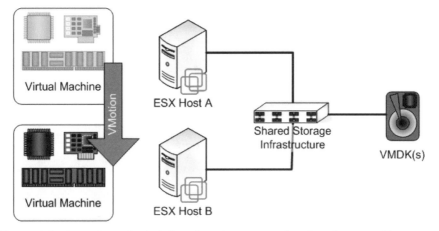

Figure 1 is deserving of a brief explanation as to what is going on. To start, a virtual machine is running on ESX Host A. The configuration files and data for this virtual machine are stored centrally on a shared storage infrastructure through one of several mechanisms that will be discussed in Chapter 5. Because both ESX Host A and B can see this same storage, the virtual machine can technically run on either system. The magic of VMotion comes when ESX Host A can move the processor, memory and network workloads to ESX Host B without interruption to the migrated workloads and while remaining invisible to the guest operating system. It is important to note that VirtualCenter is a requirement in order to leverage VMotion for your virtual machines.

A VMotion migration is actually performed with only a few seemingly simple steps. These steps are made possible solely due to the fact that the VMkernel (which we will learn about a little later in this chapter) provides an abstraction layer between the virtual machine and actual physical hardware. Even though the physical hardware platform is changing, the VMkernel makes sure the virtual machine doesn't notice anything is changing physically.

The memory state of the virtual machine is "snapshotted" on the source host. This allows the source host to first send the memory state of the virtual machine to the destination host.

After the initial memory transfer is complete the virtual machine configuration settings are sent from the source host to the destination.

The virtual machine settings are checked for availability at the destination. Enough CPU and Memory resources must be available. In addition, the destination host must be able to see the VMDK file(s) used for virtual machine data and must also have the same virtual switches configured to ensure network connectivity is maintained after the migration. If any of these checks fail, the VMotion process exits and returns to normal operation on the source host.

The final memory state is transferred from the source host to the destination host. This makes sure that any changes that occurred while the initial memory state was copied and configuration settings were verified are updated at the destination host.

Control of the virtual machine is taken by the destination host. This includes transferring the SCSI reservation for the VMDK file(s) and sending an arp request from the virtual machines NIC's to dictate the MAC address has switched network ports. This dictates the end of the process and the VMotion migration is complete.

There are several key uses for VMotion in an infrastructure that opens possibilities that aren't available in a physical infrastructure. One of the most obvious uses is for ESX host maintenance. Although most physical systems, especially the ones used for VMware ESX infrastructures, are built with many redundant components. A failure of any one of these components is not a major issue, but at the same time, should not be ignored. By using VMotion, the virtual machines running on the host requiring maintenance can be moved to alternate hosts in the infrastructure. This capability is not limited to hardware maintenance. VMware has been known to release occasional patches that require a reboot of the ESX host to take effect. Before beginning the patch process for a host the running virtual machines can be easily migrated to alternate locations using VMotion.

Another function that commonly leverages VMotion technology is balancing resource utilization across ESX hosts. As a virtual infrastructure grows both in the number of virtual machines hosted and in resource utilization within existing virtual machines overall utilization across multiple hosts in an infrastructure become unbalanced. It is not an uncommon practice to go through and reanalyze resource utilization on a monthly basis and make adjustments by shifting virtual machines across the infrastructure. VMotion can be leveraged to remove any downtime that would normally be associated with this activity.

There are several challenges with manually using VMotion for the mentioned tasks. In the event that an ESX host requires maintenance you need to know where you can safely VMotion your virtual machines to. Without proper planning it is quite possible that a host can be overloaded, which would have a negative performance impact on the virtual machines running on that host. This leads into another major challenge that also exists in the workload balancing scenario which is the fact that the VMotion process is very manual. The amount of change in some environments also requires that resources be closely watched on an ongoing basis. Failure to do so can lead to negative virtual machine performance. VI3 can simplify these uses of VMotion through a technology called Distributed Resource Scheduling, or simply DRS.

VMware DRS

VMware DRS technology takes VMotion to the next level. By leveraging VirtualCenter, DRS has the capability to make recommendations or, depending on the setting, automatically VMotion your virtual machines to balance the workload evenly across multiple ESX Hosts. By organizing groups of virtual machines into Resource Pools, you can ensure that these specific groups of servers have access to the resources they need when they need them, regardless of which host is providing these resources. The configuration possibilities of DRS are quite advanced and will be discussed in full detail in Chapter 8. Many people fear letting VMware make these decisions and there are some minor flaws with some of the logic behind the process, but overall this innovative technology is yet another thing that sets VMware apart from the rest of the virtualization world.

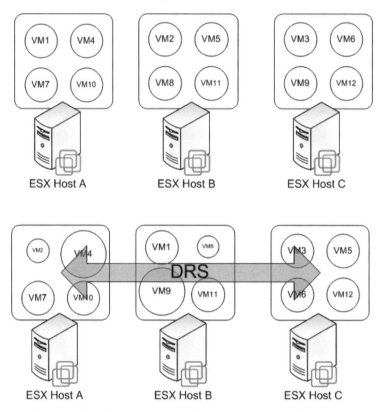

Figure 2- 2: DRS

Figure 2-2 shows a high level example of what DRS is capable of. The top row shows a group of 12 virtual machines, all using the same amount of resources. Knowing this almost never happens in the real world; the bottom row of hosts shows how specific virtual machines leveraging more resources (VM4 and VM9) are combined with servers using fewer resources (VM2 and VM8). While this is a simplistic view, we can start to immediately the benefits of what DRS can provide on a large scale.

In order to use VMotion and DRS both a source and target ESX server must be online and available, as the migration process is performed without guest impact. In order to provide resource availability to virtual machines in the event of a host failure, VMware has provided VMware HA.

VMware HA

VMware HA, or High Availability, provides automatic protection of virtual machines in the event that a host failure occurs. The recovery time in the event of host failure depends on the amount of time it takes the effected virtual machines to reboot on alternate ESX hosts. Many advanced application architectures have internal dependencies that dictate one system must be running before others can function. HA meets this requirement by allowing users to specify priority to each virtual machine configured in a host cluster. In the event of a host failure VMware HA will do its best to power everything back on properly without requiring end user interaction.

There are two key requirements to enable VMware HA in an infrastructure. First, VirtualCenter must be managing all hosts involved in the high availability cluster. The only way to have this level of control over a virtual infrastructure is through the use of this centralized management console. The most important requirement for VMware HA is leveraging a centralized shared storage infrastructure. Much like VMotion, every host needs to have access to the virtual machine configuration and data files to properly boot it in the event of a hardware failure. **Figure 2-3** will give you a rough idea of how VMware HA functions within an environment.

Figure 2- 3: VMware HA

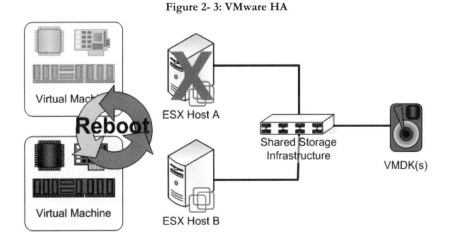

It is extremely important to note that using VMware HA will not allow your infrastructure to run uninterrupted. If a host failure occurs, each virtual machine running on that host will need to be booted on an alternate ESX Server. A small amount of downtime will be noticed for each virtual machine while it reboots. This can cause issues with application architectures that are dependent on the component that is rebooting. As an example, if a Database virtual machine has to reboot due to a host failure additional systems may need to be rebooted as a result, even though they are running on a host that hasn't experienced any issues. VMware HA does not address this issue so external processes will need to exist to resolve potential issues.

In addition, additional resource capacity to run the virtual machines must be available within the infrastructure. We will discuss properly building an N+1 virtual infrastructure in Chapter 3. If VMware HA is being used in conjunction with VMware DRS, VirtualCenter will actually have the capability to look at each existing host in the host cluster to determine the best place to recover each virtual machine based on current resource utilization. Using VMware HA on a centralized storage infrastructure can help protect against a local hardware failure, but what happens when there is data loss on the storage infrastructure, or worse yet, the entire storage infrastructure becomes unavailable. It is critical to have a solid backup recovery/disaster recovery plan and the next component of VI3 addresses just that.

VMware Consolidated Backup

The final add-on component for VI3 that we are going to mention here is VMware Consolidated Backup, or more commonly known as simply VCB. A major challenge with a virtual infrastructure has been backing up the environment in a specific backup window. While we will go into more details of all of the available backup options in Chapter 11, we feel it is important to mention the basics of VCB here.

VCB is a separate component that must be installed on its own physical Windows 2003 server, and no, it cannot be the same system as your VirtualCenter Management Server. When configuring shared SAN storage for use within a virtual infrastructure, the same LUNs must be made available to the VCB "Proxy" Server. With the proper SAN configuration VCB can be run in one of two ways. First, it can mount the VMDK files of the virtual machines as drive letters to the proxy server. The individual files on the VMDK can then be accessed by a typical tape backup agent and backed like any other file on the VCB proxy server. The second method that can be leveraged with VCB is as an image level backup. This mode will allow VMDK files to be backed up as image files, typical to how backups are managed using existing third party backup tools.

Figure 2- 4: DRS

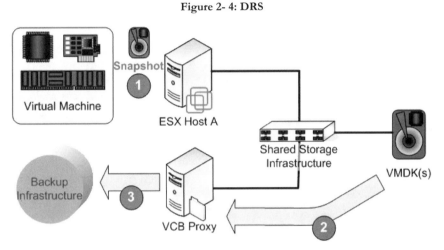

Figure 2-4 highlights the basic steps involved in a VCB backup job.

A snapshot of the virtual machine is taken. This unlocks the VMDK file(s) for use on another system.

The VMDK file(s) is mounted to a VCB Proxy server as a drive letter or a full image export is performed.

A backup server grabs the individual files or the exported image and moves it off to short or long term storage in the enterprise backup infrastructure.

The main advantage of using VCB over one of the available third party tools is that no host resources are used while backing up the infrastructure. While this may seem like the ultimate solution, there are quite a few intricacies in planning for VCB. Please make sure you blast through Chapter 11, where we will discuss this and other solutions in painstaking detail, before deciding that this is the only backup solution for you.

Now that we have described all of the things VI3 is capable of providing it is time to start digging into the details of how it works. The rest of this chapter will focus strictly on ESX Server 3. The other functionality will be fully described in the remaining chapters of this book.

ESX Server 3 Architecture

Now that a majority of the typical sales and marketing information that most people reading this book aren't interested in is out of the way, it's time to truly dig into the architecture of ESX Server 3 to see what really makes it tick. VMware ESX Server 3 is an advanced operating system with an intricate architecture. While we will not go into details of every last aspect of the internal workings, a feat that would be an entire book upon itself, we will go over the common components that are interacted with most commonly. Figure 2-5 shows a 10,000 foot view of the primary architectural components that we will discuss in this section.

Figure 2- 5: ESX Architecture

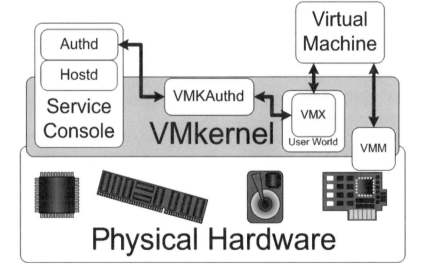

Service Console

The service console of an ESX server is commonly referred to as the Console Operating System, or COS. VMware has put forth an impressive effort to deemphasize the use of a COS in the new ESX 3 architecture and remove all references of the term from people's memory. Their long term goal is to eventually make it completely disappear entirely. To please VMware and help them in their efforts we will make every attempt to use the currently proper term "Service Console" in this book. In the event we miss an instance or two, Service Console should be considered synonymous with Console Operating System.

The Service Console is a Red Hat Enterprise Linux 3 (Update 6) based Linux distribution that is heavily modified and stripped down to provide a lightweight management interface of the VMkernel to the end user. A primary function of the Service Console is to bootstrap and turn over full control of all hardware resources to the VMkernel. The service console is assigned a default value of 272 MB of physical host memory to execute processes and manage the small amount of physical hardware that the VMkernel doesn't manage. It runs as a privileged virtual machine inside the VMkernel and is subject to resource allocation and scheduling alongside other virtual machines running on the ESX host. Overall, the Service Console is responsible for quite a few things that are vital to the proper operation of ESX.

User Interaction with ESX – The Service Console is responsible for managing the various methods to communicate with the ESX host. In order for an end user to interact directly with the VMkernel the Service Console must be used in some fashion. Several services are run in the Service Console that allow user interaction with the host using various methods such as:

- Direct Console Access

- SSH Access to the Console

- Web Management Interface (Which is also responsible for providing the SDK programmatic interface to ESX Hosts)

- Proprietary Communication Methods from 3rd Party Software

Managing Secure Access to the Host – When a user communicates to the ESX host using one of the above methods there are several security mechanisms available in the Service Console to prevent unwanted access. The Service Console manages user authentication using standard Linux authentication mechanisms. In addition, an iptables firewall is enabled by default that allows only the type of access to the system necessary for support and management. For details on properly securing an ESX host please reference Chapter 9 of this book.

Running Support Applications - There are many command line tools available that allow a user to manipulate either Service Console or VMkernel information. These applications can be used to perform most any Linux function inside the management interface. While interfacing with the Service Console you will probably run across quite a few recognizable commands that are available in any standard Linux distribution. In addition to these standard utilities VMware has provided several of their own tools to both ease Linux management and interact directly with the VMkernel for virtual machine management. Unfortunately, with VMware deemphasizing the use of the Service Console, many tools that were available in previous versions of ESX are now missing. If there is one thing that VMware should learn from Microsoft it is that you do not mess around with an administrator's command line tools because THEY feel they are no longer needed.

Manage Access to Non-Core Hardware – The VMkernel directly controls access to CPU, Memory, Disk, and Network hardware resources. In order to trim some of the fat from the VMkernel, VMware decided that any non-critical hardware resource should still be managed by the Service Console. Some devices that must be emulated on a virtual machine and accessed through the service console are:

- Serial Ports

- Parallel Ports

- USB Ports

- CD-ROM Drives

VMkernel

As previously mentioned, the Service Console is responsible for bootstrapping the VMkernel. The big question is "What is the VMkernel?"

The VMkernel is VMware's core operating system that assumes responsibility for all hardware management and resource scheduling, and other major virtualization tasks on the ESX host. The process in which the Service Console bootstraps the VMkernel is similar (but by no means identical) to the way in which Microsoft DOS was used to bootstrap Novell Netware. When the VMkernel takes over the hardware resources of the host, the Service Console is warm booted and managed as a virtual machine within the VMkernel.

The VMkernel is what makes virtualization with VMware ESX Server possible. The following is an overview of the primary functions that the VMkernel is responsible for.

Scheduling CPU, Memory, and Storage Resources – The VMkernel is responsible for scheduling and ensuring virtual machines have access to the resources they require. We will talk about several mechanisms that the VMkernel uses to prioritize resource assignment when multiple virtual machines attempt to access more resources than are available. You may also notice that the VMkernel doesn't manage network scheduling. The simple reason for that is that there is no scheduling of network resources. Due to the time sensitivity of the TCP/IP protocol, any form of delays due to scheduling will potentially cause transmission issues.

Manage Memory Page Tables – The VMkernel has some very advanced memory virtualization and tracking mechanisms that, under the proper circumstances, can actually allow you to over-allocate memory resources of a host for virtual machine utilization. We will discuss these various mechanisms in detail when we discuss memory virtualization later in this chapter.

Manage the Virtualization Storage Subsystem – In addition to having a network stack integrated into the VMkernel, the newest revision of ESX also has an enhanced storage subsystem. This has support for a limited amount of storage types and file systems. When combined with the network stack, there are several low-cost storage alternatives available that have previously eluded virtual infrastructures. Detailed specifics on storage types and file systems are highlighted in Chapter 5.

Manage the Virtualization Network Stack – Unlike previous versions of VMware ESX Server, ESX 3 has a network stack built into the VMkernel. While this increases the size of the VMkernel footprint, it opens essential functionality for low-cost storage alternatives. An additional benefit of having a network stack available directly to the VMkernel gives further flexibility to the virtual infrastructure through several virtual networking enhancements while minimizing the overhead caused from virtualization. Some of these features include, but are not limited to the following. If you do not understand all of the terms, don't worry, Chapter 6 is where all the terms will be fully described.

- Virtual Switches

- NIC Teaming

- VLAN Tagging

- Port Groups

Support for Loadable Modules – Much of the VMkernel's advanced functionality is made available through loadable modules. Having standalone modules that can be loaded into the VMkernel provide a simpler mechanism for updating the specific functional components without having to update the entire VMkernel.

Support for User World Processes – User World Processes are new to ESX 3 and are specially compiled binaries that are managed and scheduled by the VMkernel. These processes are similar to standard Linux processes with the exception that they are run in the VMkernel space and have no impact on the Service Console. The most significant benefit of this is that processes that were previously pinned in the Service Console were forced to only run on CPU0 of the physical server. Since User World applications are managed by the VMkernel, they have access to all CPUs in the physical host.

The User Worlds provide limited Linux syscall support for User World Processes. It is important to note that User Mode Processes are not standard Linux processes and must be compiled against the proper VMkernel headers to properly function. VMware has made the use of User Worlds available to members of their Community Source Program and several ISVs have begun to take advantage of this technology. Many of VMware's internal processing has also moved into the User World applications, which has lowered virtualization overhead on tasks and processes that were common in ESX 2.X.

VMX

The VMX is a User World application (vmware-vmx) and is actually the primary driver for the creation of User Worlds in the first place. In previous versions of ESX, VMX applications were run directly in the service console and were responsible for memory and CPU virtualization overhead. Now that these processes are scheduled by the VMkernel, the memory requirements of the Service Console are drastically lowered and there is no longer a tiered memory assignment/virtual machine relationship for the Service Console.

There are many functions that are often overlooked in a virtual infrastructure that are made possible by the VMX process for a virtual machine.

- Emulation of non-critical hardware resources through a Service Console Proxy (Video, CD-ROM, Serial Ports, Parallel Ports, etc)
- Bootstraps the virtual machine
- Communicates with User Interface components of ESX (Remote Console, etc)

By running "esxtop" in the service console you can actually view the various vmware-vmx worlds and how much utilization they are leveraging in the VMkernel. You may need to use the "e" command and choose a virtual machine GID to properly view the worlds, including VMX threads that are supporting that virtual machine.

VMM

The VMM, or Virtual Machine Monitor, acts as the traffic cop between a virtual machine and the VMkernel. There is one VMM process per virtual machine, and within a VMM process there is one thread per virtual CPU configured for that virtual machine. The VMM has several functions based on the type of resource being requested. The VMM has varying access to the physical hardware of the system to help enhance the overall performance of the VMkernel.

In the event that a virtual machine is requesting CPU resources the VMM determines if the instruction can be executed directly on the hardware, or if the VMkernel must be used to virtualize the call in a secure protection ring of the processor. Don't worry; we make this easier to understand in a few moments when we start talking about actual CPU virtualization.

In regards to memory, the VMM is responsible for presenting non-contiguous physical memory pages as contiguous to the virtual machine. In addition to presenting these pages, it is also responsible for maintaining maps of the "virtual" memory pages back to the physical. This tracking opens up some unique opportunities in the virtualization space that we will talk about in the memory virtualization section on this chapter.

The VMM also has the task of passing other hardware calls to their proper components. Network and storage I/O traffic is handed off to the VMkernel to be processed by their respective stacks that are built-in to the VMkernel. Non-critical hardware calls are passed by the VMM into the VMX, which emulates the hardware functionality. Hardware access of CD-ROM, Serial Ports, Parallel Ports, and USB Ports are examples of hardware devices passed to the VMX.

Like the VMX components loaded into the VMkernel, you can also see VMM processes in the esxtop Service Console application. As before, you may need to expand the world groups to properly see the various VMM threads.

Hostd

Hostd is a daemon that runs within the Service Console that is responsible for the management of the ESX host. It provides the necessary communication link between external applications like VirtualCenter and the VMkernel. Hostd uses loadable libraries to manage various aspects of managing an ESX host server such as:

- Host Information
- Host Configuration
- Virtual Machine Inventory
- Virtual Machine Control
- Organize Performance Data

As mentioned earlier, VirtualCenter communicates with the Hostd daemon when specific functions are requested that affect a host server. Additionally, applications that leverage the VMware SDK to communicate directly with a host also communicate through Hostd using a SOAP interface.

Authd/VMKAuthd

Within the ESX infrastructure, VMware needed to provide a secure mechanism to manage virtual machines and minimize the risk of external access corrupting the environment. The Authd and VMKAuthd work in conjunction to provide a secure ticketing solution that allows that secure access to the VMkernel for system management and interaction.

The Authd daemon sits in the Service Console and manages connections and authentication requests coming into the host using TCP port 902. Since we never want unsecure access to the VMkernel, the Authd process will authenticate the user requesting access, and assuming the proper credentials are specified, supplies a ticket to the remote client. In addition to assigning the ticket to the client, the Authd process also sends the ticket to a location that the VMKAuthd daemon, which is a User World process that listens on TCP Port 903, can also access. The client will communicate with the VMKAuthd daemon and the secure ticket is verified. Once the ticket is verified, the client can directly access the VMX, which if you remember also exists in the User World space. Remote console connections and virtual machine management may now occur directly with the VMX in the User World without using any Service Console resources.

The reason for the multi-step ticketing mechanism is because of the native security provided by the VMkernel and User World applications. The Authd daemon, or any process in the Service Console for that matter, has no way to directly access or turn control over to a process running in the User World. Generating a shared ticket and allowing the VMKAuthd daemon to grab it for verification is what ultimately allows the client to communicate directly into the User World space.

Now that you hopefully have a solid understanding of the magic that makes virtualization possible using VMware ESX Server 3, its time we take a look at all of the advanced functionality that the VMkernel brings. We have made several references to advanced functionality of the primary resources involved in virtualization. It's time we take an in-depth look at what all of the various VMware virtualization components opens up for your environment and how they allow you to maximize the physical resources available on your server.

Core 4 Resources – In Depth

There are four core resources that you need to strongly consider when you review and design your virtual environment. These resources are what we originally titled the "Core 4". Properly understanding and configuring these resources are essential to maintaining a stable virtual environment. This section focuses on these "Core 4" resources and how they pertain to VMware ESX Server 3 and its guests.

Processor

Assuming you are utilizing a processor that meets the requirements of ESX server, your guest will see the same physical processor that's installed on the host server through processor virtualization. By presenting the host processor type to the guest, the VMkernel does not need to perform any emulation to ensure compatibility between the virtual machine workload and the physical hardware. This information is essential when dealing with operating systems that load a different kernel that is based on a specific processor architecture. Trying to run a virtual machine's Intel instructions on an AMD processor would require emulation of the processor type and would literally destroy the performance on an ESX host with the number of processing cycles required to perform the translation.

Virtual machines are assigned virtual CPUs as they are built. Each virtual CPU acts as a slice of a physical CPU core on the ESX host. New in ESX 3 is the capability to provide up to four virtual CPUs to a single guest operating system. When we start talking about Virtual SMP a little later in this chapter, you will see why that does not equate to 4X the performance of a single virtual CPU virtual machine. Overall, any single ESX host can have up to 128 virtual CPUs active at any given time. Remember, the VMkernel requires scheduling resources for each of these virtual CPUs, and at a point the amount of overhead required for scheduling will start to degrade the overall performance of all virtual machines running on the host.

Execution Modes

ESX 3 has two different data execution modes depending on the type of workload being requested; Direct Execution Mode and Virtualization Mode. Direct Execution mode is by far the preferred method of data execution and ESX will leverage this whenever possible. This mode allows the VMM running the virtual machine to directly access physical hardware resources of the host to process data. By running an instruction directly on the underlying hardware, the VMM does not need to virtualize any processing calls and can generate near native performance of the requested instruction. The amount of instructions typically being executed in Direct Execution mode is higher than those in Virtualized Mode, but there are always exceptions. To determine the overall utilization of Direct Execution Mode calculations in a guest operating system you should look at the overall percentage of User Mode Process utilization. Direct Execution Mode is used in ESX for all processing in Protection Rings 1-3 of the CPU as shown in Figure 2-6.

Virtualization Mode is used when direct execution of an instruction is not possible. In the case of ESX Server 3.0 this is any call that requires Protection Ring 0 access to the CPU. Ring 0 of a CPU cannot be presented directly to a guest operating system in ESX. Intel and AMD are creating methods in which a virtual Ring 0 (commonly called Ring -1) can be presented to the guest for direct process execution through the VMM. ESX 3 cannot take advantage of this functionality at this point. Instead, the VMM must send the instructions to the VMkernel to execute the instruction and return it to the guest. The VMM virtualizes this process to make the guest think that it is running in an actual Protection Ring 0. Due to the fact that the instructions must be virtualized and executed within the VMkernel there is virtualization overhead associated with these calls. The amount of overhead varies depending on the type of instruction and the overall workload being processed by the VMkernel. You can tell how often a guest operating system needs to run in Virtualization Mode by capturing the total percentage of Kernel or System Mode Process utilization.

Figure 2- 6: Processing Rings

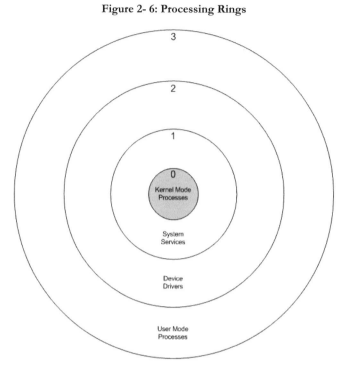

Fortunately for us, the VMM responsible for running each virtual machine knows when an instruction requires Virtualization Mode and has the capability to properly move itself into the proper execution mode. When the requirement for Virtualization Mode has been met, the VMM will move itself back into direct execution mode.

Hardware Virtualization Enhancements

As mentioned earlier Intel and AMD have new processors on the market that have virtualization enhancements integrated into the processors themselves. At this point in time VMware ESX 3.0 does support some of the functionality, but not all. As an example, in order to run a 64-bit guest operating system ESX requires the use of a virtualization enhanced processor. This allows the VMkernel, which is a 32-bit kernel to run 64-bit instructions for the 64-bit guest. Alternatively, ESX 3 does not have the capability to present a virtual Ring 0 to the guest operating system for Direct Execution Mode processing of Kernel Mode Processes.

Multi-Core

One of the greatest things to happen to processors in the recent years is the creation of Multi-Core processors. While the performance increase of multi-core processors was acceptable in ESX 2, VMware has made sure that ESX 3 is fully aware of multi-core processors and initial results show excellent performance with these new processors. One of the major challenges with multi-core processors as the chip vendors keep cramming more into less is the amount of bandwidth available for memory access. We will only continue to see performance increases with these processors if the system bus is capable of keeping the rest of the system up to speed with CPU I/O. So far, VMware has been keeping with per socket licensing as opposed to per core licensing, which has also been keeping people extremely interested in the newer processors.

Hyper-threading

Hyper-threading is an Intel technology that allows a single processor to execute threads in parallel, which Intel claims can boost performance by up to 30%. What Intel is actually doing with this technology is presenting two logical processors to the operating system for each physical processor installed. The primary use for this technology is for enhancing task scheduling in operating systems.

VMware ESX Server 3 has full support for hyper-threaded processors. The additional logical processors presented to ESX are packaged with the physical CPU and are numbered adjacently. For example, processors 0 and 1 would be physical CPU1 and its logical counterpart and processors 2 and 3 would be physical CPU 2 and its logical counterpart. This behavior is different than that displayed in a typical x86 operating system in that all physical CPUs are counted first and then the logical CPU pairs are numbered. It will be important to remember this numbering system if you attempt to use CPU affinity for pinning a virtual machine workload to a specific processor on a host.

VMware's resource scheduler is hyper-threading aware and is capable of properly balancing resource utilization across physical processors when possible. Without this intelligence it could be possible for CPU instructions to run on a physical CPU and its logical pair while a second physical processor on the system is sitting idle. The increase that a system receives from hyper-threading is dependent upon how well the application running on the system utilizes the system cache.

Be aware that some of the newer Intel processors that support multi-core processing do not have hyper-threading extensions included in the processor architecture. Please review each processor chipsets functionality before determining if hyper-threading is to be used in your environment.

Virtual SMP

As we previously mentioned, Virtual SMP is an add-on module for VI3 that provides the capability to configure multi-processor virtual machines. While Virtual SMP can provide enhanced performance to your virtual machines, there are several guidelines that should be strictly followed. Virtual SMP can just as easily negatively impact the performance of an environment.

- Administrators should never start off by configuring a virtual machine with multiple virtual processors.

- Once upgraded to a Virtual SMP virtual machine, it is extremely difficult (and in some cases impossible) to properly downgrade a Windows guest.

- Utilizing Virtual SMP slightly increases CPU overhead of an ESX host.

- Virtual SMP should only be used if an operating system and application is fully capable of leveraging SMP extensions. Single threaded applications are not Virtual SMP candidates.

While performing best practices analysis of environments we've noticed that there are quite a few people that still start off by deploying every virtual machine as a Virtual SMP system. The added virtualization overhead from this configuration can e the source of significant performance problems as the environment becomes more utilized. By only utilizing Virtual SMP on guests that are capable of taking advantage of it, the virtualization overhead of an ESX host is kept low, allowing the system utilization to be maximized.

Now that VMware has provided the capability to assign up to four virtual CPUs to a single virtual machine extreme caution must be used when virtualizing enterprise workloads. Even though VMware provides us with the ability to build enterprise level applications in a virtual infrastructure, we still feel that if that much horsepower is required that the system be built on a standalone physical machine. When host CPU workloads are pushed to their limits, there are several mechanisms that can be leveraged to make sure virtual machines get the CPU cycles they need.

Scheduling

The VMkernel was designed to provide a high level of interaction with the processors, allowing ESX to dynamically shift resources on the fly to running virtual machines. For example, if you have three virtual machines that are running in a primarily idle state on the same host as a SQL server, ESX will temporarily shift resources to the highly utilized server to accommodate its immediate needs. If a process is spawned on a low utilization server, the necessary resources are returned to the original virtual machine to effectively run the new application. Generally, a good rule of thumb is to allocate 6 virtual processors per core, although we've worked in some environments where seeing 8-10 virtual processors per physical core not out of the question. The types of processors also need to be considered when performing these sizing decisions. These numbers may be slightly lower if older hardware is being reprovisioned for virtualization, and slightly higher as new processor architectures hit the market. ESX does have a hard limit of 128 virtual processors that may be assigned within any single host. With larger systems such as 8 or 16-way hosts, this limit should be considered during the design process of your infrastructure. This limit can be broken down any number of ways mixing single processor and Virtual SMP virtual machines.

If further sharing granularity is required, ESX provides several mechanisms for manually adjusting processor allocation. This may be useful when one system requires a higher priority than others, such as a database server that is handling transactions for several different applications on the same host.

Processor Share Allocation

One of the easiest ways to modify the default processor allocations of a virtual machine within ESX is to utilize shares. Shares are a mechanism to allocate resources relative to all virtual machines running within a specific host and are used in several instances. Using this method you can assign priority to specific virtual machines when the host becomes limited on processor cycles. As you add more virtual machines to a host, the total number of shares goes up and the percentage of total shares to a particular guest goes down. A server that has 1000 shares will receive twice the priority when assigning CPU cycles as a host with 500 shares. The downside to this method is that with each new virtual machine created the allocation to existing machines decreases, which will slightly decrease their performance when the host system is under heavy load.

CPU Reservations and Limits

Within VMware ESX Server 3 you may assign a minimum (reservation) and maximum (limit) value in Megahertz for the processing resources of a virtual machine. By setting a reservation you are telling ESX to always ensure a particular virtual machine has the specified horsepower available when it needs it. This does not mean that a virtual machine must use the total reservation. If a virtual machine is sitting mostly idle, other virtual machines on the same host may use the reserved resources. If the idle virtual machine has a sudden need for CPU resources to process a workload, the reservation guarantees that the CPU cycles that were previously scheduled elsewhere are immediately available. The main thing to consider if you are going to be using CPU reservations for your virtual machines is that you must have the resources available before you can turn a virtual machine on. As an example, if you have a 4GHz processor with four virtual machines, each with a 1GHz reservation, you will not be able to power on any other virtual machines if the four machines with a reservation are all running. The default value for a newly created virtual machine is "0". This means a virtual machine has no guaranteed resources unless a reservation is set. To assign priority when virtual machines become contentious for CPU cycles and there is no reservation, CPU shares are leveraged.

Specifying a limit for a virtual machine has the exact opposite effect as setting a reservation. A limit provides a hard value in Megahertz that a particular virtual machine may not exceed. There are two key instances in which setting a limit on a virtual machine can be beneficial to the virtual infrastructure. First, by setting a limit you can tell ESX to allocate a maximum MHz value to a problematic virtual machine. This would provide a level of protection to the other virtual machines trying to compete for the same host resources as a machine that has runaway processes wasting CPU cycles. The second instance in which a limit can be helpful is for managing the expectations of application owners or developers on a low-utilization ESX host. If there are a small amount of virtual machines on a new ESX host there will be no resource contention and each VM will have access to the resources that it needs. As the host becomes more utilized by adding new virtual machines the performance of the original applications will slowly deteriorate. By setting a limit when the original virtual machines are first configured there will be no surprises later on as more VMs are introduced into the infrastructure.

Setting reservations and limits are independent of one another. You can choose to set only a reservation, only a limit, or specify both values for a virtual machine. Not setting any values gives ESX full control over the processor allocation of your virtual machines. While this is sufficient for small deployments with a low number of virtual machines, it may be crucial to manually adjust these values as the virtual infrastructure grows.

Affinity

In addition to setting processing thresholds using one of the previously described methods you can also specify which physical processor(s) the virtual machine can use. This gives you complete control of the where the processing for a virtual machine occurs. Not only can you specify that a virtual machine is guaranteed a minimum reservation of processor and that it has a high level of priority in receiving additional allocations, you can also specify the exact processor or group of processors that proves the resources. Using this methodology you have complete control over how a production infrastructure reacts on a box and can ensure that every virtual machine has the proper resources without interfering with other critical applications.

Again, processor affinity is not limited to specifying a single processor. By specifying a group of processors you can tell ESX that it is allowed to allocate resources only from the selected CPUs, leaving the remaining processors inaccessible to the virtual machine. Application servers such as Citrix servers can be pinned to different physical CPUs to minimize the amount of scheduling required for kernel level calls from multiple systems. Support servers may then be pinned to the remaining processors and be allowed to share those resources amongst each other. This allows for a layer of isolation for resource allocations. Typically, as shares are granted and removed from the entire pool of processors every guest on the host is impacted. By utilizing processor affinity, the support servers may dynamically adjust their processing resources while the Citrix servers react as if business is normal.

Using processor affinity should be considered an advanced configuration and should only be leveraged if there is a specific need. If advanced VI3 functionality such as DRS and VMware HA will be used in the environment there can be severe implications to using affinity that need to be considered. As virtual machine resources move across hosts in a pool, the affinity settings will also attempt to follow. If other virtual machines are using affinity, there may be conflicts with reservations that will not allow a virtual machine to receive all of the resources the reservation requires.

Memory

Memory easily has some of the most advanced functionality available to VMware ESX Server. Memory is used in several locations in the ESX infrastructure and VMware employs several memory saving techniques to allow for the most optimal use of the physical hardware.

VMware ESX Server requires a certain amount of memory to be assigned to the service console. Versions of ESX Server prior to 3.0 required a varying amount of memory based on the number of virtual machines that the host would run. It was not uncommon to see hosts configured with anywhere from 200-800MB of memory. In addition, environments that grew beyond expectations often had to have their memory setting changed, which required a host reboot. The reason for this dynamic memory configuration was because the Virtual Machine Monitors (VMMs) that we described earlier had to run inside the Service Console.

In the new ESX 3 architecture the VMMs now run in a User World, whose resources are assigned and controlled by the VMkernel. The default value of 272 MB of memory should be more than enough for nearly every ESX Server environment. The only time it may be necessary to increase the amount of memory in the service console is in the event that multiple monitoring or backup agents are being run in the service console. The amount of memory that must be increased completely depends on the applications and agents running.

Any memory that isn't assigned to the service console is automatically given to the VMkernel for allocation and management. The VMkernel will assign memory to each powered on virtual machine based on that machines memory assignment. In addition, each virtual machine will consume a small amount of memory for virtualization overhead. The amount of overhead memory depends on the configuration of the virtual machine itself such as the total amount of memory assigned. Alternatively, you will typically see 64 bit guests leveraging more overhead memory than 32 bit guests.

The VMkernel memory manager used some advanced techniques when allocating memory resources to virtual machines. There are several methods that the VMkernel uses to optimize the system performance, and in some cases allow a host to allocate more memory to virtual machines than is physically available to the host.

Basic Over-commitment

One of the simplest memory management techniques employed by ESX Server 3 is basic over-commitment. This method allows you to assign more memory to virtual machines than what exists on the physical host. As a simplified example, a host with 1GB of memory can have three virtual machines configured each with 512MB of memory. The premise behind this being not all memory from all virtual machines will be active at the same time. Virtual machines that are not actively using memory pages can temporarily give them to other guests that are more active. When the virtual machine that gave up the memory resources becomes more active, the VMkernel will wipe the memory pages clean and reassign them back to the original guest.

Basic over-commitment works well when the total amount of active memory doesn't exceed the amount of physical memory installed in the ESX host. When this condition is met the VMkernel must use some alternate mechanisms to allow virtual machines to continue running. Like processing resources, ESX has the capability to dynamically optimize utilization by using "shares" to provide priority to virtual machines. When memory pages become available on a highly utilized system, shares dictate which virtual machines get access to the physical memory pages and which need to use an alternate mechanism to store memory.

These methods provide basic memory management for your virtual machines. VMware ESX Server also leverages several other techniques to allow for the over-commitment and management of memory resources: Transparent Page Sharing, ballooning and swapping. While we recommend only using sharing and ballooning for production systems, swapping can be utilized to further maximize development hosts and allow more guests. Using the following techniques, it's not uncommon to achieve over allocation of 20-30% in a production environment and up to 100% in development.

Transparent Page Sharing

When a guest operating system is loaded, there are many pages in the memory space that are static and contain common pages found on all similar operating systems. The same can be said about applications that run inside the guest operating systems. The VMkernel contains a Transparent Page Table that keeps track of the memory pages in the virtual machine and maps them to the memory pages in the physical memory in which they are stored. A basic overview of this technology is highlighted in Figure 2-7.

Figure 2- 7: Transparent Page Sharing

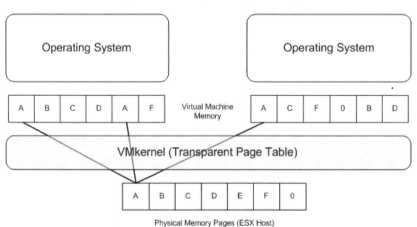

Physical Memory Pages (ESX Host)

The transparent page tables provide a mechanism to share this space among several virtual operating systems. By mapping identical virtual page numbers back to physical page numbers, guests that are using identical space in the machine page space can share these resources. This lets the system free up memory resources for over allocation without impacting any guests. The VMkernel automatically performs Transparent Page Sharing takes place automatically it is the only memory allocation method that takes place without the host running at maximum memory use.

Ballooning

When over-commitment is occurring beyond a point that Transparent Page Sharing is optimizing the system performance VMware has provided functionality to let the guest operating system decide what memory it wants to give back for sharing. This is made possible by using a memory reclamation process called "ballooning." Ballooning consists of a vmmemctl driver installed in the virtual machine that communicates with the VMkernel. This driver emulates an increase and decrease in memory pressure on the guest operating system and forces it to place memory pages into its local swap file. Once the memory is paged locally on the guest operating system, the free physical pages of memory may be reallocated to other guests. Since the ESX host sees that memory demand has been reduced inside the virtual machine it will instruct vmmemctl to "deflate" the balloon, thus reducing pressure on the guest OS to page memory. If the vmmemctl driver is not installed or running on the guest, the standard VMware swap file method is utilized. The vmmemctl driver is the preferred method of memory collection as the guest operating system gets to call its own shots.

Swapping

ESX has its own application swap file that is configured when the system is built. This file is independent of both the Service Console and page files setup within the virtual guest operating systems. VMware recommends that this swap file capacity be set to the total amount of memory that will be allocated to all virtual machines. This allows up to a 100% over allocation of memory resources using paging. This is not recommended though, as paging large amounts of data requires additional CPU resources and tends to have a negative impact on the host. When an ESX system becomes over allocated beyond the point that Transparent Page Sharing and Ballooning can recover memory, the VMkernel takes it upon itself to swap memory to the ESX page file. This differs from ballooning in the fact that the VMkernel decides what memory to swap, regardless of whether the guest is using it or not. This technique may be useful in a development environment where paging will have less of an impact on the overall performance of the environment, but should be avoided at all costs on a production host.

Idle Memory Tax

When memory share allocation takes effect, VMware provides a mechanism to prevent virtual machines from hoarding memory they may not be utilizing. Just because a particular server has four times the memory share priority than another does not mean it requires it at the time allocation takes place. VMware has a process that applies an idle memory tax. This associates a higher "cost value" to unused allocated shares than it does to memory that is actively used within a virtual machine. This allows the virtual machine to release it for use on other guests that may require it. If the virtual machine in question has a need for the memory, it still has the proper authority to reclaim it as it still has priority over the memory space. A default value of 75% of idle memory may be reclaimed by the tax.

NUMA

With the increasing demand for high-end systems today's hardware vendors needed an affordable and easily scalable architecture. To answer these needs the NUMA (Non-Uniform Memory Access) architecture was developed and adopted by several hardware vendors. NUMA functions by utilizing multiple system buses (nodes) in a single system connected by high speed interconnects. Systems that have NUMA architectures provide certain challenges for today's operating systems. As processor speeds increase memory access bandwidth becomes increasingly more important. When processors must make a memory call to memory residing on a different bus it must pass through these interconnects. This process is significantly slower than accessing memory that is located on the same bus as the processor. VMware ESX 3 is a fully NUMA aware system. These optimizations are applied using several methods.

Home Nodes. When a virtual machine initially powers on, it's assigned a home node. By default it attempts to access memory and processors that are located on its home node. This provides the highest speed access from processor to memory resources. Due to varying workloads, home nodes alone do not optimize a system's utilization. For this reason it's strongly recommended that NUMA nodes remain balanced in terms of memory configuration. Having unbalanced memory on your nodes will significantly negatively impact your system performance.

Dynamic Load Balancing. At a default rate of every two seconds, ESX checks the workloads across the virtual machines and determines the best way to balance the load across the various NUMA zones in the system. If workloads are sufficiently unbalanced, ESX will migrate a VM from one node to another. The algorithm used to determine which VM to migrate takes into consideration the amount of memory the VM is accessing in its home node and the overall priority of the VM. Any new memory pages requested by the VM are taken from its new node while access to the old pages must traverse the NUMA bus. This minimizes the impact of a guest operating system from a migration across nodes.

Page Migration. While dynamic migration of a virtual machine across nodes limits the impact on the guest, it does not completely eliminate it. Since memory pages now reside on two nodes, memory access speeds are limited by the fact that the processors do not have direct access to them. To counter this, ESX implements a page migration feature that copies data at a rate of 25 pages per second (100 kb/sec) from one node to the other. As it does this the VMkernel updates the PPN to MPN mapping of memory to eliminate virtualization overhead.

Storage

Storage in VMware ESX 3 comes in several flavors. In addition to the traditional local SCSI and Fiber attached SAN options, ESX 3 also supports new low-cost storage alternatives in the form of iSCSI and NFS. When dealing with storage for ESX 3 there are two things that need to be considered; the installation point for ESX Server itself and storage space required for storing your virtual machine data.

Install Point

A requirement of VMware ESX Server 3 is that it must be installed on a server to properly function. The installation of ESX server itself takes about 1.2 GB of storage space. You are not alone in thinking "This will not come close to filling up my 146GB SCSI drive". ESX 3 is optimized for performance and many packages that can bloat the installation are not included. Having a small storage footprint for the VMkernel and other installed packages fits perfectly into the Boot from SAN model, in which a small LUN can be presented to the host and leveraged as the installation point. This would separate the entire ESX host, including configuration files, from the physical hardware. We will go into much more detail in Chapter 5 when we discuss advanced storage planning, but feel it is important to highlight some of the primary differences between a Local install point and a boot from SAN model.

Local Installation

- Very inexpensive solution

- Easy to implement

- Eliminates external factors from affecting operation

Boot from SAN

- Separates install from hardware

- Easy recovery from hardware failure

- Better use of storage space (less wasted)

As you will see in the next chapter, there is a limit on the amount of space that can be utilized on a large local hard drive when dealing with ESX. If the decision is made to leverage local storage you are better off going with smaller but faster drives. You will also need to be prepared to waste a lot of storage space.

Virtual Machine Storage

In addition to storage space required to install and run VMware ESX Server there is also a need to dedicate storage space to virtual machines that will be run in the environment…a LOT of storage space. VMware has several supported types in ESX 3 which include: Local SCSI, SAN, iSCSI, and NFS. There are advantages and disadvantages to each solution that will be discussed in Chapter 5. As you dig further into the planning and implementation of your virtual infrastructure, you will quickly find that storage becomes one of the most expensive components in the entire environment.

VMDK Files

We say VMware requires a lot of storage for running virtual machines, but why is that? The answer lies in the virtual machine file structure leveraged by VMware ESX Server. Many people who are familiar with VMware Workstation or VMware Server (GSX) may be familiar with the practice of "Copy on Write" disks. As more data is added inside a virtual machine, the virtual machine disk file grows. This method is NOT the case inside ESX server. When a virtual hard drive (or VMDK) file is created, all space is immediately allocated. A virtual machine that has a 40GB data drive assigned to it will immediately take up 40GB of storage space on the ESX host, regardless of how much data is stored in the virtual machine.

Although we are withholding all of the good information for Chapter 5, we do feel it is important to quickly describe a VMDK file. A VMDK file is actually made up by a set of files (typically two) that acts as a physical hard drive device inside the guest operating system. Inside the virtual machine, a VMDK file appears as and is accessed like any typical SCSI drive in a physical server.

VMFS

VMware stores VMDK files inside a file system that is customized for speed and high availability called VMFS (we make an assumption that this stands for either Virtual Machine File System or VMware File System). In versions of ESX server prior to 3.0, VMFS was a flat file system with no capability to store or organize files in subdirectories. Every VMDK file was stored directly on the root of the file system. We noticed that this design made some VMware ESX implementations quite interesting when it came to data management at the VMFS level. Because VMFS was a flat file system, the only items worth storing inside a VMFS partition were either VMDK files or REDO files (which are the old name for Snapshot files, which we will discuss shortly).

ESX 3 has now introduced a new version of VMFS, which is simply called VMFS3. The file system now has a directory structure available in which subdirectories can be used to organize data per virtual machine. In addition, more information is stored within each virtual machine's subdirectory such as virtual machine configuration information and log files. Having these files available inside VMFS is what makes rebooting a virtual machine using VMware HA possible, assuming you are using a centralized storage infrastructure of course.

Snapshots

We previously made a brief mention of REDO and Snapshot files but didn't really describe them. Both REDO and Snapshot files are extremely similar. REDO files were used in versions of ESX prior to 3.0, and Snapshot files are the new standard. Since this is technically a book on ESX 3, we will leverage the use of the name "Snapshot". Creating a "Snapshot" for a virtual machine forces the VMkernel to create a Snapshot file alongside the VMDK file in the VMFS file system. As soon as this action occurs, the VMDK file is unlocked and all data changes are written to the Snapshot file. Once a Snapshot has been established, a virtual machine can be reverted to its original state, or the Snapshot data can be applied into the VMDK file. Either of these actions removes the Snapshot from the virtual machine.

New to VMware ESX 3 is the capability to create multiple branches from a single VMDK file using multiple Snapshots. We will go into more detail on this advanced topic in Chapter 5. There are actually several instances in which Snapshots can play a crucial role in your virtual infrastructure.

- Unlocking VMDK files for image level backups
- Testing application changes/upgrades before permanently applying them
- Branching several development configurations from a single template virtual machine

Network

Networking in VMware ESX 3 is another topic that is deserving of its own chapter in this book. Although Chapter 6 is completely dedicated to the advanced networking strategies of ESX 3, we feel it is important to describe some of the basic terms and give you an overview of the networking capabilities of the VMkernel. Figure 2-8 displays a basic configuration and highlights the major components involved in ESX networking.

Figure 2- 8: Network Infrastructure

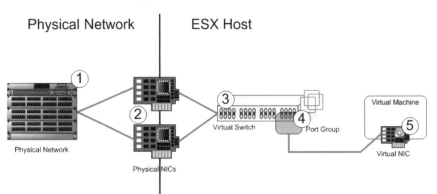

Physical Network – In order for your virtual machines to communicate with the rest of your environment the ESX hosts must be connected to the physical network. We will discuss several options in Chapter 6 to enhance performance and provide high availability to your virtual infrastructure.

Physical NIC – Multiple physical NICs can be leveraged on an ESX Server for load balancing and high availability. VMware ESX can use 10, 100, or 1000Mb networking, and VMware is currently working on support for InfiniBand networking. The maximum number of physical NICs varies based on network card vendor and speed.

Virtual switch –A virtual switch is just what its name describes—it emulates a physical switch for the guests that are configured to utilize it. From 1 to 32 physical NICs can be used to create a virtual switch on an ESX host. In addition, a special type of virtual switch can be created without any physical NICs. This type of switch will be discussed in Chapter 6.

Virtual Switches can be configured with multiple ports that again, act similarly to ports of a physical switch. When you create a virtual machine with a virtual NIC and assign it to a Virtual Switch you use one port of that virtual switch. The default number of ports assigned to a virtual switch in ESX Server 3 is 56, and the maximum number of ports that you can assign to a single virtual switch is 1016.

Virtual switches are responsible for load-balancing virtual machines across all physical NICs used to create the switch. If one physical network switch port or Physical NIC were to fail, the remaining Physical NICs in the bond that makes up the virtual switch would pick up the workload. Another feature of the virtual switch is that any traffic between VMs on the same virtual switch is typically transferred locally across the system bus as opposed to the across network infrastructure. This helps to lessen the amount of traffic that must travel over the wire for the entire host. An example of where this may be used is a front end web server making database queries to another server configured on the virtual switch. The only traffic that traverses the network infrastructure is the request from the client to the web server.

Port Group – Port Groups are logical groups of ports of a virtual switch that have common configurations. Port Groups are not assigned with a static number of available ports. Any time a virtual NIC is configured to use a specific Port Group within a virtual switch it uses one available port of the virtual switch and the Virtual NIC is added to the Port Group.

As previously mentioned, several common configurations are shared amongst all Virtual NICs assigned to the same port group. These configurations include:

- VLAN Configurations

- Security Settings

- Bandwidth Control Policies

- Load Balancing Mechanism

Virtual NIC – In order for virtual machines to communicate over the network they must contain at least one Virtual NIC. A Virtual NIC is mapped to a Port Group on a Virtual Switch which is made up of one or more Physical NICs on the Physical Network (See how it all comes together at the end?). A single virtual machine can have as many as five Virtual NICs installed. It is uncommon that a standard virtual machine configuration would need more than two NICs. We have seen some instances of virtual machines acting as routers, which would have a requirement to have a connection to multiple VLANs. The default driver presented to the virtual machine for the Virtual NIC is an enhanced version of the AMD PCNET adapter. While this adapter can run on older systems with a standard driver, the VMware Tools must be installed to take advantage of advanced functionality such as Gigabit connectivity.

This section is just a primer of what to expect in Chapter 6 where we will discuss all of the available configuration options including their advantages and disadvantages. We will also go into a bit more detail of each of the highlighted components from this introductory chapter.

Summary

If you managed to get this far then you have more than enough information to build and configure your own ESX server. By understanding the various components of ESX and how they operate, you're well on your way to managing an ESX host. In the next chapter we'll take this information and apply it to the configuration of your first ESX server. By knowing the information presented in this chapter you'll have a good understanding of the various options presented to you during the installation process and why we make the recommendations that we do. Whether you're planning an environment of 2 hosts or 50, the information in this chapter will act as a reference baseline for the rest of this book.

Chapter 3 - ESX 3.0 Implementation

Now that you have an understanding of how ESX Server works, we need to move on to making decisions about your new environment. This chapter focuses on hardware selection, hardware design, and the basics of ESX installation in your environment. It should be noted that step by step procedures for installation are found in the operations section of this book, here we are focusing on the design of the environment not the step by step configuration.

In this chapter, we'll look at the various elements affecting the performance of ESX servers. Then we'll examine various real-world server sizing strategies so that you can create your own strategy. Lastly, we'll go through the basic installation choices for ESX and describe the configuration options available to you.

ESX Server Hardware Design

Server sizing in ESX environments is quite a bit different than server sizing in traditional server environments. Since the ESX host will have multiple virtual machines simultaneously accessing the ESX server resources, the hardware tends to be much more robust than that of standard servers.

To adequately create your server sizing strategy, it's worth inspecting how server sizing works in ESX environments. To do this, we'll focus on each of the major server hardware components and how they affect the virtual environment.

Before addressing hardware, however, there are a few things that you should keep in mind.

First of all, when you design your ESX servers, you need to make sure that you have "real" server hardware. Desktop computers turned on their side do not constitute "real" hardware. VMware ESX Server has a very strict hardware compatibility list. Unlike some operating systems, you will not be able to run ESX successfully on hardware components that are not on the HCL. At this point I usually will hear the argument that since ESX is really Redhat, "We can get it to work." With ESX this simply isn't true. Even if you can get the hardware to work for the service console that is Redhat based, it does not mean that the VMkernel will recognize the hardware you are "forcing" into the system. Save yourself hundreds of hours and maybe your job, and get a server or components from the VMware HCL.

Now, let's get started with our exploration of server hardware in ESX environments. We'll begin with memory utilization.

ESX Server Memory Usage

When estimating the amount of memory you will need to account for in an ESX build, it is important to not only allow for some service console memory, but to also take into account memory sharing, over allocation of memory, and the amount of memory used by the VM's themselves. Every VM on your ESX server (that is powered on) will use some memory. The amount of "real" physical memory in use will depend on a large number of factors, all of which play into your basic design.

If ESX Server had a completely flat memory model, where no memory was shared between VM's, calculations would be simple. You would need to purchase enough physical memory for your host to supply each VM with the amount of memory you wish to assign to it and enough memory for service console operation. Some engineers actually do this to ensure that little, if any, memory swapping occurs. However since the ESX memory model is not flat and memory is shared and reclaimed in the environment, it is important that you take these memory 'tricks' into consideration.

In addition to the memory sharing, you should also take into account the types of VM's you will be hosting. Basically, you should create a list of the types of OS's you will support, the applications they will host, their environment (Prod, dev, QA etc), and the general amount of memory you wish to assign to the VM's. In Chapter 7 we discuss creating a VM standard for Memory and other configurations, but here we will describe some real world recommendations and discuss the other design attributes that go into sizing the memory on your server.

The amount of memory put into a server is closely tied to the number of processors in your system. The reasoning behind this is simple; you will create most of your estimates for number of virtual machines per host based on the number of processors in that host. This number (the number of VM's per host) will determine the amount of RAM you will need to design into that host. If you are going to use dual processor servers and are expecting 8 to 10 VM's per dual processor server, then you need to have enough memory in the server to support those 8 to 10. This is much different than using an 8-way server and expecting 45-60 VM's per host.

So how much memory is enough to support those 8 to 10 or 45 to 60 Virtual Machines? Well the design answer can be found in the following items:

- Workloads placed on the VM's and their memory requirements.
- Performance requirements for VM's (Performance SLAs).
- OS's being hosted.
- Memory standards for VM's.

Workload of the VM's

So what is a workload? Simply put, the workload is the applications or types of applications running on the VM's. Different applications (workloads) require different amounts of physical resources, including memory. But workload is much more than just the application. Imagine a development Exchange server that you use to test upgrades. This server will require less memory than a production VM hosting Exchange mailboxes for 500 users, thus there will be different loads placed on the system by these two machines.

Test and Dev Workloads mixed with production VM's

The other question about workloads is how you are going to spread them out in your environment. Some companies choose to separate the production VM's from dev and test VM's, in doing so they create specific farms or specific hosts for production and specific hosts for dev and test environments. The big advantage in this configuration is that it guarantees that test VM's will not impact the performance of production VM's (which is still kind of hard to do in a properly design environment). The obvious drawback of this model is that you could be creating an environment where all of your "eggs" are in one basket, and a single ESX server failure will increase the number of production VM's affected.

On the other side of this equation are environments that mix test and production VM's on the same hosts and within the same clusters. In this configuration, administrators generally allocate a higher number of resource shares to production VM's to help ensure that test VM's do not negatively impact production VM's. The big advantage of this model is that test and dev servers are often idle. This idle time can allow for better performance of the production VM's since fewer of the server's resources are in use all the time. Of course depending on the security or network model in your environment, this configuration (test and dev mixed with production) may not meet your requirements.

Advantages of Mixing Dev, Test, and Production Environments:
- Dev and test servers are idle the majority of the time, offering best performance for Prod VM's.

- During a host failure, a smaller number of Prod VM's are affected.

- Dev servers often require less memory resources, allowing you to allocate more to Prod VM's.

Disadvantages of Mixing Dev, Test, and Production Environments:
- A runaway process on a test box creates the possibility that performance can be impacted on a production VM.

- It may require more network ports if the prod and test networks are kept separate.

- It may not meet your company's security or network design.

The mixing of workloads and resulting improvement in overall production VM performance is a large factor in some decisions. Your VM configuration, the amount of memory you allot for each VM, and your hardware may keep you from having to install memory expansion boards in your servers, resulting in a reduction in your server costs.

Real World Recommendation: Mix workloads when possible and when security policies allow. Mix High memory VM's with VM's that require little physical memory. In addition, assign less memory, memory shares, and processor shares to test and dev VM's than you do to your production VM's.

Performance Requirements for VM's

Performance SLA's will have a large impact on the memory design in your ESX server. As stated in the previous chapter, ESX allows you to control (to some extent) how memory is shared and distributed among VM's. Memory design for your host should take into account performance SLA's for your VM's. If your VM's are required to act identically to a physical server, or as close to a physical server as possible, you may not be able to over allocate memory in your environment.

Some of this configuration may also depend on your previous decisions about mixing (or not mixing) dev and test workloads with production VM's. The idea is that you may be able to over allocate more memory if you have dev and test VM's on the host. If the host server only has Production VM's on it and your performance requirements dictate a high SLA, you may not be able to over allocate memory.

Real World Recommendation: Mix guests that have stringent SLA's and loose SLA's. This will allow you to give more shares and or allocate more memory overall to the guests that need it, without having to purchase huge amounts of memory.

Operating Systems Being Hosted

Obviously the types of operating systems being hosted will have a major impact on the memory design for the ESX Server. The memory required to host 10 Windows 2003 Server guests is much higher than the requirement for hosting 10 Windows NT Servers. Take this comparison a step farther and compare a Windows 2003 Server guest with a guest running Linux to test a simple firewall. The difference can be huge.

Recently we have been helping clients test Windows Vista at numerous sites. One item we noticed was that Vista is a complete dog below 1.5GB of memory. 1GB was barely usable, 1.5 it gets to the point of OK, and at 2GB it seemed to run fine. Compare this to a Windows 2003 Standard web server that runs just fine at about 512MB of ram.

In addition to all of this confusion, the more VM's you have that have the same types of OS's, the more you will be taking advantage of ESX's memory sharing abilities. We have found that when running all like OS's you will generally see about 20 percent memory savings due to sharing. The long and short of it is that you have to create a list of servers that will be hosted or project what will be implemented in the environment to gauge the amount of memory you will need.

Advantage of Mixing guest OS's

- Mixing guest OS's often gives you a mixed workload and therefore better performance.

- It keeps you from creating "silos" of ESX server for specific Os's.

- It creates a simple, easy to understand environment; any VM can go anywhere.

Disadvantage of Mixing guest OS's

- Savings from memory sharing will be reduced.

Memory Standards for VM's

In chapter 7 we will discuss creating a VM standard, but here we need to at least understand the theory. Much like physical hardware standards, you need to create a VM hardware standard. For memory, this will mean a standard memory configuration per type of VM being built. Much like physical hardware, people tend to over allocate memory to VM's. Often we will visit a site where the admin in charge of VM's has basically enabled every option and given every VM as many resources as possible. He may have a test Windows 2000 VM with 2GB of RAM assigned and Virtual SMP for a server that is only used to test ADSI scripts.

The problem with this type of over allocation is that it is not a linear move in cost. With a physical server 2GB of memory can be attainted very cheaply if using 512MB DIMM's. Of course to be able to support a large number 2GB VM's you will need a large amount of memory in the ESX host. This often requires that you purchase all 2, 4, or 8GB DIMM's and possibly a memory expansion board. As you can see, the cost will not be the same MB for MB.

It is important to understand and have memory standards for your environment. Once you have these standards you can use them, the workloads of the guests, OS types and environments to determine the amount of memory needed.

Real World Recommendation: Create a standard that is realistic. 2GB of memory for every VM regardless of actual requirements is not good engineering, that's called over engineering. Instead create a standard that allows you to provide good performance for all VM's and allows you to change memory configurations as needed. Often we will recommend that about 512 to 768 MB of memory per Windows 2003 VM is a good starting place. This can also be adjusted up or down depending on development or production environments (this is detailed in Chapter 5). If the server requires more memory (say 1-1.5GB), then increase the memory for that specific VM. This increase is often offset by the VM's that are running at 512 or 768MB and will keep the average at or a little less than 1GB per VM.

So Much Memory per Processor

On servers hosting nothing but production VM's, we like to recommend 4 GBs per processor core in the host ESX Server. Note that it says CORE not just processor. This falls nicely in line with the average of 4 VM's per processor core that most environments see. Additionally, when factoring in the memory allocated to the Service Console, memory saved through sharing, and any lost to virtualization overhead, you still will be able to allocate an average of a GB or so per VM. If you expect to allocate more than this, up the memory. I recently completed a project where we used 24GB of memory in dual core, dual processors servers. This equated to 6GB of ram per core, and about 1.5GB per VM on average.

If you plan on running development or test VM's only, then you have the ability to run a much higher ratio of VM's to processors. In addition, you can more easily over allocate memory to VM's in test and dev environments since these servers are often idle and performance is not as important as it is in production environments. We have found that in a number of test environments the average ratio is about 5 to 7 VM's per processor core.

The long and short is that we like the 4 GB range per processor core for most environments. It allows you enough memory to host production VM's and still allows you the flexibility to over allocate for test and dev environments.

ESX Server Processor/Core Usage

When it comes to sizing ESX Server processors and cores, don't take the time to beat yourself up over the difference between 2.8 and 3.2 gigahertz processors. Processor speeds (clock speeds) are dictated by Intel, AMD and the hardware vendors, and you're pretty much forced to take what they offer. While speed itself can be important, the real decisions should be made around processor and system bus architectures and the number of processors / cores per processor per host. In most cases, you need to figure out whether your server will be a dual or quad processor blade, a standard dual, a quad-processor chassis, Eight-way, or maybe even a 16 processor box. Then toss on top of that whether you want to run dual core or a quad core system.

In deciding how many processor cores you want in your servers, keep in mind that you will have to find a balance between number of cores in a server, the amount of VM's hosted per server, and the number of ESX servers you are willing to manage. Also consider the amount of risk associated with a hardware failure on your ESX host. There is a big difference between a 16 processor host failing with 80 or 90 VM's on it and a dual processor dual core host going down with only 16 VM's on it.

Each VM will have to share processor time with the other VM's. Even if a VM is doing nothing at all, servicing no requests, hosting no files, etc., some processor will be used. In this design, if one VM does not need much processor time, then more processing power is available for other VM's. Due to the way ESX server shares the processor and the fact that each VM's processor requests can (by default) be executed on any processor on the server, it is fairly easy to scale up ESX. But one thing to remember is that the more processors you have, the greater your risk of running into a bottleneck in another part of the system.

In a perfect world, your processor utilization would constantly be in the 80 percent range. This would indicate that you didn't waste money buying too many processors, but also that no VM's are waiting for processing bottlenecks.

Single core Vs. Dual core Vs. Quad core Vs. AMD vs. Intel....

Which one to get? AMD dual core, Intel Dual core, Intel VT dual core, AMD V dual core, Intel quad core.... The reality is that there are numerous (read- way too many) white papers, spec sheets, opinion articles, and blogs out on the Internet right now detailing which is better, which manufacturer is better, why clock speed is not as important as bus speed, why Intel beats AMD, why AMD beats Intel, blah blah blah.

In the real world of x86, the operational world where most of us happen to live, we wouldn't notice the difference between an AMD and Intel processor that are both dual core with similar clock speeds on a similarly configured server. Sure we could throw a bunch of math at them to determine how long they take to finish a certain task, or run SQL and Exchange load tests at them to find their minute differences, but the reality is that a good processor in an ESX server is a good processor. After that it really comes down to cost and personal preference. But, for argument's sake, to get some people their fill, cause a stir in the forums, and a rise in hate e-mail we receive, we will discuss the "multiple core" question here, what makes a good ESX processor and possibly some processor virtualization while we are at it.

Multiple Core Processors

These days there is much talk about multi-core processors. The advent of which really came from the increasing difficulty at making a single core processors faster. Remember that in 2004 you could purchase a 3.0 GHz Pentium processor, well you still can in 2007. So manufacturers of processors turned to two major strategies to improve (read- sell) more processors. The first was to continue to integrate new improvements onto the processors for things users use like multi-media functions. The second was to continue to increase the speed/performance of the processor by adding more cores to a single processor essentially doubling the number of threads that could run at any instant and allowing more cycles to be executed.

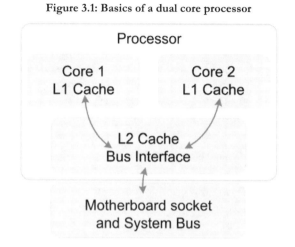

In figure 3.1 we show the basic concept behind a dual core processor. A single processor contains two independent cores. These cores interact with the system through a single bus interface (for good or bad) and share and L2 cache. From an ESX perspective the increase in the number of cores per CPU socket is a good thing. Knowing how VM's are scheduled on the processor, and understanding that each core looks and acts like a unique processor, you can see that an increase in cores allows for you to simultaneously execute more virtual machines on a single socket. This of course can increase the number of VM's you can run on a specific system or decrease the cost of the system by reducing the number of processors you need to purchase. An additional benefit of this is that VMware licenses ESX Server per Socket, not per core. Eventually this may change, but right now it is allowing you to get near quad processor consolidation ratios for the cost of a dual processor license. Buy it while the buying is good!

At the time of writing (end of 2006 beginning of 2007) dual core processors are very prevalent and quad cores are being introduced into most server lines. Maybe by the time you read this sentence, 8 core processors will be available. What you need to determine is the number of cores you want to put in a server and this decision is a balance between the number of cores and amount of memory in the system. Too many cores and you run out of memory before processor, too few cores and you have a processor bottle neck.

One point that should be made is that a core is not a processor. Based on the concept above, you can see that the cores do need to share the bus interface, meaning, that while a dual core processor offers you more processing power than 1 single core processor, it may not run even in performance to two single core processors. As for quad cores, well the verdict is still out on those at this time. Our first recommendation would be to never run a single Processor system with ESX no matter the number of cores. If you have the option of a single proc quad core or a dual proc dual core, buy the latter.

Most architects design their ESX systems using 4 to 16 cores per host. Using an average of 4 to 5 VM's per core you can accommodate (generally) 16 VM's on a 4 core system about 32 on an 8 core system (some customers see higher ratios, some lower). Designs using 4 to 8 cores per server tend to be a good balance among the number of VM's per host, cost of the host, and number of hosts that have to be managed.

Dual core, dual processor systems (4 total cores) are generally the most cost effective as you are using a traditional 2 processor chassis that is pretty inexpensive. As quad cores become more prevalent (and the cost comes down) it will be possible to get 8 cores in this chassis as long as the amount of memory you need is not outrageously priced.

If you want scale with large servers, the quad processor, quad core servers (like the HP DL 585 using AMD processors) have had excellent results as ESX hosts. The memory needs in these systems are extremely high and in some cases you may have to choose slower memory to get the required amount installed into your systems. The up side of these systems is that they can host a TON of virtual machines. I have personally seen a series of 585's with 48 GB of ram running live VM's up into the high 40s and low 50's. That's a serious consolidation ratio.

AMD vs. Intel

This is kind of like "pick your religion." Personally I am an AMD fan. I like AMD because I like to be different, and I believe in the concepts behind their memory architecture and that it may make an impact on my ESX environment. That being said I have done more projects with Intel processors and have never seen a case where either processor showed a significant advantage in number of

VM's hosted on a like configured system. Pick your processor and enjoy, worry more about the three C's: cores, cache, and cost.

Virtualization at the processor level

Where to begin, where to begin? I guess the first place to begin is that ESX 3.0 does not care about processor virtualization. It doesn't use it, doesn't care if it's there. ESX was designed, built, and in production long before the Intel VT and AMD V were in real silicon. In the current rev of ESX it actually is SLOWER for them to use the virtualization at the processor than to continue to execute Ring 0 calls the way they do now.

It is my assumption that in the future VMware will find a way to take advantage of these hardware changes, but the reality currently is that V and VT were put in place for use by Xen Source systems and possibly Microsoft's next virtualization platform.

Real-World Processor Recommendation

Processors are very fast and very cheap. Buy systems with at least 4 cores possibly 8. Never buy a system using a single socket; start at dual processors (multi-core) and work your way up. Stay in the 4-8 core range, and you are safe. If you venture into the 16 or 32 core per server arena be prepared to spend a ton of cash on memory. It can work, it's just expensive.

ESX Server Hard Drive Usage

In most environments your ESX server hard drive configuration will depend on your company's storage strategy (if they have one). The hard drive configuration for your ESX host will look extremely different if you plan on using SAN or NAS for storing VMDK files instead of local storage. In Chapter 5, we discuss storage design, if you plan on designing your SAN solution for ESX based on this book, you may want to jump ahead after reading this. This section will purely focus on the local drives and partitions for the ESX host.

In the 2.5 version of ESX, VMware introduced its boot from SAN feature. This feature was pretty much made for the Blade servers now being implemented by many organizations. Personally, I feel that boot from SAN is really not needed in the ESX world. If done correctly with a SAN your ESX server becomes an appliance that executes VM's but does not store or configuration information. Knowing this and knowing that storage on the SAN is generally so much more expensive than local storage, using the SAN for the OS of an ESX server (including swap space and all) is pretty much useless, but that's just my opinion.

Because of the way that hard drives are typically used in ESX environments, you don't need very much storage space on individual servers. Typically VMDK files are stored on a SAN solution, and the only things that are stored locally are the console operating system and its own configurations. In ESX 2.5 local VMFS based swap was used for VM swapping. This has been moved to the VMFS volume hosting the VM's (generally on the SAN). Also in 2.5 the VM configurations also were stored on the host. These too have been moved to the SAN. The ESX servers (over several versions) have become more and more appliance like.

In general, a mirrored set of drives will work for almost any installation using SAN for its VM storage. If you are going to use local disk to store VMDK's then you should plan on a couple of large raid volumes. Maybe a mirrored set for the ESX Service Console and a large raid 5 volume for VMFS storage.

Storage Installation Options

One of the first steps in the ESX setup process is configuring the installation of the console operating system. Based on a combination of VMware best practices and our personal experiences with VMware, we recommend a partitioning scheme that will create a very flexible environment regardless of how you move forward with ESX. Below is a table that is duplicated in the Operations Guide, these are our recommendations and notes, but may need to be adjusted based on your specific requirements.

Mount Point	File System	Fixed Size	Size in MB	Force to Primary	Purpose
/boot	ext3	X	250	X	Core Boot (img) files
n/a	swap	X	1600	X	Swap for Service Console
/	ext3	X	5120	X	Main OS location
/var	ext3	X	2048		Log files
/tmp	ext3	X	2048		Temporary Files
/opt	ext3	X	2048		VMware HA Logging
/home	ext3	X	2048		Location of users storage
NA	vmkcore		100		VMkernel Panic Location
	vmfs	Fill to remaining disk if you want			Local storage is only required for VM Clustering

ext3

EXT3 is the primary file system of Linux. As the Service Console is based on Redhat Linux it is the one we will use. There are two other propriety file systems which are only accessible by the VMkernel. These are vmkcore and VMFS version 3. We will cover VMFS in more detail after the install has completed in the storage chapter.

/boot

This is where core boot files with an img extension are stored. After powering on ESX, the master boot record is located and boot loader is run. In the case of ESX 3.x this is now the GRand Unified Bootloader (GRUB). GRUB then displays a menu which allows you to select what .img to execute. Img files are image files and are bootable. They are analogous to ISO files which can also be bootable. I've doubled the VMware recommendation to err on the side of caution. Previous VMware recommendations have made this partition too small. This gave people problems when upgrading from ESX 2.x to ESX 3.x through lack of disk space.

/swap

This is where the Service Console swaps files if memory is low. I've chosen to over-allocate this partition. The default amount of memory for the Service Console is 272. VMware usually takes this number and doubles it to calculate the swap partition size (544MB). The maximum amount of memory you can assign to the Service Console is 800MB. This is how I derived the 1600MB value. This means if we ever choose to change the default amount memory assigned to the Service Console – we do not have to worry about resizing the swap partition. It doesn't have a mounting point as no files from the administrator are copied there.

/ (referred to as the "root" partition)

This is the main location where the ESX operating system and configuration files are copied. If you are from a Windows background, you can see it a bit like the C: partition and folders coming off that drive like C:\Windows or C:\Program directory. If this partition fills, you may experience performance and reliability issues with the Service Console, just like you would with Windows or any other operating system for that matter.

/var

This is where log files are held. I generally give this a separate partition just to make sure that excessive logging does not fill the / file system. Log files are normally held in /var/log. But occasionally hardware vendors place their hardware management agent log files in /var.

/tmp

In the past, VMware has recommend using a separate partition for /tmp – which I have always done in ESX 2.x as well. As I have plenty of disk space I have made this larger than it really needs to be.

/opt

Several Forum members have seen the /opt directory fill up very rapidly and then fill the / partition. This location is also *sometimes* used as a logging location for hardware agents. In VMware HA has been seen to generate logging data here as well. So I create a separate partition for it to make sure it does not fill the / partition.

/home (Optional)

Technically, you don't need a separate partition. In the past VMware recommended one for its ESX 2.x in production. This was due to the fact that VM's configuration files such as the vmx, nvram and log were stored in /home. In ESX 3.x all the files that make up a VM, are more likely to be located on external storage. I still create it for consistency purposes – and if I have users on the local ESX server those users are more likely to create files there – than in a directory coming off the / partition.

vmkcore

This is a special partition used only if the ESX VMkernel crashes, commonly referred to as a "Purple Screen of Death.." If that happens then ESX writes debugging information into this partition. After a successful boot the system will automatically run a script to extract and compress the data to a "zip" file in /root. This file with tar.gz extension can be sent to VMware Support who will endeavour to identify the source of the problem. These PSODs are normally caused by failures of RAM or CPU. You can see a rogue's gallery of PSOD's at

http://www.rtfm-ed.co.uk/?page_id=246

vmfs

VMFS is VMware's ESX native file system which is used for storing all the files of the VM, ISO's and templates. Generally, we use external storage for this. The only case for using local storage for your VM's is when you do not have access to external storage. So here I am assuming you have access to external storage, and therefore, you have no need for a local VMFS partition.

Hard Drives and Controllers

Obviously the hardware on the ESX host should be utilized to its fullest extent. One of the most under-designed aspects of the server is often the drives and controllers in the host. New VMware admins tend to load up on memory and processors at the expense of really hot disk controllers and fast drives. Depending on the load placed on your ESX server you may want to investigate implementing separate controllers for the service console and the local VMFS partitions. If you plan on storing VMDK files locally, this is probably a good idea and will separate traffic bound for the VM VMDK's and increase your overall performance. If you are not going to store VMDK's locally, then local disk design is not as important. The local disk will essentially only be used by a single system (the service console), and 99% of the writes to this disk will be log files. Use a simple RAID 1 and maybe a hot spare, and your service console will be well covered. A RAID 5 is obviously possible, but it could be over kill as you are adding a lot of disk space for an OS that will only consume 5-10GB.

On the controller side of things it is probably a good idea to use a hot SCSI controller with at least 128MB of cache of using local VMFS. Most of the off the shelf RAID controllers from HP and IBM now come with 64 or 128 MB of cache. It is also important to ensure that the write cache is enabled. I have seen certain instances where these settings have come from the manufacturer disabled, and I hate paying for things that I don't get to use.

If you are using local storage for your VMDK files and would like to separate them to a separate controller, but still save some money, your best bet is to use the integrated RAID controller for the service console and the additional RAID controller for the VMFS partition that will host VMDK files. If separate controllers are not possible, then shoot for a different SCSI BUS on a local controller.

As a final thought on this, we should probably talk about drive speed. There is often an argument between buying 10K or 15K drives. My opinion is up in the air. If the local drives are only used for the service console, I would say it is ok to use 10K drives and save the money. If you are going to use local disk to host the VMDK files it wouldn't hurt to move up to 15K drives for everything. This will help to ensure optimal performance for your guest VM's and doesn't add too much cost to the overall system.

PCI Cards and PCI Slots

One of the common mistakes most engineers make when designing their hardware is choosing hardware (a form factor or model) before defining all their requirements. The engineers (or sales guys from some hardware vendor) focus on Processors, Cores, and amount of memory. But they skip the number of PCI slots, type of slots, and what you really need in the system.

For example, let's assume you have decided (after reading the book) to have 2 fiber HBAs for redundancy and two dual port nics along with the two onboard nics. This is a total of 2 fiber ports and 6 network ports on your server. Ideally (for redundancy purposes) you would maintain separate HBA's instead of getting one dual port HBA and have 2 dual port NICs instead of one quad port nic. But you have ALREADY chosen (or have had dictated to you) a model of server that only has 3 PCI slots... you obviously cannot fit 4 PCI cards (two HBA's and two NIC's) into three slots, so you wind up either with a single point of failure on the NIC's or on the HBA's and this could have been alleviated by simply defining these types of items prior to picking hardware.

PCIe,x,y,z, oh me, oh my...

So which to use and what to look for? Once you have start to dig into the PCI slots on your proposed server you will notice a number of options or specs around the PCI slots in your system, such as PCIe or PCI Express and PCI-X. Often confusing, you would think these hardware guys could come up with a better name. Anyway, PCI-X is the slower of the two and essentially is based on PCI, kind of like a PCI version 2 but PCI is 64bits wide as compared to the original PCI that was 32bit. PCI-X is even backward compatible and able to accept older PCI cards. Essentially this "older" technology is slower and shares available bandwidth on the bus. PCI Express was developed to solve some of the issues with PCI and PCI-X specifically around IO and dedicated bandwidth.

PCI-Express is a whole new ball game from a motherboard/performance perspective. While PCI-X may have similar throughput numbers on the speed side,

PCIe has a distinct advantage when you start to use multiple cards on the same bus (back to our design with multiple nics and HBA's) and can handle multiple simultaneous IO operations much better than PCI-X due to bandwidth allocation and interfaces for each PCIe device.

The long and short is the PCI-Express should be used where possible in ESX servers. If you have only a limited number of PCI-Express slots use them for your storage controllers/HBAs, and use the PCI-X slots for the NIC cards.

If you do not have the option of using PCI-Express and are stuck with PCI-X or limited PCI slots, not to worry. While one is better than the other it doesn't mean your system won't perform well, it's just not optimal but will more than likely perform just fine.

ESX Server Network Connectivity

Each ESX Server should, at a minimum, have at least 2 network cards. While it's possible in ESX 3.0 to run with only one NIC almost every server on the planet comes with 2 onboard nics. In a 2 NIC configuration both cards assigned will provide redundancy to the other with one card acting as the primary for the service console and another acting as the primary for Virtual Machine use. While this configuration will function, and provides a little redundancy, it limits other network based functions (like VMotion) that you may want to use and does not allow for physically separate management networks for the service console. For a minimal configuration with redundancy and VMotion functionality, you may want to design at least a 4 NIC configuration as seen in Figure 3.2.

Figure 3.2 Typical ESX Server Network Configuration

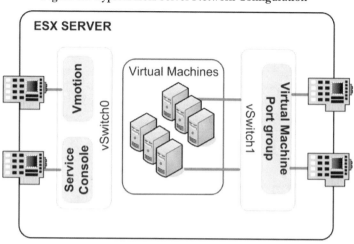

Service Console NIC Configuration

Referring to Figure 3.2, the two nics on the left are configured as part of a single virtual switch. One nic is utilized by the service console for management tasks. ESX management by virtual center, interaction with the console via SSH, etc. A port group policy (better explained in the networking chapter) is used to config-ure this nic as the primary nic for the service console. VMotion functions are assigned to another using the service console nic for failover. This would re-quire that that VMotion traffic run across the production network (not as big a deal as it might seem) and if you isolate the traffic with VLAN's that port trunk-ing be configured on the upstream physical switch ports.

Virtual Machine Port groups and Switches

In this example, the two network cards on the right combined are both config-ured as active NIC's on a single virtual switch. This configuration not only sup-plies additional bandwidth to the VMware guests, but also provides fault tolerance in the event of a NIC or upstream switch failure. It is important to size these NIC's appropriately. In this configuration we often use Gigabit net-work cards. Using 100 MB as a baseline for each VM, this configuration easily supplies enough bandwidth for 16 - 20 VM's. For sizing purposes it is good to assume at least 1 Gig NIC per 5-10 VM's. If fault tolerance is required, you will have to make a decision about bandwidth availability during a NIC failure. Is it acceptable for say 16 VM's to run from a single GB NIC if one NIC fails?

From a real world perspective I personally have looked at the utilization on 1000's of servers during consolidation analysis engagements. Generally only about 1 % ever average more than 1 or 2 Mb of utilization. Sure, a handful of heavier used servers will use more, but most traffic is intermittent with VERY short spikes of any real utilization. You will be able to see this once you analyze your own environment carefully.

Virtual Switch

While it is possible to assign standalone physical nics to virtual machines for network connectivity, there is no redundancy involved. If the NIC or connection were to fail, the guest operating system would not be able to talk to the network. To prevent this downtime, ESX allows you to create virtual switches (alluded to before). These virtual switches allow you to bond or team up to 32 physical nics for use by virtual machines. For more detailed information on VM networking please jump to Chapter 6. For now, you just need to understand that you will need at least 1 virtual switch in your environment.

Real-World Network Connectivity

We definitely recommend a minimum of a three NIC configuration for most production systems. If you plan on implementing VMotion, then a fourth NIC should be used to isolate that traffic away from the NIC's used by the VM's. If you are planning to implement servers that are larger than 4-ways, you may want to look into adding another two network ports to accommodate the amount of bandwidth that will be required by the VM's or you may need to add nics to connect to separate physical networks you need to support. A good rule of thumb is 8 to 12 VM's per Gigabit network card dedicated to VM's. If you are looking at an eight core server and possibly 30, 40 or more VM's, you should have at least two and possibly three or four NIC's dedicated to VM's.

As an alternative, you can break this down into bandwidth requirements if you wish to get very granular. This requires that you estimate the amount of bandwidth required by each VM, then add that total up to determine the number of

NIC's you need. Obviously we have done this assuming 100MB or a little less per VM in using the 8-10 VM's per NIC.

Real-World Sizing Strategies

Now that you know the basics of how server hardware components work in ESX environments, you need to think about your strategy for sizing your servers.

The objective is simple: you want to build your servers to be big enough to support your VM's and keep the number of hosts you need to manage down to a reasonable level, while still making the servers small enough that you don't break the back purchasing them.

At first, this statement may seem extremely obvious. Nevertheless, there's plenty to think about when you get ready to size your servers.

Why Should You Care About Server Sizing?

Server sizing is not about buying the fastest processors and the most memory. When it comes to server sizing, the maximum number of VM's a server can support is less important than the cost for each VM on that ESX server. If you build a 16 core server that can handle 64 VM's, but two 8 core servers would have cost you 25 percent less and would have handled just as many VM's, you may find yourself out of a job. In addition, server sizing is finding a balance between hosting as many VM's as possible, while still maintaining a manageable number of hosts and keeping the cost per VM at a reasonable level.

A proper server sizing strategy involves creating a balance between too many small servers and too few large servers. For example, it's possible to build a sixteen core server with 64 gigabytes of memory. But just because you can build one gigantic server for all of your VM's, should you? There are plenty of servers out there that have 48-64 VM's on them; however the cost per VM in these solutions begins to rival the normal cost of adding a blade into a blade chassis.

Server Sizing Options

By building several smaller ESX servers, you're able to increase the redundancy of your ESX environment. In this strategy you not only build in redundant components but build redundancy through the number of systems. If you build one gigantic $60,000 server and something happens to it, all of your VM's are down. However, if you build three $20,000 servers and you lose one, only one-third of your VM's are affected.

Your server environment will ideally balance between the two extreme options:

- Build a few gigantic servers.

- Build many small servers.

Our recommendation - take the middle road.

Option 1: Build a Few Gigantic Servers

Drive space, processors, and memory are so incredibly inexpensive these days that many people are transfixed by the idea of creating a few massive servers that can each support tons of VM's. They like the concept of only having a few servers to manage and the fact that they can spend money on large chassis, redundant drives, processors, tons of memory, NIC's, power supplies, etc.

The general issue here is that the price / performance ratio of big servers might not be there. When looking at building large servers (read- 8 and 16 processor servers – potentially with multiple cores), the cost per VM when compared to a similarly configured 4-way may be 25 percent more. Of course a benefit of having large ESX servers is that you have fewer ESX servers to manage. This will reduce time spent for monitoring the host, patching, upgrading and managing the host, and of course reduce the "number" of servers in the datacenter.

Advantages of Building a Few Gigantic Servers
- Fewer hosts to manage and monitor

- Less time spent upgrading and patching hosts

- Large chassis always have plenty of PCI and memory slots for all the additional components you need to jam into an ESX Server

Disadvantages of Building a Few Gigantic Servers
- Single point (or fewer points) of failure

- Possibly an increase in cost per VM

Option 2: Build Many Small Servers

Instead of building a few gigantic servers, you might choose to build a large number of smaller servers. This option lessens the risk that one system's failure could take out a significant number of your VM's.

When thinking about building multiple smaller servers, two advantages become apparent: redundancy and scalability. Because you have multiple servers, you could lose one without a large part of your environment being down. (This means that you might not get paged if this happens, allowing for a full night's sleep.) Also, you can schedule servers to be taken down for maintenance or to be rebooted without affecting large portions of your environment.

Furthermore, you might be able to support more VM's with the same amount of money. Or, you could look at this as being able to save money. Many ESX administrators also like the fact that building multiple small servers gives them more flexibility to dynamically deploy and re-deploy VM's as requirements and resource needs change.

Another benefit in favor of multiple, smaller servers, is the ease with which servers are managed and provisioned today. Many companies are leveraging blade servers to build large farms of redundant servers. (Think of it as "RAIS"—Redundant Array of Inexpensive Servers.)

Advantages of Building Many Small Servers
- Redundancy

- Often a lower cost per VM

- Flexibility, redeploy applications and move them around as needs shift

Disadvantages of Building Many Small Servers

- Some utilization might be wasted

- Additional ESX hosts to manage

- Really small servers tend to be limited by number of PCI Slots or amount of memory you can install

Option 3: Build Servers in the Middle Ground

Finally, you have the option to move into the middle ground. Instead of going to either extreme you can find a middle ground like a quad processor server or even a dual processor dual core server. In a number of engagements we have found that the quad processor and dual processor multi-cores are the "sweet spot" when comparing price, performance, and manageability.

With all else being equal, quad processor servers often fall right into an environment's sweet spot. Quad processor servers are more of a commodity than the 8- and 16- processors servers, which lowers their prices when compared to the larger servers. In addition, they often have the flexibility in their design to allow you to configure Network cards, HBA's, and other components for your environment. This is often a huge advantage over blades and 1U's.

One big recommendation we can make is not to make a chassis selection until you design your network and storage solution. Often in designs with clients, they want to jump right to the selection of the specific model of server. We generally steer them back to deciding the number of NIC's, types of redundancy option, number of HBA's etc. Then, once we have that information you can say for sure how many PCI slots you need, and what type. This more often than not dictates the servers you can buy. When this is done in reverse, I have seen clients purchase servers with only 3 PCI slots, then want to have full NIC redundancy for 2 additional dual port nics and have 2 Fiber Channel HBA's- four PCI cards in a three PCI slot chassis.

Generally, the disadvantage seen in quads or large dual core duals is either from a political front where someone is set on one technology over another, or the fact that your ESX environment will still be too small for quads and would be better off with just a couple of small chassis dual processors.

Advantages of Building Mid-size servers
- Often sweet spot for price per VM

- A good balance between number of VM's and number of hosts

- As flexible as small servers if your environment is large enough

Disadvantages of Building Mid size servers
- Might not provide enough redundancy in smaller environments

- Additional ESX hosts to manage when compared to large servers

Installation Alternatives for Host Servers

The first step in designing your host build is to determine what is going into your base build. Regardless of whether you hand build each ESX host or you script the entire process you need to determine what you want to accomplish with the script or the build check list. Below is a list of some of the common items/tasks in the build process and in some cases (like for the agent installs) our notes on their installations:

- Hardware agents from HP, Dell or IBM

- Management and Monitoring Agents

- Anti-virus, if you must

- NTP Configurations

- Authentication modules

- Firewall settings

At a minimum we recommend you have a solid base ESX build that includes a step for installing hardware agents, NTP configuration, external authentication configuration and of course modifications of the firewall settings to make these items possible. Anti-virus, third party management or monitoring agents are always nice to have in the host system but not a full fledge requirement unless dictated by your company policy.

Basically, for the build you have three options: script the build, build by hand, or use image based builds. We outline the build options below.

Scripted Installations

Scripted installations can cover many alternatives from using a basic VMware created kickstart installation, a custom kickstart file you have created with follow up shell scripts, or scripted builds based on deployment tools like Altiris. In any of these scenarios the goal is the same; to create a repeatable installation process that removes the "human factor" from the build. A side benefit of this is that process is quicker than a normal hand installation since no one is stopping to read a document or checklist or looking for media to put in the CD drive.

The drawback of using scripted installations (in most shops I have been in) is that there are only a handful of people, if not a single person, that has the ability to edit the files. Scripting and maintaining scripted installations of ESX will require a basic knowledge of kickstart and shell scripting for Linux. Generally ESX Server is found in predominately Windows environments, and the staff lacks this knowledge. If you plan on going down this route I suggest getting a book on Linux scripting (specifically something that covers shell and kickstart basics).

Advantages of scripting the installation
- Creates a repeatable installation that removes the human factor
- Can create a build process that is faster than being built by hand

Disadvantages of scripting the installation
- To do it right it takes a basic knowledge of kickstart and shell scripting
- Has to be maintained and possibly requires numerous scripts for numerous hardware platforms

The Operations Guide section of this book (specifically the command line chapter) has the specific step by step process for creating an unattended install. We debated having processes in for deployment tools like Altiris, but decided that keeping up with changes in various products and individual environments may be a bit too much to bite off.

Hardware Agents (Dell, HP and IBM)

While most small organizations don't take often take advantage of tools like HP SIM, Dell Open Manage, or IBM Director, we firmly believe that you should in your ESX environment. Now that you are designing this consolidated environment where 10, 20 or even 40 guests may be operating on a single server, a failure on that server's hardware becomes more of a problem than a hardware failure on a single server. In most instances these tools will allow you to be notified of the issue, if not notified PRIOR to the issue becoming a full fledged failure of the system.

I have actually received calls from people (and you may have seen this too) where they had a server with a RAID 5 configuration loose a drive. They never noticed it in a system console (no monitoring tools installed) and never saw the red light on the front of the drive. The server continued to run just fine because that is what RAID was intended for. Of course it ran just fine until the second drive failed and the system crashed. Wouldn't it have been nice to know that was coming?

Anyway, below we show some install steps for each of the three major hardware vendors. These steps were tested on a base ESX 3.0 build and the version of the agent has been noted. I recommend you check your vendor and VMware's websites to determine the latest agent you should be running as these agents sometimes change on a monthly basis. Also note that these are listed in alphabetical order... we have no preference. ;-)

Thanks to the RapidApp Engineering team that put together these steps on agent configurations for different vendors.

Dell OpenManage Agent

As of this writing Version 5 is the only version certified to run on ESX 3. The agent comes as a tar ball so you will need to copy it from a central location or mount up the CD on the host (Either of which can be scripted.

HP SIM Agents

As of this writing the current version for ESX 3.0 HP Insight Management agents are 7.5.1.A. Like all agents, as this changes, these instructions may change but could act as a good starting point. To install the Insight Management agents, download or copy the hpmgmt-7.5.1a-vmware.tgz to the ESX 3.0 tmp directory. Untar the file by typing:

tar -zxvf hpmgmt-7.5.1a-vmware.tgz

or

srvadmin-services.sh start

To check to see if the agents are running point your browser to:

https://fully.qualified.name.com:2381

IBM Director (VMM)

In order to install the IBM Director agents, you need to open the ports needed for the agent, perform the installations, then start the agents. It should also be noted that IBM Director has a module called Virtual Machine Manager (VMM) that integrates with the VMware VirtualCenter application. We recommend you configure both the host and VirtualCenter portions detailed below.

To enable the ESX firewall for ibm director:

esxcfg-firewall ---enableservice ibmdirector

HP SIM Agents

As of this writing the current version for ESX 3.0 HP Insight Management agents are 7.5.1.A. Like all agents, as this changes, these instructions may change but could act as a good starting point. To install the Insight Management agents, download or copy the hpmgmt-7.5.1a-vmware.tgz to the ESX 3.0 tmp directory. Untar the file by typing:

tar -zxvf hpmgmt-7.5.1a-vmware.tgz

from tmp/hpmgmt/751/ console prompt type:

./installvm751.sh

srvadmin-services.sh stop

or

srvadmin-services.sh start

To check to see if the agents are running point your browser to:

https://fully.qualified.name.com:2381

Conclusion

As you can see, defining what will be installed on your server is very important (there are tons of options). The Operations Guide has steps for installing all of the "normal" configurations such as NTP, firewall settings and authentication modules. Once you have nailed down what you want installed on your hosts, jump on ahead to the operations guide to build your scripted installation (don't worry, it's a script, you can always modify it later)

Chapter 4 - VirtualCenter and Cluster Design

In this chapter, we will look at ESX design options from a managed cluster perspective in addition to VirtualCenter (as a service) and its alternatives for implementation. Also, we will wander around the VMware licensing model and some of its design considerations.

Licensing

While no one really likes to talk licensing, it is a must. VMware (like any other software vendor) wants to get paid for their intellectual property, and thus we need to license the servers. Let's look at what components need to be licensed and how they are licensed, then we'll review the licensing architecture used in VI3.

Licensed Components

One thing about being in IT (that no one ever mentioned when I got into it), is that licensing, not to mention the legalities of it, is one of the biggest pain in the butt issues I deal with all the time. Every time a vendor comes out with a feature, you get a new price and a new license model. Or, you have to ask how things are licensed (like per server vs. per processor, and does server mean a virtual or physical instance, etc…?). While all the license models in the world are a little out of scope here, and quite frankly, impossible to write about since MS and other vendors change their stance about once a quarter, we will try to walk you through an ESX environment's licensed components and what they mean to you. Below we have an ESX server environment using almost every possible licensed feature for ESX.

Figure 4- 1: VirtualCenter Licensing

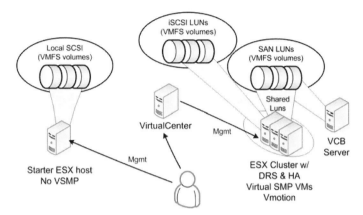

The setup in the previous image shows two different ESX environments. The ESX host on the left of the image is a standalone host, showing a basic "Starter Edition" configuration. You get a basic ESX host, the ability to create VM's and use local VMFS volumes and that is about it. These servers can have up to 4 processors (you pay per socket) and 8 GBs of RAM. There is no limit on the number of VM's, but you are limited in reality by the amount of RAM to about 16 VM's. In addition management of these servers is not centralized. They are each managed individually, with no centralized VirtualCenter Server.

Moving left to right in the image we then see a VirtualCenter server managing an environment of multiple ESX servers. When moving up to Standard Edition for the ESX host you get additional storage options like iSCSI and Fiber Channel based SAN. In addition, your VM's can now use Virtual SMP (dual and quad processor), and the limitations on the number of processors and amount of memory for the host has been removed. This is a fully functional host, but not a fully functional environment, yet.

You'll then notice that the "Standard" servers are configured in a cluster using advanced features of VirtualCenter like Distributed Resource Scheduling (DRS), High Availability Services (HA), and VMotion. Each of these is an "add-in" license to enable a specific functionality. These licenses are in addition to the basic VirtualCenter agent license, which allows the Standard Edition ESX server to be managed by a VirtualCenter agent. Confused yet? Don't be, while you can buy these piece meal, often times you will either purchase a Starter, a Standard, or VI 3 Enterprise (what used to be call an Infrastructure Node license) that includes all of the optional components, even if you don't need them all. The reason to get the infrastructure node is simple, price. If you need one or two of the add-ins, it is often about the same cost as getting the node license and much simpler from a quoting and purchasing/upgrading perspective.

Finally, on the right hand side you will see a VMware Consolidated Backup (VCB). This is another feature (that you can get with the VI 3 Enterprise license) that is licensed Per ESX server and allows for enhanced backups of VM's.

So which one do you need? 90% of you who are reading this book will need the infrastructure node licenses. But for a short who's who in the zoo, we break it down like this:

Starter Edition: This is used by one or two server shops that do not need central management, work load balancing of VM's, or high availability. Generally used when testing the waters.

Standard Edition: This is used by almost everyone and managed in almost every environment by a VirtualCenter Server. Used by those that may or may not need the DRS or HA services but do need a central mgmt console.

VI 3 Enterprise (Formerly Infrastructure node): This is used by a majority of environments with anything more than a couple of servers. These license packs allow you to take advantage of automatic VM recovery (HA services), give you the VirtualCenter mgmt license, along with DRS and VCB.

How licensed components are licensed...

ESX Host licenses are simple; they are licensed by processor socket (NOT CORE). As of this writing the ESX two processor licenses is good for a dual processor quad core server, and if you wish to support a 4 processor server (regardless of cores per socket) then you need to purchase two dual processor licenses. The amount of processor throughput you are getting for your dollar in multi-core systems is great. I expect at some point for this to change, but right now you should get it while the getting is good...

For other components it's a little trickier. The VirtualCenter Agent component along with VMotion, DRS, and HA are per host features, but generally work out to a per processor cost. What I mean by this is that an Infrastructure node license for a dual processor system is maybe $5,000 US. But a quad processor system with the same feature is $10,000 US. So while the HA, or DRS features are pretty much processor agnostic and really are VM or Host-based, their pricing is very dependent on the number of processors (and therefore the number of VM's) you have.   VCB, on the other hand is licensed by host (unless you roll it into the infrastructure node). In either case, it's still a per host license; only, it's included with the inf. node pack so we get back to the paying by the proc concept.

VirtualCenter is essentially licensed by the number of agents (read ESX servers) you have. These again tie back to the number of processors as a Quad is a different cost than a dual proc.

The basics of licensing with ESX is that everything is moving to a per processor model. So the sweet point now is that multi-core processors are offering more processing time per dollar since VMware is still charging for licenses by the number of sockets and not cores. Best bet is for you to determine the number of processors you are going to use, then get quotes based on that. Too often people get mixed up in the "I have 6 dual, dual cores, or 4 quad proc dual cores, and confuse themselves and the sales guys. Just count up proc sockets, and tell them what features you want.

Choosing a Licensing Model

Licensing in ESX 3.0 is essentially a file-based license. In the ESX 2.x era, administrators would key in a long product license code into the web interface for each ESX server they managed. Then, if the server were managed by Virtual-Center, and you wanted to use features like VMotion, you keyed in licenses (basically from a text file) to enable VC management and advanced features.

The file-based license architecture used in ESX 3.0 changed all of this. ESX licensing now has two modes: 'Host based' licenses (a file that resides on the ESX server) and Server-based licenses (a file that is hosted on a separate Windows server running the VMware license services). The concept is this, you (as a VMware customer that has purchased licenses) can go to their website and generate license files. The format of these files is the basic format used by FlexNet (formerly FlexLM) licensing. These license files can contain all of your licensed functionality (VMotion, DRS, how many processors, etc…) and determine where the license files are stored, on the host or on a centralized Windows Server running the FlexNet licensing services. It should be noted here, that when you generate the license file you must choose between the host based and server based, they can not be interchanged.

Essentially you have two options when it comes to how to maintain / host your licenses. You have the ability to host them on a central server for all of your hosts, or you can have an individual license file for each and every host in your environment.

VMware (in their documentation) allows for a 3rd model where you would store the VirtualCenter license file on the license server then also have each individual ESX server host its own license. We see no need for this except in cases of upgrades (like during the transition from a single server environment with no VirtualCenter) or some weird political issue within your organization that X business unit owns a server license, but corporate IT owns the VMotion and Virtual Center license etc… If the latter is the case then cut through the politics, if it is the former, then you are moving into a centralized model anyway.

Server Based Licenses (Centralized)

With that out of the way, let's talk about centralization. The centralized model requires a Windows server running the VMware licensing services. These services are really the FlexNet/FlexLM services, and I would suggest you install this first (prior to VirtualCenter) as it is pretty much required anyway. The server-based (Centralized) model is the most common in use in ESX environments. It allows for you to add your licenses for base ESX Functionality (licensed by processor socket) and allows for licensing for additional functionality like VMotion, DRS, HA services, Virtual SMP etc.

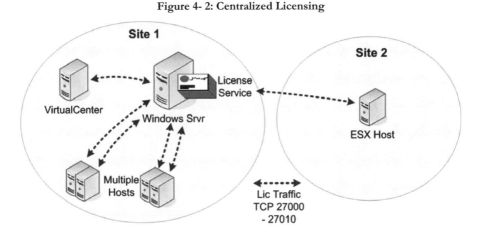

Figure 4- 2: Centralized Licensing

The nice thing about this model is that you can generate your license file for your entire environment (let's say 100 CPU's as an example); then, dole it out as your ESX servers come online regardless of the number of CPU's they have. Essentially you can have multiple hardware form factors (duals, quads, eight-ways, etc.) all pulling from the same server, and as long as you have available licenses, they will be good to go. Additionally, this centralized model makes licensing much easier to manage. You have one place to add and remove licenses and can restrict access to that server/application as needed.

In a multiple site model, you can opt to host the licenses at the corporate site and have the remotely located ESX servers connect to that server. If the WAN link between the remote site and central office is down it won't kill the remote ESX hosts. The VM's already running will continue to do so, but you cannot make configuration changes (more about that later in the chapter). If you feel that this is too much of a risk, you can put a license server at the remote site. Often license services are located on the VirtualCenter server, which makes sense, since that is the central configuration point and the tools you would most likely use to make the changes you want. VirtualCenter server placement is much more important than the license server placement, and you should finish reading the next few sections before jumping into a decision about license server placement.

The draw back to this model is that it is centralized and doesn't really allow you to earmark licenses for specific servers or business units. If in your environment

---

your business units own the licenses for ESX, then they may have reservations about centralizing them. Another drawback to this model is that it is a single point of failure, not a massive failure, mind you, but not easily made redundant. See, the license server parameters for each host is set on a host by host basis. Meaning, at time of install, you point your server to a license server, give it the port number and it knows where to get licenses from. The issue with this is that if the license server (or link to it) is down (and FlexLM isn't really clusterable) the ESX servers can't get their licenses. Now this is not the end of the world since ESX servers will continue to operate and you are not even in violation of the license for 14 days! In addition the already running VM's will continue to run, but no new hosts can be added to the clusters. We'll talk about some licensing options for high availability environments in a moment, for now just understand the limitations.

Advantages of the Server-based (Centralized) License Model
- Single management point for all licenses

- The only way to go (because of previous advantage) in large ESX environments

Disadvantages of the Server-based (Centralized) License Model
- Requires an additional Windows Server to host the services (though license services are often co-located with VirtualCenter services)

- A single server outage or down WAN link can be a single point of failure (though it does not affect already running VM's or Hosts)

If licensing model seems familiar to you it is probably because Citrix uses the same platform, only in their use of this model they tie their license file to the host name of the server on which the license service resides. VMware does not do this as it would be a royal pain in the butt when using Host-based licensing. Hopefully, they will never go to that model.

Host Based Licenses (Per Server)

Host based licenses are often used in small one or two server environments. They have the advantage of not requiring a separate server for hosting the license file but require that you install (and manage) the licenses on a per host basis. While this works (and is used) in many small environments, it is not very scalable and can become a management nightmare when licenses need to be upgraded or changed for some reason. In addition if you are going to run Virtu-alCenter to manage these one or two hosts, then you need a license service running on a Windows server for the VirtualCenter server. Since most environments beyond one or two servers use VirtualCenter (and therefore have the license services running on windows) it is easiest just to centralize the licenses on that server.

Advantages of the Host-based License Model
- Does not require a Windows Server for licensing (unless you also use VirtualCenter)

- VM's and hosts can still be started and restarted if a license server is down

Disadvantages of the Host-based License Model
- Decentralized model requiring host licenses be managed individually

License Server High Availability and Common Implementations

In most cases (in every case I have been a part of) the license services reside on the same Windows server that is hosting the VirtualCenter services. The license service itself is a lightweight, almost no resources used, type of service, and could easily reside on any server in the environment. It just makes a lot of sense to match it up with the VirtualCenter server. The other thing about a down license server is that running VM's and hosts are not affected for 14 days. Basically, you have 2 weeks to get the license server back up and running (from a legality perspective). Of course you can't add any new hosts the environment, but VM's continue to operate. Personally I think VMware has went out of their way to make this easy to live with, but maybe that's just me.

At this point it is important to understand that neither VirtualCenter nor the VMware License Services are supported in a clustered configuration. The Virtu-alCenter database may be hosted on a cluster, but the services themselves are not cluster aware. It is also important to note that VirtualCenter uses a 'Heart-beat' at 5 minute intervals to determine if the license service is still available and if there have been any changes to the licenses (remember these are just files managed by other interfaces). If the licenses have changed (or the license server goes away, same applies to the VirtualCenter server) it basically notes that the licenses affected are now in an "Unlicensed Use" state. The idea here is that if the license server returns to service (or the single license) things will go back to normal, but it may take 5 minutes because of the polling interval.

Now, let's get back to the common implementations part of this.

- VMware recommends that you: Install the License Service on the VirtualCenter server and;

- States that you can make this server a Virtual Machine and place that Virtual Machine in an HA cluster to provide redundancy.

We need to look at each of these individually and explore a couple of other options. The first recommendation makes complete sense in that if you already have a Windows server hosting VirtualCenter why not use it for the Licensing services. The second needs to be explored a little more.

License Service on a VM

The second suggestion is a little more interesting, and we should explore a bit without getting too much into HA and its internals just yet. Reviewing the next image we will notice a few interesting attributes:

- The HA heartbeat traffic for the host is done via the console interface over the physical network.

- TCP traffic for HA uses ports 2050 thru 5000 and 8042 thru 8045

- HA services run on the host itself and are NOT part of Virtual-Center; they are just configured using VirtualCenter.

- Using the image below ESX Hosts will look for licenses via their console interface, out over the physical network, back to the VirtualSwitch interface, then to a Virtual Switch, and ultimately the License Server (When the license server is a VM).

- If Host 1 fails (let's assume a server shutdown of some type) the Virtual Machine restarts on Host 2, generally within a few minutes.

- The remaining hosts contact the license server, as before, once network connectivity is re-established by the VM

Figure 4- 3: License Service on a VM

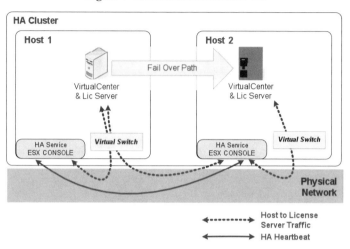

This seems to work fairly well but ignores some basic limitations of HA and hard shutdown Windows servers. If the host completely fails the VM will restart on another host (good for us). And if this VM hosts just the license services for VMware there are really going to be no problems since HA kicked in and the license service is not heavily transactional.

But if Host 1 does not completely shutdown, let's assume that you only loose connectivity to storage on Host 1, then the VM will eventually blue screen (due to loss of connectivity to its disk), but the VM and host are still running. If this happens HA failover never occurs, yet you have lost your licensing service.

HA services (the good and the bad) are gone over in more detail at the end of the chapter, but for now it's important to understand that it protects against a hardware failure on the host and RESTARTS the VM as if it had had its power cord pulled. It does not VMotion VM's off as that assumes the host is still up and running, which if HA has kicked in, it's not. Also, it is important to note that you need a host failure, and not something like a loss of storage connectivity, to make HA activate.

License Service on a Physical Machine

Another option is to place your License server on a physical machine. In this scenario you are doing this for one of two reasons. The first is that your VC server is physical, and therefore you have decided to place your license services on the same physical box. Or, you have an existing FlexNet server (for maybe a Citrix environment) and are going to go ahead and use that for VMware, too.

Figure 4- 4: License Service on a physical machine

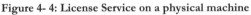
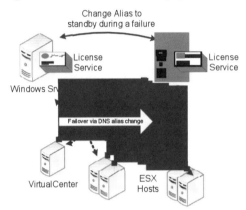

The trick with this is that you still need some type of redundancy. In most cases, we will use DNS names (read alias) for the license service (like vmwarelicense.company.com). In a physical server model you could have a standby server, with the license servers loaded and none of the hosts pointed at it. Use the DNS name (as the figure is shown below) during configuration, and in the event of a server failure, simply install the licenses on the license server and change the DNS alias. This of course would require somewhat short TTL's on the DNS side, but it would ensure that within a few minutes your licenses are back up and available.

Using Software-Based Replication for Redundancy

A final option for your redundant license server configurations (whether virtual or physical), is to use a software replication package like Co-Standby Server or NSI's Doubletake. These types of packages essentially do software base replication between two servers with a named primary and standby. In the event of one server going down, the other server is notified (via a heartbeat) and takes over the services of the primary. In some cases, these packages even take over the original host name and IP address.

This type of solution will work either physical or virtual and can even allow for you to run a physical server and a virtual standby. The drawback to using these is cost. While the level of redundancy is great, you have to shell out some dollars for these packages, and the better they are the more they hit your pocket book.

VirtualCenter Server and Services

While VirtualCenter is sometimes talked about as an add-on product for ESX, it is really central to the entire system, and needed for almost all of the advanced functionality. VirtualCenter will (in most environments) be the daily tool used to monitor, manage, and configure their ESX environment. It provides several crucial functions in each ESX environment including:

- Configuration of the ESX servers

- Resource management for the hosts and virtual machines

- Console access for the Virtual machines

- Performance reporting for VM's and Hosts

- Inventory views into Hosts and virtual machine

- Ability to logically group these objects and provide role based security

- Alerting on performance thresholds for individual VM's or Hosts.

- Interfacing for third party products in the environment

- Configuration of ESX Clusters for both HA and DRS

- Configuration of resource pools to manage VM resource utilization

So regardless of what else goes on in your environment, you will more than likely want a VirtualCenter server, and quite frankly, we see it as a must beyond one or two servers. So, to better understand what VirtualCenter does, let's look at its components, then dive into how to design the system.

Figure 4- 5: VirtualCenter Components

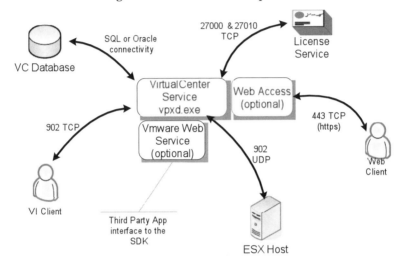

The first two components to note are the "optional" ones: the VMware Web Service and the VirtualCenter Web Access. These two should not intermingle as they are really two separate entities. The VMware Web Service is the SDK and interface for many third-party tools. If you use something like Provision Network's VDI broker or certain products from HP, these tools ask for the VirtualCenter server name and will want to really connect to the SDK. The Web Access component is a web page/s for Virtual machine management. It has limited functionality but will allow you to do some things. So while these are "optional" you might as well install them and save yourself the hassle later when some new fancy tool wants to use them.

As you can see, the rest of the components circle around the vpxd or VirtualCenter service. This service is what your VirtualCenter client (or Virtual Infrastructure Client) will connect to when managing the environment. The VPXD service also talks to a database (where it stores its information) and the License Services (to make sure you are compliant on the licensing side).

Often times in small environments all of these components (short of the ESX host) are located on the same physical machine. Administrators will install MS SQL on their Windows server and then install the VirtualCenter package including the optional services, the License Services, and the VI client. It all works and is even fairly scalable, but let's look at each of these components individually.

VirtualCenter Service (VPDX) hosting

The VC server itself needs little in the way of resources. Thinking about the diagram, and about some of the rules we are about to go over; you can tell that there will not be a lot of connectivity to the VC server. It will communicate with hosts in the environment (maybe even a lot of them), possibly have several users connected with the VI client, and maybe even a third party tool using the web service. But even with this number of connections, we may be talking only on the high side of 100 or so... not a lot of load. In addition, VMware recommends that a VirtualCenter 2 server not have more than 2000 VM's or 100 ESX hosts to maintain its performance. While most environments won't start off with anywhere near this many, it is easy to look ahead (in this era of blades) and see an environment with 100 Hosts, at about 8-12 VM's per blade and pushing that limit. Our general recommendation for sizing is as follows:

- 1 processor for up to 25 hosts, add a second processor if you plan on scaling above 25

- 512 MB base memory, then about 1 MB of memory per every VM managed and 2 MB of memory per managed host.

Following those recommendations, let's look at two sample environments and come up with their VirtualCenter server configs (remember these exclude the SQL or Oracle DB if they are running locally). If I had a 10 Host environment with 200 Virtual Machines, I would need 512+ (10*2) + (200*1) = 732 or 768 (rounded up to next 256 increment). But if the environment needed to scale to 60 hosts and 1200 VM's we would need 512 + (60*2) + (1200*1) = 1832 or 2048 rounded up to the next increment.

Granted, the equations are simplified, but as you can tell a dual processor, 2GB system will pretty much handle the load for one of their bigger supported environments. You may also notice we start out at 512. That allows us to assume there is overhead from the OS, Monitoring agents, anti-virus, etc. But in any case, you can see this doesn't have to be a powerful system. If you want to be a little more conservative, take the MB per VM and per host and increase them by 50% or 1.5MB per VM and 3 MB per host.

Physical vs. Virtual Machine VirtualCenter

Running the VirtualCenter server as a Virtual Machine is not an issue. A number of organizations do it and do it successfully. Though, in some shops, the question of running your management service, which allows you to manage and view and possibly troubleshoot your virtual infrastructure, becomes a contentious one; so let's look at some of the benefits and drawbacks.

Advantages of using a VM to host VirtualCenter
- Reduced number of physical servers

- Hardware failures covered by HA services

- Load can be shifted and the VM easily "upgraded"

- VM can be snapshot before upgrades and patches

- No need for a standby server, HA will often recover faster than you can configure and start the standby server

Disadvantages of using a VM to host VirtualCenter
- HA Services do not cover all failures (such as a storage failure)

- Internal resistance due to managing a VM environment with a VM

Running it as a VM is not a bad idea as long as you do not host the VC database on that same server. Here we are explicitly talking about the VC server and not it's DB. The databases used (SQL and Oracle) are transactional databases that do not like to have their availability based on a power off and power on. Loss of transactions can occur and in really bad cases, database corruption. We suggest that if running this as a VM, separate the Database from the VirtualCenter Server. Then the DB can be hosted on a cluster (VM or Physical) and be guaranteed higher availability easily.

If you elect to run the VirtualCenter as a Physical server then you have a number of options. Obviously, you lose some of the HA features when not running it as a VM. So, you need to plan accordingly. One of your options is to use a physical machine and a standby. The standby can even have VirtualCenter installed; then during a failure start it up, point it to the Database, and off you go. You should (on the standby) change the VirtualCenter unique ID (located in the VI Client –Administration – VirtualCenter Server Configuration –Runtime Settings) to match that of the production server, but it is a quickly recoverable solution.

You also have the option of using something like an NSI Doubletake to replicate the VC server to a standby. Again, this can be physical to physical or physical to Virtual. Thinking about it some, it can even be virtual to virtual if you so choose.

While VMware doesn't officially state that VC is cluster aware* they do have some articles on it (from the VC 1.x days), and I am sure they are planning on making VC a clusterable application though it's not available yet. In some cases, Users in the forums have posted links to cluster VC steps…

Just before going to print VMware posted an article on clustering the Virtual-Center service for 2.0. We will cover this in detail the next edition, once we have had time to test it. The article can be found at: http://www.vmware.com/pdf/VC_MSCS.pdf

VirtualCenter Database Sizing

Whenever designing the VC solution and talking to the DBA's, they always want to know how big this database is going to get. From a utilization standpoint (processor and memory) this DB has very few clients (Uh, your VC server) and probably will never have more than 10 connections to the DB from even your VC server. So, with low utilization it always comes down to a question of space. At the time of this writing, VMware has a spreadsheet they float around to help estimate size of the DB. But, it is important to note that its sizing does change between versions as they change counters and objects. So, sizing described here is based on VirtualCenter 2.0.1 Patch 2 and later.

The biggest factors impacting the size of your VC database are the number of Virtual Machines and the logging level set in VirtualCenter. The default logging level in VC is Level 1 of 4 possible levels. Each time you crank up to the next level you increase the number of *counters/metrics* being collected on each sample, thus increasing the amount of data. In addition, the default smallest collection interval is 5 minutes. If you change this and increase the frequency from the defaults, these numbers can also be skewed.

Anyway, let's look at some sizing numbers below based on the most important items with regards to the database sizes at different logging levels for Virtual-Center:

	Objects by logging level (in MB)			
	VM	Host	Cluster	Res Pools
Logging Level 1	3.52	3.01	3.52	0
Logging Level 2	10.05	10.05	9.55	7.03
Logging Level 3	26.65	49.75	9.55	7.03
Logging Level 4	37.19	71.36	21.6	196.3

These numbers are based on common configurations for hosts, and VM's, meaning the Host numbers assume a 4 processor host (or dual proc dual core) with several network interfaces and numerous disk devices etc. The VM numbers assume the average VM is a single processor with 1 disk and 1 network interface. The Cluster and Resource Pools are pretty steady numbers, but if your VM's all have 2 disks instead of 1, or if your Hosts have 8 processors instead of 4, you can fudge these numbers up by 15% for logging levels 3 and 4. At levels 1 and 2, it really doesn't matter much.

In addition to the raw database size, which you can get by multiplying your expected number of each object times the MB at the used logging level, you should really allow the DB size *2 to allow for the temp database that will also use disk space. Logging level selection is looked at in the next section, but for now let's runs through some examples.

Remember VMware does have a spreadsheet calculator on line, though it is sometimes hard to find, at the time of this writing you could download it here:

www.vmware.com/support/vi3/doc/vc_db_calculator.xls

Sample Environment 1: 10 Hosts, 150 VM's, 1 Cluster, and 2 Resource pools, level 1

Here, we do some simple arithmetic to determine the potential DB size after a year of data. Year-old data is purged so the DB will remain about the same size over time.

	# of Objects	MB/Per	Total @ 1 yr
VM's	150	3.52	528
Hosts	10	3.01	30.1
Clusters	1	3.52	3.52
Res Pools	2	0	0
		total:	561.62 MB

As you can see, we are running about 15 VM's per host and wind up with about a 560 MB database. Of that 528MB is from the Virtual Machines. Now, let's change the number of hosts (by using smaller hosts but host the same number of Virtual Machines.

Sample Environment 2: 20 Hosts, 150 VM's, 2 Clusters, and 4 Resource pools, level 1

Here we have basically doubled the size of the environment from a host perspective, creating two clusters, compared to one, but running the same number of virtual machines.

	# of Objects	MB/Per	Total @ 1 yr
VM's	150	3.52	528
Hosts	20	3.01	60.2
Clusters	2	3.52	7.04
Res Pools	4	0	0
		total:	595.24 MB

As you can see, the additional hosts are really just 10 or 15 new logical objects being monitored and barely impact the size of the DB. The greatest number of Objects (with unique metrics being monitored for each) is the VM's; therefore, they are most important in determining the size of the DB.

Sample Environment 3: 10 Hosts, 150 VM's, 1 Cluster, and 2 Resource pools, level 4

In this sample we take environment 1, which previously was at logging level 1(estimated at 560MB), and crank the logging level up to level 4. Now, most environments are never going to run at level 4 but this shows how the logging level increases the DB size dramatically:

	# of Objects	MB/Per	Total @ 1 yr
VM's	150	37.19	5578.5
Hosts	10	71.36	713.6

Clusters	1		21.6	21.6
Res Pools	2		196.3	392.6
		total:	6706.3 MB	

Notice that the environment that did have a 560 MB db is now more than 10 times that size at about 6.7GB. Of course you may be higher or lower than this (use a 10-15% plus or minus) but the trick is to realize that the logging level has a major impact on DB size by increasing the number of metrics being monitored for each item.

VirtualCenter Stat Collection and Logging Levels

Number of processors per host and VM and number of network interfaces and disk devices for hosts or VM's, all have an impact on the size of the DB, but their impact is fairly minimal when compared to the logging level and sheer number of metrics that are added as you increase the logging level. Because of this, let's look at the different logging levels, what they provide you, and why you would use them.

Beware: Changing your logging level in VC removes all of your previous VC logged data. I believe they change the fields/tables when they change the logging level; so, when you change this in VirtualCenter it removes all of your previous data.

Logging Level 1

This level provides the basic metrics for VM's and hosts, including CPU, Disk, Memory and network usage. Uptime metrics are counted along with DRS metrics. Statistical information for individual devices is not collected in this logging level.

Logging Level 2

This level grabs all of the metrics for the core four (CPU, disk, memory, and network) and device statistics that were not included in the level 1. As an example, an average quad processor, ESX server will have 6 metrics collected at level 1 during a sample interval, while level 2 collects a total of about 20 (+/- a few based on the number of devices in the host).

This level is used most often in environments that do capacity planning and charge back on VM's. It allows you a pretty granular look at the information about the core four without grabbing level 3 counters and which is a big jump in the amount of metrics monitored.

Logging Level 3

This level collects all metrics for all counter groups. The increase in from level 2 (20 metrics each sample interval) is almost 500%. The total metrics captured here is 131. This level is often used for troubleshooting or environments in ASP/Hosting models.

Logging Level 4

Level 4 is the highest logging level and collects samples for any metric supported by virtual center. Total metrics collected for a single quad processor host of average config is a small jump from level 3 to 174.

The size of the VC database, while taking up 3 pages here, is really not all that important to your overall infrastructure design. We simply wanted to provide you with some info on sizing, so when your DBA explains that you need 2 controllers, with 5 logical partitions to support your VC db, and he needs his sizing info, you can show him some simple math, and move on to your next part of the design... Like VirtualCenter system design.

VirtualCenter System Design

In an ESX 3.0 environment there are a number of communications paths you need to worry about when designing the environment. The first, and most obvious, is VC to ESX host communications. These are the "no brainers" with which most people are familiar. Essentially, the VC server sends commands to ESX hosts for execution (such as starting a virtual machine), and performance data is shipped to the VC server for each host being managed by that server.

Figure 4- 6: VirtualCenter Overview

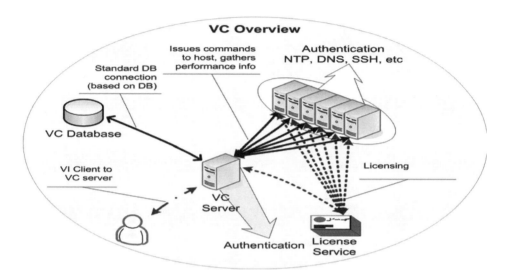

These are the communications that most people worry about, but the reality is that host servers will also communicate to DNS (really dependent on this if using HA services in the cluster), NTP, and Authentication for shell logins etc. In addition, you need to think about the connection from each host to the License server (when using a centralized license server) and for the VC server to the VC database. Finally, the VC server will also communicate with Active Directory (or possibly Windows local groups) for authorization to log in to the VC client and perform operations/issue commands within VC.

To show a simple example let's assume you want to VMotion a VM from one host server to another. In doing so the following steps (simplified) will show how almost all the communication paths are used:

1. User launches VI Client and connects to the VC server and inputs credentials.

2. VC server contacts the database.

3. VC server checks account against DB for this user's rights to log on and matches to roles in VC (Windows auth done at this point)

4. VI Client still in communication with VC server begins to load inventory in the GUI from the VC server that is reading it from the DB.

5. User selects a VM and issues a VMotion command.

6. Licensing is checked on those hosts along with prerequisite checks for VMotion compatibility.

7. VMotion begins (which we won't get into here).

8. Progress is reported to VC DB, errors/logs are written, and normal VMotion traffic happens between host servers.

9. Change is reflected is in GUI once VMotion is completed, and also VM location info is written into the DB

As you can see, there is a lot of chatter going on in this environment. Not heavy traffic, mind you, but enough to be sure that if one of the links is broken it can make for a fun night of troubleshooting.

VC Server Locations in the Enterprise

Now that we have a basic understanding of the communication paths in ESX environments we have to look at the decisions that need to be made about where to place the VC Server or Servers on your network. If you have a single datacenter or single central point that ESX will be used, then your decision is already made. But, if you will have ESX in multiple locations you will need to decide if you will have a VC server in each location with an ESX server, a VC server in only large sites, or a VC server in only a central site.

This decision should be made with the following items taken into account:

- Bandwidth available between sites containing ESX servers

- Number of ESX servers in a location

- Location of administrators for the ESX servers in any given location

- DR/BC Plans

Centralized VirtualCenter

First let's look at a centralized VC Model with both high-speed and low-speed connected sites. In this scenario, we assume that ESX servers are located at both of the remote sites and that the administrator has decided to manage them all via a single VC server and DB.

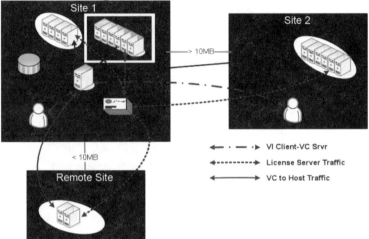

Figure 4- 7: Centralized VirtualCenter

Advantages of the Centralized VirtualCenter Model
- Single management point for all clusters/hosts
- Single place to security for your whole ESX environment
- Single server to manage, backup, patch, update, etc...
- Administrators from remote sites can still access the VC client if they have been given rights

Disadvantages of the Centralized VirtualCenter Model
- Almost unusable, if not completely unusable, over low bandwidth links
- May require changes in how templates are deployed, updated, and managed
- Not the best for DR/Hot site configurations

The Centralized VC model has a number of benefits. You have one point of management for every server, you have single place to set security in the entire virtual environment, and only one server and database to manage, update, patch, and monitor. In this configuration, remote administrators (like from Site 2 in this example) can still access the VC server from their site and manage their servers if they have been given proper permissions.

The drawback to this design is that low speed/low bandwidth links can cause sporadic issues in VirtualCenter, such as disconnected servers, slow downs in getting performance information, and sluggish response when issuing commands to be executed on the host. If a site has a small connection to the central location (like a single T-1) VC may still work, but timeouts and other issues when communicating over a T-1 used for other traffic (as seen in some environments) makes VC almost unusable.

A quick note here; recently I was at a VMware client with a 10+ Mb ATM link that was lightly used. Their centralized VC model works fairly well with just a few things/workarounds to make template deployment and updates easy to use. But, just a few weeks earlier I stopped at another client, using almost the same configuration with a 35 Mb link that was totally saturated and has had nothing but issues with the centralized model. So it's not just the link size, but its available bandwidth that you need to consider.

Finally, with centralized models your template deployments can become an issue. Generally template deployment is very bandwidth intensive process. If done over the network (like templates being centralized then copied to remote VMFS volumes) you could wind up copying gigs and gigs of data. Of course this often fails right out of the gate in low speed connections. So centralizing like this requires that you configure templates at each location anyway, to speed template deployment. In some cases, administrators will resort to NOT using the template functionality in VC and instead leaving a VM or VM's on a remote server and VMFS volume that acts as a template, but they simply clone it or copy it using shell commands.

Decentralized VirtualCenter Servers

In this design option, we use a VC server and database at each location. We assume here that we have centralized administrators for Site 1 and possibly some offshoot remote locations. Site 2 is a second datacenter with its own set of administrators and also has its own VirtualCenter server. You will notice that we show the License server hosted centrally. License services were discussed previously in this chapter, and here we have decided that the centralized licensing will be used since all sites are sharing the same licenses, instead of a bunch of individual purchases managed by site.

Figure 4- 8: Decentralized VirtualCenter

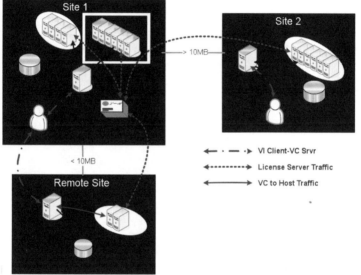

You will also notice in this image that Admin in Site 1 is connecting to the VirtualCenter server in the Remote site. If the link has low latency and plenty of bandwidth, this often works fine using the VI client. This configuration is slower than a LAN, obviously, but still usable. If this link is saturated or extremely slow Administrators will often load the VI client right on the VC server, then just use MS Terminal Services to access the server and run the VI client for managing that remote environment.

Advantages of the Decentralized VirtualCenter Model

- Works well over limited bandwidth links

- Ability to decentralize security for different environment owners

- Works best for DR/Hot Site configurations

- Templates are localized in each site and can be used "traditionally"

Disadvantages of the Decentralized VirtualCenter Model
- Multiple servers to manage, update, patch, backup, etc...

- Decentralized security points, must configured in multiple locations

- Disjointed virtual infrastructure creating datacenter based silos

The obvious benefit of the decentralized model is that it is simple. You bring up an ESX 3.x cluster in a new site, and you bring up its VirtualCenter management components and configure them. Replicate your design and procedures from place to place, and you are done. The biggest disadvantage is that the management is decentralized now, but is this really a big deal? If you think about other management tools in your environment like HP SIM, or HP Openview or IBM Director or Desktop management tools you have, are they completely centralized? Often not. In a lot of cases these are decentralized since the staff in that location handles / uses the management systems. So, while decentralizing can have its drawbacks, it is a model used more often than not in larger, multi-site environments.

An important note here about remote sites and design alternatives- from a VirtualCenter perspective, a 50 or 100Mb WAN link (non-saturated) is as good as a LAN connection. Most of the information going back and forth between hosts and the VC server is fairly light, and a centralized model for VC works just fine (barring any potential template issues previously stated) with this type of available bandwidth. The scenarios we are describing is sub 35Mb connections and specifically things like T-1s, E-1's or aggregated links of the like. In addition, it is important to note that this does not mean you can simply span an ESX cluster across sites, but that VC (as discussed here) can be used to manage clusters in different sites. Clusters and their design considerations are discussed later in this chapter.

Cluster Overview

Clusters in ESX 3.X are really simple to understand once you break it down to the basic functions of a cluster and the required components to make these functions work. From a functional stand point, a cluster is a set of like-configured ESX Servers, in the same site/datacenter, that share common storage and networks and have VMotion enabled across the hosts. There are some important configurations and requirements to make our simple definition a reality, but the basics concepts are detailed below along with a drawing of a simple 2 cluster environment.

Figure 4- 9: Cluster

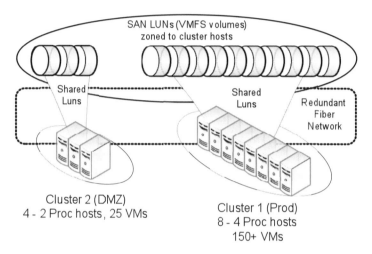

Cluster 2 (DMZ)
4 - 2 Proc hosts, 25 VMs

Cluster 1 (Prod)
8 - 4 Proc hosts
150+ VMs

Let's take a look at these two clusters and review each of the decisions that went into making these two different configurations. The first cluster (prod cluster) is a set of 8 quad processor systems, hosting 150+ Virtual Machines. As you can see, all 8 servers share the same VMFS volumes (a total of 10 VMFS volumes in this case). VM's in this cluster only reside on those 10 LUN's. The second cluster is a smaller cluster using 3 shared LUN's and 3 dual processor hosts hosting 25 Virtual Machines.

The first item to notice is the size of the servers, Dual processor vs. Quad processor configurations. When doing cluster design the first question is how many VM's do you want to host? In this case they have decided to separate the DMZ VM's from the Prod VM's. We can assume that this is due to physical network connectivity and/or security policies in the organization to keep DMZ separate from Prod. That creates two distinct pools of Virtual Machines to be hosted and therefore two distinct clusters. You see, since the configurations have to be split (from a network perspective) the configuration of the hosts, not to mention the physical connectivity to the network will be different, therefore VM's cannot be VMotioned / mixed between these hosts.

Once the physical limitation/configuration was decided on then we have to run the number of expected VM's (25 in the DMZ and 150+ in the Prod) through a simple exercise taking into account the following:

1. ESX 3.x clusters are limited to 16 servers per cluster (based on HA limits).

2. If not using HA and only using DRS, clusters are limited to 32 nodes.

3. Reality is that a common best practice is to limit cluster size to between 10 and 12 hosts.

4. Estimated average VM to Processor ratio (in this case we will assume 6)

5. The amount of redundancy we want to have in the farm from a host level (Newhart?) In this case we assume at least N+1.

6. Storage will be allocated as needed; all volumes will be VMFS and shared amongst hosts.

Hardware selections (dual, quads, 8-ways, multi-cores etc...) are discussed in Chapter 3. Here we are assuming a single core for simplicity, for a "core" discussion please jump back to chapter 3. Assuming that we will host 6 VM's per processor we know that the DMZ will need at least 4 (and a fraction) to host 25 Virtual Machines. In the prod environment we want to host about 150+ virtual machines. Using that same 6:1 ratio we can estimate that we need about 25 processors not including redundancy. Knowing the number of processors required for each environment we can then decide on the form factor based on costs and amount of redundancy.

For the DMZ we need about 4 processors to host the expected VM's. In this case we can buy 2 quad processor systems getting us 8 total processors, or we can purchase 3 dual processor systems for a total of 6 processors. In the quad processor case we have almost 4 processors completely unused. Yes, I know ESX will still use them, just not fully, but that is not the point. The point is we have just over purchased by purchasing way more machine that we need just to satisfy the N+1 need. In the dual processor configuration the active VM's can basically be hosted on 2 dual processor servers requiring a 3rd to act as the N+1 server which (in almost every case) 3 dual processor servers are much less expensive than 2 quad processor servers.

On the Production cluster we have to host 150+ VM's or about 24 or 25 processors. Again this can be done with quad processors for a total of 6 or 7 hosts. Or it can be done in a dual processor configuration requiring 13 hosts. When using dual processor configs with this cluster we are doubling the number of fiber and network connections, and their cost may come into play In addition, the concept of managing twice as many servers and being close to the 16 server limit in the cluster is an issue.

The decision in this example was made to go with a quad processor system (needing 7 hosts) plus an extra to match the N+1 requirement, while still having room to expand the cluster without starting a new one. Now that we have figured out the hardware needs, we will focus on the Cluster options in the design.

Cluster Design Options

In chapter 3 we looked at mixing workloads (like test and dev with production etc.) and how that can affect your network connectivity requirements or change the hardware you are about to purchase. Assuming that you are past the point of deciding what is going to be hosted on these servers, let's review cluster requirements then look at the design alternatives:

- All servers in a cluster will need to be zoned to the same VMFS storage.

- Servers will need to be pretty much identically configured:

- Processors will need to be similar if not identical (just do a search on VMware's site for Processors and VMotion compatibility, there's a list).

- Like major software version (3.x) – try to keep the patch level the same to minimize issues.

- Licensing will need to be identical (to allow for VMotion, DRS, HA, or any other options you wish to use).

- Network connectivity will need to be the same (physical connections to the same network or logical networks when using VLAN tagging) Virtual Switch names and configurations should be identical.

- Should all be in the same site as cross site VMotion is not the reality for any site connected via a WAN link.

Knowing these requirements we are still left with a lot of alternatives. Let's create a sample environment containing the following:

- 2 Logical networks (VLANs) test and prod on the internal network

- 1 Separate physical network for the DMZ

- 1 Mgmt network (VLAN) used for out of band mgmt (like ILO, DRAC etc), and other mgmt tools

- VM's will be required in each of the environments (Mgmt, DMZ, Test and Prod)

- 200 VM's in total with 10 VM's, 20 VM's, 65 VM's and 105 VM's respectively

Figure 4- 10: VM Environment

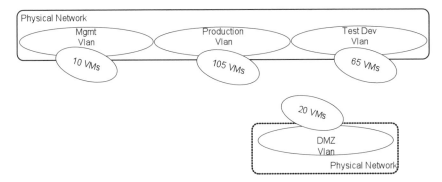

Single Cluster Design

The first option is to create a single cluster that will host VM's for all environments on the network. This cluster will require about 10 ESX servers assuming quad processor hosts with an average load of 24 VM's per server maximum and N+1 redundancy.

Figure 4- 11: Single Cluster

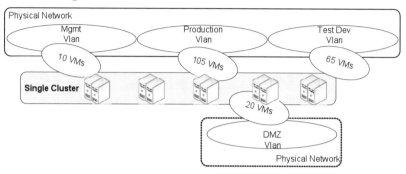

The big benefit of this design is that you have a single cluster for all VM's. This allows you to leverage a single set of servers hosting different workloads for better performance and allowing you the ultimate virtual infrastructure; any host can host any VM for any network segment. In addition, you reduce the number of hosts required and eliminate unique silos and configurations of ESX in your environment.

While this environment simplifies the mgmt of the virtual infrastructure, in the long run it does increase the complexity of the system and hosts. In our example the host is going to have physical network connections to both the internal network and the DMZ. In addition, the Virtual Switches on the internal network will have multiple port groups configured for the 3 logical VLAN's. Each time a VM is added the proper Virtual Switch will have to be selected to ensure proper network connectivity of the VM. While this sounds a little daunting it is not that much to handle, but it increases the network complexity from a trunking/vlaning perspective and may get push back from your security team for hosting DMZ VM's on the "inside" of the network.

Advantages of the Single Cluster Model
- Single type of server/configuration to manage

- Ability to optimally balance work loads

- No siloing/underutilization do to siloing

- Reduced number of hosts because capacity used for redundancy is used across all environments

- Easier to manage in the long run

- Lowest capital cost upfront

Disadvantages of the Single Cluster Model
- More complex from a host networking perspective

- Security teams will often say no to this just out of principal

- Requires more management of resources and resource pools due to the large number of environments being hosted

Silo'd Cluster Design

In this alternative a cluster is created for each of the unique network environments. It should be noted that each ESX host in the environment will still have a network connection (or two) to the mgmt or production network for its service console, but here we are just talking about VM connectivity. As you can see, we now have 4 clusters for this environment. The mgmt network will have 2 ESX hosts, the production environment will require 6 hosts, the DMZ will have 2 hosts, and the test and dev cluster will have 4 hosts. Essentially the environment is silo'd by the network to which the VM's will connect. This eventually results in 4 clusters and 14 hosts.

Figure 4- 12: Silo' Cluster

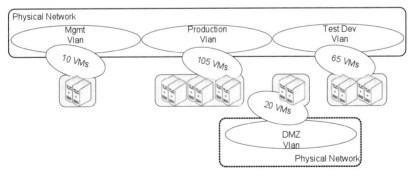

In addition to network separation, the cluster design will take into account zoning of the VMFS storage. Each environment will have its own LUN's zoned to it and should not be crossed.

The major benefit of this design is that it is the easiest to implement when you first get into ESX Server. The major drawback is that once implemented it is a real pain to get out of for both technology and political reasons. Selling this type of cluster design in an environment is easy to do; migrating to a more consolidated model later on can be cumbersome when you start talking about changing the LUN zoning, reconfiguring the switch ports servers are connected to, migrating VM's etc. In addition, when you silo servers that are alike, such as the large number of web servers in the DMZ, tool servers in the mgmt area, or unused test servers in the test environment you will not be able to optimally mix differing work load types, meaning you will run into similar bottlenecks on hosts running similar types of VM's.

Advantages of the Silo'd Cluster Model
- Simplest option from an individual host networking perspective

- Increased number of hosts because capacity used for redundancy is not leveraged across all environments

- Easiest to sell to internal teams during an initial implementation

- Requires very little with regards to resource management since A: there is more available hosts and B: no VM's from differing environments

Disadvantages of the Silo'd Cluster Model
- Multiple configurations and clusters to manage

- Not an optimal configuration for balancing work loads

- Increased under utilization due to more redundant capacity

- Highest capital cost upfront due to the increase in hosts

Middle Ground- Some Silo'd Clusters

Often a good design comprise is to only silo off some of the clusters. One that is used often is the separation of DMZ clusters from internal clusters. Using the same fictional network this option would segregate the DMZ from the Internal VM's, creating 2 clusters with 9 hosts in one and two in the other. In some ESX environments they only have internal ESX hosts and may just separate the Dev and Test VM's from prod VM's. In any of these cases, the trick is to find the economies of scale, if you have an environment that is significantly large enough to warrant its own cluster (lets say 8, 10 or 12 hosts) then the cost for redundancy is minimal and it wouldn't really hurt anything to remove it. Using our example and only siloing off the DMZ VM's we wind up with just 11 hosts (1 more than a single cluster design) and still keep the security guys happy, but we could have just as easily folded the DMZ into the Prod cluster and had the Test/Dev cluster rolled out to its own.

Figure 4- 13: Mixed Cluster Design

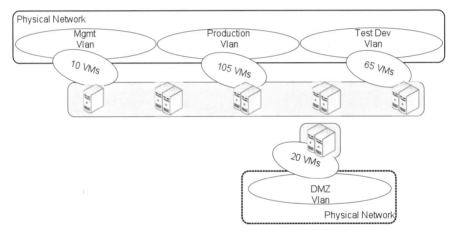

The advantage here is that it allows for minimal siloing, but still keeps cost as low as possible by leveraging the redundancy capacity across numerous environments. It also is a good balance in that it keeps different types of workloads running on the hosts to get close to optimal configuration for resource usage.

Advantages of having some Silo'd Clusters
- Relatively easy to sell to internal teams

- Reduced number of hosts when compared to the completely silo'd model

- Reduces the number of silos to manage when compared to the previous model

- Good balance between the two primary models

Disadvantages of having some Silo'd Clusters
- Some teams/app owners may feel they need their own cluster

- Just as complex from a networking perspective as the first option

- Still requires resource management in any environments mixed (in our example, prod, Test, and Mgmt).

- Siloing Test and Dev or DMZ type workloads decreases resource utilization because of similar workload characteristics in these environments

Distributed Resource Services (DRS) Enabled Clusters

When creating clusters in ESX 3, one of the options is to enable the cluster for DRS. DRS is essentially a load leveling tool that uses resource utilization from the hosts and VM's to create recommendations for Virtual Machine placement. DRS clusters are limited to 32 nodes maximum, but that number is essentially artificial as most clusters that use DRS will also use HA services (discussed next) which are limited to 16 nodes maximum. Why the conflict? Well DRS is a product written by one group and HA is a product licensed from another ISV then modified for VMware. The long and short is that if you plan on using DRS and HA that 32 node limit goes out the window, and in most cases we even stay a little below 16 nodes.

Anyway, DRS creates recommendations based on load that can be used as simple recommendations (seen in the VirtualCenter client) and acted on manually, or they can be automated at different levels and allowed to automatically balance VM load across the environment.

DRS is controlled, managed and executed by VirtualCenter, unlike HA that is managed and configured by VirtualCenter but runs independently (as an agent) on each host. DRS's essential functionality is to balance CPU and Memory load on the hosts by moving VM's from high-utilized hosts to less utilized hosts. DRS does not take into account network or disk utilization (throughput or IO).

Right now DRS's focus is on processor and memory resources which happen to be the two major bottlenecks in 99% of ESX servers.

To understand the advanced features of DRS, we first should look at how it works from the basic recommendations perspective.

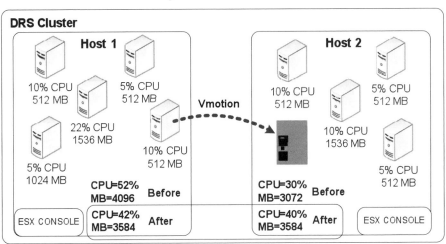

In this example we have two nodes in a DRS cluster. Host 1 has 52% CPU utilization and about 4GB of ram in use, while Host 2 has 30% CPU in use and about 3GB. VirtualCenter (and specifically the DRS components) sees this differential in utilization and attempts to determine which VM moves would balance the load. Here (a simplistic model mind you) the 10% CPU and 512MB VM gets moved to the less utilized server. This results in the two servers almost having the same load. The system does not move a VM like the 22% utilized VM, since it would just create an imbalance where Host 2 is more utilized and more moves would be needed to balance the load.

Obviously that is a simplistic look at how DRS works, but the important items to note (at this point) is that this entire process is controlled by VirtualCenter working off of performance information it collects from the ESX hosts. It is also important to note that you have some control about the aggressiveness of these moves and can control whether this process is fully automated, partially automated, or in completely manual mode, which basically just sends recommendations to the admin and he decides whether to apply the recommendation or not.

DRS Recommendations

VirtualCenter constantly reevaluates load in a DRS cluster. Basically, DRS is driven by a default interval of 5 minutes or when a host is added or removed from the cluster thereby affecting the load / capacity of the environment significantly. So in any given hour DRS looks at load in a cluster 12 times, then based on this creates a series of prioritized recommendations to level load across the cluster.

These recommendations are prioritized by DRS and shown to the administrators using a Star ranking. These "stars' also correspond (inversely) to the aggressiveness of the DRS automation mode. So, star rankings can be seen like this:

Figure 4- 15: DRS Recommendations

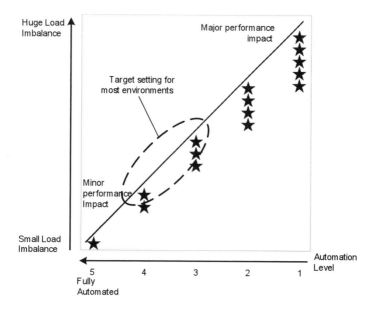

Looking at the image you can see that a recommendation with a "5 Star" rating means that there is a huge load imbalance and making this change (moving this one VM) will solve the imbalance. As you move down the ratings to a 1 star rating, you have a very minor imbalance from which you will see almost no performance impact. The automation levels are exactly the inverse of this. Meaning at level 1 automation (the most conservative) it will only automatically apply recommendations with 5 stars, while the level 5 automation will apply any recommendation (1 star or greater).

The reality is that these recommendations are movement recommendations for single VM's. In any production environment you are very unlikely to see a 5 star rating. In most cases, a 5 star rating means you have moved a VM (manually) in a DRS environment violating some type of affinity rule (discussed later) but for straight utilization it is almost impossible to have a single VM cause that much of an imbalance in your environment, so level 1 automation is almost useless and can mess up a manual change you made for a reason. If you want to be fully auto-mated, level 4 is just as good as any other.

In any case, you should gain a level of comfort with DRS automation. Maybe start at manual, look at the recommendations, apply them, then start to move the automation level up and gain a level of comfort with each automation setting.

Rules for Load Balanced or "Special" VM's

When hosting load balanced VM's running on an ESX cluster (two VM's maybe using Windows load balancing) or running multiple VM's that have dependencies on each other (like an application server that needs its database server up to be useful), you may need to set some special rules to ensure VM's are placed on proper hosts.

DRS Affinity Rules

Affinity Rules, when talking about DRS affinity, should not be confused with processor affinity in at the VM or host level. VM level processor affinity assigns a VM to a specific processor on a host. DRS affinity allows you to set rules so that multiple VM's are always on the same host, or always kept on separate hosts.

If you select the DRS rule to "Keep Virtual Machines Together" the rule wizard allows you to add multiple VM's to a list affected by this rule. Essentially, DRS will take this into consideration when making recommendations and assume that these VM's need to be on the same host, and when moved, they are always moved together. This is most often used when VM's are part of an application set such as a front end and backend server, and you want to keep the traffic between the servers local to the host on the virtual switch.

The opposite side of that rule is to "Separate Virtual Machines". This will ensure that two or more VM's are never placed on the same host by DRS. This is most often used when you have a pair of load balanced VM's to provide redundancy for an application. If DRS were to move the VM's onto the same host, and there was a host failure, you basically lose your hardware redundancy and both VM's can go down at the same time. By configuring this DRS properly you will ensure that it never moves the selected VM's onto the same host.

DRS Automation Rules for Specific VM's

DRS automation settings can be overridden on a per VM basis. Essentially, allowing you to automate the entire environment but exclude certain VM's from being moved around by DRS. This is often done for "sensitive" VM's in an environment. A perfect example of this is Virtual Machines in a pharmaceutical environment. Some of these VM's are running pharmacy apps that are governed by laws saying that the server (VM) its network configs, disk, and paths to disk etc., can be audited at almost any time. In these environments they may still want to use DRS to level load, but will need to override the DRS automation for this VM and never move it just to level load.

To set these rules you can edit the cluster settings and edit the Virtual Machine options. This then allows you to select the specific VM's to override DRS settings and set to one of 5 automation levels:

- Manual: Recommendations are created but have to be applied by a human; this is often used to allow for change control on the move for auditing purposes.

- Partially Automated: This is essentially like a level 1 or level automation for this VM, only move it if it corrects a large imbalance in cluster load.

- Fully automated: Which is essentially apply level 5 automation to this VM

- Default: Which just accepts the Cluster's DRS settings and applies them to the VM.

- Disabled: Which ignores DRS for these VM's. The VM's load is calculated as part of the host load, but no recommendations are ever made for this VM and other VM's are used to level host load.

These rules are great and allow you some granularity, but they come with a caveat. They should be used sparingly. If you have a DRS cluster with 20 VM's and have DRS automated in the cluster but have disabled it for 17 VM's or even 10 VM's, you have effectively limited the balancing ability greatly. These settings should be used judiciously and in probably no more than 25-35% of the environment at most. Greater than that and you are limiting your options greatly and incurring unneeded overhead.

Maintenance Mode

Not that this is a huge deal, but something we want to note here is a function/state of a cluster node known as maintenance mode. You can set a cluster member to maintenance mode which essentially removes its resources from the cluster's resource pools and from the available capacity in the DRS pool. This then forces DRS/VirtualCenter to migrate (VMotion) all of the VM's off of the affected server and keep VM's off of it until it is removed from maintenance mode.

This is essentially a nice way to migrate VM's, allow you to work on, upgrade, bounce etc., the Host while not impacting the VM's in the environment.

High Availability (HA) Services

High Availability services is a service provided within VirtualCenter managed clusters that provides redundancy for hardware failures within the Cluster. This service should really be called "Faster Recovery Services," but I am sure some marketing department put the smack down on that one. The reason for our alternate name recommendation is that HA does not really provide true High Availability. In IT we consider clusters (where a process fails over from one host to another seamlessly) as true High Availability. VMware's HA does not do this. VMware's HA offers a fast/automated recovery for VM's running on a host that has failed or been isolated from the network.

The HA service (as it sits today) is really a software package from Legato called the Automated Availability Manager or AAM for short. AAM is a pretty interesting product if you get to reading about it, but from a VMware perspective you see about 1/10th of the full AAM functionality. In the VMware world, VirtualCenter, instead of the AAM console, is used to configure HA services for HA enabled Clusters. Unlike DRS, VirtualCenter does not initiate VM moves but instead configures the AAM agents running on the hosts and allows these agents to manage themselves and look for host failures.

This is probably a good time to explain to you (if you don't already know) how HA failures affect Virtual Machines. Some people in the industry assume that having HA configured during a host failure means that the VM's are never offline and that when a host fails the VMotion functionality is invoked and the VM's seamlessly migrate to the other host machines. This is completely untrue. VMotion requires that the source and target host machines be up and running. And since HA only takes action AFTER a host failure, it is impossible to VMotion any VM's to another host. In addition to this, the VM's are essentially in a powered off state when HA kicks in and were more than likely powered down hard as their host has just crashed... Getting a warm fuzzy yet?

Not to worry. It takes about 15 seconds for HA services to realize a failure and begin restarting VM's on other hosts in the cluster. The really cool thing about this is that the recovery time for VM's (have them back up and running on good hardware) can generally be counted in minutes. Tests we ran in the early 3.0 days show 20+ VM's restarting from a failed host in less than 5 minutes. Try that on a physical piece of hardware with a bad motherboard.

HA Key Architecture Notables

So let's review some of the key attributes of HA services:

- Clusters using HA can contain up to 16 nodes.

- HA configurations allow you to specify the number of host failures for your Cluster (1-4).

- HA offers what it calls admission controls to protect against over utilization.

- HA has isolation detection to allow a host to determine when it has lost network connectivity.

- Key files and logs for HA can be found in the /opt/LGTOaam512/ directory (see, Legato…).

- HA does not need VirtualCenter running to restart VM's.

- HA is highly dependent on DNS, meaning all host names in the cluster must be able to be resolved via DNS. (Most HA issues are really DNS related.)

- HA does not detect (at this point) SAN storage losses or Network connectivity losses that are not Console NIC's.

When configuring/designing your HA cluster you have a few key decisions to make. The first is to determine the number of host failures you feel the system can absorb. This comes back to your decisions on N+x in your environment. As an example let's assume you have enough VM's to pretty much load up a 10 Host cluster. Your environment requires that you supply N+1 redundancy. So you build an 11 host cluster to meet the requirement. When configuring HA services you will be asked to specify the number of Host failures for which you want to guarantee VM failover. In this example your setting would be 1.

HA allows you to configure a cluster for anywhere from 1 to 4 host failures. The limitation of resides in a limit built in to provide for only 4 "Primaries" or Primary Nodes. These nodes in Legato terms are where resources can be moved. ESX incurs an overhead for each primary added, and the acceptable overhead (per VMware) falls at a maximum of 4 hosts for this purpose in a 16 node cluster.

While the number of failures allowed is an interesting number, don't just go and set it to the highest number yet. The reality is you need to take into account the day to day load of your environment. Let's assume you built the cluster we used in the previous example. You have enough VM load to run 10 hosts at 80% utilization. You then design and built the cluster with 11 hosts to provide N+1.

Here, your setting would seem to be 1 for the maximum number of failures, but let's do some math and see if you can go any higher.

Maximum number of acceptable host failures

While it is easy in the physical world to say "N+1" is required, in the virtual world it is not a one to one ratio. Your 11 server cluster (using DRS and HA) will have VM's running on all hosts to utilize their resources when available. But if we do some quick math around your 11 host environment built to handle 10 hosts at 80% we find some interesting things:

- We assume that each server has 100 units of capacity (converting % of utilization to a number).

- 10 servers have 1000 total capacity units available. 80% of this available capacity is 800 units.

- Your environment (example above) will use 800 units of capacity with 11 hosts that have a total of 1100 units available.

- 11 hosts splitting up those 800 units results in about 72.7 units each or 72.7% utilization.

- If one of these 11 servers were to fail, its 72.7 units are then split amongst 10 hosts (taking us back to 80% util).

- But don't we still have 200 units available? -more than enough to take another host failure.

The idea here is to determine if 80% is truly the maximum or, if during a failure, you can run at 87 or 90 or even 100%+ utilization... Right now our example environment has enough capacity before each server reaches 100% utilization to handle at least 2 more server failures.

The trick with determining the acceptable % is first dictating a policy in the environment for operations during a failure (IE: is it ok to run at 100% or close to it or do you have to stop at 80%, 90% whatever?). Once you do that, you can do the math yourself, determine the bottleneck in the farm as it grows (generally memory but sometimes proc), and then set the maximum number of failures.

Why is this maximum number of failures important? Well, not just because it could save your job, but because of a second option in the HA configurations, Admission Control. Admission Control allows you to dictate what happens when you reach the number of failures configured in the HA environment.

The first option is "Do not power on virtual machines if they violate availability constraints." That is really a big mouthful for "after we hit the limit number of configured failure, and another host fails, don't restart the next failures VM's." This setting essentially will force the system to obey your design decision (the acceptable amount of utilization during a failure) and keep from over utilizing the remaining hosts in the cluster during a massive failure. When this option is selected it also keeps you from reverting snapshots, migrating VM's into the cluster, and reconfiguring any VM's for more CPU or Memory.

The second option for Admission Control (the default) is to "allow Virtual Machines to be powered on even if they violate availability constraints". Basically ignoring your setting, and continue to start VM's even if your farm has sustained the number of expected failures or more.

Detection of a failure

HA is a pretty cool animal once you think about it. The VirtualCenter server allows you to configure your settings, and it takes off from there monitoring all the hosts and looking for failures. But how does it work? The bottom end of HA is an agent that runs on each host in this cluster. This agent stores information (in memory) about the nodes in the cluster and the controller in the cluster. The first node in the cluster acts as the controller. This controller interprets HA rules, can initiate failover actions, and has redundancy provided for its operations by other hosts in the cluster. This controller has a redundant setup in which another node will take over for the controller in the event of a controller failure (one of the reasons for storing HA info on each node in the cluster).

Failures of a node in the cluster are determined by a heartbeat that utilizes the Console network interface. It is HIGHLY advised that you provide redundant NICs for the console to limit failovers in the event of a single Console NIC failure. The heartbeat for HA is monitored by all hosts. Each host monitors the other hosts' heartbeats and in the event of a lost heartbeat a failure event will be triggered. The heartbeat threshold for failures is configured for 15 seconds.

Meaning a loss of the heartbeat will not be considered a "failure" for the first 15 seconds. This allows for a minor network disruption or a loss of a heartbeat packet without kicking off recovery actions.

Once a failure is detected VM's are restarted on the Hosts with the most available capacity. Load may not be evenly distributed initially, but the VM's will restart and DRS at that point can begin to load level the environment. It is at this point that some people notice that HA is "not working." In one environment they successfully configured HA, and then had a project that moved their DNS servers to new IP addresses. The ESX hosts themselves were never reconfigured, and during a failure, no VM's were restarted... I cannot state enough times how important it is to ensure your ESX servers have proper DNS settings and are able to resolve the names of all the other hosts in the cluster.

DNS, DNS, DNS

Did I emphasize it enough? Have proper DNS configurations? If not, here is another piece of information. Prior to ESX 3.01 and VC 2.1 (thankfully this now fixed) the DNS names for ESX hosts using HA have a limit of 29 characters. If the FQDN for your host is not 29 characters or less you will have problems with HA. As an example, this FQDN works just fine "esx1.ronoglesby.com" -19 characters. While this one: "prodesx12.internal.ronoglesby.com" -33 characters, does not. Beware; this has bitten more than one ESX admin. Hopefully you are not running this older version of ESX, but one never knows...

Node isolation

One interesting thing that comes from using a heartbeat for this process is that node isolation can cause some big issues. Imagine if someone (inadvertently of course) disconnected all the nics or even just the console nics on one of your ESX hosts. The cluster node at this point stops receiving heartbeats from the other nodes. When this happens, the node first needs to determine if it has been isolated. It does this by pinging the console NIC's default gateway. If no response comes back after 12 seconds it determines it has been isolated and can take action at that point to shut down VM's (this is configurable and discussed next).

Specific Virtual Machine Settings

When VM's are added to the cluster there are some default settings and behaviors you should understand. The first is that within the HA cluster you can configure VM Restart Priorities and their Isolation Response. Let's look at restart priorities first.

Restart Priority

Restart priorities are set for each VM (default is Medium) and are a relative starting priority for VM's after a failure. VM's with higher starting priorities (maybe more critical VM's) are started before medium, then medium priority VM's are started, and so on. Setting these all too high does nothing other than give equal weight to the VM's for restarts, so use judiciously.

Restart priorities are really important when you have configured the admission control to allow for more than your planned amount of failures. Assuming you have only planned for 1 or 2 failures and set the configuration accordingly, then you have 3 hosts fail, the restart priority will ensure that the more important VM's are started before you potentially run out of resources.

Isolation Response

Isolation Response is a setting that dictates what to do with the Virtual Machine when a node detects it has been isolated from the network. The default for this type of event is to power off the virtual machine. The reason behind this default is fairly well conceived. HA recovery is based on the assumption that the host has failed and the VM's need to be started up again. In the case of a node isolation, the VM's may still be running, and the host will still have a lock on the files for the VM's. By initiating a power off of the VM, the lock will be released, and the HA mechanisms can kick in and restart the VM on another host.

One interesting thing about this is to understand the timing involved and the effect on the VM. If a node has been isolated for 12 seconds it declares itself isolated then begins to follow the isolation responses for the VM's. Power Off responses are just that, like hitting the power button on a server and not doing a clean shutdown. At 15 seconds, the other hosts begin their restart steps on the VM's that just powered down. Now, not all applications behave well after a hard power down, and therefore, they have allowed for another option "Leave power on."

'Leave power on' leaves the VM running on the isolated host. Other hosts trying to restart this VM will not be able to but it may be isolated from the network (or not) and basically just sits on this host hoping everything is ok. Of course the VM with this setting may also have lost its disk connectivity (if using iSCSI over the console nic) and could be dead in the water anyway. Personally, I don't see much of a use for this unless the data inside the VM is extremely susceptible to corruption during a hard power off.

Conclusion

As you can see there are a number of small decisions that need to be made to go into your cluster design. It is imperative that you design your clusters correctly, unlike the logical groupings in VirtualCenter, a cluster is a physical object that requires physical connectivity to the network and storage systems. So decisions about the cluster are more important (and not as easily changed) than the logical Virtual Machine groups in VirtualCenter. Take your time and think out your cluster design, because after hardware selection it is the most important design aspect you will make.

Chapter 5 - Storage

In the last chapter we went through the different local partitions and storage requirements to setup ESX server. In this chapter we dive into the real meat of ESX storage: VMFS partitions for VM disk storage. VMFS 3.21 is the current version of the VM File System created by VMware. VMFS was created to provide storage for the extremely large files that make up VMs. In turn, the requirements for large amounts of storage put a special emphasis on local and SAN based storage for your VMs. This chapter delves into the various uses of storage in an ESX environment.

Storage Components

The storage infrastructure that supports an ESX environment is often one of the most complicated and misunderstood aspects of a virtualization project. Fortunately, over the years, the popularity of virtualization has made its way down to the storage teams and there is better awareness now than there was in the past.

If following the best practices of not only ESX storage configurations, but also the best practices defined for storage infrastructures, your environment should be laid out similarly to the example illustrated in Figure 5 – 1. While this diagram illustrates a typical Fiber Channel SAN infrastructure, we will find that iSCSI follows a near identical design, only using a network communication infrastructure as opposed to fiber.

Figure 5- 1: SAN Infrastructure

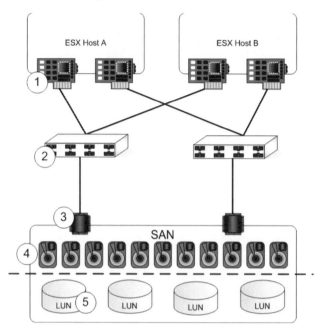

Fiber HBAs

The key component that must be installed in the ESX server for fiber-based SAN storage connectivity is a Fiber HBA. According to the VMware documentation there is a physical limit of 16 HBAs that can be installed in a single system. Again, this is overkill. Except for the most intensive transactional workloads, two HBAs should suffice for your host configuration. The most we would ever recommend putting in a single system is four, assuming you are looking to virtualize Messaging or Database applications that require more dedicated throughput.

Fiber HBAs come in many flavors. We are typically seeing 1 Gb fiber HBAs being phased out and slowly being replaced by 4 Gb fiber, but a solid majority the implementations we are performing are using 2Gb fiber. A single 2 Gb fiber adapter gives us a theoretical maximum bidirectional throughput of about 400MB/Sec, meaning you can concurrently read AND write at about 200MB/Sec each, not that you can read OR write at a total of 400MB/Sec. 1Gb adapters will be about half that speed, 4Gb adapters will give you about double.

iSCSI HBAs

When planning to use iSCSI in a production environment you will want to leverage iSCSI HBAs. These adapters are used to encapsulate Standard SCSI commands inside TCP/IP packets for remote block level storage. By providing adapters specifically for this purpose you will offload the processing required for the storage infrastructure to the hardware.

iSCSI HBAs must leverage a network infrastructure to communicate with backend storage. A true production iSCSI implementation will have its own independent network infrastructure so as not to interfere with regular network communications. Based on this fact, the maximum speed per path in an iSCSI implementation is 1 Gb with a maximum capability of two iSCSI HBAs (paths) per host. While this may not be enough for the most intense of enterprise workloads, it is definitely nothing to ignore based on the cost per performance you receive with an iSCSI infrastructure. Based on the imminent release of 10 Gb networking not far off for VMware ESX, we are expecting these speeds to increase drastically and give some significant competition to the performance of fiber-based SAN infrastructures.

SAN Switches (Used with Fiber HBAs)

SAN switches are not unlike network switches in that they provide a mechanism for a multiple hosts to communicate to a centralized storage infrastructure. The configuration and use of SAN switches typically falls within the responsibilities of the storage group in an organization. It is highly unlikely that you will come across a configuration that does not use multiple SAN switches, thus providing multiple paths to your SAN infrastructure. The importance of the storage infrastructure definitely demands a very highly available solution to keep hosts and storage arrays constantly communicating with one another.

Network Switches (Used with iSCSI HBAs and NFS)

Network switches come into play when using a form of network based storage for your virtual infrastructure such as iSCSI or NFS. It is highly recommended that a separate network infrastructure from the production communication network be used for the storage infrastructure. This ensures proper flow of incoming and outgoing network communication traffic does not interfere with disk activity, and vice versa. As a worst case scenario, a separate VLAN should be used for the storage infrastructure to ensure all the Windows broadcast garbage stays away from storage communication.

The use of network switches is discussed in significantly more detail in Chapter 6 where we discuss networking in ESX Server.

Storage Arrays

Storage arrays are the key to a centralized, redundant, and high speed virtual infrastructure. Storage arrays are used to manage and configure very large amounts of storage for enterprise applications such as Database, Messaging, and of course, Virtualization. VMware ESX supports fiber based and iSCSI based storage arrays across a wide variety of vendors.

While the speed and capabilities vary widely between the various vendors and models of storage arrays, there are several key components that are generally found regardless of who is providing your centralized storage.

Storage Processor (sometimes called controllers)

Both Fiber and iSCSI storage arrays contain at least one, and optimally two storage processors (SP). Storage processors manage the front end access of hosts back to actual SAN storage LUNs. SAN's typically come in one of two configurations: Active/Active or Active/Passive.

Active/Active arrays are ones in which a single LUN may be accessed down either or both storage processor concurrently. This allows for the greatest flexibility in load balancing I/O communication down multiple paths. It should be noted that ESX cannot take full advantage of Active/Active SANs, as there is a limitation in the VMkernel itself which only allows ESX to communicate to a given LUN down a single path at any point in time. It is possible within ESX to determine which HBA a LUN uses in an Active/Active configuration at the VMkernel level, making Active/Active arrays the optimal choice for load balancing your SAN environment for your virtual infrastructure.

Active/Passive arrays are those that only allow access to a given LUN down a single path at a time. Multiple LUNs may be accessed down alternate storage processors. The SP that is not active for a particular LUN will act as a failover SP for that LUN. It is possible to dictate which SP is preferred on a per LUN basis on the SAN, but this cannot be specified on the ESX host.

Physical Disks

Prior to virtualization, many Windows administrators could have gone their whole life thinking that a SAN consisted of some REALLY large hard drives. The truth is, SANs are made up hard drives that are typically smaller than those provided in new server deployments; there just happens to be a lot of them.

While we won't go too far into actual SAN management and configuration in this book, it is important to inform ESX administrators what it is that makes SANs so fast and fault tolerant. The simple answer is "Lots of disks". SANs provide volumes to hosts by using typical RAID striping mechanisms across a large number of disks. Typically, the more disks (spindles) that are provided, the faster the disk access will ultimately be. There is, of course, a point of diminishing return which is based on your actual SAN infrastructure and how the storage processors communicate with the disks (Typically internal Fiber or Serial Attached SCSI).

Some of the more critical data LUNs not only use RAID striping, but also mirroring to create some unique SCSI configurations such as RAID 1+0, in which each disk has a mirrored pair and the data is then striped across all mirrored pairs.

It is not uncommon for an implementation to call for multiple RAID configurations to be leveraged for various purposes in their infrastructure. As an example, a set of RAID1 volumes may be created for the sole purpose of hosting operating system partitions, as performance is not important, but redundancy is. A set of RAID5 volumes are then created for standard data partitions where speed is critical as well as lightweight protection from disk failure. The most critical of data volumes may be configured in a RAID10 configuration, which provides not only high performance, but also an extremely high level of protection of the underlying data. It is very important for the ESX administrator to understand the backend configuration of the storage infrastructure to properly match the role of the virtual machine disk files to the proper SAN volume on the backend infrastructure.

LUNs

Knowing what we now know about the backend storage infrastructure we can describe what a LUN is. LUN itself stands for "Logical Unit Number" and refers to a logical device that is presented to a host as a single physical disk. LUNs in an ESX infrastructure are typically assigned to multiple hosts to enable VMotion, DRS and HA functionality. When we discuss VMFS partitions later in this chapter you will have a better understanding as to how this is possible.

Each LUN is assigned a LUN ID when it is presented to the ESX hosts. It is extremely important that these LUN IDs stay consistent across all hosts in the ESX cluster; otherwise it is possible to run across some strange disk signature errors on certain hosts. It is also important that each LUN be given a unique ID. Any two LUNs that are assigned to the same host with the same ID will be assumed to be the same LUN. ESX will natively provide failover capabilities in this instance, and if it has to fail over it would be quite bad for your data not to exist on the second LUN. For this reason, if a LUN is presented down multiple paths to the same host, it must be presented with the same LUN ID down both paths.

A total of 256 LUNs may be assigned to any single ESX host with a maximum size of 2TB per LUN. In addition, you want to limit the number of hosts that can access a single LUN to prevent a bottleneck when accessing the data. Based on some of the other limitations of building a virtual infrastructure, the greatest number of hosts that should ever theoretically have access to a single LUN is 32, which is the maximum host size for a DRS cluster. Trying to leverage LUNs across multiple large DRS clusters is not a good idea and will eventually result in choking your bandwidth to the point that the LUN is unusable.

LUNs can be used in several ways, which we will discuss throughout the duration of this chapter.

A single LUN can be configured with a VMFS file system

Multiple LUNs can be spanned together to form a single VMFS file system

A single LUN may be configured for direct access by a virtual machine without using the VMFS file system (This is called a RAW Device Mapping, or simply RDM)

Identifying LUNs in VMware ESX Server

You may have already been poking around ESX and noticed the number for your RAID controller or Fiber cards; it looks something like this:

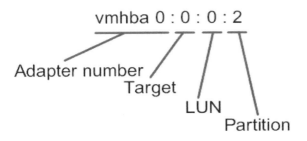

Before we get to deep into this you need to understand first how VMware identifies the HBAs in your system. This numbering scheme can be seen from either the Virtual Infrastructure Client or from within the service console. Generally when dealing with SAN LUNs or other disks presented to the server, you will see the first three sections of this identifier as ESX sees it: a simple disk attached to the system via a Virtual Machine host bus adapter (vmhba).

The first section shows the adapter number, the next section shows the SCSI target ID, and the final section shows the LUN number. When this numbering scheme has four sections, the fourth section is used for partitions on specific LUNs—not by the adapter itself.

Storage Types

So, I know I want to implement ESX, but have not decided on the storage solution yet. Which should we use in our environment: Local SCSI disks or remote SAN, iSCSI, or NFS storage? Well the answer may well be a combination of the various available technologies. While it is possible to run ESX without a local

VFMS partition, that doesn't mean it's the best solution. Also, while it is possible to use all local VMFS partitions for virtual machine storage, it may not offer the flexibility you need in your environment.

Local SCSI

In many small environments local SCSI disks are how ESX is first implemented. Then as disk needs or the environment grows, SAN connectivity is implemented and the VMs are moved to the centralized storage.

The primary reason for using local storage for your virtual machines is cost. When comparing local SCSI disk costs to that of SAN storage, local disk is much cheaper. In addition, if you are a small environment that does not have a SAN right now, the initial implementation of a SAN can be a substantial investment.

The major drawback to not using centralized SAN storage is that you lose the ability to move virtual machines quickly and easily from host to host. Touted VMware features like VMotion, DRS, and HA require that you have a SAN infrastructure in place to use them. In addition, if a host fails and you are using local storage, you must recover the virtual machine disk files from either a backup solution or some other form of network storage used for disk file backups. Where, if you had a SAN, you could simply restart the virtual machines using the existing disk files on a new host.

Configuring SCSI Controllers

The first thing you need to be aware of is that the VMkernel only supports a specific set of controllers. The current list of supported controllers can easily be found on VMware's support site and should be referenced before configuring hardware for ESX.

The next thing you will have to decide on is how to configure your controller and the options available to you. If you have a controller capable of creating multiple arrays, you have a lot of flexibility. If you have multiple controllers in your box, you are really set up.

Like database servers, it is best from a performance perspective to split up the operating system and the application. In this case (though it is a crude analogy) it is best to split up the service console from your virtual machines. Having two controllers will allow you to store your service console on one controller and your virtual machine disks and configurations on another. If you only have one controller with the ability to create multiple arrays then that is the next best option you have. Split the service console onto the first array and the VMs onto the second. Spread the VMFS partition for the VMs across as many spindles as possible. A RAID 5 would be my recommendation for the VMs while a simple mirrored set (RAID 1) is more than sufficient for the service console.

If you don't plan on storing VM disk files on your local storage, then a single RAID controller – even if it only supports a single array – will suffice. But this section is really focusing on the configuration for the local storage of VMs.

Advantages of using local SCSI Storage:
- Cost. Local SCSI storage will always be cheaper than a SAN solution

- Simple to implement; requires no special SAN experience of any additional configuration within ESX

Disadvantages of using local SCSI storage:
- Makes recovering virtual machines from a failed host more complex and time consuming

- Eliminates your ability to use features like VMotion, DRS and HA

- Reduces the overall scalability of your implementation

Remote Storage

The exact opposite advantages and disadvantages of local storage applies to Remote storage for ESX. While a remote solution requires additional expense and configurations, the benefits are enormous.

Remote VMFS partitions allow you a number of benefits over local storage. The simple use of VMotion, DRS and HA is a huge benefit to any environment. But add on top of the ability to have a fast, central repository for virtual machine templates, the ability to recover virtual machines on another host if you have a host failure, the ability allocate large amounts of storage (we're talking terabytes here) to your ESX servers, and the list goes on and on.

The real idea here is that a remote implementation offers you a truly scalable and recoverable ESX solution. The options and features available to remote storage users are enormous, while the limitations found in local SCSI storage are like an anchor around an ESX admin's neck.

In this section we will discuss Fiber and iSCSI SAN configurations as well as NFS shares for VMFS partitions. For now let's just look at the advantages and disadvantages of using remote storage for your VMFS volumes.

Advantages of using Remote Storage
- Allows for VMotion, DRS and HA functionality

- Allows for a centrally maintained template location

- Allows for fast recovery of virtual machines in the event of a host failure

- Provides a more scalable storage solution for your environment

- Allows for VMs to be clustered across hosts (Fiber Only)

- Allows for physical to Virtual Clustering (Fiber Only)

- Provides the ability for your virtual machines to use RAW disks, just like a physical machine

Disadvantages of using Remote Storage
- More complex to manage and implement

- More expensive than local storage

Fiber Channel

Fiber Channel SAN is the most common type of storage used for VMware ESX implementations due to its performance and scalability. Fiber Channel SANs provide block level access to storage LUNs which allows ESX to have direct access to the physical disk. As the name implies Fiber Channel infrastructures connect the host to the enterprise storage through high speed fiber connections. The current maximum supported speed for Fiber Connectivity in ESX is 4 Gb per Fiber HBA, which equates to roughly 800 MB/Sec of bidirectional throughput (~400 MB/Sec Read and ~400 MB/Sec Write). By loading up two 4 Gb HBAs in your system and properly balancing your data LUNs down multiple paths you can easily achieve the required performance of 95% of your infrastructure through shared bandwidth, which is quite impressive.

A major benefit of a Fiber Channel storage solution is the fact that the entire storage infrastructure is separate from the network infrastructure. The only communication flowing across a proper SAN infrastructure is disk I/O. Not only does this help from a performance standpoint, but also from a security standpoint as well.

Advantages of Fiber Channel Remote Storage
- Has been around a long time and is in use within many organizations
- High performance access for multiple servers
- Standalone infrastructure to support disk access
- Block level access to underlying LUN

Disadvantages of Fiber Channel Remote Storage
- Supporting infrastructure is more costly than alternate remote storage options

iSCSI

While it was possible to configure virtual machines to communicate with iSCSI disks in previous versions of VMware ESX, it typically had poor performance overall. With ESX 3, VMware has built iSCSI access into the VMkernel to provide the same level of block access to LUNs as a SAN infrastructure. This means that ESX can now use iSCSI SANs to create LUNs and configure VMFS file systems. At this point, iSCSI can be leveraged in one of two modes; through a hardware initiator, which requires specific hardware for storage communication, or through a software initiator that is integrated into the VMkernel network stack.

The iSCSI protocol takes standard SCSI calls and encapsulates them into TCP/IP packets for transport to a remote device. Because of this, iSCSI often requires additional overhead because of its dependency on the TCP/IP network stack. By using the proper hardware initiator with a TCP Offload Engine

(TOE), you can significantly reduce the processing overhead incurred from iSCSI by letting the hardware do the menial task of managing the TCP/IP stack. This option is not available in a software initiator, and the overhead of managing the network stack is managed by... yup, the VMkernel.

A maximum of two iSCSI HBAs can be installed in any given host; each currently capable of speeds up to 1 Gb/Sec. This equates to a theoretical bidirectional throughput of about 250MB/Sec per HBA, which is a bit slower than Fiber Channel. Technology is already well down the path of providing 10Gb networking capabilities to ESX and the VMkernel, at which point iSCSI SANs may start outperforming some of the more expensive fiber based solutions in place. It will probably be a slow and costly process for organizations to start implementing a 10Gb solution in their environments, and while VMware will support it, we don't anticipate wide adoption for some time.

It is entirely possible to configure iSCSI communication on your regular IP network, but definitely not recommended. iSCSI infrastructures should consist of a separate physical network as to not interfere with regular network traffic, and vice versa. Not only will physical separate provide the best performance, it will also provide the best security for your iSCSI I/O infrastructure.

Advantages of iSCSI Remote Storage
- Excellent cost for performance

- Provides centralized storage over a low cost communication infrastructure

- Block level access to underlying LUN

- Will soon exceed the speed of Fiber Based SAN solutions

Disadvantages of iSCSI Remote Storage
- Performance not yet to that of Fiber Based storage

- Will be costly to upgrade to 10Gb networking for higher speed

- Often a newer component to many organizations

NFS

In addition to supporting iSCSI, VMware ESX also has built in support for NAS devices through the use of the NFS protocol. This allows for a second method of providing low cost network based storage to your virtual infrastructure. When ESX 3 first came out and people started dabbling with NFS support, there was a quick judgment made that it should only be used for storing virtual machine template files and that the performance was substandard for virtual machine utilization.

It has been found, over time that NFS actually performs extremely well in a properly configured and structured environment. NFS has been around for a good 20+ years now and has proven to be a very reliable centralized file system with performance that only improves over time based on network enhancements. Initial testing results that have come back show that not only can NFS be used for running virtual machines; it is actually extremely fast when using some of the newest available hardware.

An ESX host has the capability to map up to 256 NFS volumes, but there are several reasons we wouldn't recommend this that we will discuss in the next section. For a SMB organization looking to get started in virtualization, leveraging NFS is an extremely low cost way to provide a centralized virtual infrastructure that has support for the advanced virtualization technologies such as VMotion, DRS, and HA. VMware addresses a major challenge of virtual machine sizing in NFS implementations by allowing the use of thin provisioned VMDK files. This reports to ESX that the full size of the disk is being utilized, but in actuality, data is provisioned and used only when requested by the guest. This allows virtual machines to be stored in an optimized fashion for use on NAS devices, which often have stricter limitations surrounding free space than other types of centralized storage.

Access to NFS volumes is performed through the VMkernel network stack. Like iSCSI, it makes sense to provide a separate network infrastructure for your NFS for ESX implementation. It is often not possible to do this, as NFS infrastructures have typically existed for some time in an organization. Changing the way NFS is managed specifically for a virtual infrastructure will ensure network activity meant for storage resources does not interfere with network activity for regular communication and vice versa.

Advantages of NFS Remote Storage
- NFS has been around for 20+ years and is a very stable and reliable protocol

- Often an existing component in most organizations

- Defaults to thin provisioned VMDK files for optimized storage utilization

- Provides centralized storage over a low cost communication infrastructure

- Will increase in speed as 10Gb networking is more widely adopted

Disadvantages of NFS Remote Storage
- Performance not yet to that of Fiber Based storage

- Contains more overhead than Hardware iSCSI Initiators (No TOE)

- Will be a costly upgrade to 10Gb networking for higher speed

Limitations of Network Based Storage

There is a common architectural issue with all types of network based storage in the fact that there is a single bottleneck in the uplink to the storage device. In many virtual infrastructures there could be as many as 20-25 hosts, each with multiple gigabit connections, communicating with a centralized storage infrastructure. If there is a lot of disk activity across the environment it will not be uncommon for the generated throughput to be greater than what is physically connected to the storage system. In this event you will see a spike in dropped network packets on your ESX hosts. If you notice performance problems in a network based storage infrastructure, look at the logical aspect of your throughput as a first step. It may just be that you have oversubscribed your SAN connectivity. Resolving these issues will require a plan of rebalancing network and disk I/O to fit within the constraints of the storage infrastructure, or possibly even changing to a different type of storage infrastructure for specific virtual machines altogether.

VMFS Intro

The primary storage for virtual machine information is the VMFS volume. VMFS is a unique journaling file system created by VMware as a low overhead, high performance file system. The primary concern when they created this file system was to be able to create a file system that could handle extremely large files, and provide as near to disk access speeds for virtual machine usage as possible

The VMFS-3 file system has some unique characteristics and limitations that make it different than traditional file systems.

- Ability to span across multiple disks/LUNs
- Ability for multiple ESX Servers to concurrently access files on the same VMFS-3 volume
- Up to 256 VMFS volumes per ESX system
- 2 TB per physical extent
- Up to 32 physical extents per VMFS volume
- Maximum size of 64TB VMFS size (using extents)

So what does this all mean to you? Let's review each of these features quickly and see what they mean.

Ability to span across multiple disks/LUNs

So what this really means is that you can create a single VMFS volume that spans multiple LUNs or multiple disks. The benefit here is obvious: you can create enormous volumes. It is important to note that creating a volume with multiple extents does not stripe the data across multiple spindles; it simply extends the volume onto additional disks. Thanks to the fact that VMFS-3 now uses LVM to manage volumes, losing one disk in the extent will not cause the entire volume to fail, but it can be difficult to predict which virtual machines won't work and troubleshoot issues when one of the extents fails.

Ability for multiple ESX Servers to concurrently access files on the same volume

This is really the functionality that enables VMotion and VMware HA in the event of a host failure. The idea here is that your ESX hosts can all see the same LUN(s). Because of this, the host almost becomes irrelevant when it comes to storing disk files. Since multiple servers can use the same LUN, you can simply stop a VM on one host and start it on another. Or if the host fails, you can simply point a different host to the existing configuration files.

This is made possible since the VMkernel does not lock the entire VMFS file system. The locking is done at a file level, which allows multiple hosts to access the same volumes, but only allows one host at a time to have access to a virtual machine's VMDK file.

Up to 256 VMFS volumes per ESX System

This one is pretty obvious. 256 VMFS volumes can provide a lot of space. Generally we see ESX systems with no more than 10 or 15 VMFS volumes exposed to them. So having the ability to go to 256 allows you more scalability than you may need. We will discuss why coming anywhere near this limit is definitely not a best practice when building a proper infrastructure when we talk about sizing strategies later in this chapter.

2 TB Per physical extent and 32 extents per volume

These two are pretty much interwoven. The first means you can have up to 2 TB per LUN exposed to ESX that you are going to create a VMFS volume on. And if you have a need to create a single large VMFS volume, you can have up to 32 different physical extents (read LUNs) that comprise a single VMFS volume. Using 2nd grade math we can quickly determine that the physical maximum for a single VMFS volume is 64TB when using the maximum number of maximum sized extents.

Differences between VMFS2 and VMFS3

Outside of the primary difference of VMFS-2 being a flat file system and VMFS-3 having an actual directory structure the major differences between the file systems have to do with size and reliability. Nearly every configurable maximum is increased in VMFS-3. In addition, the introduction of journaling which provides better data consistency recovery from system crashes.

A final item to note that will become quickly evident to ESX users is that the canonical VMHBA names for LUNs and volumes have been replaced with

UUID signatures for volume management. In VMFS-2 there were issues where the same LUNs were given different IDs across different hosts. VMware ESX 3 will now use the unique UUIDs for management of these volumes.

While ESX 3 does have the capability to load and read VMFS-2 volumes, it cannot perform write operations, thus making it impossible to run VMFS-2 based virtual machines on ESX 3. The VMFS-2 functionality is provided solely to allow ESX 2 to ESX 3 upgrades.

Now you understand the basics and limitations of VMFS. It's a high performance file system made to handle a small number of large files. Now it's time to get down into the how's and why's of VMFS. Let's take a look at what knowing all this information allows us to actually do.

Naming Standards for VMFS Volumes

One thing that will become quickly apparent, if it hasn't already, is that we are big fans of incorporating naming standards into any user namable component within the virtual infrastructure. When creating a naming standard for your VMFS volumes you should use something that makes it quickly identifiable not only to you as an ESX administrator, but also to a storage administrator. Naming something "VMFS0", "VMFS1", etc does not make troubleshooting easy. Use something a little more conventional such as "cx7_SAN_13", which would indicate I am using an EMC CX700 storage array and my VMFS volume is on a SAN LUN with an ID of 13. The same works for iSCSI as well. Take "fas250_iSCSI_25" as example of me using a NetApp FAS250 iSCSI LUN with an ID of 25.

Since NFS is a network file system based solution, a slightly different approach is needed to identify an NFS mount. Assuming all ESX mount points are in the same root directory on the NFS server, I use the simple naming convention of "Servername_MountPoint". This allows me to quickly and easily identify the NFS server or device and the exact storage mount point I am using to store my virtual machine data.

Default File and Directory Structure

We've stated earlier that unlike previous versions of the VMFS file system, VMFS-3 is no longer a flat file system and contains an actual directory structure. As we will find out later in this chapter, this is a key feature that is required for the proper operation of VMware HA. The root path for all VMFS volumes on an ESX host is /vmfs/volumes/. Each VMFS volume is assigned a unique UUID and has a listing under this root path. If you set up a friendly name as instructed in the "Naming Standards for VMFS Volumes" section, you will also see a symbolic link that points your friendly name back to the ugly UUID.

Figure 5- 2: Directory Structure

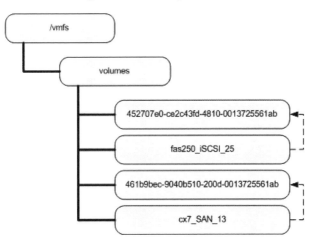

Directories

Each virtual machine or template that is created in the infrastructure is given its own directory on the VMFS volume that was specified as the virtual machine's datastore during the creation of the virtual machine. The directory name will match that of the virtual machine specified during configuration. If multiple VMDK files are specified after the initial creation of the virtual machine that span across multiple LUNs, there will be a virtual machine directory on each VMFS volume that contains a VMDK file. This model allows for easy tracking of your virtual machine's configuration information, even if it does span multiple volumes within the infrastructure. By default, there are no other subdirectories contained inside the virtual machine's configuration directory.

Files

The VMDK files aren't the only objects contained in these virtual machine directories, there are several files that are critical to the operation of the virtual machine. Since most of these files have been touched on in other areas of this book, I will only lightly discuss them here.

VMX – The virtual machine configuration file that specifies the detailed configurations of CPU Count, Memory, Disk locations, and other critical options for the virtual machine

NVRAM – Contains the BIOS configuration information for the virtual machine

LOG – Contains the log information of the virtual machine

VSWP – The VMkernel swap file that is used for the virtual machine when a host has over allocated its memory resources

VMSD – Contains information about the location and path to the VSNP files when using snapshots

VSNP – A snapshot file indicating the VMDK file is in a non-persistent mode and that changes are being written to this snapshot file

VMDK Disk Format

In order to create and assign hard drives to your virtual machines when using centralized VMFS storage you will need to leverage VMDK files. A VMDK file represents a physical hard drive device that is presented to your guest operating system. When connecting a new VMDK file to a virtual machine, the operating system sees it as a non-partitioned physical drive. This drive can be partitioned and formatted using a variety of file systems including NTFS and ext3. Up to 60 VMDK files can be assigned to any guest operating system, allowing for quite a bit of flexibility in creating a partitioning scheme in the guest operating system. When sizing a VMDK file, ESX has a limitation of 2 TB per VMDK.

A typical VMDK file consists of two files on the VMFS file system. The first is the header file, which contains critical information about the disk such as its size and geometry. It is typically a very small file and can be read in any plain text editor. The second file is the flat file which contains your actual virtual machine data. The flat file will always report as being the same size as the size of the hard drive you specified when building the virtual machine. ESX is unlike Workstation and Server in the fact that when a VMDK file is created you have no choice but to assign all disk space at the time of creation. This keeps the file system clean and sequential for VMDK file access. There is one exception to this rule and we will discuss that when we talk about thin provisioning VMDK files later in this section.

Creating VMDKs with Different Provisioning Methods

There are actually four different methods of provisioning VMDK files (outside of Raw Device Mappings, which we discuss later) in ESX server. Each of them provides unique functionality around creation time, access speed, and disk space allocation.

Zeroed Thick

Creating a zeroed thick VMDK file is the default action when creating a new VMDK file from the Virtual Infrastructure Client or with the "vmkfstools –c" command. At creation time, a zeroed thick VMDK file is completely allocated at creation time, but existing data blocks are not wiped clean immediately. When a virtual machine attempts to read data on one of these data blocks for the first time, the block is filled with random data. This means that the VMDK file can be very quickly created, and the data that may have been on the disk prior to being formatted with VMFS cannot be read by a guest operating system. Since this data must be written to the disk before it can be read by the guest, there is a small performance hit the first time the data block is accessed. This action only occurs once per data block, so if the same block were to be changed a second time, it would not need to be wiped clean.

Eager Zeroed Thick

Creating an eager zeroed thick VMDK file can only be done with the vmkfstools command and specifying the "-d eager zeroed thick" option. The difference between eager zeroed thick and zeroed thick lies in the fact that an eager zeroed thick VMDK file will have all data blocks zeroed out when it is created. This means the VMDK file will take longer to create than a zeroed thick disk. The exact amount of time is dependent on the size of the disk and the speed of the underlying storage infrastructure. Creating an eager zeroed thick VMDK file will not incur any performance penalty the first time a data block is accessed, as the data has already been zeroed out. If creating a VMDK file for a transactional system such as a database, messaging or file server, it makes sense to manually create your VMDK file with this option from the service console.

Thick

I'll start by stating that using this creation method is a major security risk and it should not ever be used. Instead of just calling it quits there and saving myself some writing, I'll actually explain why such a bold statement is necessary. When you create a thick VMDK file, it is done in the same fashion as creating a zeroedthick file. All space is allocated when the file is created, but no data is wiped clean. The downside is that it is not wiped clean the first time it is accessed either. Any data that may exist in the data blocks that make up the VMDK file can quite easily be accessed through easy to write code or easy to find undelete utilities. If you care about data integrity in your environment (typically Sarbanes Oxley or HIPPA will dictate that for you), never ever create a thick VMDK file.

Thin

A thin VMDK file is a new and unique method in an ESX environment. It is the default creation option if a VMDK file is created on an NFS volume. What it means is that data blocks are allocated and zeroed out as they are used, making it the most efficient in regards to storage space utilization. The down side of this becomes evident if you have multiple thin VMDK files on the same NFS or VMFS volume through fragmentation. Since data blocks are only assigned when they are used, if multiple files are being created, moved, etc in the same volume, your performance is going to suffer because these files will become extremely fragmented extremely quickly. This performance impact isn't as significant in an NFS environment, as the block data is abstracted from the ESX host, but it is recommended that you not use thin provisioning of a VMDK file when using VMFS volumes on your ESX host.

Snapshots

Snapshots are not an entirely new component in ESX. Previous versions used a very simplistic REDO file method to create a point in time snapshot of a virtual machine. The legacy REDO files were only linear and there was a maximum limit of two concurrent REDO files for any given VMDK file. The new snapshot format is identical to that used in VMware Workstation and VMware server. When using snapshot files you can not only create a linear checkpoint structure, but can also create complex parent-child relationships to provide significant flexibility around various recovery or testing points. Snapshots are taken at a virtual machine level, whereas REDO files were taken at a VMDK level. This means that when a snapshot of a virtual machine is created, all compatible disks are captured in that snapshot.

A single virtual machine can contain up to 32 levels of snapshots, which should provide for even the most complex configurations of a virtual machine. A typical snapshot consists of three major components:

Guest Memory State (Optional) – Performs a memory dump to disk of a running virtual machine so it may be recovered to the exact point and power state at the time the snapshot was taken. If guest memory is not included with the snapshot, the server will boot from scratch in a crash consistent state.

Guest Configuration State – Captures the configuration of the virtual machine hardware such as number of processors, assigned memory, virtual hard drive configuration, etc.

Guest Disk State – Cuts off disk access to the parent disk and creates a snapshot disk file (child). Any new file system changes are written to the snapshot file and the parent is not modified until the child snapshot is deleted or the user reverts back to the checkpoint.

Linear Snapshots

Linear snapshots are the easiest to visualize and manage in a virtual infrastructure. A linear snapshot configuration consists of the same virtual machine with several point-in-time checkpoints that do not branch in different directions. Each snapshot has one parent image and one child image, with the exception of the primary VMDK file not having a parent and the final snapshot not having a child.

Figure 5- 3: Linear Snapshots

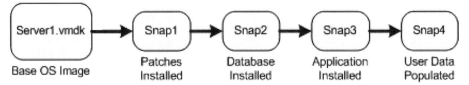

The key to applying a name to a snapshot is to describe the activity that occurred up to the point in time that the snapshot was taken. As an example from the image above, the database was installed between the time after Snapshot 1 was created and Snapshot 2 was taken. If you want to revert back to a point in time and install a different database platform, you would need to revert back to Snapshot 1, which invalidates any of the data that occurred from that point forward in a linear format. This is where nested snapshots come into play.

Nested Snapshots

Nested snapshots function on the premise that a parent VMDK can have more than one child, but a child can still have only one parent. This allows multiple configuration branches to be formed for more complex configuration and test scenarios.

Figure 5- 4: Nested Snapshots

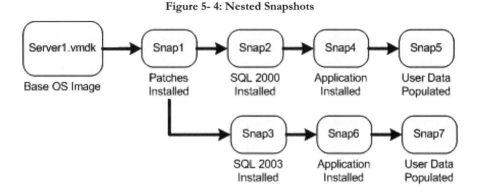

In this configuration we can see that a new branch has been made by creating a second child snapshot to the Snapshot 1 parent. This allows a tester to more easily switch back and forth between not only different database platforms, but also the application and user data that was added to that platform. By simply flipping between Snapshot 5 and Snapshot 7, the user can completely change their database environment to perform testing against otherwise identical configurations.

We can take a look at one final example to show how easily a nested snapshot infrastructure can get in what most would consider a typical test scenario for an application developer.

Figure 5- 5: Advanced Nested Snapshots

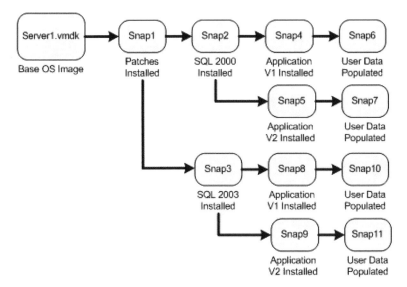

As you can see here, we have not only nested our database with two different versions like we did in our previous example, but we have also introduced two versions of our application. By changing between Snapshots 6, 7, 10, and 11, a user can very easily test four unique scenarios quickly and easily on an enterprise ESX infrastructure.

When using Snapshots, you want to be extremely conscious of the amount of free space you have in your VMFS volumes. Snapshots constantly grow as data inside the virtual machine changes. Devastating results have been known to occur if a VMFS file system is filled to its maximum capacity and snapshots are being used on virtual machines. If you intend to use snapshots for activities such as backup or creating multiple checkpoints, make sure you plan a sufficient amount of free space into your VMFS volumes to support the rate of change in your virtual machines.

Independent Mode Disks

There may be a situation in which you would like to exclude a particular disk from a server snapshot. This is typically in a case where you only want to capture the base operating system for recovery purposes and do not want to capture a large data volume. You can specify individual VMDK files that you wish to exclude by changing them to Independent Mode VMDK files using the Virtual Infrastructure Client.

Persistent and Non Persistent VMDK Files

When using Independent Mode Disks, you must specify how the data will actually be written to your VMDK files. There are two access modes that you can set on a per VMDK file basis.

Persistent Mode - This is the default access mode for all newly-created VMDK files. VMDKs in this configuration behave exactly like a drive on a physical machine would. Once you make a change to the file system, its permanently written to the VMDK file. It's recommended that unless there is a specific need to use a different access mode, that persistent be used, as it provides the best overall disk performance.

Nonpersistent Mode - VMDK files configured in a nonpersistent mode discard all changes made to the file system since the point in time in which the access mode was changed to nonpersistent. When the virtual machine is powered off (not rebooted), any changes that were made to the VMDK are ignored. This is handy in kiosk situations where multiple people have access to a machine through some form of remote connectivity.

If someone were to delete key files, you can instantly return the system to its original state. Another situation in which nonpersistent mode may be convenient is for training classrooms. Several students may be given their own virtual machines as their lab to configure a specific system. They can install applications and reboot several times. At the end of the day, a simple power off of the VM will place the machines back to their original state.

When using nonpersistent access mode, it's best to completely configure the server then change the disk access mode to nonpersistent. This ensures you always go back to the expected configuration on the VMDK file.

Raw Device Mappings (RDMs)

ESX 3 provides a way to map LUNs directly to a virtual machine without having to mess around with VMFS partitions and VMDK files. This is done by configuring a disk mapping file on an existing VMFS partition that each ESX host in a cluster has access to. When using disk mapping files, you are basically using a VMDK type file stored on a VMFS volume that instructs the VMkernel that the actual data is stored directly on a SAN LUN. The virtual machine that you want to leverage the Raw LUN will actually point to the mapping file as the location of its virtual hard drive.

The mapping file manages the metadata for the LUN that the virtual machine uses as its disk. The metadata is basically the locking information for the LUN and the physical location of the LUN. Notice here that we say LUN and not partition. Disk mapping files only support mapping directly to an entire LUN and not a partition that exists on a LUN.

Figure 5- 6: RDM

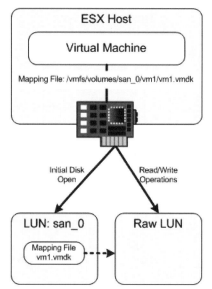

When using an RDM it is important to note that the mapping file is used to instruct the VMkernel where to write the data, not as a continuous proxy mechanism to the Raw LUN itself. When access to a disk is requested, the

VMkernel reads the mapping file, performs the necessary locking and reads the physical location of the Raw LUN. Subsequent I/O activity is then written directly to the Raw LUN itself without having to leverage the mapping file again (until the virtual machine is powered off and the disk can be unlocked and released).

The virtual machine itself will actually treat the Raw LUN as a regular physical disk and it will be partitioned directly with an NTFS or EXT file system, without having to use VMFS and VMDK files on the LUN itself. The advantage of using the mapping file is that regardless of which type of RDM you configure, you will still have the capability to perform VMotion, DRS, and HA activities of virtual machines with RDMs configured.

There are two different access modes for RDM disks inside VMware ESX, each with unique characteristics: Virtual and Physical.

Virtual RDM

When configuring a virtual mode RDM, the access to the RAW LUN is fully virtualized by the VMkernel. You have the exact same capabilities that you would if you were using a standard VMDK file such as the ability to add redo logs, and import and export the contents of the disk just like a normal VM disk file. Inside the virtual machine, you would see this disk just as you would a typical VMDK file as well. It would appear in Device Manager as a VMware SCSI disk device.

Virtual mode RDMs are often used for very large volumes that already exist and it doesn't make sense to migrate data over to a VMDK file. This is typically found on File, Database, or Messaging servers. By keeping the VMDK in virtual mode, you are afforded with the benefits of being able to add snapshots to your virtual machines and back them up by taking advantage of virtualization specific backup software.

Physical RDM

In physical mode, the virtualization of the SCSI device is limited. As a matter of fact, all SCSI commands from the virtual machine are sent to the physical device with the exception of the Report LUNs command. This mode is often used when you are required to run SAN management agents within the virtual machine that require lower level access to the physical device. When using physical mode RDMs, the disks are seen within the operating system with their physical characteristics.

Another scenario in which physical mode RDMs are typically used are when physical to virtual or virtual to virtual cluster across hosts is required. Physical mode RDMs remove SCSI locking from the list of responsibilities of the VMkernel and passes it on to the guest operating system, which is a requirement for using MSCS in a virtual environment.

It is very important to note that since near nothing is virtualized, and SCSI locking is not managed by the VMkernel, it is not possible to use VMware snapshots when using a physical RDM. This is the trade off you have to give when you need lower level access to your physical disks.

When to Use RDMs

We have already highlighted several instances of when RDMs should be leveraged. One thing we want to make clear is that RDMs should NOT be used as a means to significantly increase performance of your virtual machine. Testing has shown that there is little to no performance gain by using an RDM over a VMDK file on a VMFS partition. In addition, there is no performance gain when choosing to use a virtual or physical mode RDM. The main reason you would want to use an RDM is for flexibility. If you need to move a LUN back to a physical host, whether it is for performance or other reasons, it is MUCH easier to do if you can simply rezone an existing LUN that has a standard file system on it.

Advantages of RDMs
- Allows MSCS clustering involving a virtual machine

- Eases data migrations of large data volumes that already exist in a virtualization project

- Provides the flexibility to move data volumes quickly from a virtual machine back to physical (Sorry VMware, it happens)

- Allows low level access to the disks inside a virtual machine (Typically used in conjunction with SAN snapshot software)

Disadvantages of RDMs

- Increases the amount of micro management of storage configurations inside the virtual infrastructure

- Must keep track of physical and virtual RDMs to know which capabilities are available to specific virtual machines.

- Cannot use VMware snapshots when using physical mode RDMs

Storage Layout and Design

The gritty details of ESX storage infrastructures come out when it is time to take all of the previous concepts and actually apply them into usable configurations. This is where VMware consultants and SAN engineers truly make their money.

Sizing

Determining the number and size of LUNs required in your environment is one of the most important things that you will do when dealing with your SAN configuration for ESX. The first thing you have to do when determining the number and size of LUNs you need is to estimate how much writable disk space you will present to the ESX servers in total (i.e., how much space are your VMDK files going to take up plus room for configuration files and growth). And the second thing is how you are going to break these up into usable LUNs.

Remember, with ESX 3 you are no longer simply storing static VMDK files on a virtual machine, there are other files you need to consider as well such as configuration and log files, but most importantly virtual machine swap files. By default, every virtual machine that gets created has a default memory reservation of Zero, meaning ESX will not set aside any dedicated memory resources. To compensate for this, a VSWP file is created that is equal to the amount of memory assigned to the virtual machine. If the system becomes over-allocated in regards to memory resources, it will begin to swap virtual machines with a lower number of shares to their swap file, effectively slowing down memory access for that virtual machine.

This, of course, gets added into the virtual machine configuration directory and must be counted towards the "used" space for your virtual machine. There are several things we can do to help limit or eliminate this requirement, but it does require reconfiguration (and a power off and power on) of existing virtual machines. If the changes are applied to a virtual machine template, each newly deployed virtual machine will maintain the settings assuming the amount of assigned memory doesn't change.

Leave the default value and take the storage utilization hit. When in doubt, just leave the default values. They are called defaults for a reason.

Increase the memory reservation to be 50% of the virtual machines memory resources. This limits, but does not eliminate, the ESX host's capability to overallocate memory. At best, you can achieve an overallocation of 50% of your memory resources, which is still a VERY high number, and it doesn't use as much storage for your VSWP files. This is the overall recommended option, but does add slight management addition to your virtual machine deployment process.

Increase the memory reservation to be 100% of the virtual machines memory resource. This will eliminate any disk allocation to the VSWP file but it will not be possible to overallocate memory to your ESX hosts. The ability to overallocate resources is one of ESX stronger selling points so this option should be avoided.

Create a separate centralized VMFS volume on low cost storage and reconfigure each virtual machine to place their VSWP file on this alternate location. This option is a management nightmare and should just be avoided. You don't want to have to deal with planning more storage layout than you need to.

In addition to simply sizing the LUNs, additional thought should go into the workload characteristics of your virtual machines and how one virtual machine could potentially impact another. This will come into play when actually determining the layout of your virtual machines onto the allocated LUNs.

There are four schools of thought around how one would typically size their LUNs for virtual machine use:

Small Number of Larger Volumes

Using a small number of larger volumes is the easiest solution to manage and is probably the most common method found in a vast majority of ESX infrastructures. Using this method, LUNs that are capable of handing 12-15 virtual machines are created. A vast majority of the time it is found that the sweet spot for this configuration is within the range of 400-500 GB LUNs. If we use a typical example we see quite often of a 10 host ESX cluster of 4-way dual core systems, we can assume we can safely run 30 virtual machines per host. 300 VMs / 15 VMs per LUN = 20 LUNs. This is a very manageable number of LUNs within a virtual infrastructure. The one downside to using larger LUN sizes is often times you will find that you waste a bit more space than if you use a larger number of smaller LUNs.

Advantages of Small Number of Larger LUNs
- Easy configuration and management model

- Allows for large VMDK file configurations (100's of GBs)

Disadvantages of Small Number of Larger LUNs
- Typically find more wasted space on LUNs than with other models

- Increased bandwidth to each LUN limits load balancing capabilities

Large Number of Smaller Volumes

In this scenario a user may determine that they would like to have better control over their virtual machine VMDK configurations if they created smaller LUNs that contained the proper amount of space to store approximately 5 virtual machines. These LUNs would typically be sized somewhere between 100-200 GB. When using this methodology an end user needs to consider the sheer amount of LUNs that may be attached to a single ESX host while remembering that every host in the cluster needs to see every LUN that contains a virtual machine for the purposes of VMotion, DRS, and HA. Taking our common configuration of a 10 host cluster of 4-way dual core systems, we can assume we can run safely run about 30 virtual machines per host. 300 VMs / 5 VMs per LUN = 60 LUNs. All of a sudden the ESX administrators aren't simply doing virtualization management, but storage management as well.

Advantages of Large Number of Smaller LUNs
- Better control of utilized and unutilized space

- Lower bandwidth to each LUN which maximizes load balancing capabilities

Disadvantages of Small Number of Larger LUNs
- There are instances where large VMDK files will be required, which minimizes the overall effectiveness of the virtual machines

- Extra management by the ESX administrator to track and manage large amount of LUNs

The Hybrid Solution

Of course we are never satisfied with providing a solution that is either on one extreme or the other. A common practice that we find, and will often recommend, is the use of a tiered architecture in which several LUNs of various sizes are created and assigned to the virtual infrastructure. This solution provides a lot of flexibility by providing support for large VMDK files, while still maintaining flexibility around utilized/free space control and manageability. Without actually breaking out the Advantages/Disadvantages of this solution, assume it takes the best of both configurations and provides a solid solution that is being used at an increasing rate across many organizations.

Use RDMs Wherever Possible

There are some organizations that want to have the absolute maximum amount of flexibility at the expense of creating a management nightmare for their VMware administrators. In this scenario a few large LUNs are provided for storing mapping files and virtual machine snapshot files. The rest of the LUNs are customized on a per virtual machine basis and assigned as RDMs inside ESX. There is no wasted space, as each LUN is customized for the virtual machine it is assigned to and is configured with a native operating system partition. Regardless of which type of RDM is being used, VMotion, DRS and HA functionality will still be supported. For systems that do not require low level disk access from the virtual machine, it is also possible to add snapshots for backup and checkpoint purposes.

A MAJOR consideration when configuring this type of environment lies in the amount of LUNs that must be assigned to each host in the cluster. Let's take our traditional example with one small hitch that was previously irrelevant. We have our 10 host ESX cluster of 4-way dual core systems, and we can assume we can safely run 30 virtual machines per host. Our added hitch here is that each virtual machine has an operating system LUN and a data LUN to maximize data throughput down multiple paths for the single VM. Doing some quick math we determine that 300 VMs X 2 LUNs per VM = 600 LUNs. If we go back to the very beginning of this chapter we remember that we can only assign 256 LUNs to any given ESX host. In this specific example we either need to drastically reduce the number of virtual machines per host (which is a bad idea to leave idle cycles in a consolidation environment), or reduce the size of our cluster, which increases management and limits our failover and HA options for those hosts and virtual machines.

One thing that drives us absolutely crazy is seeing people assign one LUN per virtual machine logical hard drive and configuring it with VMFS and placing a VMDK file that fills up the entire LUN. It simply makes no sense. If you are going to do this you eliminate your capability to create a snapshot and are much better off using an RDM.

Needless to say, using RDMs should be intermixed in with a hybrid disk sizing solution and only used if there is a specific need. Remember, RDMs do not provide any noticeable performance increase in a properly configured environment.

Hosts per LUN

VMware has a published maximum of 32 paths to any given volume. If you take a look at their recommended maximum of 32 hosts in a cluster, you had better be using single path LUNs, which is not recommend as it provides no redundancy for the most critical aspect of your virtual infrastructure. We assume every ESX host connecting to fiber based or iSCSI SANs will have at least two paths, making the absolute maximum number of hosts in a cluster 16. We even go a few hosts lower in our practical configurations from Chapter 4 where we recommend no more than 10-12 hosts in a single cluster. At most, this would provide a very safe value of 20-24 paths communicating to a single LUN at any given point in time.

LUNs per host

VMware has a hard limit of 255 LUNs that can be assigned to a host at any given time. Using our sizing suggestions from above you should be hard pressed to have to manage any more than 40-45 LUNs on any given host of a cluster in a worst case scenario. This is still a fairly manageable number and provides some good opportunities for properly balancing LUNs down multiple paths to the storage infrastructure. We find that having 20-25 LUNs assigned to a single host is actually the norm.

Template Locations

Virtual machine template storage is a unique scenario in which it is worth building and configuring a lightweight NFS server simply for that purpose. Every Linux distribution under the sun has NFS included, and Windows has even started distributing an NFS server in Windows 2003 R2 or other versions of Windows with their Windows Services for UNIX download. With the amount of usage this particular volume will receive, it does not need to be a costly or high performance solution, as long as it stays running so virtual machines can be properly deployed.

Load Balancing and Failover

The various storage configurations within ESX each require unique failover considerations. Carefully following the guidelines laid out in this section will ensure the critical backend storage infrastructure is as redundant as possible for your virtual infrastructure.

Fiber SAN and iSCSI Hardware Initiator

For redundancy purposes it is recommended that at least two fiber HBAs be installed in an ESX host. While the VMkernel itself does not provide any load balancing down multiple storage paths, through creative and proper planning we can achieve manual load balancing on a per LUN basis. Fortunately, the VMkernel does provide efficient failover capability if the same LUN is seen down multiple paths.

Figure 5- 7: Multipathing

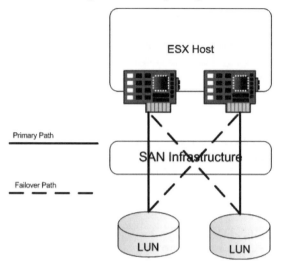

As you can see in the figure we have a simple configuration consisting of a single host with two HBAs communicating with two LUNs. By default ESX has configured a different HBA as the primary path for each LUN. This provides our load balancing method for our storage infrastructure. While this is not the most efficient load balancing in the world, it is the best we can currently get in our virtual infrastructure. If either primary path were to fail anywhere in the SAN infrastructure, the failover path would kick in within about 45-60 seconds and take over storage communication for the required LUN.

VMware provides two different internal methods to provide load balancing down multiple paths of the storage Infrastructure: Fixed/Preferred Path and Most Recently Used (MRU).

The MRU option is the default configuration that is used with Active/Passive storage devices, such as small arrays that have dual controllers in an active passive configuration. These are devices that maintain a single active path to the exposed disk and failover in the event of a component failure. The Fixed/Preferred Path option is the default for Storage that is configured for Active/Active accessibility. Generally higher-end SANs will support an active/active configuration. You will need to verify the configuration your SAN supports by reviewing the VMware documentation or working with your SAN vendor on the proper setting.

In an MRU configuration, the HBA being used to access a specific LUN will be used until it is unavailable. In the event of a failure, either in the card, the connection, or the storage processor level, ESX will automatically failover to the other HBA and begin using it for connectivity to the LUN. If the first card/path comes back online, the path currently being used will not change. As the name states, ESX will continue to use the path that it has failed over to since it is the 'Most Recently Used'. The storage array itself can often be configured to specify which of the available paths between the ESX host and the SAN controller is the "preferred path", but this functionality is not available in ESX when using the MRU option.

Advantages of using MRU
- Automatically configured to an available path

- Very little configuration required

Disadvantages of using MRU
- Possibility that all VMs will run over a single HBA

- Since the first HBA in the system is scanned first, this path is likely to be found and used first by the system for all LUNs

Contrast this to the Fixed/Preferred Path configuration option. In this configuration, the Preferred Path is used whenever it is available. So if a connection is lost, and the ESX Server fails over to another HBA/Path, it will only use that path until the preferred path becomes available again. This is used in Active/Active storage arrays in which any of the available paths can be used for storage communication at any point in time.

In an Active/Active SAN it is possible to assign alternate preferred paths on a per LUN basis. It is worth the extra time and configuration it takes to continuously analyze the balance of communication down the multiple paths of an ESX host and adjust it when necessary by changing the preferred path of key LUNs to equalize the path utilization. In Active/Active configurations this rebalancing is done through the Virtual Infrastructure Client and does not impact the availability or performance of the virtual infrastructure. Naturally, it should be documented and processed through a change control just in case you fat finger something and end up disabling a path and crippling your disk I/O by jamming it all down a single path.

Advantages of using Fixed Multipathing
- Allows you to 'manually' balance your LUNs between HBAs.

- System will automatically return to your original configuration when the path is returned to an operational state.

Disadvantages of using Fixed Multipathing
- Requires a little manual setup initially to ensure LUNs are split evenly between HBAs.

So what happens during a failure?

When an active path to a SAN disk is lost, the I/O from the virtual machines to their VMDK files will freeze for approximately 30-45 seconds. This is the approximate amount of time it will take for the SAN driver to determine that the link is down and initiate failover. During this time, the virtual machines using the SAN may seem to freeze, and any operations on the /vmfs directory may appear to hang. Once the failover occurs, I/O requests that have queued up will then be processed and the virtual machines will begin to function normally.

If all connections to the storage device are not working (assume a disastrous loss or a single path configuration), then the VM's will begin to encounter I/O errors on their virtual disks.

iSCSI Software Initiator and NFS

Load balancing iSCSI software initiated LUNs and NFS volumes is completely controlled by the standard network high availability capabilities of the VMkernel. The process in which load balancing and failover are performed for these storage types are entirely controlled by the configuration of the virtual switch responsible for managing the communication to the storage systems. You will have an immediate understanding of this process upon completion of the next chapter, in which we discuss the networking aspects of the virtual infrastructure.

Note on Windows Guests

When using Windows Server OS's in your VMs, you may want to adjust the standard disk time out for disk access. During the failover of an HBA, the default timeout in a Windows guest may cause issues within the guest OS that is used to having extremely responsive disks. For the Windows 2000 and Windows Server 2003 guest operating systems, you should increase the disk timeout value in the registry so that Windows will not be extensively disrupted during failover. The registry value can be found at the following location:

HKEY_LOCAL_MACHINE\System\CurrentControlSet\Services\Disk

The entry you wish to change, or add if it does not exist, is the TimeOutValue. Set the data to x03c hex or 60 decimal. This will configure the Windows Operating system to wait at least 60 seconds for disk operations to finish before reporting errors, which will likely consist of a wonderful blue screen.

Conclusion

As you can see, there are a lot of critical considerations and configurations that are required for a proper storage infrastructure for your virtual environment. With the introduction of network based storage platforms the entire process is complicated by the fact that we are not simply dealing with a centralized storage infrastructure, but we need to consider the importance and impact of the network infrastructure as well. We did not dig too deeply into these network configurations, but not to worry, our next chapter does plenty of that for us.

Chapter 6 - Networking Concepts and Strategies

We discussed some very high level basics of networking in an ESX infrastructure back in Chapter 2. This chapter is going to highlight the key concepts and strategies surrounding the networking capabilities of the virtual infrastructure. Here we are going to discuss the advanced networking aspects of the physical hardware, virtual machines, and network based storage configurations. The end of this chapter will focus on several usage scenarios that are common in many enterprise virtual infrastructures.

Key Concepts of ESX Networking

Here we want to start by referring back to the image from Chapter 2 and discuss in more detail on how each of the various network components of a virtual infrastructure are used.

Figure 6- 1: Network Components

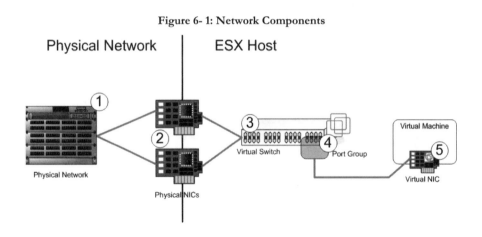

Physical Connectivity

Physical network connectivity is not required to actually run and leverage virtual machines. Having physical network connectivity will make it possible to remotely manage the infrastructure and will allow external systems to interact virtual machines running within the environment. We suspect that there is no reason for anyone reading this book to not plug an ESX host into the network and will focus on what it takes to get connected.

Physical Network

While physical network components such as switches and routers are not a direct component of ESX, we feel it is important to discuss some of the design options surrounding the configuration and use of a redundant network switch infrastructure. VMware provides several mechanisms of load balancing for configuring network components, each of which inherently provide redundancy when connected to multiple physical switches. Further details surrounding these mechanisms will appear a little later in this chapter. Knowing this information it is important to review the physical network layout to determine if it is possible to connect your physical NICs to multiple physical switches.

If connecting to multiple physical switches is not possible it is recommended that multiple blades of a switch chassis be used. This will at lease provide protection if a particular switch blade fails. Failing that, there is nothing wrong with using a single physical switch for all network connectivity for your virtual infrastructure, you just need to be aware of the implications of introducing a single point of failure into the environment.

When configuring the switch ports that you will connect your ESX hosts to you must be aware that the Spanning-Tree protocol has been known to cause delays in re-establishing network connectivity after a failed link returns to service. It is not uncommon to see 15-20 ICMP requests fail when a physical NIC within a virtual switch re-establishes its connection after a failure. To minimize the impact of the Spanning-Tree protocol, there are two things that can potentially be configured at the physical switch. The first option is disabling the Spanning-Tree protocol for the entire physical switch. There is an extremely good chance that this is not possible in most environments. The alternate, and most likely solution to resolve some of these issues would be to enable Portfast Mode for the ports that the physical NICs are connected to.

Every hardware vendor is unique and has different ways to configure various settings. We recommend working with the vendors closely if there are questions in regards to a specific configuration that is required for VMware compatibility.

Physical NICs

It should go without saying that physical network adapters are required in order to enable remote communication to not only the ESX hosts, but also the virtual machines they contain. Pretty much any modern network card that is either embedded on a server, or that can be added as a PCI card, is compatible with ESX Server. We are finally in a time where 100Mb networking is coming to an end and most organizations have implemented a gigabit network infrastructure. When you start taking a look at the nature of ESX and its intended implementation, 100Mb just doesn't cut it anymore...for any physical connection on the ESX host. Before attempting to setup your ESX host you should verify with either VMware or you hardware vendor to ensure the chosen adapters are fully compatible for ESX 3.

The number of physical network adapters installed in a system is dependent on several factors such as the level of redundancy required or the desired VLAN configuration of your solution. A typical configuration will optimally contain anywhere from 4 to 5 physical network adapters for each ESX host in the solution. It is possible to have an acceptable solution with 3 physical connections, but having only 2 is definitely not recommended. More than 5 may be required if the politics of the office get in the way of allowing the ESX server admins to take ownership of VLAN management and configuring VLAN tagging is not possible on the ESX hosts. We will discuss the use cases for various NIC configurations at the end of this chapter.

VMware has put limitations on the number of physical NICs that may be installed on a single physical host running ESX 3. While these are hard maximums, anyone who comes remotely close to half of these limits are encouraged to call a VMware service provider to show you how to actually build a virtual infrastructure. The reason behind variations between NICs typically has to do with the amount of memory required by the necessary drivers of each individual device.

Device	Count
Intel e100	26
Intel e1000	32
Broadcom	20

Virtual Connectivity

Virtual connectivity of your virtual machines, more often than not, is quite a bit more complicated than setting up the physical networking surrounding the infrastructure. It is actually possible to construct a fully functional enterprise network infrastructure using the logical components provided by VMware ESX. The three key concepts that we will focus on for this section are the use and configuration of Virtual NICs, Virtual Switches, and Port Groups.

Virtual NICs

A Virtual NIC (vNIC) is a network adapter that is configured within ESX for use by a virtual machine. Each virtual machine may have up to 4 virtual NICs configured, providing significant amounts of flexibility when connecting a virtual server to multiple subnets. Each vNIC that is assigned to a virtual machine receives its own unique MAC address, just as a physical adapter in a physical server would. In fact, if you were to look at the configuration of the network ports on your physical switch you would see that these MAC addresses are being published all the way into the physical infrastructure.

The way that these virtual NICs are presented to your virtual machine is actually done one of several different ways. By default, any newly constructed virtual machine that is configured with a virtual NIC is configured with the "Flexible" VMware adapter. The theory behind this adapter differs slightly, and improves on a design flaw from previous versions of ESX Server.

The Flexible adapter has the capabilities of both the legacy VLANCE and VMXNET drivers from previous versions of ESX rolled up into a single device.

It has the basic compatibility that is required by older operating systems, and with the proper VMware drivers installed, has the compatibility and advanced feature set that the VMXNET device used to provide.

The addressed design flaw with this solution was the fact that in legacy operating systems if you configured the system with the VLANCE driver and decided to change this to VMXNET at a later time, it was a device modification that was reported to the operating system. IP Address settings and device naming would not carry over during this change. By combining the functionality of both devices into this Flexible adapter the only modification required is a driver installation (typically with the VMware tools) in the guest operating system and the full feature set is instantly enabled without having a new device added to the system.

When working with 64-Bit operating systems VMware will instruct the guest to an Intel e1000 device driver. While it is possible to manually run 32bit operating systems with the e1000 device by modifying the VMX file of the virtual machine, it may not be officially supported by VMware, and full functionality may be questionable. If you will be running 64bit operating systems you will have no choice but to use this driver.

If using either the Flexible driver in VLANCE mode or the e1000 driver, ESX will be emulating their respective adapters. This will incur some virtualization overhead in the fact that every network call must be translated by the hypervisor to properly communicate. The Flexible driver, while running in VMXNET mode is a paravirtualized device, which means it is tightly integrated with the VMkernel's network stack and does not incur as much overhead as a strictly emulated device.

We mentioned that each virtual NIC that is configured for use with a virtual machine receives a unique MAC address. Fortunately VMware has gone through the process of registering their OUIs with the IEEE. In theory, you should never see a VMware MAC address outside one of the following ranges:

    00:05:69
    00:0c:29
    00:1c:14
    00:50:56

Virtual Switches

A virtual switch is a logical component of ESX that acts identically to a physical layer 2 switch and is used to map a Virtual NIC back to individual or groups of Physical NICs for network connectivity. In addition, virtual switches can be configured in a "private" mode that has no connectivity to the physical network, but still allows virtual machines to communicate internally to the ESX host.

Whether you are configuring your virtual switch in a public or private mode, there are several functions that are identical. Each virtual switch can be configured to support up to 1016 vNICs. This is a FAR cry better than the 32 vNICs supported in previous versions of ESX. Traffic that flows between any two vNICs on the same virtual switch will actually transfer over the system bus and will not traverse the network (assuming VLAN tagging is not being utilized, but more on that in a moment). When laying out your network design, this should be considered, as it is often advantageous to have network intensive applications talking directly to each other. When information is transferred in this manner, no network resources are impacted. All processing in this scenario is handled by processor 0 of the ESX host system. As neat as this sounds, there is a down side in the fact that if your traffic never hits the wire, typical networking monitoring and packet sniffing technologies will not be able to see the communication between VMs.

One key fact to remember is that there is a hard limit of 127 virtual switches allowed on an ESX host. This, like most of VMware's hard limits should not come into play in most normal situations. The only chance of seeing any configuration ever coming close to this limit is if an ESX host is being used alongside a VMware Lab Manager implementation.

Public Virtual Switches

Public virtual switches are easily the most utilized virtual switches in an ESX environment. In a public virtual switch, anywhere from 1 to 32 (Depending on physical hardware) Physical NICs may be bound, providing connectivity to the physical network for virtual machines. When utilizing a single Physical NIC, it is important to remember that there will be no redundancy in the network design for your virtual machines. It is also important to note that a Physical NIC can only belong to one virtual switch at a time.

Figure 6- 2: Public Virtual Switch

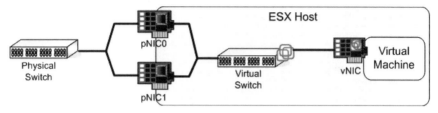

In a default configuration, all Physical NICs are configured in a redundant bond that load balances virtual machines across all adapters in that bond. We will discuss the various load balancing mechanisms later in this chapter. In addition to configuring load balancing methods, each virtual switch may be configured to handle VLAN configurations in different ways. By default, all virtual machines become extensions of the VLAN that the physical switch port is configured for. ESX provides mechanisms to handle VLANs in different manners. Alternative VLAN configurations will also be reviewed at a later time in this chapter.

Private Virtual Switches

The main difference between public virtual switches and private virtual switches lies in the fact that private virtual switches do not have a connection to the physical network. In a private virtual switch, all traffic generated between virtual machines is handled by the CPU and transferred over the system bus, as there is no other way for this traffic to travel between virtual machines. Private virtual switches provide isolation and can serve several purposes such as testing AD schema changes with a namespace that is identical to production, or building a DMZ environment in a box.

Figure 6- 3: Private Virtual Switch

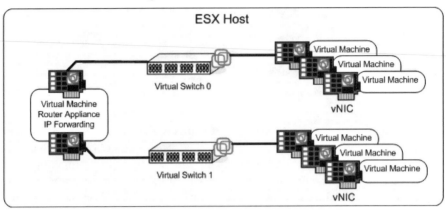

Virtual machines that are connected to a private virtual switch must be configured for the same subnet in order to communicate with each other. Multiple private virtual switches can be created within an ESX host to provide a multiple subnet environment. ESX does not provide routing capabilities internally across virtual switches. The only way that virtual machines that are on different virtual switches can communicate is by configuring a guest operating system with IP forwarding enabled. Guest operating systems must then have either static routes defined or default gateways configured that point to this "gateway" server to communicate across subnets. There are also several virtual machine appliances available for download that provide a lightweight Linux kernel with routing capabilities built in.

Port Configuration

The default configuration of a virtual switch is to enable 56 ports. Each Virtual NIC that is assigned to a virtual machine takes up one of these ports...not unlike a physical infrastructure. VMware has extended the capabilities of ESX 3 to allow significantly more ports than previous versions. Within the Virtual Infrastructure Client it is possible to configure a virtual switch to contain 8, 24, 56, 120, 248, 504, or 1016 virtual switch ports. Modifying this value does require a reboot of the ESX host to take effect, so plan accordingly. Also, if you do plan on using more than the default 56 allotted ports, consider increasing the service console memory from its default value.

Virtual Switch Configuration Options

Virtual switches, while not as intelligent as a typical physical switch, do have some configurable intelligence built in. The configuration of the virtual switch provides flexibility to the end user to provide some advanced functionality in security, bandwidth throttling, and redundancy settings.

Security

Virtual switches may be configured with several Layer 2 security policies. These configurations provide useful measures to enabled (or disable) typical configurations that can go above and beyond what can normally be done in a strictly physical environment.

Promiscuous Mode – Enabling promiscuous mode enables a virtual switch to receive all frames, not just those targeted for the virtual NICs configured within that switch. This is disabled by default

MAC Address Changes – Disabling this prevents guest virtual machines from changing the MAC address to something other than what is specified in its VMX file. This is enabled by default.

Forged Transmits – Disabling this prevents guest virtual machines from modifying the source MAC address of a frame to something other than what is currently registered on the virtual switch for that guest. This prevents IP Spoofing mechanisms. The default configuration is to allow Forged Transmits.

Traffic Shaping

Within ESX 3, it is also possible to limit the OUTGOING bandwidth through a virtual switch. It is very important to note that there is no way to limit the amount of bandwidth coming into a virtual switch. There are several basic configurations in regards to setting up bandwidth throttling.

Average Bandwidth - This setting is the sustained throughput that you would like the virtual switch to maintain for its guests.

Peak Bandwidth - This is the maximum amount of throughput allowed through a virtual switch. A virtual switch may hit its peak bandwidth to assist in properly processing all data that needs to be sent. Peak bandwidth is often configured to double the value of average bandwidth. This allows the virtual machines to properly send all packets when the system comes under load.

Burst Size - The amount of data that may be sent through a virtual switch while hitting its peak bandwidth. If the burst amount is hit, the virtual switch will drop below the peak bandwidth until the next burst cycle is available. The burst size should be configured as a byte value of 15% of the average bandwidth. This should be more than enough throughput to properly fill the peak bandwidth rate.

If the application or guest operating system being filtered starts to display errors such as dropped connections or failed ICMP requests, you should consider increasing these values accordingly.

NIC Teaming

The NIC Teaming functionality that ESX 3 provides is one of the most powerful features of the virtual switch architecture. The scenarios that may be configured through the use of the various teaming functionality provides unparalleled levels of high availability and load balancing for your virtual infrastructure.

Load Balancing

VMware ESX provides three methods for load balancing the traffic generated by virtual machines. Each method, in addition to providing load balancing for virtual switch traffic, assists in providing a redundant network design. There is also a fourth method of redundancy in which a Physical NIC within a virtual switch may be configured in a standby mode, but this does not provide any load balancing.

Virtual Port Based – When a virtual NIC is assigned to a virtual switch, it is also assigned a virtual port ID that is remembered by the virtual switch. Using Virtual Port Based load balancing, which is the default setting of VI3, leverages a round robin mechanism to assign virtual port IDs down an active physical adapter of the virtual switch. Once this virtual port is assigned to a physical NIC it will not change when the system is rebooted or goes offline. New virtual port IDs that are created are assigned to the next available physical NIC, even if it is only for temporary use.

Over time, it is possible for virtual switches to have an uneven number of virtual machines down each path, but it is significantly less of an issue than using the MAC Based mechanism that we will discuss next. Since virtual port IDs are simply assigned to the next active physical NIC, there is almost no processing or logic behind the assignment, which has the smallest impact to ESX host for managing failover. The VMkernel is responsible for managing which physical NIC in a virtual switch a virtual port, and subsequently, a virtual MAC address of a virtual NIC, will communicate with. The VMkernel will only announce the MAC address of the virtual machine down the active path to prevent issues where duplicate MAC addresses are broadcast to every physical switch port. This also allows the VMkernel to manage failover if a link failure is detected. The VMkernel will send a new ARP request down the new active path to reestablish communication to the virtual machine. In fact, with Virtual Port Based load balancing, physical NICs bound to a virtual switch may span across multiple physical switches for maximum fault tolerance.

MAC Based - MAC Address Load Balancing was the default load balancing mode for previous versions of ESX Server. Like Virtual Port Based balancing, this method does not require that any additional switch configuration be made to the physical switches that ESX is connected to, making it an ideal candidate in terms of network infrastructure compatibility. In this load balancing mode, the VMkernel has full control over which physical NIC in a virtual switch publishes the virtual machine's MAC address to the physical switch infrastructure through the use of a calculated hash based on the actual MAC address. By only allowing one physical NIC to announce a MAC address for a virtual machine, there are no duplicate MAC issues on the physical switches that prevent the virtual machine from properly communicating. Like Virtual Port Based load balancing, MAC Based configurations may span across multiple physical switches. MAC Based load balancing is introduced in VI3 for legacy and compatibility purposes. It is recommended that you use Virtual Port Based load balancing for all but the most intensive workloads.

While Virtual Port and MAC Address Load Balancing may be the easiest of the three methods to set up, they are not the most efficient at load balancing traffic.

The VMkernel uses an internal algorithm to determine which physical NIC in a virtual switch a specific virtual MAC address gets announced through. It is not possible to manually configure which virtual machines communicate down specific paths of a virtual switch. What this means is that the VMkernel simply tells a specific physical NIC to handle the traffic for a virtual NIC without regard to the amount of traffic being generated. We have seen instances on ESX where one physical NIC is generating significantly more traffic than any other within a virtual switch. When we do ESX designs in the field we do not utilize MAC Address Load Balancing to actually load balance traffic; it is used as a redundancy method and we use it when we know we have the appropriate network capacity within a virtual switch to handle an N+1 configuration. If we lose one physical NIC in a virtual switch, we should still have the appropriate capacity to provide the virtual machines with the throughput they need for operation.

IP Based - The third method that ESX is capable of providing for load balancing is based on destination IP address. Since outgoing virtual machine traffic is balanced based on the destination IP address of the packet, this method provides a much more balanced configuration than Virtual Port or MAC Address based balancing. Like the previous methods, if a link failure is detected by the VMkernel, there will be no impact to the connectivity of the virtual machines. The downside of utilizing this method of load balancing is that it requires additional configuration of the physical network equipment.

Because of the way the outgoing traffic traverses the network in an IP Address load balancing configuration, the MAC addresses of the virtual NICs will be seen by multiple switch ports. In order to get around this "issue", either Ether-Channel (assuming Cisco switches are utilized) or 802.3ad (LACP - Link Aggregation Control Protocol) must be configured on the physical switches. Without this configuration, the duplicate MAC address will cause significant switching issues. This option is only required for the most intense of network workloads, which is not very often. It is surprisingly difficult to truly max out the throughput of a properly configured ESX host based on our configuration recommendations at the end of this chapter. If you don't need to introduce this much complexity into the networking environment of your virtual infrastructure, don't use this option.

Use Explicit Failover Order – As we mentioned, there was a fourth "load balancing" option that can be configured for a virtual switch. This option is simply, don't load balance. Instead this instructs the virtual switch to simply use the highest priority active NIC for the switch and simply "failover" down the list of alternate active NICs.

Network Failover Detection

VMware ESX 3 provides two different methods for determining whether a link to a physical NIC has failed. The first method is simply if the physical NIC detects that the link between it and its uplink physical switch has failed. This works for most scenarios that ESX may be configured in.

There is an alternate method that may be used that addresses the situation of "What if my uplink switch is still active and online, but it cannot communicate with ITS uplink switch. As far as ESX is concerned, the link is active and the virtual switch stays online. The problem comes in when a node that isn't attached to that same physical switch requires access to one of the virtual machines.

Beacon monitoring provides protection in cases such as these. If you have properly configured your network, you will be using multiple uplink switches per virtual switch to eliminate any single points of failure. In the event a single port or cable fails in the core switch, the second physical switch can still manage the load of the virtual machines. The only way to detect the failure between the uplink switches and their core switch is by enabling beacon monitoring.

The idea here is that ESX Server will send beacon packets from one physical NIC to all other physical NICs in the same virtual switch. The beacon packets will then traverse the network through the switch infrastructure to the other physical NICs on the virtual switch. If there is no response from beacon packets, this means there is a network disruption somewhere upstream.

Figure 6- 4: Beacon Monitoring

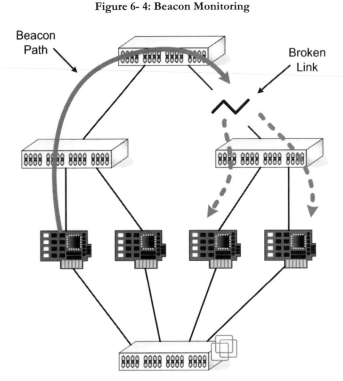

Using beaconing is only effective when the Physical NICs of a virtual switch are connected to different uplink switches. If the Physical NICs are only connected to a single uplink switch, then beaconing does you no good since you are adding beaconing overhead to traverse a path between switch ports on the same physical device. Using beaconing on a single physical switch will tell you nothing more than the fact that the device or its ports are still active, which ESX server will handle by default, without beaconing.

Unless you absolutely need to have ESX monitor your upstream network we would veer away from it. Beacon monitoring sometimes detects network failures that are not really happening.

Port Groups

The final component of the virtual network infrastructure is also one of the most important. Port groups are logical groups of virtual switch ports that share common settings such as Security, Traffic Shaping, Load Balancing, and VLAN configurations. Up to 512 port groups may be configured on any given ESX host at a time. There are three different types of port groups that may be configured on an ESX host

Service Console

Service Console port groups are used to configure access to the ESX service console for management of the physical host. Service Console port groups may not be used for any other purpose than providing access as a "vswif" device in the Linux management console. Each vswif device that is formed by creating a Service Console port group can be configured with a unique IP Address.

VMkernel

VMkernel port groups are used to configure either VMotion or network based storage access for NFS or iSCSI volumes. VMkernel port groups cannot be used to run virtual machines or allow access to the service console. A VMkernel port group that is to be used for VMotion must be explicitly configured to allow VMotion access. An IP Address must be properly configured at the VMkernel level to provide access to either VMotion functionality or to enable communication with network based storage devices.

Virtual Machine

Virtual Machine port groups are those that allow network connectivity for your virtual machines, whether through a public or private virtual switch. Every virtual NIC that is created within a virtual machine must be assigned to a virtual machine port group. Each of these virtual machine port groups, like all other port groups, contains unique settings. In the case of virtual machine port groups, different VLAN tagging configurations, as you will find out very shortly, may be assigned to various port groups. Each virtual NIC may be assigned to only one port group at a time, but a single virtual machine may have up to 4 different virtual NICs, each in a unique port group configuration. These virtual machine port groups are leveraged to define unique identities to the various network configurations for your virtual machine environment.

Virtual machine port groups are not configured with an IP Address. Instead, they either become an extension of the VLAN of the physical switch port they are connected to, or can be configured as trunk ports

Naming Standards

Port Groups are the single networking component that allows user specified names. Careful planning should go into the creation of a proper naming standard for port groups. Quickly determine the difference between "Port Group 1", "Port Group 2", and "Port Group 3" when building a virtual machine could be a very tedious process.

Implementations of ESX Server in a small or medium sized business could be as simple of a process as naming your virtual switches "Production Network", "Development Network", and "Quarantine". It is very easy, with a very quick glance, to determine the difference between these port groups with a proper naming convention.

Enterprise organizations are a difference story. Often times there are hundreds or even thousands of "Production Networks", so such a simplistic naming standard will probably not work. In these cases it often comes down to integrating naming conventions into already existing network IT policies. If applications serve as network boundaries, it may be as simple as calling your port group "Application1 Prod", and "Application1 Dev". In environments where the network is simply grown as new systems are implemented, simply naming your port groups after VLAN configurations may be sufficient. Simple names such as "VLAN 102" and VLAN 786" often suffice.

When creating and naming port groups use some common sense and integrate these naming conventions with your everyday business practices to make something that is easily identifiable to anyone responsible for building virtual machines.

Port Group Configurations

It is possible to configure port groups with the same Virtual Switch configuration options. By default, a port group will automatically assume the configuration of the virtual switch it is created on. This may be overwritten so each port group contains a unique configuration, although they belong ot the same virtual switch.

As an example, let's take a look at the following scenario represented by figure 6-5.

A virtual switch is created on an ESX host and is made up of 4 physical network adapters split across two physical switches. The virtual switch has no advanced configuration in place outside the default settings.

Two port groups are created, one for VLAN 101 and one for VLAN 102.

Each port group has two specific Physical NICs configured as Active NICs for the port group and two specific Physical NICs configured for failover purposes. Each physical NIC assigned as Active for the port group goes to a different physical switch.

Figure 6- 5: Port Groups

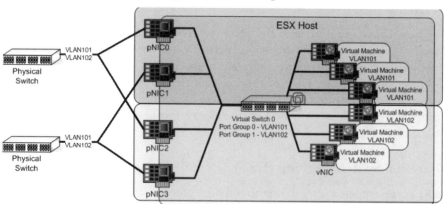

This solution is extremely redundant for several reasons. First, the virtual switch is made up of four physical NICs. Even under medium to heavy workloads the ESX host could lose up to two NICs and still have enough capacity to continue to run the virtual workload. Second, the port groups on the virtual switch are configured so that up to two failures at a minimum are required to bring the system down entirely. The port group has two physical NICs it can use for balancing traffic, each connected to a different physical switch. Even if the two primary physical NICs go down the port group will share the failover NICs with the second port group. The largest, and most unlikely event that can bring the virtual machines down is if both physical switches fail at the same time. While this is not impossible, it is quite unlikely to happen except in a major disaster or business crippling event.

One thing it is very important to note is that when you are configuring your virtual switches and port groups with the intent of using VMotion, the configurations must match across the board on all ESX hosts in the cluster. This includes the proper naming of the port groups themselves. VirtualCenter will happily let you know that there are invalid settings across these required common components if a VMotion is attempted when improperly configured.

The single configuration option that is available to port group configurations vs. virtual switch configurations is in the fact that you can assign a port group to only listen to packets tagged with a particular VLAN.

VLANs

To help better integrate with the advanced nature of enterprise network architectures there are several ways to integrate VLAN configurations into a virtual infrastructure. There are three different ways that ESX allows us to configure VLANs within a host. Each method has a different impact on how our virtual switches are configured and how our guest operating systems interact with the network. In addition, there are advantages and drawbacks to each method.

External Switch Tagging (EST)

EST is the default configuration for all port groups within an ESX host. In this mode, all VLAN configurations are handled by the physical switch. This does not require any configuration on the physical switch other than properly configuring the ports that the physical NICs of the ESX host are plugged into for the proper VLAN. This configuration is no different than if a physical server were being plugged into the network that required a specific VLAN configuration.

In the following diagram, we have two virtual switches, each consisting of two Physical NICs. The physical switch ports that the Physical NICs are plugged into are configured for a specific VLAN. By design, ESX ensures that a particular VLAN is presented all the way to the virtual machine. The only way a virtual machine can communicate on the network is if it is assigned an IP address that falls within the subnet range that defines the specific VLAN that it is connected to.

Figure 6- 6: External Switch Tagging

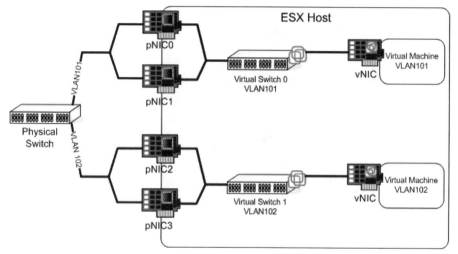

Advantages to Using EST
- Easiest VLAN configuration (No additional configuration necessary)

- Supported in every version of VMware ESX.

Disadvantages to Using EST
- Amount of VLANs that may be configured is limited by the number of physical NICs installed in the host

- Large number of NICs required for multiple VLAN configurations

Virtual Switch Tagging (VST)

VST consist of allowing a virtual switch to handle its own VLAN tagging. By configuring the uplink switch to explicitly tag packets with the 802.1q specification, all control of VLAN configurations is handed over to the VMkernel. The processing of 802.1q tags is managed by the physical network adapter hardware, so overhead from these tags never hits the VMkernel and has no impact on virtualization processing. In this configuration, each physical switch port that connects to a physical NIC is configured in a trunk mode. After the trunk is established, specific VLANs are presented down the trunk to the uplink "switch" which, in the case of the diagram below, is an ESX virtual switch. A port group must then be created for each VLAN.

Figure 6- 7: Virtual Switch Tagging

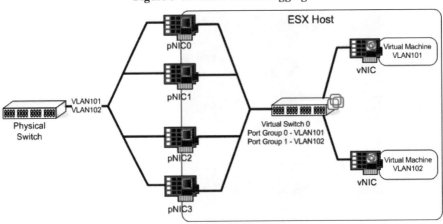

Once the virtual switch receives the VLAN information from the trunk it needs to have the capability to assign virtual NICs to specific VLANs. In order to achieve this, port groups must be configured within ESX. Since a virtual switch does not have physical ports that we can assign specific VLANs to, we need to utilize port groups as a reference to a particular VLAN. Each VLAN that is being announced down the trunk to the virtual switch must have its own port group configured before virtual machines can be utilized on the published VLAN. It is best practice to set the Port Group Labels to "VLANX", where X is replaced by the published VLAN's ID.

You will need to review your switch vendor's documentation to ensure 802.1q VLAN tagging is a function of your specific switch model. Each physical switch also has different configuration steps for properly configuring 802.1q; so again, documentation should be consulted for the proper configuration. One thing to note is that port groups cannot be configured with the "Native VLAN" for a switch. This Native VLAN is utilized for switch management and does not get tagged with a VLAN ID, and therefore is dropped by ESX. The default value for Cisco switches is 1, so any value between 2 and 4094 should work without issue.

Using VST also changes the way in which we recommend configuring virtual switches. One of the main reasons we recommend creating multiple virtual switches is so multiple VLANs can be utilized within a single ESX host. VST removes this restriction and allows a seemingly unlimited number of VLANs to be accessed through a single virtual switch. For this reason, if VST is to be utilized in an environment, we recommend configuring a single virtual switch that contains all Physical NICs in the system. This provides additional redundancy and throughput to the virtual switch, but simplifies the management of an ESX host by allowing us to configure port groups only once per ESX host.

Advantages of Using VST:
- A single virtual switch can utilize multiple VLANs, removing the dependency on multiple virtual switches and physical NICs to support multiple VLANs

- Once 802.1q trunks are established, adding new VLANs to ESX is a simple process

- Decreases the amount of network connections for ESX hosts that will support multiple VLANs

Disadvantages of using VST:
- May not be supported by all network infrastructures.

- Configuring trunk ports directly to servers is a new configuration in most environments, and is not always welcome.

Virtual Machine Guest Tagging (VGT)

The final mode for configuring VLANs for virtual machines is virtual guest tagging. In VGT mode, the virtual switch no longer reads 802.1q tags, but instead forwards them directly to the virtual machine. The guest operating system is then responsible for properly configuring the VLAN for the virtual NIC of the virtual machine. There is extremely limited support to this configuration. Most 2.4 and higher Linux kernels have VLAN tagging support built in. The only time this configuration should be utilized is if a particular virtual machine requires access to more than 4 VLANs. This number is based on the fact that a single virtual machine may only utilize 4 virtual NICs.

Figure 6- 8: Virtual Guest Tagging

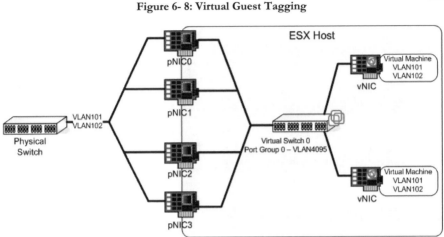

This configuration is achieved by configuring a new port group to use VLAN 4095. Any Virtual NIC assigned to this port group will then have VGT enabled.

Accessing the Infrastructure

After about 20 pages of reading about the key components it's about time we talked about how to actually communicate with your infrastructure. You will likely find that after reading this chapter up to this point that accessing the infrastructure is quite simple and anti climactic.

Service Console

Access to the service console is required for several specific reasons. First, VirtualCenter must communicate with its agent that is running within the service console operating system. This is how host and virtual machine configurations and performance metrics are captured and stored in the VirtualCenter database. Many users also find a need to install specific support applications such as hardware management or backup. This requires access to the service console to perform installations and configurations using standard RedHat Enterprise

Linux mechanisms. Others still require access to create custom automation scripts or harden the system to meet corporate IT security standards.

By default, ESX creates a Service Console port group on the host. This is represented within the service console as a device by the name of vswif0. Don't be thrown off by the name. To the service console, this interface acts identically to a typical eth0 interface of any Linux installation. ESX enables an iptables firewall on this interface to limit communication to the ESX host to only what is required for system management.

Without configuring firewall policies it is possible to connect to a host using SSH, HTTP, and through VMware's management protocol for VirtualCenter. It is possible to open additional access for items such as backup or monitoring agents by using either the CLI or through the Virtual Infrastructure Client. It is also possible to create multiple service console port groups if the console operating system is required to participate on multiple networks such as a production and a backup network.

We want to make the recommendation that a separate management network be configured for your Service Console and VMotion network connection. This will provide maximum security by setting up routing filters or potentially firewall policies to only allow specific communication to these sensitive components over certain ports or from certain workstations. Access to the service console should be treated with the highest level of security, as a compromise of the service console puts every virtual machine running on the host at risk of not only unauthorized power operations, but also potential data theft.

Virtual Machines

Assuming a virtual machine's virtual NIC is attached to public virtual switch your virtual machines will communicate with the network like any other device would. One of the most important things to note about virtual switches is that they do not have any layer 3 networking capabilities, so will not directly process packets destined for a different network. This type of communication must traverse the physical network and communicate through the physical network infrastructure. This provides a significant level of security around virtual machine communication.

There will be instances where two virtual machines are communicating with each other on the same port group of the same host. Since virtual switches operate at layer 2 of the network stack these virtual machines will communicate with each other without touching the physical network. It is important to remember this when performing troubleshooting of communication issues, as port monitoring at the physical switch may not show all traffic as expected.

In a private virtual switch virtual machines that reside within the same port group will be able to communicate with one another over the system bus due to the inner workings of the virtual switch. Virtual machines cannot communicate with one another in a private virtual switch unless there is a virtual machine that is configured on multiple port groups with IP forwarding available. This gateway virtual machine would need to be set as the default gateway for the virtual machines and will act as a router for inter communication. In a private virtual switch no communication is ever sent directly to the physical network.

Practical Configurations

With all of the options available for setting up a network infrastructure within ESX, many people are often overwhelmed when defining their network strategy. Except for the most extreme cases the best answer is often the easiest solution to implement. Just because VMware provides tons of functionality it doesn't mean you must try and integrate it into your design. It often just complicates the solution and negatively impacts performance overall, which is far from desired.

Standard ESX Installation Recommendations

We've already discussed some of the best practices around configuring your physical switches, physical NICs, virtual switches, and port groups. Now we want to take the opportunity to discuss the best way to use all of these components together in practical configurations that are commonly used across organizations of varying sizes.

Here we highlight a handful of the most practical use case scenarios for virtualization networking. There are cases that will require the use of more than four network adapters such as providing internal and DMZ virtual machines that require physical network separation, but those are not as common as the configurations highlighted throughout the rest of the chapter.

3 NICs

The use of three physical network adapters was very common in ESX 2. Unlike with ESX 3, it was not easy to configure the service console in a redundant fashion, so there was little reason in configuring more NICs than could be used. As is the case now with ESX 3, having 2 physical gigabit adapters is more than enough to handle even the most intense ESX workloads.

Many systems today come with dual port on-board gigabit network connectivity. With a three NIC configuration an additional PCI gigabit adapter should be purchased and installed in the server. One port of the on-board adapter will be dedicated to the ESX service console and VMotion activity. The remaining on-board port and the PCI NIC port should be joined together to support networking capabilities for your virtual machines. This will provide redundancy for your virtual machines only, and, by default, will not provide any failover capability for your service console or VMotion connectivity.

The configuration of the virtual switches inside the ESX host itself will depend on the physical network layout of the infrastructure. There are two different methods of configuring this setup, which is dependent on the number of virtual switches leveraged.

Two Virtual Switches

If the "management" network for the service console and VMotion connection use a different physical network infrastructure than the virtual machine network, two virtual switches will be required. In this case, it will also not be possible to provide any failover for the service console or VMotion, period. Configuring a failover NIC is only possible across port groups that reside on the same virtual switch.

The first virtual switch contains the first on-board networking port and is configured with two port groups; one for the service console and one for the VMkernel. If you do not plan on using VMotion, the latter port group is not necessary. The second virtual switch is configured with the remaining on-board NIC port and the PCI NIC port. A virtual machine port group for each VLAN presented to the ESX host should be created. This will make up the virtual machine network environment and will have integrated redundancy due to the dual NIC switch configuration.

Figure 6- 9: 3 NIC/2 Virtual Switches

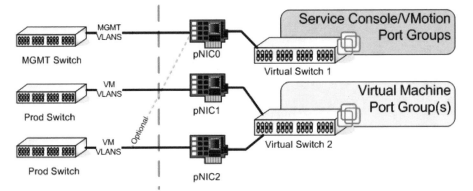

Advantages of 3 Physical NICs w/ 2 Virtual Switches
- Easy to set up and configure within ESX

- Provides physical isolation of management network and production network

Disadvantages of 3 Physical NICs w/ 2 Virtual Switches
- No redundancy for management functions such as service console access and VMotion

Single Virtual Switch

If the physical switches in the network will be providing all connectivity for management functions and virtual machine connectivity, it is possible to create a single virtual switch with at least three port groups: Service Console, VMkernel, and Virtual Machine (one per VLAN). The Service Console and VMkernel port groups should be assigned to the first on-board NIC port of the server with the two remaining NICs configured as failover adapters. The two remaining adapters should be added to a port group for virtual machine usage. These adapters will automatically be configured in a failover mode based on the fact that they both belong to the same port group. You will also need to make sure that if you intend to provide failover for the management NIC that you also configure the physical switch ports that the virtual machine NICs are connected to by presenting the proper management VLANs down all paths. If this step is ignored a failed over service console/VMotion port group will have no way to communicate to the physical network.

The reason we want to assign specific NICs in this case is to ensure that management activity such as service console based backups and VMotion activity does not impact your virtual machine network access with the exception of a NIC/Port failure in the management port group. There would be no guaranteed separation if every port group in the virtual switch had access to every NIC as a primary adapter.

Figure 6- 10: 3 NIC/Single Virtual Switch

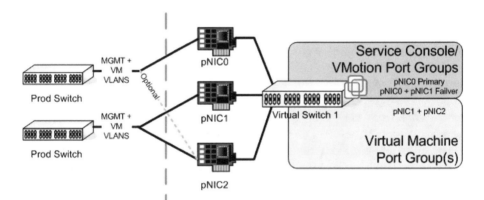

Advantages of 3 Physical NICs w/ 1 Virtual Switches
- Provides redundancy for management functions such as service console access and VMotion

Disadvantages of 3 Physical NICs w/ 1 Virtual Switches
- More complicated setup within ESX

- Potential production virtual machine impact during failover

- Not possible if Management Network is on separate physical switch infrastructure from Production Network

4 NICs

The most common configuration in an ESX 3 infrastructure is through the use of four physical NICs. Assuming your ESX host has come preconfigured with a dual-port on-board adapter you would simply add a second PCI dual-port gigabit adapter. The cost difference between a dual port and single port PCI adapter is actually quite minimal. Similarly to the various options available with a 3 NIC configuration, there are two different options when using a 4 NIC configuration based off your physical network design and/or how you wish to configure your virtual switches on the ESX host.

2 Virtual Switches

This is easily the most common of all configurations, and the one we most recommend during customer implementations. Whether you have a separate network infrastructure for management functions and production use, or you simply want to use two virtual switches, this design will provide the maximum redundancy, flexibility, and security for your virtual network infrastructure. Best of all, it's also very easy to setup and manage.

In this configuration two virtual switches are created, each consisting of two physical NICs. Each virtual switch should contain one connection to an on-board NIC port and one connection to a PCI adapter. This will ensure that even with a NIC failure, the virtual switch will maintain connectivity. On the physical network side, each on-board NIC port should connect to the same physical switch. The two PCI NIC ports should also both connect to the same physical switch, but a different physical switch than the on-board ports if possible. This provides protection in the event a switch fails. In this configuration it would take a very significant disaster to bring the network of the virtual infrastructure down.

The first virtual switch will only contain your virtual machine port groups required for virtual machine access. The second virtual switch will only contain the port groups necessary for management such as for the service console and VMotion. Each virtual switch has full redundancy based on the fact that each has two physical NICs, which in turn are optimally connected to alternate physical switches in the network infrastructure. This configuration also provides maximum security to the infrastructure by separating management and production traffic. It is difficult in this configuration to accidentally put a virtual machine on the management network and vice versa.

Figure 6-11: 4 NIC/2 Virtual Switch

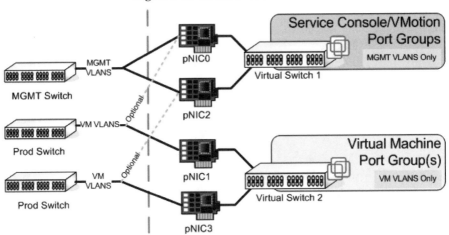

Advantages of 4 Physical NICs w/ 2 Virtual Switches

- Provides maximum redundancy for both virtual machine access and management tasks

- Most secure network configuration for your ESX environment by providing isolation of your production and management networks

- Simple setup and Easy to setup and configure within ESX

Disadvantages of 4 Physical NICs w/ 2 Virtual Switches

- There are no obvious disadvantages to this configuration

Single Virtual Switch

A 4 NIC Single virtual switch implementation is almost as simple to configure as the previous 4 NIC design. The primary difference between the two designs is in the fact that all VLANs for the entire solution are presented down all network paths, eliminating physical separation of your management and virtual machine networks.

By default, this solution will assign traffic for all port groups down all four paths of the host. There is potential for a spike in traffic such as from a virtual machine backup or a VMotion migration to impact the performance of the configured virtual machines. To prevent this, we recommend that if you are to use this solution, that you still configure two Physical NICs (Each connected to a different physical switch) as primary for your virtual machine port group(s), with the remaining two NICs (also connected to separate physical switches) as failover NICs. The two NICs that were configured for failover for the virtual machine port group(s) should be configured as the primary for the management port group(s), with their failover being the primary NICs from the first port group. A completely unnecessary amount of micromanagement goes into properly configuring this scenario so we recommend that you simply follow our previous recommendation and use two virtual switches.

Figure 6- 12: 4 NIC/1 Virtual Switch

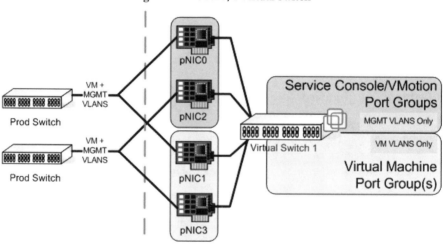

Advantages of 4 Physical NICs w/ 1 Virtual Switches
- Provides maximum redundancy for both virtual machine access and management tasks

Disadvantages of 4 Physical NICs w/ 1 Virtual Switches
- Micromanagement of Active/Passive NICs per port group if properly implemented

- No physical separation of management and virtual machine networks

- Not possible if Management Network is on separate physical switch infrastructure from Production Network

Worst Case Scenarios

There are always going to be cases in which following the best practices for a solution will not be possible. Whether it is due to hardware limitations or simple corporate policy, there are some configurations that will need to be considered for some organizations. For that reason we would like to point to the two of the most common "worst case scenarios" that we have come across.

Limited to 2 Physical NICs

We are hoping that this situation is limited to the development space, as we really hate to see someone not able to spring the extra $125 and put in a second dual port adapter into an ESX server for production use. There is nothing wrong with this scenario for development, but we need to set a few expectations.

In this situation, if at all possible, plug the two NICs into different physical switches. This will at least protect the environment in the event one of the switches was to fail. For a development environment, there is no shame in plugging both NICs into a single switch. To keep redundancy and load balancing for the virtual machines a single virtual switch configured with both physical NICs should be configured. This virtual switch will be configured with all the required port groups for virtual machine and management use.

We will forgo our traditional Advantages/Disadvantages for this configuration, since there really is nothing but disadvantages here. VMotion and virtual machine backups will potentially interfere with your running virtual machines and there is no physical separation of your management and virtual machine networks (assuming they are different networks at all in this situation).

Figure 6- 13: 2 Physical NICs

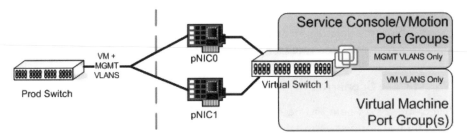

VLAN Tagging Not Allowed

There is no technical reasoning that a network engineer can conceive that should prevent the use of VLAN tagging on your ESX host (Unless of course your switches don't support it). It is strictly a political battle and should be dealt with organizationally. For the cases where a fight to the death is not possible and you have no choice but to not enable VLAN tagging for your ESX hosts there is still a solution that will technically work, but it is not glamorous.

In this scenario you will need at least one, and preferably two NICs for every VLAN that you wish to configure your virtual machines on. Each NIC or pair of NICs will need to be configured in a virtual switch with a single virtual machine port group configured. The network hardware and connectivity adds up very quickly if you have to provide connectivity to four, five, or even eight different VLANs on every ESX host in the environment.

Again, if there is any way to avoid this situation, please do. It will make your experiences with virtualization that much more successful and enjoyable.

Figure 6- 14: No VLAN Tagging

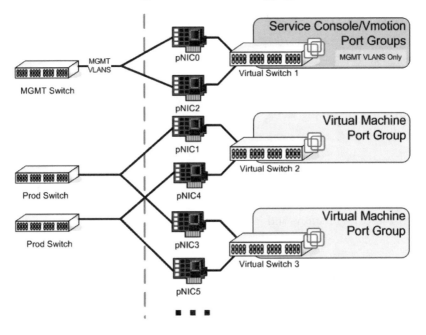

As you can see, there are many options available for properly configuring your network environment for your virtual infrastructure. We've provided the most common configurations found in virtual infrastructures of various sizes. By leveraging our examples and considering the advanced configurations discussed throughout this chapter, we are confident you now have all of the information necessary to provide a solid network design that meets the needs of your organization.

Chapter 7 - VMs and VM Selection

So far, most of this book has focused on the architecture and mechanics behind VMware ESX Server/VI3. We've described (sometimes in excruciating detail) the smallest components that make up ESX and the virtual environment. In contrast, this chapter focuses on the guest environment and VM strategies. This is somewhat important seeing how it's the whole reason anyone uses VMware in the first place.

In this chapter we'll look at how to create a Virtual Machines strategy for your organization and how to determine which servers in your environment will become guests in the ESX Server farms you create. Then, we'll get into VM standards, VM configurations and P2V migration decisions that need to be made.

Creating a Virtualization Strategy

Until a few years ago, the only people in an IT organization who had used (or even heard of) VMware were generally the developers and engineers. These original users of the VMware products used VMware Workstation and in some cases GSX Server to implement virtual machines for testing and lab development.

VMware allowed these IT pros to create quick test beds for new scripts, applications, or even to try out a new OS within their organization. Eventually, some IT departments started using VMware to host large portions of their test environments. However, even in these cases, most CIOs or CTOs still had not heard of the product. Those that had only had a passing knowledge of it.

As the practice of using virtual machines for testing grew, people started to notice (and so did VMware) that most of their other production hardware was underutilized. Most servers were over engineered from the start to save on upgrades later. In addition, more and more servers were required for everyday business, and it seemed like each new application on the network required its own dedicated server—even if all it did was run a batch job a couple of times a day.

In addition to this general production server underutilization, IT organizations also started to notice other benefits. The first thing benefit noticed was that the time they were spending provisioning, putting together, racking, configuring, and managing servers was becoming a larger part of their day. It used to be that organizations ran the same servers for long periods of time with very little change. Most management was on the application side or simple server maintenance and monitoring. Now it seems that almost every day brings a new application requiring any number of new servers—even while the old servers on the network never seem to be completely decommissioned.

As companies and datacenters grow larger, they begin to notice that the vast majority of their production servers are underutilized. Try this little exercise if you don't believe this: Walk into your datacenter and pick a rack of Windows servers. Out of the rack pick three of the servers at random. Open up the console on these servers and run performance monitor for 20 minutes on each. Look at Overall Processor Utilization and Physical memory in use. If you want, throw in a network and a disk counter. I'll bet that not one of the three is at or near 90% utilization on any one of those counters. In most cases, when I have done this (not including Citrix environments), the servers are all less than 20% utilized on all of those "Core Four" resources except memory, and in that case it is usually less than 50%.

Now we as engineers and architects used to think this was a good thing. This is because we were taught that if the servers are not near capacity, then the performance is as good as it can be on the server and there will be few if any complaints from the user about performance for those applications. The problem here lies in the fact that you may have a datacenter with several thousand processors in it all at an average of 10% utilization. Ten percent! Think of that. That's like buying a car you can only drive less than a day a week, then having to buy three or maybe four more of those cars to fill up the rest of the days of the week.

One thing to remember about processing is this: Any server that is not running with 100% CPU utilization is "wasting" time executing idle threads. Whether you have 30% utilization or 80% utilization, there are still available CPU cycles.

Every idle tick that is processed is time when the processor is doing nothing and is waiting for you to send it more instructions. Why not use this capacity? A server at 80% is just as fast as a server at 30%—it's just waiting to be used.

Once you understand that, it's easy to understand that virtualization and specifically VMware can help with this. The real question is how can it help your specific organization? The answer depends on where your organization's pain points are. There are basically a few different strategies for VMware. Some of these can combine and morph into smaller tactical solutions, but the basic concepts can be found in one of these three situations:

- Using VMware for test and development environments only

- Using VMware for underutilized production servers in addition to Test and Dev

- Using VMware for ALL servers in your environment

Let's examine each of these strategies, what they entail, and the benefits and drawbacks of each.

Using VMware for Test and Development Servers

This is kind of like saying, "let's use our old hardware for test servers." Almost no one can argue with this strategy. Using VMware for a test environment is really a no-brainer. Within any size organization a single VMware ESX server can be a huge benefit to the test environment.

VMware's ability to host a large number of underutilized servers on a single piece of hardware can reduce hardware costs for your test environment by 50-75% or more. In addition, the ability to make a Virtual Machine disk un-doable is a huge benefit. Imagine the following scenario:

A developer in your company wishes to test a new application install he has created. It works on his workstation but he hasn't tested it on any server builds yet. The catch is that each time he runs his test he has to see if the install was successful or not, and if not, he needs to start with a fresh build. Using a VMware test environment, the developer can test his install and if it has failed, it can be back to a fresh image in under a minute.

Let's take this development environment a little further. If this same developer needs to test his install against various types of server operating systems and configurations, he would ordinarily require one server of each type or else he would be forced to rebuild the server using the OS or configurations for the next test. In a VMware environment, this developer can have numerous servers all running on a single piece of hardware provisioned for just these tests. He can finish his testing sooner, utilize less of the IT staff's time, and in turn can decommission or delete the servers he used for testing if he no longer needs them. (Try doing that with a $6000 asset assigned to a specific cost center!)

Let's look at a real world example of this from one of our clients. Before VMware, this client struggled to keep up with all of their development and test servers for their core business application. They had close to 100 test and development servers alone. After we took a look at these servers, we realized that 95% of them sat completely idle doing nothing at all on a given day.

After some doing some discovery on these servers we determined that they could repurpose about 80 of these servers if we brought in two servers (with 8 cores each) for VMware. This client was also undergoing a major expansion in their Citrix farm, and the 80 "extra" servers were a huge benefit to have from a cost savings perspective.

You're probably wondering what happened to the other 20 servers. Those 20 were used for system stress testing for new applications. Since those 20 were identical to the existing production Citrix servers, we decided that we would leave these physical servers alone in order to be able to accurately test system changes (as far as performance goes) on duplicates of the production hardware that was still utilizing physical servers.

When deciding to use VMware in your test and development environments you first must answer a few basic questions and do some discovery in your environment:

What will your production systems look like?

A test environment for a company whose production environment is hosted completely on VMware will look completely different than a test environment for a production environment consisting entirely of physical servers.

For now we won't get into the advantages and disadvantages of hosting production servers on ESX. (That comes later in this chapter.) Instead just take a look at your strategy for your production environment.

If you're introducing VMware into a test environment and your production environment will be built out of completely physical servers, then you should start by determining how many of the test/development servers are used or are going to be used for performance and stress testing. Once this number is known, you can basically rule these servers out of the VMware environment. When stress testing or gauging the performance of an application or server, you want to exactly duplicate the production environment. A performance test against a VM for an application being hosted on a physical server is basically useless.

However, the remaining servers are your VMware candidates. These servers are generally used for testing the functionality of new application code, service packs, OS upgrades, etc. These are called the "functionality" test servers because they'll be used to test the functionality of the system after a change.

These servers have just become your targeted guest operating systems. Once you have identified them, you can create a quick cost/benefit analysis showing the costs of physical servers for this environment versus virtual servers. We generally find that in test environments, the cost of virtual servers is about one third to one quarter the cost of physical servers. If the majority of your servers are idle 90% of the time, this ratio may even be higher.

Advantages of using VMware for your Test/Dev Environment
- Cost effective use of hardware
- Large portions of your production environment can be replicated on a few servers
- Lower cost of hardware for the entire test environment
- Faster rollback during testing
- Faster deployment of a new test platform
- Test VMs can be decommissioned and even deleted after they are not needed

Disadvantages of using VMware for your Test/Dev Environment
- Requires that your staff have (or learn) some basic VMware skills

- VMs are not good for load /stress testing if your production environment is completely physical

As you can see, the advantages of using VMware in your development or test environment easily outweigh the disadvantages. On top of that, the second disadvantage can be completely mitigate by simply keeping an few pieces of hardware for load testing if you plan on maintaining physical production servers.

Using VMware for Underutilized Production Servers

VMware is also often used for production servers that have very little in the way of hardware requirements. In the last year or two the use of VMware ESX in production environments has grown enormously. The initial "fear" of the new technology is gone, and the reality that a VM is just as good as a physical server in most cases has become IT's reality.

Most organizations are beginning to realize that the strategy of application isolation (giving each application in the environment its own unique server) has left them with numerous servers that utilize very little of the physical hardware available. Often times you can look at a production server that hosts file shares for users or even the backend data for a specific department and will notice that the server is barely being used.

In this scenario, the IT department would utilize ESX Server to host multiple production servers on ESX hosts. This allows them to retain unique servers for their applications while reducing the overall hardware requirements across the board.

Not using virtualization technology in your environment for this use case could be career shortening. I mean apply this type of thinking in any other aspect of business. It is unthinkable. Let's look at the following scenario to see if it sounds familiar:

The accounting department in your company requests a new server for an application they've decided to implement. The application vendor states they require their own server (typical!) but that resource requirements are not very high for this server. Well even if testing shows that the application only needed 300Mhz of processing power, you can't even buy that processor anymore. Instead you have to buy a machine with a 3GHz processor and since you have certain company standards you throw in mirrored SCSI drives and a gigabyte or two of memory. Now you have a server that you paid $6000 for that you're using 10% of its processor and it's associated rack space, power, KVM, etc.

In most cases even production servers are underutilized. Since we as IT professionals have been trained to make sure that the system is responsive to the end user, we've been conditioned to think that less utilization equals better performance for the user. To us it is a "good thing" when a production server runs at 10, 20 or 30% utilization and is only using half of its physical memory. The problem here is that we (or the businesses we work for) have basically been paying for lots and lots of hardware that isn't being used. Imagine if every server in your environment ran at 50% utilization on all its resources. Now imagine that you could magically cut the number of servers in half by moving processing time, memory, etc. from one group of servers to another. You would be seen as the IT genius of the year. Why? Because it makes business sense.

All of this basically means that businesses have x% of available server resources not being used and still continue to purchase more of these same resources. It's like a company owning two buildings in downtown Chicago, both of which are only 50% full. Sure they plan to grow but they only plan to add 10 or 20% more people over all. Should they go ahead and buy a third building? Of course not. This (in business) makes no sense, but for some reason we as IT professionals have been taught this is how we do things in the Wintel world. (Part of the blame must go to the hardware vendors here, but that's another story.)

Combining numerous logical servers onto a physical piece of hardware is no longer a good idea, it's a "must do". Environments of any significant size can see a major cost savings in hardware by just putting some underutilized servers onto a single ESX server. In most large environments, the pay back for ESX is about 6 months depending on the rate of server deployment per month. For one client, the ESX payback was seen in 12 weeks, and that included factoring in consulting costs to architect the environment.

So how is it done? You can begin by looking at existing servers in your environment and even servers that are being requested. Estimates are made about the server's utilization and that helps us determine the number of guests per processor. Later in this section we'll dive into the detailed process of evaluating potential guests but for now you should understand that you will have to estimate requirements for new servers and evaluate existing servers' utilization in your environment.

Often your "newer" servers can be re-used as ESX hosts for a number of your other servers. In this strategy existing dual and quad processor servers can be re-purposed as ESX hosts. Their original operating system is migrated to a VM and other VMs are then loaded onto the "new" ESX server. This allows you to implement a server consolidation strategy with a reduced outlay in new hardware costs.

Advantages of using VMware for Under Utilized Production Servers
- Cost effective use of hardware

- Existing hardware can often be reused as ESX hosts

- Lower cost of hardware for the entire environment

- Faster deployment of new VM servers

- Fewer production network ports required

- Fewer production SAN ports required

- Less time spent provisioning and tracking hardware in the environment

- Less hardware to manage and support in the environment

- Ability to move VMs from host to host as performance dictates

- Ability to do maintenance on physical hardware without interruption to VMs

Disadvantages of using VMware for Under Utilized Production Servers
- Requires that your staff have (or learn) VMware skills

- Some software vendors do not officially support VMs

- Can require in-depth knowledge of VMware to troubleshoot performance problems

- May require you to invest in some SAN infrastructure to provide space for VMs

Using VMware for all of your systems

While this may sound like a leap for some of us, it's really not that farfetched. VMware offers a lot of benefits aside from its major one of being able to share hardware. In fact I know personally of 3 Fortune companies that have a mandate of "Virtual First". Meaning, if you want a server, their standard is a VM. If you want to deviate from that standard you need approval from on high, and a solid business or technical reason not to use a Virtual Machine.

When a business decides to use VMware for "all" their production servers, they rarely actually get every server on the network hosted on VMware. But the theory for such a deployment (or attempting such a deployment) is as follows:

Since very few servers on the network are truly utilized 100%, this means that a dual processor web server with 65-70% utilization still has cycles left. While in a consolidation model (underutilized servers only) this web server may not fit your ideal profile for migration into ESX, it still has hardware resources available and could be hosted to gain other benefits. Let's assume that you wish to move all servers into the ESX environment. If this is a true business goal, then you could move the web server onto a quad or eight-way ESX host and still have room for other VMs. You can then select VMs for coexistence with this server that require very little in the way of resources, or allow VMw'ares DRS to automatically shift load as needed. This will allow you to get your maximum number of VMs per processor even though one of the VMs uses a high amount number of resources.

The general idea behind using VMware for all of your production servers is twofold:

- You can use your hardware to its maximum extent and realize all of the benefits from that
- Disaster recovery (DR) becomes extremely simple for the entire environment

Generally when people move all (or a vast majority) of their servers to VMware, it's because most of their servers are underutilized or they have a DR plan that relies heavily on the portability of virtual machines. In either case, they begin to truly use VMware to its fullest potential. Determining if this works for your environment will depend on whether most of your servers are underutilized or if you need that VM portability for DR or other purposes.

Advantages of using VMware for All or a Majority of Production Servers

- Cost effective use of hardware

- Existing hardware can often be reused as ESX hosts

- Lower cost of hardware for the entire environment

- Faster deployment of new servers

- Fewer production network ports required

- Fewer production SAN ports required

- Less time spent provisioning and tracking hardware in the environment

- Less hardware to manage and support in the environment

- Ability to move VMs from host to host as performance dictates

- Ability to do maintenance on physical hardware without interruption to VMs

- Facilitates DR for the entire Environment

- Decreases recovery time from hardware failures for all systems

Disadvantages of using VMware for All or a Majority of Production Servers

- Requires that your staff have (or learn) VMware skills

- Some software vendors do not officially support VMs

- Can require in-depth knowledge of VMware to troubleshoot performance problems

- Requires a more complex and expensive SAN infrastructure

Candidate Identification

Once you have identified your overall VMware strategy you can move on to identifying candidates in your environment. First, you should understand that there are two types of identification:

- Identification of candidates from existing servers
- Identification of candidates for new servers being provisioned

Identification of candidates from your existing environment is fairly simple and really just a simple exercise in resource utilization. Identification of candidates for new servers is a little trickier and generally is a process that requires you test each new deployment and move on from there. Let's go into each of the scenarios separately.

Existing Candidate Identification

To identify VMware candidates from your existing servers you need to have performance data from each server, an understanding of your strategy, and inventory data from there (including peripheral devices if any).

To collect this data there are a number of tools available. IBM has their CDAT tool. UNISYS has some tool they tout, but it is really UNIX tool that they ported (in a poor way) for Windows. VMware has their capacity planner application, and another major player in this area is Platspin's PowerRecon. Since I really don't like the CDAT or UNISYS tool, here we will focus on the raw counters you need and the two available tools.

Performance Counters that Matter

Let's start with some basics on candidate identification. Candidate identification of existing servers is really simple math, and the understanding of peripheral devices. To understand this let's look at each of the core-four resources individually and their needs from a metric and inventory perspective (this next section is Windows focused but can easily be done on Linux, for simplification we use Windows metrics only).

% of Processor Time and Speed and Number of Processors

When the Total % of processor time is combined with the number and speed of processors in the target system you come up with a PERFECT number for determining CPU utilization on a potential guest. A number of people try to use the % of CPU utilization only; this only leads to false identification, and more often than not, the exclusion of older candidates that are perfect fits for VMware.

When using % of processor only you get only a piece of the story. A server with a single 1Ghz processor running at 20% is different than a server with four 3GHz processors running at 20%. To make this counter valuable you need to take the % of the overall available processor throughput. So in our examples this would look like the following:

(Speed * Number of Procs) * (%utilization / 100)= MHz in use

(1000 * 1) * (20/100) = 200 MHz

(3000 * 4) * (20/100) = 2400 MHz

Those numbers look different don't they? Exactly. In candidate identification you need to rationalize the relative counters to come up with a valuable number. Now when you dump these into a spreadsheet you can come up with a MHz in use (Average and peak if you can get both) to determine the real CPU needs for a VM.

Typically we will take into account the speed of the processors and the number of cores when doing candidate identification. If you are looking for only underutilized servers you are probably going to want to see about a 4 or 5 to 1 ratio of VMs to Cores. So if a core gets you about the total throughput of 2800 MHz (not complete throughput of the processor's rated speed) you need to do the math and calculate in peaks and average run time.

To do this lets take the 2800 MHz per core. Assume we don't want to run at more than 80% normally (80% of 2800 MHz) 2240MHz. Now let's assume that you are more conservative and want to leave 20% of the CPU for peaks, failures etc (see cluster design sections to understand failover capacity better). In that case you take 60% of the 2800MHz and end up with 1680MHz. Divide this number by 4 or 5 and you come up with 420 MHz or 336MHz. So your low hanging fruit (CPU wise) should average 420 MHz or less while still allowing for spikes of up to 40% more.

Now remember this is an average. So if 420 MHz is the average of your candidates for low hanging fruit you can have some that average 800 MHz and some 200 MHz. If you are going more aggressive and want to use all but the highest utilization physical servers you could take that average target up to 1 or 2 GHz. Our average rule of thumb is to calculate the point at which a server REQUIRES a physical server (generally averaging a full processor use or more) and identify them as potential candidates but not low hanging fruit.

Memory in Use

Memory in use is big for two reasons. The first is cost. Memory (in large amounts) is expensive. So if you have a host with 16GB of memory and put a VM on that require 8GB but little processor you have effectively used ½ of that server (by creating a bottleneck) and reduced your overall consolidation ratio. The second is that there is a limit to the amount of memory you can use in a VM. Using ESX you have a 16GB memory limit for any single VM. This means large boxes using that much memory don't often fit into "classic" consolidation models.

Much like processor the memory targets in VMs is heavily reliant on the consolidation ratio you are looking to achieve. If you have looked into the processor specs and determined you want 5 VMs per core, you then have to see if you can support that many VMs based on memory constrains. If you have 2GB per core installed (dual processor dual core server) for 4 cores and your VMs need 1GB each you have a memory bottleneck. Now if you have 4GBs per core and you need 1GB average per VM, you have a 4:1 ratio (close to your processor count of 5:1). So with memory you want to determine the amount of physical memory the servers use and find the average that works for you.

In our example we would be looking for VMs that physically USE a little less than a GB of memory. Then when the VMs are built you can assign them the next 256 MB increment up from what they already use.

To find this one of the best ways (available in almost all tools) is to grab the free memory counter (MB or Bytes) and subtract the free memory from the memory installed. So if I have a physical server with 4096 MB installed and free MB is 3275, my physical memory in use is 821. For the VM you would count this as a 1024 MB server when being migrated, but from a candidate identification standpoint it falls right into your strike zone.

A not on paging activity. Some people place a huge amount importance on paging activity. Personally I believe that if your candidate is paging (and using low amounts of memory) you can go ahead and give it more memory in its VM configuration. Having been part of projects with hundreds and thousands of physical to virtual migrations I have NEVER seen paging as a performance issue once the server was made a VM. Sure it may page, but give it some more memory. It doesn't kill the server and should not be relied on for candidate identification.

Disk IO and Throughput

A lot of time and space could be given to this discussion. But before we go into any of it I want to preface this section with the following statement:

While Disk IO and Throughput is important, it is rarely a constraint. I just finished a review of an environment with about 1800 servers in it. In this environment only about 20 servers had what we considered "high IO" and moved them into the "potential candidate" instead of prime candidate. 20 servers of the 1800 is only about 1% of the servers. And in every one of these 20 server they also have high memory and processor usage already moving them out of the low hanging fruit.

Now that I am off of my soap box let's talk about disk IO. In Windows you can grab a decent counter as Disk Transfers/Sec. This counter is the combined number of read and write operations on the disk. We use this number as the "IO" number and tend to rule out or move to "potential candidates" when servers get about 250 or 300 IOs per second. Now this is not a hard fast rule, but again we are looking for averages, if you all your VMs averaged more than 300 IOps on a single box, and you had 20 or 30 VMs you would have a lot of IO for a single server. But to have a few of these mixed in is not going to really hurt performance.

On the throughput side a good counter to look at is the Disk Bytes/sec counter. This counter is the combination of data from both reads and writes for the disk. This average is what you are looking for (later in this section we will discuss time frames but for now let's use overall average). For this counter we often find that servers fall into the 50,000 to 100,000 range. Sounds impressive right? Well, remember this is in BYTES. Converted to MB of throughput 100,000 Bytes is about 97K or less than a MB of throughput on the disk. From a candidate perspective we would try to keep this average below 20 or 30 MB. The reality is that if you are pushing 50MB or more of throughput you are more than likely also seeing high memory and processor usage.

Network Throughput

Much like disk you want to work out the averages for IO and throughput and assign accordingly. Also much like disk very few servers on your network use those gigabit connections you have connected to them. In most cases peak network and processor usage are seen during backups and tends to be 4 -10 times as high as normal load for the server.

From a counter perspective we like to look at the Bytes\Total Sec. The trick with this is that the counter is in Bytes and our Nics and Networks are rated in Bits. So you will need to do a little math here. Much like disk anything that I have seen ruled out based on the network (and I have only seen a couple) also had processor and memory constraints.

From a numbers perspective you need to be realistic. Most environments will have at least 2 NICs per server for a VM. If these are GB NICs and you have 20 VMs, then each VM should average less than 100 MB. Easy to do because in 90% of servers you will find they average less than 10MB.

Time Frames for Counters

The past few pages have went over the basic counters you need to look at for candidate identification. But it then comes down to being able to get data from the "important" times. VMware breaks this down with their tool by breaking usage data into an overall average, a peak hour average, and a business hours average (8am-5pm). In most cases simple perfmon cannot give you this info, and a tool may be required or you may need to mine this out of your existing performance monitoring database.

In any case the important numbers are from the overall average, the peak hour average, and an identification of the peak hours. The overall average gives you numbers you need to scale and plan your environment, but the peak hour allows you to determine if peak hours are important or if the average is more important.

When we say "peak hour identification" we mean what hour (on the clock) do the servers peak. You will want to make a chart of this based on your candidates to determine if a majority of them all peak during the same hours (a 1 to 2 hour time slot) or if the peaks are spread almost across the 24 hour clock. If 50% of the server peak during a 1 or 2 hour period, then you need to plan on that from a utilization perspective. If your servers peak all around the clock and somewhat evenly, then the overall average can be used since servers peaking will be a small % of the VMs with the rest in off-peak hours.

A perfect example of this is a client I had that their backup jobs all kicked off simultaneously, as in not staggered at all. Basically at 7 pm every night almost every server in the environment went from 5% utilization to 50-100% utilization. The solution to this was to either build the clusters to take 50% utilization for each VM at the same time, or stagger the backups over night starting at 7, 8 , 9, 10 o'clock, etc. Now this is an extreme case, but something to be aware off. If most of your servers (let's say 60%) peak during the 8am to 11am window, you may have to scale your farm based on their peak numbers.

New Server Candidate Identification

New server identification is a little tougher. The best process for this is to implement a good introduction process into the farm that includes some testing and a virtual to physical migration process should you need it.

The most successful companies with VMware have implemented a "VM First" policy. This policy simply states any new servers for test or production are deployed as VMs unless a technical (or sometimes business) reason can be found not to. This requires that new servers be spec'd as VMs and tested. This is easy for organizations that manage application life cycle through a Dev, UAT and

Production cycle. During UAT you will be able to get a good read on the resource usage and performance for the end user.

If a server is going right to production, the policy would state that the VM will be deployed and performance will be monitored. If performance issues arise fallback options using a V2P tool will move the server to a physical chassis. This doesn't happen often, but the ability to move back to physical is what allows it to be successful.

In either case the VM should be deployed and its resource utilization reviewed. If enormous resource needs are identified, the VM can be upsized fairly easily or moved to physical.

Candidate Assessment Tools

The two major tools that we have talked about here are Platespin's Powerrecon and VMware's Capacity Planner. We will look at an overview of each one here and then compare and contrast their benefits and drawbacks. You could pull the data you need from internal monitoring tools (if they are configured to gather what you need) but assuming you don't have those tools we are only focusing on the two industry standard external tools.

VMware's Capacity Planning

A few years ago VMware purchased a company called AOG. This company was the original vendor for Capacity planner and gained some notoriety even before the purchase for being able to collect performance and inventory data without clients on the target servers.

Capacity Planner's architecture is pretty simple; one of their collectors (a Windows Server) is installed local to within the targeted environment. Their collector software uses WMI and remote registry calls to gather inventory information on up to about 500 servers. Personally I limit these collectors to about 300 or 350 servers total. Anyway, after the inventory for hardware and applications is done a new job is started that collects performance metrics from the targeted servers. This job goes out to each server once an hour (in Windows remote Perfmon calls are made in Linux shell access is made and data from the proc file system is grabbed) and gathers four samples from the server for key performance metrics.

Over a 30 day period this data is collected. About once an hour the data (stored on the collector in CSV format) is uploaded to VMware's capacity planning website over SSL. It's this point in the process that gives some engineers pause… The data going out is inventory and performance data, which for most organizations this is no big deal, for some it is a showstopper.

The reason the data is moved to VMware is so they can process the inventory, marry it up to the performance data and even run some default reports. The idea being that VMware's partners can leverage pre-canned reports and tools without having to develop their own. The issue with this is that everyone using this tool tends to give the same results, and it's only available through VMware partners. That's right; you can't get the tool and use it, you have to find someone to sell you the licenses and do the assessment.

Advantages of using Capacity Planner
- Cost effective – it's the cheapest tool around

- Agentless, requires no change on the target systems

- Data and reports and generally reviewed by someone with experience in the VMware space

Disadvantages of using Capacity Planner
- Data is sent off-site

- Must be purchased from a partner, no self analysis

- Is only available in time chunks (30 or 90 days) no long term use

- Collectors are clunky and sometimes need to some baby-sitting to make sure data is being sent up to VMware

- Only works on Windows and Linux

Platespin's PowerRecon

PowerRecon is really starting to become a decent product. Platespin's first version of this product pretty much fell on its face. But with their latest release they have taken aim at VMware targeting some of their "bad points".

Much like Cap Planner PowerRecon will gather inventory and performance information remotely. But unlike Cap Planner, PowerRecon keeps the data in-house on a server in your environment. They then have a localized web-interface that installs with the product that allows you to run the reports and do identification without a outside consultants.

In addition they support other operating systems (like Sun) on non-x86 hardware. This could be advantageous for mixed environments that don't focus on Windows only. Also they allow you to buy this on a project bases (30-45-60 days etc) or on a permanent basis.

As you can see Platespin's product is very similar to VMware's, with the difference being that PlateSpin targeted Cap Planner's weaknesses. Solving their issues does not come cheap though, the price of PowerRecon is (at time of this writing) is about twice that of VMware's tool.

Advantages of using PowerRecon
- Agentless, requires no change on the target systems

- Data is not sent off-site

- Self use is available

- Permanent licenses can be purchased

- Works with some non-x86 systems

Disadvantages of using PowerRecon
- More expensive tool than VMware's

VM Standards

VM standards are possibly just as important as candidate identification. Much like physical hardware you need to define your "base" VM build. Now remember VMs are hardware. Your OS and other items that go into it are important, but here we are talking about the standard hardware that you will provision to VMs.

Typically one of two things happen in a new VMware environment. Either the administrator and other staff go 'hog wild' and provision VMs with dual and quad processors and 2,4 and 6 GB of memory, or they under provision VMs and become the "VM Nazi" dictating that any VM only gets a single proc and 256 MB of RAM.

The reality is that the sweet spot is somewhere in between these two extremes. In cases where companies over provision (dual procs for everything) they didn't understand the impact of this on their environment (essentially doubling their scheduling load). Conversely organizations limiting VMs to only all single procs with almost no ram are limiting their field of play and possibly hurting perform-ance of some of the VMs

The sweet spot comes when you develop a realistic VM standard that allows you to cover the needs of 80% of your VM audience with the ability to "up-grade" VMs to cover the other 20%.

Typical items that need to be address in your standard VM include:

- Number of Virtual Processors assigned
- Standard amount of memory
- Standard number of NICs and Virtual Switches connect to
- Standard Virtual Disk configuration (type, size and data disk size)
- Logical partitioning standards within the virtual disks

The standards you create are important and give you a baseline configuration for the majority of your VMs. This will help to limit support, create an envi-ronment that is easy to understand and troubleshoot, and is a best practice.

In addition to your "standard" VM configuration and the upgrade process for it, you could have a two tier system where there is a standard, and an up-sell VM that has a greater number of resources. These are often used in environments that charge back or charge an initial cost for their VMs as a way to recoup the cost a VM that uses more resources. Below is a table that shows a typical stan-dard VM configuration and a large resources VM:

Tier	Low utilization/Standard VM	High utilization VM

Range	80% of env.		20% of env. (2x cost)	
Base	Windows	Linux/UNIX	Windows	Linux/UNIX
Proc	1 vCPU	1 vCPU	2 vCPU	2 vCPU
Disk	C: 10GB (VMDK) Data: Right-sized VMDK	12GB w/single VMDK	C: 10GB (VMDK) Data: Right-sized VMDK	12GB w/single VMDK
Network	1—Backup 1—Prodnet	1—Backup 1—Prodnet	1—Backup 1—Prodnet	1—Backup 1—Prodnet
Memory	1GB	512MB	2GB	1GB

As you can see the standard is just that, a base line VM standard. If a specific VM needs more memory or processor the standard allows for that. Of note you should see that the memory gets larger as you go to the High Utilization VM but does not go crazy. Memory should really be sized properly as it is the most common bottleneck in ESX environments, and can be easily over allocated based on application owners whining about needing X amount of memory.

Physical to Virtual (P2V) Migrations

P2V migrations are a mystical and magical thing to those new to VMware. To those that have been doing them for a while they are nothing more than an imaging or file copy process followed by some driver replacement. The reality is that a P2V process, generically, is the process of getting an existing physical server into a Virtual Machine.

When spoke about in the VMware community a P2V often means a tool based process that moves the contents of an existing server's disks into a virtual machine disk file, then inserting the scsi drivers into that virtual machine file to make it bootable when attached to a virtual machine. While this is a simplification, it is really the 'gist' of the whole evolution. How you actually do this is where the decisions come into play.

There are a number of players in the space that make P2V utilities. There is the free Ultimate P2V based on using a WinPE boot CD, Ghost and some cool utilities to do the driver fixes. There is VMware's own VMware Converter, and of course Platespin's PowerConvert.

The real info you need to know is about your options. There are three basic P2V options for migrations:

- Use a P2V tool and do a "live" migration
- Use a P2V tool and do a cold migration
- Don't use a tool, and build a new VM then migrate to it

Each option has its benefits and drawbacks, but you should understand all of them BEFORE you offer up any of them.

P2V tools and Live Migrations

The term 'live migration' makes most people think of zero downtime, no interruption Physical to Virtual Migrations. The reality is that we want this type of migration, but often it does not work out very well. Early versions of these tools (starting out in about 2005/2006) were really bad. You often had to stop services (even like the Windows Server Service) just to get the live migration to work. So essentially your server was turned on during the migration, but clients couldn't access it… so why even do it then?

In the last year or so these tools have gotten better. Platespin's PwoerConvert has live migration option as does VMware's Converter. While this sounds great, you should understand that these tools have their limitation. At time of writing neither of these are recommended for actively used, transactional based servers. The risk is that you may miss a transaction in the cutover. That leaves servers that do not change that often (like web servers and application servers) as the best target for these migrations.

The process is pretty simple really, an "agent" type of software is installed on the source machine. This agent acts a lot like a backup agent helping to move files from the source machine to the target VMDK(s). Once completed the agent can be removed or left in place.

You should not that when one of these migrations takes place you are essentially copying the contents of the source server's drives to VMDK files for the new VM. This can cause issues if you have servers with hundreds of thousands of files on them as the software has to parse through each file and copy individually as apposed a simple disk/block level copy that a cold migration does.

Advantages of using Live Migrations
- When they work they reduce the amount of downtime needed to convert to virtual

- Easier for app owners to buy into conversion with small downtime window for migrations

- Migrations move the application and entire server and configurations in whole, often reducing app owner involvement to simple testing

Disadvantages of using Live Migrations
- Is not recommended for actively used transactional systems (the ones you most want to do live migrations on).

- Can take longer than a cold migration that is a simple imaging process

- Requires that an 'agent' be installed on the source machine to facilitate the file copies

P2V tools and Cold Migrations

Cold migrations are the original form of migrations. Essentially an image is take of the server you are attempting to migrate. That image is pushed into a VMDK file just as if it was a physical server you were pushing an image to. The Actual "conversion" comes after the imaging is completed by inserting the drivers in to file system within the VMDK. This makes the VMDK bootable so that the targe VM can boot up and complete the process (generally installing mouse and video drivers along with VMware Tools).

Cold migrations are the original migrations that were used in VMware environments. They are pretty much fool proof, and work on almost any type of server. The trick with these is that you need to be able to boot the machine to a dos or Win PE environment (and have the drivers to do that) and get an image into a target VM's disks.

Cold migrations are nice in that they work almost every time, require no agent in the source system leaving it in a pristine state should you need to fail back to it, and generally work very predictably (since it's a block level copy of a disk you can make assumption about timing based on the amount of disk used and not work about copying hundreds of thousands of small files).

The disadvantage of cold migrations is that app owners have heard about the "live" migrations and want to use those if possible. Most customers want to have almost no downtime and think that the live migration is the key to it all...

Advantages of using Cold Migrations
- Server is shutdown during the migration so no transactions can be missed

- Can be faster than a live migration option (from overall migration time frame)

- No agent installed on the source machine

- Migrations move the application and entire server and configurations in whole, often reducing app owner involvement to simple testing

Disadvantages of using Cold Migrations
- Can be increased downtime when compared to the Live migration

- Requires that you shutdown the server for the duration of the migration

Building "new" VMs for migrations

This is the simplest of all migrations (from a VM Administrators standpoint). Essentially you build a new VM with a fresh OS installed, and allow the application owner to migrate or install his app into the VM and handle the cutover. But while it is easiest for the VMware team it is often the most impractical from a project standpoint.

When a server is migrated using a P2V tool of some type the server is moved as an image. This means that configuration changes, application tweaks, and all the little bits of supporting tools that the application teams have installed or messed with over the years are moved over with no changes. This is great from a project perspective as it requires the least number of man hours over all in most cases, and ensures a duplicate of the existing server in the new VM environment.

Conversely if you were to create a brand new VM, the application owner would have to install the application, any supporting tools, make the configuration changes needed, test the application, then try to figure out what they missed. Obviously some servers would be fairly simple, but in the current IT world where identifying an app owner and even installation instructions for every application is a huge problem, this often adds weeks or sometimes months to individual application migrations.

Advantages of Building New VMs
- Reduces workload on the VMware team
- Supplies a fresh OS build in the new environment (with no hangovers from the physical world)
- Good time for an OS upgrade if needed

Disadvantages of Building New VMs
- Creates an enormous amount of work during the migration
- Slows the migration process down

Post Migration Clean Up

No matter which P2V tool or process you use, there will be some cleanup you need to do after the migration. When you move a physical server to the virtual world there are services and applications running (most times) that have direct ties to hardware that was once installed. So post migration you need to have a strategy to deal with these hangovers from the physical world.

Typically we will have a script that will disable items like HP SIM monitoring, or Dell OpenManage services. Also you will need to do some basic clean up of the "old" nics that are no longer showing up in the Network Properties (in Windows) but still has the old IP address assigned. Finally a major change needed in most P2V'd servers in the HAL change. Prior to migration most servers are dual or quad processor servers. Then, when moved to a VM, are setup as single or uni-processor servers. This can cause excessive CPU activity because of the mismatched HAL. Basically you need to "downgrade" the system to a uni-processor HAL. For this to work properly you would need to carry out a kernel update. In the world of Microsoft Windows this means changing from an ACPU Multi-processor to a ACPI Uni-processor HAL within the "Device Manager" tool. Again there are steps to do this on the internet and in the admin section of this book. But for now, know that it is important!

As stated, the internet (and second half of this book) has tons of lists and step by step processes covering P2Vs. This section focuses on the decisions that need to be made and knowledge needed and leaves the regurgitation of the lists to your Google searches.

VM Deployment/Templates

From a design perspective the basic decision you need to make is whether to use templates or not. Templates are essentially clones of individual VMs. Basically you can configure a single VM, install your supporting software/agents, configure the OS with specific settings for your organization, then clone that template over and over for new deployments. When you need to update the template you can simply fire it up, make your updates and resave it.

The nice thing about templates is that they essentially allow you to do disk copies of the VM, and in the case of Windows operating systems even can be integrated with Microsoft's deployment tools such as Sysprep. The major drawback we see is that this process may not match up well with your existing deployment mechanism and you could wind up just adding another tool for OS deployment to your environment. With that in mind you really have a few options:

- Use template based VM deployment

- Use existing tools (like PWE boot based tools) for VM deployment

- Hand build/other...

Using templates is not a bad thing, and in most VMware environments pretty much the norm. Using a template is a lot like using an imaging process for OS deployment, the difference here being that your hardware is never different since ESX abstracts the underlying hardware into the virtual machine's standard hardware.

The drawback is that you may already be using a tool like Altiris to do your OS builds. Or in the Linux space you may have centralized scripts that you run to ensure each new machine is built to current standards. In these cases template use would basically create two deployment mechanism instead of further simplifying your environment.

So, templates are great for VM environments, but you need to make a smart decision about them. Don't create more complexity when you don't need to. I have a client that does complete unattended installs of any OS they support. They slip stream in any patches or updates to the builds and find that deploying a VM this way is no different than their existing process. For them it makes perfect sense.

On the other side I have a client that hand builds based on a checklist whenever a server is not delivered from their vendor with their pre-loaded image. In that case templates were a perfect fit as they had no internal tool.

Chapter 8 - Managing the Environment

Often when you think of a chapter on managing an IT environment you envision a bunch of how to's and frequent tasks. In this book we are not going to go down that path. The second section of this book has plenty on configuring the alerts and setting up templates for VM deployment, etc. Instead we are going to focus on a number of items needed to manage you environment long term, such as:

- Monitoring and Alerting from an architectural perspective

- DataCenter and Resource Pool configurations

- Integration into change/configuration management

- Maintenance plans

- Costing/chargeback models

- Capacity planning

- Writing custom applications using VirtualCenter data

We see these as critical management components. While deploying VMs and setting up individual alerts are important, how you are going to architect the entire environment is the first step.

Monitoring and Alerting

It should be noted that while alerting is based (generally) on the monitoring tools in use, Alerting is a separate and equal partner in the design and should be treated as such. Monitoring (or monitor) in reference to computer science is defined as *"A program that observes, supervises, or controls the activities of other programs or systems."* So what are we observing or controlling? And how are we going to do that?

The first and most used monitoring program for VI3 environments is obviously VirtualCenter. VirtualCenter by its nature tracks performance of objects it manages such as VMs, Hosts, Resource Pools, and data centers. It is also a central point of integration for most third party management tools that support ESX and in most cases use its data to report back to their consoles. You should also know that there are a couple of drawbacks to using VirtualCenter; first it is VMware centric. Meaning if you have other systems to monitor and are using other tools it doesn't know about them. Second it has been known to have some odd database/statistics issues. For a while VC would miss collecting data on ESX servers, during these "blank periods" it would put zeros in the data base for the missing samples. Of course when the data was reported on via the console or rolled up for weekly or monthly averages, it would average in all those zeros bringing the utilization average down and making the long term performance data almost useless.

Of course, the upside of using VirtualCenter is it is VMware centric and knows about / can see into the host level resource utilization which is the most accurate information you can get in the virtual world.

The time-drift issue...

One of the reasons you want to use an ESX/VMware aware monitoring too`l is the ever present time drift in a VM. To explain time drift we need to look at how counters work at a basic level. Essentially there are two types of counters, those that rely on time, and those that don't. To differentiate between the two at a counter level is pretty easy, anything that references X per second, or a % of utilization is time based. As an example, System Context Switches in Windows OS shows the number of Context Switches per second. Or Total CPU generally referenced as % of CPU utilization is also a time based essentially showing the number of cycles used as a % of the available cycles per second. In contrast non-time based counters such as Memory - Bytes Available, is a flat number. It tells you at any given point in time how many bytes are available but is not based on what happens second to second.

So why is all of this important? Well, the counters that are based on time are essentially based on the system clock of the VM. And the system clock is based on the number of ticks the VM sees from the processor. The issue comes along when a VM is de-scheduled from the processor and how the VM sees the "real" processor underneath. Meaning the VM sees a 3GHz processor and expects to see 3GHz worth of processor ticks every second either from active processes or the system idle process. When a VM is de-scheduled from the processor to allow other VMs to run, it essentially looses processor cycles and therefore the clock in the VM is not correct (at least at a sub-second level). So to the VM a second may be a second, or it may be a second and a half. And if this is true, then a counter that reports X number of IOps or Y number of context switches is not 100% accurate. So the very scheduling mechanisms that make it possible for multiple VMs to run on a single processor also have an effect on our monitoring.

Now this is not to say that high utilization still isn't high... As an example a VM may be reporting 95-100% CPU utilization. But if it is competing for time on the processor it is executing, it may be seeing 100% of the CPU it is allocated, but only really using 50, 60 or 70% of a physical CPU. Of course if a VM is reporting that it is about 90% over 3 minutes of course there is an issue whether the clock is right or not, but from a capacity planning perspective it may be irrelevant.

Confusing huh? Well let's get into some design options to understand what we are monitoring and why.

So what needs to be monitored?

Essentially you need to start from the bottom up and work from the hardware level, through the host software (ESX Server) then up to the VM and potentially inside the VM itself. We'll look at each of these individually and what you get from each level.

Hardware Monitoring/Agents

To use a common example I will talk about HP hardware here. Often HP customers will use SIM or System Insight Manager, to monitor their hardware. The SIM agents get installed into the OS and monitor everything from CPU Fan speed, to power supplies. They then report this back to a central console. The thing with SIM is that it is hardware specific; don't try to use this on Dell. But Dell has its own software as does IBM. But it requires that the OS you install on has direct access to the hardware, which the VMs do not. So in our ESX environments we need to install agents into the ESX Service Console.

Anyway, what you want is an agent that you can report hardware failures or pending failures, etc. As of this writing the supported ESX agent levels for major vendors are as follows:

- HP Insight Management Agents: 7.5.1.A

- Dell OpenManage Agent: Version 5

- IBM Director Agent: 5.10

All of these vendors do a pretty good job of integrating with ESX these days. In almost every environment you will want some type of hardware monitoring since the VMs themselves cannot see the hardware directly and are unaware of it and running without it could be dangerous seeing how you just stacked 20 or so VMs on a single piece of hardware.

Host Monitoring

The next level of monitoring we need is at the host/ESX level. This is often handled by VirtualCenter in new environments. VirtualCenter will give you a pretty good look at an ESX host and does a decent job for daily operations. For long term capacity planning it is pretty much useless. But for host monitoring (is the processor utilization high, is memory over-committed, etc) it is pretty good. Its big lacking piece (as of VC 2.0.2) is a good way to handle alerting. Since VC's inception the ability to set alerts based on duration has not been there. Instead the alerts are based on a single threshold concept. As an example let's use processor usage:

Assume you want to get an alert when host processor usage is over 90%, but you don't want to catch spikes in utilization, you want 90% over a period of 5 or 10 minutes only. This is a dual threshold alert, it has to meet both a certain level of utilization AND for a certain number of samples/certain amount of time. The issue with Virtual Center is that it uses single threshold alarms. Meaning that it sets a threshold of say 90% on CPU, and one sample is 90% you get an alarm. Kind of a pain on the host, but very much a pain if you apply this to VMs. VMs are spiky by their nature (just like normal servers) and alerts triggered this easily can be annoying, but there is a solution, have VirtualCenter feed a more refined alerting system like MOM, Director, or HP Openview.

In most cases enterprise customers will already have a management tool in place something like Microsoft Operations Manager (or System Center as it's now called) or an HP Openview. The benefit of using one of these systems is that they tend to have more refined alerting systems that you may need, and it will limit the number of places that an alert will come from. Of course to use one of these you need a go-between type of system that will feed true ESX data to your monitoring system.

Figure 8- 1: Host Monitoring

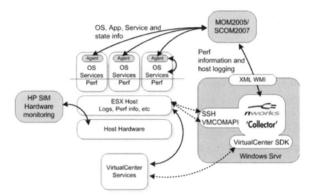

Here I use nworks as an example. Nworks is one of the better known solutions that a number of environments use. It makes a go between collector for both HP Openview and MOM. Here we show a typical nworks setup where it collects information from VirtualCenter and feeds it back to the MOM console. The nice thing about this setup is that you get both the VirtualCenter / Host information but in the same console you can see you non-VM systems and have agents for apps and services inside the Virtual Machines.

Notice that the collector in the image uses the VirtualCenter SDK. This is the most common model for VMware partners building tools and add-ons. From a host perspective it can connect via the API or directly to the host via SSH. This type of software or something like it is an absolute must in any large environment.

Virtual Machine Monitoring

Finally you will want to watch your virtual machines at some point. In smaller shops often there is no host monitoring in physical servers, so they leave VMs the same way. But if you monitor your physical servers now for items like Up/Down state, free disk space, processor usage, service state, etc. you will probably want to do the same for VMs so lets look at a few important options.

Service state, Up/Down, and applications

Anything like this you can continue to do as you normally do. If you use something like MOM or NetIQ to monitor your AD or Exchange servers and are now making them VMs go ahead. If you have an agent you use to monitor service state or up/down of the server, keep them! They work just fine. No changes are needed. Granted you may see some odd things... I had a SQL guy tell me once that his read time on some obscure counter went from 3 ms to 4.5 ms average... I asked if performance changed for the end user? No, actually he didn't even know if the counter was important. Of course it was a TIME BASED counter so it was probably skewed, but that is another story. For general application stuff, keep them running.

Perfmon type metrics

Of course for serious counters/metrics you have to be a little smarter. Like we talked about before, time based metrics are inaccurate. Not completely wrong mind you, just not 100% right. As an example; I had a client that commonly monitored for servers at 90% cpu for longer than 5 minutes. While within the VM that counter might not be perfectly accurate from a whole CPU perspective, if the VM was using 90% of what it had access to it was still a lot. And if that was not normal they wanted an alarm triggered. It worked just fine, in some cases batch jobs would stall and spin up a process and it would signal the operations team so it still worked. But for capacity planning or very accurate trending time based metrics should not be relied upon.

For non-time based metrics, go ahead and set them up. Most VMware users will still monitor for things like disk space in use (it shows the logical space inside the VMDK) or free memory etc. To list each counter that works or not here would be a 10 page table. So instead remember the time based issues and make decisions intelligently.

Resource Pools

While this may seem an odd place to cover it, I wanted to touch on these items where it seemed most appropriate. Resource pools are used to manage resources in a cluster and often times throttle resources for different types of VMs. In most cases they are implemented over aggressively and tend to hurt the environment, hopefully we can put them into their proper place here and help your long term management of the environment.

Basically Resource Pools are an extension of the existing Share and reservation systems that VMware built to control resource allocation to VMs. Only when using Resource Pools you are grouping the VM together to share resources instead of applying these settings on an individual VM level (as was done with previous versions of ESX). So it is possible to cap or "limit" resources or to guarantee a minimum or "reservation" of either of resources (specifically CPU or memory) to a VM or a resource pool. Alongside these unchanging and hard-coded limits or reservations, we can have a more dynamic control over VM's usage of CPU, memory or disk. We can use VMware's proportional "share" system which responds to changes in resource demand relative to each VM and ESX host. At an extreme level it is possible to peg a resource to a VM with such features as CPU affinities – hard-coding a VM to have exclusive access to a CPU.

Technically, I really should mention that VMware Distributed Resource Service (DRS) is an invaluable resource management tool. DRS integrates very closely with VMware High Availability (HA) so it was decided to show these two products together in the "High Availability" chapter of this book.

During this chapter I want to use an analogy to explain how resources are managed in ESX. This analogy is about an airline. Each plane will represent an ESX host, a fleet of aeroplanes a VMware DRS cluster. Every plane has fixed capacity in terms of the number of passengers it can comfortably accommodate. Each of the "seats" will represent a VM. If the airline has 200 seats per plane and ten planes that is a total of 2000 seats. But the 200 seats per plane do represent a fixed limit on capacity. Fundamentally, though these 2000 seats exist as a logical capacity, a passenger can only board one plane – just as an VM can only currently execute one server, not a cluster. Access to the plane is controlled by unique system of reservations which is intended to guarantee not that you fly – but that a certain quality of travel like business class will be provided. In contrast, economy passengers do not make reservations. They merely turn up and hope there will be capacity to fly.

Setting Limits

As stated a moment ago it is possible to impose limits upon a VM or resource pool. This can be done for CPU resources (by Mhz) and for memory (by MB). In fact, limits are imposed on VM from the perspective of memory when you first define a VM. When you create a VM you set the maximum amount of memory it can have during the "New Virtual Machine" wizard. If a VM demands more memory it cannot exceed this amount allocated to it – even if free physical memory exists. At first glance this seems quite restrictive, however, from an architecture point of view, it has to happen. If we have poorly written applications and operating systems we would want to avoid the situation where a VM was able to drain a physical host of all its available RAM – thus causing a reboot of the physical server. If we use our analogy it's not possible for a single passenger on the plane to take up all the space at the expense of the other passengers. Additionally, there are some fixed limits we cannot exceed. If there are only 200 seats on the plane we cannot allow 201 passengers to board. Similarly, if the ESX host or pool resources are totally consumed – a limit has been reached. We cannot magicly out of nowhere find additional resources- with one exception. When all memory has been depleted is possible for a VM to use its VMkernel swap file.

In contrast there are no default limits on CPU usage. If a VM demands CPU time, and that CPU time is available, then this is allocated to a VM. One reason to cap or limit a VM usage of CPU could be because you know you have a poorly written application that regularly crashes. Perhaps when it crashes it "hogs" the CPU of the ESX host. Using CPU limits is one method (amongst many) to control these kinds of VM's.

Lastly, a word about terminology - in the ESX 2.x product the word "maximum" was used instead of the word limits. VMware changed the phraseology to "limits" as this is more meaningful and more clearly describes the feature. Additionally, VMware has moved away from allocating limits on CPU's by a percentage value and now prefers to use Mhz. Mhz is a more accurate measure of CPU usage than percentages, which can be very misleading. In the context of CPU's 10% of a 1.44Mhz processor is decidedly different from 10% of 2.6Mhz processor.

Setting Reservations

In addition to limits, we can also use CPU or memory "reservations." One analogy that can help when thinking of reservations is to compare them to the plane reservations. These reservations are supposed to *guarantee* a resource in the form of a seat. Similarly a CPU or memory reservation in Mhz or MB is intended to *guarantee* the resource to the VM or resource pool. In this case there are no *default* reservations for CPU or memory, unlike the default limit on memory set when creating the VM. We can regard these reservations or guarantees as offering us a way of ensuring we meet certain performance levels. Perhaps you could even regard them as a way of meeting "service level agreements" (SLA).

Just like with a plane or hotel you must "meet" your reservation in order to board or check into a hotel. So, if you say that the memory reservation on VM is 256MB of RAM – and that amount of RAM is physically not available – you will be unable to power on the VM. VMware refers to this as "Admission Control." Similarly, if we configured a situation where a VM must get 1000Mhz of CPU time, but the physical host can only offer 500Mhz of CPU time – that VM would not power on.

Using our airplane analogy, if a passenger makes a reservation for 10 seats in business class those seats must be there. Our airline imposes a very *special* definition of customer care that states if a business class reservation cannot be met – rather than pushing our customer in economy class, we refuse admission to the flight. Here we can see the weakness of all analogies, they don't work perfectly in all circumstances. Nonetheless, I want to persist with this analogy as it is helpful in most cases.

As with CPU's in ESX 2.x VMware used to call "reservations" minimums. Again, the label change was introduced to be more meaningful.

Putting the concerns to one side for a moment there is very interesting and useful relationship between memory limits and reservations and the VMKernel swap file. The difference between the reservation subtracted from the limit – determines the size of the VMkernel swap file. The usage of the VMkernel Swap file was mentioned in the previous chapter as an indicator of potential performance problems – but here I wish to delve a little deeper into different ways of using it. Explaining how to use the VMKernel swap file is perhaps best done with a couple of examples.

Example 1: Difference between Limit and Reservation

I had a VM with a 512MB limit and 256MB reservation – on power on the VM would create a 256MB VMkernel swap file (512-256) and guarantee that the VM would receive 256MB of RAM.

Example 2: No difference between limit and reservation

If I set the limit to 512MB and the reservation also as 512MB – and powered on the VM, ESX would not create a VMkernel swap file at all. It would run the VM entirely in a memory reservation of 512MB.

Example 3: Big difference between limit and reservation

If on the other hand the VM was given a 16GB limit, and the default of 0MB was used for the reservation – a 16GB VMkernel swap file would be created.

With example 1 if I had an ESX host with 2GB of physical RAM I could run at least 8 VM's before running out of memory (2048MB/256MB). I would not be able to power on a 9th VM because there would be insufficient memory to meet the reservation guarantee. If all the VM's simultaneously wished to use memory up to the limits (512MB*8) I would find I would get swap activity. What I hope is that this would be such an unlikely event – that it would be "safe" to configure the system this way.

Perhaps you find this "memory over-commitment" a bit scary. You are concerned about the negative aspects of swap activity, and you wish to have a cast-iron guarantee that your VM's will *always* run in memory. If this was the case you could use example 2. By setting the VM's limit and reservation to be the *same* value no swap file is created – and the VM is guaranteed to always run in memory. However, on a 2GB system the effect of this policy would be very significant. I would only be able to run 4 VM's not 8 (2048MB/512MB). If I tried to create a 5th VM and power it on – it wouldn't, as all my memory would have been reserved for use by my other VM's.

I could imagine example 1 being configured by someone who is optimistic and is looking for very high VM to ESX host ratios or someone trying to run as many VM's with as few resources as possible. Alternatively, we could see example 2 as someone who is perhaps pessimistic or conservative, or someone who has so many resources there is no need to use the VMkernel swap file.

The last example, example number 3 is a warning. If you set extremely high values on memory, with no reservations – the ESX host will generate an extremely large swap file. Just like with memory reservations, you need the physical MB disk space to create the VMkernel swap file. In example 3, if you didn't have 16GB of free disk space in the LUN where the VM is stored, it would not power on as there would be insufficient resources to guarantee the *difference* between the limit and reservation.

The Share System

Between the gap between limits and reservations another system is at play. It is called the "Proportional Share" system. Shares allow you indicate that when a resource is scarce that one VM or resource pool is more important than another. To use our analogy it's like the airline treating a Hollywood star more importantly than the average guy on the street. Share values can be applied on per-VM basis or on resource pools. Unlike limits or reservations which are fixed and unchanging – shares on the other hand react dynamically to resource demands. The share value can specified by a number (usually in multiples of 1,000) or by user-friendly text value of normal, high, and low. The important thing to remember about the share value is that it is only relevant when the resource is scarce and contention is occurring. If the resource is plentiful or VM's do not have to compete over resources – the share value does nothing at all.

In my discussions with VMware I've been told that many customers do not use the proportional share system as much as VMware might like. Why might this be? Firstly, because customers frequently don't understand how shares work, and secondly, because shares only take effect when things are performing badly

– a great many people try to configure their ESX hosts and VM's so this never happens. Personally, I am a big fan of the shares system. What especially appeals to me is its dynamic nature, its ability to react to changes.

If you or your customer is still struggling with the concept of shares you might like to try a couple of other analogies. You could see the share value like shares in company that are quoted on the global stock exchanges. The amount of shares a company chooses to issue is up to it – what matters is the number or portion of your shares. The greater amount of shares you hold in a company the more of its resources you own. Therefore a big share owner of 5000 shares has much more influence than a shared holder with just a thousand shares. Perhaps you own as much as ¼ of the company or 25% of its shares.

Here's another analogy I use regularly on courses. Imagine you have 3 children – one is a baby, the next a 5 year-old and the last a teenager. When you come home after a hard day's work they all demand your time. Here your time is like the CPU, and each of your children are pesky VM's making demands on your tired brain. Being a particularly cruel parent you decide to take a permanent marker – write 3000 on the baby's forehead, 2000 on the toddler's forehead, and lastly 1000 on the teenager's forehead. You decide you're like one of the ESX hosts you manage at work, and this is your parental strategy from now on!

In this scenario when you are faced with contention (say when you come home from work) you would give the baby ½ (3000/6000), the toddler ¹/₃ (2000/6000) and your teenager just ¹/₆ (1000/6000) of your valuable time. Now when it's mid-evening you decide that the baby is tired enough to go to sleep. You're in luck tonight as he's out for the count in seconds – you now can give ²/₃ of your time to the toddler (2000/3000) and ¹/₃ (1000/3000) of your time to the teenager. When the toddler goes to bed (after much crying and wailing normally) you are facing no contention at all. Just as you're settling down to watch your favorite sit-com the teenager comes down from her bedroom – perhaps the internet connection has failed or her games console has broken. She now decides this will be an opportune time to discuss why college is a waste of time and how she should really follow her favorite drug taking band around the country. Now you can give all of your time to teenager – 1000/1000 – in persuading her that while a life of drunken debauchery might have its appeal, it won't lead her to a prosperous career in IT like yours. Finally, everyone goes to bed – contention is over and you get the opportunity to get some well-earned z's. But then at 3 a.m. a sound is heard from the baby's room which grows into crying. You're out of luck, and it is your turn and not your partner's to feed the baby. However, rest assured as long as you get to the baby quickly, it will not wake the others – and you are able to give 100% of your time to getting back in bed as quickly as possible!

All joking aside, the analogy does illustrate some points. Firstly, that share value adjusts depending on the level of contention. Secondly, that when there is no contention the share value does nothing at all. Thirdly, that when you become a parent you will have no time to yourself whatsoever!

Lastly, you should know that there is another way of setting the share value – which is by using friendly labels of "High, Normal, and Low." These offer novices a more intuitive way of dividing up resources. You will have seen these whenever you create a new VM. You can use these text labels on a VM and also in resource pools. If you are going to use these you should know what actual settings apply.

High
Allocates 2000 shares per virtual CPU

20 shares for every 1MB allocated to the VM

Normal
Allocates 1000 shares per virtual CPU

10 shares for every 1MB allocated to the VM

Low
Allocates 500 shares per virtual CPU

5 shares for 1MB allocated to the VM

As you can see, high is twice as much as normal and four times as much as low. There is also another assumption at play here. VMware assumes that the more memory you assign to a VM the more sensitive it is to a lack of memory. So when contention takes place the VM "wins" a greater slice of memory resources. This assumption might not always be the case (although it frequently is). You could have a memory intensive application that is not business critical.

CPU Affinities

One extreme method of controlling the VM's access to CPU resources is to "peg" it to a specified CPU. As was mentioned in the previous chapter, internally to physical server the VMkernel dynamically moves the VM across to work on the best CPU inside the ESX host. We can switch off this feature using CPU affinities on the properties of a VM. I would this regard this configuration as a last resort. Firstly, configuring it is very administration intensive. Not only to have to configure the VM in question to use only CPU3 for example, you also have to configure every other VM *not* to use CPU3 – to truly dedicate a VM to given CPU. Secondly, CPU affinities are incompatible with VMotion. Thirdly, as DRS is effectively an automated VMotion for performance – CPU affinities also break DRS. Removing CPU affinities on a VM running on a ESX host which is already a member of DRS cluster is possible, but very convoluted. Therefore, I consider CPU affinities a very last resort.

Resource Pools or VM Settings

There are two main ways to apply many of these settings – limits, reservations, and share values. Resource pools only affect CPU and memory resources – so if your goal is to control disk and network activity, these must be done on the properties of the VM or a vSwitch respectively. Despite this limitation, CPU and memory resources are very critical, and resource pools offer a much more effective way of applying limits, reservations, and share values. Right-clicking each VM and setting these values is by its nature very administration intensive, whereas dragging and dropping a VM to the correct VM is an easy task. If you are trying to calculate the total share value it is easier to compare a small number of resource pools, rather comparing a large number of VM's.

Resource pools can be live in two main places – hanging off a stand-alone ESX server which divides up the resources of a single host into smaller units or pools, or alternatively, resource pools can be created on VMware Cluster which divides the total resources of many servers into pools. Once you got the concept of resource pools and the way they function – they are the same if they are on a stand-alone or a cluster, but they really come into play when applied to clusters where resrouces needs and workload movement become more important. You could create resource pools based by department (sales, accounts or distribution), function (web servers, database, or file servers), or by IT Infrastructure (test, development, production).

If we apply our analogy to this we can see each of the airplanes as representing an ESX host. A DRS cluster represents the collective capacity of all my airplanes, but fundamentally a passenger can only fly on one airplane – not on two simultaneously. Our air-traffic controllers are very clever guys who can detect some airplanes stretched to capacity and move passengers from one plane to another while they are flying. This would be called VMotion in ESX.

In the Operations Guide section of this book much of this information will be repeated. We feel this topic cannot be stressed enough as these "settings" are often misunderstood. As with all of our information if you want specifics on how to configure these settings, go ahead and jump forward to the Operations Guide.

Integration into Change/Configuration Management

One of the big items forgotten in most designs is how to integrate the new virtual environment into existing change control or configuration management systems. Virtual Machines are sometimes treated like physical servers, which can limit the inherent abilities of the new system, or the new technology creates 'fear' that makes the change control for the environment overly conservative. In either case it is really a lack of understanding that causes this. So here we will point out common functions and where they often fit in change control procedures. But before we do this we will first overview the idea of a cluster and Virtual Machine from it components perspective for configuration mgmt.

Configuration Management

Configuration management requires an understanding of the entire system, of what components are dependent on each other, and how they are all interrelated. Below I have an image showing cluster from a component overview. Let's take a look at this:

Figure 8- 2: Configuration Management

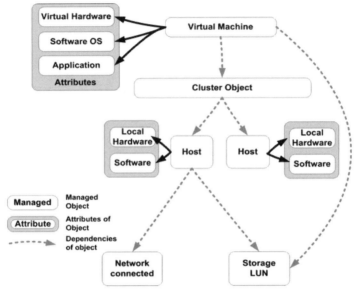

Basically a VM is not directly dependent on a specific host. From a configuration and change mgmt perspective it is really dependent on a cluster, this in turn is dependent on the hosts that are part of that cluster. Finally the hosts are dependent on the storage and networks they are connected. The So the VM is really not dependent on any specific host. So from a configuration mgmt and even change control perspective you can see the logical links being created in the environment. If you want to shut down one host, and not the whole cluster, you can do this without interruption to any VMs.

From a configuration management perspective this diagram is interesting since it shows all the levels in the VM environment and samples of the attributes you can track. Let's look at a few specific items/objects and their possible configuration items you want to track:

Virtual Machines

From an individual VM perspective you no longer need things like asset tags. This is sometimes a bit confusing as asset management databases often are tied to configuration management, so you may have to find a workaround like using the logical cluster name as the VM's asset tag. Anyway, some of the attributes we commonly see in configuration databases for VMs are:

- VM hardware configuration

- Guest Operating System information

- Storage/LUN VM is stored on

- VM cost center/info on VM charges (see the VM cost section later in this chapter)

Obviously the OS is something used whether physical or virtual. The biggest change is how hardware is account for, asset tags and of course the Storage the VMDKs are located on. This is often used to determine impacts of changes to do with SANs but can be very useful once your environment is large and you do storage changes, migrations, or upgrades.

Hosts

On the host these are often labeled as infrastructure like domain controllers or name servers. In addition another issue with configuration information is how some network teams require that you associate an IP or specific host with a specific network switch port. Of course on the hosts you may have several nics that have 10 or 20 VMs on them. Additional items you may see for the hosts include:

- Local hardware config and asset information

- Software versions and patch level

- Rack information

- Cluster membership

- Network port/switch information

- SAN port / switch information

Another alternative is to create a cluster object in the config management database, and manage the hosts as part of that. Personally I like keeping the hosts separate, and making their cluster an attribute of each host.

Network and Storage

Network and Storage attributes often don't need any additional information for VMs, but instead need a change in how servers are added. As mentioned previously often network and SAN teams will require individual host information or IPs to assign the port to your servers. SAN teams are usually ok with the concept of multiple servers connected to a single lun (from other cluster technologies) it is the Network team that often sees this as a foreign concept so make sure you cover it.

Change Management

One of the most frequently ask questions I get from clients around change control is "Should we do a change request for a VMotion". I find this funny because of all the new things going on in the environment and all the moving parts, the one that gets the most attention is VMotion. Of course I understand this since it is often a pretty mis-understood piece of technology, but also I try to point out there is a lot more to worry about than VMotion. In the Virtual-Center and cluster design chapter we went over DRS. And if you plan on using that it pretty much rules out change controls for VMotion, so let's look at some items in the environment may need change control, either from a pre-approved stand point or a change that may require more review.

Below is a list of common changes that you will need to consider (that are new to the environment):

- VMotion – Movement of a VM between hosts, no downtime, no change in storage – no impact to VM

- Host configuration change – Prior to failure or maintenance, uses VMotion to move VMs to other hosts, so that the originating server can be repaired (maintenance mode)- no impact to VMs

- Patches for ESX hosts, host hardware maintenance, etc.- no impact to VMs if VMs are moved first

- DRS – Automatic load-leveling on hosts using VMotion, could occur daily or hourly, no downtime for VMs or hosts

- Cluster change – Addition of LUNs, no downtime for VMs, rescan of storage

- Cluster change – Removal of LUNs, only affects the VMs stored on those LUNs

- Cluster change – Upgrade of hosts – Potential impact major – Downtime of VMs not always required – VMTools upgrades (during major host upgrade) requires VM restart on installation of new tools

- Addition of host to cluster – No impact to VMs.

- VirtualCenter updates – no VM changes, but possible loss of access to VMs via Virtual center

Maintenance Plans

Maintenance plans can be as varied as ESX or Windows Server builds are between different companies, but the common thread is there has to be one. Organizations without a minimal maintenance plan will often fall into the "I'm two service packs and one major rev behind" problem. With that known we believe in using weekly and monthly maintenance plans for ESX environments. For the most part these servers just run, but you still need to check things out / clean things up as needed.

Weekly Maintenance Tasks

For your VI 3 environment I would recommend starting with at least 5 and possibly 6 weekly tasks. These tasks are basics that review the existing environments logs, check volumes and look for open snap shots. Here is my basic list:

- *Review host logs for each server and note errors or possible issues for trouble-shooting.* Review forums and VMware documentation for any errors to determine if this is a benign error or something that needs correcting.

- Review VirtualCenter logs for issues or errors.

- *Review VMFS volumes for space in use and available capacity.* Any volumes with less than 10% available space should be looked at further and VM deployment should be stopped for that lun. (can be scripted or viewed in VC)

- *Review environment for VMs with open snapshots.* Snapshots that are not applied over time can grow huge amounts and cause performance issues and lock ups on the VM when applied. Weekly reviews will ensure snapshots are not 'forgotten'. (Can be scripted)

- Check local drive space on hosts for partitions filling up. Clear log files or temporary storage as needed.

- If you have "temporary VMs" used for Test/Dev check them to determine if they can be decommissioned and are not forgotten about and left to run forever.

A number of these tasks can be automated for the environment. Items like checking for disk space either locally on the hosts or on the VMFS volumes can be done using a shell script to output to a text file, then these files can simply be reviewed. How you accomplish tasks like this is not important, the importance is in actually doing them. Hopefully you can start with these tasks and add your own. The next section looks at a monthly checklist that focuses more on capacity planning and upgrades, but is no less important.

Monthly Maintenance Tasks

Some organizations will change this schedule to a quarterly schedule. Personally if it is done monthly I find that environments stay well up to date. For some reason when these tasks are moved to quarterly they are pushed off more often and or forgotten about for a while. By establishing a routine for the first or last week of the month, these tasks will happen on a regular basis and keep your environment in good shape.

- *Create a capacity report for the environment and distribute to IT and Mgmt.* Capacity plans are detailed more in the next section of this chapter. But they are imperative as your environment grows.

- *Update your VM Templates with the latest hotfixes and patches approved for the environment.* This will help to ensure that your templates are always current and when deployed need little work done to get them online.

- *Review the VMware website for new patches or fixes for your infrastructure.* You should determine if you need the patches being deployed. Security fixes are often a must, but if the patch fixes something with linux guest tools, and you have no linux guests, it's something you can wait on or not deploy at all. Make sure you document WHY you need or don't need to deploy a specific patch, this will help with audits.

- Review patches for VirtualCenter or other supporting services like monitoring tools used in the VI environment.

- Test and deploy updates as needed.

Again, you may decide to add or remove items from this list or may find that you have special tasks that need to be done. I have a client that has 4 sensitive VMs in their environment that must be tracked constantly. They have added a monthly task here, to check the VM hardware specs, review its audit logs and the logs for the host they are on.

VM Costs/Chargeback

We have been deploying VMs on ESX for clients since 2003. In the past 4 years on thing has become apparent in each environment I have visited. The environments that work out their VM cost/chargeback strategy early on tend to be very successful very quickly, the ones that don't tend to run into capacity issues or over spend (not meeting ROI targets) very quickly.

I think the reason for this is twofold; 1: clients that implement a cost/chargeback solution often have their act together in other areas and this just happens to be one of them and 2: those that don't implement a cost model often run out of capacity and run into performance and capacity issues since "VMs are free!!!".

The reality is simple economics, and while I know we in IT don't like to think like this since it gets finance involved, to be successful you have too. Look at it this way, if a project has budgeted $30K for hardware, $50K for software and $100K for consulting to implement a new piece of software, then you as the VMware guy give them 7 VMs for "free" so they free up that 30K, do you think they are just going to transfer it to you later for your next host? Nope, they are going to spend it on something else. Then when the VMware environment runs out of capacity and there are no more funds for servers or storage you are left holding the bag.

Cost of the VM

It really doesn't matter which one you implement, it's just important that you pick one. Based on your organization and the IT finance model you already have, this decision may be a foregone conclusion. But in either case, the cost model should include the following:

- Server cost

- Rack space

- UPS/Power distribution

- KVM

- ESX /Virtual Infrastructure licensing costs

- Supporting software costs (like 3rd party monitoring tools, or tools like ESX Ranger)

- SAN / NAS disk cost (if you are storing your VMs off the ESX host)

- Fiber and Network switch ports

From these basic numbers you can calculate an average VM's costs. Basically if you know all the component costs in a system, then the number of VMs you are going to host per server, simple division will give you an average VM cost (some organizations call this a slice).

The interesting thing in this model is that you have several ways to cost out the VMs to your customers. You can come up with an average cost, know that some VMs will have more disk space, or dual processors etc, but still charge everyone the same amount. This will result in a basic cost model, but seems to me to be a little "socialist". I mean if everyone is charged the same amount why would an application owner not ask for dual proc 4GB VMs? They would. So while this model can work, I believe in "up charges" for VM hardware upgrades.

To me you should attempt to drive the end-users behavior by costing/pricing VMs appropriately to their hardware allocated. This (like purchasing physical hardware) helps to drive them not to over allocate resources. Of course this model can also become very complex. The idea of up-charging for a dual processor VM over a single Processor VMs sounds nice, but its not as simple as doubling the price.

Let's assume you 'charge' $1000 for a single processor 512MB of RAM VM with 8GB of iSCSI based storage. Then a user asks for a dual processor server with the rest of the configuration the same. Essentially you have doubled one resource (processor) but changed nothing else. The proper way to do this is to understand your cost of ram, processors, storage space etc. That way when the next app owner only wants to go to 1.5 GB of RAM on a single processor system, you can properly charge for the 1 GB upgrade.

If you have a mature SAN environment in your organization you may already have a model like this in house. Storage is a shared service (like VMware) that has many options. Thirty GB of disk to the end user could be a mirror on the backend (60GB) or a RAID5 with a hot spare, or it could be replicated off site or mirrored locally based on user requirements. In any case the pricing reflects the actual hardware used and does not just double or triple based on simple sizing changes.

Finally, another reason to charge for VMs is to help stop VM sprawl. About 2 years ago Scott and I made a point to start pointing out that VM Sprawl was going to be an issue because; 1- VMs are so cheap, 2 –VMs that are free have no reason to be decommissioned, there is no incentive for app owners to go back and shut them down, thus continuing the cycle of using resources for no good reason.

In any case getting the right amount of money for the VMs and their underlying supporting infrastructure is extremely important. Most organizations handle VM purchases via inter department transfers. The best ones have accounts just for ESX shared infrastructure. The reason for this is to ensure that the money used to purchase VMs today, is allocated to purchasing the next set of capacity for tomorrow's VMs.

One-Time Cost vs Chargeback

We often get into long debates about 'chargeback' within client organizations. Some IT environments do not have a chargeback system and therefore see any type of IT "charge" as a chargeback, and thus push back strongly on charging for VMs. Frankly, whether you do an upfront cost or a recurring chargeback is up to you, but the reality is that you must do it for this technology in larger organizations.

One-Time costs are nice as they show the end-user a cost reduction right away (you would have bought this Dell PE 1950 for $5K, but instead here is a VM for $1.9K). The issue (long-term) with this model is that it never expires. Meaning someone buys a VM in 2004, by 2007 the lease is up on your hosts and storage and you are ready to refresh. Well, if the VM doesn't have something like an expiration date the end-user has a never ending upgrade path for free. So it is imperative in the upfront models to have a time out/drop dead date for VMs to ensure that you can handle/pay for future refreshes.

Chargeback on the other hand is perfect for VM environments. Whether you charge monthly, quarterly or annually, someone is looking at that bill every time and is driven to keep costs down (as we all are). Chargeback models ensure that the app owners or departments continue to pay for that system and continue to maintain the hardware and software (through paying for the service).

You can make either system work for you, the trick is that you have to have a cost model for your VMs early in your adoption to be successful. The cost model should be built in such a way that it motivates users not to over allocate resources, and pushes them to help keep VM sprawl in control.

Capacity Planning

An interesting thing has been happening in VMware environments for the last few years, people have been going back to their old ways... By that I mean I have recently audited two environments that have begun to underutilize the hardware in the ESX environment. One was averaging about 20% processor and 40% memory across their 30 hosts and the other was using even less on a 52 host 5 cluster environment. When prodded as to why this was going on, the response in both was the same; "we don't want to push the servers since any performance hit will be seen as a VM issue". Of course in both environments the average VM had a single proc with 1 GB of ram. The hosts were 8 core machines so that any VM spinning at 100% would only use 1/8th (or 12%) of available CPU. Averaging 20% normally they would have to have 6 or 7 VMs spin out of control, on the same host simultaneously...

Of course, the issue really is that they don't know about their capacity, how to plan for it, or how to articulate what is being used or what is needed to their management. So the easy thing to do is to revert to the old ways, underutilize the hardware and ask for more servers. This is the worst thing you can do. The cost of VMs will go up, and the savings your CIO or VP of Infrastructure was looking for will not materialize.

To keep you from falling into this trap, let's talk about capacity in a VI environment and how to really look it, calculate it and articulate it.

It's about the VMs!

One of the funny things about a lot of admins doing capacity planning is that they tend to look at their VirtualCenter, take a look at the little charts or the % proc used on each host and its memory, then guess (that's right guess) at their available capacity. They may even print up the cluster or resource pool reports showing 51% average processor, 75% average memory usage, 8.3 MB of average disk through put etc, then present that as a capacity report to their manager or VP.

As a VP or Manager my first (and really only) question about this report would be "So how many more VMs can I deploy?" Obviously the answer is not in that type of report. Managers and VPs don't care about the processor running at 40% and neither should you.

If a server runs at 40% average processor utilization, that means nothing. Not without a VM count to rationalize it. So if you had 4 VMs on the server running at 40% and you don't want your servers running over 80% at any given time, you essentially can deploy 4 more VMs before you reach your normal operating maximum. This is simplified but imagine, your environment ran at 40% average, and you had an average of 14 VMs on your servers. Now the average VM is using 2.85% of the processor (40/14=2.85) and if the operating maximum is 80% you can deploy 14 more VMs before hitting that limit. See why the percentages mean nothing without the VMs?

So what are you to do? Well, it's simple really. The idea is to find the bottleneck in one of the core four resources (Processor, Memory, Disk or Network). Each time you build a capacity report you have to determine which resource you will run out of first. Using the previous example of 40% processor utilization let's build on that with some memory stats and disk and network stats. We will simplify the disk and network stats here so that our Processor and Memory stats are what we are focused on.

Environment 1, 10 hosts 140 VMs:

- Processor Utilization average across hosts: 40%

- Physical Memory Utilization average across hosts: 70%

- Disk throughput average across hosts: 22.9 Mb

- Network throughput average across hosts: 31.5 Mb

- Target maximum on any resource: 80% of maximum physical resource

With these basic numbers we can come up with a capacity report that shows amount of VM capacity in use, available, and emergency capacity available. First you need to identify the average utilization of each resource for the average VM in your environment. Do this by taking the number of VMs and dividing it by the number of hosts to come up with your average VM per host count (14 in our case).

Once you have this number you can come up with averages for each of the core four resources per VM. So in our example environment you have the following:

Average VM in Environment 1

- 2.85% of processor utilization

- 5% of host memory utilization

- About 1.6 Mb of disk throughput

- About 2.25 Mb of network throughput

Knowing that we have multiple Gigabit nics in each system and 4GB fiber, we can see that disk and network are nowhere near their maxes. On the other hand the average host is at 70% memory utilized. This means that if current trends continue we can deploy 6 more VMs per host (5% memory per VM with 30% memory available average 30/5=6). Take that 6 per host average and multiple it by the number of hosts in the farm (10) and we can deploy about 60 new VMs before we run out of memory. Of course we have simplified this here, but you get the idea.

Beyond just baseline number, we also will ask VMware end users to identify their target maximums for capacity planning. So in most instances IT admins will say "we don't want to run above 80% normally". So for our previous example where memory was already at 70% the math would change slightly and instead of taking the available 30 and dividing by the VM average usage we should take 10% (80-70) and divide that by VM average usage to come up with 2 VMs per host or 20 more VMs.

I know this seems a little crazy to those new to capacity planning, but this is what is important from a management perspective, how many more VMs can you deploy? Answer that question with real numbers, and getting new capacity should be much easier.

Writing custom applications using VC data

Before releasing this book we had about a 52 page section on writing custom applications using VirtualCenter data. Sadly the book was just TOO BIG to even think about binding and we found that the section was much more about SQL queries and building an app than it was about VMware's VI3. So instead we are going to release this as a whitepaper on VMguru.com. RobZylowski (a friend and all around smart guy) was gracious enough to write all these pages on developing a VC app as an example and to not make his work public would just be a shame.

Chapter 9 –Intro to Security

Security is often one of the most important, yet one of the most frustrating, aspects of any infrastructure. Virtualization compounds security due to the overall complexity of the environment. With VMware ESX there are a lot of components introduced into a single infrastructure and it requires a lot of thought and planning to properly manage a tightly secured environment. The components we are going to discuss have to do the with the core functionality of the virtual infrastructure:

- ESX Hosts

- VirtualCenter

- Virtual Machines

- Network Switching and Routing

- Storage Infrastructure

ESX Host Security

Host level security is one of the most important aspects of the virtual infrastructure. What people who are newly introduced to ESX don't realize is that like any other host in your infrastructure, consideration needs to go into properly protecting both the service console and the VMkernel. The VMware ESX service console is a heavily slimmed down version of Red Hat Enterprise Linux 3. It is protected extremely well from many attack vectors out of the box, but it is by no means invulnerable.

Overview of user and group accounts

Access directly the host using either the service console or the Virtual Infrastructure Client will use user and group permissions that are defined by service console authentication. This authentication model is the standard authentication system that is in place on any Linux operating system. Users are created and stored in the /etc/passwd file on the ESX host. Groups, which can contain multiple users, are stored in the /etc/group file. Finally, for security purposes, encrypted passwords for the user accounts are stored in the /etc/shadow file.

The importance of knowing the low level details has been de-emphasized thanks to enhanced user management and role based policies that are integrated into the Virtual Infrastructure Client. This does not mean it is not important to have an understanding of how the authentication scheme functions within the service console; it's just that there is simply a limited need to use the service console to perform user and group management on your ESX host. In the following sections, we do want to provide more intimate details on protecting authentication to your ESX host by leveraging tried and true methods within the service console.

User Access

VMware provides two methods to access your ESX host; through the service console and by using the Virtual Infrastructure Client. The default behavior of a new user after being created with the Virtual Infrastructure Client is to have no access to the service console or be placed in any default role (which we will find out about when we talk about VirtualCenter). If you are not using Virtual-Center, you can assign a user to a role within the Virtual Infrastructure Client to give them access to perform actions against virtual machines or configuration of the environment. By default, the root user is the only account that can login using the Virtual Infrastructure Client and is assigned to the administrators role, which gives them carte blanch access to manage the virtual machine environment.

When a user is given access to the shell they will be given the capability to log in locally or remotely via SSH to the service console. Once logged into the shell they will have the capability to run a wide variety of commands that can be used to query vital information about the host. For this reason, the only users that should ever be given shell access are the highest level ESX administrators.

By default, the root user is not allowed to connect remotely over SSH to the ESX host. It is not recommended that this default behavior be changed. Any user that connects to the ESX host should first connect as their self and use one of several methods of escalating their privileges to that of the root account. This allows all user activity to be traced back to the person connecting and running commands. If root over SSH were enabled there would be no way to determine which administrator connected as the root user and executed commands at the command line.

The super user (su) command is enabled by default and allows a user to change their shell to that of the root account. Any command that is run after properly entering the root shell will execute with the privileges necessary to run any command on the system. An even more secure mechanism of allowing a user to run privileged commands is through the use of the "super user do" (sudo) application. Unfortunately, sudo does require configuration out of the box, but it is extremely powerful. It has the distinct advantage of giving a user the ability to execute single commands with privileged access without the need to enter the root shell. It can even be configured to only enable specific commands for users or groups. A quick Google search, or brief read of the security chapter of our previous book (available free online at www.vi3book.com) will provide enough information to get started with these enhanced user control commands.

Password Expiration and Complexity

Once you've identified the users that require console access and have appropriately configured them you will need to ensure the accounts themselves conform to corporate policy. VMware provides mechanisms within the service console that provide us with the ability to enhance the security of our user account policies. This becomes very important when dealing with Sarbanes Oxley compliance for your ESX hosts. Since the service console exists and can be accessed, it must be protected like every other "Linux" host in your environment. Fortunately, VMware has the capability to tighten our policies utilizing PAM modules. There are several restrictions that we commonly see across the various environments we implement. Many of the restrictions are best practice and some are actually required by law.

Like many tasks that had to be manually performed in previous versions of ESX, VMware has provided a command to significantly simplify the process of locking down local authentication. The *esxcfg-auth* command has options to chance many of the policies surrounding user passwords including the following:

- Maximum password age

- Minimum number of days before a user may change their password

- Number of days before password expiration that a warning is given

- Minimum password length

- Password complexity

Every organization is going to have different policies surrounding their account expiration and complexity policies. Configuring some of the most secure environments will entail some advanced configuration of the ESX host. As soon as the environment grows beyond a few hosts it becomes near impossible to maintain these account policies on each individual host without a centralized infrastructure. The easiest mechanism to provide centralized management of user account policies is to tie your ESX user authentication into your existing login authority, which is typically Active Directory.

Enabling External Authentication

There are several whitepapers from VMware that have been published in regards to authenticating your ESX servers against an NT4 or Active Directory environment. VMware provides documentation on configuring your ESX host to authenticate users against their Windows account information. Instead of covering the process here we will discuss usage scenarios for this setup as well as some of the benefits and drawbacks of integrating ESX authentication into your Windows password database.

There are obvious advantages to integrating your ESX environment into your Windows authentication database. Utilizing a centralized database allows your ESX users and administrators to remember a single password. In addition, the challenge of synchronizing passwords across ESX hosts disappears. The use of local authentication into the service console should be used extremely sparingly and only for the highest level ESX administrators. When VirtualCenter is utilized in a virtual infrastructure we recommend that it be utilized to do the things that it does best; one of which is centrally manage user authentication to perform day-to-day tasks.

Integration of ESX into Windows authentication makes managing large amounts of users significantly easier, but is not the best solution in every instance. Several things should be considered before attempting to configure your system to authenticate against a Windows database:

- SMB (NT4) is significantly easier to setup than Kerberos (Active Directory).

- If using a Native mode Active Directory you must use Kerberos. Accurate time synchronization is critical to the proper operation of Kerberos authentication.

- An account must still be created for each user as a point of reference for the service console. Only the passwords are referenced on the backed database.

Host Firewall Configuration and Recommendations

VMware uses an iptables firewall to limit the communication coming into and out of an ESX Host. By default, the policy is extremely restrictive and only communication required for management of the environment are enabled. There is a very good chance that several modifications will need to be made to the default firewall policy. VMware has provided quite a few default rules that can easily be enabled or disabled using the Virtual Infrastructure Client. These include the required port definitions to enable outgoing NTP queries or for the configuration of hardware based monitoring agents such as IBM Director and HP Insight Manager. There are too many default services to list as filler content for this book, and every one of the services can be easily viewed from the Security Profile configuration screen for the ESX Host.

Naturally, VMware does not have a definition for every possible incoming and outgoing service that can be available to an ESX Host. A good example of this is sending log messages to an external syslog server. In order to open the proper communication you will have to use the Service Console to run the esxcfg-firewall command to enable the proper communication. More details on this command can be found in the "Administrator's Guide" complimenting the design guide.

Finer tuned control can be applied to firewall rules by leveraging the iptables command directly without the use of the esxcfg-firewall wrapper utility. This includes limiting communication to or from a particular host or subnet. Before opening any additional network ports for the iptables firewall, take the time to ensure you are only opening what is absolutely required and that you analyze any negative impact of enabling that type of communication from either entering or exiting your ESX Host.

Syslog

As we will find out when we discuss VirtualCenter, VMware really provides no capabilities to actually audit your virtual infrastructure. VirtualCenter can only track centralized access to the infrastructure through the centralized management server. Access to individual hosts through the service console and long term tracking of Virtual Infrastructure Client access directly to the host cannot be tracked from outside of the host itself.

The best way to track access for authorized and unauthorized use is through an external syslog server. Fortunately, the service console already leverages syslog locally for its own internal log files. The problem, from a security standpoint, is that leaving these files locally can potentially allow someone attempting to maliciously access the system can cover up their tracks by manipulating these local log files. With a simple configuration file change it is simple to redirect syslog to also write to an external system (Keep in mind you will need to open up the proper firewall access on the host to allow this communication). Using an external syslog server has several very distinct advantages.

First and foremost, it provides a centralized location for the collection of all log files from every host in the virtual infrastructure. This fact alone should be sufficient enough reason for everyone implementing VMware ESX servers in their environment to consider using a syslog server. Without a centralized syslog server the only way to audit remote connectivity and root access is to check the log files on each individual host either through the service console or by connecting directly to each host using the Virtual Infrastructure client and reviewing the log files there.

Another major advantage to syslog that does not necessarily tie to security is in the fact that it can capture far more information than VirtualCenter ever likely will. Simple notifications that should be blatantly to your virtual infrastructure monitoring platform are easily and immediately captured in syslog. With a proper syslog server alerts and actions can be set up to notify and attempt to resolve some of the potential issues. The following are examples of details that can only be captured through log files/syslog.

- Unauthorized use of the root account – Allows the tracking of people trying to remotely connect as root or leverage the sudo command outside of standard security policies.

- Loss of connectivity to fiber storage – Losing a single fiber path in a properly planned infrastructure will not cause a storage outage, but going down to a single path can definitely cause performance issues and puts your environment at risk.

- Loss of network connectivity for a physical NIC – Like storage, losing one NIC will not likely cause an outage to network access for your virtual machines, but it doesn't mean you don't need to know when it happens.

- In depth information about the VMkernel – Most of this information is overkill for typical situations, but a properly configured syslog parser can give notice to the end user when something unexpected, but normally invisible, occurs.

Any typical Linux distribution can serve as a syslog server in the environment. In addition, many enterprise monitoring solutions offer syslog integration and parsing. For small to medium sized organizations looking to enhance monitoring through centralized syslog management, there are many tools available. The most popular, and ultimately one of the best out there is the Kiwi Syslog Daemon, which runs on a Windows host. It can be downloaded from the Kiwi Enterprises website at http://www.kiwisyslog.com/.

Time Synchronization

When you start centralizing your log management and system management it is critical that every system display the exact same time. If a series of events is occurring to multiple hosts at the same time it will be critical for people responsible for troubleshooting or post mortem reports to properly reassemble the chronological order of events.

VMware ESX uses the standard Linux implementation of NTP and it is highly recommended that it be enabled and configured on every host in the environment. All hosts should synchronize their time against a time source external to the virtual infrastructure such as a timekeeping appliance or an Active Directory domain controller. It is not recommended that an internal component to the virtual infrastructure such as a virtual machine or ESX host be referenced as a time source.

At this point it is only possible to configure the NTP service from the service console. You will also need to make sure that the proper firewall access is opened up on each host to allow NTP requests to leave the host. This is typically done by ensuring outgoing UDP port 123 is open.

Agent Installations and Local Process Execution

One of the most controversial subjects when virtualizing infrastructures with VMware's ESX product is whether or not the service console should be treated like a Linux installation or as a hardened appliance. Unfortunately, the answer is "both". As long as we can see, touch, and interact with the service console the appropriate actions must be taken to properly protect and audit the operating system instance. At the same time we need to be conscious of the fact that the service console is performing a very specific task and any processes running inside the service console could potentially impact the performance of the virtual machines being powered by the host's resources. Typical applications such as virus scan software are normally avoided at all costs due to the amount of potential load they can add to a host.

This information obviously begs the question, "So what is acceptable when considering running agents or processes inside the service console?" We first need to determine the different methods that software vendors and system administrators are using to perform actions inside the service console. Typically, this consist of three various mechanisms, often a combination of more than one. There is really nothing wrong with using any of these mechanisms at this point, but there are some critical items that must be considered upon determining that a specific application or product requires direct access to the service console. These guidelines will ultimately determine whether leveraging the service console for these applications is acceptable or not for your environment.

General Guidelines

Regardless of the mechanism that is used to execute code at the service console a few things should be considered before installing and using the application. The first is determining if the application truly requires the use of the service console. There are many things that can be done through the VMware SDK or other external mechanisms that do not require the use of the service console, but a software vendor may have already had something that worked for Linux that they decided to jump on the virtualization bandwagon with. The service console is heavily modified and locked down from typical Linux installations, and installing software that was written purely for a Linux installation will cause more problems than it will likely ever solve.

The second critical guideline is to determine whether benefit will truly be utilized by installing software or executing processes within the service console. The benefit of the application should also be compared against potential performance impact of the software running inside the service console and the resources it is going to require. I alluded to an example of installing antivirus software inside the service console not being recommended. This is due to the fact that even a default installation without additional configurations is highly secured out of the box. Running a nightly virus scan and performing real time file system protection typically uses a lot of system resources nearly constantly. This has a very negative effect on the ability to schedule resources for your virtual machines in a timely fashion. If an agent or process has major benefit to your organization and the resource requirement is low or execution is required in infrequent after-hours bursts, there is nothing wrong with installing an agent or executing binaries in the service console.

Scripting

Running scripts locally inside the service console is the least preferred method of interaction with the service console for several reasons. First, while scripting is easy for anyone to manipulate, it is also easy for anyone to screw up. Most scripts often require customization to work in a particular environment. A simple mistake in modifying a script can wreak havoc on the resources assigned to the service console. Add that to the fact in most organizations one or two people are intimate with the script, and others are simply responsible for making sure it runs. If one of the script maintainers leaves the company or gets hit by a bus, there will be some very upset, but newly promoted ESX administrators that have to wade through someone else's script to determine how to make further modifications. If you will be using scripting for executing processes or performing actions within the service console, make sure it is very well tested in development before rolling it into production. In addition, make sure it is extremely well documented and commented to make it easier on the next person that has to assume ownership of further script maintenance.

We do need to specify here that remotely running scripts that communicate with the virtual infrastructure from outside the hosts themselves is actually quite a common practice. With the introduction of the VI Perl Toolkit regular users can finally easily interact with VirtualCenter and automate many tasks. By moving scripts from the ESX host and to an external system there will be a loss of some lower level interaction with the host itself, but scripting really be used for these purposes anyways.

Agent Installation

Many people treat agent installations like they are a rare and deadly infectious disease. Most of the time the reasoning behind this is the fact that "It runs in my service console", which doesn't really hold any water when comparing it against what is occurring with scripting or, as we will see, binary injection. A properly written agent will use an extremely small amount of system resources and will often enable functionality that is simply not available through native means such as the SDK or VMware command line applications. There are actually advantages to manually installing an agent within the service console. First, since it must be manually installed, it is very easy to track exactly when the agent was placed on the system and who installed it. Since the installation is often either in RPM or scripted installer format, it is also extremely easy to see exactly what changes are occurring to your system. You never want to blindly execute anything in your service console. That is a recipe for disaster.

A properly written agent will not constantly run and will only leverage system resources while an action is occurring. This can be controlled several different ways such as through xinetd or other service control mechanisms. The exception to this would be some form of monitoring agent that is capturing statistics that simply cannot be provided by the SDK. These are typically very lightweight and leverage resources on regularly scheduled intervals when polling metrics. The key to installing an agent is knowing exactly what is occurring when the agent is installed. As with all service console based applications, you must be conscious of the performance impact to the host and virtual machines compared to the benefit gained from the application itself.

Binary Injection

Binary Injection is the process in which an application connects to an ESX Host, typically over SSH, to send compiled binaries for execution within the service console as a part of some form of automated action. These components are often, but not always, completely removed from the ESX Host when the process or set of processes have completed. This is how most software vendors can claim that they are "agent less" which, based on the methods being leveraged to inject binaries, is typically marketing fluff. This method is ideal for administrators new to ESX and Linux and who are not familiar with the typical methods for installing applications through scripted processes or RPM packages. It provides a simple mechanism to keep the end user away from the service console, which is definitely not a bad thing in many cases. As a matter of fact, this is the method that VMware themselves use to inject their "agent" when a host is configured to be managed by VirtualCenter.

On the other side of the coin, this method is the one you also need to be most careful with. Many users go along not knowing that these applications are touching the service console, and thus have no idea what changes are occurring on the system. Any software vendor that leverages this technique should provide a checklist of what their application is doing to an ESX Host that includes at least the following information:

- Does the injected process require root access to run, and if so, can they accommodate non root over SSH?

- What binaries are being placed onto the system, where they are being placed, and what purpose are they serving by being injected? Any software vendor not willing to part with this basic information, which can be provided without giving away intellectual property, should be approached with caution.

- When the process completes are the injected components completely removed or are they left in place for easier execution the next time the process executes?

Again, we want to emphasize that there is nothing wrong with leveraging the service console to execute processes. Often times, it enables advanced functionality that simply cannot be performed through external methods such as leveraging the SDK. With any of the methods, take special care to analyze the benefit of any service console based process against potential performance impact to the service console resources. As VMware moves closer to removing the service console entirely, make sure you test every support application, as you will find a vast majority of them rely on having access to the service console for process execution.

Patching

Like any other system in your environment your ESX Hosts are prone to vulnerabilities. VMware is extremely responsive in providing updates when new vulnerabilities are discovered. While not every patch or update requires a reboot of the ESX Host, many do; especially if any critical files used by the VMkrenel are updated. Fortunately VMware has provided the capability to put your host into "Maintenance Mode" to safely apply updates to the system. If you have VMotion and DRS properly configured in your cluster, putting a host into maintenance mode will automatically move your virtual machines off to other hosts in the cluster while you perform the necessary maintenance on the targeted host.

You should plan your updates carefully and ensure to test all functionality prior to rolling the updates into the production infrastructure. Security updates are often relatively clean and do not impact support applications or other core functionality of the system. You will, on the other hand, need to be quite a bit more careful with update releases that introduce new functionality, as these are more likely to change components that third party applications may depend on.

VirtualCenter Security

VirtualCenter is the centralized point of all management in your virtual infrastructure. Unauthorized access to this host could be disastrous as a malicious would have full control over your entire environment, including the capability to shut down, delete, and worst case, take with them any virtual machine managed by the infrastructure. Proper security of the VirtualCenter server itself as well as user roles and policies for managing the infrastructure are the key to a secured virtual environment.

Access to VirtualCenter Server

Access to your VirtualCenter server should be tightly controlled and as restrictive as possible. A user that has administrative access to the VirtualCenter server has a full set of keys to the kingdom when it comes to manipulating the virtual infrastructure since, by default, anyone who is a local administrator of this system is put into the "Administrators" group for the virtual infrastructure. Because of the volatility of this system, the administrative privileges should be extremely restrictive with only the most trusted of users having access.

It is not uncommon for the VirtualCenter server to reside on a separate management network along with ESX Host Service Console connectivity so tight network ACL controls can be put in place on this management VLAN. We will discuss this in further detail when we discuss network security later in this chapter.

When considering VirtualCenter security, many people overlook the fact that all VirtualCenter data is stored in the back end database backend. Unauthorized access to the database itself will allow a user to quite easily capture an entire inventory of the virtual infrastructure and even make modifications to certain configuration aspects of the infrastructure, including user access rights. The database server/instance should be treated just as securely as the VirtualCenter server itself.

Virtual Infrastructure Management

Whether you are using the Virtual Infrastructure Client to communicate directly with the ESX host or to VirtualCenter you will need to be aware of the structure that VMware uses to assign permissions for users to manage the virtual infrastructure. The same methodology is used whether you are communicating directly to the host or are using VirtualCenter to manage the infrastructure so we will not discuss them separately. Rather, we will point out the subtle differences in the three key components of assigning permissions to your users; Users and Groups, Roles, and Policies.

Users and Groups

I am hoping it doesn't take a lot of explaining to describe what a user and a group is, and if I do, you guys have the wrong book. If you do not leverage VirtualCenter for your virtual machine management and work on a per host level, users and groups are defined by using the standard Linux user and group configuration of the service console. Environments that are managed by VirtualCenter leverage the Windows account database of the server VirtualCenter is installed on. VirtualCenter may use either local or domain based users and groups for assigning permissions to users.

The default permissions of VirtualCenter allow anyone who is a local administrator to have full control of the virtual infrastructure. It is best to change this default behavior shortly after installation. A common practice is to create an Active Directory Global Group with the domain users that are VirtualCenter administrators. This global group must then be added to a local group on the ESX host. This local host is then given administrative privileges through the VirtualCenter client. It is not possible to assign domain global groups to roles directly within VirtualCenter; a fact that is extremely annoying. It is also recommended that a local (to the VirtualCenter server) user account be created and assigned to the administrator role within VirtualCenter. This will ensure that even if domain connectivity is lost for whatever reason, the entire virtual infrastructure does not become unmanageable. Once the initial user and group configuration is complete, the local administrators group should be removed from having any direct access to VirtualCenter.

Privileges

A privilege is a single action that can occur within the virtual infrastructure such as powering on a VM or creating a new datacenter. Overall there are over 100 privileges that are broken up into manageable categories at both the host and VirtualCenter levels. Many privileges go hand in hand, but must be configured separately. As an example you will often configure the ability to power off a virtual machine to anyone who has the ability to power them on. These are both unique privileges that would typically be assigned at the same time. The key to properly organizing these various privileges to create templates for management is done through the use of roles.

Roles

Roles are a collection of privileges that are grouped together to allow a specific type of management for users of the virtual infrastructure. As an example, a standalone ESX host has three default roles configured; Administrator, Read Only, and No Access. A user or group that has been assigned to the administrator role has full control to the virtual infrastructure, while a user assigned to the read only role can only view the configuration of the infrastructure without having the ability to make any changes. The no access role is something of a special case that is used to deny specific privileges to a small set of individual users that may be a part of a group that has access to a particular role. Within the virtual infrastructure, the most restrictive set of privileges takes precedence for users that are assigned to multiple roles that are assigned to the same object.

At the VirtualCenter level there are quite a few more roles that may be assigned for infrastructure management. Each of these roles is tailored for providing very specific capabilities to users or groups that are assigned to them. The following are the default roles that exist within VirtualCenter:

- Virtual Machine Administrator
- Datacenter Administrator
- Virtual Machine Power User
- Virtual Machine User
- Resource Pool Administrator

In addition to the preconfigured set of roles, the Virtual Infrastructure Client provides the capability to create custom roles, clone roles to base new roles off an original, or modify existing ones (with the exception of the no access, read only, and administrator roles). This capability allows you to tailor specific roles for your environment based on the needs of the users accessing the infrastructure.

Object Level Permissions

Each level of the infrastructure can have unique permissions. Any object of the virtual infrastructure such as Datacenters, Clusters, Hosts, VMs, Folders, and Resource Pools may have unique permissions assigned. A permission is defined by stating a particular user or group is assigned a role at an object level. Permissions can be configured to propagate down the tree and be inherited by child objects. The default configuration of VirtualCenter states that members of the VirtualCenter server's local administrators group is a member of the Administrators role within the virtual infrastructure and that permission is propagated down throughout the entire infrastructure. All other users are automatically given the same rights as the no access role.

There is no way to limit how far down the virtual infrastructure a propagated permission has access. If permission is defined at a datacenter level and is selected for propagation, that permission goes down all the way to the virtual machine level. If there is a reason to limit or increase the permissions of a user or group to any object, a new permission can be assigned for that particular object.

Permissions assigned at the object level always take precedence over propagated permissions.

Virtual Machine Security

Virtual machine security in a virtual infrastructure is not that different than protecting a physical machine environment. The same procedures that you would need to follow to protect your physical infrastructure should also be carried over into your virtual. Scheduling of CPU or disk intensive tasks as they relate to security, such as full virus scans require special attention to prevent an instance in which performance for an entire host or LUN is impacted.

Process and Memory Isolation

Each virtual machine is run through its own virtual machine monitor (VMM) within the VMkernel. These VMMs are unique to the virtual machine in which they are handling processor calls and do not share instructions with any other VMM. This provides a secure model to ensure than processes that are being executed within one guest instance cannot be seen by others.

Memory does not have the same level of isolation as processing resources. A major benefit of using VMware is in its capability to overallocate memory on a given host by using memory sharing techniques. Virtual machines that have identical memory pages across multiple instances will actually share the same physical memory space at the host level. If any operating system modifies the memory that is shared it will immediately be detected by the VMkernel and be rewritten to its own unique physical memory page. Due to the method and speed in which unique memory can be rewritten there is no risk in which a virtual machine can access the memory resources of another system that is unique to the secondary system. VMware not only provides high speed memory access and the capability to over-allocate resources; they manage to do it securely.

Patching

Keeping your virtual machines up to date with the newest patches should not be handled any differently than it is done in the physical environment. If anything patching becomes more critical because of the simplified process of deploying new virtual machines in minutes. Many organizations are introducing new challenges to patching because the sheer number of operating system instances being deployed is increasingly dramatically thanks to virtualization. One thing about patching that is significantly improved is that the virtual machine templates can be very quickly and easily updated. This ensures that any newly deployed virtual machine will already be as up to date as possible.

Template Management

All users should leverage the template capabilities of VirtualCenter. By properly managing and updating templates an organization can ensure that any new virtual machine that is deployed is done so in the most secure fashion. Templates should be stored in a centralized repository that each ESX host has access to. NFS volumes are often prime candidates for template storage due to the cost of storage and native integration as shared centralized storage for the entire infrastructure. Any time there is a security or maintenance update to any major component of the template it is critical that the template is not accidentally left out of the update process due to the fact that it s a powered off virtual machine.

Virus Protection

Running a virtual infrastructure provides no additional protection for your virtual machines in regards to their ability to become infected by viruses. Standard virus policies should exist for all virtual machines just as they do for physical. Special consideration does need to go into engineering the schedules for full virus scans. Full scans are often extremely CPU and Disk intensive; both of which are valuable resources to a host. I have seen entire ESX hosts grind to a halt simply because 4-5 VMs kicked off a full virus scan at the exact same time. It will be a significant pain to configure these schedules the first time, but once a policy is in place it will be relatively simple to follow for any new virtual machine that gets added to the infrastructure. If using a serial-based schedule it is also important to note the impact that VMotion and DRS will have when configuring scheduled windows at a host level. Before you know it you could be right back in the same situation where virus scanning was bringing down a host.

Network Security

Network security is often the most complex aspect of any environment, which is quite understandable. If systems had no way to communicate with one another, security would be a heck of a lot easier. Unfortunately, not only is there plenty of communication going on in a virtual infrastructure, securing it is quite a bit more difficult based on the fact that the ESX hosts themselves take on roles that have been typically reserved for the physical network infrastructure and the network administrators. When considering network security in the virtual infrastructure you not only need to think about protecting the ESX hosts, but also your virtual machines and any network based storage that is being used to house and run virtual instances.

Management Network Isolation

When we discussed ESX 3 networking earlier in this book we made quite a few references to securing your management services on a separate network from your actual virtual machines. This recommendation was made to better isolate and protect the traffic that can potentially communicate with the service console or interfere with other management services.

Console Access

The default behavior of VirtualCenter and ESX is to only allow communication through secure communications such as SSH, ssl, or encrypted communications for virtual machine management over tcp ports 902 and 903. Since the host has an iptables firewall running we can easily ensure the host only accepts traffic that is used for management of the environment.

There are several varying degrees that organizations will go to in order to protect their management interfaces for their ESX hosts. Of course, each additional layer protection adds complexity to the management of the environment.

Figure 9- 1: Secured VLANs

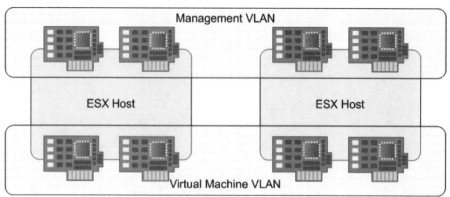

One thing is certain in that all VMware physical management NICs should be contained within their own VLAN as shown in Figure 9-1. These NICs will support communication to the host's service console from VirtualCenter or the Virtual Infrastructure Client as well as VMotion traffic between hosts.

The management VLAN itself can be secured and isolated so nearly all communication from other networks cannot enter and attempt to access the ESX hosts without authorization. In this scenario the first question that comes to many people's minds is "How do we manage the environment if it is completely isolated?" In this case the VirtualCenter server would also exist within this management VLAN. Depending on the organizations policies Authorized desktop systems could be added to the ACL to communicate with VirtualCenter and possibly the hosts. If an organization is, in my opinion, overly stringent on its security policy, management desktops with the Virtual Infrastructure Client and possibly putty installed could also be set up in the management VLAN with RDP access from authorized desktops. This significantly complicates the process of maintaining the virtual infrastructure and has scalability issues as more ESX administrators are introduced into the organization.

VMotion

More serious security concerns begin to arise when additional services are enabled for advanced functionality such as VMotion, which is not encrypted. All communication that occurs between hosts during a VMotion migration is unencrypted and can technically be picked up with a network sniffer. This where the use of an isolated VLAN as described in the previous section is critical. The fewer systems that can be used to attempt to view network activity during a VMotion, the better protected the infrastructure is as a whole. Sending VMotion traffic across VLANs should be proceeded with caution and fully investigated for potential risk before ever being configured and attempted.

Network Storage

VI3 introduces the capability to configure network based storage in the form of iSCSI and NFS for storing and running virtual machines. The traffic that travels between the ESX host and the back end storage is not encrypted or protected once it hits the wire. With this in mind it is extremely critical that the network storage be isolated in its own VLAN at a minimum. For maximum protection and performance it is recommended that the storage communication also occur on its own network infrastructure as shown in Figure 9–2. Assuming this infrastructure is properly configured, it is very difficult to accidentally configure a physical or virtual machine to share the same network as the storage network. Stringent policies around the connectivity, configuration, and mapping of physical adapters should be created and enforced to guarantee a secure communication channel between the hosts and the back end storage infrastructure.

We've gone over the fact that network storage is not encrypted, but this does not mean you are powerless from having someone find a way to connect to your network based storage resources. Configurations that can be applied to both the source hosts and target storage arrays can be used to require authentication and masking to prevent unauthorized systems from seeing storage they should not.

Protecting NFS volumes that are used for template storage is not as critical as protecting NFS volumes that are being used for running virtual machines. Regardless of what you are using NFS volumes for there is an authentication mechanism that requires the use of a username/password combination to properly access the disk resources. Users who use NFS for running virtual machines should go the extra mile to ensure the traffic between the ESX hosts and the storage infrastructure is as isolated as possible.

Properly protecting iSCSI is a bit more complicated than simply supplying a username and password, although this is highly recommended as well. iSCSI supports protecting connectivity using CHAP authentication at the storage array. Hardware iSCSI initiators and the VMware software iSCSI initiator both have the necessary functionality to authenticate against the target. The VMware iSCSI initiator does not have the capability to authenticate at a per target level so once your host is properly connected it will have access to any LUN that is zoned to the iSCSI adapter name.

Zone plays a crucial role in securing your data volumes at a SAN level and we will discuss it towards the end of this chapter when we talk about storage security in particular.

Figure 9- 2: Networked Storage

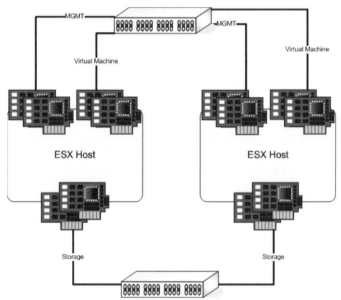

VLAN Isolation

Many ESX environments leverage VLAN tagging to support various network configurations across a large number of virtual machines. Network and security administrators often have concerns about the security surrounding the virtual switch model, especially when they have to start trunking multiple VLANs to the host. Networking capabilities for virtual switches and port groups in ESX 3 operate inside the VMkernel. Virtual switches operate at Layer 2 of the network stack only. They simply receive and forward packets to the proper virtual ports of the switch. There are no layer 3 capabilities to route traffic or bridge traffic across multiple virtual switches. The only way in which multiple VLANs can communicate with one another without leaving the host is if there is a virtual machine that is set up as a router to manage the layer 3 communication.

Physical NICs do have the capability to be configured to listen to traffic tagged for more than one VLAN. This is important if you do plan to leverage a DMZ or other secured network on your existing ESX hardware. This is the reason we highly recommended using a different set of physical NICs if you do intend to use a DMZ on your host. Physical NICs cannot belong to more than one virtual switch at a given time. Configuring multiple virtual switches helps isolate this traffic as much as possible. Overall, leveraging multiple VLANs on a single host does not pose any form of security risk by allowing traffic to bridge across various networks without following the standard layer 3 routing policies of the physical network.

Bridging Network Zones

A topic that is very commonly discussed when designing a virtual infrastructure is the layout of a secured network such as a DMZ. There are two schools of thought with this one; the first being to provide a separate cluster of ESX hosts for highly secured network access. In this case, a group of ESX hosts are configured into their own cluster and given access to VLANs that are considered "secure". They are not given any access (outside of the management interface) to the internal network. It is not uncommon to have the management interfaces configured on an internal DMZ as to completely isolate the ESX host to keep it as secure as possible. This is easily the most secure way to provide a virtual infrastructure for customer facing web servers. In smaller environments or organizations that do not have a lot of external facing or secured systems, this option could lead to underutilized hardware.

Advantages of creating a separate cluster for secured systems
- Highly secured environment for public facing or highly sensitive communication

- Removes end user error of improperly configuring a VM

Disadvantages of creating a separate cluster for secured systems

- Requires an additional cluster, consisting of several ESX hosts for redundancy

- Often leads to highly underutilized servers in small environments or environments with few sensitive servers

The second school of thought is to create an additional virtual switch with additional physical NICs that are isolated from the internal network. This allows users to leverage their existing ESX infrastructure to support public systems. There is an inherent risk involved with this configuration since a careless administrator could accidentally place an internal virtual machine onto the external network. Worse yet, they could accidentally set up a virtual machine that has connectivity to both the internal and external networks at the same time…which is quite bad. The virtual switches and virtual machines on the host should be audited regularly to ensure no breach in security policy has occurred.

Advantages of creating public or isolated virtual switches
- Can use existing host/cluster architecture and layout

- Does not change server configuration or management policies

- Maximizes ESX host utilization by running all virtual machines on a single virtual infrastructure

Disadvantages of creating public or isolated virtual switches
- Not as secure as an isolated network environment

- Leaves open the opportunity for human error in the configuration of virtual machines

When taking a look at network isolation and configuration of public access for virtual machines it is extremely important that people understand that under no circumstance should the ESX management functions (service console, VMotion, etc) EVER be plugged into a public network. Anyone who configures their environment in this fashion deserves to have all of their data stolen and be brutally criticized on Slashdot or Fark.

Using VI3 through a firewall

We have made several recommendations here to protect and isolate the management connectivity of the ESX host by providing a management VLAN for all management tasks. The best way to protect this VLAN is through the use of a firewall or ACL. ESX requires a well defined and very specific list of ports for network communication. Figure 9 – 3 displays the various network ports that are required for the various communication components of the virtual infrastructure.

Figure 9- 3: Port Mappings

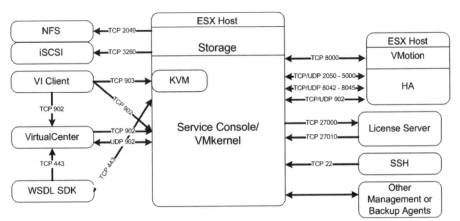

Storage Security

Any time you decide to use an enterprise storage infrastructure it is important to meet the security best practices while doing so. This is far outside the scope of this book, but what we do want to talk about are some of the extra considerations that are required when securing the centralized storage environment used in a VMware virtual infrastructure.

Highly Sensitive Data

Virtualization is one of the fastest growing technologies and with new innovations by VMware and the hardware vendors we are starting to see more and more enterprise level applications virtualized. These enterprise level systems often have more stringent requirements on the sensitivity of their data and often require additional planning around their placement in the infrastructure.

The most common practice I have seen is creating a cluster of ESX hosts particularly for the purpose of enterprise applications and secured data. The shared storage architecture of VMware means any host in the cluster has the capability to see the same LUNs. The best way to prevent a virtual machine from accessing a VMDK file or raw LUN with sensitive data is to make sure it cannot see it at all. Providing a cluster just for this purpose makes this possible. Of course, by segregating the environment into a secured and non secured environment does introduces some management challenges as increases the likelihood that some of your infrastructure will be underutilized. Secured data configurations also typically have a direct relationship to systems that have heightened security requirements over the network. This fact may help justify the use of several standalone ESX servers in a "secured" cluster.

Zoning

The ability to specify which hosts can and can't see a particular data LUN is controlled at the SAN level by using zoning. Zoning at the SAN level allows a user to specify exactly which HBAs or hosts are allowed to see a particular LUN or group of LUNs. ESX relies quite heavily on zoning, especially when multiple clusters are being used in larger environments. If you plan on using VMotion and DRS you will need to ensure that every host in a cluster is properly zoned to see the same storage or the benefit of real time migrations will be lost to those hosts.

This added level of security further enhances the iSCSI mechanism of using CHAP authentication to determine if a system has the proper access to a LUN. Not only must the host properly authenticate, but the HBA must also be defined by the SAN as having the capability to see the LUN. Once the data volumes are properly secured we need to consider the data that will eventually be stored on them.

VMDK Creation

In chapter 5 we discussed VMDK files in detail and found out that there are several ways in which they can be created. The default behavior for an ESX host is to create VMDK files in "zeroedthick" format. Any data that resides on the physical disk still exists on the VMDK file until a read operation is requested from the virtual machine. At the time of the read operation the data is zeroed out and its original contents are cleared. From a guest operating system level there is no way to read data that originally existed on the VMDK file. This is not the case when accessing the VMDK file at a block level from outside the virtual machine.

If you are using a storage infrastructure that has had multiple virtual machines configured, deleted, moved, etc, you will likely create VMDK files that contain existing data. If you perform image level backups of these virtual machines you will be able to capture this "stale" data and read it from an external system. Most people do not realize that this level of access to data from a previous system exists. The safest way to prevent this behavior is to create your VMDK files as "eagerzeroedthick" from the service console before assigning them to a virtual machine. Disks created in "eagerzeroedthick" format a zero-filled at creation time, which overwrites old data. The obvious downside to this is that it also takes more time to allocate disk files for your virtual machines. In addition, there is no way to create "eagerzeroedthick" VMDK files through the Virtual Infrastructure Client; it must be performed from the service console directly. For those that are concerned about ensuring highly sensitive data doesn't make its way into virtual machines due to the back end storage infrastructure it is highly recommended that you take the time to create VMDK files in "eagerzeroedthick" format.

VMDK Access

The ability to create snapshots and capture fully running virtual machines from the ESX host also introduces another challenge. It is now quite easy to capture and move an entire virtual machine. While this portability is actually a huge benefit, it is also a security risk. Once the virtual machine is removed from the ESX host it can be moved to any Windows workstation and very easily mounted as a drive or run on free VMware products like VMware Server as the actual virtual machine itself. Protecting access to the ESX service console will help a user from manually capturing this data, but similar practices must be put into place to protect data once it has been removed from the host. Image level backup utilities should have data encryption mechanisms. If data is not directly encrypted it should be stored on a file system that is locked down and likely encrypted as a target for backups only. Any user that can take a VMDK file in an unencrypted format will have full access to all data of that virtual machine.

Conclusion

ESX requires significant planning around security when introducing it into your environment. Combining the typical best practices of your existing physical infrastructure and taking the additional requirements for virtualization into consideration will ensure your virtual environment is as protected as is possible.

Chapter 10 - Recovery and Business Continuity

Not long after VMware and virtualization started to take off for server consolidation projects, people started to truly realize the portability and recoverability aspects of virtualization. In fact, VMware started to win awards for "Disaster Recovery Product of the Year" without actually being a disaster recovery product.

Recently, VMware has significantly modified its marketing message and has moved away from "Server Consolidation" and now focuses very heavily on "Disaster Recovery." While VI3 does provide a strong platform for recoverability, it is important to note that it is no magic bullet to simply toss a virtual infrastructure into an environment. It would be foolish to think that by simply installing a few ESX servers with VirtualCenter an organization has a recovery plan without additional effort.

In this chapter, we are going to dig beyond "Disaster Recovery" and address a larger issue that virtualization with VMware actually enables: "Business Continuity." By the end of this chapter it will be quite simple to see that Disaster Recovery is a very small part of the equation when providing highly available and recoverable systems.

What is Business Continuity?

Business Continuity, as we will address it in this book, comes down to two key points. The first aspect of business continuity is an organization's capability to meet or exceed application and system availability service levels. This is done through the use of several technologies that will be discussed in this chapter, including various methods of High Availability and Fault Tolerance.

The second aspect to business continuity is an organization's ability to recover from failures, both minor and catastrophic, with minimum business impact. In order to meet this set of requirements a solid backup recovery and disaster recovery plan is required. This also shares some territory in the High Availability space by the use of virtual machine replication, which has become quite popular over the last few months.

In short, this comes down to a simple premise of keeping your systems running and getting them back as fast as possible if something really bad were to occur.

In order to properly define business continuity, I would like to refer to the business continuity pyramid as defined by Vizioncore, Inc, one of the primary vendors in the backup and disaster recovery space for VMware.

Figure 10- 1: Business Continuity Pyramid

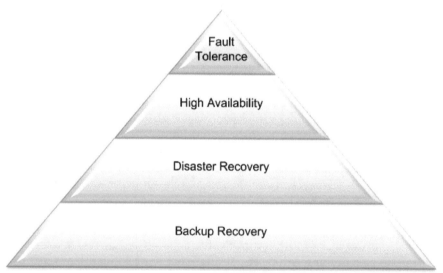

This pyramid dictates the four primary areas of business continuity on which this chapter focuses. The lower layers of the pyramid, which are the widest, dictate that more virtual machines in your environment will make use of the particular technology than at the higher layers, which get increasingly narrower.

For the purpose of this chapter we are going to begin by discussing the lowest layer of the pyramid, as this encompasses the largest number of systems, and work our way towards the top.

Backup Recovery

If we need to explain exactly what backup recovery is to the audience of this book, you probably have the wrong book in your hands. This process has been around just about as long as computers have as a way to recover data in the event of corruption or loss. Over time, this technology has matured to allow for entire system recovery, which we'll discuss further when we talk about disaster recovery later in this chapter.

As with just about anything virtualization, backup recovery can still be done using the same tried and true mechanisms that have been in place for ages, thanks to the portability and flexibility provided by the virtualization platform. Backup recovery can actually be further optimized beyond the capabilities provided by typical backup software.

Backup and Recovery Strategies

When dealing with designing a backup recovery strategy for your virtual infrastructure it is important to consider just exactly what it is you wish to backup. There are several components of the entire virtual infrastructure that require attention when creating your backup recovery plan. Each of these items does need to be addressed and managed individually.

ESX Hosts

The ESX host itself, or more accurately, the Service Console was a very critical piece of an ESX 2.X infrastructure. VMware has done several things in VI3 to deemphasize the importance of backing up various aspects of the SC, and we will mention those in context.

At this point we are assuming you are backing up the host server for recovery to like hardware. We are not discussing backing up any of the data that exists inside the virtual machines at this point. That will be discussed a little later in this chapter. There are three primary components of the ESX host that require consideration when developing your backup recovery plan for your host systems themselves: SC Configurations, VMware ESX Configurations, and virtual machine configurations. Since this isn't a database host or a file server (or sure shouldn't be) the backup job should be relatively small and easy to maintain.

Following this line of thought, you need to determine if you are going to backup your ESX servers at all. If you have a completely scripted installation of ESX, that covers all of your configurations, additional software packages for monitoring, security management, etc, and if you have decided to recover your virtual machines by storing their VMDK's on centralized storage, then you may have no need to backup your ESX servers at all.

When creating a backup plan for the SC, we want to temporarily forget about the configured virtual machines, as those will probably be recovered differently than an ESX host. Virtual machine backup and recovery has its own special set of considerations that we will look at in a minute.

Critical Components of the Service Console

As previously mentioned, there are three primary components that require backup and recovery consideration within the SC.

Service Console Configurations

VMware has taken significant steps and still continues to move forward on turning the ESX host into an appliance whose files are very static in nature. This does not mean there is no need to backup specific files that make up advanced or customized SC configurations. This is primarily focused in the area of security configurations, as this seems to be the most unique component across every organization. While every implementation will be different, the following files are those that we often find are modified to better enhance security or user access/control.

- /etc/profile

- /etc/ssh/sshd_config

- /etc/pam.d/   (Entire Directory)

- /etc/ntp/   (Entire Directory)

- /etc/ntp.conf

- /etc/passwd

- /etc/group

- /etc/sudoers

- /etc/shadow

- /etc/syslog.conf

VMware ESX Configurations

All configurations of ESX and the VMkernel are stored in the /etc/vmware directory. Like the Service Console configuration files, it can be time consuming to reconfigure ESX to its exact pre-failover state. By backing up the entire contents of the /etc/vmware directory you can easily return ESX to its original state after a base installation using the install media. VMware has enhanced the /etc/vmware directory in ESX3 by consolidating many log files and directories into a smaller number of objects.

Virtual Machine Configurations

The biggest of these modifications is that virtual machine configurations are no longer independently managed by the ESX host where they reside. All files that make up the configuration of the virtual machine are now located in the centralized storage infrastructure. This, of course, assumes there is a centralized storage infrastructure and that each host is not using local VMFS volumes to run virtual machines.

Due to this change in configuration file management; there is almost no point to backing up individual virtual machine configuration files from the Service Console. There are several methods to backup entire virtual machines, each of which backup the required configuration files. These methods will be discussed when we start talking about virtual machine backups.

At this point the plan is to backup and restore only configuration files. That means during the recovery of a server you will perform a base install of ESX using the original name and IP information, then restore that server's configuration to its previous state. With that in mind, the next step is to install the backup agent onto the console and configure it for your backups.

Which Backup Software Should You Use?

Since the SC is really a RedHat Enterprise Linux based system, you will need a backup agent that works for a Linux OS. Every major backup vendor that is worth trusting in an environment has Linux agents available, and these can be installed within the SC for use. If you manage to find a vendor that does not provide a Linux agent, or you do not want to spend the additional money for agents to place on ESX, it is possible to use a script to copy the required files and directories to another location.

Backup Schedule

Once all configurations are made and everything is running properly, changes are rarely made to the above mentioned files. Since the SC uses text configuration files for all settings, the amount of data being backed up is extremely small. For this reason, we recommend a nightly backup schedule on the files and directories that have changed. While nightly backups may not be necessary, the required capacity and amount of time to perform the job should have no impact on the performance of other backup jobs in the environment.

VirtualCenter

Backing up VirtualCenter is a relatively simple process. The only component of the VirtualCenter infrastructure that is important and difficult to duplicate without a backup is the database. Every configuration option, permission, and performance metric is stored within the database. VirtualCenter can be easily installed on a compatible operating system and returned to service by simply pointing at the existing database server.

Because of the importance of the data stored within the VirtualCenter database, it is critical that this be backed up using either a database compatible backup agent, or if VirtualCenter is running within a virtual machine, through an image level backup utility on a regular basis.

Virtual Machines

The most important asset to your virtual infrastructure is by far the virtual machines that are being run. Like just about any other system in the environment, your virtual machines probably need to be backed up. Traditionally this has been performed by an organization through the use of an enterprise backup agent from any number of vendors. Through the use of virtualization, we have the opportunity to enhance this process and better enable data recovery through several technologies.

Remember, in this section we are discussing the normal backup and recovery strategies for a guest virtual machine. The idea here is that the strategies are for "normal" backup and restorations and not strategies for disaster recovery. We should note that you may wind up using the same recovery procedures for DR that you use on a daily basis, but we will not make that our primary focus for this section.

There are two basic approaches to perform virtual machine backups. First, you can treat the virtual machines as you do any physical server in your environment and leverage processes inside the operating system to perform backups. The alternative to this method takes advantage of the portability of the virtual machine and captures an image of the virtual machine VMDK and configuration files. Of course, some of the best backup recovery designs use the best that each of these technologies has to offer.

File Level Backups

File-level backups are traditionally used to recover individual files in the event of accidental deletion, corruption, or any other number of reasons your users can find to destroy data. Recovery is typically a straight forward process of choosing the proper file or directory and choosing the proper date of the object you wish to restore. There are some applications now available that allow better application integration with Exchange, SQL, Active Directory, etc... that enable individual object recovery such as database tables or user mailboxes directly from a backup of the respective databases.

Agents

In this scenario, a backup agent is installed within the guest operating system; backup jobs are then created and run on a regular basis, and recovery is handled all by communicating with a centralized backup server.

Figure 10- 2: File Agent Backup

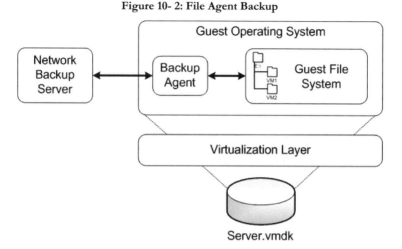

The primary advantage of this design is that it can simple integrate into your existing backup system and provide for full, partial, or file level restores to the virtual machines. The primary disadvantage is that it does not tap into the abilities of a virtual machine to be completely restored in its entirety. Instead, to do a complete restore, you would have to load an operating system onto a new virtual machine, install the agent, perform a complete restore of all files, and finally hope and pray that the applications on the server will run when the process is completed.

Advantages of Performing File Level Backups

- Allows for simple restore of individual files or directories

- Fits easily into most existing backup architectures

- Requires no VMware knowledge

- Day-to-day procedures for backup recovery do not change

- Has application awareness for transactional systems

- Only way to capture data within a Physical RDM

Disadvantages of Performing File Level Backups

- Does not take advantage of virtual machine portability

- Difficult to perform recovery of operating system components

You'll notice that the final advantage that we listed discusses capturing data from within a physical mode RDM. As we learned in Chapter 5, the use of physical mode RDM's provides the best performance for high I/O activities like Exchange or SQL. Since a physical mode RDM does not leverage the VMFS file system to store data or act as a pointer, there is no way for the virtualization layer to receive a SCSI lock for a volume. Because of this, the only way you will be able to retrieve data from a physical mode RDM is through the use of an in-guest agent that has exclusive rights to the NTFS volume. It is possible to convert your physical mode RDM to a virtual mode RDM and access it through a typical virtualization backup utility, but think long and hard before doing this, as there are potential performance implications in this situation.

Image Level Backups

Image level backups leverage processes to get "underneath" the guest operating system and capture the entire state of a server. In the physical world this was done by the use of "bare metal" backup agents. This functionality typically adds significant cost to the overall backup solution, but provides a very easy mechanism to capture and recover an entire operating system, something that is extremely difficult and sometimes impossible when using a file-level agent.

Virtualization provides us with a very simple mechanism to get underneath the guest operating system from the virtualization level. In this scenario the entire virtual machine is treated like a set of files within the ESX Service Console. Here, the VMDK, log, and virtual machine configuration files are backed up and stored remotely.

The obvious benefit of this configuration is that with the restoration of a few files you can successfully restore your virtual machine to its previously backed up state. While this may seem like an optimal solution because of the recoverability of the system, there are some drawbacks that need to be considered.

The sizes of the VMDK files tend to be very large. In some cases, we have seen people create VMDK files several TB in size (which isn't a good idea in general). When creating backups of VMDK files you obviously need to put them somewhere. The old adage "storage is cheap" does not apply when you are trying to cram several TB of space in an enterprise. Also because of the size, they tend to take a long time to copy over the network or even the SAN. We will discuss ways to optimize image size and backup speed in our "Optimizing Backup and Disaster Recovery" section of this chapter.

When looking to perform image level backups of virtual machines there are several approaches that can be taken. Each provides a very unique way to perform the required work and has just as unique advantages and disadvantages associated with it.

Guest Agents

As previously mentioned, many backup agents provide "bare metal" backup and recovery solutions that allow for the capture of an entire system image. You will typically need to pay a premium for these solutions, often times in excess of $1000 USD per server. In order to recover using an image backup from your bare metal agent you will often require a boot CD to properly enter a preboot environment that has enough functionality to connect to the network and access the backup server to recover the image. This does require a bit of manual intervention and VMware knowledge.

Figure 10- 3: Image Agent Backup

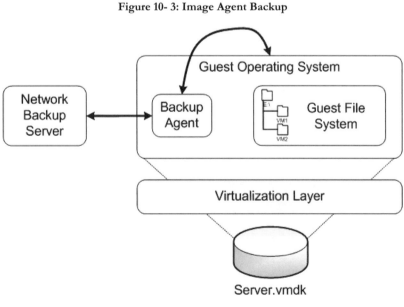

Advantages of using Guest Agents for Image Backup
- Uses same software as physical environment

- Uses same backup infrastructure as physical environment

- Daily backup procedures don't change

- Typically allows file recovery from image backup

Disadvantages of using Guest Agents for Image Backup
- Costly solution

- Manual restore process

Applications

After VMware ESX really started to hit the mainstream, the recoverability aspect of virtual machines became extremely popular. Several individuals and vendors have been able to capitalize on VMware's capabilities and have written applications specifically suited for virtual machine backup. These applications either run in or communicate with the virtualization layer to capture entire virtual machines, which often consist of at least one VMDK file, VMX configuration files, and log files. The best part of these solutions is that they can run against running virtual machines without the operating system, and most importantly the end users, even knowing that it is occurring.

Figure 10- 4: Virtualization Backup Application

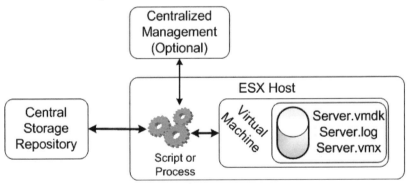

As mentioned earlier, there are several very reliable options when looking for applications to assist in the image level backup and recovery of your virtual machines. All available scripts or applications leverage the same set of steps to capture an image of a running virtual machine.

Figure 10- 5: Backup Process

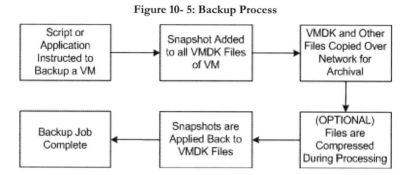

The oldest method to backup virtual machines, which is still available and actively maintained today, is a Perl script called VMBK.pl, written by Massimiliano Daneri. While scripting normally gets a bad rap, Massimiliano's script should almost be considered more of a full-fledged application. The best part is that this script is completely free. It is by far the optimal solution for smaller implementations of VMware. More information can be found on the script's home page: http://www.vmts.net/vmbk3.htm.

For larger implementations of VMware something a little more advanced is required to effectively manage the backup infrastructure. The clear leader in virtualization backups is Vizioncore's esxRanger. In addition to being an easy to use centralized Windows application, esxRanger provides advanced functionality such as enhanced compression, differential backups, integration with VCB (which will be discussed in a few minutes), VMotion/DRS support, simple recovery, and has basic capabilities for file level recovery from an image backup. While this solution is not free, it is still reasonably priced for the functionality it provides. Further details can be found at Vizioncore's website: http://www.vizioncore.com.

Appliances

A creative way to backup entire virtual machine's images, which has become increasingly popular with the release of VI3, is the use of a backup appliance. The "appliance" itself is a lightweight virtual machine (typically Linux due to distribution rights) that mounts VMDK files of the virtual machines being backed up. Once mounted inside the appliance, processes are run to copy data from the appliance operating system to remote storage for archival. The key to using appliances is in the fact that a backup appliance does not have the same speed limitations that the ESX Service Console has. This means that appliances have slightly higher speed access, primarily to disk resources, than stand alone backup applications.

In order to provide end users with the capability to configure and manage a backup architecture, there is typically a GUI component involved. This can either be in the form of a web interface or a small "GUI Helper" virtual machine.

Figure 10- 6: Virtual Appliance Backup

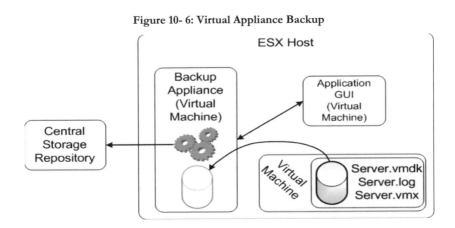

Additional benefit can be found from the backup appliance simply by the fact that it is a virtual machine. The appliance itself can participate in VMotion and DRS activity without impacting running backup jobs. This provides a layer of high availability in the event of host performance issues.

While it may seem like there are a lot of advantages of using appliances, there are also some disadvantages. Appliances run in and leverage the same resources as the actual virtual machines being hosted in the virtual infrastructure. If the appliance is performing compression of an image or doing other CPU intensive activity this will potentially impact the same virtual machines they are trying to backup. ESX does have several mechanisms to limit resource utilization, and appliances can be set up to run in resource pools, but the more you limit the appliance, the slower the backup jobs will run. The key is finding the proper schedule and balance of resource utilization to minimize the impact on the running virtual machines. This does make it slightly more difficult to get up and running.

The primary tool used when considering the backup appliance approach is esX-press by PHD Consulting. It is full of features such as differential backups, a fault tolerant architecture, archive encryption, and even includes virtual machine replication (which we will discuss in the High Availability section of this chapter) whereas this is typically a separate product from vendors such as Vizioncore or DoubleTake. More information can be found at their website: http://www.esxpress.com.

VCB

As previously mentioned in Chapter 2, VMware released add-on functionality for SAN-Based backups for VI3. This add-on is referred to as VMware Consolidated Backup, or simply VCB. We break VCB away separately in this section, as it can ultimately be run as either a file-level agent replacement or as an image capture tool.

A common misconception of many people is that VCB itself is a backup tool. This is absolutely not the case. VCB, as it stands, is a command line driven framework that allows other backup tools to access virtual machine data over the SAN. VCB does not provide data archival and retention, tape management, or advanced scheduling like any number of true backup utilities. Nor does it provide an efficient means to restore virtual machines.

This section is going to focus on the current capabilities of what VCB provides, what some of the important limitations are, and in what situations it can be leveraged best.

VCB for File Level Backup

The primary focus by VMware for the release of VCB was in eliminating (consolidating being the more backup friendly term) the amount of agents purchased and deployed to virtual machines within the virtual infrastructure. In a typical backup agent implementation, each operating system (whether physical or virtual) has a file-level agent installed. In many organizations, there is a SCt associated with each individual agent that is deployed.

VCB can help in this scenario by leveraging the centralized storage architecture of a virtual infrastructure. Instead of installing a backup agent in each individual virtual machine, VCB allows you to mount the VMDK files in a Read-Only mode to a directory on a Windows proxy server. The proxy server itself has the proper file-level backup agent and backs up each virtual machine's directory. Since the proxy server is accessing the individual files of each virtual machine, backup agents are not required in each operating system instance of the virtual infrastructure.

This solution is only compatible with Windows operating systems at this point. The Windows VCB Proxy does not have the capability to read and understand Linux partitions.

Figure 10- 7: VCB Backup

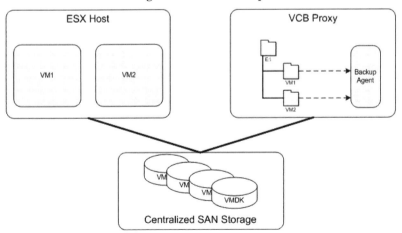

Behind the scenes, there are several things going on when VCB is executed and the VMDK files are mounted on the VCB Proxy Server.

1. VCB is executed from the command line on the VCB Proxy Server either as a scheduled task or as a pre-script to a File-Level Agent.

2. (Optional) A "Pre Freeze" script is executed on the target virtual machine. This script must be located on the virtual machine. A user can configure a custom script, but it must be called by the "C:\Windows\pre-freeze-script.bat" file.

3. (Optional) A VMware data consistency driver freezes the I/O of the virtual machine and ensures no file system writes are occurring.

4. A snapshot file is added to each VMDK file configured by the virtual machine. It is important to note that if a virtual machine has an incompatible disk, such as a physical RDM or a non-persistent disk, the process will fail and the user will not be able to leverage VCB for this system. There is no way to perform this activity on an individual disk of a VM. It is an "all or nothing" deal.

5. Once the snapshot file is applied to the virtual machine, the consistency driver allows I/O of the virtual machine to resume.

6. (Optional) A "Post Thaw" script is executed on the target virtual machine. This script must be located on the virtual machine. A user can configure a custom script, but it must be called by the "C:\Windows\post-thaw-script.bat" file.

7. The VMDK file(s) of the virtual machine are mounted as directories on the VCB proxy server.

8. The File-Level backup agent backs up the files contained within the VMDK file(s) over the SAN using the standard backup infrastructure.

9. Upon completion of the File-Level backup, the VCB CLI command to unmount the virtual machine is executed either manually or as a post-script of the backup agent.

10. The virtual machine's snapshot file is applied back into the main VMDK file and the system returns to normal operation.

Advantages of Using VCB as a Part of your File-Level Backup Strategy
- Minimize the number of backup agents deployed

- No host or guest CPU utilization to backup guest data

- No network impact since all virtual machines are backed up over the SAN

- Depending on the backup tool being used, only modified files are backed up nightly

- Allows an organization to use a single toolset for backing up the entire environment

Disadvantages of Using VCB as Part of Your File-Level Backup Strategy
- Requires Fiber SAN (iSCSI and NFS implementations are not supported)

- All virtual machines are backed up from a single host, making restoration with some backup applications more difficult

- Since VCB mounts images Read-Only, archive bit on files cannot be modified- may impact some backup applications

- Windows must have access to the shared VMFS LUNs, increasing risk of accidental corruption

VCB for Image Backup

The second way that VCB can be leveraged is to provide a VMDK image of the entire virtual machine. This type of backup is similar to a "Bare Metal" export of the entire virtual machine. This method does not mount the VMDK file or look at the contents inside of it, so is compatible with any operating system that is supported on the ESX platform.

There are several export options when performing a VCB Image backup in regards to what the final VMDK archive contains after the process completes. A user can specify to create sparse or flat VMDK files on the target. If the Sparse file is exported it should be noted that additional steps of converting the VMDK file with vmkfstools will be required before the archive can be properly recovered on an ESX host. Sparse files will tend to run more quickly, as 0-filled data is not copied and written into the archive. Flat files will match the file size of the original source VMDK, as an exact binary copy of the file (including the zeroes) is written on the destination.

There are some minor differences in what occurs behind the scenes when VCB executes an Image Backup vs. a File-Level Backup.

1. VCB is executed from the command line on the VCB Proxy Server either as a scheduled task or as a pre-script to a File-Level Agent.

2. (Optional) A "Pre Freeze" script is executed on the target virtual machine. This script must be located on the virtual machine. A user can configure a custom script, but it must be called by the "C:\Windows\pre-freeze-script.bat" file on a Windows VM or the "/usr/sbin/pre-freeze-script" file on a Linux VM.

3. (Optional) A VMware data consistency driver freezes the I/O of the virtual machine and ensures no file system writes are occurring.

4. A snapshot file is added to each VMDK file configured by the virtual machine. It is important to note that if a virtual machine has an incompatible disk such as a physical RDM or a non-persistent disk, the process will fail and the user will not be able to leverage VCB for this system. There is no way to perform this activity on an individual disk of a VM. It is an "all or nothing" deal.

5. Once the snapshot file is applied to the virtual machine, the consistency driver allows I/O of the virtual machine to resume.

6. (Optional) A "Post Thaw" script is executed on the target virtual machine. This script must be located on the virtual machine. A user can configure a custom script, but it must be called by the "C:\Windows\post-thaw-script.bat" file on a Windows VM, or the "/usr/sbin/post-thaw-script" file on a Linux VM.

7. The VMDK file(s) of the virtual machine are exported to the specified directory on the VCB Proxy Server. No VMDK files are mounted.

8. (Optional) The File-Level backup agent backs up the exported VMDK files using the backup infrastructure.

9. Upon completion of the agent backup of the archive files, the VCB CLI command to unmount the virtual machine is executed either manually or as a post-script of the backup agent.

10. The virtual machine's snapshot file is applied back into the main VMDK file and the system returns to normal operation.

Advantages of Using VCB as a Part of your Image Backup Strategy

- Simplified recovery of entire virtual machine during OS corruption

- No host or guest CPU utilization to backup guest data

- No network impact since all virtual machines are backed up over the SAN

- "Bare Metal" backups without the added cost of upgraded agents

Disadvantages of Using VCB as Part of Your Image Backup Strategy

- Hefty storage requirements since each VM is backed up in its entirety nightly

- No File-Level restore capability from image backups

- Limited number of simultaneous data streams due to I/O requirements

- Windows must have access to the shared VMFS LUNs, increasing risk of accidental corruption

Requirements for Running VCB

There are several key requirements necessary to successfully implement VCB into your virtual infrastructure. Most people will find that the worst part of using VCB is actually in the initial configuration and SAN Zoning.

Physical VCB Server

To start, a standalone Windows 2003 server is required. Previous versions of Windows will not be able to run the VCB framework. Unfortunately, you cannot install the VCB Framework on a system that has VirtualCenter installed. There are common components in both VirtualCenter and the VCB Framework that are not compatible with one another, and certain functionality within VirtualCenter will actually break. This Windows 2003 Server must have a single HBA connected to the SAN that is storing the virtual machine VMDK data. There is no multipath support, and attempting to configure the VMware LUNs down more than a single path will cause issues with running VCB backup jobs.

Temporary Storage Space

It is also a good idea to have ample temporary storage space if you intend to perform image level backups on the VCB Server. These often take up large amounts of temporary space, as an Image Level VCB Backup must actually export the VMDK file and store it locally. The size of this temporary space must be large enough to store at least 2-3 virtual machines' data at any given point in time. Also remember, VCB does not allow a user to selectively choose which VMDK files of a virtual machine to export. If a virtual machine has a VMDK attached, it is getting exported.

SAN Zoning

Once the VCB Proxy server is built and configured the SAN team will need to step in and zone your precious VMware LUNs to the WWN its HBA. The LUN ID's as seen by the Windows VCB Proxy Server must match the LUN IDs as seen by the ESX Hosts in order for VCB to function. Every storage array has a different way to configure this, but it should be a very simple process to complete (even though you will probably hear about how much of a pain it was). When all is said and done, several new hard disk devices should appear in the "Disk Drives" section of the Device Manager.

THIS FOLLOWING PARAGRAPH IS ONE OF THE BIGGEST WARN-INGS THAT WE CAN PLACE IN THIS BOOK

Do NOT choose to initialize any disk if Disk Manager is accessed on the VCB Proxy System. Although VMware claims that Microsoft writes its disk signature to a different offset than VMware does, you would be extremely foolish to put that much faith in Microsoft and your own ability to not instantly click "Yes" on any message that pops up on your screen. Although VCB opens VMDK files in a Read-Only mode, it still has full access to the zoned LUNs and an uninformed user can very easily reformat these partitions with NTFS, effectively destroying every virtual machine with a VMDK file on the LUN.

VCB Framework Installation

The VCB Framework installation package can be downloaded and installed from VMware's website for licensed customers. The installation of the VCB

Framework is very straight-forward. The only way to test whether it is working is to properly configure your SAN Zoning and run a test VCB command.

Designing your VCB Infrastructure

In order to have a successful implementation of VMware Consolidated Backup, it is important to understand the limitations and best practices behind integrating VCB with your environment. The challenge with setting up and running VCB is that it is extremely sensitive to the back end storage array being used for the virtual infrastructure. In addition, your mileage will vary based on whether File-Level or Image-based VCB backups will be occurring. The larger, and often times more expensive, storage arrays will be able to execute more concurrent backups than basic, lower cost, storage arrays. The recommendations we make in this section will be middle of the road, but it is entirely possible that you will notice differences based on your particular environment.

The general rule to building out a VCB infrastructure is to have one VCB server per ESX Cluster configured within VirtualCenter. The reason behind this is that a VirtualCenter Cluster serves as a shared storage boundary. ESX Hosts within a cluster are, assuming the environment is properly configured per the guidelines of Chapter 5, guaranteed to see the same LUNs, and most importantly, with the same LUN ID across all hosts. It is possible to have 2 ESX Clusters within VirtualCenter leveraging the same VCB server, but configuring LUN IDs requires extra special care. Having a LUN0 in each Cluster with each being unique will cause some significant challenges when VCB attempts to access VMDK data. VCB may not find the object for which it looks.

Figure 10- 8: LUN ID Assignment is Critical

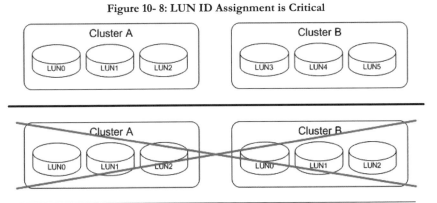

The type of backup that is being performed by VCB plays a critical role in your sizing strategy for the number of VCB Proxy Servers that are required to backup your infrastructure. When performing backups using the File-Level method, there is a limit of 60 concurrent VMDK files that may be mounted at any given time on the VCB Proxy Server. The important thing to remember here, and any time anyone mentions a limit, is that a maximum number almost never references a realistic value. The amount of data that is being backed up will ultimately drive how many File-Level backups can be run at any given time. Backup agents that have file-level differential technology will allow for more and faster concurrent backups once an entire set of full backups is created. On average, it will be safe to backup about 10-15 virtual machines without VCB starting to experience connection issues to VirtualCenter and have jobs fail with little to no information as to why. Again, higher end storage infrastructures will be able to better support more virtual machines.

When performing image-level exports through VCB there is a strong recommendation to limit the number of concurrent backup jobs to 2-4. The amount of disk I/O generated by doing block level dumps of entire VMDK files not only impacts the VCB Proxy, but could also have an adverse affect on your storage infrastructure. Since VCB has no bandwidth control, it is entirely possible to flood the VCB Proxy with enough I/O to cripple it and cause jobs to fail.

Testing in each particular environment needs to be performed to properly determine whether all virtual machines can be backed up within a specified window when leveraging VCB. Backup speeds are typically dictated by the back-end storage array, but extensive testing shows VCB has the capability to move data at a rate of about 1.5GB/minute on an average sized array. By testing the speed in your particular environment it should be relatively simple to estimate the number of VCB Proxy Servers required to backup the infrastructure. As the virtual infrastructure grows, the VCB environment should grow and scale appropriately alongside it. Often times, people overlook the VCB environment until they run out of capacity and backup jobs begin failing.

Limitations of VCB in a Virtual Infrastructure

While VCB may seem like the ultimate solution, there are several things that you need to be aware of before implementing it wide scale in your virtual infrastructure. Since VCB can move data quickly you need to consider the fact that just because it isn't using any local resources of an ESX host doesn't mean there is no impact. Remember, this data is flowing over the exact same storage infrastructure that is actually servicing your virtual machines. This doesn't impact the host itself, but it sure could impact the storage infrastructure to the point that every host appears sluggish simply because the SAN is too busy streaming massive amounts of data.

If your environment breaks the few hundred virtual machine barrier, you will find that performing 2-4 concurrent backups on a single VCB proxy is going to be a nightmare to schedule and manage. Even if you add several VCB proxy servers you need to properly split the workload to backup everything you need. This is quite a manual undertaking.

A final thing we have found is that the VMware consistency driver being used by the VMware Tools Service does not always effectively manage transactional systems such as database or email systems. If a snapshot is added to a virtual machine with one of these workloads, take a look at the Event Log of the system. There is a good chance that for every snapshot that is added, there is a database consistency check that goes along with it. While these systems have internal mechanisms to protect the integrity of their data in this circumstance, it does add unnecessary workload to the virtual machine to verify and correct potential issues.

To combat this issue, we recommend writing a small script that can take advantage of alternate technologies, such as Microsoft's Volume Shadow Copy Service (VSS), to better protect the consistency and integrity of transactional applications. While this functionality is only supported in Windows 2003 or higher, it can eliminate the consistency checks that must occur when a snapshot is added to a virtual machine.

As you can see there are quite a few options surrounding simply finding the best way to backup your virtual infrastructure. The good thing is that much of the knowledge you have just gained is also applicable to providing disaster recovery for your virtual infrastructure.

Disaster Recovery

Now that we have spent a very large portion of time discussing the various backup recovery methods and technologies let's dive into the similar topic of disaster recovery. Disaster Recovery refers to your capability to get your system(s) back online and running in the event of a catastrophic failure.

There are only a few things that are for sure about DR. First, it takes a lot of planning and preparation to do right, and second, it's never cheap when done correctly. DR with ESX server is no different. We have all heard the sales pitch as to how easy DR is with VMware, but is it really easy or cheaper? Maybe it's easier; however, I am not sure about cheaper.

To recover a VMware environment, we need to analyze three primary components. The first is the ESX Servers themselves. Without them, we won't get a single VM up and running. The second is the supporting infrastructure such as storage and networking components. The third and most important component is your virtual machines themselves. Notice we didn't mention Virtual-Center. In reality, this is not required to get your DR environment up and running. We will look at a few different ways to handle each of these and let you see which fits best into your environment.

ESX Server Recovery

It would be nice during a disaster recovery scenario to have a bunch of preconfigured DR hosts setup and ready to go. If this is the case in your company, then your virtual infrastructure disaster recovery is one step easier. Have the server built and ready for the situation, and you are ready to go. However in most business this is not the case. Basically, if you don't have a bunch of standby hardware, you are dealing with one of two solutions:

- A contract facility that will provide you with "like" hardware.

- The repurposing of existing company owned hardware.

The first option is used by a majority of companies out there. The basic idea is that they contract with someone like SunGard, so that in the event of a disaster,

SunGard guarantees them X amount of rack space and bandwidth and Y amount of different types of hardware.

The issue here is that you will most likely not get the SAME EXACT hardware. Or you may get the same model, but will it have the same HBA's in the same slots, the same types of NICs plugged into the same speed network ports, etc? If not, your unattended install for ESX that does all the cool NIC and HBA configurations just went out the Window. So when planning for the redeployment of ESX or when trying to ensure that you get the correct contract level that will ensure you get hardware as close as possible to your existing configuration, you will need to adjust your DR builds for ESX to be extremely flexible and allow for manual configuration of the server.

The second option of repurposing existing hardware is much more interesting. In repurposing, you are taking existing hardware that you own and rebuilding it as ESX servers. This gives you a little more flexibility as you will have a better idea of the hardware that will be used during DR. Some organizations will attempt to repurpose other "less critical" production servers for the critical production boxes. This is a poor plan, as you are really robbing Peter to pay Paul. You will eventually have to bring back those production servers that were "less critical".

If your organization already has multiple datacenters running their own virtual infrastructures, your DR plan may come down to prioritizing your virtual machines and turning off test, development, and non-critical production virtual machines to ensure the necessary host capacity is available to bring up the critical virtual machines. Through the use of technologies such as virtual machine and SAN replication, that we will discuss in the High Availability and Fault Tolerance sections of this chapter, this type of scenario can actually be simplified quite a bit.

Infrastructure Recovery

Just having ESX hosts available does not make for a solid disaster recovery plan. There is some consideration that needs to go into portions of the infrastructure that support the virtual environment. Since this book is not a disaster recovery book, we will only lightly touch on these topics to provide awareness that disaster recovery of virtualization does require thought outside just the virtual infrastructure.

Storage

When you need to get your virtual machines up and running at a disaster site the first thing that should cross your mind is "Where should I put them?" The virtual machines obviously need to be stored on a platform that VMware supports (SAN, iSCSI, NFS, etc) and you need to make sure you have enough storage to bring up all of the systems you require. If you are using SAN replication technologies, which are very costly, you do not need to worry as much as someone who is backing up images of virtual machines and needs to recover them to alternate storage types at a destination datacenter. The keys when taking your storage environment into consideration when planning your virtual infrastructure disaster recovery plan are to make sure you have enough storage and that it is compatible with ESX3. If you have the right recovery tools, it won't matter if you are using local SCSI, iSCSI, or a SAN from an alternate vendor.

Network

Just as important as having a place to store your disaster virtual machines is the capability to communicate with them in the event of a disaster. In most disaster recovery plans there are several configuration items that will change and will need to be addressed to get your virtual machines up and running on the network again.

There is a very good chance that the VLAN's at the disaster site do not match the VLAN's at the primary site. This means that in order to communicate on your network you will probably need to change the IP Addresses of your virtual machines. Any time you change an IP Address of a system you need to know if there are also DNS entry changes that are required. If you change the IP Address of a web server and its communicating on the network, it doesn't do any good until you let people know that website.example.com now points to a different IP Address. Having a solid runbook of each virtual machine is a critical component in knowing everything that needs to be modified or anticipated during any change made to the system, especially in a disaster scenario.

Virtual Machine Recovery

Now that there is a plan around host and infrastructure recovery we can finally look at what it takes to get our virtual machines up and running in a disaster. If your backup recovery process is leveraging the correct data capture methods, your disaster recovery process will actually be relatively simple.

Leveraging Backup Recovery as Disaster Recovery

Since there are many tools available to assist in backing up virtual machines using various methods, there is no reason that your daily backup procedures can't be used to provide disaster recovery for your virtual infrastructure also. There are a few things to be careful of if you are planning on using your backup procedures for this purpose. The way that the data is captured and archived will play a key role in the level of recoverability you have in your environment.

Inefficiencies of File Agents for DR

Using the file level recovery method for you disaster recovery plan will only truly help you if you are only concerned about retrieving application data. It will not help you if you need to recover entire operating systems. We will see towards the end of this chapter how we can properly leverage both file level and image level backups for disaster recovery, but here we just want to point out that if you want your operating systems back, don't use file agents exclusively. It is just as much of a pain in the butt to restore a virtual machine using a file level backup as it is a physical.

Image Backups for DR

If you plan things properly, and we certainly hope that we point out in this book that properly means performing image level backups of your virtual machines, then your disaster recovery process will be almost as easy as VMware says it will be.

First off, let's determine what components of a virtual machine are required in a disaster scenario. At the absolute bare minimum, your VMDK files will be required. The VMDK data is the only component that is absolutely required to get your data back. Unless you are using your own scripting mechanisms, and not doing the best job at it, you most likely will have the VMX configuration file of the virtual machine also, as well as the NVRAM file, which stores the BIOS settings for that particular guest.

If you are using a manual process as opposed to one of the available automated tools, you will need a way to get your backup files onto the destination ESX host (assuming they aren't already there). One of the best free tools available to perform large file copies to ESX is FastSCP from Veeam Software: http://www.veeam.com. If you do not have the VMX file you will need to leverage the Virtual Infrastructure Client to build a new virtual machine on a specific host. When it prompts you for disk configuration you will need to point to the directory within VMFS that you copied your VMDK data to. You will need to add a new hard drive to each virtual machine for each VMDK file you have that belongs to the system.

If you were smart enough to grab the VMX file with the VMDK file of the virtual machine, the recovery process is simplified even further. Unfortunately, the Virtual Infrastructure Client does not have any functionality to import an existing virtual machine onto a host. So, you will need to break out your trusty command line skills. You will need to log in and escalate your privileges to run a command as the root user. With the following command your virtual machine will be registered, visible and ready to start on the ESX host where you registered it.

vmware-cmd –s register /path/to/servername/servername.vmx

If you are using one of the many automated backup recovery tools available such as esxRanger or esXpress you will not need to worry about any manual intervention using either the Service Console CLI or the Virtual Infrastructure Client. These tools will take care of copying your data back to the host, registering the virtual machine, and even giving you the option to power on the virtual machine when the process is completed.

Optimizing Backup and Disaster Recovery

There are several methods that backup which storage vendors are employing that significantly enhance the efficiency of backup and disaster recovery in a virtual infrastructure. When you take a step back and look at what it takes to most effectively implement a solid set of backup and disaster recovery processes, you will see that there are three primary points that must be addressed.

- The size of the backup archives

- The amount of time it takes to create an archive

- The overall impact that creating an archive has on your virtual infrastructure

There are several advanced technologies available to us through backup software or storage hardware that assist in the three key areas identified above. When at all possible, these advanced technologies should be reviewed to see if they can be fit into your backup and disaster recovery plan.

Minimize the Size of Archives

VMware image files have a tendency to get quite large. When capturing images for backup or disaster recovery you would be foolish not to enable or leverage compression options for the archive files. There are some cases where compressing archives just won't cut it. When a virtual machine is scheduled to run nightly and has 20GB of data that is backed up, there is a lot of money going into storing these archive files. Over the period of a single week 140GB of storage space would be used just for this single virtual machine.

Thankfully, there are several options available that help alleviate these ridiculous storage requirements for virtual machine archives. You will notice that many of the technologies have been in place for years in typical file level backup agents. There is no reason these same technologies cannot be applied specifically to virtual machine archives since, well, they are just files.

Incremental Backups

In a typical file level backup architecture incremental backups only archive files whose data has changed since the last backup job was run. Since a VMDK file is constantly changing every second, it does make sense to say "Only backup my VMDK file if it has changed since the last time I ran a backup job." In fact, the only time this is possible is if the virtual machine is powered off. In order to combat this virtualization, backup vendors had to break down a VMDK file into smaller pieces.

By scanning and comparing each individual block of data that makes up a VMDK file, backup vendors have a way to backup only the portions of the large files that change between backup jobs. When performing an incremental backup of a virtual machine, only the data blocks that change between every backup job are archived.

Figure 10- 9: Incremental Backup

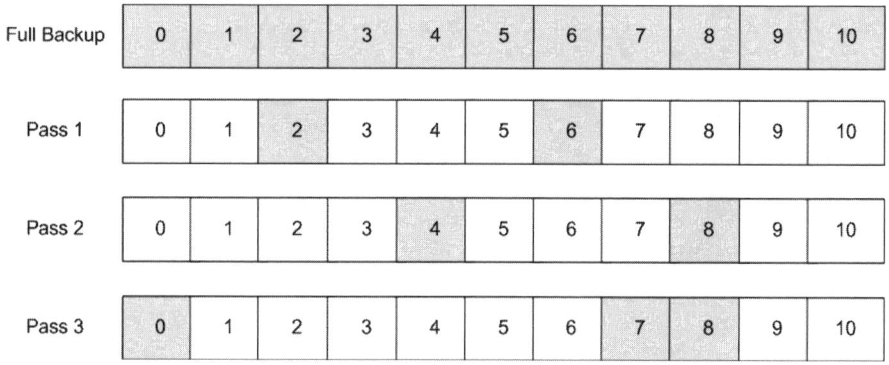

Full Backup	0	1	2	3	4	5	6	7	8	9	10

Pass 1	0	1	2	3	4	5	6	7	8	9	10

Pass 2	0	1	2	3	4	5	6	7	8	9	10

Pass 3	0	1	2	3	4	5	6	7	8	9	10

As you can see in the diagram, a full backup is required at least once; otherwise there is nothing to compare against for an incremental backup. On the first pass after the full backup there are two data blocks that change and are backed up for that particular pass. The same is true for the second pass where two more unique data blocks change. Pass 3 is unique in the fact that three data blocks changed since the previous pass

Based on the given example we can do a quick comparison of how much space is theoretically saved by using incremental backups vs. a full backup on every pass.

Nightly Full Backups

Incremental Backups

Pass	Blocks
Full	10
1	10
2	10
3	10
Total	40

Pass	Blocks
Full	10
1	2
2	2
3	3
Total	17

Incremental backups have always had one fatal flaw. In order to recover you need to have the original full backup job plus every incremental file between the full backup and the point in time to which you would like to recover. In the event that one of the incremental archives is deleted or corrupt, anything after that particular incremental file is suspect.

Going back to our diagram, if the archive file from Pass 2 was accidentally deleted and we needed to recover up to Pass 3 we have an issue. Blocks 0, 2, 6, 7, and 8 are actually safe because they are protected by recovering Pass 1 and Pass 3. The problem is that we have no idea that block 4 ever changed, so will still contain data from the full backup. While this does not seem like a major issue, remember that this is a VERY simplified example, and VMDK files often consist of thousands of blocks of which hundreds can change on a nightly basis. Corruption of a single archive file can turn your recovery result into a giant block of Swiss cheese.

Advantages of Incremental Backups
- Only captures data that changes between passes

- Maximum space savings for archival of virtual machines through software

Disadvantages of Incremental Backups
- Requires every incremental file to properly reassemble a virtual machine

- Increased probability of archive corruption

Differential Backups

Differential backups actually put a slight spin on the method of using incremental backups to archive your virtual machines. The difference between a differential and incremental backup is based on the fact that instead of comparing data that changes night to night, differential backups always perform a comparison to the original full backup. This actually makes each block modification cumulative for every pass.

Figure 10- 10: Differential Backup

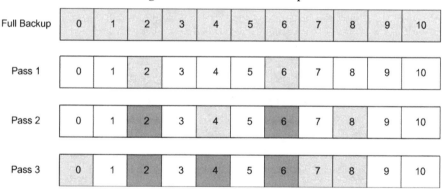

This concept is a little confusing so let's refer to the diagram. The full backup still needs to occur and will still consist of 10 data blocks. For the first pass, there is actually nothing different between an incremental and a differential backup; two blocks have changed, so two blocks are archived. The difference between differential and incremental backups comes into play for Pass 2. Remember, differential backups always compare what has changed back to the original full backup, not the previous pass. A differential backup will not only capture blocks 4 and 8, which changed between Pass 1 and Pass 2, but it will also re-capture blocks 2 and 6 since they have also been modified since the full backup was taken. Pass 3 will use the same logic and will back up all six blocks that have changed since the full backup was taken.

Let's take a quick look at our table comparing block utilization when using differential backups vs. a full backup.

Nightly Full Backups

Pass	Blocks
Full	10
1	10
2	10
3	10
Total	40

Differential Backups

Pass	Blocks
Full	10
1	2
2	4
3	6
Total	22

While it is still a space savings, it is not as good as the disk savings achieved by Incremental backups. We see that over time differential archive files will continue to grow in size. Theoretically, they can grow as large as a full backup job, although this is highly unlikely. Just don't defrag your hard drive and continue to perform a differential backup... that gets pretty ugly.

The best part about using the differential backup methodology comes into play when it's time to actually recover a virtual machine. Unlike Incremental archives where you need every single archive file, with differentials you need a maximum of two files. You will always need the original full archive. If you need to recover to a point in time, you only need the differential file that was created for that particular pass. This is possible because that differential file has every block that has changed since the full backup was taken. It does not matter if the prior pass failed, was deleted, or is corrupt.

Advantages of Differential Backups
- Simplified recovery: only need a maximum of 2 archive files to recover a virtual machine

- Low risk of corruption

- Still provides a space savings over performing a full backup with every pass

Disadvantages of Differential Backups
- Each differential archive is increasingly larger than the previous

- Over time differential files can become as large as full backups

Both incremental and differential backups have significant risks the more times they are run in between new, full backup jobs. Incremental files run the risk of corrupting significant amounts of data, and differential files grow in space very quickly. Both of these issues can easily be solved by running regular, full backups. This allows you to start with a clean slate on a regular basis. The frequency that a full backup job should run depends on the backup method you are using and how much data ultimately changes between backup passes. For information on optimizing the speed of your full backup jobs, take a look at the "Minimize Time Required to Capture Images" section later in this chapter.

Deduplication

The process of deduplication is typically used by storage vendors to remove commonalities in data across multiple files. These commonalities are stored in a high speed index file so they can be quickly scanned and compared. This technology is always run at either the block or byte level of the storage device.

The easiest way to explain deduplication is to look at a typical virtual infrastructure. Most organizations will deploy their virtual machines from a standardized template. If an organization deploys thirty virtual machines from the same template there is a very large amount of data that is identical across each of those instances. In fact, the only differences are those caused by guest customization. If a backup job leveraging deduplication backs up every virtual machine in the infrastructure it will perform a backup of the first virtual machine and build an index file of each block. As future virtual machines are backed up, any block that matches an entry that exists in the index will simply have a pointer generated that states "Block X of data = Index entry Y". This is much more efficient that backing up the entire data block.

By the time the process is complete for all 30 virtual machines it is not uncommon to notice that there is significant storage space savings involved. While the example we gave is a very simplistic example, it goes to show how much benefit can be achieved using this technology. There are some challenges that do pop up when using this scenario in the real world. The index that is generated is absolutely critical. If this were to become corrupt or deleted it will be impossible to recover any of your virtual machines, since the archives are fragmented with real data and pointers to index records. Many deduplication vendors have failsafe measures in place, but you'd better make sure you fully understand what they are and how to recover in the event that something goes wrong.

When it comes time to recover your virtual machine there is no simple process of saying "Here is my archive file, let me restore it." Once deduplication works its magic and properly indexes the data, there is no way to recover without having the entire backup infrastructure in place. This makes it slightly more complicated (and costly) since every ounce of stored data will need to be stored and replicated across multiple datacenters to have true DR capabilities of your virtual machine images.

There is a lot of movement in this area, and nearly every hardware vendor providing storage solutions is putting deduplication technology into their data protection offerings.

Advantages of Deduplication
- Most efficient use of storage space available

- Very high speed backups for virtual machines

- Backup workload is offloaded if managed by the storage hardware

Disadvantages of Deduplication
- Index vulnerability

- Entire backup infrastructure must be available to recover

Minimize Time Required to Capture Images

The second key aspect to optimizing backup and disaster recovery in a virtual environment is capturing your images as fast as possible. You do not want your backup jobs taking so much time that they extend beyond backup windows, as this could technically impact portions of your virtual infrastructure to the point that it will be noticed in your virtual machines.

The Smaller the Archive, the Faster the Backup

The easiest way to increase the backup speed of your virtual machines is to backup less data. Fortunately, we discussed several methods of doing that when we mentioned Incremental and Differential backups and deduplication technology. Keeping the archive file that is moving across the network to a minimal size will ultimately allow you to backup more virtual machines in a given backup window.

Don't Backup Useless Data

This one is definitely easier said than done. When you are dealing with modern operating systems they do some things to enhance performance of the operating system that don't necessarily play nice with virtualization. When data is deleted from an operating system the data itself is not deleted, just the pointers that tell the operating system where that data is. If you are using image level backups and delete 4GB of data just before performing a backup, you will still capture all of the data that was just removed. The question then becomes, "How do we get rid of this data?" Well right now there is an answer, but it is not optimal due to the amount of I/O required to make it happen.

There are several tools available, many of them free, which will allow you to write 0's over data that is stale to the operating systems. The most popular of these is the SDelete utility from Sysinternals. This utility is Windows based. If you want similar functionality for Linux guests you will need to take a look at some creative scripting to perform similar functionality. Zero filling your VMDK files should be considered if you have a system that reports it is using a small amount of data, but the backup archive size is consistently larger than reported.

Minimize the Performance Impact to the Virtual Infrastructure

The final aspect to optimizing your backup and recovery process is minimizing the impact that performing backups or capturing images has on your virtual infrastructure. The only way to really do this is to offload this work onto a component of the infrastructure that is removed from the ESX hosts themselves.

VCB

We've spent a significant amount of time discussing what VCB is and how it can be used. If you are looking to perform file level backups of your virtual machines, this is easily the best available option. If you intend to use VCB for image level backups you are best off leveraging a product like Vizioncore's esxRanger that can further enhance VCB by enhancing the compression of the backup archives.

SAN Snapshots

A second option to offload your image archives of your virtual machines is to keep everything entirely on the SAN. Many SAN vendors have snapshot functionality built in that can take a point-in-time snapshot of a running virtual machine and allow you to move it straight to tape or a secondary SAN. This solution is nice as it requires no additional hardware such as a proxy server. These SAN based solutions often come at an additional cost to enable the required functionality which may put the overall solution out of reach for small to medium-sized businesses.

High Availability

We finally have the opportunity to stop talking about backup and disaster recovery for a while and get to talk about the next layer of the pyramid, High Availability. Having a highly available environment gives you the capability to recover from a catastrophic failure extremely quickly. If your infrastructure is considered "Highly Available" there will still be a minimal amount of downtime while the virtual machines are recovered. This downtime should not exceed more than 10 minutes in duration for the most critical systems.

In highly available infrastructures, you should not need to recover any data from tape or other media. The virtual machines should have the capability to simply be powered on and continue running where they left stopped. There are ultimately two scenarios that you should prepare for when designing your high availability infrastructure.

Local HA

Providing highly available services still has some benefit, even if there is only a single site involved. No matter how hard they try, hardware vendors will never be able to manufacture hardware that has a 0% failure rating. In the event that one of your ESX hosts goes down due to a hardware or even software issue, you need to have the capacity to run your virtual machines on alternate hardware.

VMware HA

As we learned in Chapter 4, where we discussed your VirtualCenter design, VMware provides their High Availability service to counter such issues in your environment. VMware HA enables a heartbeat between all ESX hosts configured within a cluster. In the event that one of these hosts stops contributing to the heartbeat traffic, VMware HA assumes the host has failed. Within 15 seconds of a host failure, VMware HA starts analyzing the other hosts in your VirtualCenter cluster and begins powering on the failed virtual machines on the hosts that DRS deems best suited to handle the workload.

VMware HA is an automatic process but does require some configuration to work properly. The options chosen for your clusters around maximum number of host failures allowed, restart priority of your virtual machines, and isolation response are fully described in Chapter 4. You will want to follow the guidelines of that chapter to best design your VMware HA specific options for your organizations availability requirements.

The single downside to VMware HA is that it requires a centralized storage infrastructure to properly function. This is the only way every host in the cluster has access to all required virtual machines. If there is a larger issue in the environment such as a wide-scale storage or network failure you will need something more than simply having the capability to power the virtual machines up on an alternate local host.

Remote HA

More important than being able to recover from a local host failure is the capability to recover from a more drastic scenario such as losing your storage infrastructure. In this event, you had better hope that you have a remote high availability plan in place. This can be done using two different methods, each of which serve a different level of SLA and come at very different cost points.

Virtual Machine Replication

Virtual machine level replication is one of the hottest technologies in business continuity right now. Virtual machine replication takes the idea of incremental image backups to the next level. This functionality uses the same process of tracking blocks of data that are modified between backup passes. Instead of storing archive files off for reassembly at a later point in time, replication takes these incremental files and applies them straight into a VMDK file being stored on an alternate host attached to an alternate storage infrastructure.

The primary advantage to performing virtual machine replication is in the fact that individual virtual machines can be replicated without the need to take every other virtual machine that with which it shares a LUN. This solution is often extremely affordable when compared to providing SAN level replication. Another major advantage is that virtual machine-level replication is storage independent. That means you can replicate your virtual machines from a Fiber connected SAN at your primary location to lower cost storage such as iSCSI or NFS at the destination site. You do not need duplicate storage architecture at your disaster site.

While it may seem like the ultimate solution, it is important to note that this solution is for one-off virtual machines that aren't necessarily "SLA 1" systems.

Due to the incremental scanning processes it is not possible, or recommended, to replicate a virtual machine at smaller interval than every 10-15 minutes.

Many people ask "If I have replication, why do I need backup recovery as well?" Fortunately, this one is easy to answer. Performing image level backups still maintains a point in time to which you can recover your system. If you pick up a virus or you lose data, you can simply specify the archive you would like to recover and you are back in business. If you are leveraging a block-level replication technology that is only looking at the VMDK file and you get a virus or lose data, those same changes are going to be replicated to your destination host on the next incremental replication pass.

There are several vendors that are writing software applications to perform this level of functionality; most notably Vizioncore and DoubleTake. The low cost of these solutions make them the optimal method for small to medium sized businesses. That is not to say that large enterprises with thousands of virtual machines cannot also benefit. Replicating a field office Exchange server, using low cost storage, back to the corporate headquarters is just one example of how a low cost solution has quite a few benefits over SAN level replication. The greatest advantage of these vendors is that there is no manual intervention required in the event of a failure other than powering on the target virtual machines. All of the configuration and registration is already handled as a part of the toolset.

Advantages of Virtual Machine Replication
- Low cost point to enter high availability
- Can selectively choose which virtual machines to replicate
- Automatically manages configuration of target virtual machine

Disadvantages of Virtual Machine Replication
- Low replication pass frequency

SAN Replication Technologies

There are instances where an application or set of virtual machines require more frequent updates than every 10-15 minutes. When this situation comes up, the only available option at this point is SAN level replication. SAN replication has been in use for years and is a proven technology to provide some of the highest service levels.

SAN replication works at the storage processor level of the storage array. For this reason, SAN based replication technologies do not have any awareness of what exists inside the storage volume being presented to your ESX hosts. The significant advantage to this is that no host resources are leveraged to replicate your data volumes. If you set up replication, every byte of data on the replicated LUN will be sent to the disaster storage array. This is not an optimal solution if you have large volumes containing multiple virtual machines. What will end up happening is you will have a need to replicate one or two virtual machines, but have to copy the entire LUN, which contains every virtual machine. If you plan on using a SAN replication technology we highly recommend that you identify the systems that truly require the highest levels of high availability and you create RDM's for their operating system and data volumes.

There are two strategies for SAN based replication that are used; Synchronous and Asynchronous. Most implantations use Asynchronous replication. This means that data is committed to the source disk and is buffered and written at the destination second. Synchronous replication forces the local data write to wait until acknowledgment has been received that the destination successfully committed the data write. Asynchronous replication will yield the best performance, since it will immediately write data to your local copy, whereas Synchronous replication will give you the absolute highest level of data protection at a performance penalty. This penalty often comes down to how much bandwidth you have between your primary and secondary storage arrays. Unless you are using dark fiber or other extremely high-speed communication between sites it is highly recommended that you stick with Asynchronous replication.

One final note on leveraging SAN based replication is that there is no awareness of the virtual infrastructure at the destination site. You will either need to script a process to scan for and register virtual machines on the replicated volumes, or you will need to manually configure each virtual machine on the destination side. Just like with virtual machine level replication, the target virtual machines will be stored in a powered off, or "cold" state until they are required.

While the cost of SAN based replication is significantly higher than that of virtual machine based replication, the cost is starting to come down thanks to some of the lower cost iSCSI storage alternatives. If you do need this level of recovery, be warned now that it still will cost you.

Advantages of SAN Replication
- Higher replication pass frequency

- No ESX host resources used

Disadvantages of SAN Replication
- High cost

- Increased complexity

- Limited control over which virtual machines are replicated

Fault Tolerance

We've already discussed backup and disaster recovery of your virtual achiness, as well as making them highly available through several mechanisms. Now we want to discuss what it takes to ensure your applications stay running even when portions of the virtual infrastructure fail. This provides the highest level of availability for your systems, and the use of the technologies described in this section are the only way to truly read "five nine" availability (99.999% uptime).

Fault Tolerant Technologies

At this point in time, there is no way to achieve true fault tolerance by simply using the capabilities of your virtual infrastructure. We define fault tolerance as the capability to lose a portion of your infrastructure and still have no end-user impact or downtime as a result. The only way to make this possible is to leverage not only the benefits of the virtual platform, but also the advanced solutions provided by the physical infrastructure, operating systems, and applications running inside your virtual environment. With the move to a virtual infrastructure, you, as an engineer or architect, need to understand how these work and when they should be implemented.

Network Load Balancing

Network load balancing involved creating a publicly available virtual IP address and placing a pool of servers, typically web servers behind this. The pool of servers behind the virtual IP address not only share connection load, but also provide fault tolerance to one another. If any server in a network load balanced pool were to fail, that server would simply be excluded from the algorithm to assign connections to a particular system.

Virtual machines can benefit from this functionality just the same as physical systems. The mechanisms to configure this can be done through software, such as Microsoft's Network Load Balancing (NLB), or through hardware such as F5's BIG-IP. For the type of workload that a network load balancing infrastructure protects, it is often a better idea to scale out to multiple servers than to cram more connections or user sessions into a single virtual instance.

Clustering Services

It will probably be about a week after the first virtual machines start to go into production that the VMware administrators will be asked about clustering. More than likely, it will be even before then. There are several technologies available, and many applications have their own form of clustering. Most of them have commonalities in the way they must be configured within a virtual infrastructure, but for the purpose of this book we are going to focus on what it takes to provide clustering services for Microsoft Clustering Services (MSCS).

Cluster in a Box

A cluster in a box is a configuration in which two virtual machines running on the same ESX host are configured in a cluster. The main purpose of using clustering services is to protect against hardware failure.

Virtual to Virtual Clusters

Using a Virtual to Virtual cluster is just as it sounds: two virtual machines participating as cluster nodes to serve up a common resource. These virtual machines can be located on the same ESX server or spread across multiple ESX servers to protect against a host or hardware failure.

Properly configuring clustering requires a few components; you will need some type of shared storage, a front-end and heartbeat network, and you will need to ensure that the common data remains intact. Remember a cluster only protects against hardware failure (in this case virtual hardware) or possibly a service failure. It will not keep data from becoming corrupt.

Figure 10- 11: Virtual to Virtual Cluster Disk Configurations

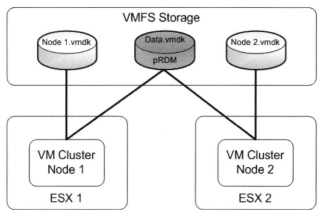

In a Virtual to Virtual cluster, the most common configuration is to store each cluster node on a separate ESX Server. This provides protection against a hardware or host failure. In addition, it would be a good idea to keep the operating system VMDK files on separate LUN's from each other. This simply removes a single point of failure for the cluster. Finally, you will still need at least one LUN to share across both hosts and act as a datastore for any number of cluster aware applications. This storage must be a physical mode RDM. A physical RDM turns over SCSI-3 reservation control to the Windows guest operating system and away from the VMkernel.

Once you have the storage properly configured you need to ensure you have adequate network connectivity. Using a product like MSCS, you are often required to have two network connections for each node, one for the production network and another for a heartbeat network.

In this configuration you should put the heartbeat network on its own virtual switch. On a physical network, these machines are generally connected via a cross over cable or isolated on their own segment. In the VMware world, we must design our hosts to accommodate the extra NIC's or VLAN's required for the heartbeat network.

Figure 10- 12: Virutal to Virutal Cluster Network Configurations

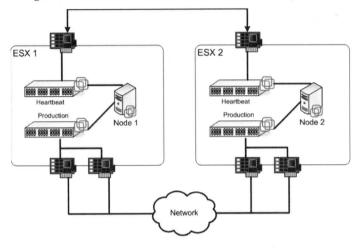

As you can see by the image, the additional heartbeat network reduces your number of available physical adapters by 1. If you think back to Chapter 6, another possibility is to utilize 802.1Q VLAN tagging for your virtual switches. This will allow you to create several port groups on the same virtual switch, eliminating the need to add additional physical NICs to your ESX hosts.

Physical to Virtual Clusters

Another way virtual machines are being used is to consolidate the number of passive cluster nodes on the network. Let's assume you have plans to implement 10 active-passive clusters in your environment. Assuming that you went with a simple configuration like a pair of dual processor systems for each cluster, you would wind up with 20 processors, which basically sit around all the time waiting for a failure that rarely occurs.

Some companies have decided that using virtual machines as the passive cluster nodes in this scenario makes perfect sense. Assuming you have 10 passive nodes, that will use very little processor and memory unless there is a failure, it is possible to consolidate these nodes onto your ESX servers and use physical RDMs in ESX to connect the virtual machines to the shared storage that the physical machines will be using.

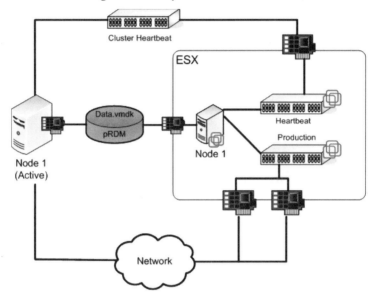

Figure 10- 13: Physical to Virtual Cluster

Using this configuration, the virtual machine passive nodes have the ability to access the production network, the shared data and quorum, and maintain a heartbeat with the active node. In this situation, it is possible to consolidate as many as 8 to 10 passive nodes onto a single dual or quad processor piece of hardware. In the event of a failure of a single node or the need to induce a failure for maintenance on the active node, the ESX Guest will pick up the load and maintain its active status until failed back.

The drawback here is that you do not retain 100% failover capacity. In other words, if you happen to have a situation where multiple active nodes fail and your ESX host is underpowered, your users may experience a decline in performance.

Business Continuity Use Cases

Rarely will an organization use only one method for providing business continuity to its virtual infrastructure. We also realize that every organization is completely different in regards to SLA requirements and business processes.

Instead of providing use cases in terms of Small/Medium/Enterprise organizations, we want to take a slightly different approach and provide examples for different application workloads and SLA requirements based on what we have found to be the most common configurations during virtual infrastructure implementation. By leveraging the examples below you should be able to successfully build a solid business continuity plan that leverages the best that virtualization has to offer.

	BR	DR	HA	FT
Active Directory Controller				
Standard Application Server	I	X		
File Server	F/I	X		
Print Server	I	X		
Web Server	I		*	X
Development Server	I			
Small Database Server	F/I	X	X	
Enterprise Database Server	F/I	X		X
Messaging System	F/I	X		X

F= File, I=Image, *=See Description

Active Directory Domain Controller

Ok, so the first one is a trick. It is also one of the most commonly asked questions about providing business continuity in a virtual infrastructure. When dealing with an individual Active Directory server running as a virtual machine there is little to no need to go out of your way to provide business continuity for it. Unless you only have one Active Directory server in your environment, in which case you should close this book and proceed to beat yourself with it until you pass out, it will always be easier to deploy a new server and follow the proper steps to create a new domain controller and allow the existing AD infrastructure to replicate the proper data to it. If you are serious about Active Directory recovery, you should look into software products such as Quest's "Recovery Manager for Active Directory" which provides enhanced capabilities to recover individual Active Directory objects.

Standard Application Server

Most organizations run a lot of applications. While there is no definite mold that these easily fit into, we have seen that often times a majority of these application servers do not have a high enough SLA to be considered for high availability or fault tolerance. What happens more often than not is these applications are simply backed up using an image-level technology. Based on the fact that an image technology is used as opposed to a file-level technology, disaster recovery is inherent to the process. If something were to happen to one of these servers, having data that is up to 24 hours old is not a major issue. A nightly backup using an image backup technology works quite well for this type of system. Make sure you use differential backups, as this can save significant amounts of space if there are not a lot of changes occurring on these servers.

File Server

File servers are unique in the fact that they can benefit from having both an image backup and file-level backup performed. In this scenario, you should consider using an image technology to backup the operating system VMDK drive. Since the operating system drive is very rarely ever likely to change, make sure you leverage a differential technology with your image backups. There is a very good chance that there is a second VMDK file hosting the data and a slightly smaller chance yet that it is an RDM. The best way to protect this system and provide the highest level of recoverability of the files being served is to use a file-level backup technology to capture the date contained in the data VMDK from within the operating system. This allows you to get the base operating system back up and running in the event of a disaster, but also gives you the best flexibility when recovering files when your users delete them on you.

Print Server

Let's face it; print servers are more often than not the bastard stepchildren of an organization. In many cases, you just find any system with extra processing capacity and throw some print queues on it. This makes them the perfect virtualization candidate. If using standalone virtual machines whose sole purpose is to manage print jobs, we don't care what files exist inside the VMDK files. All we care about is getting the print queues back up and running so your manager can print his multi-colored spreadsheet. A simple image-level backup is more than enough to protect this system. Unless you are an insurance company that I used to work for, you should not be adding enough print queues to the system to justify backing up these servers more than once a week. It's almost not even worth the effort to configure differential backups for a system such as this.

Web Server

This is where creating business continuity for an organization really starts to get fun. When you need to take off your Windows administrator hat and go argue with the network guys about what the best solution for protecting your web application is, it's a great day. In theory, web servers should remain quite static. A simple image-level backup on a regular basis is more than enough. Assuming you are running a web application that has a higher SLA requirement than most you will need to put some thought into how to keep the system available. The best solution is to build a load balanced farm so you have not only load balancing, but also fault tolerance built into the solution. There is some high availability consideration that should go into this design as well. What happens if you lose an entire datacenter and the only hosts serving your application no longer exist? For this reason alone it is worth using virtual machine replication to get at least one of your, *hopefully* identical, web servers from one datacenter and off to a disaster site. In the event that the worst happens, simply power on the destination virtual machine, update your DNS entries, and possibly whip out a few quick clones of the system to help handle the load on the disaster side.

Development Server

In every organization there is some manager who stands up in the middle of a room when discussing business continuity and says "It's a development server, who cares if we don't get it back?" Being in the software business, I can easily tell you that developers care. Their sole purpose for being at your company is to develop software. If the systems that they are depending on to perform their daily functions are disabled for too long, they will get quite upset and you will be wasting a lot of money while they watch the clock tick. I'm not telling you to fire up the SAN replication by any means, but you most definitely should not simply ignore the fact that quite a few people rely on development servers day in and day out. Since developers are notorious for doing crazy things seemingly at random, a nightly image backup of the systems they most frequently use will help protect their long hours of coding and debugging.

Small Database Server

When we start talking about small database servers we are starting to hit our limit as far as what we are truly seeing virtualized in the real world. As with most systems, an image-level backup should be taken on a fairly regular basis. This will help in the event that the database becomes corrupted or someone accidentally deletes and entire table by running a bad query. It should be noted, however, that image-level backups do not treat transactional systems well. These systems are often in a crash-consistent state, and while that shouldn't cause a major issue, it is better to be safe than sorry. For that reason, it is highly recommended that a proper file-level agent be used inside the guest operating system to backup the database the proper way. This will provide a failback in case issues arise from being in a crash-consistent state. Depending on what type of data is being served by these database systems, it may not be a bad idea to perform virtual machine-level replication to a remote site. Many times, the loss of the 10-15 minutes of data will not be the end of the world in a system such as this, and it will allow you to recover the system with minimal effort in the event of a failure.

Enterprise Database Server

If you decide to place an enterprise database server within your virtual infrastructure you better have all of your bases covered. As with a small database server, you will want to leverage an image-level backup of the operating system and use a typical file agent to properly backup the database. There is a good chance that the database files will reside on a physical RDM, so this is the only way you will be able to get at the data anyway. Instead of looking at virtual machine-level replication for these systems you should just focus on SAN replication to get your data to an alternate datacenter. If this were a true enterprise-level database system, you would have a high enough communication link to actually be able to provide clustering services between sites for the database. Personally, I have yet to see anyone brave enough to put a system that critical inside of a virtual machine.

Messaging System

Email is one of the most important applications to any organization. It's quite sad how much we depend on being able to instantly communicate with one another. If it weren't for email, I'd actually have to talk to people on a regular basis. Because of the critical nature of messaging systems they should actually be handled quite similarly to enterprise database servers. Since email is a transactional system as well, don't trust your recovery to only an image level backup; use the proper file-level agents to get your messages to safety. In fact, laws in many countries force you to backup and store your mail messages in a very specific manner. Don't interfere with doing this the right way. Again, many organizations will have mechanisms in place to have remote clustering available to keep email systems up and running. Just don't forget that you'll need more than one MX record for your domain on your DNS server. Assign a significantly lower priority to the MX record that correlates with your disaster site.

Use VMware HA

You will notice that there was no mention of using VMware HA in any example on the previous pages. This is because VMware HA should be carefully planned and configured on EVERY cluster in your virtual infrastructure when it is available. For as basic as the idea of powering on virtual machines during a host failure sounds, not having to manually perform the task and balance your own workloads while doing it will allow you to sleep comfortably at night. Make sure you review Chapter 4 to ensure you are designing VMware HA to meet your needs on a day to day basis, and don't focus on it for DR.

Book 2: VI3 Advanced Operations Guide

This book is the domain of Mike Laverick of RTFM Education. Mike's unmatched documentation on the internet led us (Ron and Scott) to seek him out and ask him to participate in this book. While we felt that our "Design Guide" hit a great target audience, we knew that the addition of a companion "Operations Guide" would make it a much more valuable resource. We, as a group, thought that the two books in one concept was a winner, and thus this second book –inside- a- book was born.

The Operations Guide

The purpose of this book is to guide you though the most popular and recommended configurations of VMware's ESX and VirtualCenter. It is not intended as complete reference. However, we do intend to add additional updates during the lifetime of this book. These will be released for free on the vi3book.com website. After all, it's not uncommon for procedures to change and for new features to be added to ESX or VirtualCenter within a release.

I used a mix of hardware when writing this guide: some old and some new. My equipment has two CPUs, four network cards, and basic connectivity to a Storage Area Network (SAN). In some cases, I had a fully redundant connection to the SAN for the purposes of capturing a real-world configuration in dialog boxes and command-line tools.

The structure of this guide was taken from the VMware authorized course "Virtual Infrastructure 3: Install and Configure" which I teach on a regular basis; the idea being that this guide could act as a companion to the course manual you might have if you attended the authorized course. It adds additional information and tips and tricks along the way. It also tries to explain various features and options in a new light which might assist you. I thought by mimicking the structure of the official VMware course this might help people whose aim is to use this guide as part of their preparation for the VMware VCP Test.

Additionally, I thought that this structure might be of benefit to those studying the product on their own.

Chapter 1: Installing ESX 3.x

You will be pleased to know that ESX is one of the easiest operating systems you will ever install. You are asked even fewer questions than the ESX 2.x installation, and the biggest part of the installation is the file copy event.

Confirm your source code ISO is good

You can download ESX 3.x from VMware's website once they have provided you with the correct serial numbers and logins.

After downloading the source ISO file, you should really check the ISO before you burn the ISO to a CD. You can do this using the Md5sum value. Md5sums allow you to confirm your ISO file has not been corrupted by the download process. The source Md5sum value is normally put under the link to the ISO or file you are downloading.

If you are running Linux on your desktop PC you will already have access to md5sum on the command-line. If, on the other hand, you are running Microsoft Windows, there are some free tools to check that your file is not corrupted. Nullriver Software has a very neat and free Windows Md5sum checker.

http://www.nullriver.com/

Additionally, rather than burning a CD, you could always use your ISO with the "virtual media" features of your server's ILO, if it has one. In the past, users have had problems with the installer engine and ILOs; however, these issues appear to have been resolved in this release. If you are using an ILO to do your installation, I would personally recommend using the "text" mode for the ESX install as I frequently find that the mouse is simply not there or too slow or disorientated. This is due to the limitations of some ILOs as opposed to the ESX installer itself. If you do use the graphical installer and your mouse does not work you can still use the keyboard:

- Tab — to move forwards

- Shift-Tab   – to move backwards

- Space-Bar   – open pull-down lists

- Cursor Keys   – to navigate lists

- Enter   – to select

Anaconda the Installer

The installation engine behind ESX is "Anaconda," which the install engine used for Redhat Linux. In fact, VMware's installer is just a lightly modified version of the same installer. Anaconda also supports scripted installations from a cd-rom, boot floppy disk or using the Pre-eXecution Environment (PXE) available on most modern network cards. We will cover scripted installation from a PXE boot server appliance in the chapter *ESX on the command-line.*

There are only two areas during installation which could cause you problems: selecting the correct network card for use with the Service Console and building a robust and reliable partition table.

The Partition Scheme

Like most operating systems, the reliability of the build will come from the installer's decisions. Critically, we want a partition scheme which will protect itself from rapidly filling event log files and "users" copying large files to the wrong location. Almost no one in the VMware Community uses the "automatic" partition scheme called "Recommended" in the installer. Nearly everyone in the VMware Community uses their own manual partition scheme based on user's personal experience.

The VMware Community has debated the advantages and disadvantages of various approaches in a very long and interesting forum thread. It was started by Steve Beaver, a very good friend of ours. If this interests you, then pop along and have a read. There are as many partition schemes as there are people on the Forum and ours is just one example. The thread is called "Taking a poll of the manual partitions people are using for ESX 3.0" and the thread ID is 425022.

http://www.vmware.com/community/thread.jspa?messageID=425022

Rather than using drive letters (C: D: E) to address these partitions, folders are used because ESX is based around the Linux/UMX world. You have been able to do something similar to this with Microsoft operating systems since Windows 2000 was released. As for the physical disks themselves, I usually recommend two 36GB or 72GB disks in a mirror.

In this example I am going to guide you through an installation to local LUNs. Later I will show you how to set-up a boot from SAN configuration. If you are installing ESX to the local storage, I recommend disconnecting the SAN cables if you can. This prevents any chance of installing ESX to SAN unintentionally – it also reduces your chances of accidentally destroying terabytes of data on the SAN while installing ESX!

Installing the ESX Operating System Locally

1. Boot to the ESX 3.x CD

   Note: Text Mode or Graphical?

2. At the welcome screen you will be given two choices. Press the [Enter] key to enter the graphical installation. Type the word "text" and press [Enter] to enter the text mode installation. If you simply wait 60 seconds, the installer will enter the graphical mode by default.

3. Choose to Skip the CD Media Test

   Note: Media Tests

   The media test checks the integrity of your CD – if you wish you may test the physical CD – but if you have already done a md5sum you should be good to go.

4. Click Next.

5. Select your Keyboard Type.

6. Select your Mouse Type.

    Note: Mouse Type

    Selecting the mouse type isn't dreadfully important, as ESX does not run with a graphic interface such as X-Windows or KDE. The question about mouse type is largely due to the installer's basis in Anaconda.

    Note: Install or Upgrade?

    The system will check for previous ESX installations. If you are upgrading or re-installing you will be given the options for an "upgrade" or installation. If you have completely blank hard-drives then you should receive no message at all.

7. Agree the EULA.

    Note: Initializing LUNs

    After agreeing the EULA you may receive a warning that the /dev/sdaN is unreadable. This reference to /dev/sdN indicates the SCSI Disk (SD), which is found first (A, B, C). Also, the dialog box should indicate on which controller this disk was found. In Figure 1.1 we can see that the controller is actually a cciss. This is a Compaq Computer Smart Raid Array 6i on my HP Proliant DL385. /c0d0 is the first controller (c0) and the first lun (d0).

    As the partition table doesn't exist, the Anaconda installer will wish to initialize the disk. This operation is potentially fatal if there is data on the drive. In this case, it is fine to accept "yes" because I know it is blank. If your ESX host is connected to SAN, be very careful in accepting yes, as this could be very dangerous.

Figure 1.1

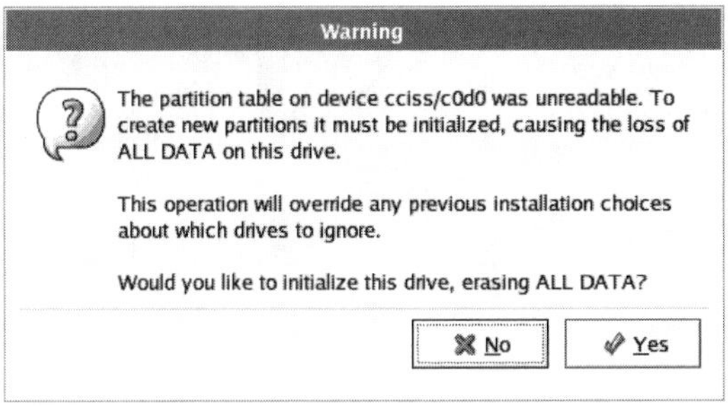

Warning

The partition table on device cciss/c0d0 was unreadable. To create new partitions it must be initialized, causing the loss of ALL DATA on this drive.

This operation will override any previous installation choices about which drives to ignore.

Would you like to initialize this drive, erasing ALL DATA?

✖ No   ✔ Yes

8.   Select Advanced as your partition scheme.

Below is a summary of a recommended partition scheme, followed by notes which explain their size and purpose. This partition scheme only uses about 15GB of space. You could easily increase these values and add more partitions. Generally, I create three primary partitions, and the rest are treated as logical drives in an extended partition. The disk management utility (called Disk Druid) automatically creates an extended partition for you using the remainder of the disk once you have created the primaries.

Mount Point	File System	Fixed Size	Size in MB	Force to Primary	Purpose
/boot	ext3	X	250	X	Core Boot (img) files
n/a	swap	X	1600	X	Swap for Service Console
/	ext3	X	5120	X	Main OS location
/var	ext3	X	2048		Log files
/tmp	ext3	X	2048		Temporary Files
/opt	ext3	X	2048		VMware HA Logging
/home	ext3	X	2048		Location of users storage
NA	vmkcore		100		VMkernel Panic Location
	vmfs	Fill to remaining disk			Local storage is only required for VM Clustering

ext3

EXT3 is the primary file system of Linux. We will use this one since the Service Console is based on Redhat Linux. There are two other propriety file systems which are only accessible by the VMkernel. These are vmkcore and VMFS version 3. After the install has completed we will cover VMFS in more detail in the storage chapter.

/boot

This is where core boot files with an img extension are stored. After powering on ESX, the master boot record is located and boot loader is run. In the case of ESX 3.x, this is now the Grand Unified Bootloader (GRUB). GRUB then displays a menu which allows you to select what .img to execute. Img files are image files and are bootable. They are analogous to ISO files which can also be bootable. I've doubled the VMware recommendation to err on the side of caution. Previous VMware recommendations have made this partition too small. This gave people problems when upgrading from ESX 2.x to ESX 3.x through lack of disk space.

/swap

This is where the Service Console swaps files if memory is low. I've chosen to over-allocate this partition. The default amount of memory for the Service Console is 272. VMware usually takes this number and doubles it to calculate the swap partition size (544MB). The maximum amount of memory you can assign to the Service Console is 800MB. This is how I derived the 1600MB value. This means if we ever choose to change the default amount memory assigned to the Service Console we do not have to worry about resizing the swap partition. It doesn't have a mounting point as no files from the administrator are copied there.

/ (referred to as the "root" partition)

This is the main location where the ESX operating system and configuration files are copied. If you have a Windows background, you can see it a bit like the C: partition and folders coming off that drive like C:\Windows or C:\Program directory. If this partition fills, you may experience performance and reliability issues with the Service Console, just like you would with Windows or any other operating system.

/var

This is where log files are held. I generally give this a separate partition just to make sure that excessive logging does not fill the / file system. Log files are normally held in /var/log, but occasionally hardware vendors place their hardware management agent log files in /var.

/tmp

In the past, VMware has recommend using a separate partition for /tmp which I have always done in ESX 2.x, as well. As I have plenty of disk space I have made this larger than it really needs to be.

/opt

Several Forum members have seen the /opt directory fill up very rapidly and then fill the / partition. This location is also *sometimes* used as a logging location for hardware agents. In VMware, HA has been seen to generate logging data here as well, so I create a separate partition for it to make sure it does not fill the / partition.

/home (Optional)

Technically, you don't need a separate partition. In the past VMware recommended one for its ESX 2.x in production. This was due to the fact that VM's configuration files-the vmx, nvram and log- were stored in /home. In ESX 3.x, all the files that make up a VM are more likely to be located on external storage. I still create it for consistency purposes and if I have users on the local ESX server they are more likely to create files here than in a directory coming off the / partition.

Vmkcore

This is a special partition used only if the ESX VMkernel crashes, commonly referred to as the "Purple Screen of Death." If that happens then ESX writes debugging information into this partition. After a successful boot the system will automatically run a script to extract and compress the data to a "zip" file in /root. This file with tar.gz extension can be sent to VMware Support who will work to identify the source of the problem. These PSODs are normally caused by failures of RAM or CPU. You can see a rogue's gallery of PSODs at:

http://www.rtfm-ed.co.uk/?page_id=246

vmfs

VMFS is VMware's ESX native file system which is used for storing all the files of the VM, ISOs, and templates. Generally, we use external storage for this. The only case for using local storage for your VMs is when you do not have access to external storage. Here I am assuming you have access to external storage. Therefore, you have no need for a local VMFS partition.

GOTCHA:

There is one major qualification to this statement: if you want to run clustering software, such as Microsoft's Clustering Software, inside a VM you will need local storage. VMware does not support storing virtual disks or Raw Device Mappings (RDMs) used in VM clustering scenarios on SAN or iSCSI based storage.

/vmimages

In ESX 2.x, we used to create a /vmimages partition or mounting point to a network location. This storage was used primarily for templates and ISOs. This partition is no longer required, as we now have more effective and easier ways of storing this data. Of course, if you are an ESX 2.x veteran who wishes to keep using /vmimages for consistency purposes then that is fine. It's just no longer required or recommended. Personally, I still like to have a portion of disk space given over to this partition location as a "working area" when I am dealing with large files. I've found my recent purchase of a SAN has made this something I use much less.

If you have done a clean install you will have a directory called /vmimages, even if you haven't created a /vmimages, which contains files used internally by VMware ESX. I will discuss this more in chapter 5 when we create VMs.

1. Click New and this will begin the process of creating partitions.

Figure 1.2 shows the new dialog box. In this case, I select /boot from the pull down list (you can type in this area). I chose ext3 as the partition type and entered 250MB as the size. I left the option as "Fixed" size and indicated with the tick that I wished this partition to be a primary partition. If I left this unchecked then the system would begin creating logical drives in an extended partition.

Figure 1.2

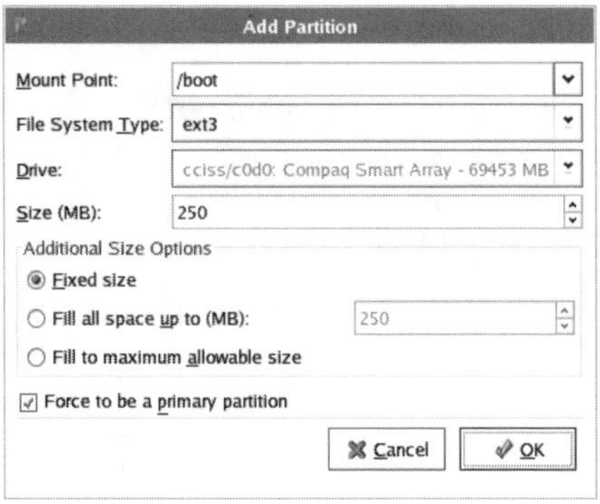

GOTCHA:

After you have built the partition table, take a few moments to confirm you created the right number of partitions of the right side. The partition table is not committed to the disk until you click "Next." This would be an ideal opportunity to spot an error and correct it. Partition errors can be corrected afterwards using fdisk, but it's much easier to get it right the first time. In my experience, a bad partition scheme usually results in wasted time spent re-installing ESX.

2. In The Advanced Options Page

    Generally, you can click Next here. But before you do make sure that the option "Install MBR to a drive" is the *same LUN* you selected earlier when you partitioned the disk. Occasionally, I have seen people select a SAN LUNs presented as the location for the MBR, and this has caused problems when their intention is to complete a local installation.

The other options aren't especially relevant to us. Force LBA32 (Large Block Addressing) would allow /boot to operate above 1024 cylinder limit (around 8GB of disk space) and is normally enabled on legacy hardware if the BIOS supports it. Only a very old server needs the LBA32 code.

The "From a Partition" is also for legacy hardware that stores BIOS information in a partition. This used to be seen on some very old Compaqs that had an Extended Industry Standard Architecture (EISA) partition. This is not the generation of equipment to which we normally install ESX server.

These options are a throwback to the fact that this is a re-engineered Linux installer. They are unlikely to be options you would use in a production environment.

3. Network Configuration

   Select your NIC which will be used by the Service Console

   Set your IP Address

   Subnet Mask

   Default Gateway

   Primary & and Secondary DNS and FQDN

   Set the VLAN ID, if you're using VLAN

   Disable option Create a default network for virtual machines

   Note: Use a FQDN

   A Fully-Qualified Domain Name and DNS name resolution are required for two core features – the VMware License Server and VMware HA. I recommend you have your DNS infrastructure set-up and in place before beginning the ESX installation so the Licensing and HA are easily configured.

   Note: Default Networking Options

   I wouldn't recommend the option "Create a default network for Virtual Machines." This would allow a VM's network traffic and Service Console management traffic to co-exist on the *same* network. It is recommended you separate this traffic for security and performance reasons.

GOTCHA:

How do you know you have selected the right network card during the install? If a server has mix of networking speeds/duplex, then ideally I would want to use a 100mps/Full-Duplex card with the Service Console, dedicating my 1000mps interfaces to the systems that really need the bandwidth, namely my VMs.

Aside from that you would have to consult documentation of your system to know which PCI Bus:Slot:Function number was related to each card. By default the install merely scans the PCI Bus and locates the card in its order of the Bus. If after installing the ESX product you find you cannot even ping the Service Console interface it could be you selected the wrong NIC during the install. If this happens to you, you may wish to consult the end of Chapter 2 entitled "Managing Service Console Networking."

4. Set your Time Zone and, if appropriate, UTC Settings.

Note: Time Zones and UTC

UTC stands for Universal Time Co-ordinate. Despite its name it is the same as Greenwich Mean Time (GMT) where zero hour begins at the Greenwich Meridian in London, United Kingdom. If you're in the UK like me you might like to know that even we don't strictly obey UTC. We partially obey GMT and BST (British Summer Time) depending on the time of the year. Sometimes we are in synch with UTC and other times we are not. For this reason, if you enable UTC and select the Europe/London your system clock will be 1hr adrift, depending on the time of the year. Also, you may wish to check the UTC tab to make sure you are correctly setting where you are, relative to GMT.

Getting time right on ESX is pretty critical. Firstly, because in most configurations this is where VMs get their time. Secondly, VMs can suffer from "clock drifting" meaning the virtual machines "clock" is out of synch with the ESX system clock. Resolving this clock drift begins with getting your time settings correct in the first place. We can synchronize the time of ESX with Network Time Protocol

(NTP) server on the internet for greater accuracy. I will cover this later in Chapter 12, *ESX on the Command-Line*.

5. Set the root password.

    Note: Creating other users on the ESX Host

    The root account is the user with highest privileges. Currently, there is no method to create other ESX users within the installer – this has to be done with the "VI client." The main reason for doing this is so you can remotely connect to the ESX host with a Secure Shell (SSH) client to get a command-line view of your ESX hosts without resorting to the ILO or RAC card on your server.

6. Watch the Status Bars.

7. You will then be left with a summary of your choices. At this stage you can still go back and change some settings, such as your IP address, if you feel you have set them incorrectly. Clicking "Next" initiates the copy process. At the end of the install clicking Finish will normally cause the CD-ROM to eject and when the system reboots you get your first boot of ESX server.

8. If you are using virtual media to access the ESX 3 ISO, remember to disconnect it before the reboot. You might find that BIOS settings cause the server to boot to the CD again.

Creating a Local ESX User Account for SSH/PuTTy Access

There is a protocol called SSH (Secure Shell) which allows us to gain access to ESX's command-line interface without the use of an ILO. A very popular tool used to create a remote SSH session is PuTTy, created by Simon Tatham. This can be found at:

http://www.chiark.greenend.org.uk/~sgtatham/putty/

Why would you want this command-line style access to ESX? Firstly, there are some tasks that *only* can be done via the command-line. In other situations, because you have a mix of command-line and GUI tasks, it is easier to choose one interface rather than work with two.

However, in ESX 3.x there are new security settings which disable SSH access to the root account. By default, in a clean install there is no access to the ESX Service Console for the root account except via the ILO. So I create a local account on ESX, use PuTTy to gain access, and then finally switch to the root account. This security change was introduced to enforce more user account traceability and an audit trail in ESX 3.

Note: User activity such as logons and changes in privilege are logged in /var/log/messages.

In the installation there is no way to create this user account, so we must use VMware's Virtual Infrastructure client to gain access.

Download and Install the Virtual Infrastructure Client

The main graphical tool used to administer either ESX server directly or via VirtualCenter is called the Virtual Infrastructure Client (VI client). We can download and install this tool from the ESX host. We can then use this tool to create a local ESX user suitable for login in remotely with SSH.

1. From your Management PC open a web-browser.

2. Type in the FQDN of your ESX host such as https://esx1.vi3book.com

    Note:

    Choose Yes to continue to access the ESX host despite the fact its certificate is not trusted. ESX creates a server certificate for each installation you do. These are auto-generated using OpenSSL and are not signed from recognized root certificate authority.

3. Select the link Download the Virtual Infrastructure Client.

4. Save or Open the VMware-viclient.exe file and install it to your management PC.

    Note: After installing the VI client you should be able open it from the shortcut on your desktop logging onto your ESX host by its FQDN, root and root's password

Create a Local User on an ESX Host

1. Click the User & Groups tab.

2. Right-Click the Window and Choose Add.

3. Fill in the dialog box as outlined in Figure 1.3.

Figure 1.3

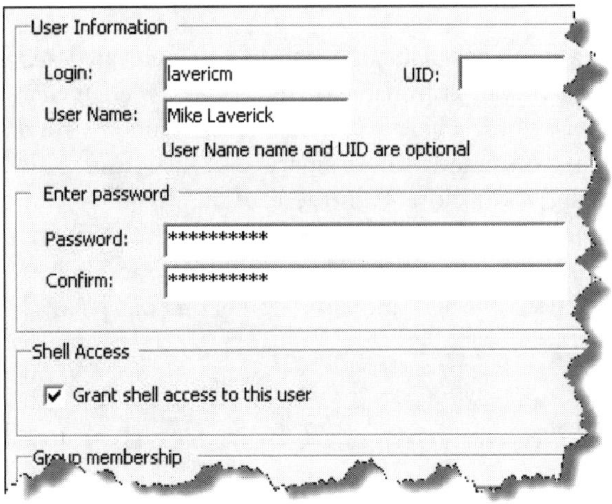

Note: Grant Shell Access

You must enable "Grant shell access" to this user for the account to have access to the Service Console via SSH. Otherwise they will only access to the ESX host with VI client.

4. Click **OK.**

Gaining Command-Line Access as ROOT with SSH

1. **Open a** SSH/PuTTy Session to the **ESX Host.**

2. **Login** with your recently created account.

3. To levitate to a higher plane of privileges type:

   su −

4. **Enter the root's password assigned during installation.**

    Note: Using the SU Command

    The SU command allows you to "switch user" and assumes, unless otherwise specified, that you would like to change to "root." The minus sign indicates you would like to use the root account's environmental settings, such as path variables. This is very important if you want to run any commands properly and not receive "command not found" error messages.

    There is a more sophisticated way to allow elevated access without even using the su command or having knowledge of the root account's password. There is a utility called "sudo" which allows you say which commands an ordinary user can run. This stops you from having to disclose even the root password; to run commands normally used by root. However, for now the method above does work. It is easy to use and still provides for traceability. I will cover a simple sudo configuration in the chapter *ESX on the Command-Line*.

Enabling SSH from your ESX host to other hosts

One of the things I like to do is connect to one ESX host and then use the SSH at the Service Console to get to my other servers – this saves me having to open repeated PuTTy sessions. However, you will be unable to use the SCP (Secure Copy) command to copy files to ESX servers from an ESX server. Under the default settings this is not allowed in ESX 3.x as the firewall denies the client (although every ESX host is an SSH server), with an error like this:

ssh: connect to host esx2.vi3book.com port 22: Connection refused

To enable this kind of access we need to adjust the firewall settings:

1. In the VI client click the Configuration tab.

2. Under the Software Panel, select Security Profile.

3. Click the Properties link in the far right-hand corner.

4. Enable the SSH Client option and click OK.

Figure 1.4

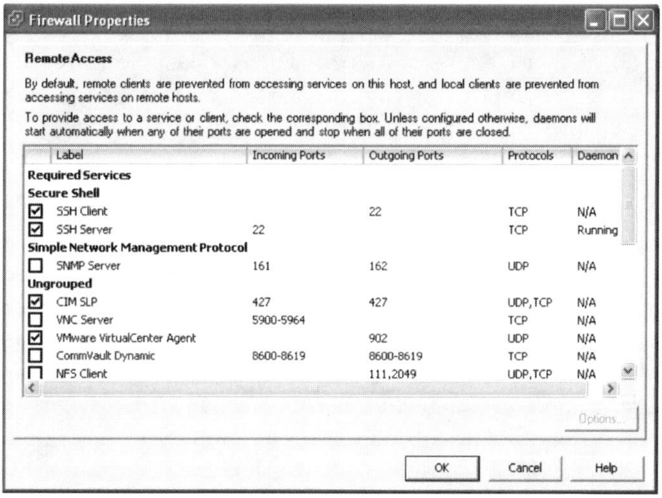

Note: Using SSH

This is all that's required for SSH. So now you could type ssh –l *lav-ericm* esx2.vi3book.com and then use su – to elevate your privileges to root rights. If you ever get confused about who you are, try the command whoami, and if you are unsure which host you're connected to, try the command hostname. You can use the command exit to leave ssh sessions.

Note: If you were using the command-line you could have enabled the SSH client using the command-line version of the ESX firewall. Please note this command, as with *all* commands, *is* case-sensitive.

esxcfg-firewall -e sshClient

GOTCHA:

Many esxcfg commands require restarting the hostd daemon if you want the VI client to refresh and show your command-line changes in the GUI. You can do this with service mgmt-vmware restart.

Configuring ESX 3.x for SAN Booting

Firstly, if you are unfamiliar with SAN technology you might wish to skip this section and proceed to Chapter 3, *Storage*. There you can learn more about conventional ESX deployments, leveraged SAN based storage. You could then return to this chapter fully armed with the background knowledge to safely continue.

Since ESX 2.x VMware has supported booting from both local storage and from SAN based storage, SAN based booting is a tempting option, especially if you run ESX servers from blades. It allows you to quickly remove a failed blade with a working one, and bring that ESX host back online quickly. Another advantage is that you can leverage your SAN snapshot features as a way of backing up your ESX server build. Before I begin an overview of preparing ESX for SAN-based booting, it's important to know some key restrictions and what is actually supported by VMware:

- Booting from SAN and using VM clustering (clustering software from Microsoft or VERITAS for example) is not supported.

- With ESX 2.x you could not use a feature called "Raw Device Mappings" (RDMs). RDMs allow a VM access to native LUNs on the SAN for existing data or storing your data using the guest operating systems native files system on a SAN LUN rather than creating a virtual disk on VMFS partition. RDM files and SAN booting are now supported together.

- ESX server can see up to a maximum of 256 LUNs (0-255). However, the Anaconda installer only displays the first 128 LUNs (0-127).

- In the past, VMware only supported booting for the "lowest order" LUN's, so if an ESX host had access to LUN's 10, 12, and 15. The LUN selected as the boot LUN would be 10. This restriction no longer applies to ESX 3 installations.

Along with these soft issues there are a number of physical hardware requirements that must also be met:

- The Fibre Channel card used should sit highest in the PCI bus for performance reasons and should be plugged into an "active" storage processor on the SAN.

- Correct LUN masking and zoning should be implemented so only that ESX host can see the correct LUN. This has some implications when you replace a blade in the enclosure. The new blade will present a different World Wide Name (WWN) value. The SAN will need reconfiguring to present this LUN to the new ESX host.

- Boot from SAN is only supported in conjunction with fibre channel switch – direct connections without a switch and Fibre Channel Arbitrated Loop are not supported.

- IBM eServer Bladecenters that ship with IDE drives onboard need these drives disabling on each blade.

Generally, the install procedure for boot-from-SAN differs little from an install to local storage. The only real difference is, rather than selecting local storage when you partition the disk or set the location of the Master Boot Record, you select a LUN on the SAN.

Firstly, before the installation I would recommend that you set the main system BIOS to boot from the CD-ROM. In the main BIOS we set the fibre channel storage controller to be above the internal RAID controller card. This stops the server booting to local internal storage.

Secondly, once the main BIOS has been correctly configured you will have to enter the configuration tool for your fibre-channel card. The fibre-channel device will need to be enabled as a boot device – and the LUN where installation files were copied selected as the boot LUN. Clearly, these settings are very hardware specific. The following instructions were developed using HP Proliant DL 385 using a Qlogic 2200 fibre channel card. If this is not your hardware I would recommend consulting your vendor's procedures for enabling SAN based booting.

GOTCHA:

One of the appeals of boot from SAN is that nothing about the ESX host itself is physically stored locally. This makes the ESX product more like an appliance, merely an engine for running VMs. There is, however, one drawback to this boot from SAN approach which is especially appealing with blade technology. If you want to setup clustering software such as Microsoft or VERITAS Clustering Services, you would need local storage on blades. VMware does not support virtual machine clustering with the boot disks of the VMs stored on the SAN. If you are configuring VM clustering and wish to be supported by VMware, the virtual disks of the VM must be on *local storage.*

Configuring the Fibre Channel BIOS Options

TIP:

Before you begin I recommend either removing physical disks or using your RAID controller card to remove any LUNs. This will ensure the only storage you see during the install is SAN based.

1. Power on your server.

2. Press **[Alt+Q]** to enter **Qlogic Cards BIOS settings**.

3. Choose **Configuration Settings** [Enter].

4. Choose **Host Adapter Settings** [Enter].

5. Set the **Host Adapter BIOS:** option to be **Enabled**.

6. Press **[ESC]** to exit the **Host Adapter Settings** menu.

7. In **Configuration Settings** choose **Selectable Boot Settings**.

8. Set **Selectable Boot Device** option to be **Enabled**.

9. Cursor down to select **Current Boot Node Name:** and press **[Enter]**.

Figure 1.5 shows the disks displayed to my server. I'm using quite an old Sun Microsystems SAN with Qlogic 2200 fibre channel card.

Figure 1.5

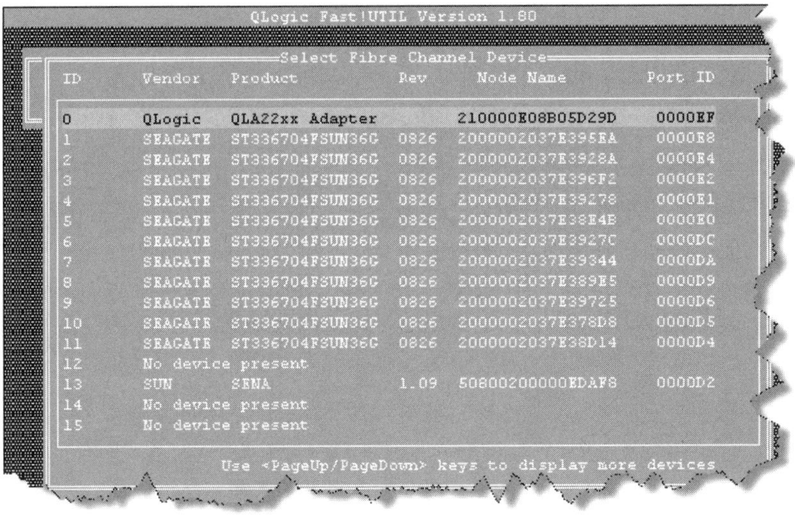

Note: Use LUN Masking

Here my ESX host can see many LUNs/Disks. You might find it easier to mask all LUNs away from the server except the SAN boot LUN. This will make selecting the right LUN much easier and clearer.

10. **Select the appropriate LUN or disk** from the list. I will use ID9 which has the Node name that ends with 20*nnnnnnnnnnnn*9725.

11. Press [**ESC**] and **Save your changes**.

12. Finally, **Exit Fast!UTIL** and **Choose to Reboot** the system.

Configure the Main System BIOS

Different systems use different BIOS providers and different keyboard strokes to gain access to the main keyboard settings. For example, on most HP systems it is F10 to enter the BIOS, but on Dell systems it is normally F2.

Below is the procedure for HP Proliant:

1. Press [**F10**] at the prompt.

2. Choose the option **Setup Utility** and press [**Enter**].

3. Choose **Boot Controller Order (IPL)** and press [**Enter**].

4. Select the **Qlogic Card** and Press [**Enter**].

   Note:

   On my system this appears as Ctlr:3 PCI Slot 3 SCSI Mass Storage Controller.

5. Choose **Control Order 3**.

Figure 1.6 shows configuring the Qlogic Card to be the primary device for boot purposes.

Figure 1.6

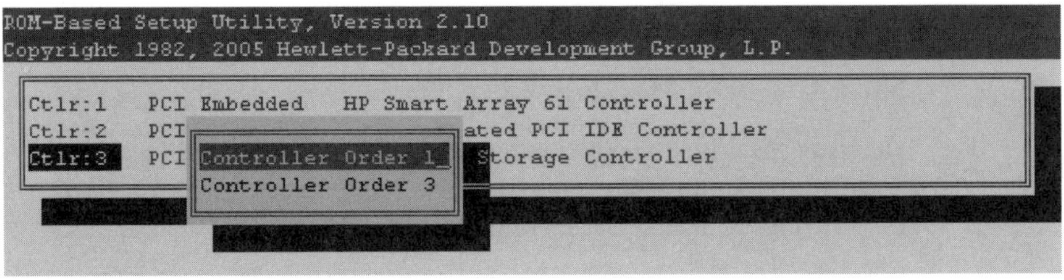

ROM-Based Setup Utility, Version 2.10
Copyright 1982, 2005 Hewlett-Packard Development Group, L.P.

```
Ctlr:1    PCI Embedded    HP Smart Array 6i Controller
Ctlr:2    PCI                              ated PCI IDE Controller
Ctlr:3    PCI  Controller Order 1   torage Controller
              Controller Order 3
```

Note: In a DELL BIOS

If you were doing this in a Dell BIOS you would choose the option called "Hard Drive Sequence" and use the +/- keys to move the Qlogic card to the top of the list.

6. Press [**ESC**] and [**F10**] to save your changes.

TIP:

Normally, I have a personal preference for the boot order on my ESX hosts which is:

• Hard Drive

- CD-ROM

- Floppy

- USB Keydrive

- PXE

This is to prevent me accidentally leaving a CD, Floppy or USB key in drive and finding a reboot boots to removable media. You might notice that the ESX CD does not ask "Press any key to boot from this CD" as some operating systems do. When it comes to boot from SAN setups I change this order to:

- CD-ROM

- Hard Drive

- Floppy

- USB Key

- PXE

This is to ensure that when I reboot the server I get to the CD the first time, and the system doesn't try to boot from a blank LUN before I have had the opportunity to install ESX there.

Installing ESX to a SAN LUN

1. Insert the ESX CD.

2. Choose **Graphical** or **Text**.

   Note: Choosing the Correct LUN

   During the installation choose the correct LUN from the SAN when you come to partition the LUN, and remember to put the MBR on the *same* LUN. Figures 1.7 and 1.8 shows the significant dialog boxes in the boot from SAN installation.

Figure 1.7

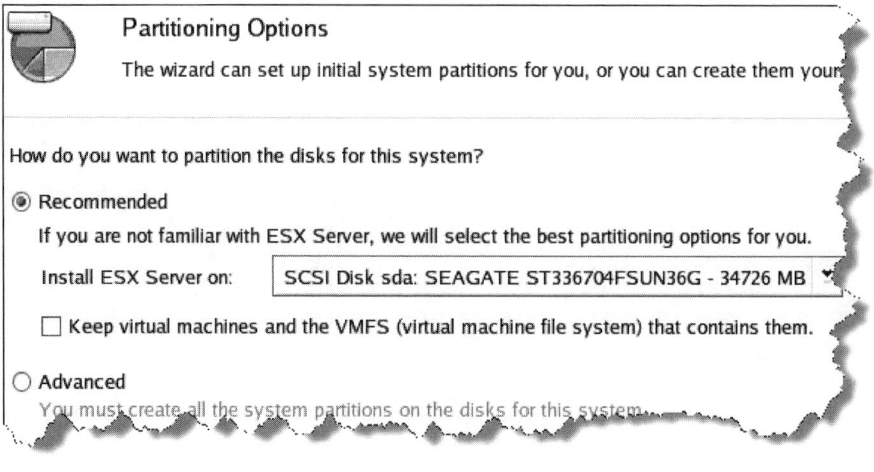

Partitioning Options

The wizard can set up initial system partitions for you, or you can create them your

How do you want to partition the disks for this system?

⦿ Recommended

If you are not familiar with ESX Server, we will select the best partitioning options for you.

Install ESX Server on: ⎢ SCSI Disk sda: SEAGATE ST336704FSUN36G - 34726 MB ▾ ⎢

☐ Keep virtual machines and the VMFS (virtual machine file system) that contains them.

○ Advanced

You must create all the system partitions on the disks for this system.

Figure 1.8

Advanced Options

These advanced options usually do not need to be changed.

ESX Boot Specification

How will the ESX Server boot?

⦿ From a drive (install on the MBR of the drive): ⎢ SCSI Disk sda: SEAGATE ST336704FSUN36G - 34726 MB ▾ ⎢

This is the standard option. Make sure your BIOS settings are correct for the drive you select.

○ From a partition

Use this option, for example, if you are using a Boot Menu tool, or if you have the option to run special diagnostic software that runs in a separate partition.

Boot Options

If you wish to add default options to boot up, enter them here:

General kernel parameters: ⎢   ⎢

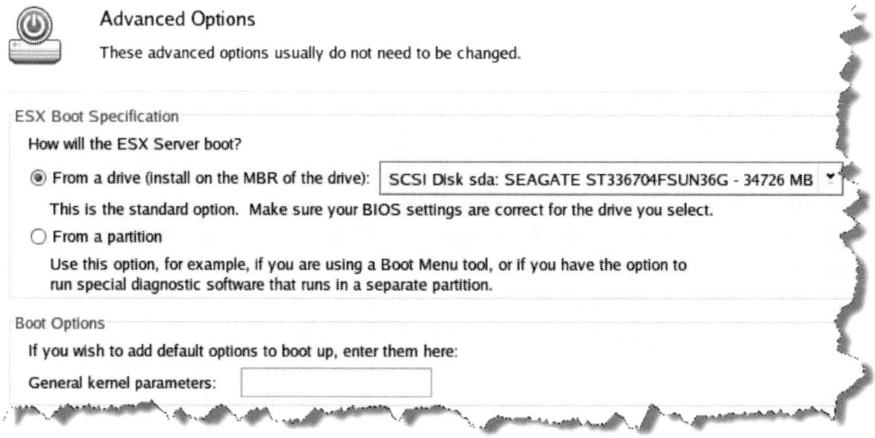

Summary

By now, I hope you are fully au fait with the ESX install procedure. In time you will probably do a few ESX installations, and all of this will become second nature to you. Eventually you will get truly bored with the idea of manual installations from a CD-ROM. Manual installations take time and only address a small part of the overall configuration of the ESX host for use in a live environment. That's where the next two chapters on Networking and Storage are taking us.

The post-configuration stages include:

- Network Configuration

- Storage Configuration such as NAS and iSCSI

- Creating ESX Users and Controlling Their Rights

- Installing 3rd Party Hardware Agents such as HP Insight Manager, Dell OpenManage and IBM Director

- Patching ESX

- Adding into VirtualCenter and Licensing

You'll be pleased to hear that much of this configuration can be automated with deployment tools, some of which are free. If you're interested in this subject then you may wish to proceed to the chapter titled *ESX on the Command-Line*. Here I cover scripted installations with "Kickstart" scripts with the source code delivered across the network with a free PXE "virtual appliance." Personally, I would advise reading the Networking and Storage chapters if you are new to the product so you are completely familiar with the post-configuration of an ESX host before you consider automating the process.

Chapter 2: Networking

What are vSwitches?

The VMkernel is a very sophisticated kernel. Not only is it adept at running VMs, it can also emulate a virtual switch, or "vSwitch." Virtual Machine's virtual NICs are "plugged in" into virtual switches. These virtual switches are then mapped to physical NICs on the ESX host. This allows many virtual machines to have networking from a single ESX host with relatively few network cards. These vSwitches are not fully-fledged HP ProCurve or Cisco Catalyst switches, so don't expect all the features of a physical switch. Nonetheless, they are VLAN aware and can control outbound traffic using a technology VMware calls "traffic shaping."

There are three types of vSwitch:

1. vSwitch with no NICs mapped to it

2. vSwitch with one physical NIC mapped to it

3. vSwitch with two or more NICs mapped to it

The first type is often referred to as an "internal" vSwitch, as it only allows communication *within* the ESX host. The internal switch could possibly be used as a staging area where you build a virtual machine before "patching" it to production network.

Alternatively, you can use them to emulate a sophisticated network environment. As one vSwitch cannot "auto-magically" communicate with another vSwitch, you could use them to create what VMware calls a "Firewall-in-the-box," linking the various switches together to VMs with more than one NIC containing Network Address Translation (NAT) software with firewall products, such as Microsoft ISA Server or Checkpoint. The only drawback of internal switches is that you cannot carry out VMotion events without first disconnecting users from the virtual machine. In a way this is understandable - they are "locked" within the ESX. They are "internal" to the ESX host, and therefore we could not 100% guarantee that users would get a continuous connection to the VM during the VMotion event.

The second type gives you basic connectivity to the outside world. This might be suitable for the VMotion network or one that doesn't require fault-tolerance such as a "test" network for test and development of virtual machines. It could be used to allow connectivity to IP based storage such as NAS, if that storage location is not offering anything "mission critical" such as access to an ISO file or VM templates.

The third type gives you fault-tolerance and load-balancing. This is ideal for VMs and IP storage where greater redundancy might be required.

You can have up to 20 physical NICs in an ESX host of any link speed. There are now 56 ports by default on vSwitch and this is configurable for up to 1016 ports. In the past, ESX 2.x users were limited to 8 gigabit or 16 100mps NICs on an ESX host and just 32 ports per vSwitch.

When two virtual machines communicate to each other on the *same* vSwitch, no physical network traffic is generated. The VMkernel moves the data in memory seamlessly from one VM to the other without ever hitting a physical network card. In this respect, you're not limited by the Ethernet access method "carrier sense multiple access with collision detection" (CSMA/CD). If you have two network intensive VMs, locate them on the *same* ESX host on the *same* *v*Switch. However, watch out for the other core resources as well as CPU, Memory and Disk performance.

Improvements in Networking open a new door of possibilities in ESX, and make certain network tasks much simpler than they have been in the past. For example, enabling IP based load-balancing on a vSwitch with multiple NIC's used to involve the hand editing of text files which can now be easily configured with a couple of clicks of the mouse.

What are Port Groups?

vSwitches can be sub-divided into smaller units called "port groups." While this technology has been in ESX 2.x onwards, it has now been expanded. In the past, ESX 2.x port groups were just a method of allowing virtual machines to interact with VLAN's. They still have this functionality but their purpose includes so much more. We have three types of port groups, each relating to a different type of traffic – with the most important probably being virtual machine traffic:

1. Virtual Machine port group

2. Service Console port group

3. VMkernel (for VMotion/IP Storage) port group

Theoretically, one vSwitch can have many NICs with many port groups, each configured for the Service Console, VMkernel IP Storage, VMotion, and VMs. Although this is certainly possible in ESX, we are still likely to want to maintain physically separate network traffic by NIC card.

GOTCHA:

Names of port groups are very important. They must be consistently named from one ESX host to another; if they are not consistently named you will have problems during VMotion and Cold Migration. Additionally, although the VI client is a Windows application, the definition of a virtual switch is stored on the ESX host in a text file (/etc/vmware/esx.conf). As such, they are also *case-sensitive*. Many people prefer scripted installations to make sure they achieve consistency.

GOTCHA:

One way of resolving this would be to rename port groups which are not a very simple procedure. However, it is not without consequences. When you rename a port group (even simply changing case, for example) virtual machines become "orphaned" from the switch because the name of the switch the VM is attached to is held in the virtual machine's configuration file (.vmx). If I have 32 virtual machines on one ESX host they would each have to be told the new vSwitch port group name. Some enterprising VMware Community forum members have written looping scripts to handle this for you, but it's perhaps best to avoid this situation in the first place.

Lastly, as we saw in the first chapter of this operations guide, ESX 3.x now has an IP firewall which is configurable through the GUI or command-line. The reasoning for this is twofold- there is now a full IP-stack on ESX which makes it fully NAS and iSCSI aware and because VMware's customers demanded one.

Creating an Internal Only Switch

1. Select your ESX host.

2. Select the Configuration Tab.

3. In the Hardware Pane, select Networking.

4. Click the Add Networking… link.

5. Choose Virtual Machine and Click Next.

6. Remove any tick next to any network adapters.

    Note:

    In Figure 2.1, when you do this, the preview window updates and states under "physical adapters" the words "No Adapters."

    Figure 2.1

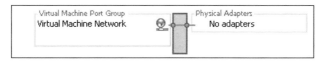

7. Click Next.

8. In the Port Groups Properties dialog, type a friendly name for this connection, such as internal0.

9. Click Finish.

Creating an NIC Team vSwitch

Creating a vSwitch with multiple NICs is as simple as adding an additional tick in a box. By doing this, you will grant every virtual machine on that switch the attributes of fault-tolerance and load-balancing. VMkernel configures this feature for you now, alleviating the use of proprietary wizards like Windows for Intel or Broadcom cards.

1. Select your ESX Host.

2. Select the Configuration Tab.

3. In the Hardware Pane, select Networking.

4. Click the Add Networking... link.

5. Choose Virtual Machine and Click Next.

6. Select two or more NICs.

7. Click Next

8. In the Port Groups Properties dialog, type a friendly name for this connection, such as production.

Figure 2.2 shows a vSwitch with a port group called production configured to use two NICs

Figure 2.2

Creating a vSwitch with VLAN Support

As in ESX 2.x, port groups can only also be used for adding VLAN support. In this case, multiple VMs connect to a single switch containing multiple port groups, each representing the different VLANs available. Actually, ESX support three different methods of enabling access to VLANs.

One method is to simply plug-in the relevant NICs to the relevant VLANs and set the VMs IP settings for that network. However, this method does consume a lot of network cards. For each VLAN you have you would need at least one NIC. If you also factor in the requirement for fault-tolerance, that would mean you need at least one vSwitch per VLAN with two NICs for each vSwitch. Once you get beyond a couple of VLANs you quickly begin to run out of network cards. However, if you only have a small number of VLANs, this "physical" approach has some benefit; it removes the need to speak to the physical switch administrator and is therefore seamless to the networking team. Unfortunately, sometimes avoiding politics and "change management" requests might be your over-riding criteria above and beyond choosing the best technological method.

The port group method requires the fewest network cards and the smallest amount of administration. The downside of this method is that you must persuade your switch administrators to enable IEEE 802.1Q VLAN Tagging on their physical switches.

In 802.1q VLAN Tagging, the network interfaces are plugged into what are called "trunk ports" on the physical switch. Trunk ports allow *many* VLAN packets to traverse them. Even with just one or two network cards, ESX can allow multiple VMs access to many VLANs. There is a very slight CPU burden on the VMkernel, but the overhead is so tiny that they are insignificant.

As each VM communicates with its port group and is about to leave the physical server, the VMkernel adds 4-bytes to the pack. This includes the flag indicating this packet is a VLAN packet and its VLAN number. This packet traverses the trunk port and is intercepted by the physical switch. The physical switch then directs the packet to the appropriate VLAN Broadcast Domain.

As with NIC teaming, no special work is required of your given guest OS (Windows, Linux, Novell, Solaris); the clever stuff is done by VMkernel, leaving the VM totally unaware it's on a VLAN.

In this example, as I am running out of network ports, I am going to remove the "production" port group to create new port groups with the VLAN information in-place.

1. Select the Configuration Tab.

2. In the Hardware Pane, select Networking.

3. click Properties... of vSwitch2 your "production" Port Group.

4. In the vSwitch2 Properties dialog, click the Production Port Group, and click the Remove button.

5. Then click Add, and in the Add Network Wizard, choose Virtual Machine.

6. In the Port Group Properties dialog, type a friendly name like accounts or vlan95.

7. In the VLAN ID (Optional) field type: 95.

8. Click Next and Finish, repeating this for other VLAN IDs by adding additional port groups.

Figure 2.3 shows this configuration with an additional two port groups called sales and distribution, representing VLAN 96 and 97, respectively.

Figure 2.3

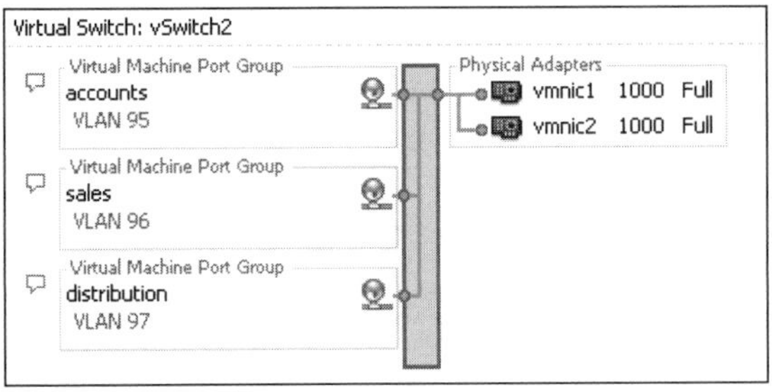

Note:

Personally, I like to name my port groups after the VLAN ID. Even though a description displays in this interface (of VLAN 95 for example), when you plug a VM into the port group all you will see is its friendly name, such as Accounts, Sales, or Distribution.

Creating a VMkernel Switch for VMotion

A very popular configuration is enabling VMkernel port group for use with Vmotion, which is moving a VM from one ESX host to another in real time without powering off the VM. VMotion is essentially a network event – cloning a VM memory from one ESX host to another until they are in the exact state. Once both VMs are identical, the original one can be switched off. This requires a VMkernel port to be configured and gigabit networking between the hosts in question.

When you create a VMkernel port group on vSwitch you will be asked to enter an IP Address, Subnet Mask, and, optionally, a Default Gateway; you may wonder why you're doing this again, since you already set these values during the ESX install. Here, we are setting up an IP configuration for the VMkernel, whereas in the installation we were configuring the IP address of the Service Console merely for management purposes.

1. Select the Configuration Tab.

2. In the Hardware Pane, select Networking.

3. Click the Add Networking… link.

4. Choose VMkernel and Click Next.

    Note:

    In this case 3 of my 4 NICs are assigned (1 to Service Console, 2 to Production, 0 to Internal). The dialog gives me the option to take NICs assigned to other switches if I wish.

5. Click Next.

6. In the Port Groups Properties dialog, type a friendly name for this connection, such as vmotion.

7. Enable X Use this port group for VMotion.

8. Set an IP Address and Subnet mask for VMotion.

Figure 2.4 shows setting the port group name, and enabling vmotion with the relevant IP settings. I am going to use 10.0.0.1/255.0.0.0 for esx1.vi3book.com and 10.0.0.2/255.0.0.0 for esx2.vi3book.com – and so on.

Figure 2.4

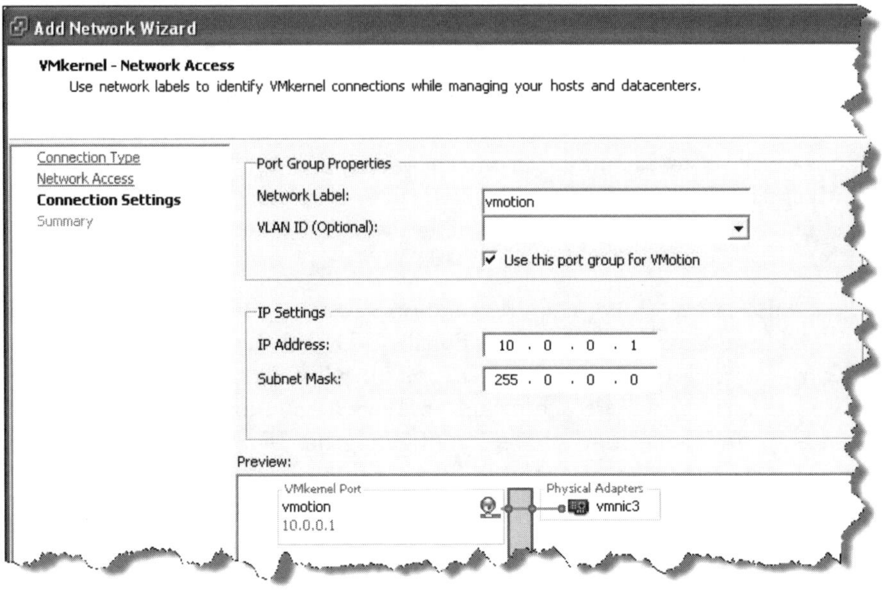

Add Network Wizard

VMkernel - Network Access
Use network labels to identify VMkernel connections while managing your hosts and datacenters.

Connection Type
Network Access
Connection Settings
Summary

┌─ Port Group Properties ─
Network Label: [vmotion]
VLAN ID (Optional):   [▼]

☑ Use this port group for VMotion

┌─ IP Settings ─
IP Address: [10 . 0 . 0 . 1]
Subnet Mask: [255 . 0 . 0 . 0]

Preview:

VMkernel Port
vmotion
10.0.0.1   Physical Adapters
                                            vmnic3

9. You will then receive this message:

    "There is no default gateway set. You must set a default gateway before you can use this port group. Do you want to configure it now"

    Note: Does "must" mean must?

    This message can be a little misleading because of the word "must." At this stage, we have been told VMware has no intention of allowing VMotion across routers. So really the dialog box should say "may need." You would only need a default gateway entry if there was a router between the ESX host and the resource being accessed.

    One example of this is when a VMkernel port group is used to access iSCSI and NAS/NFS devices (more about this in the Storage Chapter). In that case you may well need to set the default gateway to cross the router.

This pop-up dialog can be an annoyance because it reappears every time you create VMkernel port group. Sometimes I set up a bogus address just to stop it from appearing.

Broken Network Links

Network links can be broken for many reasons:

- Broken NIC

- Broken Cable

- Switch /Port Failure

Just like many popular operating systems, the VI client will show you if you have network failure by flagging an interface with a red exclamation mark in the network section. Figure 2.5 shows this.

Figure 2.5

Popular vSwitch and Port Group Configurations

Increasing the Number of Ports on vSwitch

In ESX 2.x, we were only allowed 32 virtual machines per vSwitch. You can increase the number of fixed numbers from 24, 56, 120, 248,504 and 1016. What might seem odd about these numbers is they are exactly 8 digits less than what you might expect (32, 64, 128, 256, 512 and 1032). So what happened to the other 8 ports? Well, those 8 ports are there but they are in use by the VMkernel for background monitoring processes.

Caution:

Changing this value requires a reboot of ESX for it to take effect.

1. Select your ESX Host.

2. Select the Configuration Tab.

3. In the Hardware Pane, select Networking.

4. Click Properties... allowing you to switch which one contains the port group labeled production (in my case this is vSwitch2).

5. In the dialog box click the Edit... button.

6. Under the General Tab, click the pull down list for the number of ports:

Figure 2.6 shows the pull down list for the number of ports. The message behind reads, "Changes will not take effect until the system is restarted."

Figure 2.6

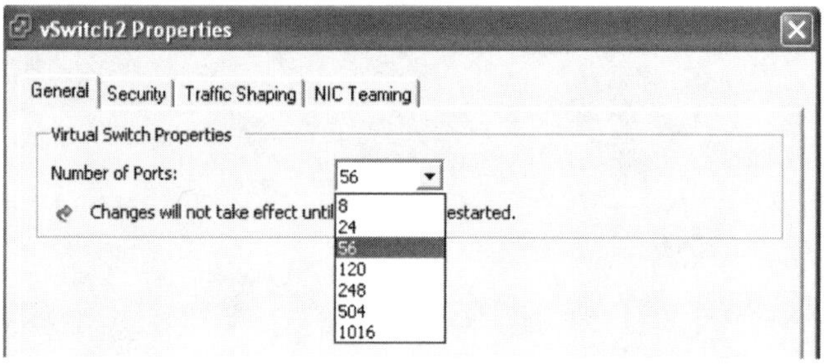

7. Click OK...

Setting Speed & Duplex on Physical NICs

The IEEE recommends setting the gigabit-to-gigabit to auto-negotiate. In fact, if you want to fix the speed and duplex in gigabit environments, this is *usually* done at the switch, not at the NIC. Even if you fix the speed and duplex settings of gigabit card, it still auto-negotiates anyway. So these settings are really only relevant perhaps in the Service Console's vSwitch (vSwitch0) where you may perhaps still be using 100mps.

1. Select your ESX Host.

2. Select the Configuration Tab.

3. In the Hardware Pane, select Networking.

4. Click Properties... of vSwitch*N*.

5. Click the Network Adapters Tab.

6. Select the NIC adapter and Click the Edit button.

7. Select the Speed & Duplex and click OK.

Note:

For ESX 2.x people - you might be interested to know you can now do this with the Service Console NIC without the need to edit /etc/modules.conf file.

vSwitch and Port group Policies

If you look at the properties of vSwitch *and the* properties of a port group, you will see very similar tabs. These are:

• Security

• Traffic Shaping

• NIC Teaming

You might ask why they appear twice. Well, the settings on the vSwitch form a "global policy," or rule, if you prefer, whereas the settings on the port group act as exceptions to that global policy. Put another way, you could have settings on vSwitch where "one size fits all," or have per port group settings to give your configuration more flexibility. The settings themselves don't differ; they merely adjust the scope of your changes. As with all security settings, before you decide to close the door you must first be sure that none of the traffic you are disabling is legitimate; the net result being you break one of your applications or services. It's worth saying that these settings are, to some degree, unique to the virtualization world, usually not available elsewhere in the physical world. Let's deal with the meaning and purpose of each of these dialog boxes in turn, starting with security.

The Security Settings Tab

Prior to the release of ESX 3.x, VMware had an audit of security which formed the basis of these new settings. Previously, these settings weren't configurable at all and if they were you had to manually edit a VMs configuration files (.vmx) to do so. VMware default settings are a compromise (as are all security settings) between security and usability. This is why you don't see *all* security options marked with the reject setting. Figure 2.7 shows the default settings on vSwitch for security.

Figure 2.7

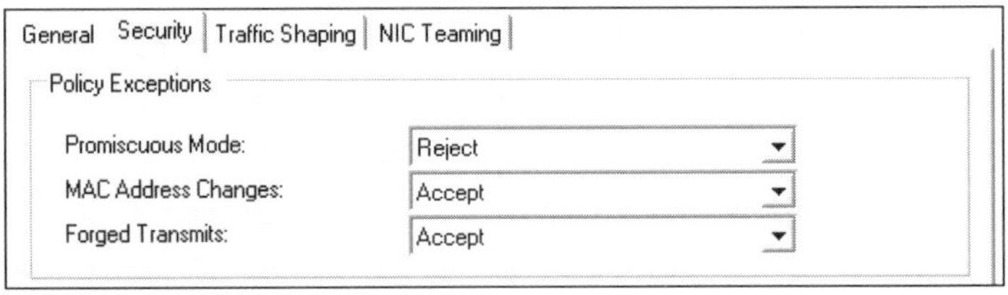

Promiscuous Mode, Default: Reject

As you might know from your "networking essentials" days, promiscuous mode describes a NIC that can collect all network packets, even ones not intended for it. It is generally used in network-sniffing applications that perhaps you use against a firewall to troubleshoot networking and such. Usually, you will find the promiscuous mode in Windows or Linux by looking at the setting of the network card. In VMware's networking architecture this behavior is not allowed. VMware wants to stop the compromised VM from being used as a tool by a potential hacker to attack the rest of the system. Of course, you could always be carrying out packet capturing for legitimate purposes. In that case, you could configure a special port group called "network-analysis" or something equally descriptive, and put a single VM on it.

MAC Address Changes; Default: Accept

Under normal operations, the MAC address of VM does not change. Of course, one thing a hacker may try to do is spoof the MAC address, as they do with an IP Address, to make other systems assume they are sending legitimate traffic.

In a VM, its virtual MAC address is automatically created by algorithm to ensure its uniqueness (the algorithm uses a combination of UUID and unique location of the VM's configuration file). This allows changing the MAC from within the guest operating system, even if the MAC address stored in the VMX file of the VM is different. I've had this situation arise when using Fedora Core 5. Once, I created a brand new VMX file for existing virtual disk. As the Fedora Core 5 operating system loaded, the operating system complained that the MAC of address of my virtual NIC was different from the one stored in the OS. The MAC address of the Fedora Core 5 is also stored in /etc/sysconfig/network-scripts/ifcfg-eth0. Fortunately, I had not altered the default security settings and communication did work, despite the warnings from the guest operating system. If I had changed the setting to 'reject' all *inbound frames* would have been dropped by the ESX host. Later, in the lifetime of this VM, I made the MAC address of the VMX file the same as the MAC address held in ifcfg-eth0. This resolved the warning messages in my VM.

There are some special cases where the MAC address of a VM does change. Microsoft Clustering and VERITAS Clustering are two good examples of services running inside a VM.

Forged Transmits; Default Accept

These are very similar to MAC Address changes, except the restriction is not on the MAC address changing, but rather on a VM being allowed to send traffic under a MAC address which is different from the virtual machines. Again, some "advanced" networking technologies, such as Microsoft's Network Load-balancing, could break if this were configured. If it is set to reject, all outbound frames generated by the VM are dropped by the ESX host.

The Moral of the Story

For the most part, the default settings are good ones – and if in doubt leave them alone. Make sure you thoroughly test your VMs if you do change the default settings.

The Traffic Shaping Tab

Traffic shaping is the ESX method of controlling outbound traffic generated by VMs heading out of the server on to your wider physical network. You might ask, "Why doesn't VMware have a method to control traffic inbound to the ESX host?" The answer is simple; for the VMkernel to analyze the traffic, it has to arrive at the network interfaces which would cause a performance hit. By then the "damage is already done," so to speak, and limiting can only happen outbound (where the VMkernel has control).

Outbound shaping limits aside, this is an interesting feature. Firstly, it allows us to whittle network performance down to incredibly small amounts – to kps even! Secondly, it acts as a "cap" to network performance. Even if the bandwidth is there, traffic shaped by virtual machines continues to just the amount you have given it. This has some interesting possibilities; the ability to emulate WAN speeds between two ESX hosts, for instance. However, this wouldn't truly reflect the latency and retransmits that typify WAN communications, but it could be used in a pinch. Traffic shaping also comes with some down sides; it's not dynamic - it can't react to changes of circumstances. Once you set the configuration you have some burst rules allowed, but limiting bandwidth based on logic is not available.

Another interesting consideration would be to ask the following question; "What traffic management do we currently do on our LAN?" The answer to this question is nearly none. Most LANs operate on a first-come, first-served basis – and we don't do any traffic management at all. Far from "throttling" our network we try give our VMs as much bandwidth as we possibly can, within reason. Another worry might be that during the hours of 9am-5pm we might wish to throttle network bandwidth used by VM – but what if we are still running backup agents within the VM and running network backups between the hours of 6pm-6am? There isn't any built-in way to indicate when the traffic shaper module is active and non-active.

So, with these caveats in place, how does this feature work? You set three values – an average, a peak, and the burst size. Figure 2.8 shows the standard settings for traffic shaping.

Figure 2.8

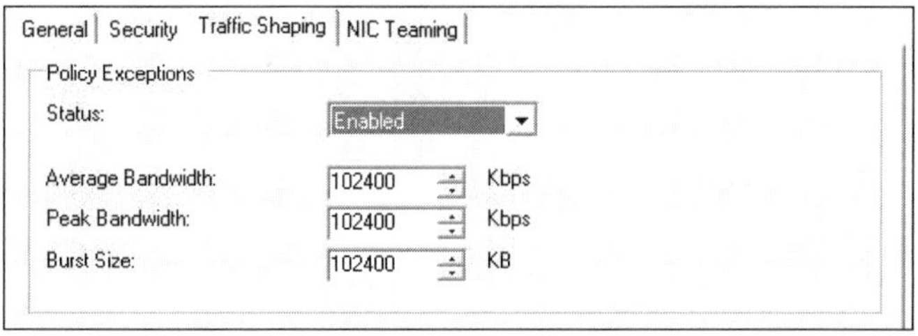

The peak acts a cap – an upper maximum over which the virtual machines cannot rise. The burst acts a little like a window size. As all bandwidth is measured by time over the amount of data we can send (57kps, 512kps), the burst size basically controls this. When the burst size is full, i.e. we have used all of our allocation, then ESX pushes the VMs back down under their average line. In this respect, peak is always more than average, and it's actually the average value that acts as throttle on network bandwidth.

The NIC Teaming Tab

This is a busy dialog box which has lots of very interesting settings. Having said this, I only change two on a regular basis. Some of the options are Boolean – by which I mean there are only two choices, such as "Network Failover Detection" and "Notify Switches." Alternatively, some of the settings have 4 options associated with them, such as the "Load-balancing" options. I want to clear the simpler settings, then move on to more complex settings, so I can gradually drill down to increasing complexity – rather than jumping in head first.

Figure 2.9 shows the standard default settings for the NIC Teaming Tab.

Figure 2.9

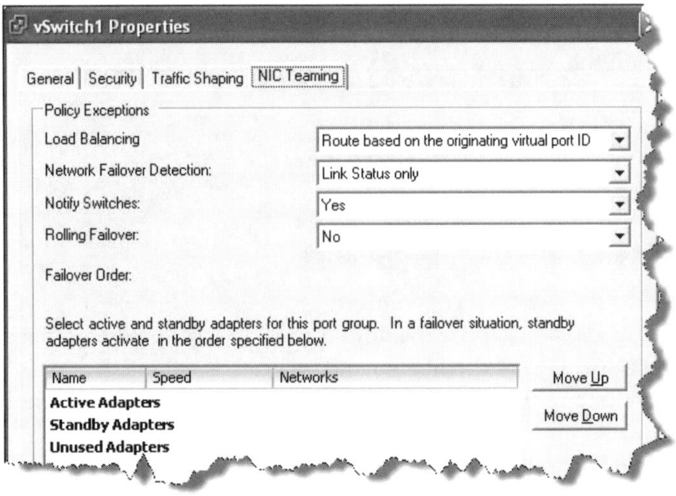

Network Failover Detection

This setting controls how ESX detects a network failure, thus triggering the movement of packets from one adapter to another in vSwitch with more than one NIC attached to it. I usually change this to "Beacon Probing" from its default of "Link Status Only." These settings control how ESX detects a network failure. The default is very similar to the guest OS systems you run. This will detect a failed NIC, failed cable, or failure of a switch/hub to which the server is directly attached. After that, "link status only" has no idea if other paths are valid. In contrast, "Beacon Probing" is able to see beyond the first uplink to the physical switch by sending a packet between the NICs in the vSwitch. This has some issues; a dropped packet, regardless of the reason, can make the system think a nic is down when it isn't. Beacon probing is rarely used in production ESX environments, and I won't be recommending it here.

Notify Switches

The "yes" default setting here indicates that when failures occur, a Reverse Address Resolution Protocol packet (ARP is the protocol that relates your MAC address to IP Address) is sent out to physical switches. This updates the lookup tables on physical switches that VMs packets must be sent to different physical NICs because the original network path is now unavailable. This is a good setting because it ensures that packets will be successfully delivered and reduces the chance of any lost packets during Vmotion. In VMotion the VMs virtual MAC address remains unchanged, once the VM has been moved from one ESX host to another; the *physical* MAC addresses have most definitely changed. Additionally, notifications are issued whenever you add or remove a physical NIC from the vSwitch. For the most part this setting is a good one and should not be changed unless you are using Microsoft Network Load-balancing (NLB) within a VM. This setting is incompatible with Microsoft NLB when NLB is set to unicast mode. However, if you are using Microsoft NLB in multicast mode there is not a problem.

Load-Balancing within a vSwitch

Once you create a vSwitch with more than one network card you have, by default, created a format of load-balancing. In this dialog box you can tweak the network settings considerably. There are in fact, four different ways of configuring multiple NICs with a vSwitch. They are:

1. Originating Port ID

2. Source MAC Address Hash

3. IP Hash

4. Explicit Failover

In reality, options 1-3 represent real load-balancing options, whereas "Explicit Fail Over" allows us to manually configure how multiple cards are used and works in conjunction with the "Rolling Failover" setting and the active/standby feature. Let's deal with Option 1-3 in the first instance.

Originating Port

Basically, this algorithm makes each VM use the next available NIC in the bundle. It's a bit like a round-robin effect; if I had a virtual switch with three NICs mapped to it, it would cycle between them. So VM1 would use vmnic1; VM2 would use vmnic2, and then VM3 would use vmnic3. After that VM4, VM5, and VM6 would use vmnic1, 2, and 3. The effect is a crude form of load-balancing on each of the NICs. Sounds good, doesn't it? In most cases, it is just fine and a default used in 90+% of environments. It should be noted though, that there is no awareness of link speeds, how heavily saturated a link is, or the latency on a given uplink. Its main merit is its compatibility with all physical switches and reduces complexity on the networking side.

Source MAC Address Hash

This method used to be the default in ESX 2.x and is an algorithm that does a computation via the MAC address. This is somewhat more intelligent than "originating port." However, as routers (and some switches) hide the MAC address of the source MAC address, it is load-balancing with limits. The algorithm simply isn't intelligent enough to work out the best "trip" for the packet with the limited amount of information it has at its disposal.

IP Hash

This is the Rolls Royce of load-balancing. It uses the source and destination IP address to work out the best trip for the packet to take. It is aware of latency because it is IP based – and it's also aware when a link is saturated. Lastly, the IP hash is aware of clients that have communicated across a router to the VM running on an ESX host. With all these attributes at its disposal, the IP hash has much better knowledge of the effect of network traffic on overall performance. The trade-off is a more complex configuration that needs to be maintained. This configuration is used in a small number of environments, and often (for our customers) found to be too complex for the benefits seen when weighed against the needs of the VMs. I mean, really, have you looked at network utilization on 95% of your servers? They often average below 5MB.

GOTCHA:

Again, as with some of the security settings, the IP Hash method is incompatible with Microsoft Network Load Balancing (NLB) in unicast mode. If you have NLB working in multicast mode there is not a problem.

Explicit Fail-Over

This is not so much a load-balancing technique as a stricter way of controlling what happens when NICs fail. If you engage it, you have two other settings: "Rolling Failover" and Active/Standby Adapter section of the dialog box.

Explicit Failover, as the name suggests, allows you to set so many adapters as "active" and so many adapters as "standby." The active ones can have load-balancing features (as long as there is more than one listed!), and the standby NICs only engage if the actives fail. Explicit failover does not wait for all the active adapters to fail before engaging the standbys. As soon as one active NIC fails, a standby is selected from the order in the list and is used.

Rolling Failover controls what happens when a failed NIC becomes available again. It's actually quite a confusing label for VMware to use. This is because far from controlling failover, it is actually used to control fail back settings. That is to say – what happens when an active NIC fails, and then later what happens when that NIC returns to an active state.

If you set rolling failover to "no" when a failed NIC comes on stream again the "active" adapter can be used immediately, taking over the role of the standby adapter. If rolling failover is set to "yes" the NIC that comes back on stream again is not used until another "active" adapter fails. The assumption here is that if you have lost an NIC, you might begin to distrust its reliability so setting "yes" would stop it being used again – unless you had another failure. One way of using this feature is when you have a team of two NICs and one is 1000mps and the other is 100mps. You would make the 1000mps card active, and put the 100mps card on standby. Rolling failover would be set to "no." Now, if the 1000mps card failed it would failover the 100mps card when the 1000mps card was active again, ESX would return to the "home" adapter.

Using this feature allows you to have very good control over which VMs use which network card because we now set these parameters on port groups. In the past, these settings were only available on a vSwitch. This was a bit "one size fits all." The downside of this kind of configuration is that could get very complicated. You might prefer to follow the "KISS" principle – keep it simple, stupid.

Using all the features together

I could create one vSwitch with three port groups – accounts, sales and distribution each with a separate VLAN ID. However, the vSwitch could have 6 physical network interfaces which are set-up with "trunk ports." Therefore, any one of these NICs could be used to send data to the correct VLAN as long as the right VMs are plugged into the right port groups. I could use "explicit failover" to allocate which was their preferred NIC like this:

Accounts port group

Active: vmnic1, vmnic2

Standby: vmnic3, vmnic4, vmnic5, vmnic6

Sales port group

Active: vmnic3, vmnic4

Standby: vmnic1, vmnic2, vmnic5, vmnic6

Distribution port group

Active: vmnic5, vmnic6

Standby: vmnic1, vmnic2, vmni3, vmnic4

Figure 2.10 shows this particular configuration. Normally, each port group has its own dedicated NICs which are configured for "IP hash" load-balancing, and Beacon Probing has been enabled. Under normal operations the accounts port group would prefer to use vmnic1 and vmnic2. This means that if there was a lot of network activity within the sales or distribution port groups it would have no impact as they prefer to use vmnic3/4 and vmnic5/6. We get excellent redundancy because there are six NICs that could be possibly used at any one time. Rolling failover has been set to "no" so if vmnic1 or 2 go offline, when they come back on stream again we get the separation of network traffic under normal operations. This configuration also allows for specific security and traffic shaping settings to be applied to accounts (and the virtual machines configured to use it) without it affecting the sales and distribution port groups.

Figure 2.10

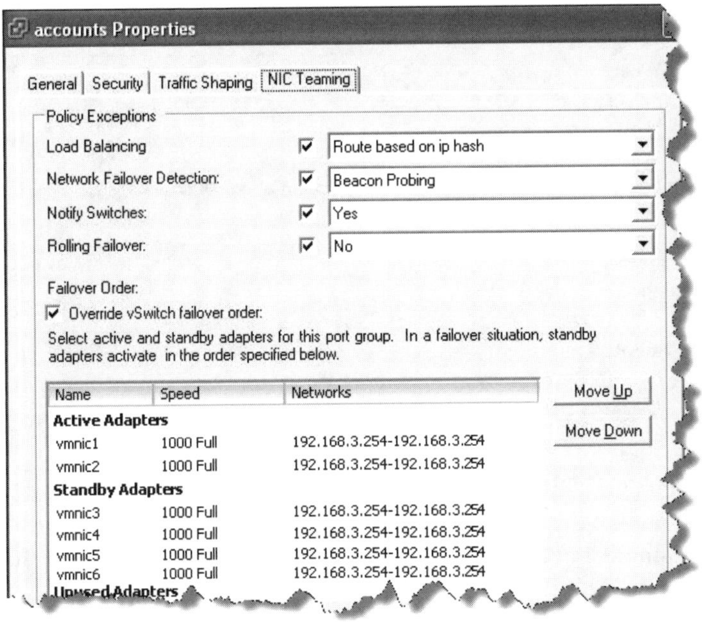

Creating Standby vSwitches

It is possible to set up a configuration by which a vSwitch has more than one adapter where some of the NICs are active and some of the NICs are standby. The idea behind this is to guarantee a degree of quality of service. So, if you lost one NIC you could replace it with the same level of bandwidth. To do this, you configure a vSwitch to have more than one NIC and set some to be Active and others to be standby; next, set NIC Teaming options for Load-balancing to be "Use Explicit Failover order." Figure 2.11 shows the configuration in question.

Figure 2.11

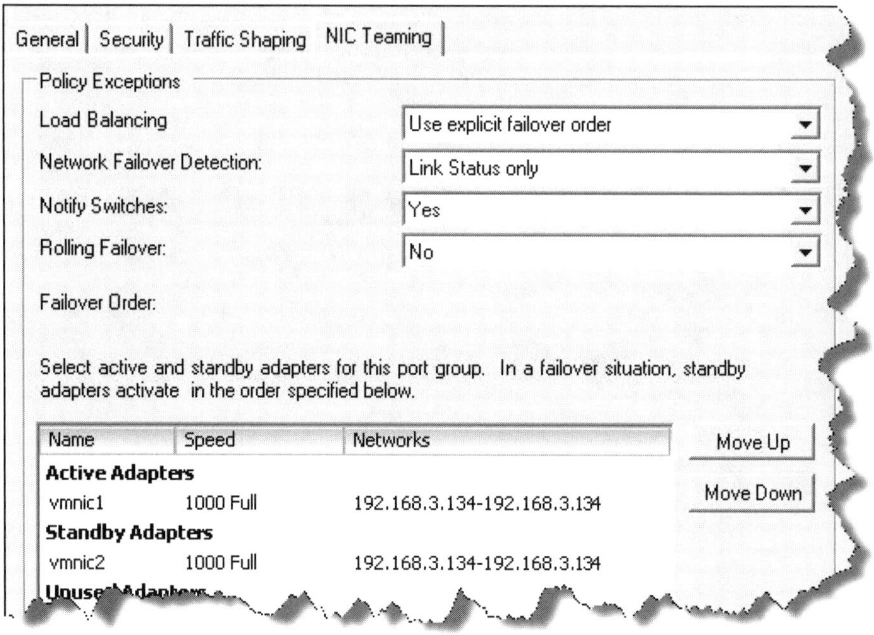

General | Security | Traffic Shaping   NIC Teaming |

Policy Exceptions

Load Balancing | Use explicit failover order ▼

Network Failover Detection: | Link Status only ▼

Notify Switches: | Yes ▼

Rolling Failover: | No ▼

Failover Order:

Select active and standby adapters for this port group. In a failover situation, standby adapters activate in the order specified below.

Name	Speed	Networks	
Active Adapters			Move Up
vmnic1	1000 Full	192.168.3.134-192.168.3.134	Move Down
Standby Adapters			
vmnic2	1000 Full	192.168.3.134-192.168.3.134	
Unused Adapters			

After clicking "OK," the VI client will refresh and indicate which NIC is active and which is standby. Figure 2.12 and Figure 2.13 show this configuration, when the vmnic1 is functioning, and when failover has occurred because it has malfunctioned, respectively.

Figure 2.12 without a failover

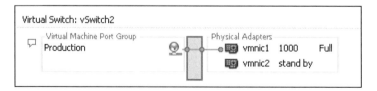

Figure 2.13 with a failover

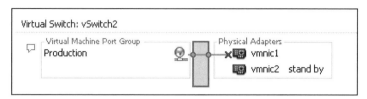

As illustrated, it is very easy to see the settings if active and standby NICs are configured at vSwitch level. It is less clear in the VI client if you enable active and standby at port group level. Figure 2.14 shows a vSwitch with many port groups, and I have configured different active and standby settings. As you can see, it is not immediately clear what kind of configuration I've created with respect to active and standby adapters.

Figure 2.14

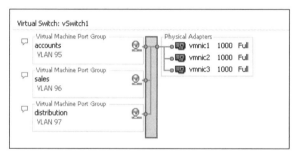

By clicking the small blue "speech bubble" icon next to each port group it is possible to view each setting. This stops you from unnecessarily navigating through layers of dialog boxes, properties options, and edit buttons to view your settings. Figure 2.15 shows the pop-up settings box.

Figure 2.15

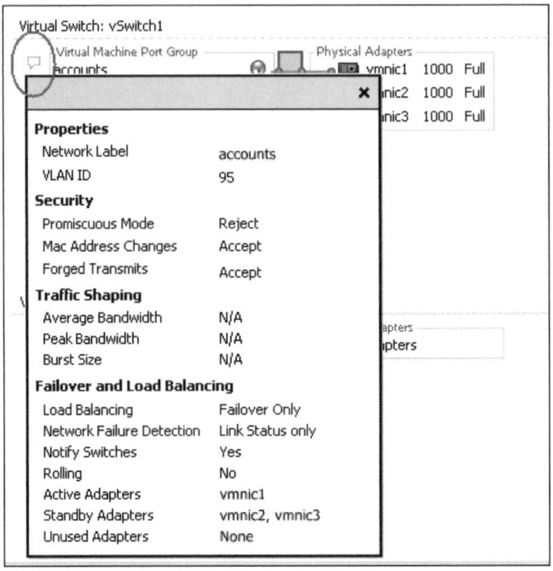

Virtual Switch: vSwitch1

			Physical Adapters		
			vmnic1	1000	Full
		×	nic2	1000	Full
			nic3	1000	Full

Properties

Network Label	accounts
VLAN ID	95

Security

Promiscuous Mode	Reject
Mac Address Changes	Accept
Forged Transmits	Accept

Traffic Shaping

Average Bandwidth	N/A
Peak Bandwidth	N/A
Burst Size	N/A

Failover and Load Balancing

Load Balancing	Failover Only
Network Failure Detection	Link Status only
Notify Switches	Yes
Rolling	No
Active Adapters	vmnic1
Standby Adapters	vmnic2, vmnic3
Unused Adapters	None

Managing Service Console Networking

Meanwhile, back in the real world, all my NICs are now fully allocated on my 4-NIC server. If I want to configure other possibilities, I might have to free up NICs by removing one NIC from production vSwitch or by removing the VMotion switch I just created to free up its NIC.

Figure 2.16 shows what my cleanly installed ESX server looks like now from a networking perspective:

Figure 2.16

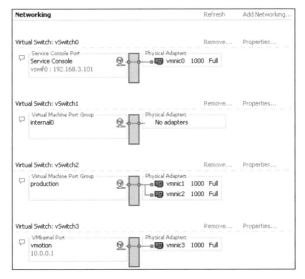

Now I want to show you some configuration settings related specifically to the Service Console, such as adding a "backup" Service Console connection and how to modify your IP settings originally configured during the installation.

Creating a "Backup" Port group for the Service Console

Up until ESX 3.x, there's always been a single point of failure on the ESX host - the Service Console network. If the single NIC (vmnic0) on vSwitch0 failed we would have no management over the ESX host except by its ILO card. Remember, if our VMs were on a different vSwitch configured with many vmNICs they would remain unaffected.

In ESX 3.x the networking architecture treats the Service Console as if it were just another VM connected to a virtual switch. This default switch is called vSwitch0 and, incidentally, the default number of ports on the vSwitch is just 24 rather than 56.

These Service Console ports have a special name; "vswif." which stands for **V**irtual **Sw**itch **I**nterface. They are serialized as you create them, with the first being vswif0, the second being vswif1, and so on.

If you have "spare" network adapters, it's very easy to protect the Service Console network by adding another vSwitch with the Service Console port group – or adding an additional Service Console port group to an existing vSwitch.

1. Select the Configuration Tab.

2. In the Hardware Pane, select Networking.

3. Select the Properties… link next to the production vSwitch.

4. Select Service Console.

    Note:

    As we already have a service Console port, the system names this Service Console 2.

5. Click Next.

6. Complete the IP Settings as befits your network infrastructure.

7. Click Next.

Figure 2.17 shows how I have created a backup Service Console port group on my VMotion switch. This is safe because it's not my primary network for managing VMs and VMotion is not event that happens very frequently. In Chapter 3, on Storage, you will learn that a second Service Console network is often required to configure the iSCSI Software Adapter. Additionally, in Chapter 10, which deals with High Availability, you will learn that this "backup" Service Console network can mitigate an unwanted event called the "split brain" phenomena in VMware HA.

Figure 2.17

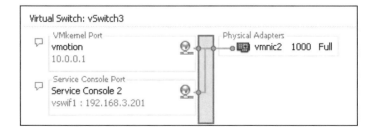

Note:

It's a good idea to confirm you can connect to this new port with ping/Putty and by pointing the VI client to this IP/Name.

Note:

As another way of "protecting" the Service Console network, try just by adding an additional NIC vSwitch; by doing so you will create a bond for the Service Console. However, most people would agree if I said this was a waste of bandwidth. If we have spare NICs we should really allocate them to the VMs. After all, they are the ones that require bandwidth and fault-tolerance.

Adding a second NIC is also a safer procedure than switching the NIC on the Service Console switch. For example, add in the second NIC (100mps) and re-move the first NIC (1000mps) and you shouldn't lose connectivity to the Service Console.

Changing the Service Consoles Network Settings

One reason to change your Service Console's settings is to change your IP Address, Subnet Mask, or Default Gateway. One of the dangers is if you make a mistake, it's a bit like sitting on a tree branch with a saw and sawing your way through the very branch that is holding you there!

If you are going to modify the primary connection for the Service Console, this could cause a disconnection. If this change goes horribly wrong, it is not the end of the world – we will be able to use the backup Service Console 2 network connection.

If you don't have a backup connection you will receive a warning. Figure 12.18 shows you the warning.

Figure 2.18

This dialog box *only* appears if you do not have a second "backup" Service Console connection.

The safest method is to connect your backup Service Console 2 network to the ESX host and then change Service Console Properties. This way you will not be disconnected in the process of changing the IP Address. If you do make a mistake you still have your "backup" connection in place.

1. Close your VI client.

2. Open the VI client using the Backup Service Console IP Address in the Server.

3. Select the Configuration Tab.

4. In the Hardware Pane, select Networking.

5. Select Properties... of vSwitch0 with the Port Group name of Service Console.

6. In the dialog box, select the Port Group of Service Console, and click Edit.

7. In the Service Console Properties Dialog box you can change your IP settings.

Troubleshooting the Service Console Networking

During the installation you may select the NIC used for the Service Console and also configure its IP settings. Occasionally, people get this wrong and select both the entirely wrong NIC and IP values. When this happens you have three options:

1. Re-install, and try again.

2. Walk to the server room and re-route the network cables to the correct switch.

3. Connect via ILO, and use command-line tools to correct your mistakes.

As you might gather, step 3 is the recommended method. Remember, if you are using the command-line it IS case-sensitive.

Correcting the "wrong NIC selected during installation" problem

We can rectify this problem by gradually adding in NICs while pinging the Service Console's IP address (assuming that the IP settings are correct). I normally use ping –t to do this – and as I add the NICs in, I can judge by whether I get a reply as an indication that I have found the correct network card. First, I type the command which lists my vSwitch configuration using the –l switch.

esxcfg-vswitch –l

This produces the output displayed in Figure 2-19. Here you can see that there is one vSwitch, which is vSwitch0, with one port group called "Service Console." The installer has selected, by default, the first NIC it could find – vmnic0.

Figure 2.19

Switch Name	Num Port	Used Ports	Uplink
vSwitch0	32	3	vmnic0

To see what NICs are available including settings such as vmnic name, PCI Bus details, driver, link speed, duplex, and vendor make and model , you can use the command

esxcfg-NICs –l

To link another NIC to the switch we can use the –L switch.

esxcfg-vswitch -L vmnic1 **vSwitch0**

I keep on doing this until I have a response. Once I have worked out, by a process of elimination, the correct NIC I unlink the NICs which were patched to vSwitch0/vswif0 using the –U switch.

esxcfg-vswitch -U vmnic0 **vSwitch0**

Using the esxcfg-vswitch –l, -L and –U command you can quickly change the preferred NIC for vSwitch0 and be up and running with the VI client in a short period of time.

Correcting your IP Settings

Occasionally people type the wrong IP address or subnet mask. One common problem that people have is not noticing that the ESX installer does some work for you by automatically setting the default gateway based on the IP address and subnet mask. If you set 192.168.3.101 and 255.255.255.0 as your IP address and subnet mask, respectively, the installer will pre-fill 192.168.3.254 as your default gateway and 192.168.3.1 as your primary DNS server.

Fortunately, if you have ILO or physical access to the server these settings are very easy to correct, either with esxcfg command-line tools or with a text editor to modify the configuration files. Again, you could use a ping –t against the IP address of the Service Console to check to see if you get responses.

To view your current IP address and subnet mask you can use the –l switch on the esxcfg-vswif command like so:

esxcfg-vswif –l

To change them, you can use the command with –i and –n switch. You also need to indicate which vswif interface you are changing; as you know you can have more than one for backup purposes.

esxcfg-vswif vswif0 –i 192.168.3.104 –n 255.255.255.0

If your problems reside with your default gateway or you incorrectly set the DNS settings, these can be fixed with a text editor. You could use a text called Vi if you wish; personally, I prefer to use a tool called nano. Linux users prefer to use Vi, as it is on every single Linux distribution, whereas nano only exists on Redhat Linux. If you do use nano remember to use the –w switch. This switches off the "word-wrap" feature which could corrupt the file if you're not careful.

If you're a novice and don't use the command-line very frequently, the nano tool should be sufficient for your infrequent usage. To correct your default gateway you need to edit the "network" file with nano.

nano –w /etc/sysconfig/network

Modify your default gateway, and exit and save using [ctrl+x] to exit nano, [Y] to accept changes, and "enter" to overwrite the original file. To make this change take effect we need to restart the networking for the Service Console with Redhat Linux's "service" command (again, the service command is not available on all Linux distributions but is available within the ESX Service Console).

service network restart

If your problems reside with the DNS settings you can edit these with

nano –w /etc/resolv.conf

Generally, if you have basic connectivity to the Service Console, many of these settings can actually be altered through the VI client. I've chosen to show you the esxcfg command because these may help in extreme cases where you simply cannot connect to your ESX host with the VI client!

If you do wish to change your default gateway, ESX host name, or DNS settings, navigate to the **Configuration Tab,** then the **Software Pane,** select DNS and Routing and choose **Properties...** in the top right-hand corner.

Using Third Party ESX Host Network Tools

By now you are probably noticing a significant administrative overhead in the area of configuring networking. Each ESX host's networking is configured separately and the VI client is not really geared up for "bulk" edits or multiple edits of many ESX hosts. This is especially burdensome considering that one of things I have stressed is the importance of consistently labeled port groups. There are two approaches to this problem right now.

In the first approach, you could script your installations and use command-line tools such as esxcfg-vswitch, esxcfg-vswif, and esxcfg-vmknic. The trouble with these tools is that they do not allow for complete configuration of all the network features. For example, none of these tools allow you to enable VMotion on a VMkernel port group. This is because their design by VMware's intention) was to use them for "troubleshooting" purposes only.

The second approach is using a third party tool that does support multiple selections for creating switches. This is also useful if you need to reconfigure ESX host sometime after their initial configuration by scripting or by hand. This tool is called VM Client and was written by Flores Eken of the Netherlands, who currently works for a consulting firm called ITQ. Flores' work is hosted on:

http://www.run-virtual.com/?page_id=160

Right now the tool is great for modifying port groups across multiple switches and setting additional information, like VLAN information. What it lacks is the ability to create vSwitches.

Chapter 3: Storage

In this module we will be looking at the three primary ESX 3.x storage options – Storage Area Network (SAN), Internet SCSI (iSCSI), and Network Attached Storage (NAS). Additionally, we will take a look at VMware's File System (VMFS) and explain how to format and extend a VMFS volume.

By their nature SAN and iSCSI systems are very proprietary. My intention here is not to teach about the configuration of HP, IBM, or EMC storage, but to explain and demonstrate how VMware can leverage this storage.

Configuring SAN based storage

One of the most common tasks required of an ESX administrator is finding out their World Wide Name (WWN). This is a 64-bit address, stamped on every Host Bus Adapter (HBA) that has a connection to the SAN. The reason storage people request this information is that they use this address to allow or deny access to LUNs on the SAN. You can see that the WWN is akin to the MAC address on a network card.

It is extremely unlikely that anyone will buy a SAN and only use it with ESX server. It is very likely that existing physical servers running an array of very different OS would have access to the same SAN. Since none of the following share a common-file-system, corruption of data is possible: ESX, Linux, Novell, Windows, and Solaris.

SAN administrators use the WWN to "mask," or hide, these LUNs to make sure the right OS sees the right LUNs. Usually the SAN vendors will have their own product specific term for this feature. For example, HP calls their technology "Presentation" or "Selective Presentation." If your SAN does not support firmware-based "LUN Masking" then you might be interested to know that ESX server can mask the LUNs through an ESX server configuration setting (Configuration Tab, Software Pane, Advanced Settings and setting called Disk.MaskLUN'S). This said, most production SANs will support LUN masking and this should always be preferred over and above any other software method.

As an ESX administrator, you might be required to provide the WWN of your server or servers so that storage people will be able to set this up. Alternatively, if you are fortunate enough to manage your own SAN you may require this information personally.

Lastly, some organizations go that extra step further. Alongside LUN masking they might also create "zones," similar to Ethernet's VLAN, for these SAN switches. It's a way of configuring the switch into smaller networks. So, not only is a server restricted by its WWN, it would also need to be plugged into the correct port within the correct zone. Additionally, this zoning can offer some performance benefits to the fabric.

Finding out your HBA's WWN

As with network cards, all storage adapters are labeled vmhba0, vmhba1 and so on. Usually the internal RAID controller card has a HBA number of 0 because this naming convention merely looks at the PCI bus and serializes the storage adapters as they are found during the installation. So in most cases, your first fiber channel HBA is likely to be vmhba1 and so on.

4. Select your ESX host.

5. Click the Configuration Tab.

6. In the Hardware Pane choose Storage Adapters.

Rescanning SAN LUNs

After new LUNs have been made available, or the storage people have done their work, you will need to force a rescan of the HBA from the VI Client. On boot-up, ESX scans all the LUNs it is able to see – but you really don't want to do unnecessary reboots of the ESX server itself just to see a new LUN. This is why the rescan feature exists.

ESX server can see up to a maximum of 256 LUNs. That's LUN 0 to LUN 255. In ESX 2.x there was a setting called Disk.MaxLUN that would stop this scanning once an ESX host had scanned from LUN0 to LUN7. This value has now been changed, mainly to reduce the number of support requests generated by VMware customers not knowing about the Disk.MaxLUN value.

The settings for Disk.MaxLUN have now been changed to 256 with a starting and scanning position of 1. On some systems, LUN0 is a management LUN and should not be used. You should consult your documentation if you are not sure.

The rescan dialog box allows you to rescan for new LUNs and also check if they contain VMFS volumes. To force a rescan:

1. Select your ESX host.

2. Click the Configuration Tab.

3. In the Hardware Pane.

4. Under Storage Adapters.

5. Select the HBA you wish to rescan,

6. Click the Rescan… from the top right-hand corner of the VI Client.

7. Click OK to the dialog box.

Note:

You can also force a rescan using the command-line tool esxcfg-rescan. Its parameters are esxcfg-rescan vmhbaN, where vmhbaN is the host bus adapter used for the rescan process. Its ability to show you the LUN discovery process in more detail can be useful.

Understanding the vmhbaA:T:L:V syntax

ESX server uses a special syntax so that the VMkernel can find its "path" to the storage it is using. This is used by local storage, SAN, and iSCSI. The syntax of vmhbaN:N:N:N is a sequence of numbers which tells the VMkernel how to navigate to the storage location in question. This syntax is not unique to ESX server; it has been in used in UNIX for many years.

It is best remembered by the acronym A:T:L:V which stands for Adapter: Target: LUN: and Volume. The target in SAN or iSCSI environment represents the storage processors (SP) on the disk array. The first three digits (A:T:L) begin their numbering at 0, whereas the last digit (V) starts with 1.

For example, vmhba2:1:18:3 would tell me I was using the third HBA (0,1,2) connected to the second storage processor (0,1) using the LUN 18 – and the volume or partition I was dealing would be the third partition (3).

Note: Remember LUN 18 is actually the 19th LUN, as we start counting from 0.

In day-to-day operations you usually won't need to know this syntax. Most people use volume and datastore labels which are available when you format a LUN as VMFS. However, you will need to know this syntax when formatting VMFS volumes and to configure other advanced storage options such as Raw Device Mapping (RDM) files. These RDM files allow the ESX administrator to give a VM direct access to LUNs on a SAN or iSCSI system. We will look at RDM files in Chapter 5 when I cover creating and modifying VMs.

iSCSI

iSCSI is a competitor to SANs. This said, frequently the people who make SANs make iSCSI equipment, too. iSCSI is very similar to SAN technology in that it is capable of presenting a LUN to server. What makes iSCSI different is the transport used to carry the SCSI commands. It uses TCP port 3260 to carry out this communication. So, watch out if you work in a restrictive firewall environment, as this port may not be opened.

iSCSI uses your normal Ethernet network infrastructure to carry the commands themselves. This means you don't necessarily need special HBAs and special switches as conventional network cards and switches will do just as well, although it is possible to buy iSCSI HBAs which are optimized for performance.

This also allows you to leverage your existing IP knowledge and equipment. In the future, because iSCSI is, by definition, "internet aware/ready," replicating data from one location to another might be much easier to achieve than it currently is with fibre channel networking.

You can use conventional network cards to connect to an iSCSI system. VMware refers to this as the "Software Initiator." VMware's software iSCSI is actually part of Cisco's iSCSI Initiator Command Reference. The software initiator inside the VMkernel works together with a vmkiscis daemon in the Service Console environment.

Alternatively, you can buy an adapter that is designed for iSCSI communication, which VMware refers to as a "Hardware Initiator" from companies like Qlogic. As the name suggests, an initiator is the side that begins the communication (the client) to the iSCSI target (the disk array). Hardware initiators have what is called a TCP Off-Load Engine (TOE chip) which improves performance by removing the load from the main CPUs. In the future, all systems will have a TOE chip which will be enabled/disabled in the BIOS. In fact, the new HP G5s already supports this multi-functionality.

Another unique iSCSI feature is its use of a different naming convention. iSCSI does not use WWN; instead it uses what is called iSCSI Qualified Name (IQN). We can regard the IQN as a DNS name, or reverse DNS. It's a convention rather than something which is hard-coded. IQN would look something like this:

iqn.2006-11.com.vi3book:iscsi1

The first part is always the text IQN followed by the domain name registration date, and ending in the name itself. In reality, it is only used to ensure uniqueness. After all, a domain name can't be registered by more than one organization at the same time. The next part is your domain in reverse. For us, vi3book.com would be com.vi3book or uk.co.rftm-ed or com.vmguru. After that, you can specify a colon and alias; in the example, the alias has been set to iscsi1. As with all aliases, the intention is allow you to use short names instead of specifying the full IQN in software interfaces.

With the software adapter the IP address, subnet mask, and default gateway are specified in a VMkernel port group on vSwitch. The IQN itself is specified when you configure the software adapter for the first time. If you are working with a hardware adapter such as a Qlogic iSCSI card, you will probably find these settings are held in the cards BIOS settings.

You will generally want to have an isolated network for your iSCSI traffic – not only for performance but also because the traffic generated, as in SANs, is not currently encrypted. VMware's iSCSI implementation does support authentication with the Challenge Handshake Authentication Protocol (CHAP) for an additional tier of security.

While iSCSI can do all the things SANs do, you should be aware of four current limitations in terms of VMware Support. Firstly, you can install ESX to iSCSI LUN for iSCSI booting purposes, but you must use a supported hardware initiator. Secondly, only the hardware initiator supports a "static discovery" of LUNs from the iSCSI system. This is not a great limitation as "dynamic discovery" is much easier to setup and works with both software and hardware initiators. Thirdly, there is no support for running clustering software within a VM using iSCSI storage. Lastly, there is currently no support from VMware for iSCSI used in conjunction with VMware's Consolidated Backup.

In this section we will focus on the use of the software adapter, as this is a method everyone can configure.

iSCSI Virtual Appliances

What is a virtual appliance? A virtual appliance is a downloadable VM which already contains an OS supported by virtualization vendor which contains a ready-to-run application or service. Sometimes these are free, especially when they are based on Linux; other times they are locked and are only used to evaluate an appliance before parting with hard cash.

There are a number of free appliances available which will emulate an iSCSI system for you. While I wouldn't recommend these for a production environment they are perfectly fine for your test and development labs or for your own personal development in the process of learning VMware, perhaps as part of your preparation for the VCP test. As with all things in life, book learning is one thing but hands on experience is quite another.

Dave Parson, from Manchester in the United Kingdom, who is active on the VMware Community Forums, has put an iSCSI emulator together as a downloadable virtual appliance. It is downloadable from these locations:

Primary Location:

http://itservices.ne-worcs.ac.uk/pub/vmware/iscsitarget.zip

Alternative Mirrors:

http://chaz6.com/static/files/vmware/hosted/iscsitarget.zip

http://chaz6.com/static/files/vmware/hosted/iscsitarget.md5

Alternatively, you might want to look at OpenFiler.com, a Linux build designed for storage which includes iSCSI support.

If you are interested in iSCSI Virtual Appliance, "iSCSI Virtual SAN" is available from the VMware Appliance Directory web site and has been created by the scarily named user, "reaper007."

http://www.vmware.com/vmtn/appliances/directory/364

Configuring iSCSI based storage

In this section, I will configure software-based iSCSI emulator, or target. After all to, configure ESX initiators there has to be something to communicate to. I would like to say that using particular software does not amount to a recommendation. I merely use them because they are easy to get.

Setting up iSCSI with Fedora Core 5 and iSCSI Enterprise Target (IET) iSCSI Enterprise Target (IET) is a popular iSCSI emulator written for Linux and is freely distributed under the terms and conditions of a General Public License (GPL). If you prefer to use a Windows platform instead, you can get a free 15-day evaluation copy of "StarWind for Windows," produced by a company called RockDivision.com. If this is the case, you can skip this section and go to the section on setting up with StarWind.

Ideally, you will set this up on a physical system, but if you are just doing this for evaluation purposes a virtual machine will suffice. I have created a VM-based iSCSI box running on ESX host. This ESX host can then connect to the VM iSCSI box and you can format as VMFS. So my VM offers up VMFS partitions to the same ESX host on which it resides! This is a bit crazy I know – but it just goes to show how flexible VMware's virtualization technology can be.

iSCSI will present a LUN to ESX just like a SAN will, so I would recommend at least one LUN for your boot disk and two or more disks to act as iSCSI Targets.

I would like to thank Geert Baeke of baeke.info and Anze Vidmar of fedoranew.org respectively for their online help in this documentation – I "borrowed" extensively from both of these links.

You can download iSCSI Enterprise Target from this location:

http://sourceforge.net/project/showfiles.php?group_id=108475

Further documentation is also available on IET's Wiki page:

http://iscsitarget.sourceforge.net/wiki/index.php/Main_Page

1. Download and Install Fedora Core 5

    Note:

    Do a standard installation of Fedora Core 5 without the GUI front-end for Linux.

2. Make sure you enable "Software Development." We will need tools like CC to compile iSCSI Target for our kernel.

3. If you do enable Fedora Core 5's firewall, you will have to enable TCP Port 3260. You can change the configuration of the firewall after the install with the setup command.

4. Confirm your current kernel release with uname –r.

5. Download and update your kernel withyum –y update kernel kernel-devel.

Note:

Yum is an automatic updater and package installer/remover for the Redhat Package Management (RPM) systems. It automatically computes dependencies required to install packages. It makes it easier to maintain groups of machines without having to manually update each one using RPM. The –y chooses "yes" to all the prompts that occur. The kernel-devel downloads a development based version of the kernel which we can use during the compilation process.

6. Confirm the prompts from yum, and then reboot to make sure your updated kernel is in use.

7. Check your kernel release again with: uname –r.

8. Using the kernel name derived from above, download the latest kernel sources with yum –y install kernel-devel-*kernel-release-value*.

Note:

In my case this was yum install kernel-devel-2.6.17-1.2139_FC5

9. Yum will download the kernel source code and put into the /usr/src/kernels directory

10. Next we will **download and untar the iSCSI Target software** to the /usr/local directory (from http://iscsitarget.sourceforge.net/).

Note:

If you want to download directly to your iSCSI box, you could use a mirror hosted at Kent University in the UK with

```
cd /usr/local
```

```
wget
http://kent.dl.sourceforge.net/sourceforge/iscs
itarget/iscsitarget-0.4.13.tar.gz

tar xvzf iscsitarget-0.4.13.tar.gz and then cd
iscsitarget-0.4.13
```

11. **Compile and Install** the iSCSI Target Software with

```
export KERNELSRC=/usr/src/kernels/kernel-
release-value

make && make install
```

Note:

In my case the export command was:

export KERNELSRC=/usr/src/kernels/2.6.17-1.2139_FC5

If you get an error stating that CC was not found this is because you did a standard install of Fedora Core 5 which doesn't include programming tools. CC is a program that allows you to compile programs from a 'C' programming language/environment

12. **Copy the sample configuration file of iSCSI-Target** to the /etc **directory**

```
cp iscsitarget-0.4.13/etc/ietd.conf /etc
```

13. **Edit the ietd.conf** file with

```
nano —w /etc/ietd.conf
```

Note:

This is quite a lengthy file that has verbose information to explain the syntax. From this file we can specify an iSCSI Target ID. It allows you to set incoming and outgoing authentication and an alias for the target itself. However, ESX only supports incoming authentication to the iSCSI Target (ESX host authenticates to the iSCSI target), not outgoing authentication (iSCSI Target authenticating to the ESX host).

14. I have two LUNs to make available without authentication. So I configured the ietd.conf in the following way:

```
Target iqn.2006-11.com.vi3book:iscsi1
# Users, who can access this target
# (no users means anyone can access the target)
#IncomingUser
#OutgoingUser
# Lun definition
# (right now only block devices are possible)
Lun 10 Path=/dev/sdb
Lun 11 Path=/dev/sdc
# Alias name for this target
Alias iSCSI
# various iSCSI parameters
# Not in use…
```

15. To **Start the Service** and to **configure it to start on boot-up** use:

```
service iscsi-target start
chkconfig iscsi-target on
```

Setting up iSCSI with Windows 2003 and StarWind

Perhaps you would prefer to use Microsoft Windows as the basis of your iSCSI emulator or appliance. As I said before, this would require you to buy the Storage Server edition of Windows 2003 from Microsoft or take an existing copy of Windows and buy a third party software add-on that would make Windows function as an iSCSI Target. (One such third-party company is RockDivision.com. They have a software product called StarWind. A free 15-day evaluation of their product lets you play with it before parting with hard cash.)

Firstly, you need to setup on Windows with more than one disk or LUN. These other LUNs do not need formatting with NTFS because they will be presented to ESX as raw storage. Next, register with Rockdivision to download their StarWind product and copy it to the Windows server you created. The software is easy to install as it is a "next, next, and next" style setup program.

Below is a very simple configuration of the software suitable for our purposes:

1. Allow the installer to **Launch Starwind**.

2. **Double-Click the StarWind icon** on your desktop.

3. Right-Click **local-host:3260** and choose **Connect…**

Note:

If you are using the free evaluation, the password for the test account is: **test**. The evaluation software ships with a RAM drive automatically configured. If you wish you can right-click this and remove it.

4. Click the **Add Device** icon.

5. Choose **Image File device**.

Note:

If you buy this product you might prefer SPTI mode. It stands for "SCSI Pass-Through Interface." This feature device allows a hard disk, LUN, or CD-ROM to be shared as an iSCSI Target with the StarWind product. Starwind can run inside a VM but only with the "Image File" method as the VM's controllers (buslogic and lsilogic) are not fully supported.

6. In the "**Image File Device Parameters**" dialog box click the **New Image** button.

7. In the new dialog box, **specify a name and path** such as **e:\disk1.img** and **specify a size such as 10240MB** – and click **Next**.

8. **Enable** the option that reads "**Allow Multiple Connections**."

Note:

We can use the multiple connections settings to allow more than one ESX host to connect to the same iSCSI LUN. You can cycle around this process as much as you like creating as many IMG files as you wish.

Setting a VMkernel port group for IP Storage

In the networking section we set up a VMkernel port for VMotion as an example. Here we are going to set up a vSwitch with VMkernel port group for IP storage with the specific aim of using it to communicate with our iSCSI systems. For clarity, I have setup my two iSCSI systems using 172.168 addresses. iSCSI1 is based on Fedora Core 5 and IET with the IP address of 172.168.2.210, and iSCSI2 is based on Windows and StarWind with the IP address of 172.168.2.211.

When configuring the networking for the software initiator, you actually allocate two IP configurations. In the vSwitch for iSCSI we configure two port groups; a VMkernel storage port group and Service Console port group. This "second" service console port group is required for using iSCSI. The configuration generally runs smoother if you have already created the second Service Console port first. This leads to less warnings and pop-up dialog boxes.

Figure 3.1 shows a default dialog box that always appears the first time you enable the iSCSI initiator if you don't *first* create the second Service Console port group. If you have already created the second Service Console port this dialog box does not appear.

I will allocate 172.168.3.101/16 to my VMkernel storage port group and 172.168.3.111/16 to my second Service Console port group.

If we were using a hardware initiator we wouldn't have to do this. For example, with Qlogic iSCSI adapters the IP address, Subnet Mask, and Default Gateway values are set in the adapter BIOS using [Alt]+[Q] to access it. If you are using ordinary network cards, as I am, you will have to create a VMkernel port group to set these values.

Figure 3.1

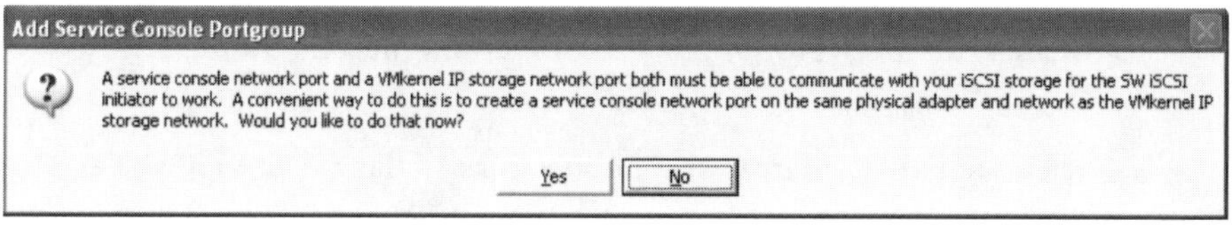

1. Select your ESX host.

2. Click the Configuration Tab.

3. In the Hardware Pane, select Networking.

4. Click the Add Networking... link.

5. Choose VMkernel and Click Next.

6. Click Next.

7. In the Port Groups Properties dialog, type a friendly name for this connection, such as ipstorage.

8. Type a valid IP Address and Subnet Mask for the VMkernel port group.

Note:

You will get a message about setting a default gateway entry for the VMkernel port group. This pop-up appears with every VMkernel port group you create if you don't choose "Yes" and set this. It can be little bit irritating. Of course, if your iSCSI systems were behind a router, you would choose "Yes" and add the default gateway entry. I often set the default gateway to be one of the iSCSI or NAS nodes on my network. This is helpful if I am on a router-fewer network and wish to stop the warning dialog box appearing. I can also use this to test my VMkernel IP configuration using the VMware ESX command called vmkping. Of course, a really easy way to check that you can communicate from ESX to your iSCSI system would be to start the ping from the iSCSI system to VMkernel storage port IP address just configured. Next we will add the second Service Console port.

9. Open the properties box for the newly created vSwitch and click the "Add" button to add a second Service Console port group.

10. Choose "Service Console" as the port group type.

11. Change the port group name to something meaningful, like iscsi-cos.

12. Set a second IP address and Subnet Mask valid for the iSCSI network.

Figure 3.2 shows how my networking has changed to reflect I now need to access the iSCSI storage system.

Figure 3.2

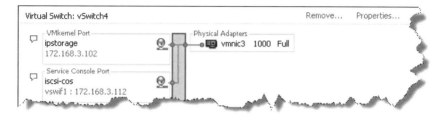

Connecting ESX to iSCSI (Software Adapter):

1. Choose the ESX Host from the list, and select Configuration Tab.

2. In the Hardware Pane, Choose Storage Adapters.

3. Select iSCSI Software Adapter and Properties...

4. In the General Tab, click the Configure button.

5. Select Enable and Click OK.

Figure 3.3 shows how the IQN data will be updated to show that the initiator is enabled and it will automatically generate a unique iSCSI Initiator (iqn.1998.01-com.vmware:esx1-1478025e5) and Alias (esx1.vi3book.com) for you.

If you prefer to use your own naming convention you can click the configure button and set your own IQN values. I usually change this after I have made the iSCSI system setup with ESX because, in some releases of ESX 3, I have seen that VI Client prompts you to do a reboot of the ESX host and I like to avoid reboots if at all possible.

Figure 3.3

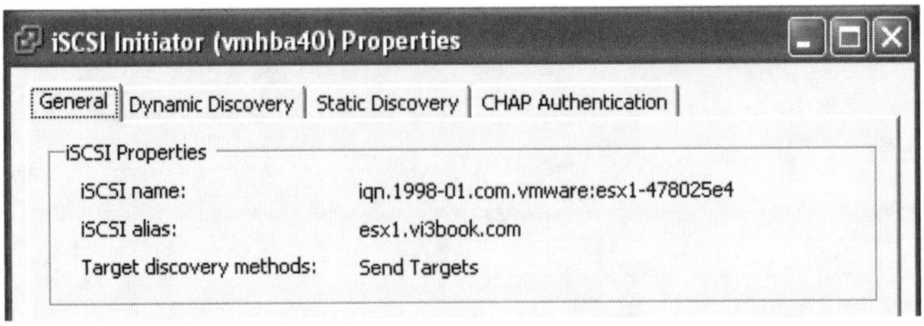

```
iSCSI Initiator (vmhba40) Properties            [_][□][X]

[General ] Dynamic Discovery | Static Discovery | CHAP Authentication |

  ┌iSCSI Properties ──────────────────────────────────────────
    iSCSI name:              iqn.1998-01.com.vmware:esx1-478025e4
    iSCSI alias:             esx1.vi3book.com
    Target discovery methods:  Send Targets
```

1. Select the Dynamic Discovery tab and Click the Add button – type in the IP Address of your iSCSI Target.

    Warning:

    It can take some time for these dialog boxes to refresh.

2. Now force a rescan by clicking the Rescan… link in the top right-hand corner – choose OK to the Rescan dialog box.

    Figure 3.4 shows the LUNs presented to ESX1 after the rescan has completed. If you select the vmhba40 software-device you should see the LUNs you presented in the IET configuration or the StarWind software. The IET iSCSI target displays separate LUNs (10 and 11) whereas the StarWind software displays each images device as separate SCSI targets (disk1 and disk2).

Figure 3.4

vmhba40					Properties
Model:	iSCSI Software Adapter		IP Address:		
iSCSI Name:	iqn.1998-01.com.vmware:esx1-478025e4		Discovery Methods:	Send Targets	
iSCSI Alias:	esx1.vi3book.com		Targets:	3	

SCSI Target 0
iSCSI Name: iqn.2006-11.com.vi3book:iscsi1
iSCSI Alias:
Target LUNs: 2   Hide LUNs

Path	Canonical Path	Capacity	LUN ID	
vmhba40:0:10	vmhba40:0:10	10.00 GB	10	
vmhba40:0:11	vmhba40:0:11	10.00 GB	11	

SCSI Target 1
iSCSI Name: disk2
iSCSI Alias:
Target LUNs: 1   Hide LUNs

Path	Canonical Path	Capacity	LUN ID	
vmhba40:1:0	vmhba40:1:0	9.00 GB	0	

SCSI Target 2
iSCSI Name: disk1
iSCSI Alias:
Target LUNs: 1   Hide LUNs

Path	Canonical Path	Capacity	LUN ID	
vmhba40:2:0	vmhba40:2:0	9.00 GB	0	

Configuring IET iSCSI Target with CHAP Authentication

So far, we have been connecting to the IET iSCSI target without any security. Security is implemented using CHAP Authentication. Very simply, a "user" is set up with a password which is required on the ESX server to allow access. It is only possible to have inbound (initiator to target authentication), as VMware does not currently support outbound (target to initiator authentication) with the software initiator.

Some systems require a password longer than 12 characters if authentication is used (this is defined under RFC 3720) and is enforced by some initiators, such as the Microsoft Initiator. However, it appears that VMware's Initiator doesn't, as I have used passwords shorter than 12 characters.

The only downside of enabling CHAP authentication for the first time is that you are required to reboot the ESX host.

1. On the IET server, nano –w /etc/ietd.conf

2. Un-remark the line:

IncomingUser

3. and replace with:

   IncomingUser *vmware 12charactersecret*

   Note:

   In this example, vmware is the user but this can be any name you like, followed by a secret which is greater than 12 characters. The secret is stored in the file as clear-text, so you must secure this file and login to the IET iSCSI server.

4. Restart the iSCSI Target daemon with:

   service iscsi-target start

5. Logon with the VI Client.

6. Select your ESX Host.

7. Click the Configuration Tab.

8. Choose in the Hardware pane, Choose Storage Adapters.

9. Under iSCSI Software Adapter select vmhba40.

10. Select Properties... and select the CHAP Authentication Tab.

11. Click Configure.

12. Choose Use the following CHAP credentials.

13. Click OK.... And choose OK to the reboot message.

In Figure 3.5 you can see that VMware does replace the CHAP Secret field with asterisks. This said the password is NOT stored in the dialog box as clear text. Confusingly, if you click "OK" to this dialog box and then return to it, the field is blank. This does not mean your change has not been recorded internally, just that it is simply not shown in the field.

Figure 3.5

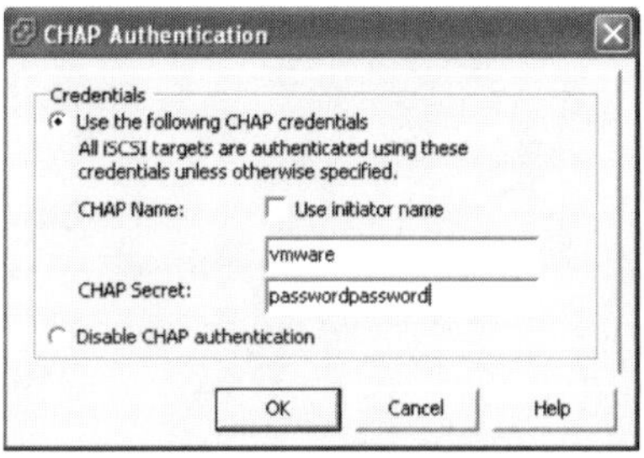

Formatting Volumes with VMFS

VMFS is VMware's own proprietary file system. It now supports directories and a maximum of 3840 files in VMFS volume and 220 files in a directory. These numbers merely represent a "soft limit" rather than "hard limit." A VMFS volume can be used in virtual machines, templates, and ISO files. It has been designed to be safe with very large files such as virtual disks. Another key property is that VMFS supports multiple-access; more than one ESX host can presented the same LUNs formatted with VMFS without fear of corruption. This is achieved by using a sophisticated file and LUN locking system to prevent corruption of data, referred to as "SCSI Reservations."

To enhance performance and reliability, VMware improved VMFS in version 3 to significantly reduce the number and frequency of these reservations. Additionally, we now see these locks as dynamic. Whenever an ESX host powers on a VM, a file-level lock is placed on that VM's files. However, periodically the ESX host must go back to confirm it is still functioning, still running that VM – and still locking those files. If an ESX host fails to update these "dynamic locks," the files are forcibly unlocked. This is pretty critical in features like VMware HA. If locking was not dynamic, the locks would remain in place when an ESX host failed, and no other host would be able to power on that VM. That VM would be locked – and HA would not work.

VMware does give guidelines for the number of ESX hosts that should be allowed access to a single VMFS volume. In ESX 2.x they stated no more than 10 ESX hosts should have access to a VMFS volume; in ESX 3.x this was increased to 32 ESX hosts.

VMFS uses a distributed journal. If a crash does occur, ESX no longer does a full "fsck" on VMFS volumes, but merely checks the journal. This is decidedly quicker – however, existing EXT3 partitions are still checked by the fsck method from Linux.

Formatting a VMFS volume is the same as if you are using local storage, SAN or iSCSI LUNs. As with any format procedure there is a huge potential for loosing data. When using the interface, take notice of any warnings that the Vi-Client produces as shown in Figure 3.6. There is no "undo format" facility in ESX 3.x, and so if you wipe terabytes of data during the process you would be resorting to your backup solution.

During the format process you will be asked to set a block size (1, 2, 4 and 8MB). These control the maximum file size which can be held in a given VMFS volume (256, 512, 1024, and 2048GB). Block sizes do greatly affect performance in VMFS and they also affect maximum file size. Sometimes this can be largely a theoretical issue, especially if your LUN size is less than the smallest file size 256GB. Generally, the larger the blocks size the better as this is good for performance and also allows you to have large VMDK files.

Figure 3.6

Please review the current disk layout:

Device	Capacity	Target Identifier		LUN
/vmfs/devices/disks/...	10.00 GB	vmhba40:0:11		11
Primary Partitions	Capacity	Description		
ntfs	9.99 GB			

Warning: The current disk layout will be destroyed. All file systems and data will be lost permanently

You will also receive the option to "maximize capacity" which sounds more complicated than it actually is. It merely means to use all of the LUN space for the VMFS volume. You can adjust this to make the VMFS volume smaller than the LUN size. There isn't any advantage to this and the free space left over is not easily accessible to the VI Client, anyway. While it is possible to create multiple VMFS volumes on a single LUN, this can affect performance. Although multiple ESX hosts can still access the VMFS volumes, doing so can impose a LUN wide SCSI reservation, which temporarily blocks access on multiple

VMFS volumes where only one VMFS volume might need locking. For these reasons I would recommend one VMFS to one LUN. In fact, I wish VMware would remove this option altogether from the VI Client.

Whenever possible, you should format VMFS volumes from the VI Client. One well-known way to optimize disk I/O is to keep the system from crossing track boundaries, known as "disk alignment." Master Boot Records frequently limits the number of hidden sectors to 63, which causes the default starting sector of disks that show more than 63 sectors per track to be sector 64. This can cause track misalignment, which defeats efforts to not cross track boundaries. The problem is further complicated by the characteristics of today's disks and controllers. Some disks don't accurately report track information to avoid other problems. Disks can also have a different number of sectors on the inner and outer tracks. "Disk alignment" is an effort to improve performance by keeping the number of sectors per second passing under the heads more or less constant. If you format volumes in the ESX installer or from the command-line using fdisk, the start sectors will not be 64k aligned. In contrast, the VI Client automatically ensures that disk alignment takes place.

GOTCHA:

If you are using RDMs to access RAW or Native LUNs, disk alignment should be done within the guest operating system. This is because fundamentally it is Windows or Linux that is in charge of the file system. Tools like Microsoft's diskpart should be used if you think your VMs would benefit from disk alignment.

1. Select your ESX host.

2. Click the Configuration Tab.

3. In the Hardware Pane, choose Storage (SCSI, SAN, NFS).

4. Click the Add Storage... link.

5. Choose Disk/LUN.

6. Select the LUN you wish to format:

   Figure 3.7 shows the two iSCSI LUNs presented by the IET iSCSI target set-up in the iSCSI section of this chapter. Notice how the

SAN identifier, together with the iSCSI IQN, allows us to see clearly the type of storage and where it is located.

Figure 3.7

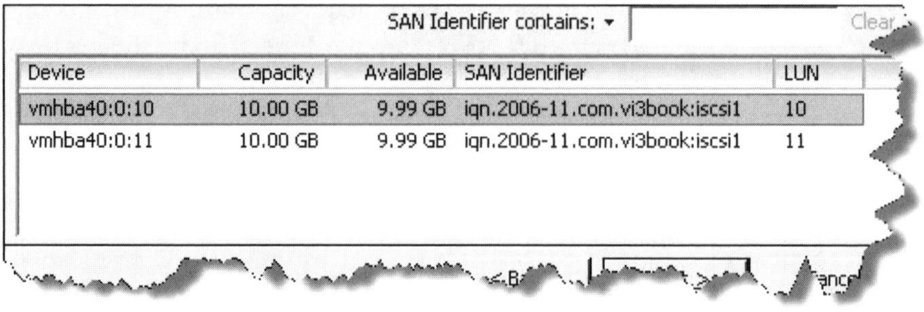
SAN Identifier contains:
Clear
Device
Capacity
Available
SAN Identifier
LUN
vmhba40:0:10
10.00 GB
9.99 GB
iqn.2006-11.com.vi3book:iscsi1
10
vmhba40:0:11
10.00 GB
9.99 GB
iqn.2006-11.com.vi3book:iscsi1
11

7. Set a datastore name such as iscsi1-lun10.

8. Set your maximum file size parameters.

   Note:

   As stated earlier its recommend to create one VMFS volume per LUN.

9. Click Finish.

Why don't I get all my space?

One common question asked is why, after formatting a 100GB LUN, you don't receive 100GB of VMFS storage. Like any file system, this storage system needs to have storage to function. In NTFS, this would be something like the Master File Table (MFT). In VMFS we refer to this as "metadata." The VMFS metadata is stored in files with the .SF extension in the root of the VMFS volume which "wastes" space on the disk. With a LUN or disk which is only 1.2GB in size, approximately 44% is wasted in metadata information. If you have a LUN of 10GB in size, about 4.8% is wasted in metadata information. If a LUN is 50GB in size, approximately 0.98% is wasted in metadata. So, the moral of the story is, the bigger the LUN, the smaller the percentage of metadata overhead.

Extending VMFS Volumes

Generally we create one VMFS partition per LUN, with the maximum size of a *single* VMFS volume being 2TB. The only way to exceed this limitation is by creating what VMware call "extents." Another reason to create an extent is if you are running out of space in a given VMFS volume.

The widespread use of SCSI-2 hardware causes 2TB's limitation, one that ESX shares with a number of x86 operating systems. SCSI-2 hardware uses a 16-byte address which then limits the maximum single LUN size. SCSI-3 equipment does not have this limitation, but we have not yet reached the tipping point for most OS vendors to move over to it completely. Fortunately, SCSI-3 equipment is backwards compatible with SCSI-2.

If you primarily use Windows, you will probably recognize extents. They function very similarly to Microsoft's "volume sets," or "spanned volumes." Most people in the VMware Community would recommend that you steer clear of this feature. I would agree with this assessment. I would only personally recommend extents as a workaround or band-aid.

In extents one LUN is stuck to another LUN to make the original VMFS larger. This could introduce performance headaches if the first LUN had a different RAID level or a different number of disk spindles. Any extents feature is only as good as the OS that underpins it – and most people would prefer a permanent "hardware" solution to this issue rather than a "software" workaround.

As great as the VMFS file system is, there are still some limitations. For example, there is no "Partition Magic" style tool for VMFS from VMware. This means that even if you have a SAN or iSCSI system that can dynamically make a LUN bigger from, say, 500GB to 1024GB, the original VMFS partition remains the original format size of 500GB. The only fix for this is either creating an extent or backup and restore. Or, if you have the free space, create a LUN that is 1024GB in size and copy the data in the 512GB LUN to the 1024GB. Afterwards, what you do with the empty VMFS and LUN is up to you. Most people would delete the smaller LUN so this capacity could be used elsewhere.

What this means from a storage perspective is that in your design you must carefully plan the LUN sizes – because changing them afterwards is difficult.

Another risky approach would be to use virtual storage and allocate more space to the ESX host than physically is available.

To extend an existing VMFS you need a free empty LUN. The VI Client makes a good job of hiding existing VMFS volumes to inhibit you from accidentally deleting valuable data. However, it does not hide any other LUNs with other OS file systems – so again be very careful, as there is no "undo extents" feature. To remove an extent, you remove the file system, along with any data.

The only real "gotcha" with extents is this scenario: let's say you later choose to extend a VMFS volume to make it bigger, and you add storage that makes the VMFS 2TB in size. It would still be formatted with the original block size. If this was 1MB you would still be limited to the maximum file size of 256GB caused by your original format.

With these caveats in mind, creating an extent is actually a very simple and easy process:

1. Select your ESX host.

2. Click the **Configuration** Tab.

3. In the **Hardware Pane** choose **Storage (SCSI, SAN, NFS).**

4. **Right-click the VMFS volume** you wish to make larger and choose **Properties.**

5. Click the **Add Extent** button.

6. Select a LUN from the list.

   Note:

   Before proceeding, confirm that the LUN is blank.

7. Click **Finish**

Configuring Multipathing with SAN

By virtue of having many HBAs in the ESX hosts and many SPs on the SAN array, it is possible to have many paths from one ESX host to a given LUN.

VMware does not currently use the multiple HBAs for load-balancing, merely for fault-tolerance. VMware takes the position that load-balancing to the storage is a more of a "storage vendors'" issue, and as a company, their expertise is in virtualization. Additionally, this would be difficult to encode from a VMkernel perspective, as they would need information about your SP's functionality to implement this. To do this, the VMkernel would have to be able to find out if a given SP was Active or Passive. An active SP can take a continual disk I/O load, whereas a passive SP only functions if the active fails. In this respect, an Active/Passive SAN would be unsuitable for load-balancing, whereas an Active/Active SAN would be a good candidate.

This aside, ESX does allow us to control which is the preferred path to a LUN on the SAN using the vmhbaA:T:L:V syntax. The first policy, which is the default, is called "Most Recently Used" (MRU) and is used with Active/Passive SPs on a SAN. The second policy is called "Fixed and Preferred" which is used with Active/Active SPs on a SAN. This second policy allows for manual disk I/O optimization.

MRU behaves in the following way: during installation, the ESX install scans the PCI bus looking for storage adapters. The first fiber-channel device found that the VMkernel has a driver for is set as the preferred path to the storage. The other paths from other SPs or HBAs are not used, except when this preferred path fails. When a failure occurs, a HBA connected to the passive SP takes over the disk I/0. The time taken to detect a failure and to use this redundant link is usually configured in the firmware of the HBA – it must be quick enough not to cause the VMkernel to think it has lost all connection to the storage. When the link on the active HBA returns (perhaps it was a failed fiber channel cable or switch) MRU does *not* return to the original HBA on the ESX host. In other words, MRU does fail-over, but not fail-back. If you wish to return to the original path, you must use the VI Client or command-line tools.

In contrast, the "Fixed and Preferred" path allows us to hard-code HBAs to service a given LUN. This enables us to configure that vmhba1 is the preferred path for LUN20 using SP0, whereas the preferred path for LUN21 is vmhba2 using SP1. This allows us to distribute the disk I/O across multiple HBAs and SPs. However, your SAN must support Active/Active on the SPs for this to work. When a failure occurs, the VMkernel is able to use any available path to the LUN, and when the link is restored it returns (Fixed) to original path. In other words, Fixed and Preferred does fail-over and fail-back.

Viewing Multiple Paths

You can view your multiple paths (if you have multiple HBAs) to a LUN within the Vi-client:

1. Select your ESX host.

2. Click the Configuration Tab.

3. Right-click a VMFS volume and choose Properties.

Figures 3.8 and 3.9 show the four paths available from two HBAs, each plugged into a different switch which is, in turn, plugged into two separate paths (vmhba1:0, 1:1, 2:0 and 2:1). We can see the vmhba1 is the active path (indicated in green) whereas the other 3 remaining paths are merely waiting for a failure to occur. Some storage people might disagree with this representation of the paths to the LUN. They may argue that if an ESX host has two adapters, it has two paths to a given LUN. Whatever your position is in this argument of 4 paths Vs 2 paths, precisely only one path is used at any one time. Incidentally, 32 is the maximum number of paths supported by VMware.

Figure 3.8

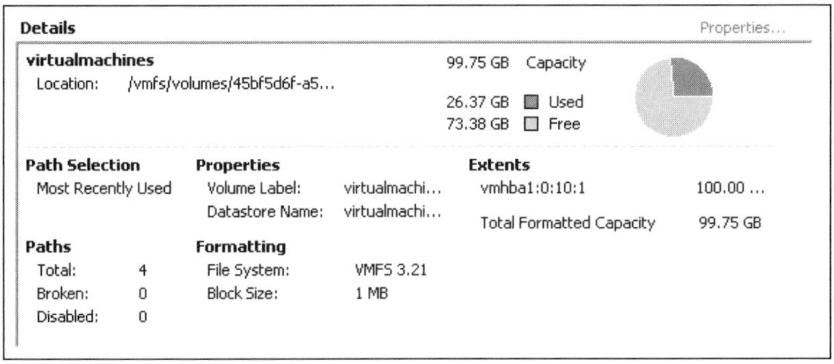

Details					Properties...
virtualmachines			99.75 GB	Capacity	
Location:	/vmfs/volumes/45bf5d6f-a5...		26.37 GB ■	Used	
			73.38 GB □	Free	
Path Selection	**Properties**		**Extents**		
Most Recently Used	Volume Label:	virtualmachi...	vmhba1:0:10:1		100.00 ...
	Datastore Name:	virtualmachi...	Total Formatted Capacity		99.75 GB
Paths	**Formatting**				
Total: 4	File System:	VMFS 3.21			
Broken: 0	Block Size:	1 MB			
Disabled: 0					

Figure 3.9

Note:

If a LUN is unformatted you can still see the paths by selecting the Storage Adapters link from the "Hardware Pane." Select your fiber-channel device and then right-click a path to a LUN (for example vmhba1:0:10)by choosing "Manage Paths."

Enabling Fixed and Preferred Paths

Warning: Only do this if you know you have a SAN which supports Active/Active storage controllers/processors!

1. Select your ESX host.

2. Click the Configuration Tab.

3. Right-click a VMFS volume, and choose Properties.

4. Click the Manage Paths button; figure 3.10 shows the current path status.

Figure 3.10

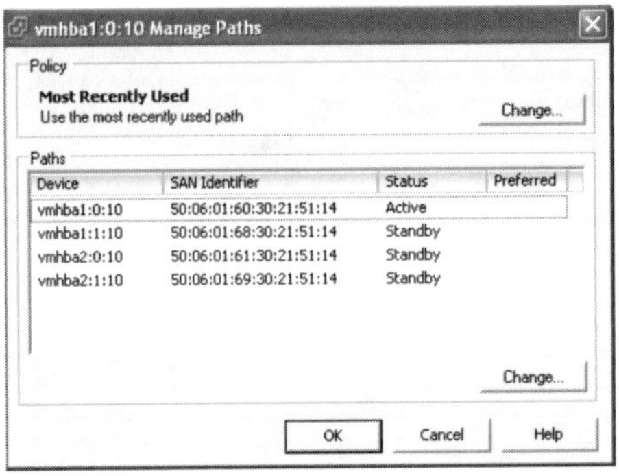

5. To Change the Policy Used, Click the Change button in the top right-hand corner of the dialog box, choose Fixed and click OK

To Change the Path Used

Click the path you wish to use, and click the Change button in the bottom right-hand corner of the dialog box. Set this path as being preferred – the disable option allows you stop a particular path from being used altogether. Figure 3.11 shows me making vmhba2 the preferred HBA for LUN 10 using SP0.

Figure 3.11

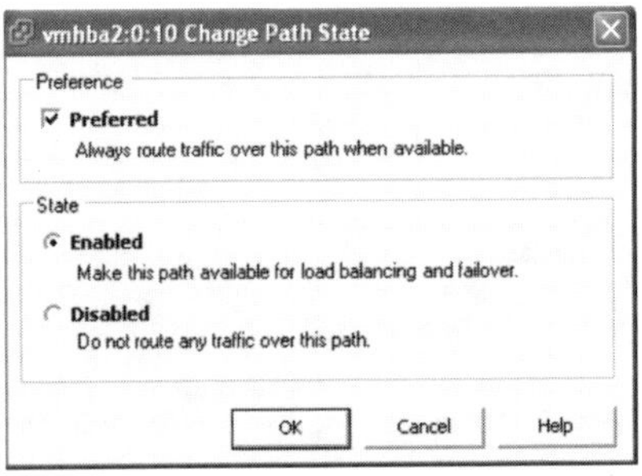

Figures 3.12 and 3.13 show the paths after changing the policy. Notice the asterisk (*) indicates which is the preferred path, and the status has changed to active for vmhba2:0:10.

Figure 3.12

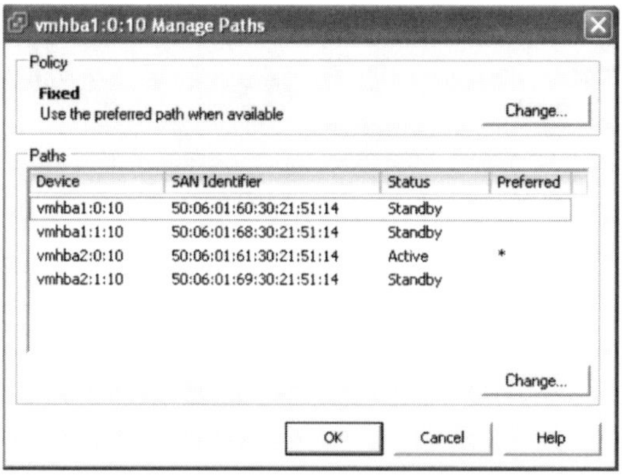

Figure 3.13

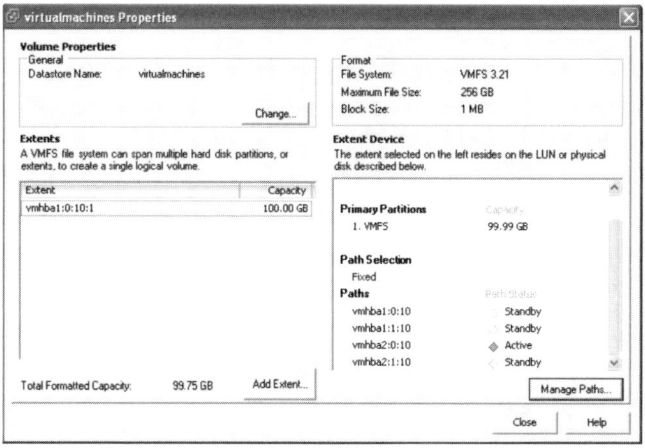

Broken Paths

Paths can and do fail, and the VI Client will alert you to this fact in the above dialog box. Figure 3.14 shows a dead path caused by a failed HBA, and Figure 3.15 shows a VMFS volume to which the ESX host has lost access.

Figure 3.14

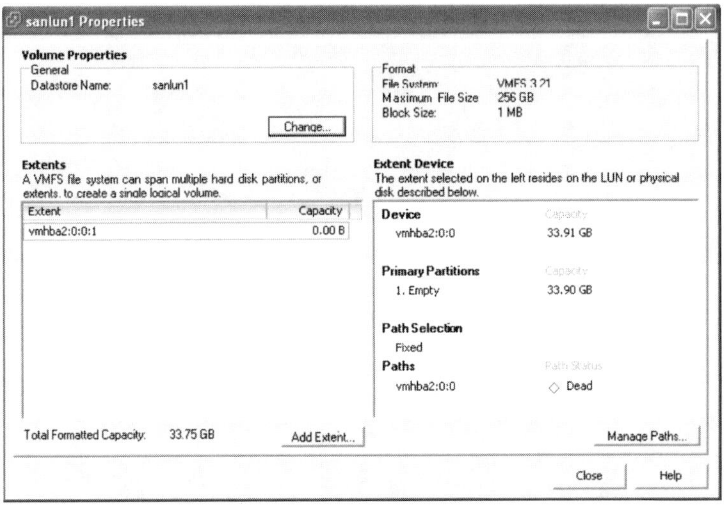

Figure 3.15

```
[root@esx1 root] # ls /vmfs/volumes/
478724-77d8fb-fc04-001560acef virtualmachines
```

Lastly, you can manage paths using the command-line tool called esxcfg-mpath. If you run esxcfg-mpath as root it will show you how to list paths, change path policies, and enable/disable paths.

Setting up NAS Storage

With the improvements and extension of the VMkernel's IP stack, VMware has introduced NAS support; more specifically Vmware supports the Linux "Network File System" (NFS) for file servers. This is where we have a file server which shares, or "exports," a folder.

Linux is supported natively by VMware using NFS and EXT3 as the files system. If you prefer to use Windows you will have to set up something like Microsoft's Services for UNIX (SFU) using NTFS partitions. Microsoft SFU emulates NFS support for a Windows Server. Fortunately, SFU is free – as long as you have paid for a valid Windows license. Alternatively, there are some very good free virtual appliances such as OpenFile and FreeNAS which you could use instead. Whatever you decide to use as the platform for NFS it's important to know that VMware ESX server only supports version 3 for NFS using TCP as transport protocol.

VMware's NAS support has three main purposes

The main purpose is to make store ISOs of guest operating systems (Windows, Linux, Solaris, and Novell) rather than locating these on SAN or iSCSI based storage, which is the most expensive you can buy. If you have lots of ISOs they can soon take up a lot of space and you may prefer to put them on cheaper NAS storage.

We could also use NAS based storage to hold our templates. The down side is every time we went to create a new VM from a template this would generate a significant amount of network activity and would not be as fast or efficient as using SAN or iSCSI. This is especially true if you also factor in the odd occasional error. For example, if deploying a new template takes 40 minutes to complete, and then it fails for whatever reason at 99%, you would have to factor in another 40 minutes to try again.

Lastly, we could use NAS to hold running virtual machines. I suspect that VMware supports this mainly for test and development environments. The cool thing about the NAS support is that we don't need to spend our hard-earned dollars on a SAN or iSCSI just for test and development environments. NAS would be sufficient. Perhaps you're one of those guys with a truck load of hardware in your basement or garage and you want to set up your own Vi-3 environment but your budget won't stretch to even a MSA1000. If this is you, then NAS could be viable. Personally, I would prefer to use an iSCSI emulator because it would allow me to use VMFS.

It is also worth mentioning that there is a great deal you cannot do with NAS based storage. So I would doubt very much if anyone would seriously use NAS in a production environment except for ISO or template storage.

Here's a handy list of what's not supported by VMware with NAS:

- Boot ESX server

- VMFS

- Raw Device Mapping Files

- Clustering inside a virtual machine

- VMware Consolidated Backup

I will begin this section with a quick overview of the setup of "exports" with NFS using Linux. After that, I will demonstrate how to set Windows up with SFU. Lastly, I will show how to add in the exports to the ESX servers.

Using RedHat Linux

In this setup I used RHEL AS Release 3 (Taroon Update 2) as my NFS/NAS Server. I configured the RHEL machine with a 10GB boot disk and 50MB data disk with a folder I created called /iso.

1. Logon to your **NFS file server** and edit the **/etc/exports** file like so:

   ```
   /iso  172.168.3.0/24 (rw,no_root_squash,sync)
   ```

   Note:

   This allows the server, any ESX server with a VMkernel storage port group in the range of 172.168.0.0, to access the mounting point called /iso. RW enables this server read and write access. The default is that the root user does not get full access to the volume. The command "no_root_squash" allows applications like VirtualCenter read/write access to the volume. Normally, root access to NFS volumes is "squashed" (in other words, denied). You can specify additional security settings using /etc/hosts.allow and /etc/host.deny files associated with the portmap service/daemon. However, these are beyond the scope of this book.

2. Sync controls how data will be written back to the disks when services disconnect from the export or when the NAS is shutdown.

3. **Start your nfs service/daemon** with:

```
service nfs start
```

4. To make these NFS services start automatically at boot-up use the chkconfig utility which allows you to make safe changes to run-levels in Redhat Linux.

```
chkconfig nfs on
```

Setting up NFS on Windows with SFU

These instructions are based on Windows 2003 with Service Pack 1. I have also successfully made SFU run on Windows 2000 with Service Pack 4.

Windows does not allow unchallenged access to shares without authentication. As Windows and the ESX Host do *not* share a common end-user database, we need some method of "mapping" the users on ESX Host to Windows. The method I have chosen is a simple mapping of the accounts using the files present on the ESX Host.

Installing SFU

1. **Copy the passwd** and **group files** from any one of your ESX servers; these are both held in **/etc**. You can use the free WinSCP tool to copy the files from the ESX host to your Windows Server.

2. **Extract the SFU package,** and run the **MSI package** called **SfuSetup.msi.**

3. Choose a **Custom Installation.**

4. **Expand Authentication tools for NFS,** and select the **User Mapping Service.**

5. Select **Next** to the **setupid** and **case-sensitive options dialog box.**

6. Under **Local User Name Mapping Service,** select **Password and Group files.**

7. **Type name and path** for passwd/group files, for example:

   c:\etc\passwd

c:\etc\group

8. Select the **Windows Domain.**

9. Select **Next, and accept the location for the install…**

   Note:

   Watch the status bar, check your email, make a cup of coffee, wonder how long you spend watching status bars… oh, and at the end of this - reboot your Windows/NFS Server.

Creating a User Mapping Between Administrator and Root

1. From the Start Menu, select Windows Services for UNIX.

2. Run the MMC, Services for UNIX Administration.

3. Select User Name Mapping node.

4. Choose Maps option, and under Advanced Maps, click Show User Maps.

5. Click List Windows Users button - and select Administrator.

6. Click List UNIX Users button - and Select root.

7. Click the Add button.

   Note:

   When the warning box appears – choose OK.

8. At the top of the console choose the Apply button.

Sharing out a folder

1. On the **Windows Explorer,** right-click a folder, and choose **Share and Security.**

2. Select the **NFS Sharing** tab.

3. Choose **Share this folder.**

4. Click the **Permissions** button, Select **X Allow root access.**

5. Change the **Type of Access to Read-Write.**

6. Choose **OK** to exit sharing dialogs.

   Note:

   Again if you're just using this share for ISOs you could leave this as read-only.

GOTHCA:

Watch out for CaseSensitivity on your sHaReNaMeS. Although Windows is not case-sensitive, it perfectly emulates NFS which *is case-sensitive*. If you want to remain sane, make them all lower-case with no spaces.

Confirming the Windows/NFS Server is functioning

Note: There are a number of tools we can use at the Windows/NFS server to see if things are working before adding in the NFS Share as IP Storage in the VI Client.

rpcinfo -p (lists listening ports on the server, notice TCP, NFS v3, Port 2049)

program	version	protocol	port	
100000	2	udp	111	portmapper
100000	2	tcp	111	portmapper
351455	1	tcp	904	mapsVC
100005	1	udp	1048	mountd
100005	3	tcp	1048	mountd
100021	1	udp	1047	nlockmgr
100021	4	tcp	1047	nlockmgr
100024	1	udp	1039	status
100024	1	tcp	1039	status
100003	2	udp	2049	nfs
100003	3	udp	2049	nfs
100003	2	tcp	2049	nfs
100003	3	tcp	2049	nfs

showmount -e (exports list on nfs2.vi3book.com)

```
/iso                                All Machines
```

ls -l

```
D:\sources\vmware\os-ISO's>ls —ls
total 11322628
1392128 -rwxrwxrwx+ 1 +Administrators  513   712769536
Feb  1  2005 wxp.iso
1251856 -rwxrwxrwx+ 1 +Administrators  513   640950272
Aug 25  2004 nt4.iso
```

Adding a NFS Mount Point

Adding a NFS mount point to an ESX host is the same whether you have used Linux NFS or Windows SFU. There is one option that does need explaining; as an ESX administrator you do have an over-ride option with permissions. Even if a NFS export has been set-up as Read/Write, you can mount it into ESX as read-only. This allows you to offer NAS as storage for ISOs but disallow it for other processes. Effectively, this would stop anyone from "accidentally" creating a VM on NAS storage when SAN or iSCSI would be preferred.

In my case, I used a FQDN name when specifying the NFS server. The Service Console is configured to resolve DNS names like this. If you have any doubts about name resolution try using nslookup at the Service Console on the name, and validate the results.

1. Next **Login** with the **VI Client.**

2. Choose the **ESX Host from the list,** and select **Configuration Tab** .

3. In the **Hardware pane**, select **Storage (SCSI, SAN, NFS).**

4. In the **right-hand side of the VI Client** click **Add Storage.**

5. In the Wizard, choose **Network File System.**

6. In the "**Locate Network File System**" page… complete the dialog box as follows:

    Server: Name of your NFS server, in my case **nfs1.vi3book.com**

Folder: Name of mount/volume you wish to access, in my case, /iso

DataStore Name: nfs1-iso (or anything you deem suitable)

GOTCHA:

Remember NFS comes from Linux – even if you're using Microsoft SFU export/share names ARE case-sensitive!

Occasionally, the NAS may be unavailable. If you want to force a reconnection to a NFS export you can do this through the Service Console with the esxcfg-nas command.

Note: If you want to check that you have communication to your IP storage, and test the VMkernel's IP stack, look at vmkping –D. Just like ping, it's a testing tool for the VMkernel.

Conclusion

In this chapter we examined the three main storage platforms available to ESX server. We also addressed how to format SAN and iSCSI LU's with VMFS. The last two chapters about networking and storage are pretty critical. Get your networking and storage sorted before you even begin creating V's and your life will be that much more trouble free. They are the absolute bedrock of the platform. Now that the ESX host server is correctly configured, we are now able to progress to the next chapter where we setup VirtualCenter.

Chapter 4: VirtualCenter

In this chapter I will look at the setup and configuration of VMware's Virtual-Center and Licensing Server. VirtualCenter is the most common method of managing many ESX servers and the VMs that run on them. I will also explain how VirtualCenter will enable you to organize your virtual infrastructure in a way that facilitates administration and delegation of responsibility. Additionally, I will discuss the configuration of VirtualCenter in terms of its own fault-tolerance. I will be covering a number of common best practices and address-ing all of the most common questions surrounding implementing VirtualCenter.

VirtualCenter is a management application which runs solely on Windows. It allows you to manage several ESX hosts in a single Window. It has a number of key features that makes it a must have for even modest sized- implementa-tions. Without VirtualCenter, these tasks can be completed but frequently they are much harder to execute and less flexible. To appreciate this you really need a list of features that are available only if you have VirtualCenter and the appro-priate add-ons:

- Centralized License Management

- Microsoft User Accounts

- Templates and Template Management

- Cold Migrations and Hot Migration (VMotion)

- VMware DRS

- VMware HA

VirtualCenter is a database application, in that it stores its information in a data-base backend. This can be either:

- Microsoft SQL 2000 with Service Pack 4

- Microsoft SQL 2003 (supported with VirtualCenter 2.0.1 or higher)

- Oracle 9iR2, 10gR1 (versions 10.1.0.3 and higher only, and 10gR2)

- MSDE 2000 (Rel A)

Out of these four different database engines only SQL and Oracle have full support from VMware. MSDE is offered for test and development environments only. It is freely distributable and has been copied to the VirtualCenter CD, so there is no need to download it from Microsoft's website. One big reason to avoid MSDE at all costs (even in a test and development environment) is what happens to the VirtualCenter MSDE database during upgrades from VirtualCenter 2.0.0 to VirtualCenter 2.0.1. The database is re-initialized meaning your previous work in VirtualCenter is lost, and you have to recreate everything you see in VirtualCenter by hand. Perhaps VMware will modify this in future releases but that is the state of play at the time of writing this chapter.

What is VMware License Server?

VMware's licensing server is a MacroVision Flexnet Licensing server which is used by many vendors to license their products. For example, Citrix's licensing server is a highly modified, stripped down version of the full MacroVision product. Theoretically, if you already have a MacroVision Flexnet Licensing server in your shop then you could reuse it with other vendors. In practice this does not always work well precisely because vendors who choose Flexnet tend to make propriety changes which then break the interoperability which we may seek. Additionally, one license server issuing licenses for many different vendors is probably going to create more "service dependency" problems than it resolves.

What is VMware Web-Access?

Web-Access is another service that can be installed along side VirtualCenter. It offers a basic user interface that allows "operator" style access to VMs without the need for the VI Client. It is also required if you wish to develop your own applications with the VirtualCenter Software Development Kit (SDK). If you don't have a requirement for this functionality it is optional. Using a "Custom" install you can choose just to install the core VirtualCenter services and opt out of the web functionality all together.

Database Configuration Issues

Before you run the installation CD for VirtualCenter you must first setup your database backend. The long-term management of the VirtualCenter database files is beyond the scope of this book. I will only address the procedures required to get up and running. You should know that the VirtualCenter database grows incrementally over time, as it continually collects performance data. Care should be taken to make sure that the database has enough free disk space into which it can grow. See chapter 5 in the first section of this book for more information on database sizing.

Configuring Microsoft SQL Server for VirtualCenter

Within your organization you most likely have your own rules about how user accounts are configured for services. It is very common for people to have datacenter policies which decree that local accounts are not allowed, and that only domain-based user accounts can be used.

In Microsoft SQL authentication comes in two flavors; SQL Authentication and Windows Authentication. Windows authentication is the strongest method. However, VMware currently only fully supports SQL authentication. Windows authentication will work but you will have to adjust the user accounts used to run the VirtualCenter services in the Windows Services MMC. However, this deviation from what VMware supports could cause you problems later when you rollout upgrades to VirtualCenter. For this reason I would recommend using SQL Authentication until such time that VMware changes its support policy.

If you are installing Microsoft SQL server for the first time then you can set the system to support *both* SQL and Windows Authentication. You can still create, in Active Directory, a unique user account with a unique password to access that database. SQL Authentication does not stop the use of domain accounts. If you are using an existing SQL server it can have SQL Authentication re-enabled using the Enterprise Administrator management console.

To create the database in Microsoft SQL 2000 and set the permissions you would carry out these steps:

1. Open Enterprise Admins and Expand + Microsoft SQL Servers, + SQL Server Group, + (Local) (Windows NT).

2. Right-click the Database folder, and choose New Database and type: vc-db (or something similar/appropriate) – and choose OK.

3. Expand the + Security tab, right-click Logins, and choose New Login.

4. Browse with … button to select the account created for Virtual-Center database.

5. Choose the option SQL Server Authentication and type in the password for the VirtualCenter Database User.

6. Set the Default Database to be the database created at point 2.

7. Click the Database Access tab, Permit access for the database, for VirtualCenter Database User, also enable the permission db_owner – and choose OK.

8. Click OK and Confirm the password again.

Installing VirtualCenter and License Server with Microsoft SQL Server

In this section I am going to guide you through the important parts of the License VirtualCenter server installation. For the most part, once you have addressed the database issue the installation is very simple. I will be installing license server and VirtualCenter software to the *same* server.

1. Insert the VirtualCenter CD or connect to its ISO.

   Note:

   If the CD fails to autorun, then you can double-click the file VMware-VirtualCenter-installer.hta.

2. Select **VirtualCenter/Web-Access.**

3. Choose **Typical,** and click **Next.**

4. In the "Database Information" dialog box, choose **Use an existing database server,** and click **Next.**

At this stage it's the Microsoft ODBC dialog boxes that are on top of the VMware dialog boxes.

5. Click the **ODBC DSN Setup** button.

6. In the **ODBC Data Source Administrator** choose the **System DSN** tab.

7. Click the **Add** button.

8. From the end of the list choose **SQL Server**, and select **Finish.**

9. In name field of the **Create a New Data Source to SQL Server** dialog box, type **VMware VirtualCenter.**

10. From the drop-down list **select your SQL server,** and click **Next.**

11. Select "**With SQL Authentication...**" and type in the user account and password for the database set up in SQL, and click **Next.**

12. Enable "**Change the default database to,**" and select the VirtualCenter Database you created earlier.

13. Click **Next** and **Finish.**

Note:

You should now be able to confirm all the dialog boxes associated with the ODBC setup – and also test that you have connectivity to the database server. This test is nearly always successful. It does *not* test your user account credentials.

14. Back at the VMware "**Database Information**" dialog box – type in the username and password used to authenticate to the SQL server – and click **Next.**

15. In the dialog box choose to "**Install a local VMware License server...**" and click **Next.**

16. In the "**License Info**" dialog box click the **Browse** button to locate the .LIC file.

Note:

This must be located locally on the VirtualCenter server. You cannot map a network drive to it. This .LIC file is copied to a directory in the VirtualCenter system – so the original can be deleted once the install has completed.

17. Click **Next** to the "**VirtualCenter Service Account**" dialog box unless you have configured a separate user account for running this service.

18. Click **Next** to accept the default port numbers used with Virtual-Center.

Note:

VirtualCenter Server uses ports 80, 443, and 902 by default. Therefore, you cannot run VMware Server on the same machine as it currently uses 80 and 902. Running a web server on the same machine is also not recommended because it could conflict with VirtualCenter. You should only enable backwards compatibility support with VirtualCenter 1.x if you require it because this adds an overhead to the VirtualCenter 2.x service.

19. **Set the Apache TomCat service** to both "**Start Automatically**" and to be **started.**

20. Click the **Install** button.

Creating DataCenters, Folders and Adding ESX Hosts to VirtualCenter

By default the "Administrators" group within Windows is used to allow access to VirtualCenter. If your user account is a member of Administrators in Windows then you will also be a full administrator in the VirtualCenter environment.

VMware's friendly name for everything that VirtualCenter stores is the "Inventory." There are four main VirtualCenter Inventory views:

- Hosts and Clusters

- Virtual Machines and Templates

- Networks

- Datastores

The "hosts and clusters" is a very "physical" view which allows you to see stand-alone ESX hosts, ESX hosts in DRS or HA Clusters together with the VMs that they are running. The Virtual Machines and Templates view is a very "logical" view showing just VMs and templates – but not the physical hosts that they are running on. The folder structures in Virtual Machines and Templates can be totally different from the structures you create in the Host and Clusters view. The networks and datastore views, in turn, show you the vSwitch port group names currently in use and the datastore names (SAN, iSCSI, and NAS). All four of the views share the common object called the "datacenter."

VirtualCenter has a hierarchical format which is akin to Active Directories domains and organizational units. The container types available are the "datacenter" and a "folder." The primary container in VirtualCenter is the "datacenter." Previous versions of VirtualCenter used the term "Farm" instead. Whatever term you prefer, we generally see these management units as reflecting distinct collections of ESX servers that share common SAN, iSCSI, or NAS storage and common LAN connectivity. Only datacenter can contain ESX hosts, although once a datacenter has been created any folder can contain an ESX host. Folders can contain practically anything – other folders, VMs, datacenters, and ESX hosts.

Figure 4.1 illustrates some of the possible permutations of datacenters and folders.

Figure 4.1

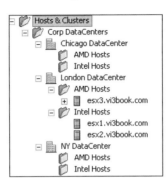

Note: If you wish to put an ESX host into a folder, you must first create a folder with a datacenter.

Similarly, in the Virtual Machine and Templates View it's possible to create folders that more accurately reflect the structure of your organization from an IT perspective. So you can create folders based on department (accounts, management, distribution), by location (New York, Paris, London), or even by person (Scott, Mike, and Ron). Figure 4.2 shows the folder structure I will be using while I write this book.

Figure 4.2

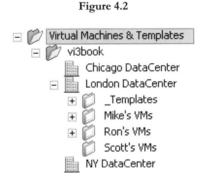

GOTCHA:

You cannot create a folder in the "Host and Cluster" view where the parent object is a VMware DRS or HA cluster.

Creating a Datacenter and Adding ESX Hosts

When you first add in an ESX host to VirtualCenter this can take some time to complete. While your ESX host is being added to VirtualCenter two critical changes are taking place. Firstly, the VirtualCenter Management Agent is installed to your ESX host. This allows VirtualCenter to communicate to the ESX host being added and therefore manage it. The agent communicates to the primary management service in ESX called hostd (its service name is mgmt_vmware) and has four main tasks:

- Relay ESX host configuration changes to hostd

- Relay VM create and change requests to hostd

- Relay resource allocations to VMs to hostd

- Gather performance information, alarms, and alerts from hostd

Secondly, a user account called vpxuser is generated. This user account is used by the VirtualCenter service to authenticate to the ESX host when it sends instructions. The actual actions themselves are executed by the root account at the ESX host. VMware uses this method to make sure that the root account credentials are never transmitted across the network during normal operations. You only need the root account and password when you first add an ESX host to VirtualCenter. This event that happens only once and the credentials of root are not stored either at the VirtualCenter server or in the database. It is therefore entirely safe to reset the root user's password without fear of complications or problems in Virtualcenter.

When you add an ESX host to the list you can use IP addresses instead of a FQDN. I personally would not recommend this. The license service and VMware HA require DNS. It is well worth resolving any name resolution problems at this stage than bypassing them with an IP address. During the adding of the ESX host to VirtualCenter, the ESX host is informed of the FQDN of your license server. If your ESX servers do not have name resolution to this license server you cannot simply enter an IP address for it. FQDN DNS name resolution is a requirement for the Flexnet License service to run.

1. Login to the VirtualCenter server using the VI Client.

2. **Right-click** "Host and Clusters," and Choose **New Datacenter.**

3. **Type in a name for your datacenter** such as Vi3book Datacenter.

4. To add-in a ESX host, **right-click the Datacenter created,** and Choose **Add Host.**

5. In the dialog box **type in the FQDN of the ESX host** and the **root account** and **password** for that ESX host.

Setting your host edition

Once your ESX host is added into the list we have to set its host edition. Virtual Infrastructure 3 can be purchased in "Starter" or "Standard;" these editions represent a bundling of different flavors with different features. To set what edition your host is using:

6. Select your ESX host from the list.

7. Select the **Configuration** Tab.

8. In the **Software Pane,** choose **Licensing Features.**

9. Next to **Host Edition,** click **Edit...**

Figure 4.3 shows me setting the host edition of ESX Server Standard.

Figure 4.3

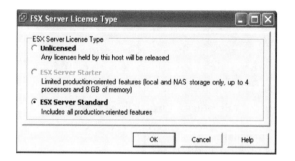

Installing a Second VirtualCenter Server for Fault-Tolerance

One concern you will have will be protecting the VirtualCenter server and the database backend to which it has been configured. The biggest single point of failure for VirtualCenter is its Oracle or SQL database, so you must back it up frequently. Depending on cost and the level of your concern there are a number of options to protect it. By far the cheapest and easiest to configure is some kind of network replication of the database files with a second database server. Alternatively, if you desired it, you could even setup your database to be protected by clustering services. Remember that if the VirtualCenter database fails, the ESX hosts carry on running and so do the VMs. However, from management perspective you would be in a tricky situation.

There are a number of ways of protecting the installation we have of Virtual-Center using conventional techniques. We could backup VirtualCenter with our backup software or we could clone the disk of the VirtualCenter server using something like Symantec Ghost or Drive Image Pro.

If you have two VirtualCenter servers they cannot be clustered; in fact they can't even be powered on at the same time when configured to use the same database. However, we can use a second VirtualCenter server (perhaps running in a VM) which would act as a "hot standby" should the "primary" VirtualCenter server fail. The setup of this "hot-standby" does alter very slightly to the setup routine outlined in this chapter. The three main stages are:

1. Power off the "Primary" VirtualCenter Server.

2. Install the "Secondary" VirtualCenter – creating a new System DSN settings.

3. Answer correctly the "existing database" dialog box.

Stages 1 and 2 are very simple. Stage 3 is straightforward as well, as long as you read the dialog box properly – and select the correct option.

1. Power off the "**Primary**" VirtualCenter server.

2. Start the installation of the "**Secondary**" server following the instructions previously discussed.

3. Choose **NO** to the dialog box that asks

    The DSN "VMware VirtualCenter points to an existing VMware VirtualCenter repository. Would you like to overwrite the data?"

    Note:

    You can proceed normally with the remainder of the installation. If you are running your primary VirtualCenter within a VM you could power it off and use the clone option to duplicate it. In my case, I opted to run VirtualCenter (Primary) on a physical server and did a clean installation of VirtualCenter to a VM from hot-standby.

Conclusion

In this chapter we looked at the setup and configuration of VMware's VirtualCenter and Licensing Service. I also demonstrated how VirtualCenter will enable you to organize your virtual infrastructure in a way that facilitates administration.

Now that our ESX host is properly configured for networking and storage and our management system is in place, we can proceed to the whole point of VMware Virtual Infrastructure – creating and managing virtual machines.

Chapter 5: Create and Modify VMs

In this chapter I will cover how to create a VM for the first time. Once we have created our first VM, Chapter 6 will address methods of duplicating the VM to save time.

I will define in more detail the virtual hardware available within a VM; examine what it is like to setup Windows and Linux within a VM, and how to install VMware Tools to your guest operating system. I will also address how to add additional "hardware" to the virtual machine – and show how it is possible to enable direct access to a SAN or iSCSI system within a VM.

I will cover how to use the new "Snapshot" facility introduced into ESX 3.x. The snapshot facility allows you to undo operations within a VM and is used in the process of backing up a VM while the VM is powered on. I cover how to un-register, remove, and delete a VM. Lastly, I will give you a quick jumpstart on how to create a VM from an existing physical server using VMware Converter.

Before you jump right in and start installing a VM you should really check out the list of supported guest operating systems, especially if your guest is a not Microsoft Windows. With operating systems like Solaris, Novell, Linux, and FreeBSD there can often be quite a surprising gap between what is officially supported by VMware and the current distribution.

http://www.vmware.com/pdf/GuestOS_guide.pdf

What defines a VM?

As you might know already a VM is firstly a collection of files. In more detail the actual files are

- .vmx – Configuration file in text format
- .nvram – The VMs virtual BIOS file

- .vmdk – The VMs metadata/descriptor virtual disk file

- .flat-vmdk – The VMs data virtual disk file (OS/Apps, Data)

- .vswp – The VMs swap file

- .delta – The Snapshot file

- .vmsn – The Snapshot Memory File

- .vmsd – The Snapshot Manager File

- .log – Log file

- .vmxf – Some kind of Internal Metadata file

- .rdm – RAW Device Mapping file with Virtual Compatibility

- .rdmp – RAW Device Mapping file with Physical   Compatibility

When you create a VM what you're actually doing is creating a text file with the VMX extension. The VMX file will hold the definition of the VM properties which include:

- VM's name

- Storage location

- Guest Operating System type

- Number of virtual CPUs (vCPU)

- Number of virtual NICs and the port groups they connect to

- Type of virtual SCSI adapter used

- Size and location of virtual disk

The VM itself presents the appearance of real hardware even though we know it is actually software – a virtual machine. When the guest operating system makes a hardware request it believes the VM is actually a physical machine with a physical motherboard. An ESX VM actually uses an Intel 440BX-based virtual motherboard with an NS338 Chip. VMware selected this motherboard because it has good compatibility and reliability with all the guest operating systems supported by ESX – so it can even cope with something very old like Windows NT 4.x. This selection of the motherboard then defines the virtual hardware that can be used within it. So what are the options allowed by this virtual motherboard? Here's a quick list of what is supported:

- 1-2 virtual floppy drives

- 1-2 virtual CD/DVD drives

- PS/2 interfaces for keyboard and mouse

- 6 PCI slots with the 6th used by the virtual video adapter – leaving 5 left over for you to configure.

- 1-4 vCPUs

- Up to 16GB of RAM

- 1 Parallel Port

- 1-2 Serial Ports

You will notice that there is no support for sound or USB. For the most part this is not a problem; if you use terminal services to connect to Windows running inside a VM you can have sound redirected to the client device. The lack of USB support (which is available in VMware Server and Workstation VMs) could cause a problem if you are running software that requires a "dongle" for licensing purposes. The most common solution is to purchase an IP enabled USB hub and redirect the USB calls to the network.

Parallel and serial devices are not fully virtualized, and their functionality is provided by the Service Console, not the VMkernel. There is a huge drawback to configuring parallel and serial devices in this way. Firstly, you will be limited by the number of physical parallel and serial ports at the back of the ESX host. You will be trouble if you have more VMs that require this kind of hardware than you have physical ports available. Secondly, if you did configure this you would be unable to VMotion that VM. VMotion, if you remember, is the process of moving a VM (while powered on) from one ESX host to another. VMware ESX server is very clever but not clever enough to unplug a dongle from the back of one ESX host and plug it in the back of another during VMotion. So again, many people purchase an IP enabled parallel or serial hub and redirect the hardware calls through the network instead.

Virtual CD and Floppy

In the world of ESX we very rarely use physical CD/DVDs and floppies. Generally, we take CD/DVDs and floppy drives and convert them into ISO or FLP files. There are a number of tools that will help you do this. After a CD or floppy disk has been "ripped" to an ISO file we then upload this to NAS, SAN, or iSCSI storage, depending on our preference.

To create an ISO file you can use tools such as your CD burning software, WinISO, MagicISO, or WinImage. There are tools in Linux such as the 'dd' and the 'mkisofs' command which will create ISO's images for you, but you should be aware that the 'dd' command does not verify that the ISO is a perfect image of your physical CD.

To copy these files to a storage address by ESX, you can use a free application called WinScp. This allows you to connect to the ESX host and then, using an explorer-like interface, drag-and-drop files to the relevant storage location. Unfortunately, for this tool to work, you would need to lower the security for the SSH daemon in ESX. This is because SSH access for root is blocked by default. However, the free WinSCP tool does not allow you to login as a lower-level user and then elevate your privileges to root. To lower security to allow root access, open a SSH session to your ESX host and then:

1. Type the command:

   `nano -w /etc/ssh/sshd_config`

2. Modify

   `PermitRootLogin no`

   to be:

   `#PermitRootLogin no`

3. Save the configuration file and exit nano

4. Then restart the ssh service with

   `service sshd restart`

Note:

In recent months I have switched away from WinSCP to Veeam SCP for ESX. At the time of writing this chapter the tool was free although you do have register an email address to download it. I've found Veeam significantly faster than WinSCP.

Keyboard and Mouse Interface

Of course, VMware has yet to produce the VMware Keyboard and Mouse like Microsoft. After all, these PS-2 connections don't physically exist; therefore you cannot plug in a physical keyboard and mouse. To interact with a VM you open a "Remote Console" session. This is similar in functionality to an ILO or RAC card or IP KVM on a physical machine. It allows you to watch a VM boot up just like a physical machine. It also allows you to send keyboard and mouse movements from your management PC to the VM.

Virtual Video Adapter

During the installation of your guest operating system the graphics will be quite poor and you might also experience poor mouse performance. During the installation a standard VGA driver is used. After the guest operating system has completed its installation we can install VMware Tools. Amongst many other things, VMware Tools adds a VMware Virtual Video Adapter Driver and VMware Virtual Mouse Driver. These significantly improve graphics and mouse operation, especially in operating systems like Windows that cannot be run without a GUI front-end.

Creating a VM

In this section I will guide you through the creation of your first VM, stopping along the way to point out some handy tips and tricks and explain some of the less obvious options in the Wizard.

GOTCHA:

One of the most common "mistakes" made by people new to virtualization is that they create VMs with the same amount of virtual hardware as they do for a physical hardware. Every VM this person creates is defined with 4 vCPUs, 4GB RAM, and 72GB virtual disks – even if the VM only uses 10% of these resources. A better practice is to define the VM with the minimums that you feel your applications or services can run with. Resources can always be increased afterwards if you set them too low. The golden rule is that it is always easier to give away resources on a need-to-use them basis than it is to take back needlessly allocated resources. A good analogy is for this is permissions. We only give the users the permissions they need as it is always easier to grant more privileges than it is to take privileges away. In this respect, this issue is also about setting reasonable expectation. Allocating too many resources to the VMs your operators manage will then set the expectation that all VMs should be configured in this way.

I will start creating my VM in the "Host and Clusters" view by selecting one of my ESX hosts.

Creating a VM

1. Select your ESX host.

2. Right-click and choose New Virtual Machine.

3. Choose Custom (so you see all options).

4. Type in a friendly name for your VM.

    Note: Use the Right Characters

    I recommend avoiding spaces and special characters and restricting yourself to using only alphanumeric characters. I advise using just lower-case as well. If you are ever at the command-line you may have to type the name of the VM. This is much harder if you have used a mix of cases, special characters, and spaces.

    In this dialog box you should also see the datacenter name within which your ESX host is located. If you have created folders for virtual machines in the "Virtual Machines and Templates View" you will be able put the VM into the relevant location. Figure 5.1 shows me selecting the correct folder to hold my VM.

Figure 5.1

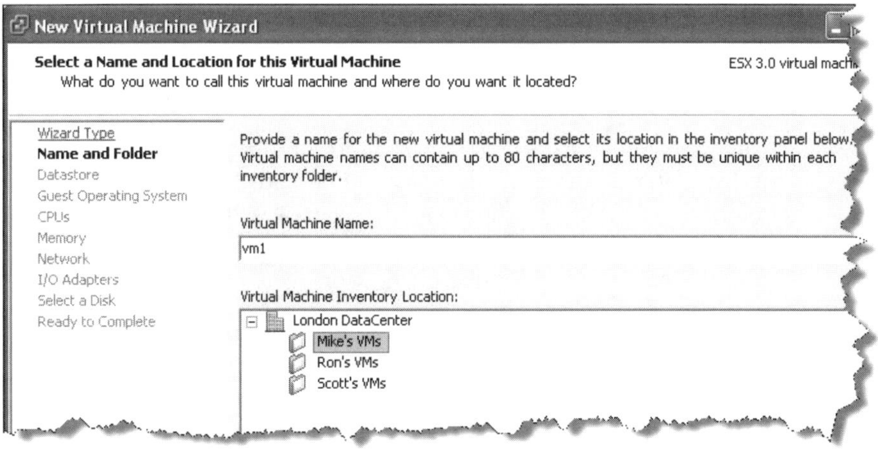

5. Next we Choose a Datastore to for the VM's files.

   Note:

   This dialog box tells you two very useful things. Firstly, it tells you how much free space you have on a datastore. Virtual disks can be quite large files so you will want to select a datastore that has enough free space for your VM. Secondly, the "Access" columns should tell you if the datastore is available to more than one ESX host – or on a shared storage. Shared storage is a requirement for VMotion, VMware DRS, and VMware HA.

6. From the pull-down list, Choose the Guest Operating System that will be run inside the VM.

   Note: Why select the right operating system type?

   This is important for two reasons. Firstly, it will assist the system when you install VMware Tools. VMware Tools ship as a Microsoft Installer package for Windows guests and as a Redhat Package Management (RDM) file and as a.gz zip file for Linux guests. By selecting the correct operating system in the list you will find the right version of VMware Tools is installed to the guest OS. Secondly, selections of the guest OS will sometimes dictate the remaining defaults in the wizard. For example, if you select Windows 2000 from the list, the default for the virtual SCSI adapter will be a Buslogic device. If you select Windows 2003 from the list this default changes to LSIlogic.

7. Configure the number of vCPUs in the VM for the guest operating system.

    Note:

    I would recommend starting with 1 vCPU and then adding more if you think later on that it might assist. Microsoft does not officially support "downgrading" from many CPUs to 1 CPU. There are of forcing a downgrade of CPUs. These methods are not officially supported although they frequently do work.

    Adding an extra vCPU does not necessarily improve performance, especially if your applications or services are not "multi-threaded." In order to leverage the real benefit of multiple vCPUs, the physical hosts may need physical sockets or cores. This is because of the way the VMkernel schedules processes that are to be executed. I will elaborate more on this subject in chapter 7 when we cover Resource Monitoring and Management.

8. Next Configure the VM's memory size.

9. The amount set here will act as a limit or maximum to be allocated to the VM. Even if you have free memory available, the VM will never exceed this amount.

10. Next choose which network connections will be used in the VM.

    Note:

    It is possible to configure a VM without a NIC at all. The usefulness of such a VM would be pretty limited, but it is an option that is available.

11. Next we select the Storage I/O Adapter type.

    Note:

    There are two types of virtual SCSI adapter in the VM – BusLogic and LSIlogic. Windows NT and Windows 2000 default to the BusLogic, whereas Windows XP, Windows 2003, and Windows

Vista default to LSIlogic. In contrast most Linux distributions default to the LSILogic Driver.

12. Next, in the Select a disk dialog, we choose Create a new virtual disk.

13. The option to "Use an existing virtual disk" could be selected if you had copied a virtual disk from another VMware product like VMware Workstation or Server (this process is covered in Chapter 12: ESX on the Command-Line). The "Mapped SAN LUN" option is used to give a VM direct access to SAN or iSCSI LUN. Later in this chapter I will cover this option in the "Adding Devices to a VM" section.

14. Next Specify Disk Capacity and Location.

Note:

When a virtual disk is created it takes up ALL the space you allocate here. ESX virtual disks do not "grow" as more data is created inside them. The term that is frequently used for this format is "monolithic" virtual disks. This format offers the best performance – as a flat file the virtual disk will be created in contiguous blocks within the VMFS volume.

How big should a virtual disk be? Well, it depends on what you are putting into it. One gotcha is giving a VM a large amount of memory, but a very small virtual disk for the operating system. You might find you lack space for the swap space for your given guest operating system. Now that the amount of memory is a configurable value this needs some consideration. What free space would there be for a swap file or partition if you started with 250MB of RAM and then later changed to 2GB RAM? Virtual disks can be made larger, and there are methods for making them smaller. I cover these in Chapter 12: *ESX on the Command-Line*.

15. Finally, the option to "Specify a datastore" allows you to store the VM's virtual disks at an alternative location. Perhaps you have two virtual disks – one for the boot disk and the other for data. Many people like to put their boot disks and data disks on different LUNs which have different RAID or backup levels.

16. Specify any Advanced Options, choose SCSI 0:0.

Note:

In SCSI systems, adapter 0 and id 0 are used to indicate the location of the boot disk (SCSI 0:0). A VM conforms to all the SCSI conventions with the adapter using SCSI ID7. If you remember the VM presents to the guest operating system the appearance of real hardware. You can have up to 4 virtual SCSI adapters if you wish, with up to 15 virtual disks attached to each adapter. Although the range is from 0:0 to 0:15 (which is actually 16 SCSI ids), id 0:7 is used by the controller itself.

I will cover the mode options of "independent," "persistent," and "non-persistent" when I delve into the "snapshot" feature later in this chapter.

17. Lastly, check your selections in the summary page – and click Finish.

First Power on and Installing the Guest Operating System

When you first power on a VM its boot order is:

1. Floppy

2. CD

3. Hard Disk

4. PXE

The second time you power on a VM the boot order is changed to:

1. Floppy

2. Hard Disk

3. CD

4. PXE

As you can see, on the first boot up the assumption is that you will probably be booting to a CD-ROM ISO to install the guest operating system. The second time you boot it is assumed that the VM is going to boot from the hard disk.

This stops the annoyance created by some vendors' operating systems where their CDs do allow the operator to skip booting from the CD. It also means that if you want an easy life you should really connect an ISO to the VM *before* the first power on to avoid having to use the VM's BIOS [F2] or [ESC] keystrokes to change the boot order. If you fail to connect a CD at the first boot you will find that the VM boots to PXE and searches for a DHCP server. If, subsequently, the CD is connected and then VM rebooted – because the boot order has been changed the VM would still not boot to the CD!

To attach an ISO to the VM you have 3 choices:

- You can use the ESX server's physical CD

- the CD-ROM drive or ISO on your management PC

- or an ISO on a centralized datastore.

The last option is the best in terms of what's best for performances, flexibility, and low administration cost. As discussed previously in the storage chapter, the ISO could be copied to an SAN, iSCSI, or NAS storage.

1. Right-click your new VM.

2. Choose **Edit Settings.**

3. In the list of devices choose **CD/DVD Drive 1.**

4. Choose the option **Datastore ISO file.**

5. Select a datastore where you have copied the ISOs of your guest operating system – and select the ISO.

6. Before leaving the "**Virtual Machine Properties**" box, ensure you enable the option "**Connect at Power On.**"

7. To open a Window on the VM, **right-click your VM,** and choose **Open Console.**

8. You can power on the VM using **VM, Power On** in the console window.

Installing Windows Vista

Installing Windows Vista is just like installing any other flavor Windows. The new version of Windows needs a terrific amount of memory and disk space to perform well. I gave my first installation 1GB of memory and 16GB virtual disk. After a plain vanilla installation I had nearly 512MB RAM when running idle and used 7.15GB of disk space.

There are, however, issues currently outstanding with running Vista on ESX 3.0.1 and older. Although the BIOS of the VM is able to boot the ISO of Vista, during the Windows installation Vista fails to find the CD/DVD which VMware emulate. The problem has been since been resolved in ESX 3.5. Figure 5.2 shows the error message in question:

Figure 5.2

It appears that there is no driver on the Vista DVD. I came across this issue in my first installation of Vista and had to use the forums to find a work-around as currently there is not a KB article from VMware. There are 3 main ways of fixing this issue. Helpfully, some people have already put the driver into a flp file for us. It is located here:

http://sti.epfl.ch/intranet/informatique/virtualisation/drivers-vista-rtm-esx.flp.zip

http://www.rtfm-ed.co.uk/downloads/winvistacddrivers.flp

If you want to read the original forum post about this issue it is located here:

http://www.vmware.com/community/thread.jspa?threadID=62141

To use this new driver, wait until you receive the Load Driver prompt, then:

1. **Press Ctrl+Alt** to release your keyboard and mouse.

2. In the VM console window, Choose **VM** and **Edit Settings.**

3. Select **Floppy Drive 1.**

4. Choose **Use existing floppy image in the datastore**, and click the **Browse** button.

5. **Select the FLP image downloaded** from above locations listed.

6. Select **Connected.**

7. Click back into the **VM console window**, and click **OK.**

   Note:

   The Windows Vista installer should read from the floppy disk and find CD-ROM Drive (A:cdrom.inf).

8. Click **Next,** and continue with the installation.

VMware Tools

After the operating system is installed, we generally install VMware Tools. This is a software package that is installed to the guest operating system. It contains three components.

- Drivers
- Service or daemon
- Configuration Applet or script

Drivers

During the installation of VMware Tools, the installer copies across 6 drivers for the following devices: VMware SVGA II, VMware Pointing Device, VMware SCSI Driver (replaces Microsoft BusLogic Driver if used in Windows NT and 2000), AMD Enhanced NIC Driver (vmxnet.sys replaces the pcntpci5.sys), a file system synchronization driver (used during VCB backups), and a memory control driver (vmmemctl). These devices and the drivers that accompany them significantly improve performances, especially the vmxnet.sys network card driver. Therefore VMware Tools is highly recommended. The memory control driver is used to control memory usage when physical RAM is scarce. I will discuss in more detail this driver in the performance chapter.

Service or Daemon

The "heartbeat" service or daemon is installed as part of VMware Tools. This service is used to alert the administrator that the guest operating system inside the VM has malfunctioned. Under normal operation a VM should have a small green icon next to it in the Inventory. If a VM "hangs," blue-screens (BSOD), or in Linux experiences a kernel panic, you should see this icon change to a red exclamation mark next to the VM. The guest operating system error stops the VMware Tools heartbeat service which then triggers an alert or an alarm.

You may get benign alerts occurring when you first power on a VM because the guest operating system is still loading, and the heartbeat service has yet to start.

Configuration Applet or Script

If you install VMware Tools to Windows you should find you have an icon in the taskbar tray near the clock. If you install VMware Tools to Linux without a GUI then you have a script that you can run instead. The applet or script is used to configure VMware Tools after the installation process has completed. VMware Tools have many configuration options available including:

1. Enabling Time Synchronization

2. Scripts triggered by power events

3. Modify Connected Devices

Installing and Configuring VMware Tools for Windows

1. Logon to your Windows VM.

2. In the **Console** window, choose **VM** in the menu.

3. Select **Install VMware Tools.**

4. Click **OK** to the dialog box.

   Note:

   In the background the system connects to ISO called window.iso held in /usr/lib/vmware/isoimages/windows. Windows should autorun this CD and execute the "VMware Tools.msi" file.

5. Choose **Typical.**

   Note: Typical Vs Complete Vs Custom

   A typical installation only configures features that are required with VMware ESX. A complete installation configures features for all VMware platforms – ESX, Server, and Workstation. A custom installation allows you to select which components outlined above you require. Interestingly there is a "hidden" driver option in the custom installation called "Descheduled Time Accounting." This driver only has experimental support at the time of writing. It is used to improve the quality of time synchronization in a VM.

Installing and Configuring VMware Tools for Linux

In Linux there are two VMware Tools packages. The first is in a Redhat Package Management (RPM) format. The second is in zipped format of tar.gz. After extracting the tar.gz file to a temporary location a script is used to install and configure VMware Tools. If you are running a graphical front-end to Linux there is a utility called VMware-Toolbox which allows further configuration. Lastly, ensure your Linux installation includes the tools required to use a C-compiler (such as gcc), as VMware Tools will need to compile the VMware drivers for your kernel.

Installing VMware Tools with the Redhat Package Management file

1. Logon as root to the Linux VM.

2. Use Control+Alt to regain control of the mouse and keyboard.

3. In Console, choose VM, VMware Tools Install.

   Note:

All this does is switch on the CD-ROM and point to the appropriate ISO file which contains the VMware Tools, located at /usr/lib/vmware/isoimages/linux.iso.

4. Next, mount this ISO file with mount –t iso9660 /dev/cdrom /mnt/cdrom as if it was a CD-ROM.

5. Execute the RPM file with the following command:

```
rpm -Uvh --nodeps VMwareTools-3.X.X-
XXXXX.i386.rpm
```

Note: The Meaning of RPM Switches

U stands for upgrade. Although this is a clean install, the same command could be used to upgrade VMware Tools to a newer version.

V is used to show for verbose information during the installation. H shows "hash marks" or status-bar like information which will tell us the progress of the installation.

Lastly, --nodeps forces an install regardless of software dependency errors. Here I have used a mixture of short switches which only need one – sign whereas longer friendly switches need two -- signs.

6. After the install process has completed you can use /usr/lib/vmware-config-tools.pl to configure the VMware Tools package.

Installing VMware Tools with a script

1. Logon as root to the Linux VM.

2. Use Control+Alt to regain control of the Mouse and Keyboard.

3. In Console, choose VM, VMware Tools Install.

Note:

All this does is switch on the CD-ROM and point to the appropriate ISO file which contains the VMware Tools. This is located at:

/usr/lib/vmware/isoimages/linux.iso

4. Next, mount this ISO file as if was a CD-ROM.

```
mount /dev/cdrom /mnt/cdrom
```

5. Copy the gziped version of the VMware Tools to the /tmp directory.

```
cp /mnt/cdrom/*.gz /tmp
```

6. Unzip this gz file.

```
tar —zxvf /tmp/vmware-linuz-tools.tar.gz
```

Note:

The z switch indicates that the tar command should uncompress the files. The x switch indicates that files should be extracted. The —v switch gives you a list of files being extracted.

7. Change into the vmware-linux-tools directory created by the unzip process, and run the installation script.

```
cd /tmp/vmware-tools-distrib
./vmware-install.pl
```

8. Accept the default locations for the file copy.

Note:

The script will create directories for locations that do not exist currently.

9. Choose Yes, to allow the system to run the script. "/usr/bin/vmware-config-tools.pl"

Note:

This script configures VMware Tools for the first time. If you wish, you can run vmware-config-tools.pl with the -experimental flag, and this will allow you to enable the "Descheduled Time Accounting" driver as in Windows.

Adding Virtual Hardware

Hot Adding Virtual Disks

It's not possible to show you every possible VM configuration – a VM is simply too flexible to make this viable. However, I wish to give one popular example–that of giving a VM direct access to a SAN or iSCSI LUN. We will see other VM configurations later in this book; for example, running clustering services such as Microsoft or VERITAS Clustering Service within a VM which requires a special configuration.

If you wish to change the virtual hardware configuration (increasing CPUs, RAM or NICs) of your VM, in most cases you will have to power it down. However, in some guest operating systems you can "hot add" a virtual disk. This includes Windows XP Professional with Service Pack 2, Windows 2003, and many distributions of Linux.

Additionally, you may wish to allow your VM direct access to a SAN or iSCSI LUN, achieved by a special mapping file called a "Raw Device Mapping" (RDM). This metadata text file essentially "tells" the VM which LUN to access. Of course, the VM doesn't actually connect directly to the SAN or iSCSI system. Instead the VMkernel intercedes on its behalf using VMkernel drivers to access the SAN or iSCSI via the ESX host's physical HBA.

There are many reasons to do this. Firstly, while some companies are happy to store their data within the virtual disk format, more conservative companies prefer their data to be stored in the operating systems native file system. Secondly, you may have existing data held within NTFS, EXT3, or other propriety files systems to which you merely wish the VM to have access. This is quite common after a P2V process. Thirdly, RD's are required for some clustering scenarios – such as running a clustering service between two VMs on separate ESX hosts (referred to as a "cluster-across-boxes"). I will cover the various VM clustering options in Chapter 10 when I discuss high availability solutions. Lastly, you may wish to leverage your guest operating system's native disk and file system tools to carry out certain tasks. For example, Microsoft Diskpart tool allows you to "stretch" a NTFS partition to fill free space. This can be an advantageous feature if your SAN supports "stretching" a LUN to increase its size.

There are two compatibility modes when you create an RDM file – physical and virtual compatibility. Physical compatibility allows the VM to treat the raw LUN as if it was a physical machine and is primarily used in VM clustering scenarios. There are no special features or options with physical compatibility. Virtual compatibility, on the other hand, allows the VM to treat a raw LUN as if it was a virtual disk. It allows for advanced features such as different disk modes and VMware snapshot files.

RDM files have the extension of .vmdk just like virtual disks and can be stored alongside the VM's other files or a different datastore if you wish.

To add in a RDM on a running VM:

1. Right-click the VM and choose Edit Settings.

2. Click the Add button.

3. Choose Hard Disk from the list of devices.

4. Choose Mapped SAN LUN as the type of disk.

5. Select the LUN you wish to present to the VM from the list.

6. Choose to Store the RDM with a Virtual Machine.

7. Choose Physical compatibility.

8. Choose a SCSI node, for example SCSI 0:1.

9. Click Finish and Close the edit settings dialog box.

Note:

If you are running Windows you will need to rescan disks using Computer Management, Storage, right-click Disk Management, and choose Rescan Disks.

Hot Adding Virtual Disks to Linux

Adding hard disks to a Linux VM while it is powered is also possible. However, the process of rescan the virtual SCSI bus is not particularly easy. Fortunately there is a script which is freely available which allows rescan for new storage devices after adding virtual disk. The tool is a BASH shell script called scsi-rescan.sh and was originally written by Kurt Garloff of Germany. You can find Kurt's script on the internet at his website under "Rescan SCSI Bus." http://www.garloff.de/kurt/index_e.html

Additionally you can find the script at Alex Mittell's website:

http://users.ox.ac.uk/~alexm/

Alex is a highly active member of the VMware Community Forums and also a member of the London VMware User Group, where he has given presentations. He's perhaps better known for his free Vi-3 backup utility called VISBU.

After adding the virtual disks to the Linux VM, download the scsi-rescan.tar.gz file, and extract it with the tar command.

```
tar –xvf scsi-rescan.tar.gz
```

Once the file has been extracted then execute the scsi-rescan.sh script. If it fails to execute try using the sh command.

```
sh scsi-rescsn.sh
```

This should run the script producing an output like so:

```
Host adapter 0 (mptspi) found.
Scanning hosts  0 channels 0 for
SCSI target IDs  0 1 2 3 4 5 6 7 , LUN's  0
Scanning for device 0 0 0 0 ...
OLD: Host: scsi0 Channel: 00 Id: 00 Lun: 00
     Vendor: VMware   Model: Virtual disk    Rev: 1.0
     Type:   Direct-Access                   ANSI SCSI
revision: 02
Scanning for device 0 0 1 0 ...
NEW: Host: scsi0 Channel: 00 Id: 01 Lun: 00
     Vendor: VMware   Model: Virtual disk    Rev: 1.0
     Type:   Direct-Access                   ANSI SCSI
revision: 02
1 new device(s) found.
0 device(s) removed.
```

Using the command fdisk – l will give you a list of all mounted, un-mounted, and un-partitioned drives like so:

```
Disk /dev/sda: 2147 MB, 2147483648 bytes
255 heads, 63 sectors/track, 261 cylinders
Units = cylinders of 16065 * 512 = 8225280 bytes
   Device Boot      Start        End      Blocks    Id
System
/dev/sda1    *          1         13      104391    83
Linux
/dev/sda2              14        196     1469947+   83
Linux
/dev/sda3             197        261      522112+   82
Linux swap / Solaris
Disk /dev/sdb: 2147 MB, 2147483648 bytes
255 heads, 63 sectors/track, 261 cylinders
Units = cylinders of 16065 * 512 = 8225280 bytes
Disk /dev/sdb doesn't contain a valid partition table
```

This means fdisk /dev/sdb could be used to partition and format the new virtual disk.

Using the Snapshot Manager

Currently, snapshots are applied to ALL virtual disks and RDMs in a VM. That would include both system drives that contain operating systems and application information – and also drives that store end-user data. Reverting a snapshot, which takes a VM "back in time," is therefore a potentially catastrophic event resulting in a loss of data. Some users have reported on the severe problems with committing snapshots above the 2GB size. There is a known issue if you have VMDK files within a VM that have the *same name* but are stored in *different VMFS datastores*. This problem is outlined in the VMware KB article 5096672. Lastly, some forum members have criticized the poor management of the Snapshot management file. This normally happens because of a failure to commit a snapshot file above the 2GB range. Due to some poor experience, the general opinion in the VMware Community is that while the snapshot's feature is generally a good one, it should be used sparingly until these issues have been properly resolved.

The new "Snapshot" feature replaces the old "redo" files of ESX 2.x. However, they have the same functionality and extra features. Snapshots allow you to capture the state of a VM at a point in time (which includes both disk and memory states) and allows you to go back (revert to snapshot) to a needed point. A good example of using snapshots might just be a fundamental change to a VM where you are unsure of the consequences of your actions; for example, applying a new service pack. In this way we are using the snapshot to deliver a type of "undo" functionality. This has been available in ESX since version 2.x, but now we can have up to 32 levels of undo within a given VM, whereas in the previous release we were restricted to just 1 level. Snapshots can be created and deleted even when the VM is powered on. This is another improvement on ESX 2.x which previously forced us to power off the VM to then change the "disk mode" of a VM.

So in ESX 3.x we can make a change, click create snapshot, make another change, click make a snapshot, and so on we go. In this respect working with a VM is a bit like working with a file – saving as you go along – so you can go back to the last known good state of the file if something goes wrong.

Using snapshots during backup is also popular. When a VM has a snapshot applied, all the read and write events that would normally be sent to the virtual disk are actually sent to a "delta" file. Under normal operations (without a snapshot) the virtual disk is locked by the file system and cannot be manipulated. However, when snapshot is applied to a VM, the virtual disk is unlocked and can be copied to another location for backup purposes.

After creating the snapshot all the new changes in the disk and memory are actually going to a "differences," or delta, file. In this respect, when you "capture the state of a VM at a point in time" you are actually creating something more like a "bookmark" that you can use to return to a point in time.

Despite these really useful features, snapshots are not without their gotchas and best practices. Snapshots grow incrementally over time in blocks of 16MB. If you allow a VM to run on the "delta" file for a long period of time it could become quite large. The other concern, depending on how much disk I/O your VM generates, is the amount of free space required to continue running on the "delta" file. VMware recommend not allowing any snapshot to grow beyond 2GB in size for performance reasons.

Additionally, time sensitive operations could be disrupted by the "revert to snapshot" feature. Let's take an extreme example, such as taking a snapshot of VM *while it is copying a file* to another system through the network. Some hours or days later when you choose to revert to the snapshot this VM would still think it was copying a file. However, the destination system would still be in your time and the network file copy would fail. There are many systems that are time sensitive, especially authentication services like Microsoft Active Directory – so this is one to watch carefully.

CAUTION:

Using the snapshot feature incorrectly can result in loss of data. I recommend you take a test VM and play with this feature until you are entirely comfortable with it.

GOTCHA:

The Revert to Snapshot icon does *not* currently ask the operator "Are you sure?" Therefore it is incredibly easy to accidentally click and send the VM back in time!

TIP:

If you power down a VM first, it is much faster to take a snapshot because no memory contents need to be saved. When you revert the snapshot your VM is returned to its powered off state.

Creating a snapshot

1. Login to the VM.
2. In the menu choose **VM, Snapshot,** and **Take snapshot.**
3. **Type in a name and description** for the snapshot.

Figure 5.3 shows my dialog box. I am going to use this snapshot to demonstrate making a mistake and going back to a good state.

Figure 5.3

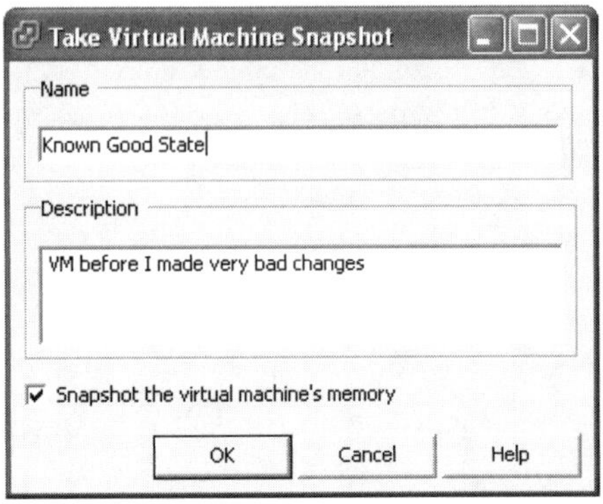

Note:

Now I make some changes I did not want. When I demonstrate this to customers in a Windows VM I tend to copy "Program Files" repeatedly. After doing this I then demonstrate the "Revert to snapshot" feature.

If you do this you might like to know you can see the "delta" file growing. To do this you can open SSH window on the ESX host in /vmfs/volumes or in the Vi Client using the "Browse Datastore" feature (as shown in Figure 5.4) by selecting your ESX host, clicking the "Summary" tab and then right-clicking a datastore in the resource pane and choosing "Browse Datastore."

Figure 5.4

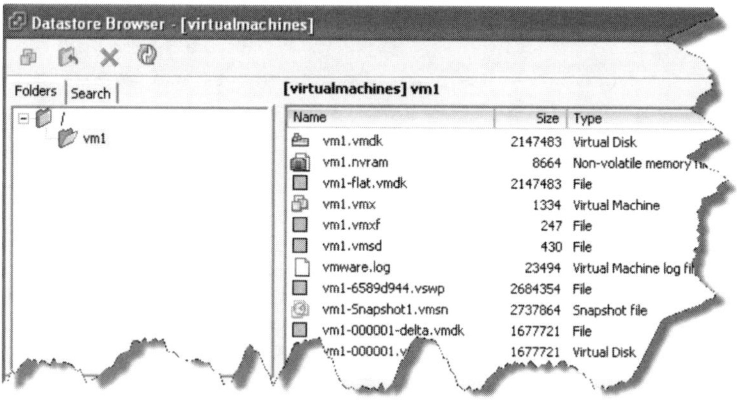

Datastore Browser - [virtualmachines]

Folders | Search | **[virtualmachines] vm1**

Name	Size	Type
vm1.vmdk	2147483	Virtual Disk
vm1.nvram	8664	Non-volatile memory fil...
vm1-flat.vmdk	2147483	File
vm1.vmx	1334	Virtual Machine
vm1.vmxf	247	File
vm1.vmsd	430	File
vmware.log	23494	Virtual Machine log fil...
vm1-6589d944.vswp	2684354	File
vm1-Snapshot1.vmsn	2737864	Snapshot file
vm1-000001-delta.vmdk	1677721	File
vm1-000001.v...	1677721	Virtual Disk

Revert to a snapshot

There are two ways to control reverting to a snapshot. There is a silent method which does not give any prompts or warnings and the snapshot manager which assists in dealing with multiple snapshots.

Silent Method:

1. Choose **VM** in the menu.

2. Select **Snapshot,** and then **Revert to snapshot.**

   Note:

   As stated previously, because of the lack of prompts, be very careful with this option.

Snapshot Manager Method:

1. Choose **VM** in the menu.

2. Select **Snapshot** and then **Snapshot Manager.**

   Figure 5.5 shows my VM. Notice how the snapshot name and description assist me in remembering what state the VM will be before the revert process. The edit button allows me to change the name and description if this is unsuitable.

Selecting the snapshot I called "Known Good State" and clicking the "Go" button would allow me to move the VM back in time before I copied "Program Files." If I selected the "Delete" button it would take the contents of the "delta" file and *merge them into the VM's virtual disks* – finally deleting the delta file at the end.

Figure 5.5

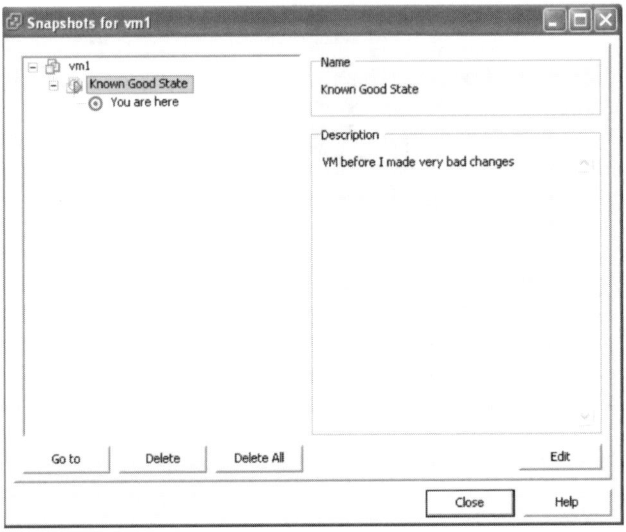

3. When you click the "**Go To**" button you will be warned that your current state (with all my bad copies of program files for example) will be lost. This is not a problem as I don't wish to keep those changes anyway.

4. Choose **Yes.**

5. **Close the Snapshot Manager** window – in a short while your VM will be returned to its original state.

Warning:

Although we have gone back in time, or "Reverted to Snapshot," the snapshot feature is still engaged. If you re-enter the Snap Manager window you would still see the name of the snapshot. This can be very useful for repeated attempts at configuration processes where you have 5 or 6 steps and you are not sure of the correct procedure because of poor documentation from a software vendor.

It also mean that it is very easy to unknowingly leave a snapshot engaged. You can tell if you have a snapshot enabled from the Vi Client: ff the "Revert to Snapshot" button is dimmed, you are not using a snapshot; if it is colored then you are using a snapshot.

Deleting a snapshot

I've found that some of my customers struggle with this particular feature of the snapshots. Not least because we all feel uncomfortable with delete buttons – we fear we might lose the stuff we want to keep. It's worth saying very clearly that when you delete a snapshot using the snapshot manager you are not going to lose your changes in the "delta" file. Customers have more problem with the delete button's terminology rather than anything else.

Here's an analogy I use with my customers to help them conceptualize the dialog box. When you click "Create snapshot" it's like you have used a camera and taken a "photograph" of your VM at that time. Half-an-hour later you think you might make another change – so you take another "photograph" of the VM. When you click "Revert to snapshot" you are going back in time that half-an-hour; it is like a little bit of time-travel. When you choose "Delete snapshot" you are going back to those old "photographs" and deciding you no longer need them – because they are so old and out-of-date. Just because you delete an old "photograph" of VM it doesn't mean you will lose the current image you are using.

Here's what actually happens when you hit the delete button. VMware ESX server takes the contents of your snapshot and copies the data in the delta file into your virtual disk. Once the "delta" file has been merged with the virtual disk the delta file is then deleted. Some people prefer the old terminology of ESX 2.x which used the words "commit" to merge the file into the virtual disk, and "discard" to remove the file and revert back to last known-good state of the VM.

When I demonstrate this to customers I usually make a change I would normally wish to keep – such as password reset. I then delete the snapshot – and prove that my password change has taken affect. This helps to re-enforce in the minds of the customer that the delete button doesn't mean "lose my changes" but "keep my changes."

1. Within the VM make a change you wish to keep, such as a password reset.

2. Choose **VM** in the menu.

3. Select **Snapshot** and then **Snapshot Manager.**

4. Select your snapshot, and choose the **Delete** button.

5. Choose **Yes** to confirm you are happy to delete the snapshot.

   Note:

   In the VM you can prove the changes have been kept by logging in and out – and checking the password. If you browse the contents of the datastore you should find the delta files have been deleted but your changes have not been lost.

Changing Disk Modes

When you define a virtual disk you are asked to set its "disk mode." There are effectively 3 different modes:

- Non-independent mode (Default)
- Independent Mode with Persistent
- Independent Mode with non-persistent

Only the non-independent mode allows the snapshot feature. The persistent mode treats the virtual disk as a normal disk would be – any I/O is committed to the disk immediately, and snapshots are not allowed. Of course, you must still shutdown the guest operating system properly to flush the contents of memory to the disk. This is due to file-system caching, present in many modern operating systems.

On the other hand, the non-persistent mode marks the virtual disk to be volatile. Any changes made after this switch stops any I/O events from entering the disk. Every time you power the VM off and on your changes are lost. Some customers use this with test and development VMs or with training VMs that always need to be reset to a given state. What actually happens is changes accrue in a "delta" file, but at power off they are never merged into the virtual disks. Taken to the logical conclusion this could be very useful in a Virtual Desktop Infrastructure (VDI) environment. Imagine a situation where you only have one VMDK file of Windows XP wasting valuable space on the SAN, and each use receives a "delta" version. At the end of the working day these VMs are powered off and reset to the golden state before the users made changes.

Lastly, changing disk modes does require the VM to be powered off.

1. Right-click the VM and choose **Shutdown down guest** from the menu.

   Note:

   The "Power off" does a hard power down akin to pulling out the power cord or hitting the reset button on some physical machines. It does not gracefully shutdown the VM. The "Shutdown down guest" option does require VMware Tools.

2. Choose to **Edit Settings** of the VM.

3. Select the **Hard Disk** in the list of devices.

4. Choose **Independent** and the **Persistent** mode.

5. Click **OK** to the Virtual Machine properties box.

6. **Power on the VM.**

Configuring VMware Tools

VMware Tools has a number of configurable options, especially in Windows. Most of these options are self-explanatory but it might be useful to discuss some of the most important ones.

Time Synchronization

The most common configuration for time synchronization is to enable the Network Time Protocol (NTP) service on the ESX host. The NTP service that provides accurate time to ESX is either on your own network or on the internet. Using VMware Tools the VM synchronizes its time with the ESX.

In VMware Tools for Windows and for other guest operating systems this is not a default. The reason being is many guest operating systems have their own time synchronization feature which would conflict with VMware Tools; in the case of Windows this is the service "Windows Time." You cannot have two time synchronization services within the same machine – the services would conflict with each other, and the VM would not be a trusted source for time. To use the time synchronization feature from VMware Tools you must disable these guest operating systems methods first.

This VMware Tools version of time synchronization happens once every minute and is not currently configurable. For this reason, some time sensitive VMs might still need their time set from systems that update their time at a more frequent interval.

To enable a Windows VM to use VMware Tools time synchronization, use the VMware Tools icon in the taskbar tray area. In other guest operating systems we enabled it by editing the .vmx file of the VM.

Enabling VMware Tools time synchronization in Windows

1. In Administrative Tools and Services

2. double-click the Windows Time service, and choose Stop.

3. From the Start-up Type pull-down list choose Disabled.

4. Close the Service console.

5. Double-click the VMware Tools icon in the tray, and enable "Time synchronization between the virtual machine and the console operating system."

Note:

Special considerations must be followed if your VM is running an Active Directory and is a domain controller. The VMware KB article 1318 outlines this.

"If you use a virtual machine as a primary domain controller for a Windows network, the primary domain controller must run the Windows Time service as a time server, to provide time to secondary domain controllers and other hosts on the network. However, that primary domain controller does not need to use the Windows Time service as a client to receive time synchronization input for its

own clock. You can still use VMware Tools to synchronize the virtual machine's clock while running the Windows Time service in a server-only mode."

This is done by engaging the Windows Registry option called "NoSync."

For this information and more detailed explanation of time inside a virtual machine consult the following VMware Documents:

VMware Time Sync and Windows Time Service:

http://kb.vmware.com/selfservice/microsites/search.do?cmd=displayKC&externalId=1318

Timekeeping in VMware Virtual Machines (PDF):

www.vmware.com/pdf/vmware_timekeeping.pdf

Enabling VMware Tools time synchronization in other guest operating systems

1. Shutdown your VM.

2. Open a SSH session on your ESX host, elevate your rights to root using the su – command.

3. Use nano or your preferred text editor to open the VM's VMX file. An example follows.

   nano -w /vmfs/volumes/virtualmachines/vm2/vm2.vmx.

4. Scroll to the end of the file, and find the tools.syncTime = "FALSE" option, modify this to read

   tools.syncTime = "TRUE"

5. Save the file, and Exit your text editor.

6. Power on your VM.

Configuring Scripts

As mentioned before, we can have scripts executed when a VM's power status changes. There are a couple of examples of configuration power-state scripts. Firstly, it is sometimes quicker to reboot operating systems like Windows by stopping services before the calling to reboot the VM. Running application services like Microsoft Exchange where you could use a .bat file with Microsoft net stop command to stop services is a good example.

Secondly, there are sometime annoyances like dialog boxes that stop successful reboots or shutdowns; rather than having to logon to the VM and deal with these prompts you could script them away. In my work, I deal extensively with Microsoft Terminal Services and Citrix MetaFrame. If an administrator uses the "Restart Guest" option in the Vi client, they could find that pop-ups appear within Windows dialog boxes (Figure 5.6 and 5.7 illustrate this). At a request to reboot or shutdown the VM triggered from the Vi Client, the request merely times out if there is no-one to answer these dialog boxes.

Figure 5.6

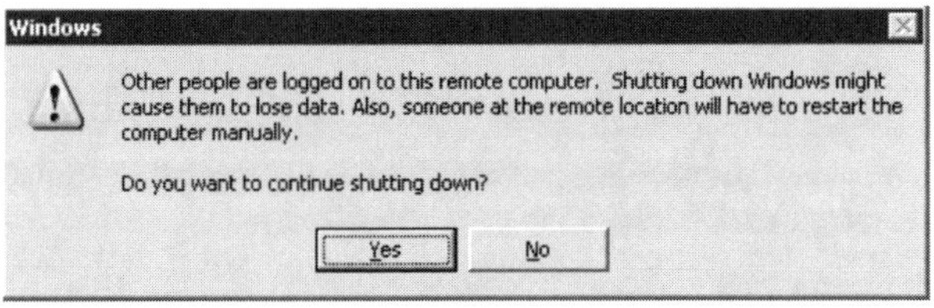

Figure 5.7

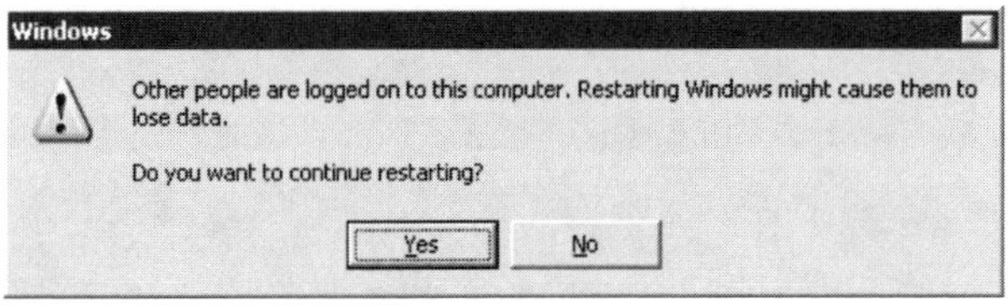

To fix this problem I used Microsoft tsshutdn command with the power-down script.

1. Login to your VM.

2. Browse to **C:\Program Files\VMware\VMware Tools**.

3. **Right-click** the **poweroff-vm-default.bat** file, Choose **Properties** and remove the "**read only**" attributes.

4. **Right-Click** and **Edit the file**.

5. Add to the bat file:

    tsshutdn 0 /reboot /delay:300

    Note:

    tsshutdn has many options. The two 0 values stop any warnings or delays and starts the shutdown immediately. If I used tshutdn 120 /powerdown /delay:30 this would give the users 120 seconds to log off, and then power down would begin 30 seconds after all log-offs had completed. The messages go to all users whether you are using the Microsoft RDP or Citrix ICA protocol.

    GOTCHA:

    Shutdown and reboot guests use the *same* script in VMware Tools. This means if you used the above workaround – and signaled the VM to shutdown – it would in fact reboot. The only way to shut-down the guest would be to login and do a manual shutdown within Windows.

Using the Shrink Feature

In ESX 3 the shrink feature has been depreciated – in fact, it's no longer sup-ported by VMware in a ESX 3 VM. This is a shame because it is actually a use-ful feature. Shrink optimizes a disk before exporting (copying) it to another storage system by deleting deleted files. As you might know most guest operat-ing systems do not actually delete files physically from either a physical or a vir-tual disk. Files are marked for deletion in the file system database and then are over-written by new files. The downside for us is that when we come to copy a virtual disk elsewhere, say prior to a backup, we get both our real data and our deleted data. Shrink used to write out the deleted files with zero values thus re-ducing the overall size of the disk – hence the term "shrink."

However, all is not lost. Many community forum members use a tool called sdelete from what used to be sysinternals.com. Microsoft purchased the website and its tools in July 2006. You will now find them re-named as Windows Inter-nals and sdelete is listed under "File and Disk" utilities.

http://www.microsoft.com/technet/sysinternals/default.mspx

There are plenty of secure delete style tools available for other guest operating systems such as Linux, Solaris, and Novell Netware.

Auto-Start and Stop VMs

ESX has the ability to gracefully power off and on your VMs if choose to do a shutdown or reboot of a ESX host. It is very easy to configure:

1. Select your ESX host, and Choose the Configuration Tab.

2. In the "Software Pane" select Virtual Machine Startup/Shutdown.

3. In the top right-hand corner select Properties…

4. In the dialog box, under System Settings enable "Allow virtual machines to start and stop automatically with the system."

5. Under shutdown action drop-down option Choose "Guest Shutdown."

   Note:

   "Guest Shutdown" requires the use of VMware Tools. This sends a signal to the VM to begin its shutdown process.

   You can use the up and down buttons to control the order of shutdown and start-up for VMs that share service dependencies.

Additionally, you can modify the start-up and shutdown interval used between VMs to reflect the fact that some VMs services will take longer to start than others. As an option, you can ask the system to over-ride the start-up daily by monitoring for the start VMware Tools, which may begin sooner than the 120 second default value. Lastly, the edit button allows you to set individual settings for each VMware over-ride to the global "System Settings."

Figure 5.8 shows the Virtual Machine Startup and Shutdown dialog box.

Figure 5.8

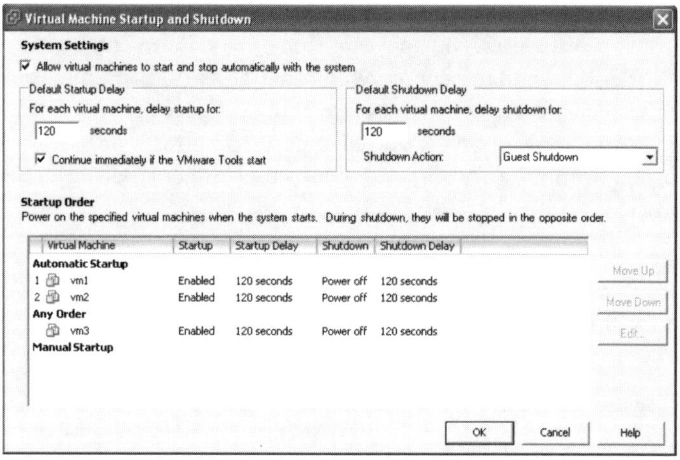

Virtual Machine Startup and Shutdown

System Settings

☑ Allow virtual machines to start and stop automatically with the system

Default Startup Delay
For each virtual machine, delay startup for:

`120` seconds

☑ Continue immediately if the VMware Tools start

Default Shutdown Delay
For each virtual machine, delay shutdown for:

`120` seconds

Shutdown Action: [Guest Shutdown ▼]

Startup Order
Power on the specified virtual machines when the system starts. During shutdown, they will be stopped in the opposite order.

Virtual Machine	Startup	Startup Delay	Shutdown	Shutdown Delay
Automatic Startup				
1 vm1	Enabled	120 seconds	Power off	120 seconds
2 vm2	Enabled	120 seconds	Power off	120 seconds
Any Order				
vm3	Enabled	120 seconds	Power off	120 seconds
Manual Startup				

Move Up
Move Down
Edit...

OK   Cancel   Help

GOTCHA:

While it is possible for ESX to stop and start VMs whenever you reboot an ESX host, it is more useful in an environment that does *not* have features such as VMotion, VMware DRS, and VMware HA. If you have these features in place then the auto-start and stop feature will not do much for you. In fact, this feature "breaks" as soon as a VM is moved from one ESX host to another by either VMotion, DRS, or HA. This is not a bug, but design. After all, as soon as we have VMotion, DRS, and HA we start to care less about where our VM runs, as long as it does run. If you manually VMotion a VM away from the ESX host that has this list configured and then return back to the ESX, it is dropped in the default location of manual start-up.

P2V of Physical Machine with VMware Converter

In fairness, P2V should be a book in its own right and is really beyond the scope of this chapter. However, I felt any chapter about creating VMs that did not at least give a brief note of converting physical machine to virtual machine, would look rather remiss in a book that extols the virtues of vitalizing existing physical environments!

In the real world, many companies opt for what is termed a "P2V Jumpstart." This is where experienced consultants from your P2V vendor visit your organization for about a week. During that week they introduce and set up the software required – and assist you in your first few P2V events. This workshop approach works better than, say, conventional classroom training which tends to be rather unrealistic. After all, there are many different types of servers, operating systems, and applications. You really need to know your hardware, operating system, application software, and your environment before embarking on the P2V process.

You're not restricted to using VMware's software in this process. The leading vendors in the third-party market are:

- VMware Converter (nee VMware P2V 2.x)

- PlateSpin PowerConvert

- LeoStream P2V

Additionally, some hardware vendors like Dell, IBM, and HP have gotten in on the act, offering their own tools for converting the physical systems into VMware VMs. Another alternative is to check out so-called "free" P2V solutions –however, these free "solutions" do not ship with any warranty or commercial support. Additionally, they are unlikely to have fancy post-configuration P2V features. Some interesting tools include:

- Ultimate-P2V (www.rtfm-ed.co.uk)

- MOA Project (www.sanbarrow.com)

- Easy P2V (www.ezp2v.nett)

You might wish to investigate how these various tools actually achieve the "cloning" process. Some vendors install an agent into the existing physical machine which then allows it to be visible to management console used for cloning. The advantage is that you can remotely convert the physical machine while it is powered on, which can be important because of uptime challenges that P2V inherently introduces. The disadvantage is that you have "altered" the original physical host. Many organizations have an ideological problem with this approach – they argue this could affect fail-back procedures and prefer the physical machine to be "closed" during the conversion process.

Other P2V solutions make the physical server from a boot from a CD and duplicate the server. This is advantageous because you can be 100% sure that every file will be copied as there are no open files, and no changes are made to the original server. The disadvantages are server downtime and the possibility that the vendor's boot CD will not recognize the hardware (critically NIC and storage controller). The best P2V vendors will offer a combination of both – like VMware Converter.

Lastly, many of these tools are geared up for Windows P2V events although some of them do offer Linux based conversions, too. So if you're working in a heterogeneous operating system environment you might want to research the guest operating systems supported. VMware Convertor is Windows application which is installed to your management PC. It is currently limited to "experimental" support for Linux.

In this section I am going to look at a very small part of the P2V process – the conversion software – and outline some very simple "clean-up" routines also. I will be using VMware Converter. VMware Converter ships in two formats – "Starter" and "Enterprise." The Starter Edition is agent-based and is free. The Enterprise Edition can use an agent or boot CD. Both the Agent and Boot CD possess the same user interface so if you have access to both there isn't any learning curve.

There are some other important limitations of Starter about which you should be aware. There are two ways of using VMware Converter with Vi-3.

1. Installing the full VMware Converter software into the physical machine.

2. Triggering the install of the VMware Converter agent and managing it remotely with a management PC.

The Starter Edition only supports method 1 whereas the Enterprise Edition supports both. This means if you use starter you have to install about 15MB of software to your physical machine and be at the physical machine to do the conversion. This said, RDP and ILO connections are unaffected.

Lastly, although I am emphasizing the physical to virtual functionality of converter, you should know that it has lots of other cool features such as:

- Converts VMware VMs across multiple VMware platforms – and therefore is compatible with ESX 3.x, 2.x, Workstation 4 and higher, Player, and Server. It is also backwards compatible with versions GSX (since re-marketed as VMware Server).

- Converter third party formats like Symantec Backup Exec Recovery, Norton Ghost, Microsoft Virtual Server, and Microsoft Virtual PC.

GOTCHA:

After a P2V process has completed, some editions of Windows will need reactivating. Windows will see the new virtual disk as a brand new hard drive, and the GUID associations with the old hard drive will be reset.

VMware Converter with the Agent (Enterprise Mode)

Before you begin verify you can login to the physical server with administrator credentials and ensure you have no mapped drives or other network connections to the physical server on your management PC.

1. **Download** VMware Converter.

2. **Install VMware Converter** to your **management PC.**

3. **Run VMware Converter,** and click the Licensing Button.

4. **Browse to your license file.**

   Note:

   If you are using the Starter Edition, install the VMware Converter product to the physical machine.

   You can run Enterprise Edition of VMware Converter in a VM.

5. Click the **Import Machine** button.

6. **Step 1**: Choose a source.

7. Select the option **Physical Computer.**

8. Choose the option for a **Remote Machine.**

TIP:

If you cannot get communication or authentication working you can always resort to installing the whole of VMware Converter to the physical server and use the "local machine" option instead.

Note:

Type in the name or IP address of the physical server. Then type in the Administrative Credentials for the Physical Machine. These must be expressed in the format of DOMAIN\Username if you do not know the local administrator account or password.

Once VMware Converter has connected to the physical machine, the converter will install an agent to the physical machine. At the end of the conversion process the agent can be automatically uninstalled or manually uninstalled- it is it up to you. The agent installs itself as service called VMware Converter Service in Windows.

9. Select the option **Automatically uninstall the files when import succeeds.**

10. **Select the Physical Volumes.**

Note:

You need not necessarily copy your data – you can just select your OS partition. Additionally, you can choose to resize disks as well.

11. **Step 2**: Choose a Destination.

12. Choose **VMware ESX server or VirtualCenter virtual machine.**

13. **Enter the name** of your **ESX Host** or **VirtualCenter server and user account details.**

14. **Type in the name of the new VM,** and **Select the folder** in VirtualCenter to hold the VM.

15. **Select an ESX host** location for your VM.

Note:

You must initially select the ESX host, not a DRS or HA cluster label. Once the VM is powered on, as long as the VM fulfils the requirements of DRS and HA, they will manage where the VM runs.

16. **Select a VMFS or NAS datastore.**

17. Select which **Network Port Group you wish to use.**

Note:

I would recommend initially using an internal switch or having the virtual NIC disconnected to avoid any potential IP or NETBIOS name conflicts.

18. Enable **Install VMware Tools.**

19. Click **Next** and **Finish.**

Note:

You can watch the status of you conversion from the converter windows in a percentage. Additionally, the "Task Progress" tab will give you an overview of the steps the converter is completing.

Note:

I would recommend choosing "NO" to the option of powering on the P2V'd VM at the end. There is some clean-up and post-configuration we can do from the Vi Client before the first power on.

VMware Converter with the "Cold-Clone" Boot CD (Enterprise Mode)

The Enterprise edition of VMware Converter also comes with the option to download a boot CD. This allows you reboot a physical server and clone the disk while the system is offline. The boot CD is actually a modified version of Microsoft WinPE environment. Previous editions have used a Debian CD and then later the Knoppix Live CD. I don't know what prompted VMware to move in this direction but I think the reason was threefold:

• It is substantially easier to add additional drivers for networking and storage.

- WinPE's competitor is the highly popular BartPE – however, to run BartPE according to Microsoft, you should really purchase a license for Windows XP or Windows 2003. Many people do, not which is very naughty of them as it upsets Microsoft a great deal. WinPE has the advantage that VMware can distribute it under a legally water-tight license agreement – to customers who perhaps don't even use Windows.

- It allowed VMware developers to write a very easy and intuitive UI, consistent both in Agent and Cold-Clone modes.

GOTCHA:

Firstly, VMware Converter supports all the flavors of Windows – and is happy if the disk is basic or dynamic. It will not convert volumes configured with Microsoft's software implementation of RAID. Secondly, you need at least 264MB of RAM for cold-cloning to work. If your memory size on the physical system is more than 364MB, the boot CD will create a RAM drive which improves the performance of the CD.

1. **Download the ISO** from VMware's website.

2. **Burn to a CD using your burner software** (if your server supports ILO or RAC boards with Virtual Media you could just use the ISO file as is).

3. At the prompt **press any key to boot from the CD…**

4. At the dialog box choose **Yes** to "**Would you like to update network parameters at this time.**"

   Note:

   Confirm your DHCP server has leased the boot CD an IP address. If you don't have access to a DHCP server, input your static configuration.

5. Click **Import Machine.**

6. **Step 1:** Import Preparation.

7. Choose to **Select volumes, and resize to save or add space.**

8. Select the **Boot Partition of your physical server.**

9. **Step 2**: Select a Destination.

10. Choose **VMware ESX Server or VirtualCenter virtual machines.**

11. **Provide login name and credentials** to access **your ESX host or VirtualCenter Server.**

12. **Type in a name for your new VM,** and select a location.

13. **Select an ESX host** to run the VM.

    Note:

    Remember, as with agent-driven conversions, you must initially select the ESX host, not a DRS or HA cluster label.

14. **Select a datastore location** for the VM.

15. **Choose a network port group** for the VM.

16. Allow the system to **Install VMware Tools.**

    Note:

    When the conversion is over select File and Exit in the Converter.

Post-Configuration Changes

After any P2V conversion there is a significant amount of clean-up work that needs to be completed. Here's a brief check-list of the kind of tasks you may need to consider:

- Remove Stale Devices.
    - o   Shutdown the VM.
    - o   Edit the Settings of the VM.
    - o   Remove legacy devices like Serial Ports and Parallel Ports.
- Remove Stale Software such as:
    - o   Hardware Drivers (Graphics, Sound, NIC's, RAID Controller). Doing this first reduces the time spent on remov-

ing stale hardware, as de-installing drivers sometimes removes the references in hardware management tools.

- o Remote Access Software such as VNC

- o Hardware Agents such as HP Insight Manager, IBM Director and Dell OpenManage

- Remove Stale Hardware with Device Manager.

    - o Run Device Manager with this batch file:

    @echo off

    cls

    set devmgr_show_nonpresent_devices=1

    start devmgmt.msc

    - o In Device Manager, change the view to Show Hidden Device (Windows 2000's Add Hardware Devices has a similar option).

- This truly shows you the old hardware – which you can right-click and choose Uninstall.

Figure 5.9 shows the stale hardware of P2V's VM. You can see the old hard-drives (a Western Digital and a Maxtor) together with various USB sticks that have inserted into the physical server. We can also see an old Sony CD-RW drive – and last, the old 3COM network card.

Figure 5.9

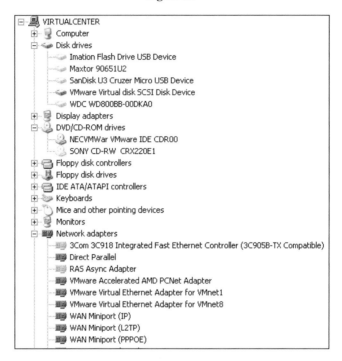

- **Reconfigure Networking**

  After the P2V your old network card has gone, and your new network card(s) from VMware will have no IP settings.

As you can tell the post-configuration process is not insignificant. Much of this process could actually be scripted. RTFM Education's website has a white paper and some sample scripts that have been developed to address this issue. An interesting one uses Microsoft's DevCon utility to compare the Virtual Machine to the Physical Machine – and automatically remove the stale hardware that appears in Device Manager. Research using the ESX 2.x. platform showed the script could remove about 60 to 80 unwanted devices in most Windows environments.

http://www.rtfm-ed.co.uk/?page_id=8

Removing, Adding and Deleting a VM

It is possible to remove a VM currently registered on ESX host and listed in VirtualCenter and add it to another ESX host in a different VirtualCenter environment. The important thing to note is that the only requirement is for shared storage. Effectively this achieves a manual moving of a VM from one VirtualCenter environment to another. If you have re-installed an ESX host or VirtualCenter - you might need to add VMs to the host in order to power them on.

Removing a VM does not delete the files that make up a VM, it merely removes the VM from the ESX host and VirtualCenter lists. A similar concept exists when you remove virtual disks inside a VM which is called "Remove from Virtual Machine" and "Remove and delete files from virtual disk."

To Remove a VM

1. Power off the **VM.**

2. Right-click a **VM**, and Choose **Remove from Inventory.**

3. Choose **Yes.**

To Add a VM

1. Select an ESX host.

2. From the Summary page, right-click the datastore where the VM resides and choose Browse Datastore.

3. Locate the VM's VMX file which is held within its directory.

4. Right-click the VMX file, and choose Add to Inventory.

5. In the Wizard, name and choose a folder location for your VM, and next your way through the remaining dialog boxes.

GOTCHA:

Adding and removing a VM is a relatively simple task – but beware of doing this from one ESX host to another. In other words, unregistering a VM from one ESX host and registering it to a different ESX host. When the VM is powered a prompt will appear asking what you would like to do with a change in the VM's UUID. The UUID stands for the "Universal Unique ID." It's often used by management systems to track pieces of hardware separately from the OS it runs. Physical servers have a UUID and this allows us to wipe Windows from a physical server and install Linux – but still have the management system recognize it as the original piece of hardware. In simple terms, the UUID is hardware identifier which has no dependencies on the operating system installed. VMs also have UUID value which is held in the VMX file and is generated from the real UUID of the ESX host.

In most cases it is best to choose "Keep" to retain the VM's identity in management systems of this type. If you were *moving a VM you should create a new UUID*. This means a VM manual moved retains its original identity or UUID. If you were manually *copying a VM, you should create a new UUID*. What we need to avoid is two VMs with the same UUID as this would cause problems in management systems that use the UUID.

Figure 5.10 shows the UUID prompt that occurs in this scenario. If you move a VM using VirtualCenter either powered on (VMotion/Hot Migration) or powered off (Cold Migration) the UUID is unaffected.

Figure 5.10

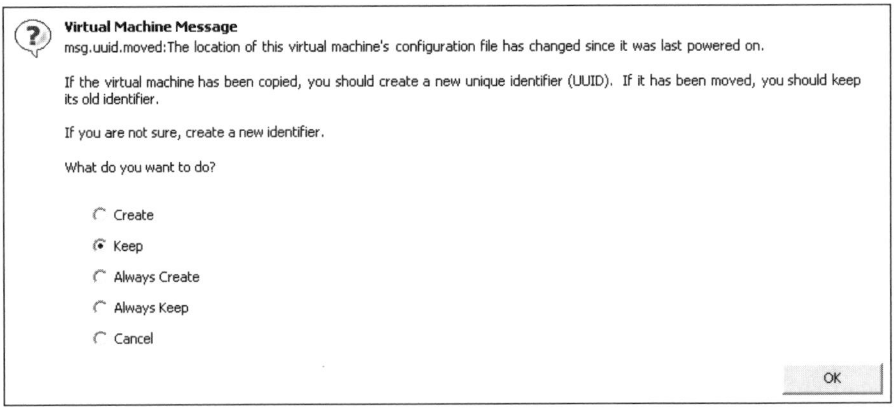

Virtual Machine Message

msg.uuid.moved:The location of this virtual machine's configuration file has changed since it was last powered on.

If the virtual machine has been copied, you should create a new unique identifier (UUID). If it has been moved, you should keep its old identifier.

If you are not sure, create a new identifier.

What do you want to do?

- ○ Create
- ● Keep
- ○ Always Create
- ○ Always Keep
- ○ Cancel

OK

Deleting a VM

Deleting a VM is a permanent operation. There is no undo button or recycle bin in ESX. If you accidentally delete a VM it is gone for good. Your only resort would be restoring it using your backup strategy. Similarly, there are no triple "Are you sure?" style dialog boxes or please confirm with a 4-digit pin number. You are asked once "Are you sure?."

1. Right-click a **VM.**

2. Choose **Delete from Disk** – and read the dialog box!

3. Choose **No**, if you are at all unsure!

VM Console Resolution Annoyance

Lastly there is an occasional annoyance with the VM console window - in fact you may have already experienced this issue in your use of the Vi Client with a VM. It usually happens during the power on and boot process as the guest operating system returns different resolutions as it loads its graphics drivers.

The problem looks like Figure 5.11 below:

Figure 5.11

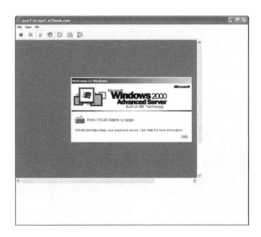

Generally, there is no "fix" to this problem at this moment. In my experience I've found that if you first "maximize" and then "restore" the VM console window like above, and then in the menu choose **View, Fit to Window,** this fixes the problem. If I don't first maximize and then restore the window I find that VM console creates a window which is 640x480 and sized to where the scroll bars are the above screen shot. This can be troublesome as it appears that the only way to return it to 800x600 or higher is by configuring it in the guest operating system display options. In the case of Windows this means opening the "Display Options" from the desktop.

Conclusion

As you have seen, VMs are infinitely more flexible than physical machines. Virtualization isn't just about taking your existing physical servers and converting them to VMs, although we did indeed touch on that subject in this chapter. It's about liberating you from the constraints of physical hardware.

Chapter 6: Rapid VM Deployment

Within a VM there are many methods to automate the VM's creation. Some companies persist in using PXE booting within the VM to leverage their existing deployment tools such as Microsoft RIS, Alteris, or HP's Rapid Deployment Pack. Additionally, there are free virtual appliances which are geared up to deploying various operating systems to a VM, one being the Ultimate Deployment Appliance. Quite often this is done to save time by removing the need for validating existing configurations. Another reason may be merely political – making it easier to implement VMs by changing as little as possible about existing business practices or procedures.

We can create a new VM exclusively to VMware VirtualCenter merely by duplicating an existing VM – a process referred to as cloning or templates. Some older users of VMware refer to this as a "golden master," but whatever term you choose to use – template, clone, image or golden master – they all mean the same thing; you've taken an existing VM and copied it.

Before you create a template you need to ask yourself a couple of questions. Firstly, how big would you like the guest operating system boot partition to be? When you create a new VM *from* a template there is no easy way to adjust on-the–fly the size of the VM's hard-disk. Secondly, how much software beyond installing the operating system and VMware Tools will you include in your base OS? For example, you might wish to consider including other things such as a service pack, hot fixes, anti-virus, and possibly even a backup agent. Most people baulk at the idea of including products such as Active Directory, Citrix Presentation Server, or Microsoft SQL which experience has shown to create more problems than they solve. Sometimes vendors do not support it, and if they do their products often need extensive pre and post-preparation. The length and reliability of such steps are sometimes so long and unpredictable that such products are often installed by secondary scripts after the VM has been created. This can sometimes mitigate the template process being "blamed" by application owners as being the source of their problems.

Creating a template of a VM doesn't just duplicate the VM's virtual disks. Additionally, the VM's .vmx configuration file is duplicated and renamed with .vmtx extension. This means that all the settings behind your VM are being duplicated, too. This saves time by reducing the number of wizards and dialog boxes you need to answer and complete.

GOTCHA:

This can also include undesirable settings like connections to removable devices such as CD-ROMs or floppy disks – as well as connections to internal switches. These settings are undesirable because they cause problems with VMotion and DRS. Disable these devices before taking your template.

In the past, one of the challenges of templates was keeping their software up to date. This is the same challenge PC deployment people face when using disk cloning software to build new PCs. It is relatively easy to build a PC and duplicate it with PowerQuest Drive Image Pro or Symantec Ghost. The tricky thing is keeping the library of images current. The same problem bedevils templates in VMware, not least because whenever a new build of ESX is released VMware Tools also requires a software upgrade, too. A new feature called "convert to template" significantly eases the management of templates – and makes it incredibly easy to keep the software inside a template with regular updates such as:

- Windows Updates

- YUM Updates

- Anti-Virus Definitions

There are three main ways to create a template:

- **Clone to Template**

  This copies the VM and converts it to the template format. If you have used previous versions of VirtualCenter, they are just like a conventional template in VirtualCenter 1.x. During the creation of the template you have the ability to compact, which significantly reduces the size of the disk, but both compacting and creating a VM from this format is slower than if it was in its original format. Of course, a good reason to compact a template is to save on disk space. To use the compact format it is recommended you use a VMFS volume as the storage location.

- **Convert to Template**

    This simply marks a VM as a template. It is much quicker than us-
    ing "clone to template" as no copy process is generated at all. It
    takes seconds to mark a VM as a template and seconds to convert
    it back to being a VM. First you build the VM and convert it to a
    template, and when the software inside the template becomes stale
    and out of date, you can quickly unmark it back to being a VM
    again. Power on and run your software update. Lastly, once you
    are satisfied that the software is as current as it can be you convert
    it back to the template format. The whole process takes seconds,
    allows you to keep your templates up to date with the latest soft-
    ware, and doesn't generate any file copy events at all.

    Another way to consider this template format is merely as a VM
    that you can't power on or a VM which is only used as the source
    for creating new VMs.

- **Clone**

    There is nothing particular special about the clone option; it merely
    copies the VM. You do lose out on the features of "clone" or
    "convert" to template such as being able to copy and compress the
    source – and being able to quickly update the "base" VM. To
    clone a VM you would need rights to the VM, as you would with
    the other two options. But as templates can be stored and moved
    into other locations where different permissions reside, templates
    are often easier from a delegation or permissions perspective, too.

Unlike VirtualCenter 1.x., there is no specific location for templates in the VI
Client interface. Most users tend to create a folder to hold them in the Inventory View of "Virtual Machines and Templates." Of course, where they get
physically stored – iSCSI, SAN, or NAS – depends on your resources. Generally, the template LUN is presented to all ESX hosts in a given datacenter to
allow centralized management and access to the templates themselves.

GOTCHA:

To create a template or clone, the VM must be powered off first. You cannot
create a template from a VM that is using a VMware Snapshot or if it is in a
suspended power state. However, you can duplicate a VM while it is powered

on by engaging a snapshot and then exporting the virtual disks using the vmkfstools command. Usage of the vmkfstools command is covered in Chapter 10: *ESX on the Command-Line.*

Creating a Folder for Holding Templates

1. In the VI Client switch to the View called Virtual Machines and Templates.

2. Right-click your DataCenter, in my case the London DataCenter.

3. Choose New Folder.

4. Type in a name. In my case I used _Templates to make sure it was always at the top of the list in the view.

Using Clone to a Template

GOTCHA:

You cannot create a template while a snapshot is engaged on the source VM. You will find the options to Clone, Clone to Template, and Convert to Template are greyed out.

1. In the Inventory View, "Hosts and Clusters."

2. Select a VM you powered off as your source for the template.

3. Right-click the VM, and select Clone to a Template.

   Figure 6.1 shows me typing in a friendly name such as "base-w2k3-sp1-build" and selecting the _Template Folder as the location in the inventory.

Figure 6.1

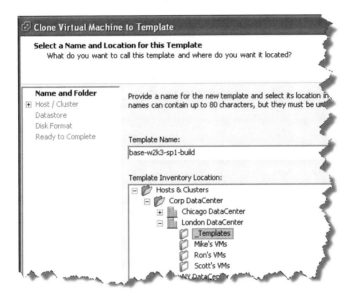

Note:

I will choose esx1.vi3book.com as the location for this template. A record is kept in the VirtualCenter indicating with which ESX host the VM was originally registered. This is not a problem so long as the template is stored on shared storage visible to the ESX hosts that will use that template. Even if that ESX host is re-installed you can still browse the datastore where the template was stored and register the .vmtx file with another ESX host.

4. Select the physical location for storing the template files.

Note:

I recommend an LUN or NAS export presented to all your ESX hosts. Figure 6.2 shows "Choose a datastore for the template" dialog which will assist you in selecting a good storage location for the template. It will show you the amount of free space, file system format such as VMFS, and, critically, if that volume is available for single host or many hosts.

Figure 6.2

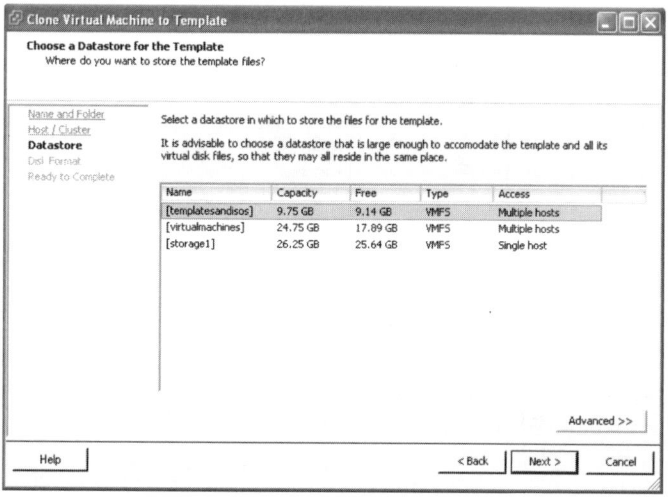

5. At this point you have the choice of Normal (all storage formats) or Compact (VMFS only).

Note:

I like to keep my templates as small as possible. I'm going to use the Compact format. The compact is slower to create and deploy a template, but does save a large amount of precious space. The downside of compact is that is not easy to maintain the template and stop the software inside of it from becoming out of date.

6. Click Finish.

Figure 6.3 shows that templates appear with special icon – making them easy to identify in the inventory.

Figure 6.3

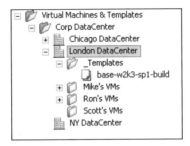

Using Convert to a Template

Remember, this method offers a very quick way of making a template – and unmarking it back as a VM to update your template as software changes. The only thing that feels "odd" is if you ever do this in the inventory view of "Hosts & Clusters." If you convert a VM into a template in the "Host and Clusters" view, the VM seems to disappear from the list. This isn't a bug, it is by design. You will find your VM in the inventory view of "Virtual Machines and Templates."

1. In the Inventory View, "Hosts and Clusters"-

2. select a VM you powered off as your source for the template.

3. Right-click the VM, and select Convert to a Template,

   Note: Notice how the VM disappears from the list.

4. Change the Inventory View to "Virtual Machines and Templates." It will be located in the same VM Folder where it was created. Figure 6.4 shows my vm1 converted into the template format. It could be renamed, and drag-and-dropped into the _Templates folder for consistency purposes.

Figure 6.4

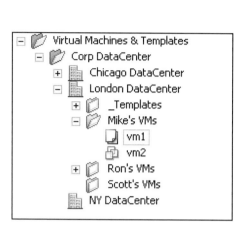

Note:

If you right-click a VM in this format you will find you have a "Convert to Virtual Machine" menu option. This allows you to quickly return the template to a VM, so you can easily keep the software within the VM up to date.

Creating a New VM from a Template

Before you rush ahead and clone or create a new VM from a template, you need to make a onetime change to VirtualCenter, especially if you're creating a Windows VM. Windows cannot be duplicated without resetting a number of attributes such as:

- NetBIOS name

- Domain Membership

- IP Settings

- SID (Security Identifier)

If you are creating new Linux VMs from a template you will have less attributes to reset such as hostname and IP settings. Fortunately, VMware has integrated Microsoft's System Preparation (sysprep) tool into VirtualCenter. VMware also has some open-source scripts that help change some attributes inside Linux. Unfortunately, Microsoft does not allow third-parties like VMware to distribute sysprep as part of their product code. Instead, we must manually copy sysprep to the VirtualCenter. If you fail to do this, options in the VI Client will not appear and will be greyed out. Specifically, the "Guest Customization Wizard" option will be unavailable.

This copying of sysprep triggers VMware's "Guest Customization Wizard" which appears during the process of creating a new VM. It allows us to reset Windows attributes prior to the first proper boot of Windows. VMware uses the information gathered in the guest customization wizard to create an "answer file" to the mini-installation wizard which normally runs after running sysprep manually. VMware uses a "disk mount" service in the VirtualCenter to access the virtual disk of the VM to inject sysprep and the answer file.

There are two "features" of sysprep of which you need to be aware. Firstly, it contains a password reset of the administrator account option which does not work consistently across all platforms of Microsoft Windows. This is outlined in the VMware KB article 1965. Password reset does not work with Windows 2003 regardless of the service pack used and will not work when you try to reset the password using the Guest Customization Wizard. More specifically, this happens if you engage the option to "Delete All User Accounts" which is required for resetting the Administrator's password when it is not blank. Figure 6.5 shows this error message.

Figure 6.5

As you can see, resetting the password and using the "Delete All User Accounts" option works in Windows 2000 but not in 2003. The only way to reset passwords in Windows 2003 is if the original source of the template has no password set for the Administrator account. This is not allowed in most people's local policy of Windows 2003. I imagine anyway that most datacenters would baulk at such a configuration – it would be too easy to create a new VM from a template with no password set on the Administrator account. Additionally, it has a negative impact on other services such as the Encrypted File System (EFS) feature.

Personally, I don't use the password reset option in the Guest Customization Wizard. I prefer to set a complex password on my original source VM – and then manually reset the new VM's password before handing it over to the application owner. If you wish to use the password reset then the configuration changes with each version of Windows.

Windows 2000: Set a password for administrator.

Reset password during customization.

Enable "Delete All User Accounts."

Windows 2003: Leave the password blank.

Reset the password during customization.

Do not enable "Delete All User Accounts."

Windows XP: Leave the password blank.

Reset the password during customization.

Do not enable "Delete All User Accounts."

Secondly, if you wish your sysprep VM to join a Microsoft Domain, you must run a DHCP Server with a scope for subnet where the VM resides. When the sysprep "mini-installation" process is running it is set to be a DHCP client (even if you specify a static IP configuration during the guest customization wizard), and static IP configurations are not applied until the first full boot of

Windows. Therefore, without a valid IP configuration from a DHCP server during the sysprep process, the VM would not successfully join a domain. These "features" are attributes of sysprep – and not bugs in the VMware template process.

Lastly, at various times in VirtualCenter history, VMware has seen it fit to move the storage location in the file system of the VirtualCenter server. In a clean installation of VirtualCenter 2.x the correct location should be in:

C:\Documents and Settings \All Users\ Application Data\ VMware\ Windows\ resources\ sysprep

Adding Sysprep Support to VirtualCenter

You have some choices about how you want to run sysprep in conjunction with VirtualCenter. You can use just one version, sysprep 1.1 for all flavors of Windows, or alternatively, you can hunt down the various versions of sysepep distributed with Windows and have each version of Windows (2000, XP, 2003) use its own version.

You can find sysprep within the support\tools\deploy.cab file on most modern copies of Windows CD such as Windows 2000, Window XP, and Windows 2003. If you are running Windows Vista you will find sysprep in the \Windows\System32\ directory. You should be aware that at the time of writing there is no support the 64-bit versions of sysprep.

You can also find copies of sysprep on the Microsoft Website by searching the below listed file names:

Sysprep 1.1

Q257813_W2K_spl_X86_EN.exe

http://www.microsoft.com/downloads/details.aspx?familyid=0C4BFB06-2824-4D2B-ABC1-0E2223133AFB&displaylang=en

Windows XP Service Pack 2

WindowsXP-KB838080-SP2-DeployTools-ENU.cab

http://www.microsoft.com/downloads/details.aspx?familyid=3E90DC91-AC56-4665-949B-BEDA3080E0F6&displaylang=en

Windows 2003 Service Pack 1 Version

WindowsServer2003-KB892778-SP1-DeployTools-x86-ENU.cab

http://www.microsoft.com/downloads/details.aspx?FamilyID=A34EDCF2-EBFD-4F99-BBC4-E93154C332D6&displaylang=en

To begin using SysPrep:

1. Extract your version(s) of sysprep.

2. Copy them to:

C:\Documents and Settings\All Users\Application Data\VMware\VMware VirtualCenter\Windows\resources\sysprep

Creating a New VM from a Template

1. In the **Virtual Machines and Templates** view, locate your template.

2. **Right-click the template,** and choose **Deploy this virtual machine from template.**

3. **Type in a name for the new VM,** and **select a folder location.**

4. **Select an ESX host** on which the VM will run.

5. **Select a datastore** for where the VM will be stored.

6. Choose to **Customize using the guest Customization Wizard.**

Note:

This option will be unavailable and greyed out if sysprep has not been copied to VirtualCenter and your VM is running a Windows guest operating system.

The remainder of the dialog boxes should be fairly self explanatory to anyone who is familiar with Windows. If you have a copy of Windows that requires an OEM number (like all copies of Windows 2003 do) it is a good idea to input this now – otherwise the sysprep mini-installation wizard stalls waiting for user input. At the end of the Customization Wizard you will have the option to save your inputs for further use. This saves you from having to fill in the Guest Customization Wizard every time you use it. To do this, use the third option in the deploy wizard called "Customize using an existing customization specification" and enable the option at the bottom of the dialog called "Use the Customization Wizard to temporarily adjust the specification before deployment."

Administrators will find the dialog boxes differ when creating a template from Linux guest operating system. VMware has a built-in script that executes inside the Linux guest to reset its IP and hostname settings.

Using the Customization Specification Manager

Occasionally, you will accidentally save a custom configuration – which you would rather delete – or have existing custom configurations which you want to modify. The custom configuration manager allows you to manage these from one single UI. It allows you to:

- Copy an existing custom configuration

- Edit an existing custom configuration

- Rename an existing custom configuration (using the properties option)

- Export to an XML file

- Import from an XML file

This import feature is useful to previous users of VirtualCenter 1.x which used an XML format for storing custom configurations. You will find it in the VI Client under Edit and Customization Specifications. Figure 6.6 shows this simple application's basic functionality.

Figure 6.6

Summary

In this chapter I've tried to show you the options that you have for provisioning new copies of Windows or Linux. This is a major feature of VMware Virtual-Center. Research has shown that the provisioning process (the process of deploying a new server) can take weeks. With VMware templates we can have a new server online in a matter of hours. In fact, what might need reviewing are the other procedures that create bottlenecks in the process. Very often these are not technical issues but IT management processes such as the time it takes to request and process things like DNS Registrations, change management requests, and approvals and security audits. Alongside I/O virtualization and VDI, some people think the "next big thing" to hit IT will be management applications that automate the whole workflow process.

Chapter 7: Access Control

You're probably quite familiar with the principles of allowing privileges from other systems you manage. If you are preparing for the Vi-3 exam you might want to spend some time making sure you are entirely happy with the difference between the built in roles used to assign privileges.

This chapter discusses the configuration of ESX and VirtualCenter for user rights. It is not unusual in large datacenters to have tiers of responsibility. Just as with ordinary users, we cannot depend on the good will of members of the IT department to stick within their job function. The only way to enforce change control is with tools that allow delegation.

Whether you use ESX in a stand-alone or with VirtualCenter the model for security is the same, the only difference being from where the users and groups come. With ESX in a stand-alone mode users and groups are created locally to the ESX host. If you use VirtualCenter your users and groups can be located in Active Directory, NT4 Domains, or users local to the VirtualCenter member server.

The model of security involves three components. Users or groups are added to VMware roles and these roles are assigned privileges. If you are a fan of the AGLP acronym you can think of VMware's model as GRP. Groups are added to roles, and roles are assigned privileges. In fact it's not possible in the GUI to bypass this method. It is impossible to assign to users or groups privileges without first using a role.

While we are on the subject of AGLP, I have found that VirtualCenter currently works in a very specific way with groups. The following approaches simply *do not* work:

- Using Global groups directly
- Using Global Groups added to Domain Local groups

What does work is the following:

- Users local to the VirtualCenter

- Groups to the VirtualCenter

- Domain Users in the Domain

- Accounts added to global groups, added to local groups on the VirtualCenter server

VirtualCenter would not duplicate the same privileges if you take the "hot standby" approach unless it is a duplicate of the primary. This can raise some interesting challenges.

As VirtualCenter has a system of folders, datacenter objects and sub-folders a system of inheritance does exist. So if you set role on a folder it will pass your privileges down the folder hierarchy. It is possible to stop this inheritance further down the hierarchy if you so wish. Of course, this system is not intended to be as sophisticated as file system's permissions system – but it is generally fit for its purpose. As with other systems you may have used, your position in the IT Management hierarchy has nothing to do with these hierarchies. So I might give a senior manager, who is not technical, read-only rights at the top of the tree – and give a Server Engineer administrator rights in a datacenter.

The Vi client does a very good job of hiding and disabling features for which the user has no privileges – so in the Inventory the user will find objects are hidden; ESX host names are not displayed; right-click menu options are greyed out and buttons on toolbars are disabled depending on your privileges.

In total, there are eight predefined roles. Three of these are available to a stand-alone ESX host and VirtualCenter, whereas the remaining 5 roles are only available to VirtualCenter. You can create your own custom roles with your own privileges. The eight predefined roles are as follows:

- No Access

- Read-Only

- Administrator

- Virtual Machine Administrator

- Datacenter Administrator

- Virtual Machine Power User

- Virtual Machine User

- Resource Pool Administrator

The first three (No Access, Read-only and Administrator) are common to both ESX and VirtualCenter. This book is not the place to discuss every single permissions difference between one role and another – clearly some roles such as "read-only" are self explanatory to anyone with experience of setting permissions and rights in other systems. But I would like to summarize the key differences. I recommend consulting VMware technical documentations for an exhaustive definition list of the privileges that make up a specific role.

No Access

This role is usually used for "exceptions to the rule." For example, say we have a group called "London" which contains 100 users, but 3 of those users should not have access to the resource in question. Rather than creating another group with 97 users, I add in the group – and then add in the 3 users (Bob, Harry, and Sue) and choose the "No Access" option. The effective permission for Bob, Harry, and Sue despite their group membership would be No access.

Administrator

This account has the highest privilege of all users. By default the Windows group of Administrators is the default group used with this role. This may not always be desirable – as a full administrator in Windows may not necessarily be a full administrator in VMware. There has to be default to allow access. In ESX 3.0.1 it is not possible to remove the last full administrator – however, in ESX 3.0.0 this was possible. ESX 3.0.1 fixed this "bug." By default, the root account on an ESX host is a member of the administrators group

Virtual Machine User

This role only assigns a privilege to VMs. Used on a datacenter with inheritance it would allow the user to power on, off, reset and suspend a VM. It would also allow the user to open a remote console on a VM. Frequently, Windows or Linux operators are given this privilege unless a more appropriate method can be used to deliver them to their environment. For example, it may be more viable to allow telnet ssh access to Linux operators and RDP access to Windows operators.

Virtual Machine Power User

This type of user has the capacity to change some (but not all) of a VM's settings. It allows access to some "advanced" VM options such as creating and reverting snapshots.

Resource Pool Administrator

We have yet to cover resource pools – but put simply it is possible to create pools of CPU and RAM and allocate groups of VMs to the pool. It offers a quick and easy way to assign resources at a group level rather than modifying the settings of each and every VM. The system allows me to delegate management responsibility to the pool. Given the highly specific nature of this role, it is usually assigned to the resource pool object itself rather than elsewhere in the inventory.

Datacenter Administrator

This role allows the user to create new datacenter objects. However, the user has very limited rights to interact with the VM. Specifically, the datacenter role has no privileges to create remote console sessions.

Virtual Machine Administrator

This role allows full control over a VM's properties – right down to the permission to delete VMs from the ESX host and VirtualCenter. Given the name you might think that wherever you set this role that would be all the user could do, but you would be wrong. Depending on where in the hierarchy this role is set, it is possible for this role to add and remove ESX hosts from VirtualCenter.

Now that we have a correct understanding of the roles and what privileges they possess it is time to configure them. To carry out the next series of tasks you will need a collection of test users and some groups. Of course the possible permutations of privileges are infinite, and it is not my intention to show every permutation, but to give you a feel for how it is both to assign and use roles within VirtualCenter and ESX. In my case I created a Windows group called "Vi3 Authors" and added two user Windows accounts – Scott and Ron.

In this demonstration I decide to allow "Vi-3 Authors" access to Mike's VMs within the Virtual Machine and Templates view.

1. **Right-click the folder in VirtualCenter** where you wish to apply your permission.

2. Choose **Add Permission**.

3. Under **Users and Groups**, click the **Add button**.

4. **Browse your system for your user group** and click **OK**.

5. Under **Assigned Role** select the role; in my case I selected Virtual Machine User.

    Note:

    In the same dialog we also have the option of deciding if these privileges "Propagate to Child Object." Disabling this option would apply the privileges to this folder only and not sub-folders.

Copying and Creating Custom Roles

One of the problems with the "Virtual Machine User" role option for me is the fact that this privilege also allows Ron and Scott to connect the VMs in my folder to removable devices such as CD-ROMs and floppy drives and modify connections to vSwitch port groups. I know that modifying these settings can cause warnings and errors with VMotion, and I would rather they did not have this privilege. I can easily duplicate the "Virtual Machine User" role and re-move this privilege from the copy.

1. Click the **Admin button** on the toolbar.

2. Right-click **Virtual Machine User** from the list, and choose **Clone**.

3. **Rename the clone to a unique and meaningful name** such as "Custom Virtual Machine User – No Removable Devices."

4. **Right-click the custom role**, and choose **Edit Role**.

5. Expand the + signs, and **navigate to + All Privileges, + Virtual Machine, + Interaction**, and **remove the tick** next to **Device Connection**.

6. **Return to your original folder where the built-in privilege was set**, and **select the Permissions tab**.

7. **Double-click the group** you assign the original role to, and select **Custom Virtual Machine User – No Removable Devices**.

   Note:

   Changes in privileges like this take immediate effect (as long as you use ESX 3.0.1 and VirtualCenter 2.0.1 or later) without the user being required to logout and login again. You should find that while users do not have right to *configure* the CD or floppy devices the privilege does not inhibit their rights to *connect* the CD or floppy devices.

Figure 7.1 shows me allocating my custom role to Mike's Group.

Figure 7.1

Removing Custom Roles

Removing a custom role is very easy; if you do it without first assigning an existing role to a user or group VirtualCenter will ask you to allocate another role first. This only happens if the role you are removing is currently in use somewhere in the VirtualCenter inventory. This is done to ensure that you don't deny your user rights altogether – crashing them out of the Vi Client through lack of any rights whatsoever.

Figure 7.2 shows the "Delete Role" dialog.

1. Click the **Admin button** on the toolbar.

2. Right-click custom role from the list and choose **Remove**.

3. Choose **OK**, to confirm you wish to delete it.

4. In the **Delete Role** dialog box select **Reassign affected users to**, and select an appropriate role.

Figure 7.2

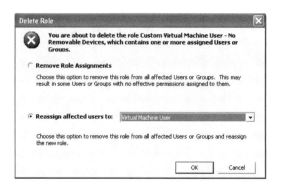

VM Creation Rights

If you want to grant a user the right to create new VMs, a combination of privileges is required. Firstly, they need privilege of "Virtual Machine Administrator" in the folder hierarchy of Virtual Machines and Templates. Secondly, as you may remember from creating a new VM, you have to be able select an ESX host or DRS/HA cluster on which it will run. As a consequence groups and users will need "Virtual Machine Administrator" rights on either datacenters, individual ESX hosts, folders containing ESX hosts or DRS/HA clusters. The instructions below enable the ability to create VMs.

Allow Rights to a Folder in Virtual Machines and Templates

1. **Right-click** a folder in "Virtual Machines and Templates" where you wish to apply your permission.

2. Choose **Add Permission**.

3. Under "**Users and Groups,**" click the **Add button**.

4. **Browse your system for your user group**, and click **OK,**

5. Under "**Assigned Role**" select the role. In my case I selected **Virtual Machine Administrator** for Mike's **Group**.

Allow Rights to Host & Clusters

1. **Right-click** in the "Hosts and Cluster" view one of the following: Datacenter, ESX Host, A Folder containing ESX hosts, A DRS/HA Cluster

   Note:

   In my case I select the "Intel Hosts" folder.

2. Choose **Add Permission**.

3. Under **Users and Groups**, click the **Add button**.

4. **Browse your system for your user group**, and click **OK**.

5. Under **Assigned Role** select the role. In my case I selected **Virtual Machine Administrator** and I choose **Mike's Group**.

   Note:

   Figure 7.3 shows how you can use Admin view to see where in the Inventory you have used your roles.

Figure 7.3

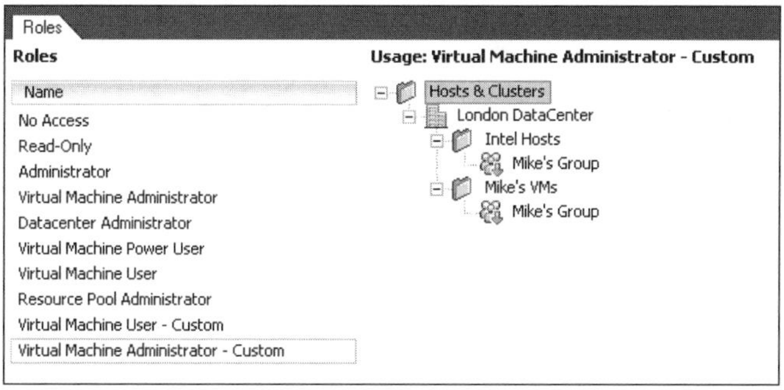

Using VMware Web-Access

On the ESX host and the VirtualCenter server there is web-service which runs. This is used to allow an "operator" style UI where operators can manage their VMs. The beauty of this service is that it only allows operators to manage VMs and nothing else, and it avoids the need to install the Vi-Client to every operator's PC. Web-Access requires no setup routine at all. All that is required is web-browser and the URL of the VirtualCenter or ESX hosts. If you point your web-browser at the VirtualCenter system, you will need to supply a Windows user account to login whereas if you point your web-browser at the ESX host, it will need local users created on it for it to work.

It has a number of neat features – firstly, the capacity for the operator to receive a console view of their VM and have this go into a full-screen view. Secondly, it has the ability to cut and paste a URL which points directly to the VM and to paste this to an email or a shortcut.

1. Open a web-browser to your VirtualCenter server, in my case this address.

   https://virtualcenter.vi3book.com/ui

   Note:

   Both ESX and VirtualCenter web-access generates a certificate using OpenSSL during the installation. The performance of web-access can be improved by either installing the built in certificate to your web-browser or creating a trusted certificate using your own Certificate Authority.

   Note:

   With Internet Explorer 7 you will have to allow pop-ups to this web-site.

2. Login with your VirtualCenter user name – I recommend testing this with a user account you have set up with limited permissions as it is more realistic.

   Figure 7.4 shows the standard layout of the web-access when managing a VM with the capacity to power on, off, suspend, and restart a VM on the toolbar. Additionally, we have the ability to manage devices such as the NIC, CD, and Floppy. The console tab will give you a view of your VM – it requires the install of an activeX control in Internet Explorer to work. Enabling the console view also enables the dimmed icon between the restart button and the NIC icon. This icon allows you to take the console view into a full screen (use [CTRL]+[ALT] to return to a normal view).

Figure 7.4

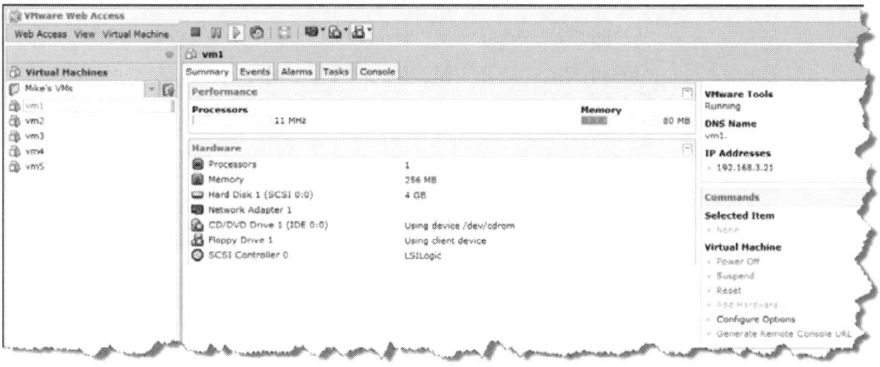

3. To generate a URL for a particular VM to be sent to use by email, under the Command Pane:

   Select Generate Remote Console URL.

4. Highlight the text in the light blue Generate URL box (like the sample shown below) and paste into an email.

   https://virtualcenter.vi3book.com/ui/vmDirect.do?view=d3NVcmw9aH
   R0cDovL2xvY2FsaG9zdDo4MDg1JnZtSWQ9VmlydHVhbE1hY2hpbm
   V8dm0tMjQ5JnVpPTM2_

Session Management

Now that we have multiple users connected via various privileges and interfaces it seems like a good time to mention session management. From the Vi Client it is possible to see who is logged on, disconnect Vi client users, and send a "Message of the Day." This message of the day is shown *every time* a Vi Client is connected and does not change until it is modified by the administrator.

1. Select the **Admin** button on the toolbar.

2. Select the **Session** tab.

Figure 7.5 shows users Administrator and Mike are both logged on. The message of the day which I have input is displayed at every logon. As the note states, modifying the text and clicking the change button transmits the messages to all sessions including your own.

Right-clicking a user like VI3BOOK\Mike and choosing "Terminate Session" sends a message to the user and closes their Vi Client.

Figure 7.5

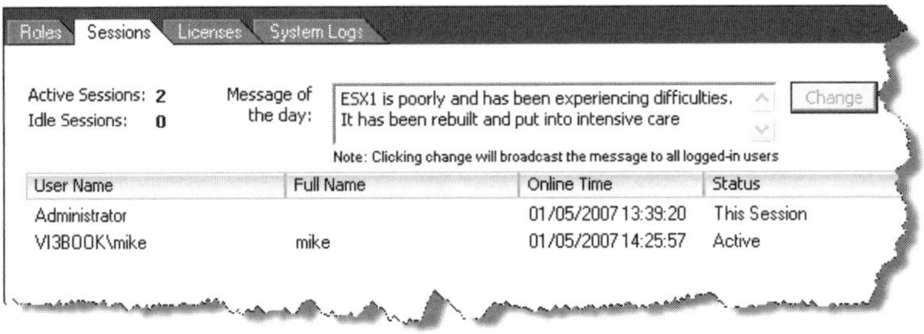

Session management also exposes itself when two users connect to the *same* VM using the VMware console. Figure 7.6 shows the alert that appears in the console title bar.

Figure 7.6

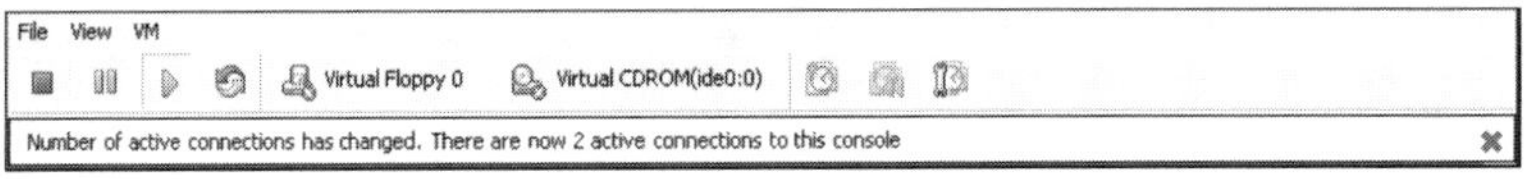

When this happens, it is possible for another user to interact with the VM at the same time as no attempt is made by VMware to "lock" the keyboard or mouse by the first user to open a console. In this respect a VM console is very much like an ILO/RAC or IP-KVM. This warning also appears if you open a console window and *also* open a console using the console tab available for each VM as shown in Figure 7.7.

Figure 7.7

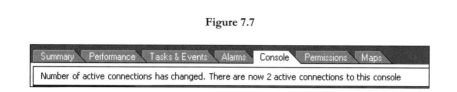

Conclusion

In this chapter we have seen how it easy it is to delegate responsibility to others within your group or team. Web-Access is useful so long as your team only needs operator style access to VMs. It also stops you from having to unnecessarily install the Vi Client to lots of PCs.

Chapter 8: Resource Monitoring

There are two very common mistakes that many administrators make when evaluating performance in VMware. Firstly, there is a tendency for an administrator to use the guest operating system's performance analysis tools such as Microsoft's Task Manager and Performance Monitor or Linux tools like VM's tat and top. Unfortunately, all of these tools have been designed for the guest operating system when it runs directly on physical hardware, not on virtual hardware. In the world of virtualization these tools have very limited usage. I still use Task Manager to identify crashed applications and use the "end task" button to kill processes. What I don't use is Task Manager's graphic chart to see what the percentage utilization is for the virtual CPU. All performance analysis is time critical- such as Page swaps/sec and CPU cycles/sec. The problem is that the VM does not see the CPU's physical clock – and therefore averages and such can be skewed. It is possible to run Performance Tools inside the VM *if* they have been written with the VMware Guest Operating System SDK (Software Development Kit). For example, Richard Garsthagen has two utilities called VM PerfMon and VM Time based on the VMware Guest OS SDK. These tools can be downloaded for free from the following site:

http://www.run-virtual.com/

Secondly, many administrators assume that poor performance is caused by the VM itself. However, a slow network response, for example, could be caused by configuration settings in the guest operating system. A couple of examples are bad DNS server search orders or poor settings in application software. All the tips and tricks you have learned to improve performance in the guest operating system still apply inside VM, such as disabling unneeded services. On its own, virtualization does not inherently improve performance or the reliability of your guest operating system – unless your VM is running on significantly better hardware than the previous existing physical systems.

Of course there is another way of measuring performance, and it's called "user experience." How fast or slow does a given system "feel" – and can you judge that against an agreed sense of "acceptable usage"? For example, what is an acceptable login time to a desktop PC against a domain controller running in VM? Is it 10 seconds, 30 seconds, 1 minute or 1 hour? Appealing though this approach might be to a modern IT department wedded to the concept of being "user focused," the problem with this is manifold. Firstly, as my login example demonstrates, it is a highly qualitative approach and extremely subjective. Secondly, user expectations are constantly rising to whatever resources we are allocating – what is fast today is regarded as slow three months later. Lastly, it tells us nothing about the cause of the problem.

Identifying performance bottlenecks can be tricky in a virtualization environment. After all, we have many VMs, all executing on the same underlying hardware. How do you identify which VMs are the cause of poor performance and which are not? Many people choose to move VMs to an isolated ESX host and do their performance analysis there. This way you can see if it is that particular VM which is the source of the problem – or its relationship to others. If a VM is still performing badly when it has access to *all* the resources of an ESX host, then this might indicate the problem is within the guest operating system layer, rather than at the virtualization layer.

The key to fixing performance problems in any environment is knowing what tools are available to collect performance information. The only reliable, cast-iron guaranteed method of monitoring performance is using VMware or 3rd party tools that collect performance information *outside* of the VM. This will lead you to identifying the constraining resource. Invariably this will be one of the "four core;" CPU, Memory, Network, or Disk. It's important to be familiar with how to monitor the resources of VMs before we embark on making changes. If we don't know the source of our performance problems – how would we know what to change – and critically how would we verify that our changes have resolved our problem? Before we look at the tools for monitoring performance we need to understand how the VMkernel allocates resources to the VMs.

CPUs

VMkernel Load-balancing or Scheduling

When VMs run they execute their instructions on the physical CPUs of the ESX host. Within the ESX server the VMkernel is configured to monitor load on the CPUs, looking for a CPU that is doing less work than others. If the

VMkernel spots a significant disparity in the load on one physical CPU compared to another it will "schedule" that VMs threads to execute on a less busy CPU. This monitoring is configured at intervals of every 20 milliseconds and places a burden on the VMkernel. However, the performance gained by carrying out this analysis more than offsets the burden. The value of 20 milliseconds is configurable, and you may decide to make it less frequent if you feel your CPU load across an ESX host is relatively uniform. So if you don't experience large fluctuations in CPU activity you can change the frequency. The setting is called Cpu.MigratePeriod and is held under the Configuration Tab and Advanced Settings. The scheduler is designed to distribute CPU requests intelligently within the ESX host and reduce contention as much as possible. Contention is the word we use to describe a scenario where resources are scarce and two or more VMs "fight over" the resource, such as a CPU.

Single vCPUs or multiple vCPUs

Single vCPUs execute their threads on a single physical socket or core at any one time. In contrast, a dual or quad vCPU executes its instructions on more than one physical socket or core.

If you are using hyper-threading on Intel Xeon processors, the VMkernel treats each logical CPU in the Xeon chipset as if it was a physical processor. So a two socket processor with hyper-threading enabled would actually appear as if you had four physical processors. When it comes to dual or quad based VMs the VMkernel scheduler always makes sure it runs the VM on two different logical processors in two different sockets. There are some cases where hyper-threading actually degrades CPU performance, especially when the CPU I/0 is exceptionally intensive. You might have already experienced this with resource-intensive products such as Oracle, Microsoft SQL, and Exchange. I have seen this personally in the terminal service environments with Citrix Presentation servers. For the most part, hyper-threading is a good feature to enable – but watch out for some high-end and processor intensive threads which would prefer to use the whole physical socket, rather than just a logical processor within it.

Here's a good analogy for hyper-threading. Imagine you have a narrow country lane which you would like enable for two-way traffic. Rather than widening the road you draw a line down the center of the road. This is what happens with hyper-threading. The CPU package is able to take bi-directional communication. However, the actual width of the road or CPU hasn't widened. So although you might get two small cars (small CPU transactions) up and down this road – if a large vehicle comes along it will have to use both lanes anyway (a single large CPU transaction).

It is possible to have some per VM controls on how VM executes on a processor with hyper-threading available.

Controlling Hyper-threading Sharing on a VM

1. Right-click a VM, and Choose Edit Settings.

2. Click the Resource Tab, and Select Advanced CPU.

Figure 8.1 shows the ability to use three options:

Any: More than one VM can execute on the logical CPU.

None: VM receives all of the CPU not shared with other VMs.

Internal: VM with two vCPUs gets exclusive access to a CPU and its logical CPUs. This setting does not affect VMs with 4-vCPU's.

Figure 8.1

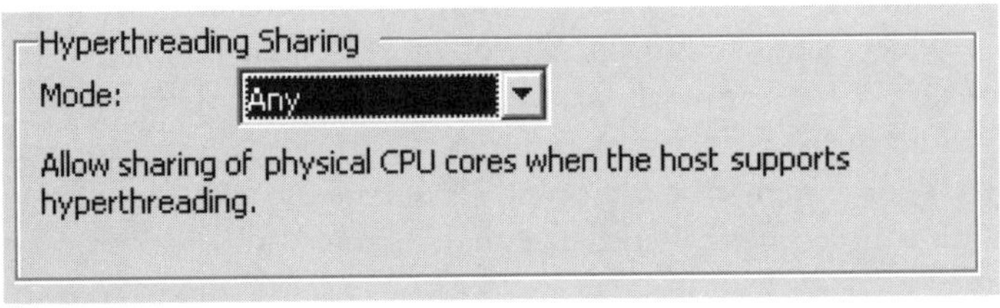

In conclusion, to get the benefit of virtual SMP you do need plenty of cores or sockets. There is little point in creating a dual based VM if you only have two sockets or two cores. All this will do is give the VMkernel's scheduler more work to do and increase the chances of two VMs competing for a resource. Very simply, the more sockets or cores you have, the more opportunities the VMkernel schedule has of finding a CPU not in use or not heavily used – which then makes the VM perform better. The term that is sometimes used is having plenty of "hardware execution contexts," or in another way, plenty of sockets or cores to run a dual or quad vCPU.

To really leverage the value of vSMP you need four sockets/cores for dual VMs and eight sockets/cores for quad based VMs. Remember, Microsoft does not officially support "downgrading" an instance of Windows from dual or quad to a single CPU VM. Additionally, not all applications and services are multiprocessor (or multithreaded) aware – so sometimes adding an additional vCPU could make no difference to performance at all. Due to these issues I would recommend the decision to use vSMP should be taken with care, on a case-by-case basis. One way of finding out the impact of such a change could be to clone an existing uni-processor VM and upgrade the duplicate to be a dual or quad VM. You could then decide to delete or roll-back to the old VM should your test show to improve the situation or make it worse.

Lastly, in years to come this kind of concern might become less significant. Intel has, in their R&D labs, already created a multi-core processor that has up to 100 cores in a single socket under its "Tera-scale" computing research program. This CPU was created for experimental purposes only and will probably never see production market. It might not be so long until each VM executes on a dedicated core of its own.

CPU, Guest Operating System Kernel Updates and Idling

Excessive CPU activity can be caused with VM after P2V process. When you P2V a multi-processor physical machine, it is possible to "downgrade" to uniprocessor VM. For this to work properly you would need to carry out a kernel update. In the world of Microsoft Windows this means changing the ACPI Function from an ACPU Multi-processor to an ACPI Uni-processor within the "Device Manager" tool. This replaces the "Hardware Abstraction Layer" file (hal.dll) and the ntoskernel.exe files. The incorrect HAL or ACPI functionality can cause a VM to make CPU demands even when it is not doing any legitimate CPU requests. This is because without the correct HAL the VMkernel cannot "idle" the VM correctly. In other words the VMkernel doesn't know how to manage the VM correctly when it is in an idle or inactive state.

Microsoft has made moves in recent releases of Windows to inhibit even the administrator's ability to change the HAL. Ostensibly this has been done to "protect" novice administrators from changing the HAL, as it can cause a "blue screen of death" (BSOD) which puts the operating system in a state from which it cannot (without a great deal of effort and skill) be recovered. Fortunately, you can side step such "protection" using CLI tools freely available from Microsoft. One such excellent hardware management CLI is "DevCon." You will find it as part of the Driver Development Kit (DDK) from the mdsn.com part of Microsoft's website.

For example, this DevCon script would forcibly downgrade a multi-processor HAL Windows 2003 or Windows XP VM to use just a uni-processor HAL. The part that does the work is "devcon update %windir%\inf\hal.inf ACPIPIC_UP" which instructs the Windows kernel with HAL to use:

```
@echo off
cls
rem Author:      Mike Laverick
rem URL:     http://www.rtfm-ed.co.uk
echo =====================================================
echo ==Downgrading ACPI to Uni-
Processor===================
echo =====================================================
echo.
echo Please Wait
devcon sethwid @ROOT\PCI_HAL\0000 := !E_ISA_UP !ACPI-
PIC_UP !ACPIAPIC_UP !ACPIAPIC_MP !MPS_UP !MPS_MP
!SGI_MPS_MP !SYSPRO_MP !SGI_MPS_MP  > nul
devcon sethwid @ROOT\ACPI_HAL\0000 := !E_ISA_UP !ACPI-
PIC_UP !ACPIAPIC_UP !ACPIAPIC_MP !MPS_UP !MPS_MP
!SGI_MPS_MP !SYSPRO_MP !SGI_MPS_MP
devcon sethwid @ROOT\PCI_HAL\0000 := +ACPIPIC_UP
devcon sethwid @ROOT\ACPI_HAL\0000 := +ACPIPIC_UP
devcon update %windir%\inf\hal.inf ACPIPIC_UP
echo Done!
echo.
echo ===============================================
echo ==Script Completed================================
echo ===============================================
```

```
echo.
echo ==========================================
echo ==Press any key to reboot the Virtual Ma-
chine===============
echo ==========================================
pause > nul
devcon reboot
```

In the case of Windows 2000 the HAL references in the INF file are slightly
different so to downgrade the HAL for it would require a slightly different
script:

```
@echo off
cls
rem Author:      Mike Laverick
rem URL:      http://www.rtfm-ed.co.uk
echo ==========================================
echo ==Downgrading ACPI to Uni-
Processor====================
echo ==========================================
echo.
echo Please Wait
devcon sethwid @ROOT\PCI_HAL\0000 := !E_ISA_UP !ACPI-
PIC_UP !ACPIAPIC_UP !ACPIAPIC_MP !MPS_UP !MPS_MP
!SGI_MPS_MP !SYSPRO_MP !SGI_MPS_MP
devcon sethwid @ROOT\ACPI_HAL\0000 := !E_ISA_UP !ACPI-
PIC_UP !ACPIAPIC_UP !ACPIAPIC_MP !MPS_UP !MPS_MP
!SGI_MPS_MP !SYSPRO_MP !SGI_MPS_MP
devcon sethwid @ROOT\PCI_HAL\0000 := +ACPIAPIC_UP
devcon sethwid @ROOT\ACPI_HAL\0000 := +ACPIAPIC_UP
devcon update %windir%\inf\hal.inf ACPIAPIC_UP
echo Done!
echo.
echo ==========================================
echo ==Script Completed================================
echo ==========================================
echo.
echo ==========================================
echo ==Press any key to reboot the Virtual Ma-
chine===============
echo ==========================================
pause > nul
devcon reboot
```

You can find copies of these scripts on my website. So if you find yourself in the unenviable position of downgrading the HAL you can do the normal "without warranty" disclaimers application and of course ensure backup, or snapshot your VMs before using them. They are under the section labeled "Sample P2V Post-Configuration Scripts for P2V and Sample ISO File."

http://www.rtfm-ed.co.uk/?page_id=8

Memory

Transparent Page Sharing (TPS)

ESX server deploys a number of memory management techniques to boost the amount of available RAM – and to dynamically manage the system should physical memory become scarce. The first and most important of these is "Transparent Page Sharing." If you run more than one copy of Windows or Linux on an ESX host, the VMkernel can identify that very similar information is likely to be duplicated in memory. So in the case of two instances of Windows there is likely to be more than one copy of files such as explorer.exe, svchost.exe, lsass.exe, spools.exe, and so on. The same scenario exists for every guest operating system supported by ESX in a VM. The VMkernel spots these duplicates and produces a single read-only copy. The read-only attribute is important from a security perspective, as it prevents the possibility of one VM modifying the memory contents of another VM. If a VM needs to modify the contents of its memory – the VMkernel seamlessly generates a read-write copy of the file – and instructs the VM where to find the file in memory. This is all done without the guest operating system or the VM realizing it is it taking place. In other words, the sharing of pages of memory is invisible (or transparent) to the guest operating system. It can be achieved because it is the VMkernel that is really in charge of the hardware, not Windows or Linux. VMware's own research has shown that around 30% of the guest operating system memory is duplicated between VMs when they are running on ESX. The values for the other guest operating systems are somewhat lower (because of Windows' systemic memory hungriness) but *all* VMs benefit from TPS to a greater or lesser degree.

The net result is a massive savings in the amount of RAM required to run a VM. In my own experience I have seen savings of 1-1.5GB on a server with as little as 2GB of physical RAM. The TPS feature also helps to "offset" the memory wasted by actually having a virtualization layer in the first place. After all, 272MB of RAM is lost when the Service Console loads. The VMkernel is round about 25MB in memory. Running one VM with one vCPU consumes 54MB of memory, with 64MB of memory consumed for a dual-VM. TPS helps offset this "virtualization overhead," sometimes even cancelling it out altogether.

The vmmemctl driver

When you install VMware Tools into a VM, alongside an improved network and mouse driver the VM has a memory control driver installed as well. Its file name is vmmemctl. It is normally referred to by VMware as the "balloon driver." This is because they use the analogy of a balloon to explain how this driver works. The most important thing to know about vmmemctl is that it is only engaged when memory is scarce and VMs are "fighting over" that resource – in other words, when contention is occurring. By itself it doesn't "fix" the problem of a lack of resources or unexpected peak demands for memory. In fact, its biggest use is as an indicator that there is a memory problem, so it is useful as a counter which draws the administrator's attention to potential problems. It is the symptom of a problem, not the source.

How does the vmmemctl driver work? Well, during normal operation where memory is plentiful and VMs are not in contention, the driver does nothing. It sits there inside the VM, deflated like a saggy balloon at the end of the party. However, when memory is scarce and the VMs are fighting over the resource, the vmmemctl driver begins to inflate. In other words, it begins to make demands for pages of memory. This generally occurs in a VM which you have marked as having a low priority on the system. The guest operating system obeys its internal memory management techniques – freeing up RAM by flushing old data to its virtual memory (page file or swap partition) to give the vmmemctl driver ranges of memory. Next comes the clever bit – rather than hanging on to this newly allocated memory, the vmmemctl driver hands over its memory to the VMkernel. The VMkernel in turn hands over this memory to the other VMs that really need it. When memory demands return to normal and are no longer scarce, the balloon driver deflates and gracefully hands back the memory it claimed to the guest operating system. On its own the vmmemctl driver doesn't fix the problem which is a lack of memory. It does, on the other hand, give us a clear indicator of a potential problem. Additionally, it allows us to configure (along with other tools covered in the next chapter) the system for worse case scenarios by offering guaranteed levels of service to VMs that need it if memory becomes low.

The VMkernel VM Swap File

There are a number of approaches for handling the allocation of memory to a VM. These will be covered in more detail in the next module. It is possible to configure a VM to guarantee that a VM always runs in memory – and never uses virtual memory. To do this you would need quite a large amount of memory, depending on how much you allocate to a VM when you create it. It is also possible to configure a VM for what is referred to as "memory over-commitment." This is where we allocate more memory to VMs than is actually *physically* present on an ESX host. This allows for very high VM to ESX ratios without the need to buy more memory. The difference between what we allocate and how much physical memory we have is made up by VMkernel, VM swap file. Naturally, some anxieties surround this idea, not least the issue of performance. We all know that despite caching on SAN controllers and the increases in disk spindle speeds – memory is faster because there are no moving parts. It is important to know that in the world of ESX the VMkernel VM Swap File is only used as a "last resort." In other words, in order to get repeated read-write activity on the swap file, *all* memory would have been used on the ESX host. This is significantly different to the way our guest operating systems use their swap files and partitions. In Windows it not unusual to see page faults and swaps even on a server with lots of physical RAM. This is because Windows always has seen physical RAM and swap space as if it were one single block of memory. In the case of ESX, one would only expect to see swap activity in the extreme case where all RAM had been depleted. As with the balloon driver, swap activity is a symptom rather than the cause. It is an indication that an ESX is low on memory or VMs have been poorly configured with more memory reservations than they actually need.

Disks and Networking

Performance considerations on these resources have been covered earlier in this book. In the storage chapter I showed how correctly configuring the SAN or iSCSI for multi-pathing and selecting the correct RAID level can greatly affect performance. In the networking chapter I discussed the merits of "Traffic Shaping." I don't wish to restate those recommendations again, but I will cover the metrics and counters that would be used to diagnose bottlenecks in these resources.

Identifying Resource Constraints

CPU

Beside the overall amount of CPU used and the amount each VM is using – there is actually a much more revealing measure of actual VM performance called the "ready" value. The ready value means the VM is "ready" to execute processes and is waiting for the CPU to allocate a slice of CPU time. It is perfectly fine for a VM to be using 99% CPU, as long as its ready value remains low. A high CPU used value merely indicates a VM is processing – it doesn't necessarily mean the VM is performing badly. It could be benign CPU cycles caused by an application which is inherently CPU intensive. If however, the % ready value grows then this usually indicates the VM is ready to run but the CPU is not ready to supply the CPU time it demands. Does VMware give any guidelines on what appropriate CPU ready values should be? Yes, they say anything constantly over 5% should be looked at as a potential bottleneck.

Often there is a close relationship (an inverse proportion in some case) between the % of CPU used by a VM and the % ready value. As a VM is allocated more CPU time, its ready value should go down, and as the % of CPU time allocated value goes down, the ready value should grow. For this reason many people say that the "ready" value should be called the wait value – as it indicates how long a VM is waiting for the CPU to respond.

If you wish to see very high CPU ready values, take two VMs doing a very CPU intensive task and use the "processor affinity" options behind a VM and peg them to the same physical CPU. The net effect of this would cause "contention" as the two VMs fought over the same resource. VM processor affinity is a tool used in resource management which we will cover in the next module – as you can see, it could have a catastrophic impact on performance if configured incorrectly. CPU affinities also constitute a VMotion barrier.

Memory

Memory problems in a VM could be caused by an application or guest operating system mishandling its memory allocation. It's not uncommon for malign applications or services to demand an allocation of memory – and not gracefully hand them back. We label such applications or services as having a "memory leak." The source and cause of these memory problems lay not with the VM but poorly written operating systems and more frequently, even more poorly written application code. Despite the existence of transparent page sharing (TPS) and ballooning – it is beyond the scope of any virtualization platform to make bad code good. In my experience the most badly written code tends to come from application code developed in-house rather than from ISVs.

As stated earlier the ESX VMkernel prefers to use physical RAM in all cases. Only when physical RAM is scarce and VMs are fighting over access to RAM, does the per-VM swap file and the "ballooning" driver become engaged. Once you know this you can use the charts or ESXTOP to look for any persistent swap I/O and for any ballooning. Any swap or balloon driver activity indicates a memory problem.

Network

Before you blame a VM or an ESX host for slow network response, it's worth asking yourself – would this system be as slow if it was running on a physical host? Frequently the source of network bottlenecks exists in your physical network or at the slowness node of, for instance, a branch office. Additionally, networking problems could easily be the cause of mis-configuration of network settings within the VM. Perhaps your VM has the wrong default gateway or DNS settings which are causing long round trips or long DNS queries. Occasionally, when I teach a course I watch people troubleshoot networking problems. They check all the settings of the VM, but sometimes fail to even use the tools they are very familiar with such as ipconfig, ping, and so on. Network troubleshooting should be begin with the basics first, before we over-complicate the process by checking the VM's settings.

It is legitimate to capture, analyze and measure the amount of packets sent or received to a VM. A network packet sent from a VM or received from a VM is unchanged (unless Traffic Shaping is engaged).

There is a close relationship between network activity and physical CPU usage. This is because the load-balancing mechanism of IP Hash (covered in Chapter 2) in itself causes the VMkernel to use the physical CPU. Additionally, lots of small TCP transactions inside a VM can cause the physical CPU to be busy – as the VMkernel works harder to remove packets from the physical NICs to the virtual NICs via the vSwitch. As a consequence, increasing physical CPU availability will help increase network performance.

If network performance is poor in the VM then confirm four configuration settings. Firstly, confirm that VMware Tools has been installed. VMware Tools replaces the driver for the virtual NIC with one which is "idealized" for virtual networking. Secondly, that the physical NICs selected for that VM's vSwitch are 1000mps interfaces. Thirdly, if you are using 100mps ensure that you have set the correct speed and duplex. Lastly, ensure that no operator has incorrectly engaged the "traffic shaper" module. The traffic shaper module is designed to throttle a VM which malignly wishes to "hog" the network pipe at the expense of other VMs.

Disk

Generally, we use disk reads and writes to check what volume of disk activity is occurring – and disk queue lengths as an indication that storage is a bottleneck. In this case it is reasonable to use guest operating system tools to monitor disk activity – as MB written to a virtual disk is no different than MB written to a physical disk. VMFS is such a light, low-weight file-system that it can be disregarded as the source of a bottleneck.

Before you consider any changes to the VM's settings, confirm that you have correctly configured and optimized your storage. In chapter 3 we discussed the importance of correctly setting the multi-pathing. You may also wish to experiment with different RAID levels as these can have an impact on storage performance. Additionally, you may wish to double-check that the guest operating system has been correctly configured. Perhaps the VM is running out of disk space and is thrashing the disk looking for free space. Alternatively, a lack of memory inside the VM will force it to engage its virtual memory which increases disk activity.

Using VirtualCenter Charts

I've spoken at some length of the various counters that could expose a bottleneck in the system. Now let's look at where you can view these values and parameters. The best way of assessing performance generally is using the Performance tab in the VirtualCenter inventory. There are other places where you will see more high-level information. For instance, if you select your datacenter, and select either Virtual Machine tab or the Host Tab, you will get a view of information like CPU, Host Memory usage, VM memory usage – and information about your ESX host's resources such as amount memory, number of NICs and uptimes. Figure 8.2 shows this basic information.

Figure 8.2

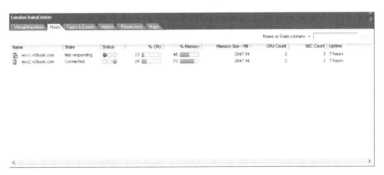

However, if you really want to "drill down" and see performance stats in detail you will find yourself going to the performance tab.

In this section I am going to focus exclusively on CPU charts. Once you have the principle of how the interface works you will be able to find the data you are seeking for any resource. The last thing to mention is that the performance tab only appears on certain object types in the Inventory. These are:

- DRS and HA Clusters (Covered in Chapter 10)

- ESX Hosts

- Resource Pools (Covered in the next Chapter)

- Individual VMs

The default counters used vary depending on which of the 4 objects you select – but these can be customized. Below is a brief summary:

- DRS and HA Cluster – shows CPU Usage in MHz using 1 counter.

- ESX Host – shows CPU statistics using 4 counters.

- Resource Pools – uses the same counter as DRS and HA Clusters.

- VMs – shows CPU statistic using 3 counters.

All of these counters collect information every 20 seconds. This is the fastest refresh that charts can offer and is referred to, slightly confusingly, as "Real Time." This currently cannot be made any faster, and I would have thought collecting performance stats any quicker than this rate would constitute a performance hit in its own right! Information can be collected over a much longer period than this for purpose of tracking endemic trends; the defaults allow you to view information over a day, week, month, and a year. Additionally, the custom option allows you to set your own time frame; for instance, you could use it if you collect and view performance trends on a quarterly basis.

GOTCHA:

All performance data is time critical. It's absolutely imperative that time is correctly set on both the ESX host *and* the VirtualCenter Server. Failure to do so can result in the performance tab failing to return any information at all. The message you receive is:

"Performance data is currently not available for this entity."

In Chapter 12: *ESX on the Command-Line*, I will show you how to setup an NTP server to be the source of time, configured to speak to a publicly available NTP server – and then how to configure an ESX host to be a client of your internal NTP server. Alternatively, you can manually correct the time settings on your

ESX hosts using the date command at the Service Console. If you have to correct time latency issue, do remember to wait to allow time for statistics to be collected.

CPU Charts

I'm going to explain how to use the Vi Client charting features, using CPUs as the resource. Learn the principles here, and you can apply them to any other resource as well, such as memory, network, and disk.

The best view to see overall CPU utilization is on the properties of an ESX Host. Figure 8.3 shows the performance tab for an ESX host. Let me walk you through some of the common options.

Figure 8.3

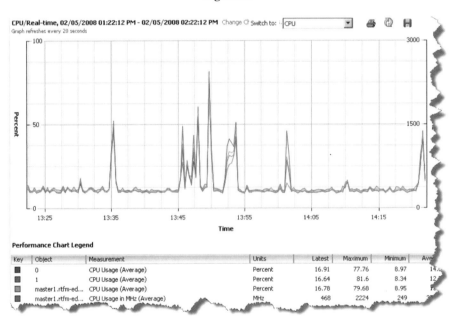

Description:

- In the top left hand corner, we have the resource being monitored (CPU) and its frequency (in real-time every 20 seconds) and period (12.52pm to 1:52pm).

- The blue "Change Chart options" allows the changing of the resource from CPU to be CPU, Disk, Memory, Network, System, or Cluster Services. System shows how the ESX VMkernel is operating and Cluster Services only appears if the ESX host is in a DRS or HA Cluster.

- The blue floppy disk icon allows you to save the chart data in a Microsoft Excel .XLS format – the XLS file contains raw data in an Excel chart that is also embedded in the spreadsheet.

- The icon to the left of the blue floppy disk icon allows you to manually refresh the data – and the icon to the left allows you to detach the chart from the Vi Client into a separate Window.

- Below that is the chart itself. Moving the mouse over it will tell you the values for each of the options, in this case as a percentage. This is the small pop-up box in the center of the chart. As you move your mouse across the chart these statistics update.

- Lastly, below that we have the Performance Chart Legend. If you select an object in the list (like I have with CPU Usage in MHz) it then highlights that counter in the chart. This is why it is it is slightly darker than the rest. If you know Windows well, this is like pressing ctrl+h while in Performance Manager.

If you want to see how the VM is behaving you need to select your VM in the inventory and choose the Performance tab. Within the Vi Client this is the only place the all important %ready value appears on the properties of the VM, not the ESX host. This is a bit of shame as it would allow you to see the %CPU and %ready values for many VMs.

Note:

In the next chapter we will look at the command-line performance tool called esxtop. Esxtop does allow you to see the %ready value on VMs and compare and contrast them.

To see the %ready value on a VM:

1. **Select a VM** in the list.

2. Choose the **Performance Tab**.

3. Click the **Change Chart Options...**

4. **On the right-hand side** of the dialog box under **Objects and Description,**

5. **de-select the check box next to the VM's name,** and select the **vCPU underneath.**

6. Next, under **Counters and Descriptions,**

7. **scroll down the list of counters,** and select **CPU Ready.**

8. Click **OK.**

If you want to generate some large CPU activity for testing purposes we can do this by using Microsoft Calculator. Yes, Microsoft Calculator can be a very CPU intensive application depending on what you're calculating.

- Open Microsoft Calculator in the VM.

- Change to the scientific view.

- Type 9999999.

- Then click the n! button.

Every so often Windows complains that this calculation will take a long time – and would you like to stop the process or continue the calculation. The calculation continues until you stop it or it is completed.

The n! button calculates factorials. A factorial is the product of a positive integer and all positive integers less than itself. For example, the factorial of a 4, written 4!, is $4 \times 3 \times 2 \times 1 = 24$. So calculating the factorial of 999999 results in a lot of calculations!

I picked up on this method of quickly generating CPU activity from Brian Madden's article "Citrix buys Application Performance Management vendor Reflectent. Is this a YAM?", which you can read online at:

http://www.brianmadden.com/content/content.asp?ID=589

Figure 8.4 shows my VM running with a calculator working on a factorial. The spike at 2 p.m. happened when I just powered on the VM. After 2:20 p.m. I ran calculator.

Figure 8.4

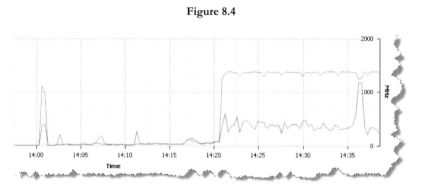

The Chart Options Dialog Box

A few moments ago we were in the chart options dialog box. That's where we added in the %ready value for the VM, focused on its vCPU. This is quite a "busy" dialog box with lots of options. Let me walk you through the settings, just like I walked you through the chart. Figure 8.5 shows us the chart settings on an individual VM.

Figure 8.5

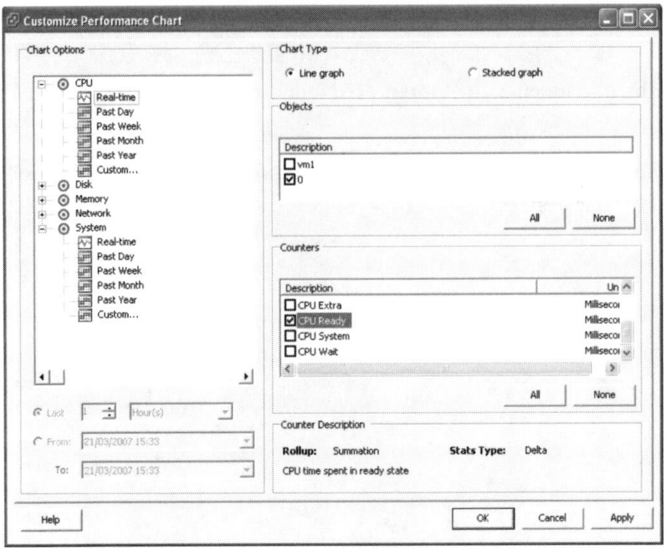

On the left-hand side of the dialog box, under chart options, we have the core resources of CPU, Disk, Memory, and Network. Expand one of these and then select an interval (Real-Time, Past Day, Past Week, Past Month, or Past Year). Unfortunately, it's not currently to possible show CPU, Disk, Memory, and Network together in four little charts for comparison purposes. This would be useful for working out something like whether disk activity was actually a symptom of excessive swap activity within the guest caused by a lack of memory. Selecting the interval of custom activates the "Last" and "From" options in the dialog box.

On the properties of a VM we also have the "System" options. In the context of a VM this allows you to see its average uptimes and the regularity of its heartbeat. These can be taken as a very general measure of the "availability" of a given VM. Clearly long uptimes with regular heartbeats mean our VM is alive and healthy – poor uptimes and an irregular heartbeat, or no heartbeat at all, is generally a sign that your VM is feeling a bit poor – and is need of intensive care or resuscitation. One reason for not receiving a heartbeat at all from a VM is because VMware Tools Service has failed to start or not been installed at all.

Over on the right-hand side of the dialog box, under chart types we can see the chart's appearance. On individual VM we only get two types (Line Graph and Stacked Graph). If you select the ESX host and Change Chart options you have three types (Line Graph, Stacked Graph, and Stacked Graph [Per VM]). Personally, I've always thought line graphs are clearer and easier to interpret.

Under objects we have description. Every resource CPU has objects – usually either the entire VM or its individual vCPUs. In turn every object has attributes or "counters" which tells the performance statistics that we have. Sometimes both of these options cannot be simultaneously displayed. So if we have VM1 and 0 selected together and also try to select CPU ready – you will receive the error message in Figure 8.6

Figure 8.6

Under counters we can select additional metrics to gather more data about performance. There are many, many counters on every single resource – far too many for us to outline here. You do get very brief information in the counter description pane but these aren't always very helpful. For example, the dialog box in Figure 8.5 defines CPU Ready as being "CPU Time spent in Ready State." I would recommend consulting VMware documentation and learning them on a case-by-case basis dependent on your performance challenges.

Configuring Alarms and Alerts

Alarms and alerts are built-in to VirtualCenter. Unfortunately, they are few in number and you cannot define new condition criteria of your own. There are built-in Alarms and Alerts which are defined at the top of the inventory in "Host and Clusters." These settings are inherited down the inventory and applied to all ESX hosts and VMs. If you wish to modify these "defaults" you must modify them at the point at which they were inherited. If you wish to create new alarms and alerts with different settings you must delete the built-in ones and create ones of your own on the relevant folder.

Modifying existing alarms

A good example of modifying an existing alarm might be the built-in alarm on ESX hosts called "Host connection state." Currently the default settings on this alarm only contain one condition (red) which occurs when an ESX host becomes "Not responding;" "disconnected" is an additional condition. These messages can occur when rebooting an ESX host or if you have a network failure. Initially, an ESX host will enter a "Not responding message," and after a timeout it enters a "disconnected" state. You can force an ESX host to enter the disconnected state forcibly – by right-clicking the ESX host and choosing disconnect.

1. In the Inventory, select "Hosts and Clusters."

2. Select the Alarm Tab.

3. Click the "Definitions" button.

4. Double-click at the Alarm called "Host connection state."

5. Select the Triggers Tab.

6. Change Warning to be "Not Responding."

7. Change Alert to be "Disconnected."

8. Click OK.

Setting Custom Alarms for ESX Hosts

In my case I have a mix of different servers with different levels of memory and CPU resources. One of my problems is that default values for an alarm or alert at 75% and 90% are being triggered too late for my hardware. Within my London DataCenter I have created a folder for my Intel servers and AMD servers. I will apply custom alarms for each folder.

1. In the Inventory choose Hosts and Clusters.

2. Select the Alarm Tab.

3. Click the Definitions button.

4. Right-click Host CPU usage, and Choose Remove.

5. Right-click Host Memory Usage, and Choose Remove.

6. Select the folder that contains your ESX host.

7. Select the Alarms tab.

8. Click the Definitions button.

9. Right-click and choose New Alarm.

10. In the Alarm name dialog field type in a friendly name such as "Host CPU usage – Intel."

11. Click the Triggers tab, and select Add.

Figure 8.7 shows that by default this adds "Host CPU Usage" – but if you click next to it you will get a pull-down list of additional triggers including some that are not created by default during installation ("Host network usage" and "Host disk usage").

Figure 8.7

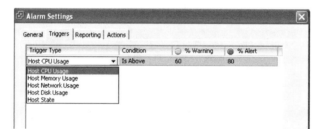

12. Adjust the initial warning and alert to be the appropriate values – in my case I lowered the values to 60% and 80%.

I repeated the same task with my AMD folder as well. The resulting configuration is outlined in Figure 8.8 which shows that "Host connection state," "Virtual Machine CPU Usage" and "Virtual Machine Memory Usage" are inherited from "Hosts & Clusters" (highlighted in blue). In contrast, my new definitions are inherited from the Intel Hosts folder level.

Figure 8.8

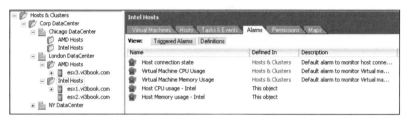

Note:

I can repeat this configuration, removing the default alarms from "Host & Clusters" for Virtual Machines. Instead I can define new ones just for the London DataCenter, leaving Ron and Scott freedom to do what they wish for the NY and Chicago DataCenters. Again, Figure 8.9 shows that when you add in custom alarms and alerts you will find additional conditions are available including network, disk usage, and the VM state (where a VM is powered on, off, and suspend). To see this, change the Alarm Type from "Monitor a host" to "Monitor a Virtual Machine."

Figure 8.9

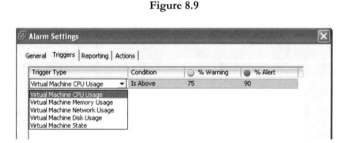

GOTCHA:

Be careful when using Virtual Machine state with powered on or powered off. If you do this you can create yellow or red alerts on the VMs which are not a problem. The system is doing its job giving you an alarm even when a condition is met. As most VMs are powered in a production environment on it's not a terribly useful alarm condition. The same can happen if you set an alarm on

VMs that are powered off.   This generates an alarm on VM which isn't even powered on.   This could be an irritation in test and development environments where many VMs are powered on when needed.

Configuring Tolerances and Frequency

Tolerance and Frequency settings in the Reporting Tab allow you to control how "chatty" an alarm can be.   Figure 8.10 shows this dialog box. This can be useful to stop unwanted SMTP/SNMP alerts.   Set in the reporting tab, tolerance affects alarm conditions that are set by a percentage (as opposed to Boolean conditions which are logical such as VM or Host State conditions).   So it is possible to send an alert when a warning reaches 75% but not send another warning until it changes by another 5% below or above 75%.

Figure 8.10

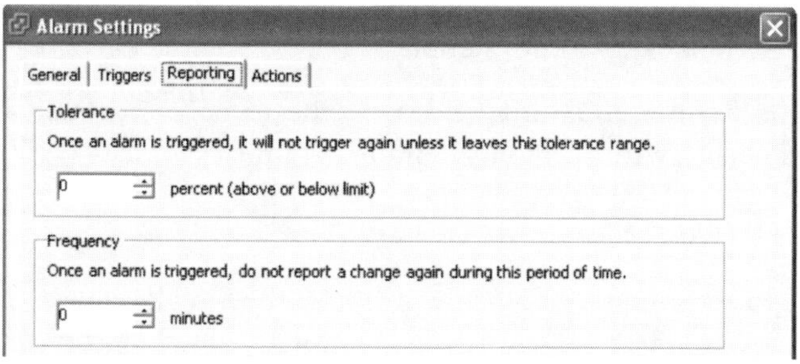

Frequency allows a user to modify how often VirtualCenter checks on an alarm that has already been triggered.   So we can ignore an alarm for, say, 60 minutes before it sends out another.

Configuring Email Alerts

Configuring VirtualCenter to issue emails generated by alarms requires VirtualCenter to know the SMTP detail's server name and both the sender's (From:) and recipient's (To:) email addresses. These settings are configured in the VirtualCenter Management dialog box. Incidentally, it's from this dialog box that some global VirtualCenter settings can be configured. Figure 8.11 shows the dialog box in question.

Figure 8.11

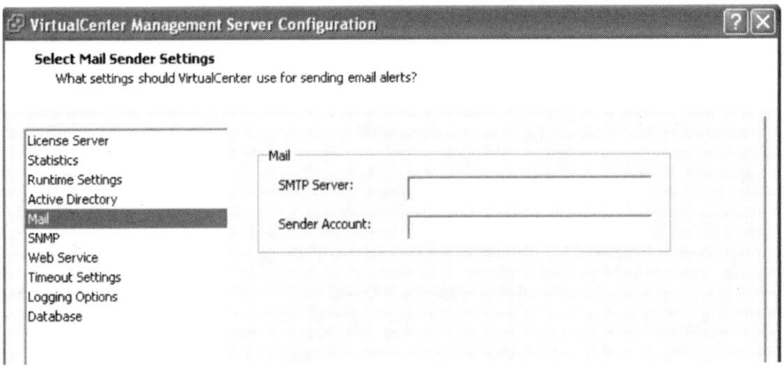

1. In the menu choose Administration and VirtualCenter Management Server Configuration.

2. Select the **Mail** section of the dialog box.

3. In the **SMTP Server** field, type the name of your mail server, smtp1.vi3book.com for example.

4. In the **Sender Account** field, type the name of account used to send emails, virtualcenter@vi3book.com for example.

GOTCHA:

Due to the absence of a password field, the SMTP requires authentication switched off. In fact, for this to function correctly your SMTP server has to be configured as an "Open Relay." If this SMTP server is internet facing it will be a magnet for spammers, so make sure whatever you set here is an internal-only email system.

5. Next open an alarm such as "Host State Connection."

6. Choose the **Actions** tab.

7. Click the **Add** button (the default is "Send a notification trap").

8. Click into the **Value** column, and type the "To:" recipient email address.

Note:

You can also enable this to send an alarm from Green to Yellow (our "Not Responding" alarm) as well as from Yellow to Red (our "Disconnected" alarm).

Configuring SNMP Alerts

SNMP is the Simple Network Management Protocol. Generally, large corporations make the investment into commercially available SNMP such as HP OpenView or Computer Associates UniCenter applications. If you are merely wishing to test that SNMP is correctly configured or use free software, there is a whole host of free SMNP management tools. This demonstration shows you how to use a free tool called Trap Receiver from Network Computing Technologies to test the SNMP configuration. You can download the Trap Receiver software at:

http://www.ncomtech.com/

1. Download and Install Trap Receiver to the VirtualCenter Server.

2. Run the Trap Receiver Application from the Start Menu choosing the Start the Service button.

3. Open an Alarm definition. In my case I choose my alarm called Virtual Machine CPU usage in the London DataCenter.

4. Select the Action Tab.

5. Click the Add button.

6. Choose Send a notification trap, and Click OK.

   Note:

   Notice that you can set more actions for VMs than you can for an ESX host – including such responses as run as script, power on or off a VM, suspend a VM, or reset a VM. Theoretically, we could have an alarm that said if a VM went to 99% of its vCPU that it would be reset.

Note:

To generate an alarm I ran a cpu intensive application within one of my VMs. This generated responses in the trap receiver application. Figures 8.12 and 8.13 show the responses.

Figure 8.12

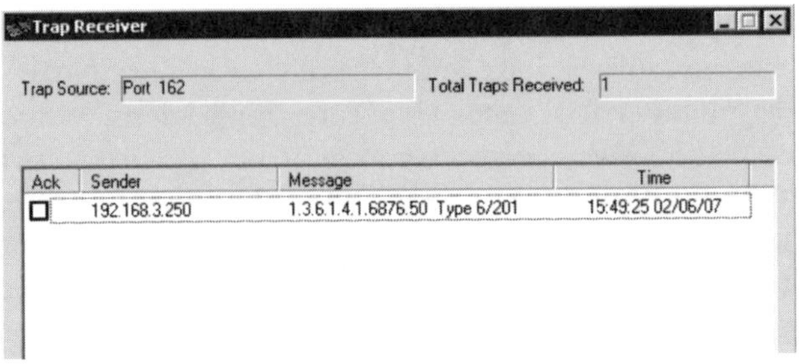

Figure 8.13

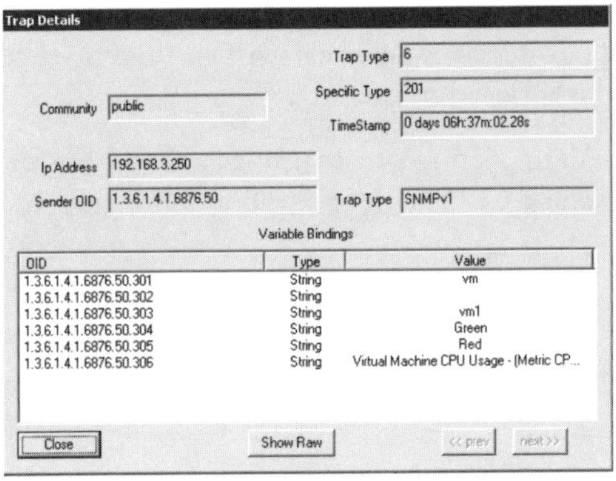

7. **Note:**

In reality it is unusual to run an SMNP Management tool on the VirtualCenter server itself but instead run it on a separate system altogether. If you wish to do this you need to modify VirtualCenter's default SNMP management settings held in the VirtualCenter

Management Server Configuration dialog box (accessible from the Administration menu).

Disabling Alarms

There is no easy way to temporarily turn off an alarm for an individual VM. The most we can do is temporarily disable an alarm if we feel that it is incorrectly generating unwarranted alerts.

1. Locate an alarm; for example, I went back to the London DataCenter where my VM alarms were held and modified an alarm I created called Virtual Machine State.

2. Double-click the **Alarm**.

3. Under the **General** Tab remove the tick next to **Enable this Alarm**.

Events and Tasks

As you probably have noticed already, the Vi Client's "Recent Task" pane is useful in showing ongoing processes and in a multi-administrator environment allows you to see tasks triggered by other VirtualCenter administrators. A record of all tasks and events is kept in VirtualCenter, and the tab called "Tasks & Events" appears at every point in the Inventory. As you navigate down the inventory you gradually see less and less focused information on a particular VM. Figure 8.14 shows a type event view on a VM. Notice the warning, which indicates an attempt to carry out a VMotion was tried but failed because of a networking problem. This is probably a vSwitch Port Group naming problem.

Figure 8.14

If a warning message appears on the Vi Client which you fail to make a note of you will generally find it in Tasks & Events.

Scheduled Tasks

VirtualCenter does have the ability to automate some repetitive tasks without the need to learn a scripting language.   Scheduled tasks are configured with a point-and-click interface and all you do to automate is:

- Power State of a VM

- Clone a VM

- Deploy a VM from a Template

- Create a New VM (not from a template)

- VMotion a VM

- Relocate a VM (Cold Migrate and/or Move its files)

- Snapshot a VM

- Add an ESX Host

Scheduled tasks are very easy to configure, so I won't even show them here.   I just wanted you to know they were available.   The only "gotcha" with scheduled tasks is how to express the time for event to happen.   Most users would expect the system to use a 24-hour format.   Instead you type in a time, say 10:00.   You must follow this by manually typing whether this is in the morning or evening with 10:00 a.m. or 10:00 p.m. in the interface.   Another slight gotcha is you only add an ESX host to a datacenter object, not a folder within a datacenter with the scheduled tasks feature.

Log Files and Support Data

VirtualCenter and ESX both have logging information; this could be useful in troubleshooting scenarios and for liaising with VMware Support.   Additionally, this can become a management issue – how long will logging data be retained and how frequently will the logs be rotated.

VirtualCenter Logs

Access and Export your VirtualCenter and ESX logs by:

1. Clicking **Admin button** in the Vi Client.

2. Select the **System Logs** tab.

3. Your logs for both VirtualCenter and ESX hosts can be exported and submitted to VMware Support by clicking the **Export Diagnostic Data button**.

Figure 8.15 shows me selecting in the Inventory that I want to collect. Use the browse button to save the export location.

Figure 8.15

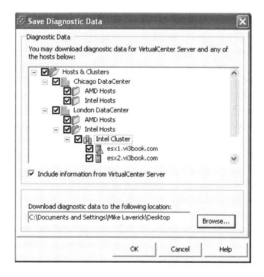

Note:

This starts a task in the "Recent Tasks" view called "Generate Diagnostic Bundles." Additionally, you can create VMware Support log bundles directly at the VirtualCenter server itself if you click:

Start > Programs > VMware

Select **Generate VirtualCenter Server log bundle**.

This method generates a zip vcsupport-M-DD-YYY-HH-MM.zip on the VirtualCenter's desktop.

ESX Host specific Log File Generation

The main location for ESX logs is in /var/log. This location is used to store log files for the Service Console and the VMkernel. Files that begin VMK are VMkernel logs, whereas all other files are Service Console log files. Individual log bundles and VMware Support files can be generated at the service console using a script:

1. Logon to the Service Console as root.

2. Type cd to make sure you are /root.

3. Type:

   vm-support

   Note:

   This tool gathers up all your logs and configuration information – and zips it all up in a handy tgz file. These files are then uploaded to VMware's FTP (rather than being sent in emails) which is disclosed to you when you open a Service Request (SR) with VMware Support.

   Note:

   Log rotation is handled at the command-line on a per ESX host basis using the "logrotate" utility.

Chapter 9: Resource Management

This chapter discusses the tools available to you for tweaking the performance of VMs. We can adjust resource parameters for CPU, Memory, and Disk on a per VM basis, or we can drop groups of VMs into "resource pools" to manage their CPU or memory. Resource pools merely allow us to treat VMs as groups, rather than individuals – and quickly apply resource settings to them – thus lowering your administrative burden.

It is possible to cap, or "limit," and also guarantee a minimum, or "reservation," of either CPU or memory to a VM or a resource pool. Alongside these unchanging and hard-coded limits or reservations, we can have a more dynamic control over VM's usage of CPU, memory or disk. We can use VMware's proportional "share" system which responds to changes in resource demand relative to each VM and ESX host. At an extreme level it is possible to peg a resource to a VM with such features as CPU affinities – hard-coding a VM to have exclusive access to a CPU.

Technically, I really should mention that VMware Distributed Resource Service (DRS) is an invaluable resource management tool. DRS integrates very closely with VMware High Availability (HA) so it was decided to show these two products together in the "High Availability" chapter of this book.

In this chapter I want to use an airline analogy to explain how resources are managed in ESX. Each plane will represent an ESX host, and a fleet of airplanes will represent a VMware DRS cluster. Every plane has fixed capacity in terms of the number of passengers it can comfortably accommodate. Each of the "seats" will represent a VM. If the airline has 200 seats per plane and ten planes that is a total of 2000 seats. But the 200 seats per plane do represent a fixed limit on capacity. Fundamentally, though these 2000 seats exist as a logical capacity, a passenger can only board one plane – just as a VM can only currently execute one server, not a cluster. Access to the plane is controlled by a unique system of reservations which is intended to guarantee not that you fly – but that a certain quality of travel like business class will be provided. In contrast, economy passengers do not make reservations. They merely turn up and hope there will be capacity to fly.

Setting Limits

As stated a moment ago it is possible to impose limits upon a VM or resource pool. This can be done for CPU resources (by MHz) and for memory (by MB). In fact, limits are imposed on VM from the perspective of memory when you first define a VM. When you create a VM you set the maximum amount of memory it can have during the "New Virtual Machine" wizard. If a VM demands more memory it cannot exceed this amount allocated to it – even if free physical memory exists. At first glance this seems quite restrictive, however, from an architecture point of view, it has to happen. If we have poorly written applications and operating systems we would want to avoid the situation where a VM was able to drain a physical host of its entire available RAM – thus causing a reboot of the physical server. If we use our analogy it's not possible for a single passenger on the plane to take up all the space at the expense of the other passengers. Additionally, there are some fixed limits we cannot exceed. If there are only 200 seats on the plane we cannot allow 201 passengers to board. Similarly, if the ESX host or pool resources are totally consumed – a limit has been reached. We cannot magically out of nowhere find additional resources - with one exception. When all memory has been depleted is possible for a VM to use its VMkernel swap file.

In contrast there are no default limits on CPU usage. If a VM demands CPU time, and that CPU time is available, then this is allocated to a VM. One possible reason to cap or limit a VM usage of CPU is that you know you have a poorly written application that regularly crashes. Perhaps when it crashes it "hogs" the CPU of the ESX host. Using CPU limits is one method (amongst many) to control these kinds of VMs.

Lastly, a word about terminology - in the ESX 2.x product the word "maximum" was used instead of the word limits. VMware changed the phraseology to "limits" as this is more meaningful and more clearly describes the feature. Additionally, VMware has moved away from allocating limits on CPUs by a percentage value and now prefers to use Mhz. MHz is a more accurate measure of CPU usage than percentages, which can be very misleading. In the context of CPUs, 10% of 1.44 MHz processor is decidedly different from 10% of 2.6 MHz processor.

Setting Reservations

In addition to limits, we can also use CPU or memory "reservations." One analogy that can help when thinking of reservations is to compare them to the plane reservations. These reservations are supposed to *guarantee* a resource in the form of a seat. Similarly, a CPU or memory reservation in MHz or MB is intended to *guarantee* the resource to the VM or resource pool. In this case there are no *default* reservations for CPU or memory, unlike the default limit on memory set when creating the VM. We can regard these reservations or guarantees as offering us a way of ensuring we meet certain performance levels. Perhaps you could even regard them as a way of meeting "service level agreements" (SLA).

Just like with a plane or hotel you must "meet" your reservation in order to board or check into a hotel. So, if you say that the memory reservation on VM is 256MB of RAM – and that amount of RAM is physically not available – you will be unable to power on the VM. VMware refers to this as "Admission Control." Similarly, if we configured a situation where a VM must get 1000 MHz of CPU time, but the physical host can only offer 500 MHz of CPU time the VM would not power on.

Using our airplane analogy, if a passenger makes a reservation for 10 seats in business class those seats must be there. Our airline imposes a very *special* definition of customer care that states if a business class reservation cannot be met, rather than pushing our customer in economy class, we refuse admission to the flight. Here we can see the weakness of all analogies; they don't work perfectly in all circumstances. Nonetheless, I want to persist with this analogy as it is helpful in most cases.

As with CPUs in ESX 2.x, VMware used to call "reservations" minimums. Again, the label change was introduced to be more meaningful.

Putting the concerns to one side for a moment there is very interesting and useful relationship between memory limits and reservations and the VMKernel swap file. The difference between the reservation subtracted from the limit determines the size of the VMkernel swap file. The usage of the VMkernel Swap file was mentioned in the previous chapter as an indicator of potential performance problems – but here I wish to delve a little deeper into different ways of using it. Explaining how to use the VMKernel swap file is perhaps best done with a couple of examples.

Example 1: Difference between Limit and Reservation

I had a VM with a 512MB limit and 256MB reservation – powering on the VM would create a 256MB VMkernel swap file (512-256) and guarantee that the VM would receive 256MB of RAM.

Example 2: No difference between limit and reservation

If I set the limit to 512MB and the reservation also as 512MB and powered on the VM, ESX would not create a VMkernel swap file at all. It would run the VM entirely in a memory reservation of 512MB.

Example 3: Big difference between limit and reservation

If, on the other hand, the VM was given a 16GB limit, and the default of 0MB was used for the reservation a 16GB VMkernel swap file would be created.

With example 1, if I had an ESX host with 2GB of physical RAM I could run at least 8 VMs before running out of memory (2048MB/256MB). I would not be able to power on a 9th VM because there would be insufficient memory to meet the reservation guarantee. If all the VMs simultaneously wished to use memory up to the limits (512MB*8) I would get swap activity. What I hope is that this would be such an unlikely event that it would be "safe" to configure the system this way.

Perhaps you find this "memory over-commitment" a bit scary. You are concerned about the negative aspects of swap activity, and you wish to have a cast-iron guarantee that your VMs will *always* run in memory. If this was the case you could use example 2. By setting the VM's limit and reservation to be the *same* value no swap file is created – and the VM is guaranteed to always run in memory. However, on a 2GB system the effect of this policy would be very significant. I would only be able to run 4 VMs not 8 (2048MB/512MB). If I tried to create a 5th VM and power it on – it wouldn't, as all my memory would have been reserved for use by my other VMs.

I could imagine example 1 being configured by someone who is optimistic and is looking for very high VM to ESX host ratios or someone trying to run as many VMs with as few resources as possible. Alternatively, we could see example 2 as someone who is perhaps pessimistic or conservative, or someone who has so many resources there is no need to use the VMkernel swap file.

The last example, example number 3, is a warning. If you set extremely high values on memory, with no reservations the ESX host will generate an extremely large swap file. Just like with memory reservations, you need the physical MB disk space to create the VMkernel swap file. In example 3, if you didn't have 16GB of free disk space in the LUN where the VM is stored, it would not power on as there would be insufficient resources to guarantee the *difference* between the limit and reservation.

The Share System

Another system is at play in the gap between limits and reservations, called the "Proportional Share" system. Shares allow you indicate that when a resource is scarce that one VM or resource pool is more important than another. To use our analogy, it's like the airline treating a Hollywood star more importantly than the average guy on the street. Share values can be applied on per-VM basis or on resource pools. Unlike limits or reservations, which are fixed and unchanging, shares react dynamically to resource demands. The share value can be specified by a number (usually in multiples of 1,000) or by user-friendly text value of normal, high, and low. The important thing to remember about the share value is that it is only relevant when the resource is scarce and contention is occurring. If the resource is plentiful or VMs do not have to compete over resources the share value does nothing at all.

In my discussions with VMware I've been told that many customers do not use the proportional share system as much as VMware might like. Why might this be? Firstly, because customers frequently don't understand how shares work, and secondly, because shares only take effect when things are performing badly – a great many people try to configure their ESX hosts and VMs so this never happens. Personally, I am a big fan of the shares system. What especially appeals to me is its dynamic nature, its ability to react to changes.

If you or your customer is still struggling with the concept of shares you might like to try a couple of other analogies. You could see the share value like shares in a company that are quoted on the global stock exchanges. The amount of shares a company chooses to issue is up to it – what matters is the number or portion of your shares. The greater amount of shares you hold in a company the more of its resources you own. Therefore, a big share owner of 5000 shares has much more influence than a share holder with just 1000 shares. Perhaps you own as much as ¼ of the company, or 25% of its shares.

Here's another analogy I use regularly in courses. Imagine you have 3 children – one is a baby, the next a 5 year-old and the last a teenager. When you come home after a hard day's work they all demand your time. Here your time is like the CPU, and each of your children are pesky VMs making demands on your tired brain. Being a particularly cruel parent you decide to take a permanent marker – write 3000 on the baby's forehead, 2000 on the toddler's forehead, and lastly 1000 on the teenager's forehead. You decide you're like one of the ESX hosts you manage at work, and this is your parental strategy from now on!

In this scenario, when you are faced with contention (say when you come home from work) you would give the baby ½ (3000/6000), the toddler ⅓ (2000/6000) and your teenager just ⅙ (1000/6000) of your valuable time. Now when it's mid-evening you decide that the baby is tired enough to go to sleep. You're in luck tonight as he's out for the count in seconds – you now can give ⅔ of your time to the toddler (2000/3000) and ⅓ (1000/3000) of your time to the teenager. When the toddler goes to bed (after much crying and wailing normally) you are facing no contention at all. Just as you're settling down to watch your favorite sit-com the teenager comes down from her bedroom – perhaps the internet connection has failed or her games console has broken. She now decides this will be an opportune time to discuss why college is a waste of time and how she should really follow her favorite drug-taking band around the country. Now you can give all of your time to teenager – 1000/1000 – in persuading her that while a life of drunken debauchery might have its appeal, it won't lead her to a prosperous career in IT like yours. Finally, everyone goes to bed – contention is over and you get the opportunity to get some well-earned z's. But then at 3 a.m. a sound is heard from the baby's room which grows into crying. You're out of luck, and it is your turn and not your partner's to feed the baby. However, rest assured as long as you get to the baby quickly, it will not wake the others – and you are able to give 100% of your time to getting back in bed as quickly as possible!

All joking aside, the analogy does illustrate some points. Firstly, that share value adjusts depending on the level of contention. Secondly, that when there is no contention the share value does nothing at all. Thirdly, that when you become a parent you will have no time to yourself whatsoever!

Lastly, you should know that there is another way of setting the share value which is by using friendly labels of "High, Normal, and Low." These offer novices a more intuitive way of dividing up resources. You see these whenever you create a new VM. You can use these text labels on a VM and also in resource pools. If you are going to use them you should know what actual settings apply.

- **High**

    Allocates 2000 shares per virtual CPU:

    20 shares for every 1MB allocated to the VM

- **Normal**

    Allocates 1000 shares per virtual CPU:

    10 shares for every 1MB allocated to the VM

- **Low**

    Allocates 500 shares per virtual CPU:

    5 shares for 1MB allocated to the VM

As you can see, high is twice as much as normal and four times as much as low. There is also another assumption at play here. VMware assumes that the more memory you assign to a VM the more sensitive it is to a lack of memory. So when contention takes place the VM "wins" a greater slice of memory resources. This assumption might not always be the case (although it frequently is). You could have a memory intensive application that is not business critical.

CPU Affinities

One extreme method of controlling the VM's access to CPU resources is to "peg" it to a specified CPU. As was mentioned in the previous chapter, internally to physical server the VMkernel dynamically moves the VM across to work on the best CPU inside the ESX host. We can switch off this feature using CPU affinities on the properties of a VM. I would regard this configuration as a last resort. Firstly, configuring it is very administration intensive. Not only do you have to configure the VM in question to use only CPU3 for example, you also have to configure every other VM *not* to use CPU3 – to truly dedicate a VM to given CPU. Secondly, CPU affinities are incompatible with VMotion. Thirdly, as DRS is effectively an automated VMotion for performance – CPU affinities also break DRS. Removing CPU affinities on a VM running on a ESX host which is already a member of DRS cluster is possible, but very convoluted. Therefore, I consider CPU affinities a very last resort.

Resource Pools or VM Settings

There are two main ways to apply many of these settings – limits, reservations, and share values. Resource pools only affect CPU and memory resources – so if your goal is to control disk and network activity, these must be done on the properties of the VM or a vSwitch, respectively. Despite this limitation, CPU and memory resources are very critical, and resource pools offer a much more effective way of applying limits, reservations, and share values. By its nature, right-clicking each VM and setting these values is very administration intensive, whereas dragging and dropping a VM to the correct VM is an easy task. If you are trying to calculate the total share value it is easier to compare a small number of resource pools, rather than comparing a large number of VMs.

Resource pools can be live in two main places – hanging off a stand-alone ESX server which divides up the resources of a single host into smaller units or pools, or alternatively, they can be created on VMware Cluster which divides the total resources of many servers into pools. Once you have the concept of resource pools and the way they function (they are the same if they are on a stand-alone or a cluster, but they really come into play in clusters where the need to divide resources up logically might more pressing) you could create resource pools based by department (sales, accounts or distribution), function (web servers, database, or file servers), or by IT Infrastructure (test, development, production).

If we apply our analogy to this we can see each of the airplanes as representing an ESX host. A DRS cluster represents the collective capacity of all my airplanes, but fundamentally a passenger can only fly on one airplane – not on two simultaneously. Our air-traffic controllers are very clever guys who can detect some airplanes stretched to capacity and move passengers from one plane to another while they are flying. This is called VMotion in ESX.

Putting It All Together: Creating Resource Pools

In this example I am going to run two VMs with a CPU intensive process. Initially, there will be no contention. I will introduce contention by forcing them to run on the same physical CPU. Then I will create resource pools with different share values to show both how resource pools help you control resources and demonstrate that the shares feature does work dynamically.

Creating CPU Intensive Events

1. On the *same* ESX host power on two Windows VMs.

2. On the root C: create two VBS files called cpubusy.vbs.

3. Cut & Paste the following code to the cpubusy.vbs script:

```
Dim goal
Dim before
Dim x
Dim y
Dim i

goal = 2181818
Do While True
      before = Timer
      For i = 0 to goal
            x = 0.000001
            y = sin(x)
            y = y + 0.00001
      Next  y = y + 0.01
WScript.Echo "I did three million sines in " &
Int(Timer - before + 0.5) & " seconds!"
Loop
```

Note:

This is a script I use regularly to create CPU activity in a VM when I am teaching Vi-3 to students. It was actually written by VMware and is freely available on their website. You can find it on the download page from VMworld 2006; it comes from the Performance Troubleshooting Lab that ran there.

http://download3.vmware.com/vmworld/2006/labs2006/vmworld.06.la b04-PERFORMANCE-MANUAL.pdf

4. Right-click the cpubusy.vbs file within each VM, and choose Open in a command-prompt.

GOTCHA:

Don't double click the file, as this will produce dialog boxes from the wscript.echo command.

The idea of the script is that it shows very crudely how quickly the VM is doing the calculation.

Note: VMkernel CPU Load-Balancing/Scheduling

At this point you will find both VMs will generate alarms and alerts – and that both receive the same amount of CPU time. As you may recall from chapter 8 on Resource Monitoring, the VMkernel does a great job of scheduling these VMs so they don't run on the same physical socket or core. Figure 9.1 shows how both VMs are running on separate physical sockets (PCPU is 100.00 on both CPUs) – and although they are each consuming a lot of CPU time (VM3 is using 99.78 and VM1 is using 98.50), the %ready value is quite low (2.33 and 3.90 respectively). Effectively, the VMkernel is dynamically trying to stop contention occurring between the two VMs.

Figure 9.1

```
22:37pm up 6:19, 50 worlds; CPU load average
PCPU(%): 100.00, 100.00; used total: 100.00
CCPU(%): 0 us, 1 sy, 98 id, 1wa; cs/sec 77

Name  %USED...     %RDY
Vm3   99.78        2.33
Vm1   98.50        3.90
```

Creating Contention

One of the good features of VMware is the proportional share system. However, to see it "at work" we have to create some contention. As you might recall from this chapter, share system only operates if contention is occurring and the resource in contention is scarce. We can easily generate CPU contention by forcing two VMs to run on the same CPU socket, core or logical processor. This effectively stops the VMkernel scheduler from moving VMs from one CPU to another.

1. On your first VM, **Edit the settings**.

2. Click the **Resources Tab**.

3. Choose **Advanced CPU**.

4. Choose the **Run on processor(s)** option, and select just one CPU.

    Note:

    Repeat this process for the second VM running the CPU busy script, which will create contention. What you should see is both VMs start to process fewer "sines" per second. In other words, they are running slower. Figure 9.2 shows how only one physical CPU is now busy (the first CPU is almost idle at 2.05, whereas the second CPU is at 100.00). Additionally, we can see that each VM is getting roughly half of the CPU (49.95 and 49.83 respectively). This happens because by default every VM gets 1000 CPU shares each, and I have two running VMs which are very busy. That means there is a total of 2000 shares, with each VM getting 1000 each – resulting in 1000/2000, or ½ or 50%.

Lastly, notice how %RDY value has massively increased in size. Clearly CPU affinities can be very dangerous – as there is no warning from the Vi-Client about creating this kind of configuration. In fact, this kind of CPU contention is precisely what we are trying to avoid.

Figure 9.2

```
23:38pm, up 7.20, 50 Worlds, CPU load average:
PCPU(%): 2.06, 100.00; used total: 51.03
CCPU(%): 0 us, 1 sy, 98 id, 1 wa; cs/sec 96

Name   %USED...     %RDY
Vm3    49.95        52.40
Vm1    49.83        52.23
```

Creating Resource Pools

In this section I will create two resource pools, one called Production and the other called Test & Dev. We will give the production resource pool 3000 CPU shares and the test & dev resource pool 1000 shares. This won't be enough to stop the contention created by the CPU affinity feature – but will show that resource pools do offer an effective way of allocating more resources to one group of VMs than to another.

1. **Right-click the ESX host.**

2. Choose **New Resource Pool.**

3. Type a friendly name such as **Production.**

4. Under **CPU Resources and Shares**: select **Custom** and type **3000**.

Next create a second resource pool:

5. Choose New Resource Pool.

6. Type a friendly name such as Test & Dev.

7. Under CPU Resources and Shares: select Custom and type 1000.

8. Next, drag-and-drop one VM to Production and the other VM to Test & Dev.

Figure 9.3 shows the final configuration.

Figure 9.3

Note:

You should find that if you look at the cpubusy.vbs script that one VM is running much faster than the other, in my case VM1. Merely by calculating the CPU shares value I can take a good guess what the actual CPU utilization will be. We allocated a total of 4000 shares (Production's 3000 plus Test & Dev's 1000). This should mean that a production VM should receive 3000/4000 shares or ¾ or 75%, whereas the Test & Dev VM should receive 1000/4000 or ¼ or 25%. Figure 9.4 shows the current utilization. We can see that the physical CPU is still very busy. VM1 is receiving 74.92% of CPU time, whereas its partner in the other resource pool is receiving 25.05%. We can see that as VM1 receives more CPU time, its ready value has come down to 15.05%, whereas VM3 which gets less CPU time is running at 48.01%. In a production environment neither of these ready values would be regarded remotely as "acceptable." Remember, this is an academic exercise where we are deliberately creating contention to show the effectiveness of resource pools.

Figure 9.4

```
0:38am, up 9.20, 50 Worlds, CPU load average:
PCPU(%): 6.16, 95.05; used total: 51.06
CCPU(%): 4 us, 1 sy, 91 id, 3 wa; cs/sec 110

Name   %USED...      %RDY
Vm3    25.05         79.19
Vm1    74.92         27.92
```

Share Values on VMs within a Resource Pool

Lastly, you might wonder if you can create resource pools within resource pools. The answer is that you certainly can. You might also ask what happens to the share value set on VMs within a resource pool. The answer is they are still effective, too. So it is possible to give one VM more shares of a resource pool than another VM. For example, let's give the Production resource pool 3000 shares and Test & Dev resource pool 1000 shares. This would mean they would have 75% and 25% split of the CPU time. If within the Test & Dev resource pool one VM had 1000 CPU shares and another VM had 2000 shares – the 25% allocated to the Test & Dev resource pool would be divided accordingly. If contention occurred and CPU resources were scarce, this would mean our first VM would receive about 8% of the CPU time and our second VM would receive 16%. The moral of the story is that VMs get their resources not from the physical server directly, but indirectly from the resource pool. As a consequence, share values are calculated within the boundaries of the resource pool.

Admission Control: Insufficient Resources to Power On?

"Insufficient Resources" - It's not uncommon for people who are new to VMware ESX server to receive this message - indicating either insufficient memory or CPU required to power on a VM. It can happen with stand-alone ESX hosts and the VM's settings, ESX hosts with Resource Pools, and ESX Clusters with Resource Pools. It can be deeply frustrating because on first glance it often looks like you have plenty of resources. For example, you know you have an ESX host with 4 quad-core CPUs (16 cores altogether) and 32GB or 64GB of RAM – and yet still your VM won't power on. The technical term that VMware uses to refer to this behavior is "Admission Control" – what are the resources required to power on your VM?

The source of these problems is always the same. It happens because a VM is given a reservation which is larger than the free resources currently available. Remember that reservations act as a guarantee to the VM or resource pool that a certain level of resources will always be available. In most cases it's impossible to allocate reservation which is greater than the resources that are free. This would be a bit like our example of an airline selling more seats than it has physically available (a policy which is actually common practice in most airlines!). So the "Insufficient Resources" message is like arriving too late at the airport and finding you failed to make your reservation. Planes and hotels are not easy resources to expand. So instead of adding more seats in the plane or building more rooms in the hotel your admission is refused.

This issue is best addressed by a couple of examples. We will create this error message – and then look at ways of resolving it.

Example 1: ESX Host without Resource Pools

In this example I will take an ESX host with N amount of free memory – and then try to allocate more RAM to the VM as a reservation and see what happens. First, let's see what amount of resources I have available on ESX2.

1. Select an **ESX host**.

2. Click the **Summary Tab**.

3. View the amount of resources available in the resources pane.

   Figure 9.5 shows that this ESX host has 2GB of RAM, with 391.00MB currently in use. By my calculations that's about 1657MB of free unreserved memory.

Figure 9.5

4. Next take a VM, and power it off.

5. **Right-Click**, and choose **Edit Settings**.

6. Under the **Hardware Tab** set the limit on the **amount of RAM to,** say, 512MB.

7. Then click the **Resources Tab**, and set the **Reservation to,** say, 256MB.

8. **Next attempt to power on the VM.**

In the first instance this should be successful. But if you create another VM and go to power it with the same setting again and again, each one will reserve 512MB of RAM out of the available memory present.

Figure 9.6 shows the result of running more and more VMs which eat up the server amount of free resources. You might ask why VMware allows this to happen. Put simply, VMware has no idea how you will run your ESX host and what VMs you will have powered on at different times – also they have no idea that you might change the total amount of resources available, such as when you add an additional ESX host to a cluster.

Figure 9.6

Clearly here your only option would be to reduce the reservation value so there is enough memory to power on the VM.

Example 2: ESX Host with Resource Pools

One way of conceptualizing resource pools is to see them as taking a server and carving it up into slices of CPU or Memory. In this respect resource pools are logical divisions of resources, whereas servers represent a physical boundary. We might decide to take a physical server to create a resource pool with 25% of its resources and another resource pool that is 50% in size. This would leave 25% unallocated outside of the resource pool.

We can get a very similar situation as in Example 1 where we reserve to the resource pool 1GB memory, but try to allocate more than what is free in the pool. The critical thing which will determine if a VM will power on is if the resource pool has an "expandable reservation" setting. If the resource pool is expandable it can reach out and use the free 25% previously outlined. If the resource pool is not expandable then it is "locked" within the confines of its own reservation. So perhaps the production resource pool would get 50% of the RAM in its reservation, with the resource pool set to be expandable, but the Test & Dev resource pool would only get 25% of RAM, set to non-expandable. Once all the memory allocated to Test & Dev had been used from the reservation a VM would not power on.

In the following example I will create a similar power-on error using a resource pool. I will reserve to the Test & Dev resource pool 1GB of RAM and then modify the settings of my VM located in the resource pool more RAM than is available. I will leave the default setting in place which allows the reservation to be expandable, then I will power on the VM to see what happens. After that I will power off the VM, and I will then change the resource pool to non-expandable.

1. Right-Click the Test & Dev Resource Pool and choose Edit Settings.

2. Under Memory Resource, move the Reservation slider to 1024MB and Click OK.

Next we will modify a VM that uses practically all the resources of the pool.

3. Next, take a VM and power it off.

4. Right-Click, and choose Edit Settings.

5. Under the Hardware Tab set the limit to 512MB.

6. Then, click the Resources Tab, and set the Reservation to 256MB.

7. Power on the VM.

8. Define other VMs in this way and begin to power them.

    Note:

    Figure 9.7 shows the "Summary Tab" on a resource pool – notice that memory usage is 1130MB, but the reservation is only 1024MB. The reason the VMs were able to power on was that free unreserved RAM of 315.29. The VM was allowed to use this free and unreserved RAM because the resource pool was "expandable."

Figure 9.7

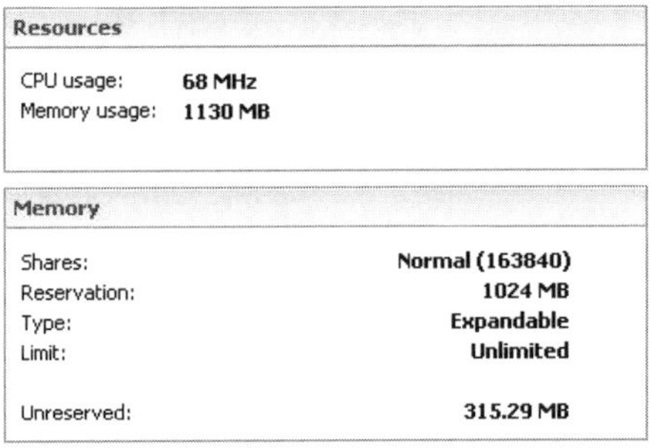

Resources	
CPU usage:	68 MHz
Memory usage:	1130 MB

Memory	
Shares:	Normal (163840)
Reservation:	1024 MB
Type:	Expandable
Limit:	Unlimited
Unreserved:	315.29 MB

9. Now power off the VM.

10. Right-Click the Resource Pool, and Choose Edit Settings.

11. Under Memory Resource, remove the tick next to Expandable Reservation.

You should find now that you get the same message we saw in Figure 9.6. As you went to power on VM1, VM2, VM3, and VM4 they began eating up the pools reservation in blocks of 256, 512, 768, and 1024. When you went to power on VM5 it would fail as there would be insufficient RAM in the resource pool left to meet your reservation. It would be like a 4 seat plane – and you were the 5th person arriving. There would be insufficient resources (seats) to make your reservation.

We can apply this to our airline analogy. The resource pool is like the Hollywood star's reservation to fly him and ten members of the staff. When he arrives at the airport he decides his personal stylist and hairdresser also need to come. At the check-in desk, the clerk recognizes that he's a premium flyer, and his reservation is expanded. Before she smiles sweetly and says that's fine Mr. X, she first must check that there are two extra seats free in business class. In my case, I am a less privileged person. When I arrive at the check-in desk the clerk checks my status and decides I'm an ordinary Joe. My reservation is not marked expandable – and my mother-in-law has to wait in the booking hall. She doesn't even look to see if there are spare seats on the flight. She knows I'm not business class, and the request to expand my reservation is politely declined. In the UK, we would call this "Computer says no....."

If you are facing this scenario there could be a number of solutions to the problem. The list below is ordered by the change that would require least impact on the rest of the system. The first would only require a change to a VM that is affected by the lack of RAM, the last would require all VMs to be powered off, to give them less generous reservations of RAM:

- Decrease the amount of memory reserved for the VM

- Increase the reservation of RAM to the resource pool

- Enable the Expandable Reservation option

- Move the VM to a resource pool that has greater resources

- Decrease the amount of memory reserved for other VM's in the same resource pool

Summary

In this chapter I have explained the different controls you have available such as limits, reservations, shares, CPU affinity, and resource pools. I have also outlined some of the advantages and disadvantages of each method – and given you a practical example of using resource pools and creating contention to demonstrate the effectiveness of them and the proportional share system. Lastly, I showed how VM reservations of memory and CPU can cause a VM not to power on – referred to by VMware as "Admission Control." Additionally, I gave some guidelines on how to resolve these power-on issues.

Chapter 10: VMotion, DRS, and HA

VMotion

How does VMotion work?

To say we are moving a VM from one ESX host to another is essentially a bit of a lie. In fact, we very rarely "move" data around at all. If you cut and paste a file in a folder to another folder what actually happens is the operating system copies the file to the new location. Once this is completed the original is deleted. Essentially, this is what happens in VMotion. The critical thing to stress is that the VM's files are *not* copied, but its *memory* contents are.

The VM on ESX1 is duplicated on ESX2, and the original is deleted. During VMotion what ESX creates is an initial pre-copy of memory from the VM running on ESX1 into a VM on ESX2. During the copy, a log file is generated to track any changes during the initial pre-copy process (it is referred to as a memory bitmap).

Once the VMs are practically at the same state, this memory bitmap is transferred to ESX2. Before the transfer of the bitmap file the VM on ESX1 is put into what is called a "quiesced" state. This quiesce process massively reduces the amount of activity occurring inside the VM that is being "moved." It allows the memory bitmap file to become so small that it can be transferred very quickly. This state also allows for rollback if a network failure takes place. In this respect VMotion has a transactional quality. VMotion is either successful or unsuccessful – what we don't get is two VMs on two different ESX hosts who believe they are the same. After the memory bitmap has been transferred the end-user is switched to using the VM on ESX2 – and the original VM is removed from ESX1.

During this switch from one ESX host to another there *may* be some dropped packets. Although the VM's physical MAC address does *not* change the physical MAC address on the ESX host does. The VMotion process triggers a Reverse Address Resolution Protocol (RARP) packet to make sure all network devices on the same subnet as the VM are aware that packets destined for the VM IP address should be directed towards a new MAC address. In my experience these one or two lost packets are not enough to disconnect even a real-time networking system like Microsoft's Remote Desktop Protocol (RDP) or Citrix's Independent Computing Architecture (ICA) protocol. In some cases where I have been pinging a VM with ping –t (a constant ping) I've seen packets merely being delayed rather than dropped. Fundamentally, you will probably see more packets dropped daily on your WAN than you ever will with VMotion.

VMotion Requirements on the ESX Host

VMotion has a number of requirements for it to function both on the VM and between ESX hosts (source and destination) – a lack of these requirements can be a good reason to resort to a cold migration instead.

Here is a comprehensive list of ESX Host requirements:

- Shared storage/LUN Visibility between the source and destination ESX hosts (SAN, iSCSI or NAS) - this includes the VMFS volume where the virtual disk(s) are and any RDM LUNs.

- A VMkernel port group on vSwitch configured with 1000mps on the VMotion network- this VMkernel port group requires an IP address and a subnet mask.

- Access to the same "production" network.

- Consistently labeled virtual switch port groups (case-sensitive).

- Compatible CPUs.

If any one of these requirements cannot be met then VMotion could fail. Fortunately, most of the requirements can be purchased (shared storage and gigabit bandwidth) or re-configured (same production network and consistently labeled switch port groups). The requirement for 1000mps networking is not necessarily a hard one. I have successfully carried out VMotion with 100mps at full-duplex – and I have also seen it fail. In the main, these have been test and development environments where full VMware support is not required. If you want full VMware support you will need 1000mps networking. The cause of the failure with 100mps is a network timeout, merely which the amount of memory in VM is large and frequently changing – and that 100mps pipe cannot bring the state of the two VMs close enough to trigger the VMotion.

There is one show stopper and that is compatible CPUs. Remember, although 99% of a VM is isolated from physical hardware – the one exception is that vCPUs do see specific *attributes* of the CPU. One reason to do a cold migration then is because your servers do not share CPU compatibility. New CPUs are constantly being released so it's inevitable that you will face some CPU incompatibility at some stage in your use of VMotion. Of course, many people attempt to purchase the same make and model of server, and indeed I've heard stories that some hardware vendors will even keep in stock CPUs that match your server's specification. I think it's likely that in the future the attributes that cause CPU incompatibilities will grow – as you purchase new hardware and as VMware exposes more of these features to a VM to improve performance, stability, and security. Here's a current list of attributes that would cause VMotion to fail due to CPU incompatibilities:

- **Processor Vendor: Intel Vs AMD**

- **Family: PIII Vs PIV, Opteron Family Numbers**

  We cannot carry out VMotion events from Intel processors to AMD processors. Within a given vendor there are "family" differences that would prevent VMotion from Intel Pentium III and Intel IV; similarly, within AMD there are family differences within the Opertons that would prevent VMotion.

- **SSE3 Instructions**

  SSE3 stands for "Streaming SIMD Extensions," and SIMD stands for "Single Instruction Multiple Data." These allow for improvements in processing for multi-media applications and have their roots in the MMX (Multi-Media eXtensions) feature found in some early Intel Pentium II processors.

- **Hardware Assist: Intel VT and AMD-V**

  These are recent enhancements that allegedly improve performance specifically for virtualization activity. They represent the first stages by Intel and AMD to create processors designed for virtualization. Right now the jury is out on whether they make such a massive impact for operating systems like ESX, but they are a step in the right direction and do represent a VMotion barrier.

- **Execution Disable: Intel XD and AMD NX**

  These attributes are designed to secure processors from attacks and exploits used by hackers.

There are, of course, other processor differences – such as the number of cores, sockets, clock speed, and amount of onboard cache; these attributes are ignored in VMotion, so are not a concern.

You will soon know you have some kind of CPU incompatibility if you attempt a VMotion where one exists. Before attempting the VMotion, ESX "validates" the destination. If a CPU incompatibility is discovered then VMotion is not allowed to even start. Figure 10.1 shows the dialog box warning that I receive when I attempt a VMotion between one of my Dell PowerEdge Servers with an Intel Processor to a HP Proliant DL385 with AMD Opteron Dual-Core Processors.

Figure 10.1

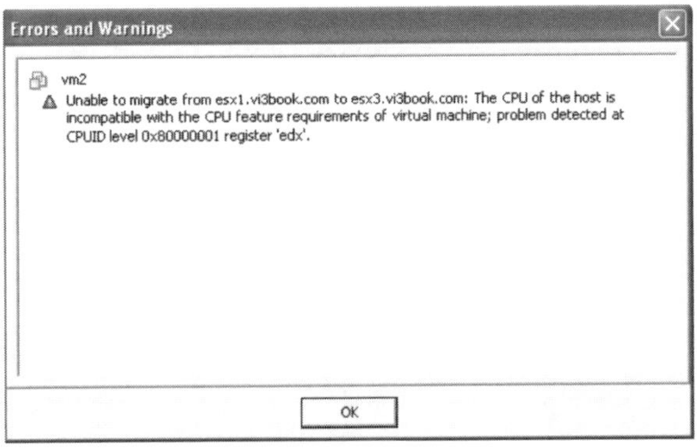

Errors and Warnings

vm2
⚠ Unable to migrate from esx1.vi3book.com to esx3.vi3book.com: The CPU of the host is incompatible with the CPU feature requirements of virtual machine; problem detected at CPUID level 0x80000001 register 'edx'.

OK

VMotion Requirements on the VM

There are some requirements for the VM. Fortunately, these are configurable and unlikely to cause you many headaches once you have resolved them. In dialog boxes like the one above you get two types of messages – warnings and errors. Warnings can be bypassed; they are merely cautions that a problem *could* occur, whereas errors must be resolved before continuing.

Here is a definite list of errors and the reasons why:

* **Active connections to use an internal switch**

  By "active" we mean that the VM is configured and connected to the internal switch. VMotion cannot guarantee that the same internal switch exists on the destination host, and would offer the same uninterrupted connectivity to the VM.

* **Active connection to use a CD-ROM or floppy which is not on shared storage**

  By "active" we mean that the VM is configured and connected to the CD or Floppy Device. VMotion cannot guarantee that the CD or Floppy will still be accessible on the destination host.

* **CPU Affinities**

  VMotion cannot guarantee that the VM will be able to continue to run on the specific CPU number on the destination.

  GOTCHA:

  CPU affinities are disabled in DRS for this reason. CPU affinities can also cause problems with DRS. If you setup CPU affinities on VM on a stand-alone ESX host and later join it to a DRS cluster you will find it cannot be VMotion-ed. There is a workaround to "loosing" your control over CPU affinities in DRS without necessarily powering off the VM, entering maintenance mode and removing the ESX host from the DRS cluster. The loss of configuration options over CPU affinities only applies in the "Fully Automated" mode. It is possible to temporarily switch the cluster to "Partially Automated" or "Manual." This will re-enable the CPU affinity feature on the VM which will then allow you to remove the CPU affinity problem. This is very irritating, and so I would recommend avoiding CPU affinities unless you have a totally compelling reason to use them.

- **VMs in a Cluster Relationship**

  Firstly, the virtual disks and RDMs used in VM clustering must be on local storage for VMware Support; as we have seen, shared storage is a requirement for VMotion. Secondly, if you think about it, the uptime is delivered by the VM cluster. If you want to move a VM cluster you could power off one node and cold migrate it and then power it back on. If you repeated this practice with the second node effectively you would have moved the cluster without downtime (of course, the reliability of this approach is only as good as your clustering software). Thirdly, because there is a potential loss of packets on the heartbeat network during VMotion there could be unwanted cluster failover. Lastly, clustering software is highly dependent on SCSI reservations to lock storage to decide which node is active and which node is passive. If you attempted a VMotion event in active node, the SAN array would have received a SCSI reservation on the quorum disk from the WWN of the *source* host. Once the VMotion had been successful, the array would receive a renewal for that lock from the WWN of the *destination* host. It will reject that reservation because the destination node didn't have the reservation in the first place.

  Perhaps one solution to this issue would be I/O virtualization, where a WWN "alias" could be presented directly to the VM. In this case the lock would be created by the VM, *not* by our physical ESX host with a physical fiber channel card. Emulex is working on adapters that have this functionality.

- **RDMs**

  This is where the destination host does *not* have visibility to the RDM LUN. I would like to make it clear that RDMs are not in-compatible per se with VMotion. In fact, one of the major reasons they were introduced in ESX 2.5.0 was to allow VMotion of VMs that were natively accessing storage, as previously the mechanism which was used to allow native access "broke" VMotion. The issue here is of LUN visibility and VMotion's requirement of shared storage. That means visibility of VMFS *and* Raw LUNs to both ESX hosts.

Here's a definitive list of warnings and the reasons why:

- **Configured to an internal switch**

  By "configured" we mean that the VM is set to use the internal switch. However, on the VM under Network Adapter and Device Status, Connected and Connected at Power On are not enabled.

- **Configured to use a CD-ROM or floppy which is not on shared storage**

  By "configured" we mean that the VM is set to use the CD or Floppy, but that on the VM under CD/DVD Drive or Floppy Drive and Device Status Connected and Connected at Power On are not enabled.

- **Snapshots**

  There could be warnings when deleting or reverting snapshots when the VM is moved. Personally, I have carried out VMotions with snapshots engaged – and never had a problem. After all, the files that make up a snapshot would be on shared storage. Nonetheless, the Vi-Client does warn you about having snapshots applied.

- **Lack of a heartbeat signal**

  This can happen if you have failed to install VMware Tools. It can also happen if you have just powered on a VM, and the VMware Tools service/daemon has yet to start. Additionally, I have found that this might temporarily interrupt the heartbeat signal if you have recently carried out a VMotion on the VM.

Figures 10.2 and 10.3 show you all the errors and warnings in single dialog boxes.

Figure 10.2 – All the Errors

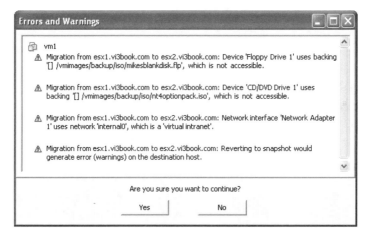

Figure 10.3 – All the Warnings

GOTCHA:

Just as these errors, warnings, and requirements can stop a manual VMotion, they can also stop automatic VMotion generated by VMware DRS, so it's important to resolve this wherever possible.

Configuring and Using VMotion

VMotion does require a VMKernel Port Group with a valid IP address and subnet mask for the VMotion network. A default gateway entry is not required as VMware does not support VMotion across routers or WANs. Earlier in this book, I configured a VMotion switch as an example of a VMkernel Port Group. In case you missed that part or have changed your configuration since then, I will repeat these instructions again, to save you having to flip back to the networking chapter. If you are running out of network cards on your server(s) then you could just create an additional VMkernel Port Group on an existing vSwitch.

- **Select your ESX host**.

- Click the **Configuration Tab**.

- In the **Hardware Pane**, select **Networking**.

- Click the **Add Networking...** link.

- Choose **VMKernel**, and **Click Next**.

- In the **Port Groups Properties** dialog, type a friendly name for this connection, such as **vmotion**.

- Enable **X Use this port group for VMotion**.

- Set an **IP Address** and **Subnet mask** for **VMotion**.

- You may then receive this message;

  "There is no default gateway set. You must set a default gateway before you can use this port group. Do you want to configure it now"

  Note:

  This message can be a little misleading because of the reference to the word "must." At this stage I've been told VMware has no intention of allowing VMotion across routers, so really the dialog box should say "may need."

  Having said this, a VMKernel port group like this could be used to access iSCSI and NAS/NFS devices. In that case, you must set a default gateway to cross the router.

VMotion by Drag-And-Drop

To initiate VMotion you can use drag-and-drop. This even allows you to drop your VM to the correct resource pools if you have them. You can also drag-and-drop multiple VMs by using shift+click to select multiples. The VMotion will do each VM in series (one after another) to preserve bandwidth on the VMotion network and prevent network timeouts.

1. **Select your VM** and **drag-and-drop** to the **ESX Host/Resource Pool.**

2. Choose to **Keep virtual machine files and virtual disks in their current location.**

3. Then **select** either **High** or **Low Priority.**

Note:

You get two priority settings – high and low. These do not control how quick the VMotion event is, but rather they set controls for the VM's availability. High only allows the VMotion to occur if there is no chance of the users being disconnected from the VM. In contrast, low allows the VMotion to go ahead even if a possible disconnect occurs. I would use high on a sensitive VM which is stateful, whereas I would use low on a non-mission critical stateless VM. Stateful services are ones which have almost continual IP communications such as Terminal Services, Citrix MetaFrame, or Voice-Over-IP. Stateless applications are ones which have only periodic IP communications such as databases, email, and web servers.

VMotion without Drag-and-Drop

You can start a VMotion without using drag-and drop either by right-clicking a VM and choosing Migration, or in the Summary Tab and Command Pane using the option "Migrate to New Host." This method asks more questions; you will be asked to select an ESX host as the destination and also where you wish to add it to a resource pool. Personally, I prefer to use the drag-and-drop method as you are asked less questions in the migration wizard.

Discovering CPU Incompatibilities

The Vi-Client does a very good job of stopping what could be a catastrophic event – that of moving a VM to one ESX host to another – where CPU incompatibilities exist. If this "validation" check wasn't done before the VMotion stopped then a VM would probably crash when it arrived at the destination. The VI Client fails by not telling you in a meaningful way what these CPU incompatibilities are. All the VI Client will tell you in the Summary tab of an ESX host are things like the number of CPUs, their clock speed, Vendor, and Family. Critically, it doesn't tell you anything about the incompatibilities that exist *within* the physical CPU such as SSE3, NX/XD, Intel-VT, or AMD-V.

Buy for Compatibility

One of the easiest ways to avoid CPU incompatibilities is to buy for compatibility. Simply put, this means being careful in your purchases to ensure that each ESX host has identical CPUs. This is attractive to organizations that have the purchasing power to buy blocks of servers. It's inevitable that over time you will be not able to buy the same hardware as two years ago. If this happens, we can see these new servers as representing a new "cluster" of ESX hosts that share common attributes. It's not an approach that will help in a company which is used to buying hardware on an as-needed basis.

Read the Manual

There are number of ways of finding out the attributes of your CPUs and whether your server hardware possesses compatibility issues. In recent months, both Dell and HP have released "compatibility documents" that will allow you to compare your hardware. I've yet to see an IBM document on this topic – but I dare say there will be a Redbook on the subject shortly.

For Dell Visit:

http://www.dell.com/downloads/global/solutions/vmotion_compatiblity_matix.pdf

For HP Visit:

ftp://ftp.compaq.com/pub/products/servers/vmware/vmmotion-compatibility-matrix.pdf

While these are very useful, and are the first step, they don't really help if you already have a mix of hardware vendors who use the same CPUs. Perhaps your organization deliberately does not buy from the same server vendor for strategic reasons. Perhaps there was a recent shift from purchasing hardware from HP to Dell or IBM to HP. It's entirely possible for there to be compatibility between these vendors if the chipset you are using is the same.

Using CPU Vendor Tools

Both AMD and Intel have their own tools for reporting the CPU types present in a system. I've chosen to mention these here for completeness. The downside of these tools is that they may flag attributes that are not a problem with VMotion. You can download the relevant tool from the following links.

Intel:

http://www.intel.com/support/processors/tools/piu/

AMD:

http://www.amd.com/us-en/Processors/TechnicalResources/0,,30_182_871_9706,00.html

Using cupid.iso

Located on the ESX CD in the /images directory is a file called cupid.iso. This can be attached using an ILO or RAC board via "virtual media" or burned to a physical CD. The cupid.iso file is bootable and will show you the CPU characteristic of your processor. The iso is also freely available on VMware's website if you do not have access to the ESX media. You will find it under "CPU Compatibility Tools."

http://www.vmware.com/download/vi/drivers_tools.html

Figure 10.4 is a capture of the information from a HP Proliant DL385 with 1 AMD dual-core processor fitted.

Figure 10.4

```
Test: 56983: CPUID CHANGE: 340063
Reporting CPUID for 2 logical CPUs..

All CPU's are identical

Family: of model: 21 Stepping: 2

Vendor: AMD
Processor Cores: 2
SSE Support: SSE3
Supports NX/ED: Yes
Supports 64-bit Longmode: Yes
Supports 64-bit VMware: Yes
```

From this image we can see that "All the CPUs are identical" within the ESX host. This is interesting because there are some rare cases, such as after a reseller CPU upgrade, that one physical server may have different CPU types. Additionally, we can see the vendor is AMD, and my single socket contains two processor cores. There is full support for NX/XS and full support for 64-bit guest operating systems. The reference to "longmode" is actually an Intel mode. Only Intel 64-bit chips with VT Technology are supported for 64-bit guest operating systems – Intel uses the term "longmode" to describe this type of CPU.

Using 3rd party Tools – VMotion Info

Richard Garsthagen is currently Technical Marketing Manager for VMware in EMEA. He's formally a VMware Certified Instructor (VCI); in fact, he was the first instructor in EMEA for VMware. In his spare time, Richard is an enthusiastic blogger (www.run-virtual.com) and evangelist for the VirtualCenter Software Development Kit (SDK). The VirtualCenter SDK allows anyone to develop their own tools for VirtualCenter in practically any programming language they like. Richard recently wrote an application called VMotionInfo, which uses the SDK to unveil the CPU attributes of your server hardware. The really cool aspect of Richard's application is that it can be run against existing ESX hosts, without having to reboot them – as we have to with the cupid.iso method.

Figure 10.5 shows a screen grab of Richard's application taken from his website and Figure 10.6 shows a screen grab of my servers.

Figure 10.5

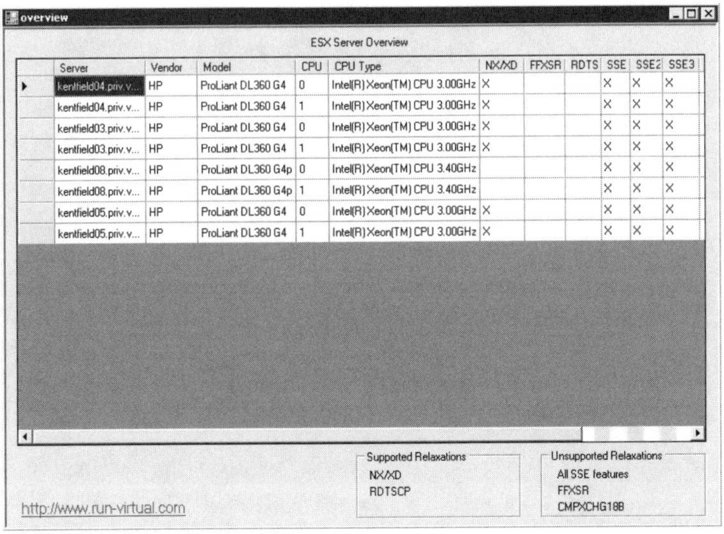

ESX Server Overview

Server	Vendor	Model	CPU	CPU Type	NX/XD	FFXSR	RDTS	SSE	SSE2	SSE3
kentfield04.priv.v...	HP	ProLiant DL360 G4	0	Intel(R) Xeon(TM) CPU 3.00GHz	X			X	X	X
kentfield04.priv.v...	HP	ProLiant DL360 G4	1	Intel(R) Xeon(TM) CPU 3.00GHz	X			X	X	X
kentfield03.priv.v...	HP	ProLiant DL360 G4	0	Intel(R) Xeon(TM) CPU 3.00GHz	X			X	X	X
kentfield03.priv.v...	HP	ProLiant DL360 G4	1	Intel(R) Xeon(TM) CPU 3.00GHz	X			X	X	X
kentfield08.priv.v...	HP	ProLiant DL360 G4p	0	Intel(R) Xeon(TM) CPU 3.40GHz				X	X	X
kentfield08.priv.v...	HP	ProLiant DL360 G4p	1	Intel(R) Xeon(TM) CPU 3.40GHz				X	X	X
kentfield05.priv.v...	HP	ProLiant DL360 G4	0	Intel(R) Xeon(TM) CPU 3.00GHz	X			X	X	X
kentfield05.priv.v...	HP	ProLiant DL360 G4	1	Intel(R) Xeon(TM) CPU 3.00GHz	X			X	X	X

Supported Relaxations
NX/XD
RDTSCP

Unsupported Relaxations
All SSE features
FFXSR
CMPXCHG16B

http://www.run-virtual.com

Figure 10.6

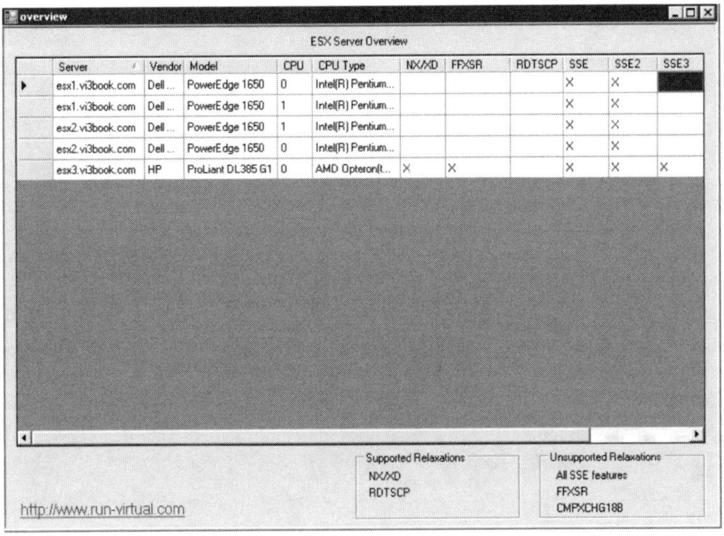

ESX Server Overview

Server	Vendor	Model	CPU	CPU Type	NX/XD	FFXSR	RDTSCP	SSE	SSE2	SSE3
esx1.vi3book.com	Dell ...	PowerEdge 1650	0	Intel(R) Pentium...				X	X	
esx1.vi3book.com	Dell ...	PowerEdge 1650	1	Intel(R) Pentium...				X	X	
esx2.vi3book.com	Dell ...	PowerEdge 1650	1	Intel(R) Pentium...				X	X	
esx2.vi3book.com	Dell ...	PowerEdge 1650	0	Intel(R) Pentium...				X	X	
esx3.vi3book.com	HP	ProLiant DL385 G1	0	AMD Opteron(t...	X	X		X	X	X

Supported Relaxations
NX/XD
RDTSCP

Unsupported Relaxations
All SSE features
FFXSR
CMPXCHG16B

http://www.run-virtual.com

Managing CPU Incompatibilities – CPU Masks

There are some CPU incompatibilities that we can do nothing about – such as the difference between an AMD CPU and an Intel CPU. Beyond this there are tools from VMware we can use to enforce compatibility at the expense of the CPU attribute. The term we use is a "CPU Mask." A CPU mask allows us to "hide" or "mask" attributes of the physical CPU from the VM. In this scenario we might mask the Intel-VT attribute or the AMD NX attribute to allow VMotion to occur between two ESX hosts that don't share the same CPU attributes. You can see the CPU mask like putting a pair of blinders on the VM, as you would on a horse. If the VM cannot see the NX attribute, for example, it will not use it.

CPU masks are property of VM and can be found under Edit Settings, the Options Tab, and Advanced. As Figure 10.7 shows, it is possible to Disable Acceleration (Intel-VT or AMD-V) and Hide the Nx flag from the guest. The advanced button allows you to create custom CPU masks (say to hide the SSE3 attribute) for the VM specified in hexadecimal. Currently, there is little or no documentation on the Advanced button. It was enabled in the VI Client reluctantly under user pressure.

At VMworld 2006, there was a useful presentation delivered by Matthias Hausner entitled "Migrating between Apples and Oranges with VMware VMotion in VMware Infrastructure 3." It contained some useful material about the Advanced button and emerging CPU incompatibilities.

http://download3.vmware.com/vmworld/2006/tac1356.pdf

In May of 2007, VMware updated a knowledge based article surrounding this long running issue of CPU attributes. This KB article (1993) has been improved to offer more information about custom CPU masks.

http://kb.vmware.com/selfservice/microsites/search.do?cmd=displayKC&externalId=1993

Lastly, there is a thread where forum members discuss their relative successes and failures at creating their own custom CPU masks.

http://www.vmware.com/community/thread.jspa?threadID=50828

Figure 10.7

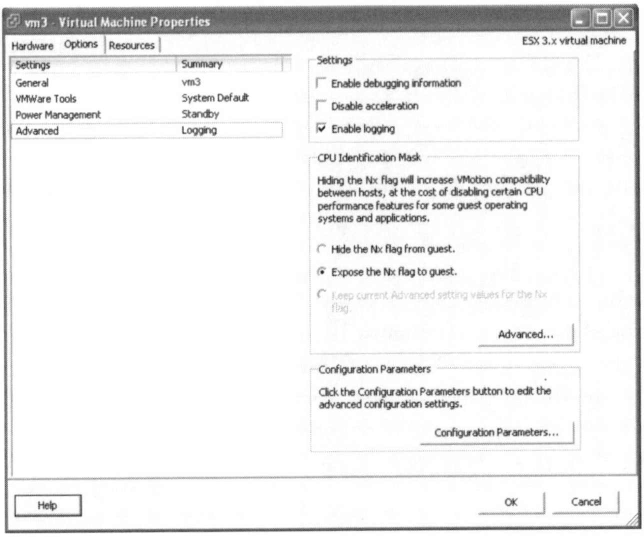

Resolving VMotion Errors and Warnings

Now that we are fully familiar with the typical VMotion errors and warnings you can receive, hopefully you should be well on the way to fixing these issues when they arise. However, I thought it would be useful to round-up these in one easy place so you know the most efficient ways.

The most popular errors are ones concerning active connections to removable devices. So the simplest way to turn these errors (which cannot be bypassed) into warnings (which can be bypassed) is to disconnect them. Most likely you will want to remove all errors and warnings.

Removing CD-ROM and Floppy Errors & Warnings

The best way to remove all CD-ROM floppy errors and warnings is to disconnect the devices within the VM, and then set them to use a "client device." This removes any path statements to either local resources such as /dev/fd0 or

/dev/cdrom and also any path statements to ISOs or flp files held on a local datastore such as /vmfs/volumes/storage1. To configure this:

1. Right-click the VM.

2. Choose Edit Settings.

3. Select Floppy Device 1.

4. Remove any ticks next to Connected and Connected at power on.

5. Select Client Device.

6. Select CD/DVD Drive 1.

7. Remove any ticks next to Connected and Connected at power on.

8. Select Client Device.

9. Click OK to Virtual Machine Properties dialog.

Removing CPU Affinities

You should really remove any CPU affinities you have on VM prior to joining the ESX host it resides on into DRS Cluster. CPU Affinities and DRS clusters are incompatible with each other, and the configuration options for CPU affinities are removed from the interface in a fully-automated mode. If you join your ESX host to DRS cluster and then build your VMs you will discover that you cannot configure the CPU affinity feature at all. The root of this compatibility with DRS stems from the incompatibility with VMotion. To disable CPU affinities and return your VM to being able to execute on any CPU, change the configuration this way:

1. Right-click the VM.

2. Choose Edit Settings.

3. Select the Resources Tab.

4. Choose Advanced CPU in the dialog.

5. Select the option of No Affinity.

6. Click OK to the Virtual Machine Properties dialog.

Removing Internal Switch Errors and Warnings

If you have configured VMs to use virtual switches that are internal, there will be errors and warnings with those VMs. Remember, the goal of VMotion is to move a VM while powered *and* while users are connected. If you remember, one of the requirements of VMotion is access to the same networks for both the VM network and the VMotion network. There are two "workarounds" to this issue. Firstly, you could temporarily configure the VM to a "production" portgroup where communication would be enabled. Secondly, you could temporarily disconnect the VM from the internal switch, carry out the VMotion, and then reconnect it to a portgroup at the destination. This temporary disconnection produces a warning, rather than a hard error – and does allow you to click next to continue the VMotion.

Both of these workarounds are more than likely to disconnect users and therefore do not *strictly* meet the requirements for a true VMotion. This said, you might prefer these workarounds compared to the alternative, which is to shutdown the VM (which most definitely disconnects users!) and then "cold migrate" the VM to the new ESX host. Whatever your approach, you are likely to have to reconfigure the VM's networking and confirm that users can still connect as normal after the move has been completed. Where possible I would avoid internal switches if VMotion and DRS are important to you as they create more problems than they resolve in this aspect of the product.

To temporarily disconnect a VM from an internal switch use the following configuration:

1. Right-click the VM.

2. Choose Edit Settings.

3. Select the Network Adapter.

4. Remove any ticks for Connected and Connected at Power On.

Moving Virtual Machines - Cold Migration

When all hope is lost and you simply cannot work around the VMotion requirements, there is always cold migration. Cold migration has none of the stringent requirements of VMotion. The only requirement is that both ESX hosts reside in the *same* datacenter. If both ESX hosts have visibility to the same storage then cold migration can be incredibly quick and the VM downtime kept to the minimum. If the two ESX hosts do not share storage then a cold migrate can take a much longer time. In the worst case scenario, where only local storage is available, it would generate network traffic on vSwitch0 as a cold migrate would use the Service Console network interface to move the VM's file from one host to another. In the best scenario your cold migrate might be only throttled by the speed of your SAN as it moves the VM's file from one SAN LUN to another in the same disk array.

Another compelling reason to use cold migrate would be if you have a VM restriction which is not reconfigurable. For example, you might wish to move a VM cluster. As this requires that VMDKs and RDMs are stored locally for full VMware Support, then VMotion is impossible. In this case you would enact the following:

- Shutdown the secondary node in the cluster.

- Temporarily remove (but not delete) the quorum and shared RDMs. This would have to be done, otherwise the cold migrate would attempt to move them also, and they would be "locked" by other VMs in the cluster group.

- Cold migrate the VM.

- Re-add the quorum and shared RDMs.

- Power the VM Cluster back on.

As long as there is at least one cluster node up at any one time you would still achieve the VM uptime you require. To do this successfully, the quorum and shared disks would have to be on shared storage. So a Cluster-In-A-Box scenario, where all the quorum and shared virtual disks are possibly held on local storage, would have to be completely powered off and cold migrated.

Figure 10.8 shows the errors generated if a VMotion of "Cluster-In-A-Box" was attempted.

Figure 10.8

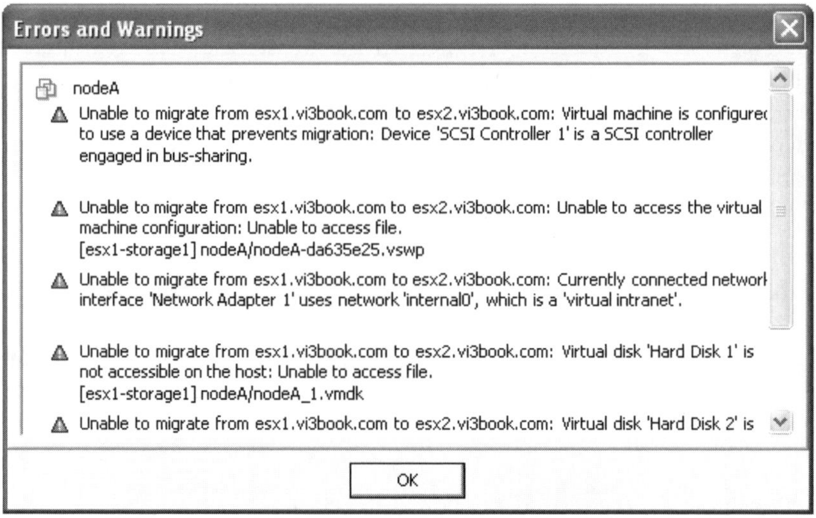

Errors and Warnings

nodeA
⚠ Unable to migrate from esx1.vi3book.com to esx2.vi3book.com: Virtual machine is configured to use a device that prevents migration: Device 'SCSI Controller 1' is a SCSI controller engaged in bus-sharing.

⚠ Unable to migrate from esx1.vi3book.com to esx2.vi3book.com: Unable to access the virtual machine configuration: Unable to access file.
[esx1-storage1] nodeA/nodeA-da635e25.vswp

⚠ Unable to migrate from esx1.vi3book.com to esx2.vi3book.com: Currently connected network interface 'Network Adapter 1' uses network 'internal0', which is a 'virtual intranet'.

⚠ Unable to migrate from esx1.vi3book.com to esx2.vi3book.com: Virtual disk 'Hard Disk 1' is not accessible on the host: Unable to access file.
[esx1-storage1] nodeA/nodeA_1.vmdk

⚠ Unable to migrate from esx1.vi3book.com to esx2.vi3book.com: Virtual disk 'Hard Disk 2' is

OK

Cold Migration triggered by CPU Incompatibility

In this example I am going to do a cold migrate from one of my Dell Intel servers to my HP AMD server. The VM will remain on the same storage. Occasionally, this produces a warning about possible changes in the VM as it moves from one processor type to another. Figure 10.9 shows this dialog box. This is a benign change and should not be a cause for concern.

Figure 10.9

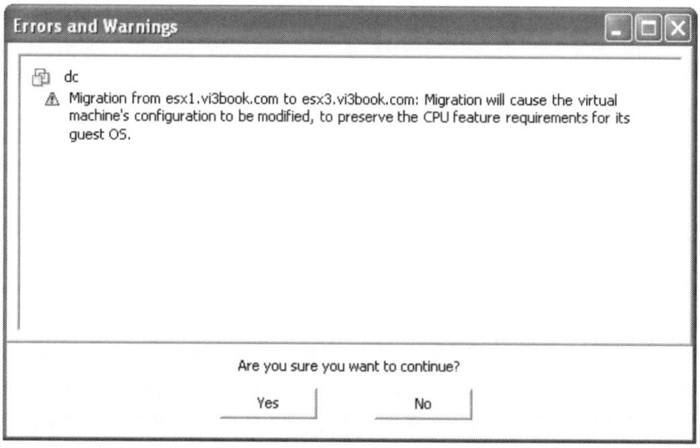

This was caused by moving by VM from an old Intel server to a new AMD server. New attributes such as NX/XD and Hardware Assist could be exposed to the VM whereas previously they were not present.

1. Shutdown the guest operating system in the VM.

2. Drag-and-Drop the VM to the destination ESX Host/Resource Pool, and confirm that Validation has succeeded.

3. Choose to Keep virtual machine configuration files and virtual disks in their current location.

   Note:

   If your VM is located on storage which is not shared you will find this option is unavailable. You will be only be able to choose the second option to "Move virtual machine configuration files and virtual disks."

4. Choose High Priority.

5. Once the move is complete, power on the VM.

Cold Migration for Storage Relocation

The second "hidden" usage of cold migrate is as a file management tool. It is possible to use the migration wizard to keep the VM registered on the same

ESX host, but move the files from one datastore to another. Perhaps one of your LUNs is full and you wish to free up space. You could move a VM from one LUN to another without necessarily using it to move the VM from one ESX host to another.

1. **Shutdown your VM**. In my case, I am using nodeA.

2. **Drag-and-drop your VM to the destination ESX host/Resource Pool**.

   Note:

   You might have to confirm various warning messages if your VM cluster is configured for an internal switch as would be the case in a Cluster-In-A-Box scenario.

3. Figure 10.10 shows how the use of local storage prevents both VMotion and the "Keep virtual machine configuration files and virtual disks in their current location" in the Cluster-In-A-Box scenario.

Figure 10.10

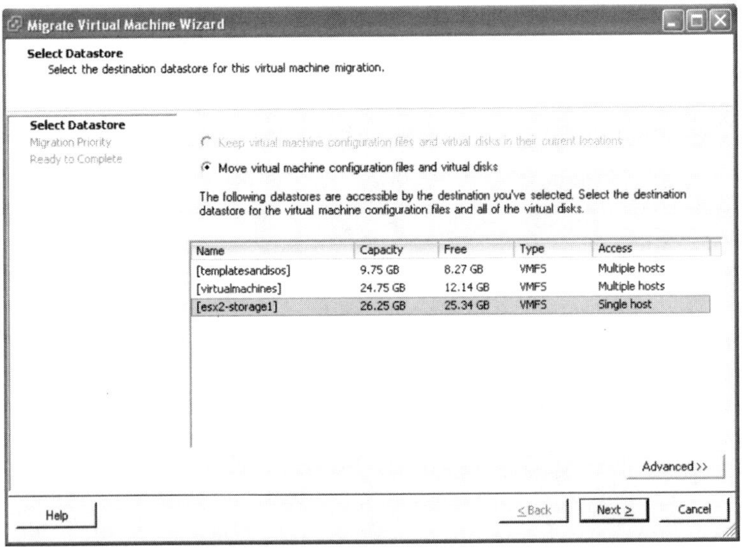

4. **Select the required datastore** – in my case, esx2-storage1.

5. Click **Next**.

6. Choose **High Priority**.

Data-Motion

One format of moving a VM occurs between ESX 2.x.x and ESX 3.x.x and is sometimes referred to as Data Motion, or DMotion, amongst community forum members. It is hoped by many of us in the VMware Community that DMotion will be enabled *between* ESX 3.x.x hosts.

Incidentally, "DMotion" is not an official VMware term. One method of upgrading from ESX 2/VirtualCenter 1 to ESX 3/VirtualCenter2 is by moving a VM from an ESX2 VMFS2 storage to ESX3 with VMFS3 storage. This can be done without shutting down the VM. The process moves the VM from one ESX host (Version 2) to another (Version 3) as well as moving the VM's files. This is achieved by engaging an ESX 3.x.x snapshot on the VMFS3 volume, which then unlocks the disks stored in the VMFS2 files system so they can be copied to the new storage. Even though "DMotion" is not an official term, we can see its origins in the name given to snapshot delta files created during this data motion.

DMotion-scsi0:00_vm2-delta.vmdk

DMotion-scsi0:00_vm2.vmdk

Configuring Data-Motion

As you might imagine this necessitates quite a number of requirements:

- Meet all the requirements for VMotion on both hosts
    - o VMotion enabled on ESX2 and ESX3
    - o vSwitch labels

o   Visibility to LUNs

o   CPU Compatibility

o   Resolve any VM based errors and warnings (connected CD-ROM, configured for internal switches and so on)

- Software Requirements

o   ESX 3.0.1 or higher

o   VirtualCenter 2.0.1 or higher

When you come to do the move you will be warned that you may not be able to move the VM back to the source ESX server. Additionally, despite the fact your ESX hosts will have to have CPU compatibility, you will receive a warning shown in Figure 10.11.

Figure 10.11

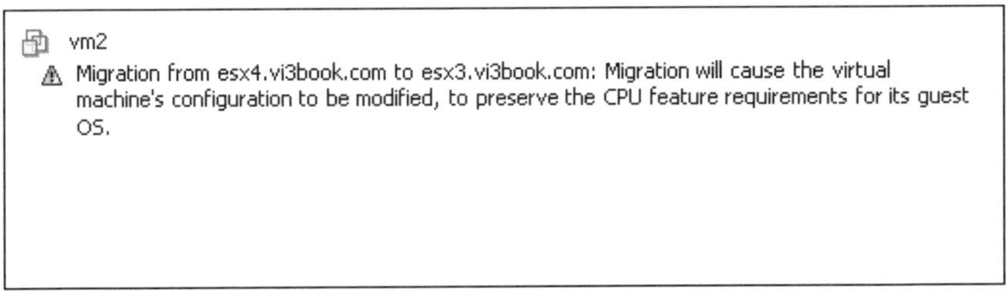

vm2

⚠ Migration from esx4.vi3book.com to esx3.vi3book.com: Migration will cause the virtual machine's configuration to be modified, to preserve the CPU feature requirements for its guest OS.

This happens because a VM running on an ESX 2.x.x host sees *less* CPU attributes than an ESX 3.x.x. This message can also appear even when you use a cold migration of the VM. After the DMotion process has completed, the VMX file is modified to include CPU masks. Below is an example of the CPU mask introduced when I DMotion'd a VM from ESX 2.5.4 to ESX 3.0.1 on two identical HP Proliant DL385s.

```
cpuid.1.eax = "----xxxxxxxx-------------------"
cpuid.80000001.ecx = "xxxxxxxxxxxxxxxxxxxxxxxxxxxxxxx0"
cpuid.80000001.edx = "xx0xxxxxxxx0xxxxxxxxxxxxxxxxxxxx"
```

These CPU masks can be also viewed in the VI Client. Figures 10.12b shows the CPU Identification Mask on this VM (Edit Settings, Options Tab, Advanced, and Advanced Button).

Figure 10.12

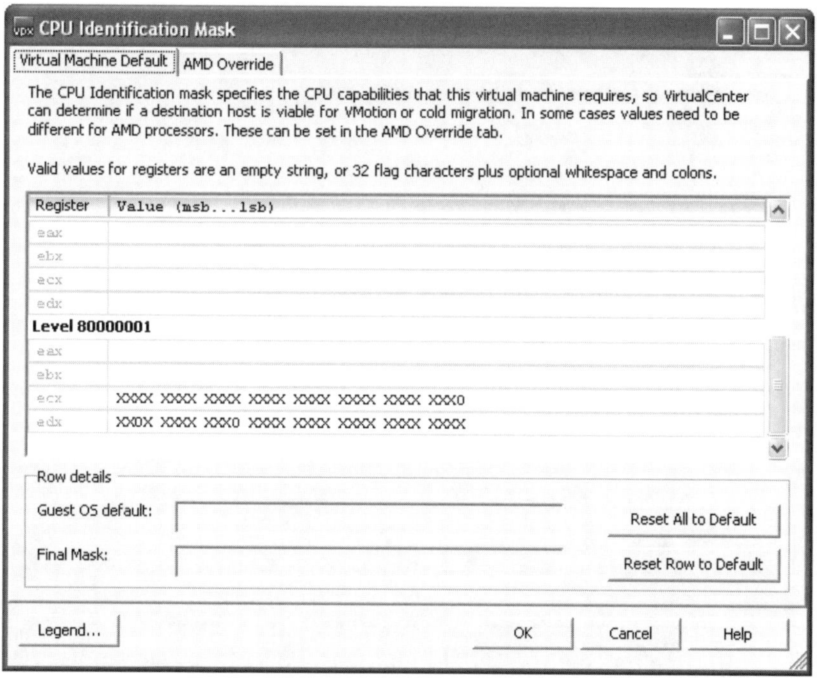

DMotion is very similar to Vmotion with the following exception; because ESX 2 and ESX 3 do not share a common file-system your only option in the migration wizard is relocate the VM's storage. Figure 10.13 shows how the "Keep virtual machine configuration files and virtual disks their current locations" option is unavailable. Consequently the event is labeled in the VI Client as "Relocate Virtual Machine storage" event.

Figure 10.13

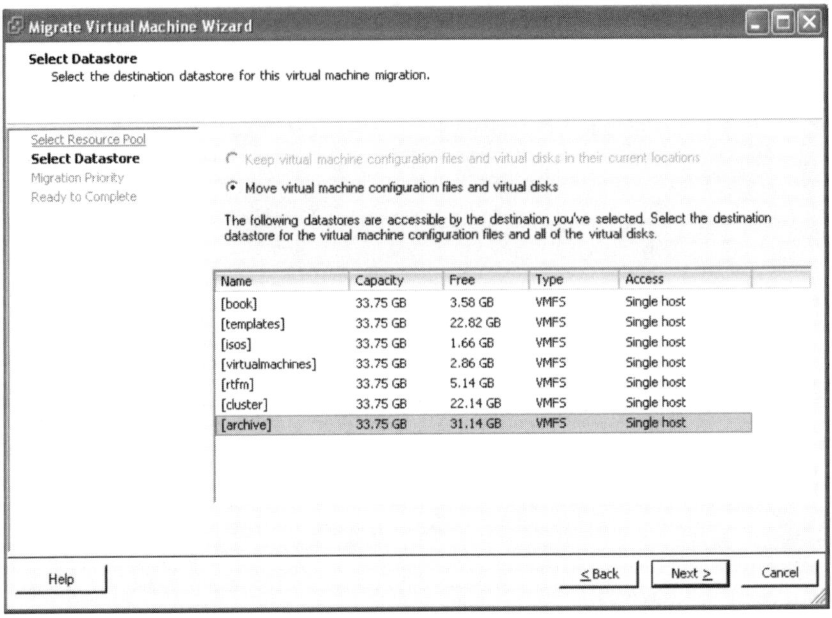

At the end of the process you should find that the VM has been moved to the new storage location, and that the snapshot files have been committed. The process will also convert the ESX 2.x.x VM into a format such that all the VM's files are held in a single directory.

VMware DRS

DRS Overview

In the simplest case, all VMware DRS is an automated VMotion. This is triggered by the system recognizing an imbalance in the resources used on each ESX host. DRS re-balances the "cluster" of ESX hosts. A lot of people mistakenly believe that what they should see is an "even" number of VMs on each ESX host. This is not the intention of DRS. After all, different VMs create different amounts of resource demands. What we are looking for is a relatively even load on ESX hosts. VMware has tested up to 32 ESX hosts in a single DRS cluster. They recommend not exceeding 16 ESX hosts. As we will see later, VMware HA has much lower tested values, tested to 16 ESX hosts. As you are likely to use both DRS and HA together, it's perhaps worth settling for a limit of no more than 16 hosts in any DRS and HA cluster. DRS is very conservative and currently will not allow more than 60 VMotions per hour. DRS only checks for an imbalance in the cluster once every 5 minutes. Many customers worry that they may get a "DRS storm" when an ESX host fails. The argument goes something like this: an ESX host fails, triggering VMware HA which would then cause VMs to power on the remaining ESX hosts. This creates an imbalance in the cluster which then triggers a VMotion or DRS "storm." This simply does not happen, because DRS would wait at least 5 minutes before checking the cluster, and it would only offer recommendations based on your "migration threshold." This allows the administrator to control how aggressively it tries to rebalance the cluster.

Another major feature of DRS, apart from dynamic load-balancing, is "initial placement." This allows DRS to decide where to place or power on a VM for the first time. These two features of DRS closely integrate with VMware's HA software. So if an ESX host crashes say because of hardware failure – HA is in charge of detecting the crash and making sure VMs are started on other nodes in the cluster. In turn, DRS will re-balance the cluster. If the failed server comes back online again and re-joins the DRS cluster then its free capacity will be recognized, and VMotion events will be triggered to utilize the server.

DRS possesses three different levels of automation:

- **Manual**

    The Administrator is offered recommendations of where to place a VM.

    The Administrator is offered recommendations of whether to VMotion a VM.

- **Partially Automated**

    DRS decides where a VM will execute.

    The Administrator is offered recommendations of whether to VMotion a VM.

- **Fully Automated (Default)**

  DRS decides where a VM will execute.

  DRS decides whether VMotion or not, based on a threshold parameter, obeying any rules or exclusions created by the Administrator.

  Note:

  Setting to DRS manual and partial does not break VMware HA. If an ESX host fails, your VM gets powered on without asking where to power it on. If an ESX host failure occurs, the VM is powered on – and only later do you get recommendations to rebalance the cluster.

At first glance, many Administrators would choose manual as they prefer to be "in control" of their systems. However, this might not necessarily be a good decision. Firstly, if you want to power on 10 or 20 VMs simultaneously answering 10 or 20 "initial placement" dialog boxes can become irritating. Secondly, will you always have the VI Client open to see recommendations and then act on them? Thirdly, if VMotion events are included as part of change management requests then you would waste time waiting for such requests to be processed. By the time you get approval for the VMotion the performance will have changed, rendering the request invalid. Perhaps it's time to learn to lose control and have VMware move VMs for you. If you have particularly politically sensitive VMs that shouldn't be moved without prior approval, we can exclude them from the DRS process.

In addition to these 3 different levels of automation, we can set a "Migration Threshold." This allows you to say how aggressive level DRS will balance the cluster of ESX hosts. You have 5 threshold levels beginning with "conservative" and ending with "aggressive" – with the default being in the middle of these two extremes. When VM is selected as a candidate for VMotion by DRS, it will be given a "star" rating – and the threshold level ties in directly with this. So level 5 is conservative and will only trigger VMs which have a 5-star recommendation.

- **Level 1 – Conservative**

  Triggers a VMotion if the VM has a 5-star rating. 5-star recommendations are rare, and you receive this recommendation when one of your "affinity rules" is breached. Alternatively, another cause of a 5-star recommendation could be putting an ESX host into "maintenance mode."

We will discuss affinity rules and maintenance mode shortly.

- **Level 2 – Moderately Conservative**

  Triggers a VMotion if the VM has 4 or more stars.

- **Level 3 – Default**

  Triggers a VMotion if the VM has 3 or more stars.

- **Level 4 – Moderately Aggressive**

  Triggers a VMotion if the VM has 2 or more stars.

- **Level 5 – Aggressive**

  Triggers a VMotion if the VM has 1 or more stars.

  DRS Rules and Regulations

As stated earlier, while DRS Automation Levels allow you to specify a global rule for the cluster such as "Full Automation," it is possible to have per-VM exceptions to this rule. This allows us to flag sensitive VMs as requiring administrator intervention. It is also possible to completely exclude VM's from DRS because of incompatibility reasons. A classic example of this is excluding a VM cluster because it lacks compatibility with VMotion and therefore DRS, too.

These automation levels which affect the entire cluster allow us to impose some rules and regulations. The first of these are referred to as "Affinity" and "Anti-Affinity" rules. This allows us to configure a scenario which states that two or more VMs must either be "kept together" (affinity) or "separated" (anti-affinity). So perhaps two VMs are very network-intensive and should have affinity so they remain on the same vSwitch in the same ESX host. Why? Well, because when two VMs communicate on the same vSwitch no Ethernet collisions occur – and networking is as fast as the VMKernel can manage. Perhaps you decide to keep two CPU or memory intensive VMs separate from each other so that they do not compete for those resources. Another reason to keep VMs apart is that they share the same role. It doesn't make much sense to have two identical VMs on the same ESX host which could fail – but to distribute them across many ESX hosts does make sense. This would stop an "eggs in one basket scenario" where all your Domain Controllers, Web Servers, or Citrix Servers ended up on the same ESX host.

GOTCHA:

It is possible to configure affinity rule conflicts. The VI Client will allow you to configure a rule where VM1 loves VM2, and VM2 loves VM3, but that VM3 hates VM1. This becomes like a plot line in a soap-opera. Fortunately, the VI Client will warn you that you are creating a logical impossibility.

Resource Pools and DRS Clustering

Just as stand-alone ESX hosts can have resource pools, so can DRS clusters. In fact, it probably makes it more compelling to use resource pools in a VMware cluster, as you are more likely to want to carve up the aggregate of many ESX hosts in a cluster into small pools of resources. When you add an existing ESX stand-alone host with resource pools into a DRS cluster you will be asked what you would like to do with them. You have two options – to remove and start again or to "graft" them to the DRS cluster. If you choose this second option you will see in the DRS Cluster the name of the resource pool followed by "Grafted from esx1.vi3book.com..." indicating where the resource pool was originally created. Personally, I like to remove existing resource pools and de-fine new ones. After all the limits, reservations, and share values imposed on a stand-alone ESX host are unlikely to be relevant to a cluster of ESX hosts that provide six times the resources. If a resource pool on stand-alone ESX host does not contain any VMs, it is not "grafted" to the DRS cluster – it is simply removed.

GOTCHA:

Make sure you have VMotion configured correctly before you begin. A good test is to check you can VMotion every single VM in your system. DRS currently makes no checks for VMotion whatsoever when it is enabled. In fact, you can even set up DRS without VMotion being enabled on a VMkernel port group! The most common mistake I have seen is the simplest – forgetting to put a tick in the check box to "Enable VMotion" on a VMkernel Port Group. You can confirm VMotion is enabled by looking at the Summary tab of each of your ESX hosts. Lastly, if you ever have problems with DRS or even HA a manual VMotion will at least check that you have fulfilled the requirements of all three features.

A good way to check if you have the basic relationships in place – shared networking and shared storage - is using the maps feature. Maps allow you to see a graphical representation of your system. Figure 10.14 shows my two ESX hosts – both have access to the same storage and networking. Maps can be saved in a JPEG, BMP, or EMF format for documentation purposes using in the VI Client under File, Export, and Export Maps.

Figure 10.14

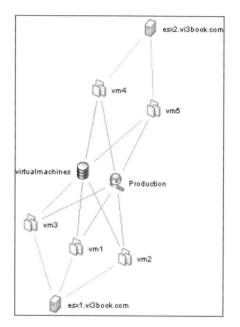

Note:

While currently VMware offers no method of converting maps into a Microsoft Visio format, there are companies who have software that will. Veeam software has recently released a Reporter tool which does precisely that.

http://www.veeam.com/veeam_reporter.asp

Figure 10.15 shows a situation where a VM is not on shared storage in the DRS cluster. Notice the red X next to the ESX host.

Figure 10.15

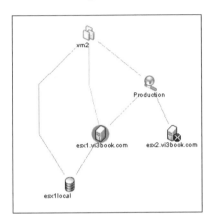

Setting up a DRS Cluster – Manual

In this scenario, we will initially setup the cluster in manual mode. This is so you can experience the recommendation system and have full control before switching to fully automated mode. I won't be showing the partially automated mode in this chapter as it is merely a hybrid of manual and fully automated.

I will be creating my DRS cluster with the Intel Host folder. This makes sense because only my Intel Server has the CPU compatibility required for VMotion and DRS.

Creating the DRS Cluster

1. In the Inventory view of Hosts & Clusters.

2. Right-click and choose New Cluster.

3. Type in a friendly name for your cluster, such as Intel Cluster and select VMware DRS.

4. Change the automation level to Manual.

5. Click Next and Finish.

Adding ESX hosts

1. Drag and Drop your first ESX host into the cluster.

2. Accept the default which removes any existing host-based resource pools.

3. Next, drag-and-drop your second ESX host into the cluster.

Note:

Continue step 3 if you have additional ESX hosts which fulfill the VMotion requirements.

Viewing the Cluster Resources

Figure 10.16 shows the main summary tab for my Intel Cluster. Here we can see that DRS is enabled and that my two ESX hosts are offering 2 CPUs with a collective amount of 5GHz of CPU time and 4GB of RAM. Under the VMware DRS pane I can see that there are already some recommendations generated by DRS as there is a blue link stating "Migration Recommendations: 3." Below that, we have the DRS Resource Distribution. The first chart shows how balanced my hosts are. The two blue and yellow columns represent two ESX hosts that are imbalanced. One is not using much CPU or memory (it lies in the 0-10 and 10-20 range), and the other is using much more resources (it lies in the 50-60 and 60-70 range). It would be more ideal if these columns were closer together which indicates my two ESX hosts are consuming the same amount of resources. The second charts how many resources are available in the cluster. My VMs are mainly idle and therefore 90% of the cluster resources are not in use. It would be more desirable if these columns were further to the left – as this would indicate that I would be getting more VMs from the resources I possess.

Figure 10.16

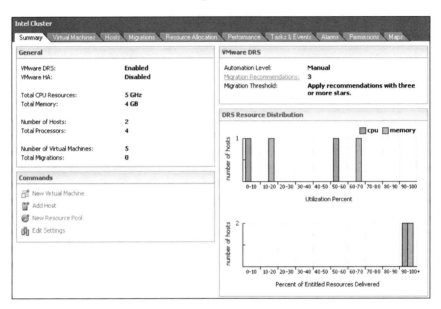

Figure 10.17 shows a DRS cluster where full automation has been enabled, and DRS has been allowed to balance the ESX hosts. Here we can see that both hosts are equally using RAM, but are not completely balanced for CPU usage.

Figure 10.17

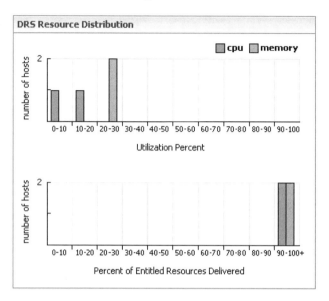

Applying Recommendations

You can see recommendations under the "Migrations" tab on a DRS cluster. Alternatively, if you already have recommendations you can click the "Migration Recommendation" hyper-link as shown in Figure 10.18 above which will take you to the same location.

1. Click the Migration Tab.

2. Select a VM with the highest star rating and click the Apply Recommendation.

TIP:

If you are not seeing the migration tab you can sometimes trigger it by adjusting your threshold to be more aggressive. Alternatively, try running the cpubusy.vbs file in *one* of the VMs. Lastly, try using VMotion to overburden one of your ESX hosts to create an imbalance in the cluster.

Figure 10.18 shows a typical migration tab summary, with each VM flagged with a star-rating together with the reason, in this case "Balance average memory loads." Incidentally, it is possible to select multiple VMs and apply the migration recommendation. DRS will do each VMotion one after the other in series.

Figure 10.18

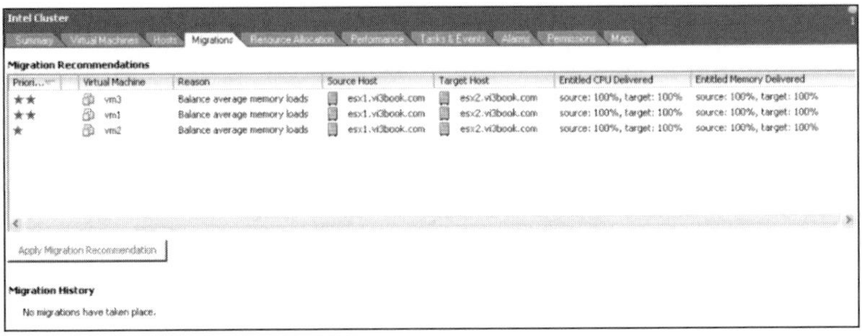

Initial Placement Questions

If you power off a VM, and then power it on again using either manual or partial automated modes, you should be confronted with a dialog box.

1. Power off and Power on a VM.

2. Select the ESX host you would prefer the VM to run on.

3. Click the Power On button.

   Note:

   The dialog box is sorted in order of recommendation – making the ESX host at the top of the list the most appropriate ESX host to power the VM on. Figure 10.19 shows that ESX2 is hardly using any CPU resources and is only using 19% of its memory, compared to ESX1 which is using 48% of its memory.

Figure 10.19

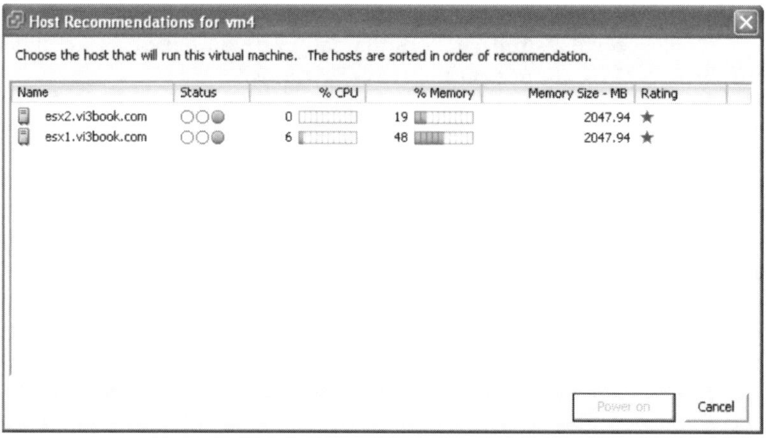

Configuring DRS Cluster Rules

As stated before, we have two types of control on individual VMs. We can create affinity (keep VMs together) and anti-affinity (separate VMs) rules. Additionally, we can set a custom automation level on sensitive VMs. Remember, the only time you receive a 5-star recommendation is when one of your affinity rules is broken.

Creating an Anti-Affinity Rule:

1. **Right-click** the Cluster.

2. Choose **Edit Settings**.

3. Select **Rules**.

4. Click the **Add** button.

5. **Type in a friendly name for the rule**, like VM1 hates VM2.

6. Under the **Type** option choose "**Separate Virtual Machines.**"

7. **Select VM1** and **VM2** and Click **OK**.

8. Click **OK** to create your rule.

Figure 10.20 shows a situation where VM1 and VM2 are residing on the same ESX host. This is in breach of my anti-affinity rule that stated they should be kept apart – so the reason for the migration is to "Satisfy anti-affinity rule." Of course, you will receive a similar recommendation if you have created an affinity rule, and the two VMs are not on the same ESX host.

Figure 10.20

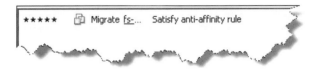

GOTCHA:

VirtualCenter *does* check your affinity rules when you first power on a VM. However, it *does not* check your affinity rules to either alert or stop the administrator from carrying out manual VMotion events which breach affinity rules. If an administrator carries out a manual VMotion it is entirely possible to accidentally trigger a 5-star recommendation by manually putting two VMs together or apart that should be kept separated or together, respectively. Interestingly, if you use fully automated mode this still happens, but what DRS does is automatically carry out another VMotion to undo this administrative "error."

GOTCHA:

As stated before, rule conflicts are possible. Figure 10.21 shows this occurrence.

Figure 10.21

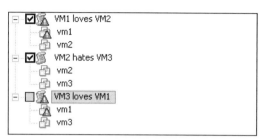

Custom Automation Levels

As you might remember, VM clustering in any of its forms is incompatible with VMotion and DRS. A good example of custom automation levels is completely disabling DRS on VMs that run some kind of clustering software.

1. **Right-click** the cluster.

2. Choose **Edit settings**.

3. In the dialog box, select **Virtual Machine options**.

4. Select **nodeA** and choose **Disabled**.

5. Select **nodeB** and choose **Disabled**.

Figure 10.22 shows nodeA and B disabled from the DRS functionality.

Figure 10.22

Virtual Machine	Automation Level
nodeA	Disabled
nodeB	Disabled
vm1	Default (Manual)
vm2	Default (Manual)
vm3	Default (Manual)
vm4	Default (Manual)

Note:

Even with this option to exclude the VM clusters from DRS, in a manual or partial automation mode, you are still asked which ESX host to power on nodeA or nodeB. You will find there is only one server on the list because the VMDK and RDM files are on local storage for VMware Support purposes. This isn't a problem, it's just an unnecessary dialog box.

DRS Automation Levels and Maintenance Mode

Maintenance mode is an option available next to shutdown and reboot on an ESX host. You have probably shutdown and rebooted your ESX host a couple of times since you started reading this book, so you might ask, "Why leave this topic until now?" Well, the main reason is that maintenance mode becomes really interesting and cool when combined with DRS. It was felt it might be relevant to cover what maintenance mode is for in the context of DRS.

Stated very simply, maintenance mode is an isolation state used whenever you need to carry out critical ESX host tasks such as firmware, ESX host, memory, and CPU upgrades. This isolation state will prevent other VirtualCenter users from creating new VMs and powering them on your ESX host. It will also stop any manual VMotion events created by an administrator or automatic VMotion events generated by DRS. Maintenance mode does survive reboots – this allow the administrator time to confirm that their changes have been effective (like adding a new hardware device such as a NIC or a HBA) before VM's can be execute on the ESX host.

How maintenance mode works will differ depending on whether or not the ESX host is in a cluster. If it is causing you a problem, maintenance mode can be cancelled at any time by right clicking the task in the task pane and choosing cancel.

Below is a list of what maintenance mode will do depending on your configuration:

- **Stand-alone ESX host** (Creates a pop-dialog box warning)

Administrator must VMotion all VMs to another ESX host manually. If VMotion is not available administrator must power off all VMs before maintenance mode is triggered.

- **Manual or Partial DRS Automation** (Creates a pop-dialog box warning)

  Generates recommendations which have to be applied to evacuate the ESX host of all currently running VMs. Figure 10.23 shows a migration recommendation triggered by maintenance mode.

Figure 10.23

Priority	Virtual Machine	Reason	Source Host	Target Host
★ ★ ★ ★ ★	vm1	Host is entering maintenance mode	esx2.vi3book.com	esx1.vi3book.com

Figure 10.24 shows a very rare occurrence in a production environment. This is a recommendation triggered by maintenance mode where DRS has no choice but to break one or more affinity rules. It happens frequently on two node DRS clusters. Here, VM1 and VM2 must be kept separate on ESX1 and ESX2, but ESX1 is forced into maintenance mode. DRS has no other option than to provide a recommendation that would break an anti-affinity rule. The small icon in the 2nd column after the star rating (highlighted in the screen capture) indicates when this is happening.

Figure 10.24

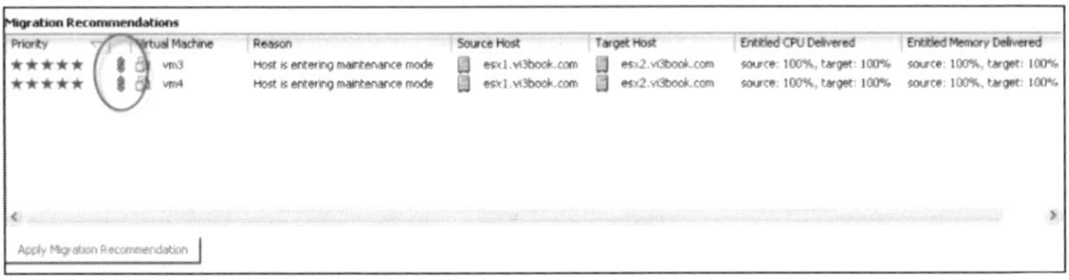

Migration Recommendations

Priority	Virtual Machine	Reason	Source Host	Target Host	Entitled CPU Delivered	Entitled Memory Delivered
★ ★ ★ ★ ★	vm3	Host is entering maintenance mode	esx1.vi3book.com	esx2.vi3book.com	source: 100%, target: 100%	source: 100%, target: 100%
★ ★ ★ ★ ★	vm4	Host is entering maintenance mode	esx1.vi3book.com	esx2.vi3book.com	source: 100%, target: 100%	source: 100%, target: 100%

Apply Migration Recommendation

- **Fully Automated DRS** (No Dialog Box Pop-ups)

  DRS automatically moves the VMs of the ESX host to other nodes in the cluster, obeying your rules and regulations where possible.

Configuring Full Automated DRS using Maintenance Mode

1. **Right-click** your cluster.

2. Choose **Edit Settings**.

3. **Change the Automation Level** to **Fully Automated**.

4. Click **OK**.

5. Now **select one of your ESX hosts in the cluster**, in the **Summary Tab** select **Enter Maintenance Mode**.

   Note:

   This should trigger an automatic VMotion of all your VM's from that host on to other ESX servers.

Maintenance Mode Hangs

One of the most common problems people experience in maintenance mode is that it hangs and does not complete. When using maintenance mode, either when an ESX host is in stand-alone mode or in a DRS/HA cluster mode, the VMs currently residing on the host must either be moved (via VMotion) or powered off. If a VM cannot be moved or powered off, the maintenance mode waits for you to resolve the problem. Unfortunately, the VI Client currently doesn't prompt you that maintenance mode is waiting nor does the VI Client tell you *why* maintenance mode is hanging. If you carefully read the maintenance mode dialog the VI Client does warn you about the requirements for maintenance mode to complete. Figure 10.25 is the dialog box that appears.

Figure 10.25

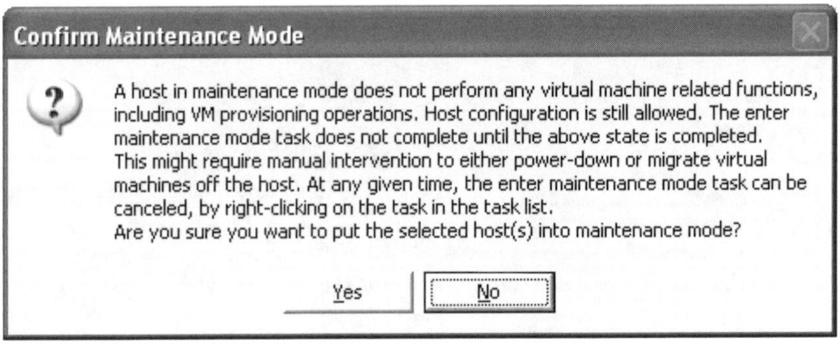

Confirm Maintenance Mode

A host in maintenance mode does not perform any virtual machine related functions, including VM provisioning operations. Host configuration is still allowed. The enter maintenance mode task does not complete until the above state is completed. This might require manual intervention to either power-down or migrate virtual machines off the host. At any given time, the enter maintenance mode task can be canceled, by right-clicking on the task in the task list.
Are you sure you want to put the selected host(s) into maintenance mode?

Yes   No

This is usually caused when DRS is in a fully automated mode but is unable to move all the VMs to other ESX hosts in the cluster. When this happens, maintenance mode just sits there – no warnings or pop-ups appear. If you try powering on a VM you will receive the message:

"The operation is not allowed in the current state."

I've seen this message in class, and I must admit the first time it happened, it had me stumped. It turned out that one of the students had attempted to enter maintenance mode earlier – and then carried on with other tasks. This meant that at first glance the "Task" pane view at the bottom of the VI Client did not show the message "Entering maintenance mode…."

While in the process of entering maintenance mode you will find you cannot carry out many tasks except for ones that would resolve the problem like the following:

- Manual VMotion

- Powering off a VM

- Cancelling Maintenance Mode

Nine times out of ten you will find that there is a property of the VM which stops the automated VMotion triggered by attempting maintenance mode. One tip is to try a manual VMotion, as this should create a meaningful pop-up message that will lead to resolving the problem and finally completing the entry into maintenance mode. Typically DRS' inability to move a VM is caused by the VM errors mentioned earlier that are listed here:

- Connected removable to local storage or devices

- Connected internal switches

- RDM's to LUN not presented to other ESX hosts

- VM Clustering

- CPU Affinities

Where are my VMs running?

There is a short answer to this – we don't know. Once you have engaged fully automated mode you will not really know (depending on how conservative or aggressive you have configured DRS in the settings) from one hour to the next where your VM will be running. For some people this is a difficult concept as they are so tied to the physical world. Remember ESX is not grid or parallel processing – so fundamentally a VM only executes on one host at one time. If you want to know on which ESX host VM is currently running there are two main methods.

Firstly, on any object that contains your VM (root container, datacenter, folder, or cluster) select the tab called "Virtual Machines;" right-click the descriptive names of one of the columns such as "name," and enable the option "host." Secondly, if you find your VM in the inventory in the Summary tab and the General pane, there should be a field that specifies its state and on which ESX host it is currently executing.

Resource Pools on a DRS Cluster

Of course, it's possible to create resource pools on a DRS cluster. In fact, it probably makes more sense that you would want to carve up the resources of a cluster into smaller pools. Resource pools on a DRS cluster work in exactly the same way as an individual host. Although the VI Client gives the impression that the Resource Pools "hang off" the cluster what happens is that these resource pools get created on each ESX host. Fundamentally, a VM is executed on an ESX host, not across ESX hosts. This would require some type of "grid computing" hardware which currently is cost prohibitive for most organizations. Therefore, when a VM demands its reservation for memory, for example, that reservation must be found physically on an ESX host. Remember that resource pools and DRS clusters represent a logical grouping of resources – we are still constrained by the physical limits of each of our servers. Lastly, when a VM is moved from one ESX host to another in DRS, its resource pool membership remains the same. Again, many people commonly think that the resource pool represents a physical location – when in fact it is merely a software concept that allows allocating resources and controlling performance of our VMs.

When you create resource pools in DRS cluster what actually happens is the resource pool is created on each ESX host. After creating resource pools on DRS cluster, if you subsequently open the VI Client on each ESX host (which is not recommend as it could cause integrity issues with the cluster) you will see every host in the DRS cluster shares the same resource pool names.

Resource pools are used to manage internal ESX processes as well. On every ESX host there is a system "root resource" pool. Contained within this resource pool are child resource pools used to manage the VMkernel tasks. There is no practical usage of this within the ESX host for a production environment. But for completeness it was felt you should know about them. You can see the ESX host root resource pool by doing the following.

1. Choose your ESX host.

2. Select the **Configuration** Tab.

3. Select **System Resource Allocation**.

4. Click the **Advanced** option.

Figure 10.26 shows the child resource pools. The nursery resource pool has a special function. It's where baby processes are born and reared, and they move to other resource pools once they are old enough to play with the grown-ups.

Figure 10.26

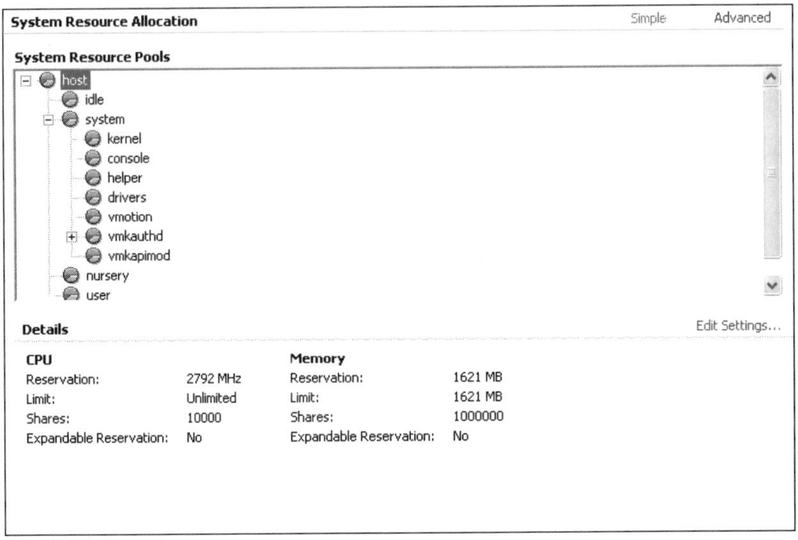

VMware HA

VMware HA is not actually an original VMware product. VMware procured a license for Legato's Automated Availability Management software and re-engineered it to work with VMs. Legato is now owned by VMware's parent company EMC and has been re-branded as EMC Autostart. However, the directories in /opt still retain the original Legato folder structure. VMware has made substantial changes to AAM and has access to the source code, so we expect improvements in VMware HA in the future.

VMware's VirtualCenter Agent interfaces with a VMAP API which acts as an intermediary layer to the AAM software. VirtualCenter is required to *configure* HA but is not required for HA to function. So, even if your VirtualCenter is down or dead then HA will continue to do its job. The architecture of HA is a peer-to-peer with each ESX host in a "mesh" topology constantly checking each other for functionality. This check is done via the Service Console vSwitch.

VMware HA has a very simple goal: when an ESX host crashes so do the VMs on the failed host. However, within 15 seconds the other ESX hosts in the same HA cluster detect that the ESX host has failed and power on the VMs on the remaining hosts. If DRS is enabled it will then re-balance the cluster. DRS will also detect when the failed host is available again and re-balance the cluster. Critically, what VMware HA does not do is manage crashed VMs. To deal with that scenario you need either VM cluster (covered earlier in this chapter) or script triggered by an alarm to reboot a failed VM. When an ESX host fails the selection process currently goes alphabetically through the remaining servers and powers on a VM on the first server that has sufficient resources to run that VM. This is intended to get the VM powered on and back online as quickly as possible. DRS is very conservative in its checks. Don't expect just because an ESX host crashes that suddenly you would get a lot of VMotion events or recommendations. VMware plans to improve this selection by name first and capacity second in future versions of VirtualCenter. The long term plan is to improve the algorithm so selection is calculated by selecting the ESX with the most unreserved capacity.

As with VMotion and DRS, HA also requires shared storage and shared networking. The only thing that HA does not require is CPU compatibility. After all, the VM is powered off when the ESX host fails and powered on a new ESX host when HA detects the failure. HA requires DNS forward (name to IP address) name resolution. There is some documentation from VMware that states that reverse DNS name resolution is also a requirement. This is true but only if you add ESX hosts into VirtualCenter by the IP address. If you add your ESX hosts to VirtualCenter by FQDN then all you need to do is forward lookups. Perhaps the best practice is to cover your bases and ensure before forward and reverse that lookups are configured in DNS. As with the license server, sort out your DNS issue before you even begin, and the setup and configuration should be relatively painless. Lastly, there is currently a limit with DNS names longer than 29 characters. VMware has promised to fix this issue in future releases. As an experiment I switched off my DNS servers after the cluster had be configured. Figure 10.27 shows the effect of no DNS name resolution on VMware HA.

Figure 10.27

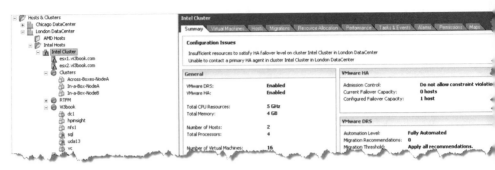

HA and Resource Management

HA also introduces some careful re-consideration of resource management. After all, if I have 7 ESX hosts in a cluster running 70 VMs – and then I lose an ESX host – will the remaining ESX host be able to run the *same* number of VMs on 6 ESX hosts rather than 7? One practical response is to design a system that has +1 redundancy. So instead of 7 servers, we would have 8. If one failed we would still be able to achieve the same performance with fewer nodes. Of course, the buck has to stop somewhere. Could we tolerate 2, 3, or 4 ESX host fails, and still run the same number of VMs? The HA software allows us to set such tolerances of ESX host failure during its configuration but the question is both an operational and design issue.

Another response to this question of resources is to only power on the remaining ESX hosts the right number of VM's needed to give "acceptable usage." Perhaps you have 2 domain controller VMs running across 10 ESX hosts in HA cluster. You know from testing and experience, that for acceptable usage you only need 10 up and running at any one time. VMware HA allows you to disable VMs from HA altogether and also set "priorities" for which VMs are started first.

HA and the "Split Brain" Phenomena

If you are experienced in the world of conventional Windows or Linux Clustering you might already be familiar with the term "split brain." It's a kind of clustering schizophrenia. It describes a situation where more than one node thinks that other nodes have failed. This is like some people believing they are Napoleon, and everyone else is crazy; the host believes it is fine and that the others are the problem.

As mentioned earlier, the mesh topology that HA creates is driven by the Service Console vSwitch. If an ESX host in an HA cluster experiences an NIC failure or cable break then this can trigger the "split brain" scenario – this is sometimes referred to as the "isolated host." This isolated ESX host would mistakenly believe that the other 7 ESX hosts had crashed, while all the other ESX hosts believe that the bad ESX host has crashed as well. In fact, the VMs are running perfectly fine on all ESX hosts.

What is VMware HA's default behavior when split brain occurs? The default is that the isolated host (the ESX host with the failed Service Console network) powers off all its VMs. This causes the VM's files to be "unlocked" in the shared storage. This then allows the other ESX hosts to assume control, and power on the VMs that were previously running on the isolated host. The assumption in the default is, if split-brain occurs, then begin HA failover to the remaining ESX hosts. VMware HA does have an over-ride option for this default, allowing the Administrator to configure a VM to stay powered on, when the split brain event happens.

One way to protect yourself from the split brain phenomena (apart from regular trips to an expensive psychotherapist) is make sure that the ESX hosts have redundancy on the Service Console networking. One method would be to use a second NIC behind vSwitch0, and perhaps patch it to a different physical switch. This would protect HA from NIC, cable, and switch failures. Alternatively, you could add a second Service Console port group to a switch used for another aspect of your virtual infrastructure such as VMotion.

Setting up VMware HA

I'll assume you already have a DRS cluster setup and therefore all that HA needs is enabling on an existing cluster. If this is not the case then you will need to create a cluster and drag-and-drop your ESX hosts into it.

When you enable an ESX host cluster, VMware will trigger the AAM software on each host – one at a time. This can cause some benign alerts. Clearly, we cannot have an HA cluster with just one ESX host. Until the second ESX host is configured, the cluster will have alerts and warnings on it. These will not disappear until you have at least two ESX hosts in the cluster enabled for HA.

1. Right-click the Cluster.

2. Choose Edit Settings.

3. Click Enable VMware HA.

   Note:

   This will add an additional set of HA options in the pane to the left-hand side of the dialog box.

4. Under the option "General," select VMware HA. This will open some settings associated with the cluster.

Figure 10.28 shows the main configuration options for HA.

Figure 10.28

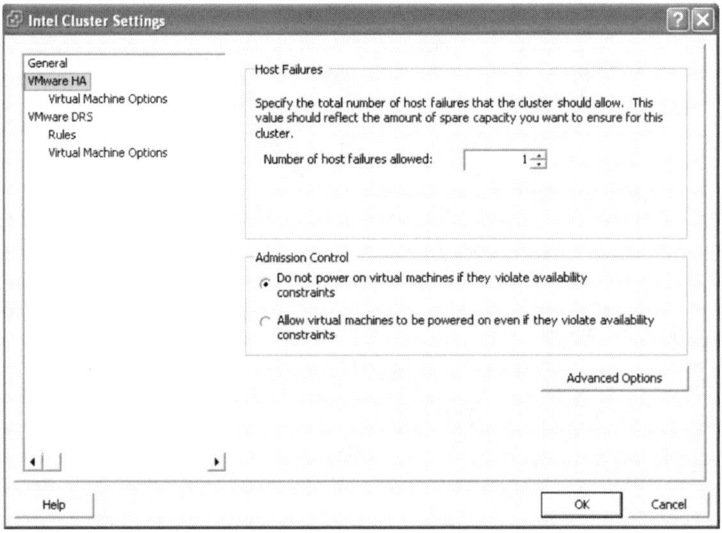

We can control the number of ESX host failures we tolerate until the HA clustering stops powering on VMs on the remaining hosts. The maximum number of hosts we can tolerate is 4. Remember VMware recommends no-more than 16 ESX hosts per HA cluster, so in reality this means we could tolerate a quarter of the ESX hosts failing. If a 5th ESX host failed, HA would not power up the lost VMs on the remaining 3 nodes in the cluster. You might ask why the number 4 is used here. In Legato's AAM, the system is based around primary and backup AAM servers. The maximum number of primaries is 4, and if one fails an election process would promote a backup to be a primary. If all 4 primaries were lost simultaneously (although this is an extremely unlikely event, I can see it happening only if you had a blade enclosure failure), then the AAM software would be broken.

The more hosts you have the better utilization you get from a resource perspective is another way of looking at this issue. If I have 2 nodes I can only load them to 45% each. If one failed the remaining ESX host would have to have 90% capacity (with 10% reserved for the Service Console and the virtualization overhead) to provide the same resources. If I have 4 nodes, I can load them at 65% each. If one failed the remaining three ESX hosts would each provide 25% of the resources needed to make up for the loss of one ESX host? The moral of the story is the more ESX hosts you have, the more you can load them – and still tolerate an ESX host failure. Remember though, at the end of the day, a VM executes on a given ESX host. If that VM has a memory reservation – it must be found in physical memory. So although the DRS cluster might have 1GB of free memory left in the cluster and 4 ESX hosts, this 1GB of memory is actually not completely available. The "spare capacity" in cluster is a logical representation of capacity, not a physical representation of where that memory actually resides.

Below the "number of host failures" allowed we have options associated with "Admission Control." These are the rather confusingly labeled options called "Allow virtual machines to be powered on even if they violate availability constraints" and "Allow virtual machines to be powered on only if they do not violate availability constraints." What do these very long sentences mean? Perhaps they are best explained with a scenario. If you had two ESX hosts with the "number of host failures allowed" set to 1 and one of them failed the default is set in such a way that you wouldn't be able to power on any new VMs. If the second option was engaged, then you would. The assumption is in the default.

There is little point in powering new VMs if you have had host failures as there would be fewer resources.

Under VMware HA we have Virtual Machine options. This allows us to set different start-up priorities for VMs and also configure the "isolation response" should an ESX host suffer from the split brain phenomena.

VMware HA and VM Clustering

To gain full support from VMware, the virtual disks and RDMs used with VM Clusters (using such software as Microsoft Clustering Service) must be on *local storage*. This effectively excludes them from being used with VMotion, DRS, and HA. The software is so compatible that you do not need to dedicate hardware to your VM clusters. You can still run them; they just won't benefit from these advanced VMware features.

Testing VMware HA

There are a couple of ways to test HA, but by far the most convincing is to remove the power from one of the ESX hosts. If you feel uncomfortable with a hard test, issuing a reboot (without maintenance mode) should cause the ESX host to emulate the same hard failure.

If you wish to simulate the isolation response where an ESX host appears to have failed because of lost of service console connectivity you can use the following command:

esxcfg-vswif -d vswif0

This disables the Service Console vswif interface. The command esxcfg-vswif -e vswif0 will re-enable it again.

Monitoring a DRS and HA Cluster

Both DRS and HA will give you status information about the integrity of the cluster. In fact, you may have already seen these notifications during the configuration of HA.

On the cluster icon itself you will find different icons to represent the state of the cluster. The red icon indicates a configuration problem, and the yellow icon indicates the server with the DRS or HA issue. In HA this happens every time you add a second host in the cluster. It takes some time for each of my ESX servers to be enabled for HA, and when you have an HA cluster of just one server then HA misreports this as the failure of the cluster.

The most common reason for the red icon on a DRS or HA cluster is administrators incorrectly using the VI Client. Once you have VMware clustering enabled you should not "point" the VI Client directly to the ESX host; this bypasses VirtualCenter. The only reason to do this is if your VirtualCenter environment has malfunctioned – and in that case you would be better served by resolving the VirtualCenter server.

If the cluster icon has a yellow exclamation mark this indicates that resources are scarce and reservations may not be met. In this case you could experience admission control style problems. The most common reason for this is a number of ESX hosts have become unavailable and as a result the cluster has experienced a drop in total capacity.

Summary

In this chapter we have looked at the many ways you can offer high availability to both the VM and the ESX host – by either VM clustering or HA clustering. We also looked at how DRS and HA are so closely integrated with each other you are unlikely to want to use them in isolation from each other. Lastly we looked at how correctly setting up VMotion and DRS can make it very easy to bring a physical server down for hardware maintenance while keeping your VMs online at all times.

Chapter 11: Backup and VMware Consolidated Backup

GOTCHA:

The most common error with VCB is operator error caused by mistyping directory paths or job names. In most cases, the errors will come from typing d:\backup rather than d:\backups or something similar.

Warning:

Please validate and confirm your backup and restore process works. The authors of this book do not accept any liability for data loss.

Methods of Backing Up

A VM is encapsulated in a few files. This introduces new ways of backing up beyond the conventional method of installing backup agents inside the guest operating system. Virtualization offers us the tempting possibility of backing up a VM without conventional backup agents. This means we can offload the network traffic generated by backup to external dedicated systems. Additionally, not installing backup agents into the guest operating system is more cost-effective. Before examining VMware's "Consolidated Backup" (VCB), it's worth comparing and contrasting the various backup choices at your disposal.

Backup Agents inside the VM

In this scenario, organizations continue installing backup agents inside the VM as we have done with our physical machines. This allows for normal, differential, and incremental backups without modifying existing procedures and methods. The powerful aspect of this approach is that we do not have to revalidate our disaster recovery or business continuity strategy to the same degree than if we select a brand new method previously untried and untested within the organization.

The major downside is that we would not really be leveraging the power of virtualization to improve those backup and restore procedures. Additionally, you may be forced to adopt this approach within the guest operating system because VCB is not fully supported with your guest operating system. VCB is able to execute a "file-level" approach which allows for backing up the *individual* data files within a VMDK file. Unfortunately, this currently excludes Linux, Solaris, and Novell guests. In other words, "file-level" backup with VCB is a Windows guest operating system feature only. Ostensibly this is because VCB runs on physical Windows hosts (referred to as the VCB Proxy) and Windows natively only understands NTFS, FAT, and FAT32 file systems.

Backup Agents inside the Service Console

It is possible to install a Linux backup agent to the Service Console because it is a modified version of Linux Redhat. One advantage to this method is that you will need less backup agents – this is decidedly cheaper than installing backup agents for each VM.

The downside is that this method will only allow you to backup the VM's virtual disks and associated files. It will not allow you to backup individual files within the VM. This is costly from a per-MB perspective and would take some time to setup and configure. Additionally, the backup would be throttled by the Service Console network and would put an unwanted CPU burden on the Service Console.

SAN LUN Replication and Network Replication

Another way of "backing up" is to use your SAN vendor's tools to create "snapshots" LUNs within a SAN or between two SANs. This can be configured within a SAN, a server room, or greater distances if you have access to "Dark Fiber." Dark fiber links are fiber channel connections within a city or between cities. If dark fiber is unavailable, you may have to resort to network-based replication using software such as DoubleTake. Dark fiber links will replicate data synchronously whereas network links will replicate asynchronously.

The difference is the former has little or no latency whereas the latter definitely will have latency. This can mean there is a difference of the data at the primary location from the backup location. This approach has some strong appeals; the SAN becomes the biggest single point of failure, not least because everything about our virtual environment is more or less stored on a SAN. Again, this approach is not without its downsides.

Firstly, dark fiber links are not universally available and can be very costly. Currently, the technology is only available to the organizations with the largest IT budgets such as banks, pharmaceuticals, oil companies, and governmental bodies. Secondly, the backup is not especially "granular." If you wish to restore an individual file that's been lost within VM, then SAN LUN Replication would not be the fastest approach to restoring it.

Third Party Backup Vendor

Another approach is a more blended one which may involve some or all of the options previously discussed, in part orchestrated by backup vendor. As virtualization grows in size the mature backup vendors are beginning to respond by developing their own custom solutions. This is worth investigating to see if your existing vendor has updated their software to be VM aware. At the very least your vendor should be supporting VCB as part of their software.

Additionally, there are a number of independent software solutions in the new third-party space surrounding virtualization. These companies are essentially "start-ups" who have sprung up in recent years or even months. Quite often they offer unique features because their main market is backing up VMs. They set themselves apart from the conventional backup vendors because they specialize in the field of virtualization. You will notice I'm not mentioning any product names here. This is because one of the authors of this very book works for one of these companies! We didn't want to come across as partisan in this chapter. This is why we'll concentrate on VMware's VCB in the main. I will discuss VCB integration with third parties using another vendor's backup software later.

Free Backup Solutions

There are a number of scripts which circulate the VMware forums and blogs. These quite often leverage the free tools that ship with ESX server. They are generally a Service Console approach and as a consequence usually backup the VM locally before copying it across the network to a secondary storage system. The merit of this approach is essentially a cost based one. It's attractive to people with modest size implementations where the volume of data to backup is similarly modest.

The downside of this approach is your support will be non-commercial and community based. However, if this approach fits your requirements, Alex Mittel of Oxford University, UK has written a very good backup script called "visbu."

Download Visbu:

http://users.ox.ac.uk/~alexm/

Community Forum Support:

http://www.vmware.com/community/thread.jspa?threadID=70253

Using VMware Consolidate Backup (VCB)

In contrast to the above methods, VCB backups the VM directly from the SAN. Strictly speaking, VCB is not a backup solution but a collection of APIs and drivers that enable third party vendors to backup a VM. With VCB there is no network hit on the ESX host during the backup process. The backup traffic is offloaded to a dedicated Windows 2003 server. SAN connectivity with the VCB software installed is referred to as the "VCB Proxy."

Two types of backup are supported with VCB; File-Level backups, and Full VM backups. With file-level backups the virtual disk of the VM is mounted to a folder on the VCB Proxy. The backup operator can select individual files inside the virtual disk. With a full VM backup the virtual disk is backed up alongside all the other files that make up a VM including the NVRAM and log files. As you might expect, file-level backups are ideal for normal, differential, and incremental backups of data. In contrast, full VM backups are ideal for archiving the operating system state of a VM. With a full VM backup the virtual disks of a VM are "exported" into the 2GB sparse format to ensure that data as well. This export process ensures that free space is not included in the backup process.

Both approaches support a "hot backup" of the VM while the VM is powered on. A special "sync" driver is installed to the VM during the install of VMware Tools. This sync driver is able to reduce the activity generated in the file system within the VM. However, you will most likely still want to stop services inside the VM to ensure that files are unlocked in the file system during backup time.

As with other backup processes, there are downsides. Although the backup process is via the SAN, the restore process is across the network. This can slow the restore process significantly. Restoring from a "Full-VM" can be achieved quite neatly, but restoring an individual file means copying them from the VCB Proxy via Windows shares to the original destination. Additionally, VCB only works on a physical host with Fiber-Channel. SAN connectivity it is not supported with iSCSI SAN even when used with hardware initiators.

VCB can be used independently of a third party backup tool for "Full VM" backups, but most people will want to use it in conjunction with their third backup vendor. This is usually achieved with an integration module. Unfortunately, the help that is provided with the integration modules is not always very clear and in some cases inaccurate. The quality of the scripts can vary significantly too, with some people resorting to writing their own scripts that they can understand and troubleshoot rather than debugging or re-engineering scripts that have been written by others. If you decide to use the integration modules that are shipped free with VCB expect to spend some time on the VMware Forums reading posts and asking others for help. There are some supported backup vendors for which there are no integration scripts, and you may be forced to create your own.

Installing VMware Consolidated Backup

Installing VCB is very easy; however, care must be taken with VCB Proxies connection to the SAN. Firstly, as you probably know, by default Windows 2003 will try to access hard disks and LUNs directly by writing a "disk signature" and mount them as part of its system. This is potentially damaging to the VMFS file structure. Ideally, you want to build this server without connectivity to the SAN until you have turned off this automount feature. There are a couple of ways of disabling the SAN connectivity. If you have physical access to the server, disconnect the SAN cables; alternatively, in the BIOS, temporarily disable the fiber-Channel host bus adapter. Once you have successfully installed Windows 2003 turn off automount using the "diskpart" utility.

Secondly, VCB currently does not support more than one HBA inside the VCB Proxy. The problem arises because Windows chooses by default to see two HBAs as presenting two LUNs, rather than multiple paths to the same LUN. Currently, the work-around is to disable the second HBA if you have one or disconnect it.

Turning off "Automount" on the VCB Proxy

1. Login as administrator to the Proxy.

2. Open a command-prompt with Start, Run, and cmd.

3. Type this command:

   `Diskpart`

4. At this diskpart prompt type this command:

   `Automount`

   Note:

   As automount is enabled by a default, this command should disable automount and give you the status information of "Automatic mounting of new volumes is disabled."

5. Exit diskpart by typing this command:

   `Exit`

Note:

You can now re-enable the SAN connectivity. If you open "Disk Management" console in Windows and are asked at any point to write a "disk signature" the safest approach is to cancel the dialog box prompt and wizard. Even safer still is not open Microsoft Disk Management tool at all. However, you may need to do this to configure other storage devices.

Installing and Configuring VCB

1. Download latest version of the VCB package from the VMware Website and Run the Installation Package.

2. Acknowledge the prompt to install the **VMware Virtual Volume Storage Bus Driver**.

   Note:

   This VCB LUN driver gives the VCB Proxy read-only access to the LUN and VMFS contained within; without this driver the Windows 2003 would not be able to access the files system to begin the backup process.

   To use the command-line tools you will need open a command-prompt to the install directory of VCB. You may also wish to add this to the "path" entry to the environmental variables of Windows.

   a. Right-click **My Computer**.

   b. Choose **Properties**.

   c. Select the **Advanced** Tab.

   d. Click the **Environment Variables** button.

   e. Under **System Variables** select **path**.

   f. Click the **Edit** button.

   g. Add semi-colon to the end of the current path and type:

   h. **C:\Program Files\VMware\VMware Consolidated Backup Framework**

Note:

Speech marks around "the path" are not required. You can confirm the path is known correctly by opening a command prompt and running one of the VCB utilities such as vcbMounter. If the path statement has been input correctly in Windows "Environment Variables" the utility should run without error messages such as "Bad command or file name."

Licensing VCB

As with any product, VCB must be licensed correctly. VCB can be enabled for each ESX server by selecting the host in the Vi Client.

3. Select the Configuration Tab.

4. In the Software Pane, choose Licensing Features.

5. Select the second Edit... button.

6. Enable VMware Consolidate Backup in the dialog box.

VCB on the Command-Line

Most people who use VCB on a daily basis use integration scripts provided by their vendor or VMware. This means they do not need to know the VCB command-line utilities. However, because this is a book about VMware we want you to have a good knowledge of these command-line tools should you wish to write your own scripts. It might also assist you in troubleshooting and debugging scripts that have been provided by your backup vendor.

Some of the VCB commands are available on both the VCB Proxy and the Service Console – and some are only available on the VCB Proxy or the Service Console.

These utilities are on both the VCB Proxy and the Service Console:

*   vcbVmName   - Returns the identity of the VM

*   vcbSnaphot   - Applies a snapshot

- vcbMounter   - Mounts virtual disks, and can trigger a Full VM backup

- vcbExport   - Exports a virtual disk in other formats

These utilities are ONLY available on the Service Console:

- vcbUtil   - List resource pools and folder location

- vcbRestore   - Restores a Full VM backup across from the VCB

This utility is ONLY available on the VCB Proxy:

- mountvm   - Mounts virtual disks to a Windows folder

Warning:

When executed on the Service Console these commands *are* case-sensitive – but when executed on the VCB Proxy they are not. However, even in Windows some of the command-line switches are case-sensitive.

In this chapter, we won't be covering all the VCB commands and all the switches – only the most useful and commonly used which are vcbVmName, vcbMounter, vcbRestore, and mountvm.

Viewing VM Unique Identifiers

To backup a VM you need to be able to identify it in the VirtualCenter or ESX host inventory. A VM has 4 identifiers:

- The VM's name as displayed in VirtualCenter or ESX

- The VM's IP address

- The VM's UUID

- The VM's MOREF (Managed Object Reference)

    Note:

The MOREF value is more commonly used by the VirtualCenter SDK (Software Development Kit). It is generated at the VM's first power on but after that it does not change.

While the VM's name and IP address are friendly and easy to determine they are also subject to change. The UUID and moref values are clearly less friendly but are guaranteed to be unique and unchanging. You can query VirtualCenter using the vcbVmName command from the VCB Proxy.

All the VCB commands have a similar syntax which uses these switches:

- -h to specify the name of an ESX host or VirtualCenter system

- -u to specify the username

- -p to specify the password

For example, to query VirtualCenter to find out the details of a VM called mike01, you carry out the following steps.

1. Login to the VCB Proxy as Administrator.

2. Open a command-prompt.

3. Type this command:

```
vcbvmname -h virtualcenter.vi3book.com -u lav-
ericm -p password -s name:mike01
```

Note:

Here the account lavericm is a user who has privileges in Virtual-Center.

This would produce the output as follows:

```
[2007-07-12 14:15:09.884 'App' 3600 info] Current work-
ing directory: C:\
[2007-07-12 14:15:10.462 'BaseLibs' 3672 warning]
[Vmdb_Unset] unsetting unknown path: /vmomi/
Found VM:
moref:vm-810
name:mike01
uuid:5034aae8-35c6-51a0-8f18-4264a177ee65
ipaddr:192.168.3.14
```

Note:

As you can see the UUID value is quite long. If I am using it I will often use the Window "Command-Prompt" copy and paste facility to capture this text to the clipboard. I also use this function to complete the very long paths that are sometimes typed into dialog boxes and configuration tools.

As you've probably realized, you can use vcbVmName with –s search as follows.

-s moref:vm-810

-s uuid:5034aae8-35c6-51a0-8f18-4264a177ee65

-s ipaddr:192.168.3.14

Note:

The ipaddr can be specified as a raw IP address of FQDN/Hostname if you have name resolution configured on the VCB proxy.

The vcbvmname command can also be used to check the power state of all the VMs in the VirtualCenter environment as follows:

vcbvmname -h virtualcenter.vi3book.com **-u** lavericm **-p** password **-s any:powerstate**

Mounting and Unmounting VM's with vcbMounter

Another utility allows us to mount and unmount virtual machine's virtual disks from the command-line. This is normally done prior to a backup. The process mounts the VM's virtual disks to a folder on the VCB Proxy. These files then can be backed up as if they were local to the VCB Proxy, when in fact they are being remotely accessed using the VCB Framework Software through the HBA.

During the mounting process the vcbMounter applies a snapshot to the VM. This allows the virtual disks to be "unlocked" in the VMFS file system. The same principle works for RDM as well, but only if you have them set with "Virtual Compatibility" mode. When vcbMounter unmounts the VM's file, this snapshot and its deltas are merged into the virtual disk, and then deleted. You can see this process in action if you have the Vi Client open at the same time you run the vcbMounter command.

To mount a VM's files for a file-level backup by its name in VirtualCenter you would use the following:

vcbMounter -h virtualcenter.vi3book.com **-u** lavericm **-p**
password **-a name:**mike01 **-r** d:\backups\mike01 **-t file**

As you can see, the –a switch allows you to set the attribute by which you identify the VM. The –r switch allows us to set the mounting point. If d:\backups didn't exist it would return an error; you must specify some kind of path for vcbMounter to work correctly. The –t switch allows us to set the type of backup. For Windows guests you can use both file and fullvm as types; with all other guest fullvm is the only option currently allowed.

The result of this command would look like this:

```
Opened disk: blklst://snapshot-861[virtualmachines]
mike01/mike01.vmdk@virtualcenter  xxxx/xxxx
Proceeding to analyze volumes
Done mounting
Volume 1 mounted at d:\backups\mike01\digits\1
(mbSize=4086 fsType=NTFS )
Volume 1 also mounted on d:\backups\mike01\letters\C
```

You can see the VM is mounted twice for one virtual disk – once by drive letter (\letters\C) and another by a number representing the disk (\digits\1).

Figures 11.1 and 11.2 show the activity generated in the Vi Client by running the vcbMounter command.

Figure 11.1

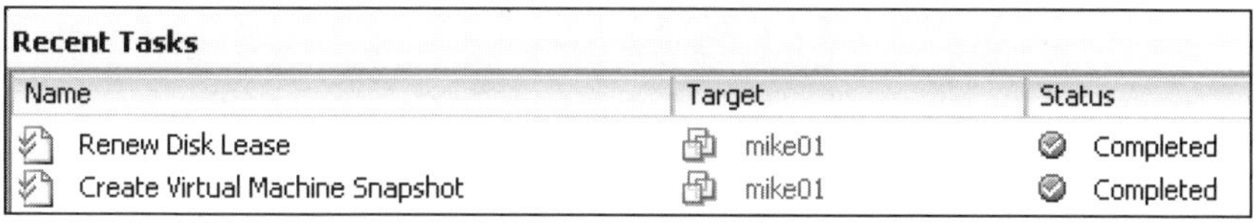

Recent Tasks		
Name	Target	Status
Renew Disk Lease	mike01	Completed
Create Virtual Machine Snapshot	mike01	Completed

Figure 11.2

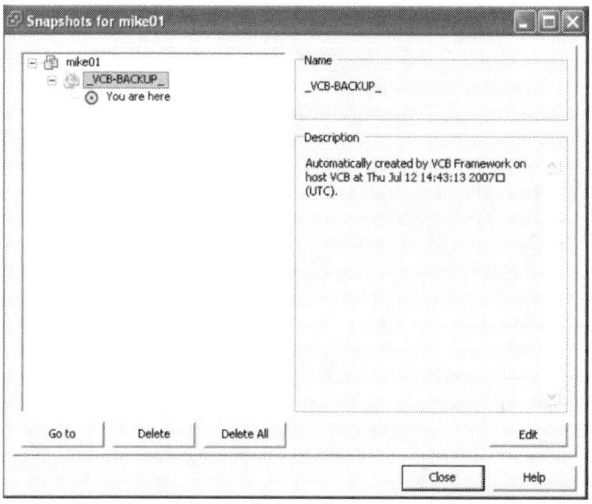

Lastly Figure 11.3 shows the hard-drive of my VCB Proxy and shows the contents of mike01's virtual disk.

Figure 11.3

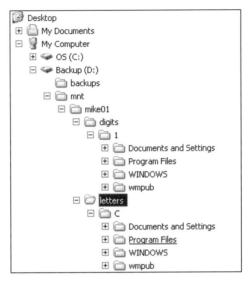

As you would expect, vcbMounter also allows you to unmount the VM's virtual disk. This creates a new disk re-lease and deletes the snapshot. You can unmount the virtual disk with this command:

```
vcbMounter -h virtualcenter.vi4book.com -u lavericm -p
password -U d:\backups\mike01
```

Note:

-U is a case-sensitive switch and directs vcbMounter to unmount the specified directory. The command-prompt would merely show the unmounting process with an output of this result:

```
Unmounted d:\backups\mike01\digits\1\ (formatted)
Deleted directory d:\backups\mike01\digits\1\
Deleted directory d:\backups\mike01\digits\
Deleted directory d:\backups\mike01\letters\C\
Deleted directory d:\backups\mike01\letters\
Deleted directory d:\backups\mike01
```

The Vi Client would show more information. Figure 11.4 shows the virtual disk's release and the snapshot's removal.

Figure 11.4

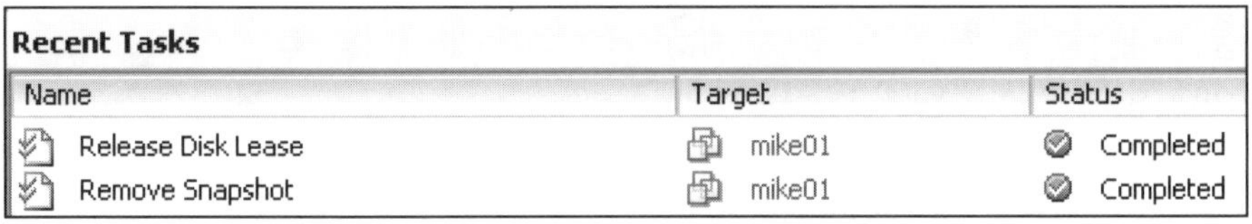

Recent Tasks		
Name	Target	Status
Release Disk Lease	mike01	Completed
Remove Snapshot	mike01	Completed

Completing a Full VM Backup

If you wish to do full VM backup the vcbMounter can achieve this for you. If you were attempting a full VM backup where you backup the VM's files then you would use fullvm as the type using –t switch. A full VM backup will backup all the files that make up a VM including the following:

- nvram

- vmx

- vmdk in the 2gbsparse virtual disk format

- log files

Two additional files are created; the catalog and unmount.dat file. The unmount file is used to automate the unmount process. The catalog file contains Virtual-Center metadata information so when the VM is restored the VM returns to the same ESX host, Resource Pool, and Virtual Machines and Templates location. A typical catalog file would look like this with mike01 being stored on VMFS volume called "virtualmachines":

```
version= esx-3.0state= poweredOn
display_name= "mike01"
uuid= "5034aae8-35c6-51a0-8f18-4264a177ee65"
disk.scsi0:0.filename= "scsi0-0-0-mike01.vmdk"
disk.scsi0:0.diskname="[virtualmachines]
mike01/mike01.vmdk"
config.vmx= "[virtualmachines] mike01/mike01.vmx"
host= esx3.rtfm-ed.co.uk
timestamp= "Thu Jul 12 16:04:24 2007"
```

```
config.suspenddir= "[virtualmachines] mike01/"
config.snapshotdir= "[virtualmachines] mike01/"
config.file0= "mike01.VM'sd"
config.file1= "mike01.vmxf"
config.file2= "mike01.nvram"
config.logdir= "[virtualmachines] mike01/"
config.log0= "vmware-15.log"
config.log1= "vmware-16.log"
config.log2= "vmware-13.log"
config.log3= "vmware-14.log"
config.log4= "vmware-17.log"
config.log5= "vmware-12.log"
config.log6= "vmware.log"
folderpath= "/Datacenters/Lab DataCenter/vm/Mike's VM's"
resourcepool="/Datacenters/Lab DataCenter/host/Lab Clus-
ter/Resources"
```

Warning:

Snapshot files created manually by an operator in the Vi Client are not backed up.

The syntax of vcbMounter command would be exactly the same as in the previous example except it would have -t fullvm as the type:

vcbMounter -h virtualcenter.vi3book.com **-u** lavericm **-p** password **-a name:**mike01 **-r** d:\backups\mike01 **-t fullvm**

In this case, the d:\backups is both the mounting point and also the destination of the backup of the VM. You might notice when vcbMounter runs, the format used is "compact" by which VMware means the 2gbsparse format. Rather than taking the virtual disks name they convert the disk into a format that is more unique, "scsi0-0-0-mike01.vmdk." This information is used to identify the virtual disk on the SCSI Bus.

Completing a Full VM Restore

Clearly the restore process means copying back our backup to the ESX host, and restoring it from the 2gbsparse format to the "monolithic" or "thick" format. We could do this manually using WinSCP or Veeram's FastSCP utility and then using the vcbRestore command at the Service Console. However, there is a more seamless way to complete this process.

Although Windows 2003 only does windows file sharing (SMB/CIFS) by default, we can install Microsoft's Services for Unix (SFU). This allows Windows to share out files using the Linux NFS protocol. The NFS protocol is natively understood by the VMkernel. Once SFU is installed and configured, we can then create VMkernel Port Group, perhaps on the Service Console's vSwitch0, and then NFS Mount point to our "backup" directory on the VCB Proxy. This allows us to use the vcbRestore command to pull the files down from the VCB Proxy and restore the VM.

The setup and configuration of SFU was covered in the Storage chapter. I've chosen to repeat those instructions again here with some slight modifications.

Windows does not allow unchallenged access to shares without authentication. As Windows and the ESX Host do *not* share a common end-user database, we need some method of "mapping" the users on ESX Host to Windows. The method I have chosen is a simple mapping of the accounts using the files present on any ESX Host.

Installing SFU

1. **Copy the passwd** and **group files** from any one of your ESX servers. These are both held in **/etc**. You can use free WinSCP tool to copy the files from the ESX host to your VCB Proxy.

2. **Extract the SFU package** and run the **MSI package** called **SfuSetup.msi**.

3. Choose a **Custom Installation** .

4. **Expand Authentication tools for NFS,** and select the **User Mapping Service**.

5. Select **Next** to the **setupid** and **case-sensitive options dialog box**.

6. Under **Local User Name Mapping Service**, select **Password and Group files**.

7. **Type name and path** for passwd/group files. For example,

   c:\etc\passwd

   c:\etc\group

8. Select the **Windows Domain**.

9. Select **Next, and accept the location for the install**...

   Note:

   Watch the status bar, check your email, make a cup of coffee, wonder how long you spend watching status bars... oh, and at the end of this - reboot your Windows/NFS Server.

Creating a User Mapping Between Administrator and Root

1. From the Start Menu, select Windows Services for UNIX.

2. Run the MMC, Services for UNIX Administration.

3. Select User Name Mapping node.

4. Choose Maps option, and under Advanced Maps click Show User Maps.

5. Click List Windows Users button - and select Administrator.

6. Click List UNIX Users button - and Select root.

7. Click the Add button.

   Note:

8. When the warning box appears choose OK.

9. At the top of the console choose the Apply button.

   Note:

   A safer method would be to create a mapping of root to a lower-privileged Windows user with rights to the backup directories on the VCB Proxy.

Sharing out a Folder

1. On the **Windows Explorer, right-click the** folder, and choose **Share and Security.** In my case I shared the d:\backups directory.

2. Select the **NFS Sharing** tab.

3. Choose **Share this folder.**

4. Click the **Permissions** button, Select **Allow root access.**

5. Change the **Type of Access to Read-Only.**

   Note:

   Our ESX hosts only need read only rights to the Backups share just for purposes of restoring lost or deleted VMs.

6. Choose **OK** to exit the sharing dialogs.

GOTHCA:

Watch out foR CaseSensitivity on your sHaReNaMeS. Although Windows is not case-sensitive, it perfectly emulates NFS which *is case-sensitive*. If you want to remain, sane make them all in lower-case with no spaces.

Confirming the Windows/NFS Server is functioning

Note:
There are a number of tools we can use at the Windows/NFS server to see if things are working before adding in the NFS Share as IP Storage in the Vi Client.

rpcinfo -p (lists listening ports on the server, notice TCP, NFS v3, Port 2049)

```
program version protocol   port
100000     2      udp      111       portmapper
100000     2      tcp      111       portmapper
351455     1      tcp             904   mapsVC
100005     1      udp            1048   mountd
100005     3      tcp            1048   mountd
100021     1      udp            1047   nlockmgr
```

100021	4	tcp	1047	nlockmgr
100024	1	udp	1039	status
100024	1	tcp	1039	status
100003	2	udp	2049	nfs
100003	3	udp	2049	nfs
100003	2	tcp	2049	nfs
100003	**3**	**tcp**	**2049**	**nfs**

showmount -e

Exports list on vcb.vi3book.com

/backups   All Machines

Adding an NFS Mount Point

For this to work we will need a VMkernel Port Group with a valid IP address to connect to the VCB Proxy. I locate my VCB Proxy on network as the Service Console vSwitch so the restore process does not interfere with my VMs.

1. Select the Configuration Tab.

2. In the Hardware Pane, select Networking.

3. Click the Properties… of vSwitch0.

4. Click the Add button.

5. Choose VMkernel, and Click Next.

6. In the Port Groups Properties dialog, type a friendly name for this connection, such as vcb-backups.

7. Set an IP Address and Subnet mask.

8. Choose Next and Finish.

   Note:

   If you are more comfortable with the command-line you can add this vmkernel port group from the command-line with the following:

   ```
   esxcfg-vswitch -A "vcb-backups" vSwitch0
   ```

```
esxcfg-vmknic -a "vcb-backups" -i 192.168.3.113
-n 255.255.255.0
```

In the next step we will add in the backup mount point.

9. In the Hardware pane, select Storage (SCSI, SAN, NFS).

10. In the right-hand side of the Vi Client click Add Storage.

11. In the Wizard, choose Network File System.

12. In the Locate Network File System page… complete the dialog box as follows:

    Server: Name of your NFS server, in my case vcb.vi3book.com

    Folder: Name of mount you wish to access, in my case, /backups

    DataStore Name: vcb-backups (or anything you deem suitable)

GOTCHA:

Remember NFS comes from Linux – even if you are using Microsoft SFU export/share names ARE case-sensitive!

Occasionally, the NAS maybe unavailable. If you want to force a reconnection to an NFS export you can do this through the Service Console with the following command:

```
esxcfg-nas —r
```
Note:

Now that you are more familiar with the command-line you could add the NAS connection from the command-line with the following:

```
esxcfg-nas -a backups -o vcb.vi3book.com -s /vcb-backups
```

Test Full VM Restore

Warning:

Do not start this process with the next step until you can verify you have a backup of the VM.

1. Locate you backed up VM in the Inventory.

2. Power Off the VM.

3. Right-click and choose Delete from Disk in the menu.

4. Open up a PuTTy session on the ESX host configured for NFS mount point serviced by SFU running on the VCB.

5. Ensure you have root level access. Then issue the vcbRestore command as follows:

    ```
    vcbRestore -h virtualcenter.vi3book.com -u lav-
    ericm -p password -s /vmfs/volumes/vcb-
    backups/mike01/ -o on
    ```

    Note:

    -s specifies the subdirectory where the VM's files are located. The –o on switch tells vcbRestore to power on the restored VM when the process has completed.

    Remember in the Service Console all commands are case-sensitive, so you must type vcbRestore with a capital R.

6. During the restore process the vcbRestore tool reads the catalog file and registers the VM with the ESX host, as shown in Figure 11.5.

Figure 11.5

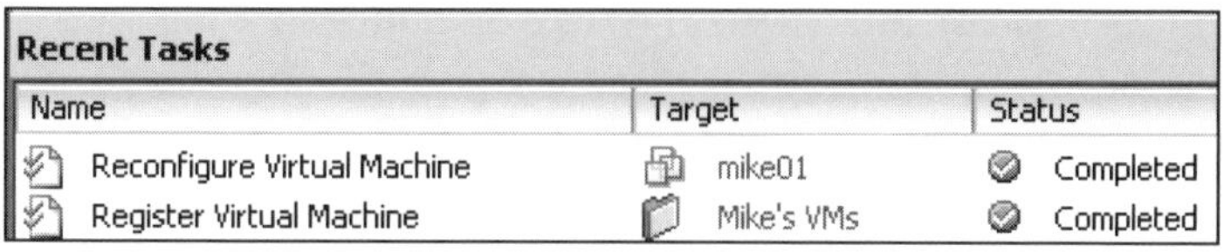

Recent Tasks		
Name	Target	Status
Reconfigure Virtual Machine	mike01	Completed
Register Virtual Machine	Mike's VMs	Completed

At the Service Console the vcbRestore utility will give you a progress bar to indicate what is happening.

```
Converting
"/vmfs/volumes/virtualmachines/mike01/mike01.vmdk" (VMFS
(flat)):
0%==================50%================100%
********************************************************
```

In this case the utility is also converting the 2gbsparse disks back into a "monolithic" or "thick" disk.

Towards the end of the restore process you might find that the friendly name of the VM is temporarily unfriendly UUID as the path to the VMX file. If you wait for vcbRestore to complete fully it does reconfigure the VM to show its friendly name. Figure 1.6 shows this unfriendly name.

Figure 11.6

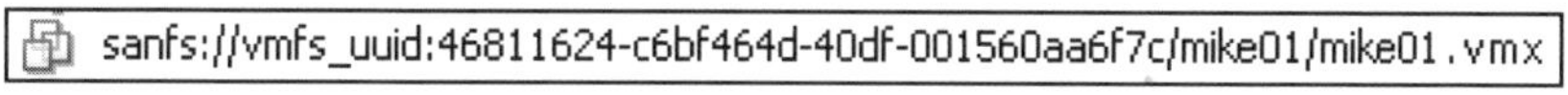

sanfs://vmfs_uuid:46811624-c6bf464d-40df-001560aa6f7c/mike01/mike01.vmx

Mounting a Virtual Disk to Retrieve an Individual File

The VCB Framework does come with a mountvm utility. This allows you to mount the backed up version of the virtual disks to a folder so that you can navigate the file and folder structure within it. It has a very simple syntax:

```
mountvm -d d:\backups\mike01\scsi0-0-0-mike01.vmdk
-cycleId d:\mnt\mike01
```

The –d switch indicates a path to the virtual disk you wish to use. The –cycleID generates a unique ID for the mounted disk in Windows; it "cycles" it so it's always unique. The last path statement is the mounting location.

If you navigate to the mounting location you would find the file system of the virtual disk there. It is possible to then copy files to the VM using conventional Windows shares.

Once you are finished with the virtual disk it can be unmounted with the mount command:

```
mountvm -u d:\mnt\mike01
```

Integration Modules and Commercial Backup Tools

Most third party vendors who support VCB will provide you with an integration module. Alternatively you may find them on VMware's website. This usually takes the form of a zip file which you extract to the VCB directory. Once extracted you run an install batch file which allows you to configure the files for your product. The core file is the config.js file which is held in the /config directory of your VCB installation. This will typically include the path to your mount directory and authentication credentials are required to initiate the backup process. Additionally, there is normally a readme.html file which will walk you through the setup.

It's perhaps worth saying that integration scripts and their README files vary in the quality, reliability, debugging, and error trapping. It is very much recommended to do research around the default scripts provided for how you can manually correct and improve them. This is beyond the scope of this book because there are simply too many vendors for us to test and verify. Additionally, scripts are quite frequently re-released and so anything in a published book regarding this aspect of the product is likely to become outdated quickly.

In this scenario, the VCB Proxy is both the backup server and backup client since the VCB Proxy is backing up files that are mounted locally. If your backup software doesn't install the backup client then it should be installed manually.

As an example of a typical integration scripts I've decided to demonstrate this using Symantec BackupExec 9.1. This version of BackupExec is supported by VCB. The main reason I selected this vendor is because they are very popular, and I had an existing evaluation copy which I could install to my VCB server. This should not be regarded as an endorsement or recommendation of Symantec software – but as a typical demonstration of configuring integration scripts.

Instructions for Backup Exec 9.1

Setup the VCB Integration Module

1. After installing VCB and if required Microsoft SFU, install Backup Exec.

   Note:

   You will need complete a wizard after the installation when you first run the BackupExec software. I like to setup a directory on my backup partition called D:\BackupExec Files as a location for disk-to-disk backups.

2. Download the Integration Module for BackupExec to the VCB Proxy from VMware's website at this url:

   http://www.vmware.com/download/vi/drivers_tools.html#backup

3. Extract the backupexec directory in the zip file to C:\Program Files\VMware\VMware Consolidated Backup Framework directory.

4. Open a command-prompt to the C:\Program Files\VMware\VMware Consolidated Backup Framework\backupexec directory.

5. Run the setup script by typing this:

   ```
   Install
   ```

6. Press [**Enter**] to accept the path for the VCB Framework Software.

7. Press [**Y**] to confirm the configuration path.

8. Choose [**Y**] to review the VCB Framework Configuration File.

Note: Entries in the configuration file marked with two double-forward slashes // are comments. You must remove the // entries for the changes to take effect. If not the default options will be used.

In my case I un-remarked

// BACKUPROOT="C:\\mnt";

and replaced it with the disk partition and directory of personal preference. For example, I used the following:

BACKUPROOT="D:\\backups";

9. Next **modify the HOST entry specifying your VirtualCenter or ESX host.** In my case I modified:

HOST="bu02.eng.vmware.com";

and replaced it with the name of the VirtualCenter or ESX host system:

HOST="virtualcenter.vi3book.com";

10. **Lastly I modified the USERNAME and PASSWORD entry with an account that has rights to connect to VirtualCenter** for backup purposes.

11. **Then in Notepad,** choose **File and Save** and **File and Exit.**

12. Choose [**Y**] to review the **BackupExec Configuration file.**

Note:

This file allows you to alter the temporary location used to store your pre- and post-scripts during the backup process. The default setting is held in the /generic/config.js file. I choose not to make any changes here – but wanted to you see that could be changed if required.

13. **In Notepad,** choose **File and Save** and **File and Exit.**

14. Choose [**N**] view the readme-backupexec.html file.

15. **Reboot the VCB Proxy to allow BackupExec and Windows to be updated with the new environmental variables.**

Note:

You can just restart the BackupExec services and close and re-open your command-prompt. However, for peace of mind I decided to opt for a full reboot after running the install script.

Setting up a Backup Job for Full-VM backup

1. In the BackupExec Management Console select Job Setup.

2. Under Backup Tasks select New Job.

3. Under the Source/Selection window in the Selection List name type a friendly name for selection to be backed up like this:

    Backup mike01.vi3book.com VM – Full VM Backup.

4. Under View Format click Text radio button.

5. Click the Insert button.

6. Type in the path to the mount point, using a FQDN to describe the directory name followed by -FullVM like this:

    D:\Backups\mike01.vi3book.com-FullVM

    Note:

    The integration script for BackupExec currently does not allow for multiple VMs to be backed up with one single job. At the moment this means that each VM requires its own backup job. The scripts could be modified to allow many VMs to be contained within one backup job. Examples of how to do this are available on the internet. One example is listed here:

    http://searchservervirtualization.techtarget.com/tip/0,289483,sid94_gci1233940,00.html

7. Click OK to the Advanced Selections Dialog box.

    Figures 11.7 and 11.8 show the respective BackupExec dialog boxes.

Figure 11.7

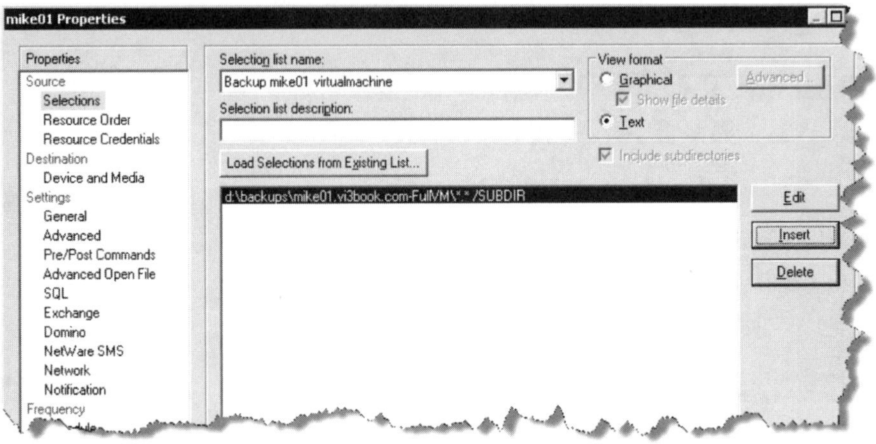

Note:

The reference to *.* /SUBDIR is added automatically by BackExec because the Advanced File Selection dialog has the option "Include Subdirectories" enabled by default.

Figure 11.8

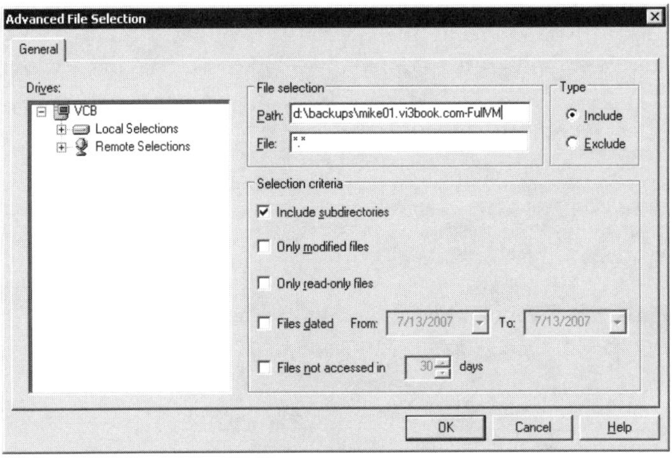

8. In the Backup Job Properties Box, select Settings and General.

9. Specify a Job Name.

Note:

Type something memorable and short as you will need to supply this later on in other parts of the job. In my case I called the job mike01-FullVM.

10. Select your Backup Method – in my case I selected COPY – Back Up Files.

Note:

Not all backup methods are supported. Consult the readme.html file associated with your vendor's integration script. For example, BackupExec supports the following:

Copy - Back Up Files

Full - Allow incrementals and differentials using modified time.

Differential - Using modified time

Incremental - Using modified time

Daily - files that Changed Today

working set - All files last accessed in (x) days

Note:

Although the backup type specified above may allow it, do not enable the "Use the Windows Change Journal if available" option. It is not supported.

Figure 11.9 shows the options selected in Backup and Settings in the BackupExec Management console for Settings, General.

Figure 11.9

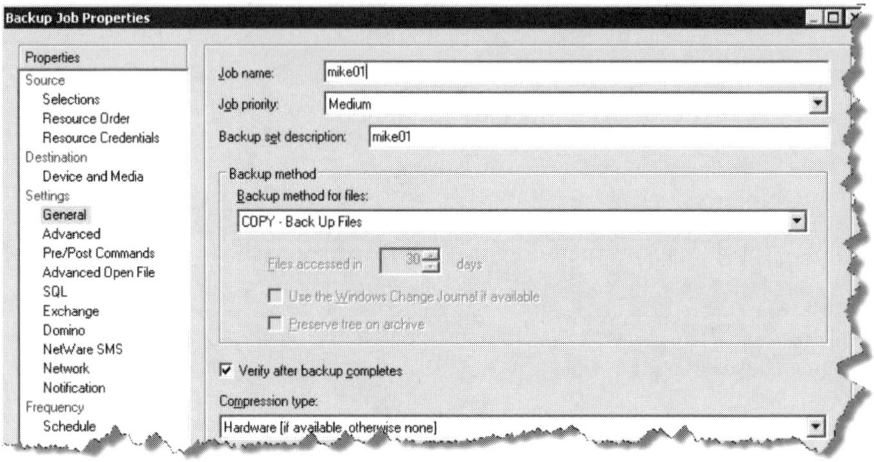

11. Next, in the Settings and Pre/Post Commands,

12. Add the following entries to the Pre and Post edit boxes respectively:

"C:\Program Files\VMware\VMware Consolidated Backup Framework\backupexec\pre-backup.bat" mike01-FullVM mike01.vi3book.com-FullVM

"C:\Program Files\VMware\VMware Consolidated Backup Framework\backupexec\post-backup.bat" mike01-FullVM

Note:

Here mike01-FullVM is the name of the backup job and the FQDN-FullVM indicates the path to the mounting point to the following:

d:\backups\mike01.vi3book.com-FullVM

Warning:

You must supply the speech marks for the path to the scripts. Using spaces in the jobname and the FQDN are not supported. The reference to -FullVM is required and hard-coded so the pre-backup script knows which type of backup to trigger.

Note:

Essentially, these are variables that are passed to vcbMounter. It is vcbMounter that will create the snapshot, mount the VM's files to d:\backups\mike01.vi3book.com-FullVM, and then begin the export process. Once the export completes, vcbMounter will then merge and delete the deltas in the snapshot. From that point BackupExec will take over backing up the exported version of the VM held in the d:\backups directory. In respect, the pre- and post scripts in the integrator are automating the vcbMounter backup process.

GOTCHA:

The README file that accompanies the backupexec integration modules incorrectly makes reference to a pre-command.bat and post-command.bat. This is incorrect and the correct file names are currently pre-backup.bat and post-backup.bat. Additionally, the README file does not warn you about using speech marks for long file names and directory paths with spaces.

13. Enable the run options including the option called "Allow pre and post-job commands to be successful only if completed with a return code of zero."

14. Increase the timeout for the cancelled command to be a larger value. In my case, I allow a 60 minute timeout.

Note:

This allows enough time for the post-script to trigger a merge and delete of the snapshot delta without the backup terminating the script due to a timeout. Figure 11.10 shows my selections and path statements.

Figure 11.10

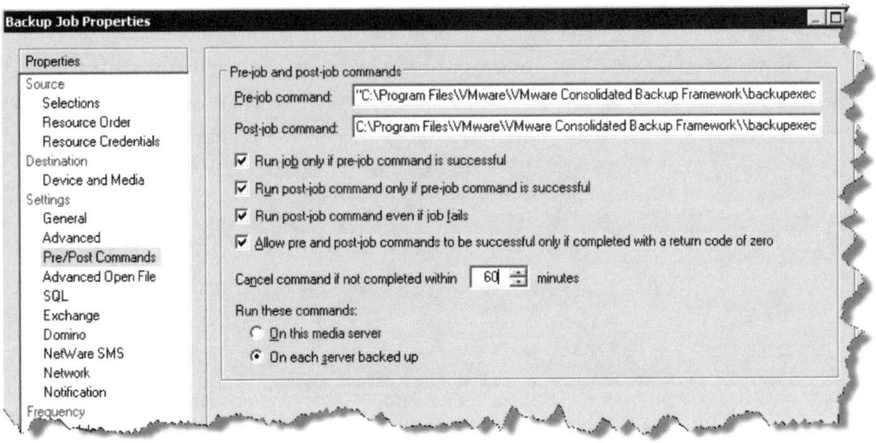

15. Lastly, select a destination device or media for the BackupExec backup. I prefer to do disk-to-disk, followed by disk-to-tape backups for offsite usage. Select your destination using Destination and Device and Media.

16. Click the Run Now button.

GOTCHA:

Be careful not to revert or commit the VCB Snapshot during the backup process.

Note:

The process begins by applying a snapshot and exporting the VM to the d:\backups\ directory. Once the export has completed, the snapshot is merged and deleted – and the VM is fully operational at all times.

Next, BackupExec backups up the files in the d:\backups export directory. In my case this would be:

d:\backups\mike01.vi3book.com.

After the backup process is completed you will have two versions of your VM. The exported version in held in d:\backup and the BackupExec version with the .bkf extension. You could delete the exported version held in d:\backups, as the BackupExec would restore the VM to that location anyway, ready for a Service Console vcbRestore.

Test Restore of a Full-VM Backup with BackupExec

First we will wipe all traces of the original VM from both VirtualCenter and from the exports directory on VCB Proxy.

1. Power on the Test VM and use the right-click Delete from Disk option.

2. Delete the Exported VM from the D:\Backups Directory.

3. Open the BackupExec Management Console.

4. Select the Restore Tab.

5. In the edit box under "Selection List" type a friendly name for the Restore Job like "Restore VM Mike01 FullVM."

6. Expand the + next to the name of the VCB Proxy and Select the Backup Job you wish to restore.

7. Click Run Now.

   Note:

   This should restore your VM back to the d:\backups directory, in my case D:\Backups\mike01.vi3book.com. Once the BackupExec restore has completed we can now restore it through the network using the NAS connection configured earlier.

8. Logon to the Service Console with root privileges.

9. Restore the VM with the vcbRestore command as follows:

   vcbRestore -h virtualcenter.vi3book.com -u lavericm -p password -s /vmfs/volumes/vcb-backups/mike01/ -o on

Setting up a Backup Job for File-Level with BackupExec

A file-level backup allows you to navigate inside a VM's virtual disk and select individual directories or files. Rather than specifying the file selection manually it is possible to enable a GUI-based browse of the VM's disks prior to running the backup job. You might find a graphical method of selecting files easier to manage than having to type long paths to files and directories. Once the files are selected in the selection list, the backup job can be run without the browse facility. In this example I have added a second disk to the mike01 VM and copied some sample files there.

1. Under Backup Tasks select New Job.

2. In the Backup Job Properties Box select Settings and General.

3. Specify a Job Name.

   Note:

   Type something memorable and short as you will need to supply this again later on in. In my case, I called the job mike01-File.

4. Select your Backup Method. In my case I selected COPY – Back Up Files.

5. In the BackupExec Management Console select Job Setup.

6. Keep BackupExec open.

7. Open a command-prompt and change into the C:\Program Files\VMware\VMware Consolidated Backup Framework\backupexec directory, the run:

   browse-start mike01-file mike01.vi3book.com

   Note:

   This should produce the following output:

```
Opened disk: blklst://snapshot-959[virtualmachines]
mike01/mike01.vmdk@virtualcenter.vi3book,com:902?xxxx/xx
xx
Proceeding to analyze volumes
Done mounting
Volume 1 mounted at
D:\backups\mike01.vi3book.com\digits\1 (mbSize=4086
fsType=NTFS )
Volume 2 mounted at
D:\backups\mike01.vi3book.com\digits\2 (mbSize=2039
fsType=NTFS )
```

```
Volume 1 also mounted on
D:\backups\mike01.vi3book.com\letters\C
Volume 2 also mounted on
D:\backups\mike01.vi3book.com\letters\D
```

8. Return to BackupExec.

9. Under the Source/Selection window in the Selection List name type a friendly name for the list of files to be backed up. Below is an example:

Backup mike01.vi3book.com VM – File Backup of D:

10. Ensure that under View Format that Graphical and Show file details is selected.

Note:

You should now be able to navigate the directory tree of d:\backups and find the files to be included in the file selection list.

Figure 11.11 shows my directory structure where I have selected everything in the D: drive of the VM except the IT directory.

Figure 11.11

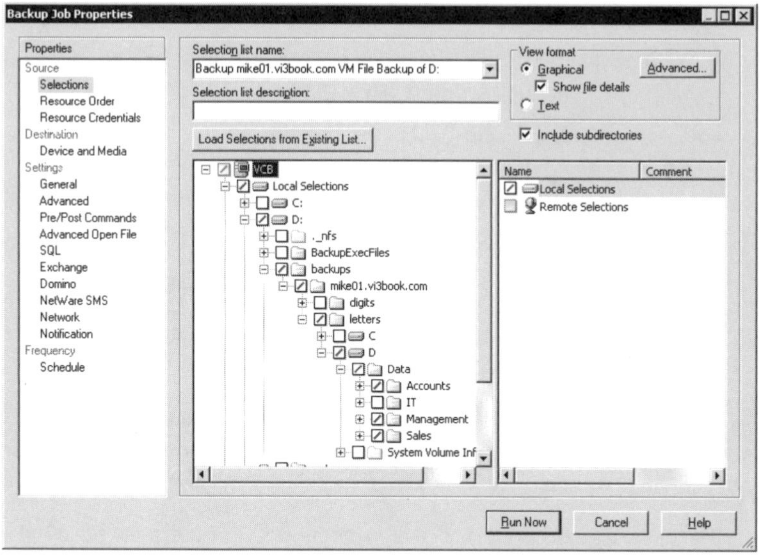

Figure 11.12 shows the View format which includes both the included and excluded directories.

Figure 11.12

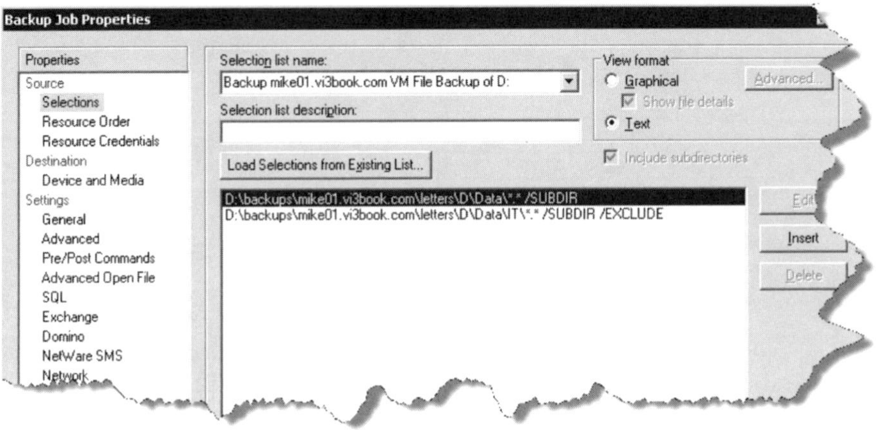

Next in the Settings and Pre/Post Commands

11. Add the following entries to the Pre and Post edit boxes respectively:

    "C:\Program Files\VMware\VMware Consolidated Backup Framework\backupexec\pre-backup.bat"

    mike01-file mike01.vi3book.com

    "C:\Program Files\VMware\VMware Consolidated Backup Framework\backupexec\post-backup.bat" mike01-file

    Note:

    Here mike01-file is the name of the backup job and the FQDN indicates the path to the VM mike01.vi3book.com.

12. Enable the run options including the option called "Allow pre and post-job commands to be successful only if completed with a return code of zero."

13. Increase the timeout for the cancelled command to be a larger value. In my case I allow a 60 minute timeout.

14. Select a destination device or media for the BackupExec backup. I prefer to do disk-to-disk followed by disk-to-tape backups for off-site usage. Select your destination using Destination and Device and Media.

15. Before you run the backup, unmount the VM from the command-line using the following:

```
browse-end mike01-file
```

Warning:

You must unmount the VM's files before starting the backup after running the browse-start command. Otherwise the pre-backup script will attempt to apply a second snapshot and mount the VM for a second time. This will cause the backup to fail.

16. Click the Run Now button.

Note:

The process begins by applying a snapshot and mounting the VM to the d:\backups\ directory. Next, BackupExec backups up the files in the d:\backups mount directory.

17. After the backup process is completed the mount point is un-mounted, and snapshot deltas are merged into the VM. This will leave you with backup files with .bkf extension.

Test Restore of a File-Level Backup with BackupExec

Restoring lost data files with VCB is a little less slick than a full backup. There isn't a handy vcbRestore-like utility to assist you in the process. The procedure is one of restoring the backup VCB proxy and then manually copying the lost files back to the VM. Another approach is to install a backup agent to the VM and restore the files that way. If you wish install a backup agent remotely to a VM after the main installation of BackupExec select the following in the menu.

1. Tools

2. Serial Numbers and Installation

3. Click Next in the Wizard.

4. Remove the tick next to Local Install.

5. Enable the tick next to Remote Install.

6. Right-click Windows Agent/Option Computers and Choose Add Computer.

7. Locate your VM in the list, and Click OK.

8. Enable Advanced Open File option and Remote Agent for Windows Servers.

However, I feel this in a way negates the whole point of tools like VCB, where we are trying to avoid the financial and network penalties of installing a backup agent. Fundamentally, the method is up to you. If you click the restore tab in BackupExec you should see a new catalog to select. Figure 11.13 shows the individual files I backed up from the D: drive of my test VM.

Figure 11.13

Conclusion

This concludes the chapter on backup and VMware Consolidated Backup. As you can see, new doors are opening in the world of backup triggered by virtualization. The problem is that door isn't quite fully open at the moment. The Holy Grail will be both backup and restore via the SAN offloaded to a backup proxy similar to VCB.

Chapter 12: ESX Command-Line Configuration (including installation)

About three and half years ago when I first picked up ESX I knew nothing about the command-line environment of Linux. Although I grew up on DOS and Netware, my command-line skills had weakened about the time I started to use Windows 95 and NT4. So the old adage holds true: use it or lose it. It's odd how some of the things I used to teach students, like .bat files and text manipulation, come in handy with ESX on the command-line, too. As they say, "What goes around comes around."

Anyway, at the end of 2003, I bought a secondhand book on Redhat Linux 9.2 (the version used by the Service Console in ESX 2.0) from EBay, and began to learn the basics you need to mange any operating system; how to navigate the file system, how to copy files around, how to edit a text file, how to fdisk and format a disk. I still would not regard myself as a Linux guru, after all my operating system is ESX, not Linux, but I know enough to get around and do my job. What I don't know – I can learn by using this thing called the Internet. I frequently ask my buddies on the forum about Linux stuff which I would regard myself as being a bit "fuzzy" on. So the moral of the story is, if you're a Windows guy – then have no fear. Commands are just words you type to carry out actions. What you don't know – you can learn because you're not stupid. But perhaps it would be a good idea to brush up your command-line skills before jumping head first in the ESX Service Console.

There are two main reasons to come to grips with the command-line environment of ESX: the Service Console. Firstly, it can be an excellent troubleshooting tool. Indeed, it might be your only option for troubleshooting if you cannot create a connection between the VI Client on your workstation and your ESX host. Secondly, learning the command-line environment could be useful for automation purposes – scripting laborious tasks especially in the area of ESX host installation and configuration.

There are a couple of caveats surrounding this chapter. Firstly, although the Service Console is based around Redhat Linux I do not intend to write a complete guide to Redhat Linux; rather we intend to drill down into very specific

ESX host tasks that largely have nothing to do with Linux. I would recommend that if you are a complete novice with Linux then purchase a book on Redhat Linux to become familiar with the basic tasks such as moving, copying, and deleting files. There are lots of free tutorials on the Linux command-line from the web – and in no time at all you will be restarting services and killing processes just as you would with any other operating system. A more complete and longer guide to the command-line is available for free from www.rtfm-ed.co.uk. This chapter was taken from that original guide and improved to make automating the ESX process more readable and focused.

Secondly, while the command-line environment surrounding ESX is very rich, it may not be the appropriate environment for certain scripting tasks. For example, if your goal is to write a script that manipulates and manages a VM, writing an ESX script will not be the best way to begin. As we saw in the previous chapter, the location of your VMs could be constantly changing because of VMotion, DRS, or HA events. In this case you would be best placed to investigate the programming environment of VirtualCenter's Software Development Kit (SDK).

The structure of this chapter is taken from the overall structure of the operations guide. We will begin with a look at automating the installation of ESX using scripts. At the end of the installation we will look at the commands used to create and configure vSwitches and iSCSI and NAS based storage. The goal will be an attempt to configure an ESX host from a blank machine to the point that it could be added to VirtualCenter and used to create VMs. At the end of the chapter there will be a roundup of some of the most useful commands used for troubleshooting and interacting with VM's from the command-line.

If you are reading this book in preparation for the VI-3 test, don't worry. We have heard no reports stating you need a strong familiarity with the command-line. This chapter is merely here for your knowledge – as a little knowledge is dangerous thing.

Try not to feel too intimidated by this chapter. The generation that grew up with graphical interfaces feels put off by command-line environments. Remember, commands are merely words that carry out instructions. Personally, I see both graphical and command-line tools as dangerous in the wrong hands. There is nothing intrinsically safer about a graphical environment – in fact, familiarity is often their weakest element. When was the last time you clicked OK, when you should have clicked cancel?

Scripted Installation of ESX

There are many reasons to automate the installation of ESX. Firstly, installing to blades using CDs can be a challenge. Secondly, automated installs guarantee consistency; this is especially useful if you have datacenter policies for partitioning and for ensuring consistently named port groups which are required for VMotion, DRS, and HA. Lastly, automating the ESX install will allow you to quickly rebuild a system if you are in a DR scenario.

There are many ways of automating ESX's installation. ESX uses the "Anaconda" installer popular with many Linux distributions. It can be automated with a configuration file containing "kickstart" (KS) commands. The automated install can use the source code via the physical CD-ROM, Floppy boot disk or remotely by FTP, NFS, or Pre-Execution Environment (PXE). I've decided to put the emphasis on PXE booting because in my experience people doing automated deployments often desire "diskless" installation where neither CD or floppy media is required – and wish to build an environment where the build they wish to deploy can be selected from a menu.

Another way of approaching this is to use your hardware vendor's ESX deployment tools such as IBM RDM or HP RDP. For those people with HP hardware an excellent site which covers the usage of HP RDP for ESX 2.x and 3.x is:

http://www.brianshouse.net/hp/

We will use a popular PXE virtual appliance downloadable from VMware's Virtual Appliance directory. This will save you considerable time configuring all the appropriate services and files required to set up a PXE boot server in a Linux environment. I decided to use the Ultimate Deployment Appliance v1.3 (UDA) as PXE server for a number of reasons. Firstly, it is very small to download. Secondly, it offers a way of serving up the files from the ESX ISO without manually copying files. Thirdly, it has an easy to use GUI which allows you to reconfigure the appliance with little Linux knowledge. Lastly, although the appliance is not geared up to work with ESX 3, with a few modifications it can be re-engineered to do so – and it can also be used to deploy a whole range of other operating systems including Windows, Linux (Fedora, Ubuntu, Suse), and Solaris X86. UDA was built to run on "free" virtualization with either VMware Server or VMware Workstation and a Windows server is needed to host the ISO files.

You can download UDA and read information about its development here:

http://www.vmware.com/vmtn/appliances/directory/232

Additionally, we can use ESX's own web-based wizard to generate a "base" kickstart.cfg file which we can modify with additional parameters to customize your installation.

GOTCHA:

Later in this chapter we will see how we can modify the kickstart script to handle the post-configuration of the ESX host. There are some limits to what we can achieve through the command-line. There are two notable restrictions. It is not possible to enable VMotion on a VMkernel port group using the ESX host "esxcfg-vswitch" command.

Additionally, although we can set the name of the license server to the ESX host, we cannot set the Host Edition level. So an ESX host remains unlicensed until enabled for Starter or Standard Edition in the VI Client.

Configuring the Ultimate Deployment Appliance (UDA)

LATE TO PRESS:

I have been liaising with Carl Thijssen, the creator of UDA. Carl has agreed to create templates for ESX, and introduce some features which I feel will greatly improve his appliance. UDA 1.4 is currently in beta but promises to include such features as:

- *A kickstart creator for ESX 3*

- *Local mounted ISOs which will dispense with the need for a Windows File Server*

- *The ability to set which NIC is used for the installation*

- *To hard-code kickstart scripts to servers by MAC Address*

I hope to add a PDF to vi3book.com covering the new features of UDA 1.4 when it is fully released.

UDA contains all the services and daemons required to do a PXE installation. It has a static IP address (10.0.0.104) and contains a DHCP scope for issuing DHCP request to PXE clients. Using its graphical web-interface it allows you to mount ISO images held on Windows/SMB shares and create a menu of pre-defined scripted installations using the Fedora Core 5 template.

Its configuration for our purpose involves 7 stages:

- Share out a Windows Folder containing ESX ISO images

- Download, Power On, Reset Passwords

- Reconfigure IP and DHCP Scope

- Setup Mount Point and Select ISO to Mount

- Create a Fedora Core 5 Template

Windows Shared Folder

This server should be in the same IP range as the UDA and ESX hosts. It could be the very same machine that is running the UDA appliance:

1. On a Windows File server setup a Windows share which contains the ESX 3 ISO.

    Note:

    You could also add additional ISO's supported by UDA if you so wish.

2. Click the Permissions button in the Sharing Tab.

3. Remove Everyone/Read, and Set the Permissions to be Full Control for an individual user account.

Note:

This account must be "local" to the Windows File Server. In other words, it cannot be an Active Directory or NT4 Domain User account.

Download, Power-On, and Reset Passwords

1. Download the Appliance and Extract the VMDK files.

2. Using VMware Workstation or VMware Server build a new VM using the "Existing Disks" option.

3. Power on the UDA VM.

4. Login to the Appliance with root using test as the password.

5. Change the password of root with the passwd command.

6. Open a web-browser on http:/10.0.0.1

Note:

You will need to give yourself a temporary 10.x.y.z address to communicate to the UDA if you don't use this range on your existing network.

7. Click the Web-Interface link and login as admin using admin as the password.

8. Click the password link, and reset the admin password.

Note:

You will find you have to logon again with the new password.

Reconfigure IP and DHCP Scope

TIP:

I found having my ESX hosts, my Windows File Server, and the UDA all on the same network made troubleshooting network problems much easier.

1. In the web-appliance, click the Network link.

2. Change your IP address, subnet mask, and default gateway as appropriate.

   Note:

   After clicking OK you will be disconnected, and you will have to connect under the new IP address.

3. Click the DHCP server link; replace the IP data with information valid for your network. Below is a sample of my DHCP file:

   ```
   ddns-update-style ad-hoc;
   if substring ( option vendor-class-identifier,
   0, 9) = "PXEClient"
   {
     filename "pxelinux.0" ;
     next-server 192.168.3.150 ;
   }
   subnet 192.168.3.0 netmask 255.255.255.0 {
   option routers 192.168.3.150;
   option domain-name-servers 192.168.3.130 ;
   range 192.168.3.20 192.168.3.30 ;
   max-lease-time 300;
   }
   ```

   Note:

   Next-server is the IP address of the UDA appliance, not the Windows file server.

4. Click OK. UDA should stop and restart DHCP service.

Setup Mount Point and Select ISO to Mount

1. Click the **Mount Points link** at the top of the page.

2. Choose **Create New Mount** – fill in the form to access the share. Figure 12.1 shows my settings.

Figure 12.1

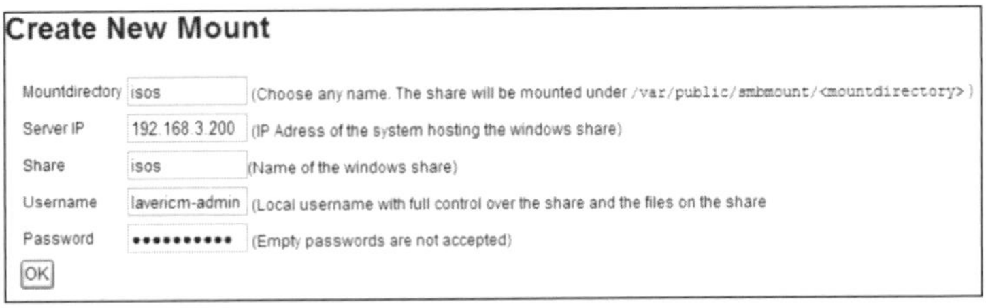

Create New Mount

Mountdirectory	isos	(Choose any name. The share will be mounted under /var/public/smbmount/<mountdirectory>)
Server IP	192.168.3.200	(IP Adress of the system hosting the windows share)
Share	isos	(Name of the windows share)
Username	lavericm-admin	(Local username with full control over the share and the files on the share)
Password	••••••••••	(Empty passwords are not accepted)

[OK]

Note:

I found that UDA prefers a RAW IP rather than hostname or FQDN, even when name resolution was setup using a host's file on the UDA itself. After clicking OK you should receive an OK-DONE message. If not re-check your IP, share names, and username and password. Clicking Mount Point again will show you the shares you have currently mounted.

3. Next in the web-admin tool, **click the OS link.**

Note:

As you can see, currently UDA 1.3 does not yet have predefined template for ESX 3. I found that Fc5 – Fedora Core 5 worked just fine.

4. Click the **Configure link for Fedora Core 5**, and in the following page **select an ISO from your mounted share**. Figure 12.2 shows my list.

Figure 12.2

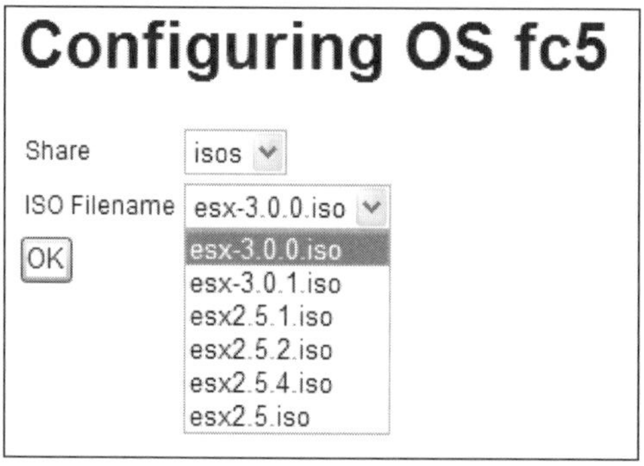

Configuring OS fc5

Share   isos ▾

ISO Filename   esx-3.0.0.iso ▾

[OK]   esx-3.0.0.iso
           esx-3.0.1.iso
           esx2.5.1.iso
           esx2.5.2.iso
           esx2.5.4.iso
           esx2.5.iso

5. After clicking **OK**, you should find that in the OS page it now reads "**Mounted**" in green.

Create a New Template

1. Next click the Template link.

2. Click Create New Template.

3. Type in a friendly templateID name.

   Note:

   This must be exactly 5 characters in length, so something like ESX01 or RTFM1 will work.

4. Choose from the OS type Fc5 (Fedora Core 5).

5. Type in a description such as: Dell: esx1.vi3book.com

Enabling ESX Scripted Installer

UDA is ready to do its work – but the problem is the KS template it created is only valid for Fedora Core 5. We need to replace it with a KS file which is valid for installing ESX 3.

As mentioned earlier, ESX has its own wizard for creating the kickstart.cfg file. It is a web-based tool, but it is not enabled by default on the ESX host. You must first edit a configuration file (struts-config.xml) on the ESX server to enable it. If you don't make this change, the following message appears when you try to access the web-page:

"Scripted Install is disabled

Message: Your ESX Server is not configured to support scripted installations. To support scripted installations, please refer to the VMware Web Access Administrators Guide."

1. Open a command-line view on an ESX 3.x host and change in the directory where the struts-config.xml is located:

    ```
    Cd /usr/lib/vmware/webAccess/tomcat/apache-
    tomcat-5.5.17 /webapps/ui/WEB-INF/
    ```

2. Make a backup of the configuration file with

    ```
    cp struts-config.xml struts-config.xml-backup
    ```

3. Edit the configuration file with

    ```
    nano —w struts-config.xml
    ```

4. **Comment out the line** that begins

    ```
    <action path="/scripted install …. Dis-
    abled.jsp
    ```

    Note:

    You comment things out by beginning the comment <!—and ending the comment with -->. If you read the line just above, it will tell you why we are doing this.   Basically this stops the warning message outlined above.

    ```
    <!—Note : Please comment the line below, if
    enabling Scripted Install Functionality.  -->
    ```

5. **Next remove the comments to enable the line that begins just below** with

    ```
    <!---
    <action path="/scriptedInstall"
    ```

```
type="com.vmware.webcenter.
scripted.ProcessAction">
```

and ends with

```
<forward name="scriptedInstall.form7"
path="/WEB-INF/jsp/ scriptedInstall/form7.jsp"
/>
</action>
-->
```

6. **Save the file** and **exit nano.**

7. **Restart the webAccess service** with

```
service vmware-webAccess restart
```

Creating a base ESX KS.cfg File

Depending on your selection, the web-based wizard displays 6 pages, each with a specific purpose.   The layout and design of these web-pages are not completely intuitive – but they do work.   For example, you are asked about licensing twice on three separate pages rather than just one (one page for the EULA, another for the license mode and third for your license server name and port number).   However, this said, the scripted installer web-pages does a great job of creating a base kickstart file which we can modify for our purposes:

*   Page 1: Deployment Method, Time zone, root password

*   Page 2: Input IP Settings of ESX Host

*   Page 3: Accept EULA

*   Page 4: Disk Partition Scheme and Licensing Mode

*   Page 5: Licensing Server Information

*   Page 6: Download completed kickstart file

1. Open your web-browser to the URL of your ESX Host.

2. Click the hyperlink called <u>Log in to the Scripted Installer.</u>

3. In Page 1 of 6, Change the installation method to be Remote.

4. In the Remote Server URL type: http://<ip>/fedora/fc5/

   Note:

   The IP address I am specifying here is of the UDA appliance (not the Windows file server), so adjust appropriate to your IP scheme. Also the path here must be completed with /fedora/fc5/ as this is the default location that UDA will look for your kickstart script – the final / is also required by the ESX scripted installer tool.

5. For Network Method, select Static IP.

   Note:

   This IP and directory location is where the physical ESX host will PXE boot to. As ESX is based on the Anaconda Installer and so is Fedora Core 4 and 5 we can reuse the work done by the UDA.

6. Choose No, to the option to "Create a default network for VMs."

   Note:

   Set your VLAN and Time Zone according to your network and geographical location.

7. Set a default root password.

8. Click Next.

9. In Page 2 of 6, enter the IP settings for the ESX host.

10. In Page 3 of 6, tick to Accept the EULA.

11. In Page 4 of 6, create the partition table for the appropriate disk.

    Note:

    If you are unsure what partitions to create check back to the first chapter about installing ESX which discussed appropriate partitioning schemes.

12. Under "drive" column ensure you select the right type of device to partition. In my experience my old Dell PowerEdge Servers, which merely have an Adaptec SCSI controller, always see the local disk or LUN as /dev/sda. In contrast my HP DL385 Proliant server with a Smart Raid Array 6i sees this device as /cciss/c0d0.

GOTCHA:

As well as reading the important warning here – be cautious if you are doing the install with a SAN connected to the ESX host. The way local storage device is recognized can be very different from what you might expect. I have seen cases where the internal disk or LUN is listed *after* all the SAN LUNs and the device name is /dev/sdh rather than /dev/sda

Figure 12.3 shows the layout of my partition table. In this case I opted to create a local VMFS partition in case I decided to use VM Clustering on this host.

Figure 12.3

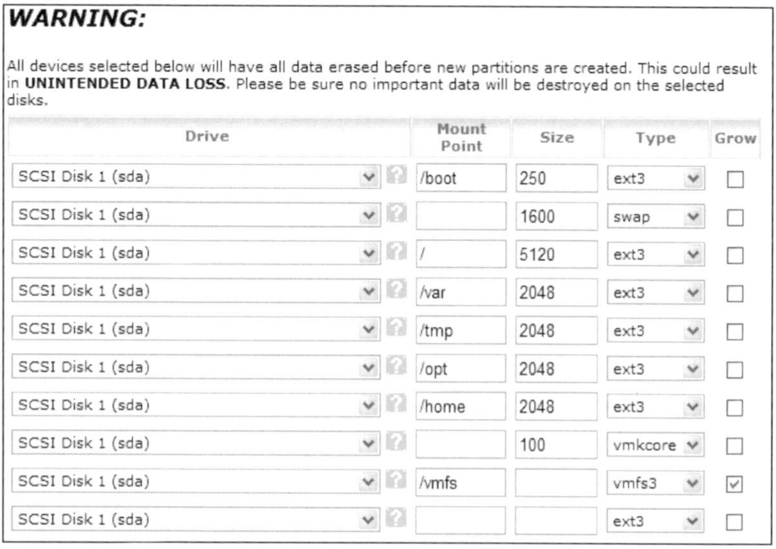

WARNING:

All devices selected below will have all data erased before new partitions are created. This could result in **UNINTENDED DATA LOSS**. Please be sure no important data will be destroyed on the selected disks.

Drive			Mount Point	Size	Type		Grow
SCSI Disk 1 (sda)	✓	🔲	/boot	250	ext3	✓	☐
SCSI Disk 1 (sda)	✓	🔲		1600	swap	✓	☐
SCSI Disk 1 (sda)	✓	🔲	/	5120	ext3	✓	☐
SCSI Disk 1 (sda)	✓	🔲	/var	2048	ext3	✓	☐
SCSI Disk 1 (sda)	✓	🔲	/tmp	2048	ext3	✓	☐
SCSI Disk 1 (sda)	✓	🔲	/opt	2048	ext3	✓	☐
SCSI Disk 1 (sda)	✓	🔲	/home	2048	ext3	✓	☐
SCSI Disk 1 (sda)	✓	🔲		100	vmkcore	✓	☐
SCSI Disk 1 (sda)	✓	🔲	/vmfs		vmfs3	✓	☑
SCSI Disk 1 (sda)	✓	🔲			ext3	✓	☐

Note:

The tick next to the "Grow Option" indicates that this partition will be created with the remainder of the disk or LUN. Personally, I would not recommend creating VMFS using the scripted installation. Firstly, as mentioned earlier in this book only the VI Client can correctly cope with the "disk alignment" issue. Secondly, although a scripted install will create a VMFS partition in the LUN, it does not format it. You would be forced to manually format this partition with vmkfstools –C command.

13. You might find it easier to create VMFS volumes at the end of the install processes automated with the %post section of the kickstart.cfg file.

14. Click Next.

15. In Page 4 of 6, type in the name of your license server and what port it is listening on (the default is 27000) and select your license type, in my case Standard.

    Note:

    This page appears because we choose to leave the default of "Use License Server" in the License Mode section.

16. On Page 6 of 6 click the Download Kickstart File button.

Modifying the Base Kickstart File

When viewing the KS file in Windows I recommend using the old DOS editor (edit.com) or WordPad. You will want to avoid notepad as it does not lay out the KS file in a readable way. Of course, if you're using Linux on your desktop then Vi or nano will suit your purposes perfectly well. The KS file contains five possible sections. We can customize it beyond the defaults asked in the web-access scripted install tool on the ESX host:

- Command
- %packages
- %pre
- %post
- %vmlicense_text

The command section contains the main instructions to complete the installation. Some of these are vanilla and would be found in Linux installations, and some are specific to ESX, including the network, clearpart, part, vmaccepteula, and vmlicense sections. %Packages are used to install additional components. Scripts can be called in %Pre and %Post processed run just before and after an installation. Of these, the %Post is the most important – as we can call a script here that will run VMkernel commands to handle such things as the creation of vSwitches, iSCSI Software Initiator and NAS configuration. Lastly, %vmlicense is only used in a host-based licensing scenario. If you are using this format you can append the contents of a host LIC file to the KS script below the %vmlicense section.

Many of the commands you might be looking for can be viewed in the default kickstart script that is left on an existing ESX host after a manual installation. It is held in the /root directory and is called Anaconda.cfg. A complete list of KS changes is perhaps too lengthy to dwell on here. If you are looking for a comprehensive list of all the entries possible in the KS file visit:

https://www.redhat.com/docs/manuals/enterprise/RHEL-3-Manual/sysadmin-guide/s1-kickstart2-options.html

GOTCHA:

There are some edits we need to make to the base kickstart file to make it work correctly. If you have more than one disk or LUN, or your ESX host can see LUNs on a SAN, you will have to instruct Anaconda where the MBR record should be written. This is done by modifying the # Bootloader section.

Additionally, if you want to stop a prompt for which network card should be used for the kickstart installation we need to edit a configuration file in UDA.

1. Open your ks.cfg file in WordPad, Vi or nano.

2. Locate the # BootLoader section.

3. If your install LUN is presented to anaconda as /dev/sda then modify:

   ```
   bootloader --driveorder=sda --location=mbr
   ```

4. If your install LUN is presented to anaconda as /cciss/c0d0 then modify:

   ```
   bootloader --driveorder=cciss/c0d0 --
   location=mbr
   ```

5. Save the ks file, and select all the text and copy.

6. Back in the web-interface of UDA, click Template Link, and Choose Edit Configuration file.

7. Select all the text and paste your ESX based KS file – replacing the default Fedora Core 5 KS file generated by UDA.

8. To stop kickstart prompting the operator to select which NIC to use for the installation:

    a. Open an SSH session to the UDA

    b. Login as root with your password

    c. cd /var/public/tftproot/pxelinux.cfg

    d. nano –w default

    e. add the ksdevice=eth0 instruction to the end of each of your templates like so:

      append   ks=http://192.168.3.150/kickstart/esx01.cfg initrd=initrd.fc5 ramdrive_size=8192 ksdevice=eth0

GOTCHA:

This reference to eth0 merely tells the kickstart installer which NIC to use for the installation. It has nothing to do with selecting the NIC used for the Service Console vSwitch. Currently the only way to adjust this is using the %post section and esxcfg commands to reassign the NIC interfaces.

Note:

The configuration of UDA is now completed so you are ready to test the PXE ESX installer. I recommend you choose a server you are willing to sacrifice if your installation fails, and for safety reasons detach the SAN cables. Most servers will use F12 to trigger the PXE boot process without any need for changing the boot order in the BIOS.

Secondly, if you have a blank disk or LUN with no existing partition table – the installer will ask if it is OK to initialize the LUNs it sees. This can also happen if your SAN is attached. This can be very dangerous if /dev/sda is not a local LUN but a SAN-based LUN that contains data. Figure 12.5 shows the warning box.

Figure 12.4

```
                    Warning
The partition table on device ccisss/c0d0 was
unreadable. To create new partitions it must be
initialized causing the loss of ALL DATA on
this drive.

This operation will override any previous in-
stallation choices about which drives to ig-
nore.

Would you like to initialize this drive erasing
all ALL DATA?

Yes    No
```

Additional Notes:

If you wish to edit by hand the various files used by UDA you will find them located here:

- **Your Template files:** /var/public/www/kickstart/

- **UDA Built-in Templates:** /var/public/www/templates

- **UDA PXE Menu:** /var/public/tftproot/message.txt

- **Default Help Message:** /var/public/tftproot/help.txt

- **pxelinux.cfg File:**/var/public/tftproot/pxelinux.cfg/pxelinux.cfg

GOTCHA:

If you shutdown or reboot the UDA appliance it does not automatically re-mount your shares. Remember if you have just powered on your UDA to request a remounting of the shares.

Configuring Networking

Generally, everything we have created in the VI Client can be also achieved from the command-line. The only exceptions are:

- Enabling VMotion on a VMkernel Port Group

- Settings advanced policy settings such as load-balancing, traffic shaping, and security settings

There are two main reasons to be familiar with the networking commands; firstly, for troubleshooting Service Console connectivity, and secondly for use with the %post section of a kickstart script.

Networking involves the use of three main commands:

- esxcfg-vswitch - handles generic vSwitch operations

- esxcfg-vswif0 - handles Service Console networking

- esxcfg-vmknic - handles VMKernel networking

These are quite sophisticated commands used in a particular order to achieve the results you are looking for. esxcfg-vswitch is the main command – and it has a mix of parameters in lower and upper-case. Lower-case parameters manipulate the switch, whereas upper-case switches manipulate the portgroup. So to add a vSwitch it is –a and upper-case –A that creates a portgroup. In one way this is nice because it's easy to remember, but beware; it is incredibly easy to forget this subtle distinction and accidentally create a switch rather than a portgroup attached to a switch.

GOTCHA:

Lastly, one important thing to mention about the esxcfg commands is that if you use them – and then check your changes in the VI Client – you may find that the VI Client will show out-of-date information. In order for the VI Client to display any changes made with the esxcfg commands, you may need to restart the hostd daemon on the ESX host if the various refresh options in the VI Client refuse to update your administrative views.

This is easy to do with:

```
service mgmt-vmware restart
```

Unfortunately, every time you restart the hostd daemon you may find you will be disconnected from your ESX host. I recommend you become familiar interpreting with the esxcfg-vswitch –l command, so you can make many changes in one go – and then restart the hostd service at the very end of the process.

Viewing your Switches & Service Console Networking

1. To view your switches type the command:

```
esxcfg-vswitch —l
```

Note:

This shows me I have one vSwitch (vSwitch0) using one NIC (vmnic0) with one portgroup called "Service Console" which is not using VLAN.

2. To view your Service Console network settings type:

```
esxcfg-vswif —l
```

Note:

Nothing to state here – but I think it's interesting that it doesn't show me my all important default gateway settings which would have been nice. If you want to know your default gateway settings and DNS settings you will find these held in /etc/sysconfig/network and /etc/resolv.conf respectively.

3. To View your network card's vmnic name, PCI settings (b:s:f), driver, link, speed, duplex, and description:

```
esxcfg-nics —l
```

Creating a vSwitch (Internal)

1. To create a new switch type:

```
esxcfg-vswitch —a vSwitch1
```

2. Then add a portgroup

```
esxcfg-vswitch —A internal vSwitch1
```

Note:

Remember to use lower-case -a for adding a switch, and upper-case -A for adding a portgroup. As stated earlier in the network chapter, I recommend using lower-case and no space for port-group names.

3. If you run the command **esxcfg-vswitch −l** you will see this information:

Figure 12.5

```
vSwitch Name
vSwitch0

        PortGroup Name
        Service Console

vSwitch Name
vSwitch1

        PortGroup Name
        internal
```

4. **If you wish to see this reflected in the VI Client** then type:

```
service mgmt-vmware restart
```

Note:

This is how my switch configuration looks now:

Figure 12.6

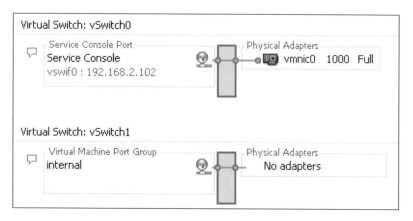

Creating a vSwitch (Single NIC)

1. In this case we will create a new switch and port group in one line with:

   ```
   esxcfg-vswitch —a vSwitch2 —A production
   ```

2. Next patch an NIC to the vSwitch with:

   ```
   esxcfg-vswitch -L vmnic1 vSwitch2
   ```

   Note:

   Again this is a case-sensitive option. —l lists switches, whereas —L links nics to switches.

3. If you run the command **esxcfg-vswitch —l** you will see that vmnic1 has been added to vSwitch2

4. **If you wish to see this reflected in the VI Client** then type:

   ```
   service mgmt-vmware restart
   ```

   Note:

   This is how my switch configuration looks now:

Figure 12.7

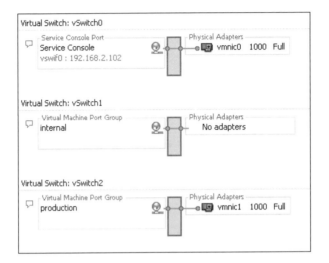

Creating a vSwitch (Multiple NICs)

Note:

It is very easy to create a NIC-Team, just re-run the previous command with a different NIC using:

1. esxcfg-vswitch -L vmnic2 vSwitch1

2. If you run the command esxcfg-vswitch –l you will see that two NICs have been added to vSwitch1

3. If you wish to see this reflected in the VI Client then type:

```
service mgmt-vmware restart
```

Note:

This is how my switch configuration looks now:

Figure 12.8

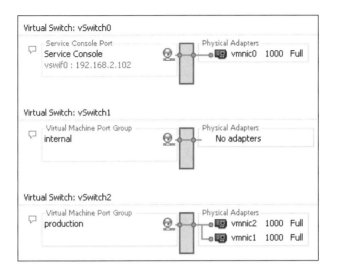

Deleting a Switch from vSwitch

I'm now running out NICs for the next part of this chapter. So I am going to delete my vSwitch2 to free up my NICs.

1. Type the command:

```
esxcfg-vswitch —d vswitch2
```

GOTCHA:

Notice how it doesn't ask "are you sure?", but then again neither does the VI Client.

Creating PortGroups for VLAN Networking NIC Team

1. We have to create a switch, create a portgroup for each VLAN, allocate our NICs and then set the VLAN ID:

```
esxcfg-vswitch —a vSwitch2
esxcfg-vswitch —A accounts vSwitch2
esxcfg-vswitch —A rnd vSwitch2
esxcfg-vswitch —A sales vSwitch2
esxcfg-vswitch —L vmnic1 vSwitch2
```

```
esxcfg-vswitch —L vmnic2 vSwitch2
```

2. **The next part is to set the VLAN id** for each network (account, rnd, and sales):

```
esxcfg-vswitch —v 10 —p accounts vSwitch2
esxcfg-vswitch —v 20 —p rnd vSwitch2
esxcfg-vswitch —v 30 —p sales vSwitch2
```

Note:

In this case —v is used to set the VLAN ID, and —p is used to modify the properties of an existing portgroup.

3. **If you run the command esxcfg-vswitch —l** you will that VLAN ID column has values beneath it

4. **If you wish to see this reflected in the VI Client** then type:

```
service mgmt-vmware restart
```

Note:

This is how my switch configuration looks now:

Figure 12.9

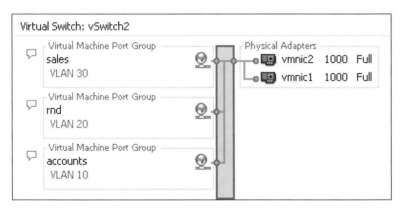

Creating Vmkernel Switches

You will need a good name for the portgroup – because the esxcfg-vswitch command just shows as any ordinary switch. In this example I will create a vSwitch good for VMotion. Remember that the command-line tools do not support enabling a VMKernel portgroup for VMotion.

- You need to use **esxcfg-vmknic –l** to see it:

1. First create the Switch, Portgroup, and Assign an NIC:

```
esxcfg-vswitch —a vSwitch3
esxcfg-vswitch —A "vmotion" vSwitch3
esxcfg-vswitch —L vmnic3 vSwitch3
```

2. Next use the esxcfg-vmknic command to add in a VM Kernel NIC and set the IP and Subnet Mask:

```
esxcfg-vmknic —a "vmotion" —i 10.0.0.1 —n
255.0.0.0
```

3. Then set the vmkernel default gateway with:

```
esxcfg-route 10.0.0.254
```

   Note:

   Remember that VMware does not support VMotion events across routers. However, you may need a default gateway if this vmkernel portgroup was being used to access iSCSI or NAS based storage.

4. If you run the command esxcfg-vswitch –l you will see the VM Kernel port has been added

5. If you wish to see this reflected in the VI Client then type:

```
service mgmt-vmware restart
```

Note:

This is how my switch configuration looks now:

Figure 12.10

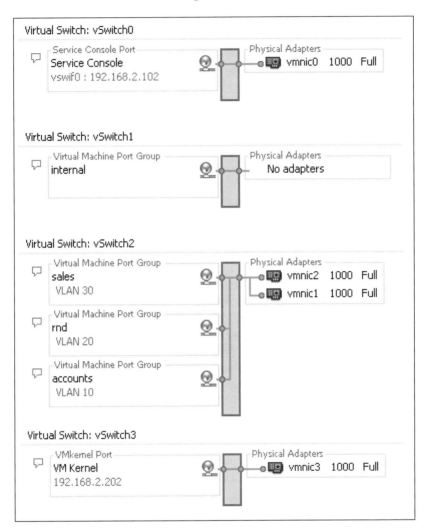

Changing your Service Console IP Settings

You can do this through a putty session but it is likely you will be disconnected unless you have more than one vswif interface (with a different IP address). It is entirely possible to have two vswif interfaces on two separate IP addresses – and use one connection to change the IP address of the other. You do run the risk of losing SSH connectivity if you screw up – so perhaps doing this through your ILO is a safer-bet and less hard work. You might also wish to include a new DNS entry for your ESX host before you make this change...

1. To view your current IP and Netmask type:

    ```
    esxcfg-vswif —l
    ```

2. To **change your IP and Subnet Mask** type:

    ```
    esxcfg-vswif —i 192.168.3.203 —n 255.255.255.0
    vswif0
    ```

    Note:

    You change your default gateway by editing

    ```
    nano —w /etc/sysconfig/network
    ```

    and then restart your networking with

    ```
    services network restart
    ```

3. Your DNS settings are located in **nano —w /etc/resolv.conf**

Setting the Speed and Duplex of NICs

We have always been able to change the speed and duplex of the vmkernel NICs but in the past the only way to change the Service Console speed and duplex was by editing the /etc/modules.conf file. You can now change both the Service Console and the vmkernel NICs through the GUI. There could be a chicken-egg/catch22 situation here though. If your Service Console NIC has the incorrect speed/duplex you may be unable to connect with the VI Client to change it. That's when knowing the Service Console commands come in handy. It can also be useful to reassign a 100Mps card to a Service Console and then fix its speed/duplex.

1. Work out which NIC has been assigned to the portgroup "Service Console" with:

    ```
    esxcfg-vswitch —l
    ```

2. To view your current speed & duplex:

```
esxcfg-nics -l
```

3. To set the speed/duplex of vmnic0 to 100Mps/Half-Duplex type:

```
esxcfg-NIC's -s 100 -d half vmnic0
```

4. To reset to auto-negotiate:

```
esxcfg-NIC's -a vmnic0
```

Recreating your vswif0 Interface

Recreating your ESX vswif0 interface can be useful in a couple of scenarios. I have seen "in place upgrades" sometimes breaks the Service Console network. Secondly, if a novice uses the VI Client to change the Service Console network it may become inoperable. Thirdly, during the installation of ESX you must select the NIC used for vSwitch0. If you select the wrong NIC you might find you have no network communication to the ESX host via the VI Client. In this case being able to modify IP settings with esxcfg-vswif –i and –n is useful, and being able to unlink and link an NIC is essential as well.

1. Logon locally to the ESX host or use your ILO card

2. Create a new switch:

```
esxcfg-vswitch -a vSwitch0
```

3. Create a new portgroup:

```
esxcfg-vswitch -p "Service Console" vSwitch0
```

4. Assign an NIC:

```
esxcfg-vswitch -L vmnic0 vSwitch0
```

5. Assign a vswif interface and set its ip/sn:

```
esxcfg-vswif -a vswif0 -p "Service Console" i
192.168.3.101 -n 255.255.255.0
```

Removing an NIC from vSwitch

Removing an NIC from a vSwitch is relatively easy; it uses the case-sensitive –U switch to unlink an NIC from a switch:

```
esxcfg-vswitch -U vmnic vSwitch2
```

Deleting a PortGroup from vSwitch

Deleting a portgroup is done with the –D switch. Perhaps you accidentally created a portgroup with –A when you should have used –a:

```
esxcfg-vswitch -D production vSwitch
```

Managing the ESX Firewall

Managing the firewall by the VI Client is really easy – it's a tick box style interface. If you use the GUI interface and then query with the command-line tool you get "friendly" information about what is enabled. If you purely use the command-line tool you will just get TCP port numbers and directions (outgoing and incoming). The GUI tool also has some handy "built-in" friendly names for popular applications, vendor specific agents like CommVault Dynamic/Static and many others. In ESX 2.x it was possible to set 3 levels of security (high, medium and low). We can achieve a similar configuration with ESX 3.x:

- High: incoming/outgoing blocked

- Medium: incoming blocked, outgoing not blocked

- Low: firewall off, no blocking of incoming/outgoing traffic

Viewing your current Firewall Settigs

1. Type the command

```
esxcfg-firewall -q outgoing
esxcfg-firewall -q incoming
```

Note:

You can also use esxcfg-firewall –q on its own. This gives you lots of stuff... most useful at the bottom:

```
Incoming and outgoing ports blocked by default.
Enabled services: CIMSLP ntpClient aam VCB
swISCSIClient CIMHttpsServer snmpd sshClient
vpxHeartbeats LicenseClient sshServer
CIMHttpServer
```

Changing Your Security Level

If you wanted to weaken your security to medium you could use the following:

1. Type the command

    ```
    esxcfg-firewall --allowOutgoing –blockIncoming
    ```

    Note:

    You should get warnings like so:

    ```
    2006-07-06 14:39:53 (1965) WARN :  Setting
    firewall default firewall/blockOutgoing to 0
    ```

    ```
    2006-07-06 14:39:53 (1965) WARN :  Setting
    firewall default firewall/blockIncoming to 1
    ```

Enabling a Single Service/Client/Agent

If you want to SSH from one ESX host to another ESX host or SCP from one ESX host to another you need to enable the SSH Client on port 22. If you do this via the GUI and then do an esxcfg-firewall –q you will see friendly information like so:

Figure 12.11

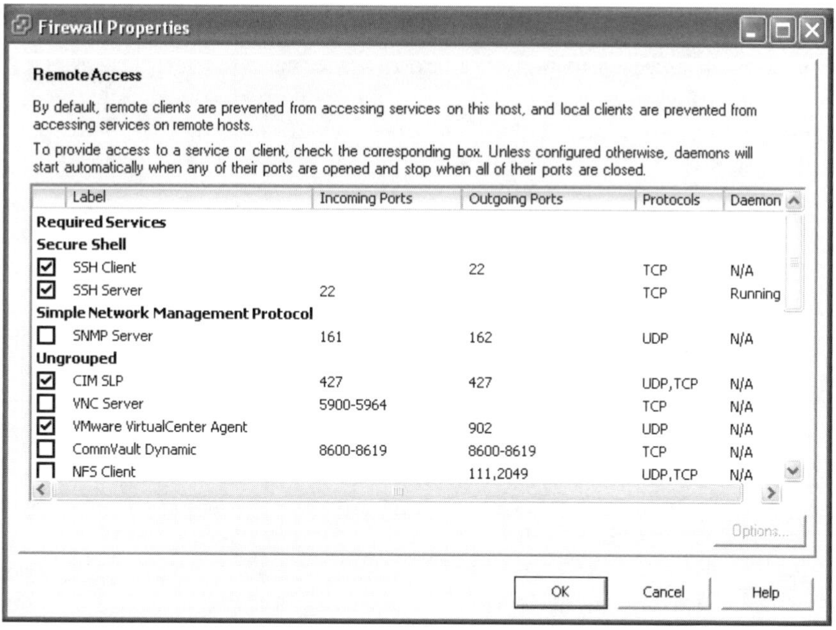

Enabled services: AAMClient CIMSLP LicenseClient
sshServer CIMHttpsServer CIMHttpServer **sshClient**
vpxHeartbeats
Dgfdfgdsdsdsd
Opened ports:

To do the same from the command-line you would type the command:

```
esxcfg-firewall -e sshClient
```

Note:

To disable, type:

```
esxcfg-firewall -d sshClient
```

Enabling non-Standard Ports

This is useful if there is an application or service which is not listed for use with –e or –d. Alternatively you might work in an environment where all port numbers have been changed to non-standard ports as part of your datacenter policies. It is possible to open a specific port by number, transport (udp/tcp) and direction (in/out). For example, to enable port 22 outbound from the server type the command:

```
esxcfg-firewall -o 22,tcp,out,ssh
```

Note:

The ssh at the end is a friendly label. If I run esxcfg-firewall –q again at the bottom it states:

```
Incoming and outgoing ports blocked by default.
Enabled services: AAMClient CIMSLP LicenseClient
sshServer CIMHttpsServer
IMHttpServer vpxHeartbeats
Dfsdfdfdfsdfsdf
Opened ports:
ssh                 : port 22 tcp.out
```

Typical vSwitch Errors

- As stated earlier, one of the most common mistakes with the networking esxcfg command is getting your case-sensitivity muddled up! Below is a quick summary of the command-line switches used in this chapter and their purpose:

- -a   add vSwitch

- -A   add portgroup

- -l   list vSwitches

- -L   link vmnic

- -d   delete vSwitch

- -D   delete portgroup

Another common error is trying to change properties of vSwitch that are in use. Typically the errors look like this:

"Failed to remove vswitch: vSwitch3, Error: PortGroup "Legacy eth0" on Virtual Switch "vSwitch3" is still in use: 1 active ports, vswif0" or "Legacy vmnic2, Error: Unable to delete portgroup "Legacy vmnic2," for the following reasons: 1 active ports"

In the first example, the operator tried to delete the vSwitch that is hosting our Service Console. To delete it we would need to add a new Service Console port and connect with it to then delete the old Service Console Connection. The second error happens if you have powered on VMs which are actively connected to the vSwitch portgroup. Powering those VMs off, or configuring them for a different vSwitch portgroup, will normally allow the command to work.

Configuring Storage

This section assumes you have already set up NAS and iSCSI storage correctly, **and** that you have created a VM Kernel vSwitch/Port Group outlined in the previous module. You are now ready to connect to iSCSI or NAS-based storage. This module repeats some of the vmkfstools command listed earlier. Sorry about this repetition but this gives more detail than a simple explanation of the commands.

Configuring NAS Storage

Remember that you must have a VM Kernel Switch to do this. There must be connectivity to the NAS via the Service Console NIC because authentication is driven through the Service Console NIC. My NFS server is called nfs1.vi3book.com, and it has one export on it /ISOs.

Mounting NAS Exports/Shares

Type the command:

```
esxcfg-nas -a ISO's -o nfs1.vi3book.com -s ISO's
```
Note:

The command should respond with:

```
Connecting to NAS volume: ISO's
ISO's created and connected.
```

Note:

-a is used to add followed by the friendly label, -o to specify the nfs server, and —s to specify the export/share.

Listing NAS Exports/Shares

```
esxcfg-nas —l
```

Note:

You should receive a response like so:

```
ISO's is ISO's from nfs1.vi3book.com mounted
nas-VM's is nas-VM's from nfs1.vi3book.com mounted
templates is templates from nfs1.vi3book.com mounted
```

Restoring NAS Connections

If the NAS become unavailable you may have to restore the mount by force. This sometimes happens to me if I start-up my ESX hosts before the NAS is up.

1. Type the command:

    ```
    esxcfg-nas —r
    ```

2. Followed by:

    ```
    esxcfg-nas —l
    ```

Using vmkping to carry out tests

Vmkping is a tool that tests your vmkernel switch IP configuration. I'm mentioning it here rather than in the vSwitches section (where it might have been a more appropriate reference) because it can also reveal information about your NAS connectivity.

1. Type the command:

    ```
    vmkping —D —v
    ```

    Note:

    This runs vmkping in a **d**ebug mode with **v**erbose information. It pings the following interfaces:

    IP address allocation to VM Kernel network(s)

    VM Kernel Default Gateway(s)

    NAS mount(s) and iSCSI systems

Connecting to iSCSI Storage (Software)

My iSCSI box is a Fedora Core 5 with iSCSI Enterprise Target installed and configured. Its name is iscs1.vi3book.com iSCISi has 2 LUNs available, it supports dynamic discovery, and its IP is 172.168.3.210. I used the iqn of iqn.2006-06.com.vi3book:iscsi1 on this iSCSI Target. The esxcfg-swiscsi is more limited than the esxcfg-nas command.

- —e enable
- —d disable
- —q query if the adapter is enabled or disabled
- —s force a scan
- —k forcibly remove iscsi sw stack

Enabling the iSCSI Adapter

1. Type the command:

    ```
    esxcfg-swiscsi —e
    ```

    Will return:

```
Allowing software iSCSI traffic through
firewall...
Enabling software iSCSI...
/usr/sbin/vmkload_mod
/usr/lib/vmware/vmkmod/iscsi_mod.o
Using /usr/lib/vmware/vmkmod/iscsi_mod.o
Module load of iscsi_mod succeeded.
```

Note:

This will enable the iSCSI Software Adapter like so:

Figure 12.12

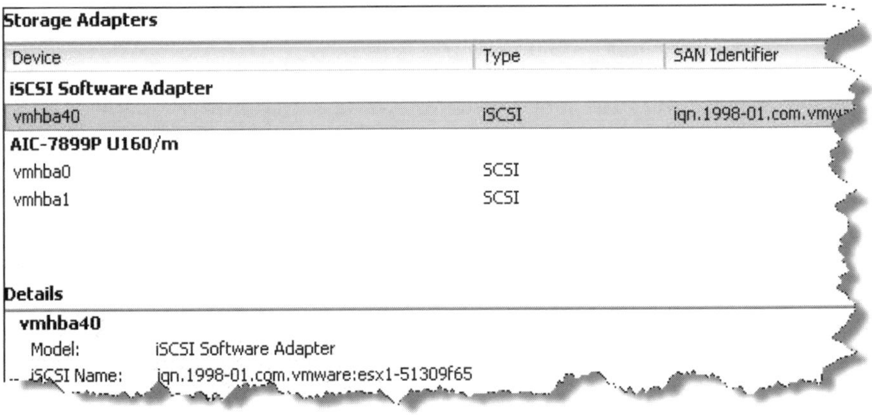

Storage Adapters		
Device	Type	SAN Identifier
iSCSI Software Adapter		
vmhba40	iSCSI	iqn.1998-01.com.vmw
AIC-7899P U160/m		
vmhba0	SCSI	
vmhba1	SCSI	

Details

vmhba40
Model: iSCSI Software Adapter
iSCSI Name: iqn.1998-01.com.vmware:esx1-51309f65

Setting the iSCSI Target IP with Discovery Mode

Note:

Remember that the Software iSCSI adapter does NOT support static discovery, so to add in an IP for the iSCSI Target for Dynamic Discovery (referred to as the SendTargets method) we use the –D and –a switches.

1. Type the command:

```
vmkiscsi-tool -D -a 172.168.3.210 vmhba40
```

Note:

-D sets the mode of Discovery, rather than static. —a is used to add an iSCSI Target, followed by the IP address of iSCSI Device and the HBA that will be used.

2. To list the targets configured use:

```
vmkiscsi-tool -l -T vmhba40
```

Note:

This should report the IQN name and the Target IP address and port number

Forcing a Rescan of the iSCSI Adapter

1. You might wish to list the current LUNs/Disk currently visible with:

```
ls -l /vmfs/devices/disks
```

Note:

I have two internal disks on an internal SCSI Controller (vmhba0:0 and vmhba0:1).

I also have JBOD with six disks inside (vmhba1:1-6).

2. **Force the rescan** with:

```
esxcfg-swiscsi -s
```

Note:

This should produce the following result:

```
Scanning vmhba40...
Rescanning vmhba40...done.
On scsi2, removing:.
On scsi2, adding: 0:0 0:1.
```

3. If we run the ls command again we can see the 20GB LUNs from my iSCSI box:

Using the vmkiscsi command

Note:

The vmkiscsi command has lots of switches. Here are some of its options:

- To view the discovery settings:

```
vmkiscsi-tool -D vmhba40
```

Will return:

```
=========Discovery Properties for Adapter
vmhba40=========
iSnsDiscoverySettable    : 0
iSnsDiscoveryEnabled     : 0
staticDiscoverySettable  : 0
staticDiscoveryEnabled   : 0
sendTargetsDiscoverySettable : 0
sendTargetsDiscoveryEnabled  : 1
slpDiscoverySettable  : 0
Discovery Status: Done.
DISCOVERY ADDRESS         : 172.168.3.210:3260

Static Discovery not supported for this adapter
```

- To list LUNs:

```
vmkiscsi-tool -L vmhba40
```

Will return:

```
Target iqn.2006-06.com.vi3book.com:storage.lvm:
---------------------------------------------
OS DEVICE NAME    :vmhba40:0:10
BUS NUMBER            : 0
TARGET ID            : 0
LUN ID               : 1


---------------------------------------------
OS DEVICE NAME        : vmhba40:0:11
```

```
BUS NUMBER                  : 0
TARGET ID                   : 0
LUN ID                      : 11
-----------------------------------------------
```

- To view physical settings of iSCSI "nic":

```
vmkiscsi-tool -P vmhba40
```

Will return:

```
=========PHBA Properties for Adapter
vmhba40=========
VENDOR                      : VMware
MODEL                       : VMware-Isoft
DESCRIPTION                 : VMware Software
Initiator
SERIAL NUMBER               :

=========Node Properties for Adapter
vmhba40=========
NODE NAME VALID             : 1
NODE NAME                   : iqn.1998-
01.com.vmware:esx2-1f199fe7
NODE ALIAS VALID            : 1
NODE ALIAS                  :
esx1.vi3book.com
NODE NAME AND ALIAS SETTABLE: 1
```

Creating a VMFS Volume

Using FDISK to Create Partition

1. Logon to the Service Console as ROOT type:

```
fdisk /vmfs/device/disks/vmhba40:0:0:0
```

Note:

Under ESX 2.x we would have needed to know how Linux addressed this disk/LUN with /dev/sd. Syntax. This is no longer required.

2. Type N to create a new partition.

---

3. Type P for a Primary partition.

4. Choose 1 for the Partition Number.

5. Accept the defaults for First Cylinder and Last Cylinder.

Note:

This creates a partition which uses all of the free space on the disk. Fdisk defaults to being a Linux type of "83" which describes an ext3 partition. This case is not good for our VMFS partition which use a partition type of "fb"

6. Type P to print out the partition table (make a mental note of the partition number here).

7. Type T to change the File System Type.

8. Type the Hex Code of fb: (the code for a VMFS partition).

Note:

This should give the result:

```
Changed system type of partition 1 to fb (Un-
known)
```

9. Hex codes tell the system what file system partition will support – 07 NTFS, 82 Linux Swap, 83 Linux File System, FB for VMFS and FC for VMware Core Dump. At this stage the VI Client would identify the partition as VMFS unformatted.

10. Type W to write your partition table changes to the hard drive – it will give you this status information:

```
The partition table has been altered!

Calling ioctl() to re-read partition table.
Syncing disks.
```

Note:

If you re-run fdisk /vmfs/device/disks/vmhba40:0:0:0 and choose P to display the partition table

1. Logon to the Service Console as ROOT.

2. To format the new partition with the VMFS file system type:

```
vmkfstools —C vmfs3 vmhbaA:T:L:V
```

In my case the hard disk partition is located on the Adapter 40, TARGET 0, LUN 0 on Volume/Partition 1.

So I would type:

```
vmkfstools -C vmfs3 —S iscsi-lun0
/vmfs/devices/disks/vmhba40:0:0:1
```

Warning:

Please note it is an UPPERCASE C you type here. A lowercase c creates a vmdk file. You can specify —b flag to set a block-size. You would need to do this if you thought any one of your virtual disks were going to be greater than 256GB in size.

We can use 1MB, 2MB, 4MB, or 8MB. When entering a size, indicate the unit type by adding a suffix of m or M. The unit type is not case sensitive. vmkfstools interprets either m or M to mean megabytes.

- 2m allows 512GB max file size

- 4m allows 1024GB max file size

- 8m allows 2048GB max file size

Note:

This should give the result like so:

```
Creating file system on "vmhba40:0:0:1" with blockSize
1048576 and volume label "iscsi-lun0."
Successfully created new volume: 44a7bcf0-8b87cb86-9403-
00065bec0eb6
```

Note:

I repeated this for my other iSCSI LUN 1

```
fdisk /vmfs/devices/disks/vmhba40:0:1:0
vmkfstools -C vmfs3 —S iscsi-lun1
/vmfs/devices/disks/vmhba40:0:1:1
```

Note:

If we re-run ls –l /vmfs/volumes we will see this lots of juicy information. The VI Client looks like this:

Storage					Refresh
Identification		Device	Capacity	Free	Type
iscsi-lun0		vmhba40:0:0:1	19.75 GB	19.14 GB	vmfs3
iscsi-lun1		vmhba40:0:1:1	19.75 GB	19.14 GB	vmfs3
isos		nfs1.rtfm-ed.co.uk:isos	74.53 GB	19.60 GB	nfs
local2-esx1		vmhba1:4:0:1	68.25 GB	21.39 GB	vmfs3
local-esx1		vmhba0:1:0:1	33.75 GB	4.43 GB	vmfs3
nas-vms		nfs1.rtfm-ed.co.uk:nas-vms	74.53 GB	19.60 GB	nfs
templates		nfs1.rtfm-ed.co.uk:templates	74.53 GB	19.60 GB	nfs

Changing the Volume Label

Note:
To do this you need to know the UUID of your VMFS volume.

1. Type the command:

    ```
    ls —l /vmfs/volumes
    ```

    Note:

    The UUID is the value in blue. So the fixed and unchanging volume id is actually something like:

```
/vmfs/volumes/44a38c72-156b2590-be15-
00065bec0eb7
```

2. Type the command:

```
ln -sf /vmfs/volumes/44a38c72-156b2590-be15-
00065bec0eb7
vmfs/volumes/esx1-local
```

Note:

The LN makes symbolic links (a bit like shortcuts), −s makes/changes a "symbolic" link, -f over-writes the existing symbolic link.

Viewing VMFS Volumes/Partition Information

Type the command:

```
vmkfstools -P /vmfs/volumes/local-esx1
```

Note:

This returns information like so:

```
VMFS-3.21 file system spanning 1 partitions.
File system label (if any): local
Mode: public
Capacity 73282879488 (69888 file blocks * 1048576),
41889562624 (39949
locks) avail
UUID: 44a6c956-66056236-c671-00065bec0eb6
Partitions spanned:
        vmhba1:4:0:1
```

Note:

For NAS data store it would look like this:

```
NFS-1.00 file system spanning 1 partitions.
File system label (if any): iso
Mode: public
Capacity 80023715840 (19537040 file blocks * 4096),
25076690944 (6122239 blocks) avail
UUID: ab184e34-6f68911d-0000-000000000000
Partitions spanned:
        nfs:iso
```

Viewing Available Physical Disk Space

Note:

1. Logon to the Service Console as ROOT

2. Type:

   ```
   df -h (the linux method)
   ```

   or

   ```
   vdf -h (the VM Kernel Method)
   ```

```
Filesystem                              Size    Used   Avail  Use%  Mounted on
/dev/sda2                               2.0G    1.3G   630M   67%   /
/dev/sda1                                46M     15M    29M   35%   /boot
/dev/sda5                               2.0G     33M   1.9G    2%   /home
none                                    132M       0   132M    0%   /dev/shm
/dev/sda7                               494M    8.1M   461M    2%   /tmp
/dev/sda6                               992M    249M   693M   27%   /var
/dev/sda9                                28G    1.4G    25G    6%   /vmimages
/vmfs/devices                           591G       0   591G    0%   /vmfs/devices
/vmfs/volumes/2cf78959-22cd65c7
                                         74G     54G    19G   73%   /vmfs/volumes/isos
/vmfs/volumes/44a38c72-156b2590-be15-00065bec0eb7
                                         33G     28G   5.1G   84%   /vmfs/volumes/local-esx1
/vmfs/volumes/44a6c956-66056236-c671-00065bec0eb6
                                         68G     46G    21G   68%   /vmfs/volumes/local2-esx1
/vmfs/volumes/44a7be3d-ab15e6a9-4abe-00065bec0eb6
                                         19G    626M    19G    3%   /vmfs/volumes/iscsi-lun0
/vmfs/volumes/44a7c03d-159649b5-0e6a-00065bec0eb6
                                         19G    626M    19G    3%   /vmfs/volumes/iscsi-lun1
/vmfs/volumes/554f516c-ba779540
                                         74G     54G    19G   73%   /vmfs/volumes/nas-vms
/vmfs/volumes/a857137a-a6f3c023
                                         74G     54G    19G   73%   /vmfs/volumes/templates
```

Note:

The partition table for /sda does NOT follow the recommendations for ESX 3.x – this partition table was taken for an upgraded ESX 2.x server.

Note:

If you wish to see how the vmhba syntax relates to /dev/sd you will find that you can still use old ESX 2.x command "vmkpcidivy -q vmhba_devs." However, it has been hugely depreciated – and instead you should use:

```
esxcfg-vmhbadevs —q
```

While returns:

```
vmhba0:0:0 /dev/sda
vmhba0:1:0 /dev/sdb
vmhba1:2:0 /dev/sdc
vmhba1:3:0 /dev/sdd
vmhba1:4:0 /dev/sde
vmhba1:5:0 /dev/sdf
vmhba1:6:0 /dev/sdg
vmhba40:0:0 /dev/sdh
```

```
vmhba40:0:1 /dev/sdi
```

Note

If you want to see all of the information together (vmhba ID, the linux /dev name, LVM id and VMFS volume label) you can use this perl script:

```
#!/usr/bin/perl
@array = `/usr/sbin/esxcfg-vmhbadevs -m`;

foreach (@array)
{
        ($vmk, $cos, $uuid) = split;
        ($tmp, $label) = split (/:/,
`/usr/sbin/vmkfstools -P /vmfs/volumes/${uuid} | grep
"File system label"`);
        print "$vmk \t $cos \t $uuid \t $label\n"; }
```

This produces an output like so:

```
vmhba0:1:0:1 /dev/sdb1 7458-66sb-fsc0-43fs isos
```

Note:

This only shows me my VMFS, not my NAS datastores.

Managing Storage Devices

You can use a couple of commands to handle storage devices. Some of these have already been mentioned like the command esxcfg-swiscsi -s to rescan the iSCSI Adapter(s). For those of you who come from ESX 2.x background it looks like cos-rescan.sh has been discontinued; its functionality has *probably* been integrated into the –s switch.

Forcing a rescan of Fibre Channel Device

To force a rescan of the fibre channel device, type the following command:

```
vmkfstools -s vmhba1
```

Note:

You can also use **esxcfg-rescan vmhba***N* to be rescanned as well which gives this kind of output:

```
Rescanning vmhba1...done.
On scsi1, removing: 2:0 3:0 4:0 5:0 6:0.
On scsi1, adding: 2:0 3:0 4:0 5:0 6:0.
```

Managing SCSI Reservations of LUN's

Occasionally, things go wrong with the SCSI Reservations or locking of LUNs. One example is when, through a configuration error, an SCSI reservation (lock) is put on an LUN, which subsequently doesn't get released. Until an LUN is released you won't be able to manage the file system. Typically, these types of reservation problems happen in VM clustering scenarios where the clustering software inside a VM malfunctions. This SCSI Reservations or locking can be controlled manually by using the –L switch on vmkfstools...

```
-L reserve .
```

This reserves the specified LUN. After the reservation, only the server that reserved that particular LUN can access it. If other servers attempt to access that LUN, they will get a reservation error!

```
-L release .
```

This releases the reservation on the specified LUN. Any other server can access the LUN again.

```
-L lunreset
```

This resets the specified LUN by clearing any reservation on the LUN and making the LUN available to all servers again. The reset does not affect any of the other LUNs on the device. If another LUN on the device is reserved, it remains reserved.

`-L targetreset .`

This resets the entire target. The reset clears any reservations on all the LUNs associated with that target and makes the LUNs available to all servers again.

`-L busreset .`

This resets all accessible targets on the bus. The reset clears any reservation on all the LUNs accessible through the bus and makes them available to all servers again.

This command uses the device parameter and so uses the following:

`/vmfs/devices/disks/vmhbaA:T:L:V syntax`

Using USB storage Devices

USB device drivers are loaded automatically by default. This can be disabled by modifying /etc/modules.conf and remarking out with # the line which begins alias usb-controller usb-ohci. If someone has done this – then you can load the modules (drivers) manually and access the device as needed using the insmod command.

You will need to think about what file system to use on a removable USB device. You can read but not write to an NTFS partition at the Service Console, and only FAT32 is supported for read/write. Windows does not inelegantly understand the Linux file system of EXT3. However, there are some free EXT3 drivers for Windows (the one I use currently only works on NT4, W2K and WXP, not W2K3).

http://uranus.it.swin.edu.au/~jn/linux/ext2ifs.htm

You might prefer to use EXT3 if you wish to convert virtual disks in a more portable format suitable for transfer to a removable hard-drive. In my case it was very easy to configure. I plugged the USB device into the server. It came up with a message – and said it allocated the id of /dev/sdc to the disk so all I had to do was mount it with:

```
mkdir /mnt/usbdisk
mount /dev/sdc1 /mnt/usbdisk
```
Note:

If this doesn't happen you might find the information documented below useful:

Systems using the USB-UHCI device driver with the USB 2.0 interface can cause ESX Server to show a false warning message during the boot sequence. The error looks like this on boot-up:

```
Mar 29 11:04:10 VM'server1 rc.sysinit: Initializing USB
controller (usb-uhci): succeeded

Mar 29 11:04:10 VM'server1 modprobe: Hint: insmod errors
can be caused by incorrect module parameters, including
invalid IO or IRQ parameters

Mar 29 11:04:10 VM'server1 modprobe: /lib/modules/2.4.9-
vmnix2/kernel/drivers/usb/usb-ohci.o: init_module: No
such device

Mar 29 11:04:10 VM'server1 modprobe: /lib/modules/2.4.9-
vmnix2/kernel/drivers/usb/usb-ohci.o: insmod
/lib/modules/2.4.9-mnix2/kernel/drivers/usb/usb-ohci.o
failed

Mar 29 11:04:10 VM'server1 modprobe: /lib/modules/2.4.9-
vmnix2/kernel/drivers/usb/usb-ohci.o: insmod usb-ohci
failed

Mar 29 11:04:10 VM'server1 rc.sysinit: Initializing USB
controller (usb-ohci): failed
```
Note:

It is safe to ignore this message, but if you want to configure your system so that this warning does not appear the next time you boot your ESX Server machine, follow these steps. VMware KB Article 1659 outlines the issues involved:

http://www.vmware.com/support/kb/enduser/std_adp.php?p_faqid=1659

If you want to use a USB hard-drive to copy files from the ESX server to it – and you have these errors -then a general work around is to boot to a Knoppix Boot CD and do it that way. Remember if you are copying virtual disks – convert into the correct format first.

If you have no errors like me, this is how you can go about using USB hard-rives and devices.

There are 3 USB host controller interface types (OHCI, UHCI and EHCI). To list what type of USB controller you have, you can use the command below:

```
lspci -v | grep HCI
```

Note:

My server returned:

```
00:0f.2 USB Controller: ServerWorks OSB4/CSB5 OHCI USB
Controller (rev 5) (prog-if 10 [OHCI])
        Subsystem: ServerWorks OSB4/CSB5 OHCI USB Con-
troller
```

so once I know my server I know I need to load the OHCI driver, not the UHCI or EHCI driver.

1. Logon to the Service Console as ROOT.

2. [Optionally] Load up the USB Device Drivers:

```
insmod usbcore
insmod usb-storage
modprobe usb-ochi or modprobe usb-uhci or mod-
probe ehci
```

3. Use the **dmesg | grep usb** to print out a list of active devices and scroll up to locate Initializing USB Mass Storage Driver....

usb.c: registered new driver usbdevfs

usb.c: registered new driver hub

usb-ohci.c: USB OHCI at membase 0xd20c6000, IRQ 18

usb-ohci.c: usb-01:00.0, Advanced Micro Devices [AMD] AMD-8111 USB

usb.c: new USB bus registered, assigned bus number 1

usb-ohci.c: USB OHCI at membase 0xd20c8000, IRQ 18

usb-ohci.c: usb-01:00.1, Advanced Micro Devices [AMD] AMD-8111 USB (#2)

usb.c: new USB bus registered, assigned bus number 2

usb.c: registered new driver hiddev

usb.c: registered new driver hid

Note:

The system assigns an SCSI device ID to the USB device (even though it's likely to be IDE Laptop Disk if it's a portable hard-drive). The critical bits are references to the SDG. This tells me the USB device has been added to the end of all my other SCSI disks (sda, sdb, sdc). This will help me in the next stage which is creating a mount point and mounting the partition on the USB disk.

Adding additional hard-drives to the system can upset this allocation of sd$n$.

4. **Create a mount point** with:

```
mkdir /mnt/usbdisk
```

5. Mount the first partition on the disk with:

```
mount /dev/sdg1 /mnt/usbdisk
```

Note:

If you are unsure about the partition scheme on the disk you can use **fdisk –l /dev/sdg** to print the partition table.

6. **List Files** and Start using the disk with

```
ls –l /mnt/usbdisk
```

7. **Unmount the USB device when finished** using:

```
cd /
umount /mnt/usb
```

Managing Groups & Users

Creating User and Groups

You can create groups and users local to the ESX host using the groupadd, useradd and set passwords with passwd command. If I wanted to create a group called "esxops" I would use:

```
groupadd esxops
```

To create a user with the login name of herolds, and friendly name of Scott Herold I would use:

```
useradd –c "Scott Herold" herolds
```

By default all users created this way are disabled until you set a password for them. You can do that with:

```
passwd herolds
```

Note:

Without changing the password libraries used in ESX, passwords can be of any length and complexity, even dictionary words.

If you want to set a password during the creation of the user, you can do this by specifying an MD5 hashed version of the password. Below is a sample where the long string in little 'quotes' represents the password of *password*

```
useradd -p '$1$Rg69B9QA$JUtqStBrjNFbyzyP9zTsf0' -c "Mike
Laverick" lavericm
```

If you want to know an MD5 hash for a given password all you have to do is create a user, and set the password. Then cat the contents of /etc/shadow. This will list the username and their corresponding MD5 hash like so:

```
lav-
ericm:$1$Rg69B9QA$JUtqStBrjNFbyzyP9zTsf0:13587:0:90:7:::
bob:$1$ZIx4R9BE$PDniTkVdtrnyOH0uJUEcI.:13589:0:90:7:::
herolds:$1$CHrrCI79$Zt.YgyzbMjhFNuM62pUg30:13589:0:90:7:
::
ron:$1$QYIt/f1V$8iHZEezwJ7WtTwkWMb0xX1:13589:0:90:7:::
```

The MD5 hash is value-highlighted in bold between the two colons. Users Bob, Herolds, and Ron all have the same password of "vmware" but MD5 hash is not a clear text representation of the password. So even if you use the same password the MD5 hash always changes.

MD5 hash is useful in post-configuration options in kickstart scripts for creating users without showing the password in the kickstart script itself.

Configuring SU

By default, anyone who knows the root password can use the SU command. SU can be used to Switch User, and is most commonly used to become root. We can offer some security against that by configuring the special group called "wheel." When the wheel group is configured only its members have the rights to use su – command. Additionally, a log of users who do elevate their rights is logged in /var/log/messages.

Effectively, this means that to use SU you must know both the root password and also be member of the wheel group. Root access can then be quickly granted or denied by changing group membership without forcing a password reset on the root account.

1. Logon to the Service Console as ROOT.

2. Edit the /etc/hosts.allow file with:

```
nano -w /etc/hosts.allow
```

3. Add the line:

```
vmware-authd:    <IP>: allow
```

Note:

Where <IP> is the IP address of your server.

4. We can then add a user to the Wheel group with:

```
usermod -G wheel herolds
```

Note:

usermod is used to modify existing users – so here user herolds is being added to the wheel group. If you want to add users to groups as you create them you would use:

```
useradd -p '$1$Rg69B9QA$JUtqStBrjNFbyzyP9zTsf0'
-c "Scott Herold" herolds -G wheel,esxops
```

This creates a user called Scott Herold with a password of password and added to the wheel group. You can add a user to additional groups by separating them with a comma.

You can view group membership by cat /etc/group. Within this file you will see the groups followed by a list of users separated by commas.

5. Next we will edit the /etc/pa.d/su file to enable the wheel feature

```
nano -w /etc/pam.d/su
```

6. remove the # comment on the line:

```
#auth        required
/lib/security/$ISA/pam_wheel.so use_uid
```

7. Save and Exit nano.

   Note:

   If you login with an ordinary user account and attempt to use su –
   and you are not a member of the wheel group you receive this
   message:

   ```
   Password:
   su: incorrect password
   ```

   But if you are member of the wheel group – access is granted.

Configuring Sudo

Sudo is a delegation system. If you are familiar with Windows, it is not unlike
the "Run As.." option which allows you to run tools and utilities under the context of another user. More specifically, this allows the root administrator in
ESX to allow ordinary users to use high-level commands normally only available if you are logged in as root - without having to disclose the root accounts
password. This is even more flexible than the su - command which requires
you to know the password of root to proceed. Sudo is configured by text file
called /etc/sudoers and has its own editor called visudo. The visudo utility is a
hybrid of the Linux VI text editor tool, but additionally it locks the
/etc/sudoers file (to prevent administrative conflicts during configuration) and
ensures that the syntax of the file is correct after you save and exit. This syntax
checking is the single biggest reason to use visudo instead of vanilla text editor.

SUDO has a number of features. We can use wildcards to allow us to configure
the sudoers file once, and then copy it to many servers. We can create com-
mand-alias, which acts as grouping of commands. For example, we could create
a command alias called "ESXCMD" that represents all the esxcfg commands.
When we come to grant the right to run the esxcfg commands we only have to
mention "ESXCMD" once in the sudoers file rather than list every command.
Once this has been done we can use our user groups in ESX to say which

commands alias are accessible to our operators. Below is a simple example of how I would give my ordinary ESX operators access to advanced commands:

1. **Logon to the Service Console as ROOT.**
2. Type the command:

   Visudo
3. Press [I] to enter **Insert Mode.**
4. Below the entry which begins # Host alias specification add the Host_Alias option:

   # Host alias specification
   Host_Alias ESXSERVERS = 192.168.3.0/24

   Note:
   This IP address which is specified in the CIDR format allows the sudoers file to be portable to other ESX host in the same network ID.
5. Locate the entry which begins # Cmnd alias specification and add some test command alias options:

   # Cmnd alias specification
   Cmnd_Alias ESXCMD = /usr/sbin/esxcfg-NIC's, /usr/sbin/vmkfstools
   Cmnd_Alias NOEXEC = /usr/sbin/esxcfg-vswitch, esxcfg-vswif

   Note:
   Here I am creating two command aliases. ESXCMD will be used to allow a group called esxops access to the commands vmkfstools and esxcfg-NIC's. In contrast NOEXE will be used to stop access to the esxcfg-vswitch and esxcfg-vswif.
6. Below the lines:

   # Uncomment to allow people in group wheel to run all commands
   # %wheel   ALL=(ALL)   ALL

   Uncomment the # so the %wheel users are not restricted and add another group entry to control the ESX operators.

   # Uncomment to allow people in group wheel to run all commands
   %wheel   ALL=(ALL)   ALL
   %esxops ESXSERVERS = ESXCMD, !NOEXE

   Note:
   The exclamation mark next to the NOEXE command alias means do not allow access. I created esxops group earlier with the groupadd command:

7. Press [**ESC**] to exit insert mode and enter command mode.
8. Type **:w** to save your changes.
9. Type **:q!** to exit the visudo.

Testing your configuration:

Firstly, make sure that you have a user in the group you gave access to with sudo.

Login as the user:

Type the command **sudo /usr/sbin/vmkfstools**

Type the command **sudo /usr/sbin/esxcfg-NIC's**

If you have been following this guide to the letter these two commands should execute perfectly well. The next two commands should result in an error message:

Type the command **sudo /usr/sbin/esxcfg-vswitch**

Type the command **sudo /usr/sbin/esxcfg-vswif**

```
"Sorry user X is not allowed to execute '/usr/sbin/
esxcfg-vswitch -l' as root on esx1.vi3book.com"
```
User X can use sudo -1 to see which commands they could run.

Note:

In this case I choose to use the wheel group as a way of granting access to SU. This example could be modified to limit the wheel group to set off commands, and deny them access to the SU command.

SSH Login Banners

Many businesses have security policies that enforce a pop-up message warning about unauthorized access to a given system. In some locations such warnings are required if you wish to take legal proceedings against offenders who breach security. Without such a warning offenders can sometimes be acquitted on a mere legal technicality. To enable a banner for SSH access:

1. **Create a message file** with something like:

   ```
   nano —w /etc/ssh/banner.txt
   ```

   Note:

   Cut and paste your business standard message.

2. **Save and Exit nano.**

3. **Then edit sshd_config** to use the banner message:

   ```
   nano —w /etc/ssh/sshd_config
   ```

   locate the #banner entry

   remove the comment and add

   ```
   banner /etc/ssh/banner.txt
   ```

4. **Save and Exit.**

5. **Restart SSH** with:

   ```
   service sshd restart
   ```

   Note:

   The banner message appears after the user has supplied a user-name, but before the user supplies a password.

   Note:

   The sshd_config has an AllowUsers and DenyUsers option if you wish to allow a user Service Console access but not via SSH:

   ```
   AllowUsers lavericm ron herolds
   ```

```
DenyUsers beavers klinek
```

Users beavers and klinek would be able to log on but only at the physical console using say an ILO card.

Setting up LDAP Authentication on ESX

The Service Console is Light-weight Directory Access (LDAP) aware; it is possible to configure ESX to authenticate against Active Directory or any other LDAP complainant directory service. This allows you to centralize access from LDAP system and password resets. To understand why might you want to do this you need to understand how Service Console user accounts work.

Even with VirtualCenter, if you want to give every employee in the IT department access to the Service Console with PuTTy you would have to create many accounts within ESX. This can be a burden. If we have 10 ESX hosts with 10 employees, I would have to create 100 users altogether – ten accounts on each server. This is because the Service Console model for users is essentially a workgroup model. No attempt by default is used to authenticate to an external database of users.

If a user needs to change their password they would have to login 10 times to 10 different ESX hosts, and use either VI Client or the Linux command "passwd" to reset their password. Even if we used the same user name 10 times on 10 different ESX hosts – and the same user name in Active Directory – the user could have potentially 11 different passwords to remember (10 on 10 ESX hosts, and one in Active Directory).

The next disadvantage comes when I want to disable access for a single employee leaving the business. I would have to disable or delete the user 10 times on ten different ESX hosts.

Configuring ESX to authenticate against LDAP would solve *some* of these problems. Active Directory could then be used to reset passwords and disable user accounts. However, it does not fix the first problem – creating the users on each ESX. Nor does the system support deleting the user accounts when they no longer required. There are a number of ways of dealing with this problem. You could buy commercial software which synchronizes named users and groups in your directory service – this software automates the creation and deletion of users as you create and delete them in your LDAP service. Alternatively, a number of talented users on the forum have written scripts that do all this for you for free.

However, these end-user scripts do not come with commercial support, and some large companies might balk at the thought of using scripts that manipulate their LDAP environment for obvious reasons. Steve Beaver, who reviewed this very book, wrote one such excellent script. Steve currently works in Florida, and has co-authored a book about scripting in VMware. You can find Steve's ldap_search tool hosted on Scott's www.vmuguru.com site.

For now we will focus on creating users on the command-line in the Service Console, and reconfiguring ESX to speak to Microsoft Active Directory (Windows 2003 with Service Pack 1).

VMware now provide a handy tool called esxcfg-auth which will allow us to set up the PAM. This is easier than it used to be as the utility edits all the files for us, rather than us having to do that manually.

GOTCHA:

Before you even bother using the esxcfg-auth command, confirm with the ESX host that you can use ping or nslookup against the name of your Active Directory domain. Secondly, verify that the time of the Active Directory server is the same (offset by any time zone difference obliviously) as the ESX host. PAM has a very low tolerance of time difference between the LDAP server and the LDAP Client (the Service Console).

1. Open a session at the Service Console as ROOT.

2. Confirm you have DNS name resolution to the Active Directory domain with

    ```
    nslookup mydomain.com
    ```

3. The syntax of the esxcfg-auth command is:

    ```
    esxcfg-auth --enablead --addomain mydomain.com
    --addc mydc.mydomain.com --enablekrb5 --
    ```

```
krb5realm=mydomain.com --krb5kdc
mydc.mydomain.com --krb5adminserver
mydc.mydomain.com
```

Note:

The switches --enablead, --addomain and --addc are required; if you wish to support Kerberos authentication then you must use the --krb5realm which requires --krb5kdc and krb5adminserver. If you use Kerberos the escfg-auth command will automatically open kerberos and activeDirectorKerberos. Use esxcfg-firewall –q to view these as "Enabled Services."

So if I have a domain called vi3book.com with a domain controller called dc1.vi3book.com I would type:

```
esxcfg-auth --enablead --addomain vi3book.com -
-addc dc1.vi3book.com --enablekrb5 --
krb5realm=vi3book.com --krb5kdc dc1.vi3book.com
--krb5adminserver dc1.vi3book.com
```

Note:

Actually, naming a server like dc1 is quite poor practice. If DC1 was down we would find that users would not be authenticated. It is actually better practice to allow DNS lookups to find "Service Records" (type SRV) which assist in locating the Knowledge Consistency Checker (kdc). A better format for this command would be:

```
esxcfg-auth --enablead --addomain vi3book.com -
-addc vi3book.com --enablekrb5 --
krb5realm=vi3book.com --krb5kdc vi3book.com --
krb5adminserver dc1.vi3book.com
```

4. Next create a user at the Service Console *without a password:*

```
useradd testuser
```

Note:

Remember if you create a user with useradd which does not possess a password it is disabled by default. Next, open "Active Directory Users and Computers" and create a user in the Organization

Unit structure with the *same name as the user created with useradd* – set a password which corresponds with your datacenter policy.

You can easily validate your setup by changing the password in Active Directory and disabling accounts. If you disable testuser in Active Directory the user receives the Access Denied Message.

GOTCHA:

Currently esxcfg-auth only covers Active Directory authentication for console access. It does not work with the VI Client. If you want VI Client authentication to Active Directory you really need VirtualCenter.

Resetting a lost root password

If you forget or lose the root password, it is very easy to reset. There is no need for any special "root" kits or hacking tools. We simply reboot the ESX host and run it in a different run-level. Run-levels allow different levels of functionality to Linux/Unix based OS and are set in /etc/inittab. For example, run-level 3 allows high levels of functionality but does not run any GUI front-end. Whereas run-level 5 would allow high levels of functionality with a GUI front-end (if one had been installed). Run-level 1 runs the VMkernel or the Linux kernel in single user mode without prompting the user for a login or password. It logs you in automatically as root with a challenge. For this reason it's absolutely critical that you physically secure your servers, and password to protect any ILO, RAC or IP-based KVM system from unauthorized access.

To reset a lost root password:

1. Reboot your ESX host.

2. At the GRUB menu move the cursor to stop the timeout operation.

3. Select Service Console Only (troubleshooting mode).

4. Press [A] to pass arguments/parameters to the boot loader.

5. Type [1] to set temporary use of run-level 1 at the end of the prompt that reads

    ```
    mem=272M tblsht 1
    ```

6. then press [Enter].

7. Allow the boot process to continue.

8. At the sh-*n.nnn#* prompt type the command:

```
passwd
```

this will reset your root password as fits your datacenter policies.

9. Type the command:

```
Reboot
```

This will restart your ESX host.

Setting up NTP on ESX

The Network Time Protocol (NTP) client is used to keep the ESX host physical clock in synch with a more accurate time source. This is critical configuration because in 99% of the time VMs receive their time updates via VMware Tools from the ESX host. I say 99% of the time because there some circumstances where the time configuration of a VM is different. A case in point is running Active Directory inside a VM and the domain controller is Primary Domain Controller Emulator (PDC). You should consult the VMware KB article 1318 which outlines the special considerations required to make time synchronization work for AD.

http://www.vmware.com/support/kb/enduser/std_adp.php?p_faqid=1318

As we saw, time can create dependencies with other systems such as authenticating to LDAP service such as Active Directory at the ESX host.

Most ESX hosts are not given access to the Internet for security reasons so it is likely you will need to point them to an internal NTP service which then in turn communicates to the Internet for a publicly accessible list of NTP servers. When you select a pool of NTP servers on the Internet as your time source it is recommended you select one close to your geographic location. Most NTP servers on the Internet will use a geographical DNS sub-zone to indicate this, such as "europe.pool.ntp.org."

You might find these URLs useful when looking for a publicly accessible NTP service:

http://www.pool.ntp.org/

http://www.ntp.org/

NTP servers are listed by their stratum number. The smaller the number the close your source NTP server is to the most accurate time source currently available from an atomic clock. NTP is UDP-based using port 123, so this will need opening on the connection to the Internet for this work.

Setting up a Simple NTP Server/Client on Linux

In this case the Linux service is going to be an external time source client and also server time to my ESX hosts. My example uses Redhat Linux as the NTP Server/Client.

1. Edit the /etc/ntp.conf file and locate the line:

   ```
   # restrict 192.168.1.0 mask 255.255.255.0
   notrust nomodify notrap
   ```

2. Uncomment the line and adjust the network ID to reflect the ESX host Service Console network. In my case:

   ```
   restrict 192.168.3.0 mask 255.255.255.0 notrust
   nomodify notrap
   ```

3. Locate the section of the ntp.conf which begins

   ```
   # server mytrustedtimeserverip and add the list
   of NTP servers.  Below is my list of publicly
   accessible NTP hosts from ntp.org:
   # server mytrustedtimeserverip
   server 0.uk.pool.ntp.org
   server 1.uk.pool.ntp.org
   server 2.uk.pool.ntp.org
   server 3.uk.pool.ntp.org
   ```

Note:

Here I change the entry to reflect my IP settings.

4. Save the ntp.conf file.

5. Start the ntp daemon and ensure it starts with every subsequent reboot with:

```
service ntpd start
chkroot ntpd on
```

Note:

You can check your configuration with ntpq –p. If you do not receive a positive response, check that your firewall within Linux allows UDP 123 outgoing and that your physical firewall has rules enabled to allow your NTP server access to the internet. Additionally, you might also wish to check DNS name resolution to the external Internet-based NTP servers.

Enabling the NTP Client on an ESX Host

1. Open a Session to the Service Console as ROOT.

2. **Open the ESX firewall to allow the NTP Client** with:

```
esxcfg-firewall -e ntpClient
```

Note:

Confirm this was successful with esxcfg-firewall –q

3. You can enforce time synchronization with the command-line tool:

ntpupdate –u ntp1.vi3book.com

Note: Positive Responses

In my case

```
19 Mar 10:50:02 ntpdate[3308]: adjust time
server 192.168.3.211 offset 0.010533 sec
```

Note: Troubleshooting Negative Responses

If you fail to receive a positive response – try ping ntp1.vi3book.com. If you receive responses check that the firewall on the NTP Client/Server is open for UDP 123 Inbound. You can confirm this by checking if the service is accessible by using telnet 123 ntp1.vi3book.com from a machine that is on the same network as the ntp.

4. **Edit the /etc/ntp.conf** file and locate the line:

```
# restrict 192.168.1.0 mask 255.255.255.0
notrust nomodify notrap
```

5. Uncomment the line and adjust the network ID to reflect the ESX host Service Console network. In my case this would be:

```
restrict 192.168.3.0 mask 255.255.255.0 notrust
nomodify notrap
```

6. **Locate the section of the ntp.conf which begins:**

 # server mytrustedtimeserverip

and add list of NTP servers. Below is my list of internally accessible NTP hosts for vi3book.com

server mytrustedtimeserverip

server ntp1.vi3book.com

server ntp2.vi3book.com

Note:

We can list more than one NTP server or use DNS round-robin to provide fault-tolerance to the NTP source. You may also wish to add these entries to your /etc/hosts file to cover yourself from potential DNS failures.

7. Save the ntp.conf file.

8. **Start the ntp daemon and ensure it starts with every subsequent reboot** with:

```
service ntpd start
chkroot ntpd on
```

Note:

Again, you can check your configuration with the ntpq –p command.

Renaming an ESX Host

Occasionally, you might need to change the identity of an ESX host. There is a simple method from the VI Client and a more convoluted method from the command-line. The advantage of renaming an ESX host from the command-line is that you do not have to reboot your ESX host to make the change take effect. Remember if you rename an ESX host but do not update DNS then you could experience name resolution issues. Secondly, the old name of your ESX host will still be listed in VirtualCenter. It would be good practice to remove the old host from VirtualCenter, and add in the host under its new name. If you prefer to rename an ESX host with Vi-Client:

1. Logon to the VI Client.

2. Click the Configuration Tab.

3. Under the Software pane select DNS and Routing.

4. Click the Properties…

5. Under "Host Identification" change your name and domain as you deem appropriate.

   Note:

   A reboot is not enforced, but is required for your changes to take effect. This process also regenerates any SSL certificates created for the Web Access Service during installation.

From the command-line the same procedure can be achieved by editing files, and some simple commands to restart services and processes:

1. Logon to the Service Console as ROOT and type:

   ```
   nano –w /etc/sysconfig/network
   ```

2. Edit the **HOSTNAME= entry**

3. Exit nano and type:

```
nano —w /etc/hosts
```

4. Edit the entry that reflects the name of your server.

5. If you are changing your Domain Name and DNS settings

```
nano —w /etc/resolv.conf
```

Note:

You may wish to check you can ping a name in the new domain.

6. The command hostname will tell you current FQDN. We can use hostname to change the current hostname with:

```
hostname esx10.newdomain.com
```

Note:

This steps saves you having to reboot the ESX host.

Configuring VMs

Understanding Different Virtual Disk Formats

Understanding the available disk formats is important for a whole number of operational tasks. A good example would be converting virtual disks from VMware Workstation or VMware Server into a format recognized by ESX. We can create virtual disks of different formats at the Service Console using vmkfstools with the –d switch. There are in fact eight different formats of virtual disk:

- **zerodedthick** (default)

  This disk is fully allocated at the time the virtual disk is created. This type of disk takes up the space on the disk you specify. So a 10GB zerodedthick disk would take up 10GB of space. Old deleted data is not purged from the disk except when the VM begins to write to the physical disk. This format is used on SAN and iSCSI based storage.

- **eagerzeroedthick**

  This type of disk is similar to zerodedthick, except space is allocated during the creation of disk. The vmkfstools zeroes out space the disks takes up as it is being created on the command-line. This format must be used in the cluster-in-a-box scenario and takes much longer to create than any other format.

- **thick**

  This disk is fully allocated at the time the virtual disk is created – however stale data on the disk is not over-written. The free space is over-written as needed.

- **thin**

  Space for this format of disk is created on a on-demand, as-needed basis. This format is used if you store your virtual disks on NAS based storage.

- **2gbsparse**

  This format splits the disk up into a series of files no larger than 2GB. Each of the 2gbsparse files are linked together by a smaller text file (metadata) which describes the geometries of the original disk. This format is "safe" for moving to and from other operating systems like Microsoft Windows which historically has certain tools which corrupt files larger than 2GB. This format is sometimes used in VMware Workstation. Actually the size of the 2gbspares file is the amount of data in the virtual disk. So a 10GB virtual disk with 4GB of data would result in 6 files being created (5x2GB disks plus the metadata file). However, the actual space taken up on the physical disk would be only 4GB. This format is frequently preferred for backing up the virtual disk and general archiving purposes.

- **RDM (Raw Device Mapping File)**

  As we saw earlier in Chapter 5 and Chapter 10, an RDM file is not really a virtual disk although it does have the .vmdk extension. The RDM is actually a metadata file which tells the VM how to access

LUNs natively on an SAN or iSCSI system. RDMs can be created through the VI Client. This format uses virtual compatibility, treating the native LUN as if were a virtual disk, and enables features such as VMware's "Snapshot" Feature. Again, RDMs of this format can be used in backup scenarios for backing up VMs while they are powered on. A common misconception is that RDMs offer a performance benefit. They do not. Instead the term "RAW" is used to indicate "native" where the VM formats the LUN with its native files system.

- **RDMP** (RDM in Physical Compatibility "Pass-Through" Mode)

  This is a hybrid of the RDM which access the LUN using "physical compatibility." As we saw in Chapter 10 in the "physical-to-virtual clustering" scenario this allows direct access to an LUN via the ESX host and weakens VMkernel locking procedures in favor of the locking procedures used by the clustering software.

- **RAW**

  This format is not supported in ESX 3.x.x and is there for legacy purposes when it was supported in ESX 2.x.x. This format predates even the RDM format which was introduced into ESX 2.5.x.

You can quite easily work out the format of your virtual disk (Virtual Disk, RDM or RDMP) using either via the VI Client, however the command-line will tell you a great deal more information about your virtual disks. To find out more you can view the metadata or file descriptor information. All virtual disks actually have two files – the metadata file, followed by the virtual disk's file or files. Using the Linux command "cat" we can print to a console the contents of a virtual disk's metadata file.

The print out below this paragraph shows a 2bsparse file set. It will have as its "createType" what is called "twoGbMaxExtentSparse." In the extents description it shows a sparse virtual disk is assembled from a sequence of files listed with a serial number and the word "SPARSE" as the format. As with a conventional physical disk the file will also tell about disk geometries (Cylinders, Heads and Sectors) and what kind of SCSI adapter type it uses.

```
# Disk DescriptorFile
version=1
CID=00000000
```

```
parentCID=ffffffff
createType="twoGbMaxExtentSparse"

# Extent description
RW 4192256 SPARSE "w2k3-s001.vmdk"
RW 4192256 SPARSE "w2k3-s002.vmdk"
RW 4096 SPARSE "w2k3-s003.vmdk"

# The Disk Data Base
#DDB

ddb.adapterType = "lsilogic"
ddb.geometry.sectors = "63"
ddb.geometry.heads = "255"
ddb.geometry.cylinders = "522"
ddb.toolsVersion = "5153"
ddb.virtualHWVersion = "3"
```

This information isn't tremendously exciting or thrilling but it becomes useful when seen used in practical examples.

Creating Virtual Disks

1. Power off your target virtual machine…

2. To create a virtual disk use the vmkfstools command:

    ```
    vmkfstools —a lsilogic -c 10240m
    /vmfs/volumes/local-esx1-storage/vm1/vm1_1.vmdk
    ```

    Note:

    This is lower-case –c which creates a file, upper-case –C creates a vmfs file system. Here I am following the file-naming convention that VC would normally apply. The first disk would be vm1.vmdk, and subsequent disks would be serialized with vm1_1.vmdk and vm1_2.vmdk

    The command actually creates two files vm1_1.vmdk (metadata, of a couple of KB) and an vm1_1-flat.vmdk which is 10GB in size. I could have used 1g instead of 10240m on the command-line.

The –a option allows users to indicate which device driver should be used to communicate with the virtual disk. Failure to set this could cause a question in the virtual machine on power-up depending on what SCSI Adapter controller is used in the VM. Personally, I always use LSILogic as the driver unless it is unsupported in the guest OS I am working with.

3. **Next we need to add this into the virtual machine.** We can do this by **editing the VMX file:**

```
nano —w /vmfs/volumes/local-esx1/vm1/vm1.vmx
```

4. add the lines:

```
scsi0:1.present = "true"
scsi0:1.fileName = "vm1_1.vmdk"
scsi0:1.deviceType = "scsi-hardDisk"
```

Note:

scsi0:1 means it is the next disk after the boot disk, on the first virtual SCSI adapter. True means the device is connected, filename indicates the virtual disk (metadata file only), and the device type indicates this virtual SCSI disk, not a virtual IDE drive. It's worth saying that IDE drivers are not supported in ESX 2.x.x or 3.x.x and this can sometimes cause problems for VMware Workstation users who have used that format – more about this topic shortly.

5. **Save** your VMX file **and Exit nano.**

6. Power on your virtual machine with:

```
vmware-cmd —l
```

Note:

That's a lower-case L for lima. This produces a list of registered VMs on the ESX host. We can use the vmware-cmd command with "start" option to power on a VM:

vmware-cmd /vmfs/volumes/44a38c72-156b2590-be15-00065bec0eb7/vm1/vm1**.vmx start**

Note:

In the past we used to be able to use the friendly volume label. This is no longer supported as outlined in VMware KB 2122:

http://www.vmware.com/support/kb/enduser/std_adp.php?p_faqid=21 22

Creating and Managing RDMs

There are two types of RDM – virtual compatibility mode and physical compatibility mode. These are normally set by radio button options in the VI Client. On the command-line the way these are specified is with two different switches. Remember that the main uses of RDMs are:

- Accessing existing data on a SAN/iSCSI

- Clustering inside VM'sVM's

- Running some (but not all) SAN Management Tools inside a VM

RDM for Virtual Compatibility

1. Before you begin, you may wish to check which LUNs your ESX server has access to with:

   ```
   ls -l /vmfs/devices/disks
   ```

2. Type the command:

   ```
   vmkfstools —a lsilogic -r
   /vmfs/devices/disks/vmhba40:0:0:0
   /vmfs/volumes/esx1-storage1/vm1/vm1_2.vmdk
   ```

   Note:

   This creates an RDM metadata file in /vmfs/volumes/esx1-storage1 using my iSCSI Lun on vmhba40:0:0:0. It creates two files as in the –c example, a metadata file called vm1_2.vmdk and a vm_2-rdm.vmdk file. Usefully, VMware automatically appends –rdm to the end of the file for us. The metadata file MUST be stored on a VMFS partition – it cannot reside on an NAS DataStore. You do have to specify the last 0 in vmhba40:0:0:**0**. This last 0 indicates you wish to use the entire LUN. You cannot create an RDM file to a specific partition WITHIN an LUN.

3. Next we need to add this into the virtual machine. We can do this by editing the VMX file:

```
nano -w /vmfs/volumes/local-esx1/vm1/vm1.vmx
```

4. add the lines:

```
scsi0:2.present = "true"
scsi0:2.fileName = " vm1_1.vmdk"
```

RDM for Physical Compatibility

Physical compatibility (required for physical to virtual clustering) is set up in a very similar way. With physical compatibility the SCSI Reservations/Filtering normally imposed by the vmkernel are "loosened" such that other systems that also want to impose SCSI reservations will work (such as clustering systems).

This is sometimes referred to as a Pass-Through RAW Device Mapping. In this case the switch is –z

- vmkfstools –a lsilogic -z /vmfs/devices/disks/vmhba40:0:1:0 /vmfs/volumes/esx1-storage1/vm1/vm1_2.vmdk

  Note:

  In this case the VMware labels the corresponding file vm1_2-rdm**p**.vmdk. We know this is a RAW Disk Mapping file with **p**hysical compatibility.

Viewing RDM Information

In the past it wasn't easy to view the contents of an RDM file, although you were able to use vmkfstools –l to list files. The command would allow you to see which files were virtual disks and which were RDMs.

There is now a switch to query the metadata file which then reports information:

1. Running:

   ```
   vmkfstools —q /vmfs/volumes/esx1-
   storage1/vm1_1.vmdk
   ```

   Will return:

   ```
   Disk vm1_1.vmdk is a Non-passthrough Raw Device
   Mapping
   Disk Id: vml.0100000000020202020564952545541
   Maps to: vmhba40:0:0:0
   ```

2. Running:

   ```
   vmkfstools —q /vmfs/volumes/esx1-
   storage1/vm1_2.vmdk
   ```

   Will return:

   ```
   Disk vm1_2.vmdk is a Passthrough Raw Device
   Mapping
   Disk Id: vml.0100010000020202020564952545541
   Maps to: vmhba40:0:1:0
   ```

   Note:

   You can also cat the contents of the metadata file as well – but the VM MUST be powered off first!

3. To cat the contents, type:

   ```
   cat /vmfs/volumes/esx1-storage1/vm1_2.vmdk
   ```

   Which returns:

   ```
   # Disk DescriptorFile
   version=1
   CID=0a8fee69
   parentCID=ffffffff
   createType="vmfsRawDeviceMap"
   ```

```
# Extent description
RW 8388608 VMFSRDM "vm1_2-rdm.vmdk"

# The Disk Data Base
#DDB
ddb.toolsVersion = "7172"
ddb.adapterType = "lsilogic"
ddb.geometry.sectors = "63"
ddb.geometry.heads = "255"
ddb.geometry.cylinders = "522"
ddb.virtualHWVersion = "4"
```

Exporting & Importing Virtual Disks

Those of you with some ESX 2.x experience will know importing (into a VMFS volume) and exporting (out of a VMFS volume) virtual disk has two main functions.

Firstly, it serves as a safe method of converting disks into a format that can be taken to/from "foreign" file systems such as NTFS and ESX3. Historically, these file systems have tools that could corrupt files bigger than 2GB in size. In the past, these two formats have been referred to as "Monolithic" and "COW" (copy-on-write). COW is no longer a favored term as it is technically inaccurate – instead we refer to it as the "Sparse" format. That is more or less still the same. However there is a new switch in vmkfstools (-d) that will allow you to control the format of the disk. The –d switch is not always required; it depends on whether you are exporting or importing.

Another purpose is for transporting virtual disks safely to/from other vPlatforms such as Workstation on Linux or Windows or VMware Server (nee GSX) on Linux or Windows. Additionally, perhaps you don't have VirtualCenter; you still have a stand-alone ESX servers – and you still use the import and export method of ESX 2.x.

GOTCHA:

For those of you from an ESX 2.x background you should be aware that the old vmkfstools –e switch is depreciated and the way you now do an export is confusingly with the –i switch with the new –d 2gbsparse switch.

Exporting "Zeroedthick" Virtual Disks (nee Monolithic) into the "Sparse" (nee COW) Format

In my case I am using /vmimages partition but you could use any EXT3 location or even export directly to a mount NFS or SMB share.

1. Type the command:

   ```
   vmkfstools -i /vmfs/volumes/esx1-
   storage/vm1/vm1.vmdk -d 2gbsparse
   /vmimages/vm1.vmdk
   ```

   Note:

   You should get a response like this:

   ```
   Destination disk format: sparse with 2GB maxi-
   mum extent size
   Cloning disk '/vmfs/volumes/local-
   esx1/vm1/vm1.vmdk'...
   Clone: 3% done.
   ```

   Note:

   The disk is now in a portable format... you could tar it up and copy somewhere else for backup purposes – connect with WinSCP on your workstation and bring the files down to your PC. If you have VMware Workstation on your PC you could configure a virtual machine to use this disk.

Importing Virtual Disk from the Sparse Format

For those of you familiar with ESX 2.x this process hasn't changed much at all. What is different is that VMFS now stores directories, and the VM's configuration files are held in a directory. The question now is: where do you restore the disk to? The easiest way to do this is first to create a VM with a virtual disk that is very small; this will then set-up up the directory structure for the configuration files. Then delete the small virtual disk. Next trigger the vmkfstools import to the vmfs volume and directory making sure you create a vmdk file with the same name of the smaller virtual disk created and deleted a moment ago.

1. Type the command:

```
vmkfstools -i /vmimages/workstationdisk.vmdk
/vmfs/volumes/esx1-storage/workstation1/ work-
station1.vmdk
Destination disk format: VMFS thick
Cloning disk '/vmimages/media.vmdk'...
Clone: 10% done.
```

Copying Files from one ESX host to another

SCP (Secure Copy) is the utility to use. This example copies a vmdk in its
sparse format. Remember to use ESX as SSH client; this must be enabled in
the ESX firewall first from the location that starts the SCP. You can use esxcfg-
firewall –e sshClient. You will also need to do this if you want to ssh from one
ESX host to another.

1. Type:

   scp /vmimages/vm1*.vmdk esx2.vi3book.com:
   /vmimages

   Note:

   Don't forget the colon: after the name of your server. If you do
   not specify a user (lavericm@esx2.vi3book.com) then SCP assumes
   you are using the root account at the destination.

   Note:

   It will warn you that the first time you copy the destination host

   ```
   " The authenticity of host 'esx2.vi3book.com'
   (192.168.3.102)' can't be established.
   RSA key fingerprint is
   92:4b:ba:b5:ca:31:6f:e7:8c:2d:00:6e:cf:c6:b6:ea
   ."
   ```

   This is because the certificate of the corresponding machine is un-
   trusted and cannot be verified. To get rid of these first time messages you need to assign your own certificates or acquire them
   from a 3rd party.

2. Choose **Yes** to continue.

Note:

The system will then warn you that:

" **Warning:** Permanently added "esx2.vi3book.com
," 192.168.3.102' (RSA) to the list of known
hosts."

3. At the prompt which reads "**root@esx2.vi3book.com pass-word:**" type the **other servers root password**, in my case ************

Note:

In this screen grab I copied the tar file for upgrade of esx 2.x to 3.x The system will give you a status bar like this:

```
vmware-esx-3.0.0.tar.gz 67% 309MB 9.2MB/s 00:15
```

Note:

By default root access is not enabled, unless you weaken security in the /etc/ssh/sshd_config file.

Renaming Virtual Disks

Renaming virtual disks used to be a simple process. You could just use the mv command and edit your VMX file accordingly to point the VM to the new file name. Now virtual disks have two files - their companion vmdk metadata file and the –flat.vmdk which has made it slightly more complicated. Fortunately, we now have a special vmkfstools switch to rename files and keep the metadata in synch with the –flat file. I guess you could manually edit the metadata file – but why bother when vmkfstools does it all for you? This tool is especially useful when a virtual disk is in the 2gbsparse format which is assembled from many files – and where manually renaming them would be a burden.

1. Before my rename the metadata in the vm1.vmdk looked like this:

```
# Disk DescriptorFile
version=1
CID=a896726b
parentCID=ffffffff
createType="vmfs"
```

```
xdgkdkfdlkfjldkjflkjsdf
# Extent description
RW 4194304 VMFS "vm1-flat.vmdk"
Xdgkdkfdlkfjldkjflkjsdf
# The Disk Data Base
#DDB
ddb.adapterType = "lsilogic"
ddb.geometry.sectors = "63"
ddb.geometry.heads = "255"
ddb.geometry.cylinders = "261"
ddb.thinProvisioned = "1"
ddb.virtualHWVersion = "4"
ddb.toolsVersion = "7172"
```

2. Type the command:

```
vmkfstools -E /vmfs/volumes/esx1-
storage1/vm1/vm1.vmdk m1-os.vmdk
```

3. After the rename the metadata looks like this:

```
# Disk DescriptorFile
version=1
CID=a896726b
parentCID=ffffffff
createType="vmfs"
xdgkdkfdlkfjldkjflkjsdf
# Extent description
RW 4194304 VMFS "vm1-os-flat.vmdk"
Xdgkdkfdlkfjldkjflkjsdf
# The Disk Data Base
#DDB
ddb.adapterType = "lsilogic"
ddb.geometry.sectors = "63"
ddb.geometry.heads = "255"
ddb.geometry.cylinders = "261"
ddb.thinProvisioned = "1"
ddb.virtualHWVersion = "4"
ddb.toolsVersion = "7172"
```

Note:

Next you would manually edit the VMX file to reflect your changes.

Resizing Virtual Disks

According to VMware documentation on the forum, the –x switch is only supported for making virtual disks larger – not smaller. This has been the case in ESX 2.x. This surprised me – because in the past I have successfully used –x to make a virtual disk smaller. This however, was way back in the mists of time, circa ESX 2.0 (around 2004). So perhaps they withdrew it as a function as it is very easy to corrupt files when you make virtual disks smaller. If you want to clone a big virtual disk to a small one perhaps you could use a disk cloning utility like Symantec Ghost or PowerQuest DriveImage Pro.

While it is relatively easier to increase the size of the VMDK file, Windows does not give you an easy way to reduce or increase the size of a partition. Therefore 3rd Party tools may be required to complete the procedure – especially if the partition is the boot partition. There are five main methods:

- Partition Tools – you can use Power Quest Partition Magic on a Client based OS, to resize the partition or Power Quests Volume Manager on Server based OS.

- If you have Windows 2003 (or Windows 2000 with the Resource Kit) you can go through a procedure using Microsoft's Diskpart utility. It's not a very friendly process and is quite convoluted. Its main advantage is that it is cheap – as you do not need 3rd party tools to achieve it. Its disadvantage is that it is not available for NT4, as far as I am aware. For more information about this you could visit Dominic Rivera's rather useful vmwareprofessional.com website.

- DR method – Backup OS System State to another location – Create a new OS disk file and restore the data.

- Ise the Knoppix Boot CD (http://www.knoppix.org) and the qparted disk repartitioning tool.

- Drive Cloning Method using Symantec Ghost or PowerQuest Drive Image Pro – Create a new disk of the appropriate size – and restore the data using a disk to disk restore method.

My personal favorite is the last one – as it can be used to make virtual disks safely larger and smaller. I've also used it to convert VMware Workstation IDE drives into SCSI Disks. My second favorite method is using the Knoppix Boot CD, mainly because it is free and handles many different file systems.

It's worth knowing the alternatives in case you cannot get your preferred method to work. You should expect a number of reboots within the guest operating system – at least one created by the Partitioning tool, and the one called for by the guest operating system (especially Windows). This can be somewhat annoying!

GOTCHA:

Backup up the VM in case the following procedure fails!

Note:

I noticed that Knoppix is susceptible to disconnections from the Remote Console especially when you are shutting down the VM after booting from the ISO.

1. Shutdown the VM.

2. Type the following command:

    ```
    vmkfstools –X 6144m –force /vmfs/volumes/local/
    vm1.vmdk
    ```

    Note:

    If you follow this command with ls –l –h you will see it is bigger. Again I could have specified 6g instead of 6144m. It's the –flat file that changes size – the metadata file stays the same but has new geometry information

3. Start-up the VM, and check that it boots properly

    Note:

    You may get "error loading operating system" messages if the vmdk file has become corrupted.

4. Connect to the ISO which contains the Knoppix Boot CD - Using the Console attach to this ISO file making sure you enable X Connected at Power On.

5. Power on the VM.

6. Change the boot order on the VM to give the CD-ROM the highest priority. Allow the system to boot to Knoppix CD or use the [ESC] key to select the CD-ROM as a the boot device.

7. Click the Knoppix KDE button.

8. Choose System Tools.

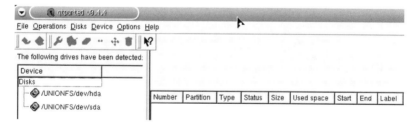

9. Choose Qparted.

Note:

Qparted will display the partition/disk layout of the virtual machine.

In this case, the IDE CD-ROM and single SCSI boot disk (sda.)

10. Select /inionfs/dev/sda

Note:

This then shows the partition table on that virtual disk.

In this case a single C drive of 4GB with free space on the hard-drive of 2GB added by using vmkfstools –X 6096mg.

11. Select Partition No 01

12. Right-click and choose &Resize.

13. In the dialog box drag to increase or decrease the size of Partition 01.

14. Click OK

15. Click File, and choose &Commit.

Note:

Confirm the warnings by clicking the Yes button – and watch the dialog boxes go by - and Confirm the Success dialog by clicking OK.

16. Shutdown the Virtual Machine.

17. Disconnect the CD-Rom.

Note:

This will allow the VM to boot to the VMDK file rather than to the CD-Rom.

18. Reboot the Virtual Machine.

Note:

In Windows 2003 you will see check disk events – this appears to be normal. Additionally, you will find Windows 2003 will detect the hard-drive as if it was a new device and request a reboot.

Converting Workstation VMs to ESX VMs using VMware Converter

In the past we used very long and convoluted manual methods to convert Workstation virtual disks. VMware released a beta tools some months ago called "VMware Importer" used mainly to covert Microsoft virtual disks and VMware Server/Workstation disks into the ESX format. This import functionality has been rolled up into the recently released "VMware Converter" tool. The VMware Converter tool is free in its non-enterprise format, called "Starter Mode."

GOTCHA:

Currently VMware Converter is fully supported for Windows VMs including the 64-bit versions of Windows 2003 and XP. However, converter only has experimental support for Linux. This is what the release notes currently say:

"Support for the following guest operating systems is Experimental. VMware Converter 3 can clone source images containing these operating systems, but the destination virtual machine may or may not work without additional configuration after import. In particular, if the source image contains unsupported hardware, you may need to modify the configuration of the destination virtual machine before using it"

- Linux

- Windows NT 3.x

- Windows ME

- Windows 98

- Windows 95

- MS-DOS"

It's worth mentioning that the only operating system listed here that is officially supported on ESX 3.x.x is Linux.

1. Download and install VMware Converter your PC where your VMware Workstation resides.

2. Load VMware Converter, and click the button labeled Continue in Starter Mode.

3. Click the Import Machine icon.

4. First select the source VM.

5. Choose Next.

6. Choose Stand-alone machine.

7. Click the Browse button and locate the VMX file of the VMware Workstation VM.

8. Retain the default of Import all disks and Maintain Size.

9. Then select the destination location.

10. Choose VMware ESX server or VirtualCenter virtual machine.

11. Enter the name of your VirtualCenter server, and user account details.

12. Type in the name of the new VM, and Select the folder in VirtualCenter to hold the VM.

13. Select an ESX host or DRS/HA Cluster to location for your VM.

14. Select a VMFS or NAS datastore.

15. Select the Network options.

16. Enable Install VMware Tools.

Note:

The option to customize the VM runs a guest customization wizard which allows you retain your original VM, and sysprep the converted VM.

17. Click Next and Finish.

Note:

You can watch the status of your conversion from the converter windows in a percentage. Additionally, the "Task Progress" tab will give you an overview of the steps the converter is completing.

GOTCHA:

When you first power on the converted workstation you will be asked to deal with the UUID value. This is because the VM has been cloned to a new physical location outside the scope of VirtualCenter. If you ran the guest customization wizard you should choose to generate a new UUID; if you intend to decommission the old VMware Workstation VM you should opt to keep the UUID. This is the difference between a clone to copy, and a clone to move a VM.

Manually Converting Workstation VMs to ESX VMs

If VMware Converter doesn't work for you, this manual method always works without failure. One reason might be that you are trying to convert a guest operating system which is only experimentally supported with the VMware Converter tool. This manual process of conversion does take a significant number of steps. An alternative to this process is using a free utility called IDE2SCSI which is available on the sanbarrow.com website as part of the MOA project.

This long title actually explains an occasional problem some users have bringing virtual disks from VMware Workstation into ESX server. In contrast to ESX, VMware Workstation supports 4 different formats which include IDE or SCSI and the disks can either be single "growable" disk (type 0) or a "growable" disk split in 2GB chunks (type 1, or what ESX user would called 2gbsparse). Other formats can be created from the command-line using the VMware Workstation utility vmware-vdiskmanager.exe which include:

- Type 0 - single growable virtual disk

- Type 1 - growable virtual disk split in 2Gb files

- Type 2 – pre-allocated virtual disk

- Type 3 – pre-allocated virtual disk split in 2Gb files

By "growable" VMware means the files dynamically take up more space on the disk as data is written to them. In contrast a "pre-allocated" disk is more like the ESX default format where a 10GB virtual disk uses 10GB of space. Growable disks are popular in VMware Workstation where local disk space on a PC or laptop may be limited. Additionally, one thing to beware of is that the default and recommended virtual disk format is IDE in VMware Workstation 5.x. VMware Workstation sets IDE whether you choose a Typical or Custom when creating the VM. This can cause further problems when bringing a Workstation disk into ESX.

These are barriers or problems some people experience in bringing VMware Workstation VM'sVM's into an ESX environment:

- IDE format is not supported in ESX but is a default in VMware Workstation

- ESX does not appear to like the Type 0 disk from VMware Workstation

- Virtual disks must be copied to ESX in the 2gbsparse format, and converted into one of the other formats (eagerzerodthick, eagerthick, or thick)

- Occasionally, the guest operating system lacks a driver for lsilogic or buslogic

This procedure is a good example of using VMware Workstation command-line tools together with ESX to move a VM into ESX – it also draws upon our capacity to access information in various virtual disk metadata files. I've had to use these occasionally with Virtual Appliances which are created in an IDE/pre-allocated format which means they cannot immediately be used on the ESX platform – and where VMware Converter refuses to work with that guest operating system.

Such a virtual appliance is the Ultimate Deployment Appliance (UDA) covered earlier in this chapter. A VM with this kind of disk IDE and Single Growable would have vmdk metadata like so:

```
# Disk DescriptorFile
version=1
CID=a9a0b01d
parentCID=ffffffff
createType="monolithicFlat"

# Extent description
RW 4194304 FLAT "uda13-flat.vmdk" 0

# The Disk Data Base
#DDB

ddb.virtualHWVersion = "4"
ddb.geometry.cylinders = "4161"
ddb.geometry.heads = "16"
ddb.geometry.sectors = "63"
ddb.adapterType = "ide"
ddb.toolsVersion = "0"
```

VMware KB 1881 is a knowledge base article which outlines the basics of manual conversion. It is an old KB article but it is still relevant. These are the stages it outlines, and I have added a few more to make it 100% accurate and complete:

- Duplicating the IDE Type 0 disk to a IDE Type 1 format

- Gather information about the IDE Type 1 disk to carry out step 3

- Adding a SCSI disk to the VM using the Type 1 format

- Editing the VMware Workstation VMX file to add a SCSI adapter

- Powering on the VM to confirm access to the SCSI Device

- Editing either the Type 1 or Type 2 disk to make it into a 2GB Sparse SCSI disk

- Transfer metadata information from the SCSI disk to the IDE Type 1 disk created in Step 1

- Uploading the disk created at Step 6 to an ESX host

- Create a new VM in ESX

- Use vmkfstools to import the 2gbsparse disk copied at step 7

Step 1: Duplicating the IDE Type 0 disk to a IDE Type 1 format

1. We begin first by backing up the virtual disk/machine.

2. Next we need to create growable 2GB sparse VMDK using the VMware Workstation vmware-vdiskmager utilities; in the case of UDA1.3 the following would:

3. Open a command-prompt and type:

```
cd\Program Files\VMware\VMware Workstation
```

4. Type the command:

vmware-vdiskmanager.exe -r <path>\uda13.vmdk **-t 1** <path>uda13-growable2gb.vmdk

Note:

The command-line tool will give you progress information. The –r switch indicates we are converting the disk, the first path indicates the source vmdk file, and the –t is the type switch indicates we need a type 1 Mware Workstation disk (a vmdk in the growable 2gbsparse format).

Step 2: Gather information about the IDE Type 1 disk to carry out step 3

1. Type the contents of the growable 2gbsparse disk with:

   ```
   type <path>uda-growable.vmdk
   ```

2. This should print out information like this to the command-line:

   ```
   # Disk DescriptorFile
   version=1
   CID=a9a0b01d
   parentCID=ffffffff
   wcreateType="twoGbMaxExtentSparse"

   # Extent description
   RW 4192256 SPARSE "uda13-growable-s001.vmdk"
   RW 2048 SPARSE "uda13-growable-s002.vmdk"

   # The Disk Data Base#
   DDB
   ddb.virtualHWVersion = "4"
   ddb.toolsVersion = "0"
   ddb.geometry.cylinders = "4161"
   ddb.geometry.heads = "16"
   ddb.geometry.sectors = "63"
   ddb.adapterType = "ide"
   ```

3. To create a similar sized virtual disk in the SCSI format we need to sum the size of the growable disk by the number sectors. These are numbers I have formatted in bold. Basically add up all these values for each of the sparse files. In my case that's 4192256+2048=4194304.

Step 3: Creating a SCSI disk to the VM using the Type 1 format

1. Open a command-prompt andy type:

   ```
   cd\program Files\VMware\VMware Workstation
   ```

2. Type the command:

```
vmware-vdiskmanager.exe -c -s  4194304 -a lsi-
logic -t 1 <path>uda13-scsidisk.vmdk
```

Note:

The switch −c is used to create a new virtual disk, and −s sets the size of the disk sectors. The −a switch sets which adapter type the disk will use (lsilogic/buslogic). If you are doing this for Windows beware that different Windows flavors support different drivers as part of the i386 code. For example, Windows 2000 and NT4 support the Buslogic Driver whereas Windows XP and 2003 support the LSIlogic Driver. You may have to be ready to supply a driver to the Windows operating system. In my case I chose lsilogic as I prefer it − the Fedora Core 5 operating system is the guest OS of UDA 1.3 − and support LSIlogic adapter.

This should take a the fraction of the time our clone/covert did previously, as it merely has to create a file with the correct geometries but does not have to copy any data.

Step 4: Adding in the SCSI Disk, Power On and Check SCSI Disk is found

1. In VMware Workstation click Edit Virtual Machine Settings.

2. Click Add.

3. Click Next, Select Hard Disk and Click Next.

4. Choose Use an Existing Virtual Disk.

5. Browse to the SCSI disk created in Step 3.

6. Click Next and Finish.

7. Using a text editor (not Windows NotePad!) edit the VMX file for the VM and add an SCSI Device by adding after scsi0:0.present = "TRUE"

```
scsi0.virtualDev = "lsilogic"
```

8. Power On the VM.

   Note:

   You can check the SCSI disk is present by using fdisk /dev/sda in Linux. If you are using Windows, the operating system should detect this new device and plug and play it. Use Device Manager and Disk Management to check that the Windows operating system can see the new SCSI disk.

   Regardless of your operating system, this disk is un-partitioned and will not be mountable by driver letter or mounting point.

9. Shutdown the VM.

10. Remove both the IDE and SCSI Disk (but don't delete them).

Step 5: Modify the Metadata of the IDE "Growable 2GBSpare Disk"

1. In a text editor (not Notepad!) open the .vmdk file of the SCSI disk.

2. In a text editor (not Notepad!) open the .vmdk file of the Growable 2GB disk.

3. Select and copy all the text in the SCSI disk below the # Disk Data Base Line, in my case:

   ```
   ddb.virtualHWVersion = "4"
   ddb.geometry.cylinders = "261"
   ddb.geometry.heads = "255"
   ddb.geometry.sectors = "63"
   ddb.adapterType = "lsilogic"
   ```

4. Paste this over the equivalent lines in the Growable 2GB Disk.

5. Close and Save your changes to the metadata of the Growable 2GB Disk.

Step 6: Transfer to the ESX Host, Create VM and Covert Virtual Disk

1. Using WinSCP or a similar tool, copy the Growable 2GB Sparse files to the ESX Host.

    Note:

    The location of /vmimages is a good place – but check you have enough space in whatever partition you choose before copying as you will want to avoid filling the / partition.

2. Create a new VM but with a 1MB virtual disk – Choose Custom, and make sure you select the right SCSI Controller type for your SCSI virtual disk (lsilogic or buslogic).

    Note:

    This will create the directory structure for the VM. We actually don't need the 1MB virtual disk, but it is impossible to create a VM with the VI Client without some kind of virtual disk.

3. Logon to the Service Console as ROOT.

4. Delete the 1MB virtual disk with the rm command, for example:

    ```
    rm /vmfs/volumes/virtualmachines/uda13/uda13.
    vmdk —f
    ```

    Note:

    The —f forces rm to delete both the metadata file and the — flat.vmdk file as well.

5. Use vmkfstools to import the "growable 2gbsparse" disk with:

    ```
    vmkfstools —i /vmimages/uda13-growable.vmdk
    /vmfs/volumes/virtualmachines/uda13/uda13.vmdk
    ```

6. Power on your VM in VMware ESX server.

Deleting Virtual Disks

There is a special command for deleting virtual disks – however we could easily use the Linux command:

```
rm namofvirtualdisk*.vmdk -f
```

This would delete the metadata and also the –flat.vmdk file... but vmkfstools can do it too with the command:

```
vmkfstools -U /vmfs/volumes/local/vm1.vmdk
```

Note:

It deletes both the metadata and the –flat file – and doesn't currently ask "Are you sure???."

Using VMware-cmd

VMware-cmd works by manipulating the VMX and sending instructions to the VM via the VMX file. There is lots you can do with this command beyond what is feasible in this document. For further information, look at the Scripting Guide for ESX. It also returns 1 for positive results, and 0 for failures – so you can use it for shell scripts with if statements:

Listing Registered VMS

To list Registered VMs, type:

```
vmware-cmd —l
```

Note:

List paths and names of VMX files, useful for when you have to type long paths to the VMX file. You can highlight an entry in the list and copy it to your command-line. Unfortunately, vmware-cmd no longer supports volume names – instead you have to use the UUID path to the VMX file.

I will give one example of vmware-cmd with the UUID. After that I will replace the string with <UUID> because it is so long!

Registering and Un-registering a VM

To register or un-register a VM, type:

```
vmware-cmd -s unregister /vmfs/volumes/<UUID>/vm1/
vm1.vmx
```

Note:

This also includes register as a command. S stands for set. This un-registers a VM from an ESX host (stand-alone).

Unfortunately, it does NOT un-register it from VirtualCenter. Instead you are left with an "orphaned" VM that needs right-clicking and "Remove from the Inventory."

This happens because what vmware-cmd –s is manipulating is what used to be called the vm-list. It's not manipulating the VC database.

Note:

Why is the command still useful? If you had a server failure which you had to rebuild, you then need to "register" the VMX file with an ESX server to be able to manage it. If you had 40 VMX you wouldn't want to do that by hand using the GUI and the datastore browser utility.

Power Options on a VM

If you use trysoft option, the Guest OS will be shut down gracefully. The trysoft is a "mode" option – it tries to run the normal scripts but uses a hard shutdown/startup if the VM is not behaving properly. There are two other "modes" – soft which runs scripts but never does a hard start or stop, or "hard" which powers off/on a VM as if you had hit the power switch. Sometimes people use trysoft first, and then if the VM refuses to power off, they follow it with hard power off.

1. To power on a VM type:

    vmware-cmd /vmfs/volumes/<UUID>/vm1/vm1.vmx
    start trysoft

2. To power off a VM type:

    vmware-cmd /vmfs/volumes/<UUID>/vm1/vm1.vmx
    stop trysoft

3. To suspend a VM type:

    vmware-cmd /vmfs/volumes/<UUID>/vm1/vm1.vmx
    suspend

    Note:

    There isn't much in the way of status/progress here. The old-style "Remote Console" from ESX 2.x days used to give you a dialog box with a status bar.

4. To resume a suspended VM type:

    vmware-cmd /vmfs/volumes/<UUID>/vm1/vm1.vmx
    start trysoft

    Note:

    There is no resume switch on vmware-cmd – just a power-up which retrieves the suspend file, and resumes the machine.

5. To reset a VM type:

vmware-cmd /vmfs/volumes/<UUID>/vml/vml.vmx **reset trysoft**

Note:

This is a soft reboot of the virtual machine.

6. To find out the **Power Status** of a VM use:

vmware-cmd /vmfs/volumes/<UUID>/vml/vml.vmx **getstate**

Note:

It will return "On"; "Off"; "Suspend" and "Stuck" if the VM is waiting for interaction.

Finding the Heartbeat

To find the heartbeat, type:

vmware-cmd /vmfs/volumes/<UUID>/vml/vml.vmx **getheartbeat**

Note:

You should see a number. Repeat the command. If the number increments the machine is alive. If it stays the same it is dead; it doesn't have a heartbeat.

Finding the Status Of Devices

The Vmware-cmd tools are able to find the configuration of the VMX file, and also change entries in the file. To find out the status of the CD-ROM you would use:

vmware-cmd /vmfs/volumes/<UUID>/vml/vml.vmx getconfig ide0:0.deviceType

Note:

The CD-ROM is an emulated (but not Virtualized) IDE 0:0 channel. This is how the CD-ROM is addressed in a Windows Environment. A safe way of learning the VMX variables is just print the VMX file to the console with:

```
cat /vmfs/volumes/esx-storage1/vm1/vm1.vmx | more
```

Note:

Cat is the same as the "type" command in Windows. It merely prints the contents of files to the command-line.

As long as you know the name of the variable in the VMX file you can change anything you like from the command line. For example, there is a variable called ide0:0.fileName = which controls the path for the CD-ROM, be it physical or an ISO image. There is a variable called ide0:0.deviceType = which controls whether it is the physical or ISO image (atapi-cdrom for the physical and cdrom-image if it is an ISO file). In this example we will attach an ISO to the CD-ROM and Connect the CD-ROM to the VM. You may wish to have VC Console open while you're doing this – to see visually the effect of your changes.

I assume that initially the CD-ROM is connected to the physical CD:

1. First, Disconnect the current device with:

    ```
    vmware-cmd /vmfs/volumes/<UUID>/vm1/vm1.vmx
    disconnectdevice ide0:0
    ```

2. Change the system to use an ISO file instead of a physical CD with:

    ```
    vmware-cmd /vmfs/volumes/<UUID>/vm1/vm1.vmx
    setconfig ide0:0.deviceType cdrom-image
    ```

3. Then set the image file to use with:

    ```
    vmware-cmd /vmfs/volumes/<UUID>/vm1/vm1.vmx
    setconfig ide0:0.fileName
    /vmfs/volumes/ISO's/w2k3.iso
    ```

4. To Refresh the OS - Reconnect the device with:

    ```
    vmware-cmd /vmfs/volumes/<UUID>/vm1/vm1.vmx
    connectdevice ide0:0
    ```

Note:

Now that the CD is set as an ISO file, you merely need to do stages 2 and 3 to switch from one ISO file another. The whole process could be put in SH script like so:

```
vmware-cmd /vmfs/volumes/<UUID>/vm1/vm1.vmx
disconnectdevice ide0:0

vmware-cmd /vmfs/volumes/<UUID>/vm1/vm1.vmx
setconfig ide0:0.deviceType cdrom-image

vmware-cmd /vmfs/volumes/<UUID>/vm1/vm1.vmx
setconfig ide0:0.fileName
/vmfs/volumes/ISO's/w2k3ent.iso

vmware-cmd /vmfs/volumes/<UUID>/vm1/vm1.vmx
connectdevice ide0:0
```

Scripted Installation Revisited

Now that we have a good knowledge of the main configuration commands, we can use this to further automate our scripted installations using the %post section of the kickstart.cfg file. We can use %post section to create a script file that executes when the ESX first boots. This script file contains the esxcfg commands. We can then use the %post section to set the permissions on this file to give it the Read, Write, and eXecute attributes. What is critical is that the post-script file must be executed *after* the ESX host has loaded the VMkernel. If the VMKernel is not loaded, or if the esxcfg post-script executes *before* the VMKernel has fully-loaded, it will fail.

I would like to thank the http://www.brianshouse.net/hp/ website. I lifted some of this content from his samples used with the HP RDP product.

Below is a basic sample from a %post section of a kickstart.cfg. A fuller version can be downloaded for free from http://www.vi3book.com/downloads/ks.cfg. If you do open this file in Windows make sure you use WordPad and not notepad, as notepad will corrupt the file. Anything between <<EOF1 and EOF can contain Linux or VMkernel commands. All this sample below shows is how to create an internal switch with a Virtual Machine Port group called internal.

```
%post
cat > /tmp/esxcfg.sh <<EOF1
#!/bin/sh
```

This first part creates a file called esxcfg.sh inserting the line #!/bin/sh which is associated with the Linux scripting SHell. Everything between <<EOF1 and EOF is included in the esxcfg.sh file. These act as text delimiters to indicate the beginning and of the file. The cat command is the similar to the type command in Windows and allows us to redirect the contents (>) of the script into the esxcfg.sh file.

```
# Configure ESX Server
# Create vSwitch1 with a port group of Internal
esxcfg-vswitch -a vSwitch1
esxcfg-vswitch -A internal vSwitch1
EOF
```

This part adds a vSwitch called vSwitch1 with a port group called internal. No network card is added with the esxcfg-vswitch –L command.

```
# Make esxcfg.sh eXcutable
chmod +x /tmp/esxcfg.sh
```

Chmod is used to modify permissions in the Linux file system. As you might gather this changes the attributes of esxcfg.sh to make it executable.

```
# Backup original rc.local file
cp /etc/rc.d/rc.local /etc/rc.d/rc.local.bak
# Make esxcfg.sh run from rc.local and make rc.local re-
set itself
cat >> /etc/rc.d/rc.local <<EOF
cd /tmp
/tmp/esxcfg.sh
mv -f /etc/rc.d/rc.local.bak /etc/rc.d/rc.local
EOF
```

You can see the rc.local file as akin to the old autoexec.bat of DOS days – it's one of the last scripts to run in the boot process. By adding our script to the end of the file we can guarantee that it will execute properly. Another alternative to rc.local is the script held in /etc/rc.d/rc3.d/S99local - both files will do the job. As mentioned before, the critical thing here is that the script must execute **after** the VMkernel has loaded as the Service Console (based on Redhat Linux) would not know how to process our esxcfg- style commands.

Conclusion

In this chapter I have not covered every single command, utility or script available. I have tried to cover the most popular and the most useful. We now have a series of very quick ways of installing and rebuilding ESX either from a PXE boot server or with a USB key. Additionally, we now have a good knowledge of the networking commands which will help you in troubleshooting service console connectivity. Try to see this chapter as a good jumpstart to automating ESX host configurations or troubleshooting. There is plenty more to learn about the Service Console. Dive in and explore!

Chapter 13: Updating and Patching

GOTCHA:

As with any update downloaded from VMware's website you should use MD5sum against your download to check that it has not been corrupted during any internet download process.

During the lifetime of VI-3 it is inevitable that VMware will issue new releases, updates, and patches. Indeed they already have, from ESX 3.0.0 to 3.0.1 and VirtualCenter 2.0.0 to 2.0.1. There are three levels of release numbers from VMware which follow the convention of "Product Name" X.Y.Z:

- An increment to the X digit is classed as a *major release* and generally reflects a brand new product. Without some kind of software assurance agreement in place your old licenses will not cover a new product such as ESX 2.0.0 to ESX 3.0.0.

- An increment to the Y digit is classed as a *minor release* and mainly includes high severity patches – but can also include new features such as ESX 3.0.1 to 3.1.0.

- An increment to the Z digit is classified as a *maintenance release,* and they usually roll-up a number of bug fixes that cannot be held back for a minor release.

As with all software – if your versions are all of the same release then you should have no problems at all. If you blend your releases together you will find you may receive intermittent, unpredictable, and unusual software errors. Choosing the correct order of your update is critical for peace of mind. I would recommend this order for your updates:

1. Update VirtualCenter.

2. Update the VI Client(s).

3. Update the ESX hosts.

4. Update VMware Tools inside the VM's.

5. Apply any individual patches.

Depending on the software there are manual methods for processing the updates and methods which automate some of the updates. For bulk purposes, I will show you all of them so once you have mastered the manual methods you will understand the more automated methods. Automated or bulk methods exist for ESX Hosts and VMware Tools and individual patches can be scripted and chained together to ease their deployment.

Of course another way of approaching this issue is never to update VMware software and always carry out a clean installation. It's possible to evacuate the ESX host of all its VMs to other hosts in a DRS cluster by entering maintenance. Once that was completed we could power off the ESX host, and remove it from the VirtualCenter inventory. We could wipe the original ESX and reinstall the new software, ideally with a kickstart script. Finally, we would add it back into the Inventory licensed and with VMotion enabled. This would leave us just with maintenance patches and upgrading VMware Tools for our VMs. It's a convoluted process that's for sure – but it does deliver the goal of clean installations without VM downtime.

Updating VirtualCenter

In the absence of later versions of VirtualCenter (2.0.1) than this book uses, I've chosen to update from VirtualCenter 2.0.0 to VirtualCenter 2.0.1. I will also assume you have followed VMware recommendations to run the License Server and VirtualCenter on the same system. If you are running VirtualCenter and SQL in VMs, I would recommend a backup or using snapshots to protect yourself during the update process.

1. Insert or attach to the VirtualCenter 2.0.1 CD/Media and begin the installation.

2. Choose VirtualCenter Management Server 2.0 from the list.

   Figure 13.1 shows the message shown indicating a previous version of VirtualCenter has been discovered.

Figure 13.1

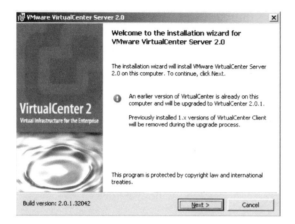

3. Choose Next.

4. Complete the installation as normal, supplying the credentials for the database.

    The installer should prompt you with this message shown in Figure13.2. Notice how you choose NO, to not over-write your data. Choosing Yes destroys your existing database!

Figure 13.2

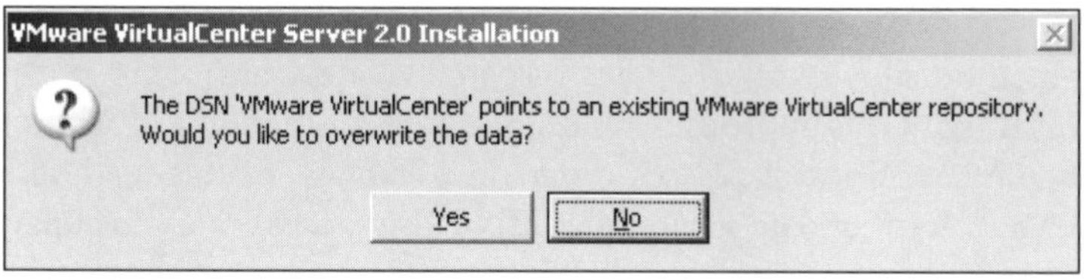

5. Choose No.

6. The remainder of the install is followed as normal – accepting the location of your served license file specified in the previous installation.

Updating the VI Client

If you primarily use the VI Client with VirtualCenter I recommend taking the VI Client that comes with the VirtualCenter CD. After a VirtualCenter or ESX update you will receive an automatic message to update your client if you point your VI Client to a VirtualCenter server or ESX host. Personally I prefer to take this update from VirtualCenter.

1. Insert or attach to the VirtualCenter 2.0.1 CD/Media and begin the installation.

2. Choose Virtual Infrastructure Client from the options.

3. Accept the message to upgrade the client.

Updating ESX 3

There are two approaches to upgrading ESX. You can put an existing server into maintenance mode, rebooting – and update using the ESX CD-ROM installer. The installation ISO will detect the existence of an older version of ESX and then offer you an update option. For most people this method works well and is reliable. This does require physical access to the ESX host or the use of virtual media with ILOs, Ills, or RAC cards. It also means the ESX host has to be powered off for a long period of time.

Another method allows you to update or patch an ESX host while it is powered on. However, with this approach you cannot have any running VMs on the host during the update. For this reason, the main advantage of this method is that it enables a "headless" update where physical or ILO access might be unavailable.

In this method the administrator downloads a zipped up version of the source code in a .tgz format from VMware's website. It can be extracted and stored on a conventional storage to which the VMkernel has access such as an SAN, iSCSI, NAS, or you can give the Service Console access to an NFS, FTP, or HTTP "depot." Depot is the term VMware uses to describe some kind of central storage point for the ROMs contained in the tgz format.

This package can be run in conjunction with ESX patch tool called esxupdate. You can learn more about patching and esxupdate by reading a very simple guide on VMware's website:

http://www.vmware.com/pdf/esx3_esxupdate.pdf

It's important you download the correct tar package. There are two. One is used with upgrades from ESX 2.x.x to ESX 3.x.x and contains an upgrade.pl script. The second is a "full" version of the product which merely contains ROMs suitable for our kind of update from one flavor of ESX 3.x.x to another.

1. **Download the tgz update file** from VMware's download page.

2. **Upload to your storage location**.

   Note:

   Choose a storage location which will be accessible to the ESX host. Personally, I prefer to put my update packages on an SAN location. This is wasteful from a storage perspective. I know every one of my ESX hosts will have access to it and delivery of the update will not be inhibited by my Ethernet network.

3. **Extract the tgz file** with the following:

   ```
   tar –xzvf esx-3.0.1-full-*.tgz
   ```

   Note:

   Where –X is used to extract a file(s); -z to uncompress file(s); -v with verbose information; -f force an extract even if the file has a colon in it.

4. **On the Server you wish to update**, Enter **Maintenance Mode**.

   Note:

   If you have DRS configured for fully-automated this should trigger a VMotion event, evacuating the ESX host of all its VMs. Alternatively, you may need to power off or manually VMotion VMs from your ESX host to other ESX hosts.

5. **Login to the Service Console** as **ROOT**.

6. Issue the command to force the update.

```
esxupdate -r file:/vmfs/volumes/nfs1/32039 —n
update
```

Note: Switches

`-r`

is not required but does stop an unwanted warning. If you don't specify the –r switch you will get the warning *"INFO: No repository URL specified, going with file: <path to where you currently located>"*. If you run esxupdate without the -r switch then esxupdate assumes you are *not* using an FTP, NFS, or HTTP deport and simply processes the files in the current directory location. If you specify -r you can trigger the update from anywhere on the command-line and esxupdate does not issue a warning about a non-specified update path.

```
32039
```

is the build number of ESX. In this case this is the build current number for ESX 3.0.1.

`-n`

instructs esxupdate not to do a reboot at the end of the installation process.

Note: End of the Update Message

At the end of the process you should find esxupdate ends with:

```
INFO: --- TOTALS: nnn packages installed, 0
pending or failed, 0 excluded INFO: Install
succeeded - please come again!
```

7. **Reboot the ESX host** – after the reboot, you may **Exit Maintenance Mode.**

Updating VMware Tools

After you have updated ESX server and have your VMs running once more – you will soon notice that VMware Tools need upgrading as well. I frequently run on old versions of VMware Tools in my development lab. I tend to move backwards and forwards from one release of ESX to another – and so I have never really bothered with keeping in synch with VMware Tools. The same cannot be said with a production environment. If you want support from VMware it's important that VMware Tools is updated, especially if you are seeking support with a guest operating system issue.

If you wish to see the status of all your VMs and their VMware Tools the easiest way of doing this is the following:

1. **Select a high-level container** such as a cluster, datacenter, or folder.

2. Select the **Virtual Machine** tab.

3. **Right-click** the **column headings**.

4. Select **Tools Status** from the list.

   Note:

   VMware Tools status will report information like the following:

   Tools OK

   Not Running

   Not Installed

   ToolsOld

   Additionally, if you look on the "Summary" tab of each VM it will state "VMware Tools: out of date."

There are two ways of upgrading VMware Tools. You can trigger a semi-automatic update while logged into VirtualCenter. The update has to be manually triggered but no interaction is required within the VM. Alternatively there is a "bulk method" of upgrading VMware Tools from the command-line of the VirtualCenter server using a tool called vmware-vmupgrade.

Semi-Automatic Updates of VMware Tools

1. **Right-click the VM** in the Inventory.

2. Choose **Install VMware Tools**.

3. In the dialog box pop-up place a tick in the box.

Note:

You *may* need to reboot at the end of the process. I found my Windows NT4 guest did reboot, but my Windows 2003 did not.

Bulk Updates with the VirtualCenter VMware-upgrade command

VMware-upgrade will deal with VMs that report "ToolsOld" and also "Not Installed." This "bulk method" only works for Windows guest operating systems. If it detects a Linux, Novel, Solaris, or Windows NT4 guests it will simply skip it completely. VMware-upgrade was originally designed to upgrade VMs from ESX 2.x to 3.x where both the virtual hardware and VMware Tools need to be upgraded. Fortunately, it can still be used to update ESX 3 VMs with a new version of the VMware Tools.

The only downside of the bulk update tool is you must power off your VMs beforehand. All of this is a major annoyance, but it must be remembered that a

VMware Tools install or update generally requires a reboot within the guest operating system for the update to take effect anyway.

There are a number of ways triggering the update of VMware Tools.

- **Update large numbers of VMs:**

  Use a path to an ESX host held in the "Host & Clusters" view in the VirtualCenter inventory. This uses the –h switch in vmware-vmupgrade.

- **Update groups of VMs:**

  Use a path to the VM held in the "Virtual Machines & Templates" view in the VirtualCenter inventory. This uses the –n switch in vmware-vmupgrade.

During an update the tools go through a number of stages. Notice at the end of the update process your VM is left in its original state – powered off. If you wish to automate this process you could look at the VirtualCenter Software Development Kit (SDK) to automate the power off before the update, trigger the update, and then power back on your VMs. Perhaps a more clumsy way which involves no scripting knowledge would be to use VMware Schedule Tasks to handle the power off and on events and Windows Scheduled Tasks to execute a batch file containing your vmware-vmupgrade.exe commands. Below is the list of the main stages the update tool executes:

- Find ESX host or VM in the inventory

- Confirm the VM(s) are powered off

- Sets a VMware Tools update

- Powers on VM (adjustable using the –m switch)

- Trigger a VMware Tools update inside the powered on VM

- Power off the VM (adjustable with the –t switch)

Per-ESX Host based VMware Tools Update

1. Power down the VMs you wish to update.

2. Logon to the VirtualCenter Server.

   Note:

   It is possible to use Microsoft's Remote Desktop Connection software if you have enabled it on your VirtualCenter server.

3. Open a command prompt to the following:

   ```
   C:\Program Files\VMware\VMware VirtualCenter
   2.0
   ```

4. Type (all one command):

   ```
   vmware-vmupgrade.exe -u vi3book\administrator -
   p vmware -h "London DataCenter/Intel
   Hosts/Intel Cluster/esx1.vi3book.com" —m 2 —t
   10
   ```

   Note:

   The lines above have been wrapped for readability – when you type the command it should be one continuous line of text.

   The switches –u and –p are required, and they set the user name and password to authenticate against VirtualCenter. The –h switch is also required, and it sets the path to an ESX host within the Inventory. In this case all powered off VMs running on esx1.vi3book.com will be updated.

   The switches –m and –t are optional and set how many VMs can be simultaneously updated and how long VMs are allowed to stay powered on (in minutes). This deals with the issue of VMs that will not power down gracefully.

Per-VM based VMware Tools Update

1. Power down the VMs you wish to update.

2. Logon to the VirtualCenter Server.

3. Open a command prompt to the following:

```
C:\Program Files\VMware\VMware VirtualCenter
2.0
```

4. Type (all one command):

```
vmware-vmupgrade.exe
-u vi3book\administrator -p vmware
-n "London DataCenter/Mike's VM's/vm1"
-n "London DataCenter/Mike's VM's/vm2"
-n "London DataCenter/Mike's VM's/vm3"
-n "London DataCenter/Mike's VM's/vm4"
-n "London DataCenter/Mike's VM's/vm5"
-n "London DataCenter/Mike's VM's/vm6"
```

Note:

As you can see, with the –n switch we can specify multiple VMs, and yes, you must specify –n each and every time!

Unfortunately, in this release it is not possible to specify simply a folder or have VirtualCenter assume that every VM in that folder (and subfolder) is updated with a new Version of VMware Tools.

GOTCHAS:

There are some frequent errors people see with vmware-vmupgrade. Firstly, remember the VMs have to be powered off first. If not the tool will give you this error message:

"London DataCenter/Mike's VM's/vm1: Cannot upgrade. VM is not powered-off"

Secondly, people often forget to input the / to indicate the end of one object in the VirtualCenter inventory and the start of another. If you do this you will get the following type of error message:

"Failed to upgrade: failed to find object at London DataCenter\Mike's VM's\vm1"

Lastly, the most common error is failing to authenticate with VirtualCenter correctly:

"Failed to connect to VirtualCenter server: vim.fault.InvalidLogin"

Patching ESX

Currently, individual patches are free to download from VMware's website. They come in three flavors:

- **Security**

    These patches prevent a potential security breach and should be installed immediately.

- **Critical**

    These patches prevent data loss or service failures and should be installed immediately.

- **General**

    These patches are non-urgent and affect a small number of users. They include bug fixes and driver updates. You should assess the relevance of these updates before downloading and applying them.

If you wish to use esxupdate to apply these patches – you need to download the versions compatible with the tool. Generally they contain two files – a descriptor file in an XML format and an RPM file, and we can use a script to chain the various updates together. With each patch for ESX server you will be given an advisory on whether powering off the VMs is required or a reboot of the ESX host is required. They are currently phrased in this way:

"All virtual machines on the host must be either shut down or migrated using VMotion before applying the patch. No reboot of the ESX Server Host is required after applying this patch."

Or

"There is no need to shut down the virtual machines on the host or to migrate them using VMotion before applying the patch. No reboot of the ESX Server Host is required after applying this patch."

Or

"All virtual machines on the host must be either shut down or migrated using VMotion before applying the patch. A reboot of the ESX Server Host is required after applying this patch."

It's actually quite difficult to remember this differing advice especially if you are planning to do a bulk update. So I feel it's probably safest to take a conservative approach and say that no update to the ESX host is executed without first entering maintenance mode – followed by an ESX host reboot.

Manual Case-by-Case Patching

1. Download the patches from VMware's website you wish to apply.

    Note:

    These are currently held here:

    http://www.vmware.com/download/vi/vi3_patches.html

2. Upload to a central storage location (SAN, iSCSI, NAS, FTP or HTTP).

3. At the Service Console untar the update with the following:

    ```
    tar -xvzf ESX-nnnnnnn.tgz
    ```

4. To find more information about the patch you can use the esxupdate command to read its info and xml file with the following:

    ```
    esxupdate -r
    file:/vmfs/volumes/nfs1/patches/ESX-5031800 -l
    info
    ```

Note:

This return information is formatted as follows:

```
Product              : VMware ESX Server
Vendor               : VMware, Inc. (sup-
port@vmware.com)
Release:             : ESX-5031800
Release Date         : Mon Feb  5 13:54:51
PST 2007
Summary              : RHSA-2006:0749 tar
security update
Description          :
This patch contains Red Hat security fix for
tar command.

CVE-2006-6097: GNU tar 1.16 and 1.15.1, and
possibly other versions, allows user-assisted
attackers to overwrite arbitrary files via a
tar file that contains a GNUTYPE_NAMES record
with a symbolic link. This is not properly han-
dled by the extract_archive function in ex-
tract.c and extract_mangle function in
mangle.c.

Upgrade paths     : 3.0.1-32039
Repository URL    :
file:/vmfs/volumes/nfs1/ESX-5031800
RPMs included     : tar-1.13.25-15.RHEL3
```

5. To install the update use the following:

```
esxupdate -r
file:/vmfs/volumes/nfs1/patches/ESX-5031800 up-
date
```

Bulk ESX Patching

Forum and London User Group member Michael Knight has created a script which will untar the patches for you and then put them in date order – and then apply the patches in bulk. You can download this script from http://www.rtfm-ed.co.uk which is held under the "Useful Tools" section of the site.

To use Michael's script make sure you download your tar files to /var/updates directory and then execute the script. Alternatively, you can edit the script to specify the required path.

Summary

Generally, VMware software is very reliable and very secure. However, like any software vendor errors and bugs are bound to happen. In this chapter we have addressed the issue of patching and updating VI-3 from the perspective of automating the process as much as possible with VMware scripts and tools such as esxupdate and vmware-vmupgrade. We have also seen how many of these tasks can be automated using scripts that are freely available on the Internet.

Index